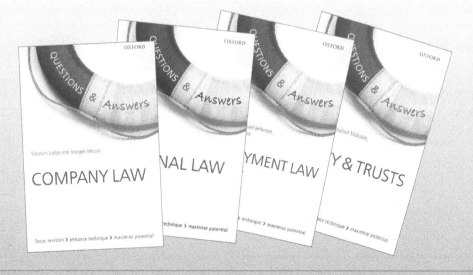

SMITH & HOGAN'S ESSENTIALS OF CRIMINAL LAW

John Child

Lecturer in Law, University of Sussex

David Ormerod QC

Law Commissioner for England and Wales, Professor of Criminal Justice, Queen Mary, University of London, Barrister, Bencher of Middle Temple, Door Tenant at 18 Red Lion Chambers

OXFORD
UNIVERSITY PRESS

Great Clarendon Street, Oxford, OX2 6DP,
United Kingdom

Oxford University Press is a department of the University of Oxford.
It furthers the University's objective of excellence in research, scholarship,
and education by publishing worldwide. Oxford is a registered trade mark of
Oxford University Press in the UK and in certain other countries

Published in the United States of America by Oxford University Press
198 Madison Avenue, New York, NY 10016, United States of America

British Library Cataloguing in Publication Data

Data available

Library of Congress Control Number: 2014959004

ISBN 978-0-19-968956-9

Printed in Great Britain by Ashford Colour Press Ltd

Preface

Smith and Hogan's Essentials of Criminal Law is a new textbook designed for undergraduate students beginning their study of criminal law. Being targeted at that audience means that the book is focused on teaching and learning, devoting space to explanations of criminal law concepts in a step-by-step manner and avoiding assumed knowledge. Our analysis always begins with the current law, ensuring that this is the focus of debates that may then consider historical and/or future developments. The book highlights complexities, and/or points of common confusion so readers can understand the problem areas. The text is complemented throughout by numerous visual aids, including flowcharts, case boxes, and offence charts, in order to help those who learn more effectively through visual representations. We also address student concerns with assessment by providing guidance in each chapter focusing on potential problem questions. Within each chapter we also include sections dedicated to debate about reform, focusing on potential essay questions.

Our focus on teaching and learning and the accessible presentation is supported by the quality of the content, with the book maintaining the ideals for which *Smith and Hogan* criminal law books are renowned: exposing and analysing the complexities of the law, setting the law in the context of surrounding academic debate, and highlighting potential reform options that might steer the law towards greater coherence and fairness. Our aim is to provide readers with an understanding of the essentials of criminal law, in a way that is accessible to all students.

Guide to the Book

This book includes a range of features designed to help support and reinforce your learning and offer useful assessment advice. This guided tour shows you how to fully utilise the textbook and get the most out of your study.

Chapter table of contents

Each chapter begins with a clear breakdown of the topics you will cover, including page numbers for easy reference.

Did D complete the actus reus and mens rea of the principal offence (alone or with P)? — Yes

No

Did P commit the principal offence? — No

Tables and figures

Tables and figures are presented across the book. These will help your learning and revision, graphically presenting some of the key concepts and principles to be considered in your study of criminal law.

Evans [2009] EWCA Crim 650

D, V's half-sister, supplied her with heroi dose, D stayed with V but did not alert t drugs. V died and D was charged with GN creation of a dangerous situation when s

Key cases

All key cases are highlighted across the chapters with a brief summary of the main facts and judgment.

Don't be confused...
The cases discussed in this section ar ing to assault or battery. However, t interesting. It should be remembere for section 47, as it is a constructive

'Don't be confused'

Throughout the chapters these boxes highlight common pitfalls to avoid and other areas of confusion for those new to the law.

Judge and jury...
Where the jury are not given a legal juries in identical cases: one jury's u is mitigated by asking the jury to ap own individual understandings, but

'Judge and Jury'

Throughout the chapters these boxes provide clarification on the role of the judge and jury in relation to offence and defence elements.

'Extra detail'

Throughout the chapters these boxes offer you additional insights into the law and suggest sources for further reading.

> **Extra detail…**
> *Devonauld* could be seen as a ca
> and to gain material to humiliate
> latter.
>   Few cases of this kind have com

'Assessment Matters'

Throughout the chapters these boxes offer you advice on how to approach a given topic in essay or exam assessment.

> **Assessment matters…**
> Our discussion of section 76 has g
> before, when learning and discussi
> answer to a set of facts is uncertain d
> edged. Your task is to analyse the sta

Reform

In the penultimate part of each chapter you will find a section on law reform. These sections include noted academic criticism of the law and other recent calls for reform. These sections will help prepare you for essay question assessments.

> **7.10 Reform**
>
> With much of the law in this area
> unsurprising that there have been
> amendments.[175] The Law Commiss

Eye on Assessment

Each chapter ends with a section dedicated to assessment advice, including how to approach problem questions and correctly apply your knowledge of the law.

> **7.11 Eye on assessment**
>
> In this section we discuss the potent
> within a problem question. The same
> have discussed in previous chapters.

online resource centre

Each chapter is accompanied by a suite of online revisions and assessment features. Please see page viii for further details.

Guide to the Online Resource Centre

This book is accompanied by an Online Resource Centre which provides you with various resources to reinforce your learning, help your revision, and prepare you for essay or exam assessment. These resources are all free of charge and designed to maximise your learning experience.

www.oxfordtextbooks.co.uk/orc/smithandhogan/

Multiple-choice questions

A selection of multiple-choice questions, arranged by chapter, allow you to assess quickly your knowledge of the various topics in criminal law.

Legal updates

An indispensable resource providing access to recent cases and developments in the law that have occurred since publication of the book.

Web links and further reading

A selection of annotated web links and further reading references chosen by the authors allow you to delve deeper into topics which are of interest to you and prepare for essay assignments. All web links are checked regularly to ensure that they remain live.

Examination questions

Each chapter is accompanied by two sample examination questions with answer guidance from the authors to help hone your assessment skills.

Video tutorials

A selection of author videos are available explaining key topics and principles, as well as highlighting areas of common confusion for those new to the study of criminal law.

Outline Contents

Detailed Contents

Table of Cases

CASES OF OTHER JURISDICTIONS

Australia

Canada

Table of Legislation

1

Introduction

1.1 Focusing on the substantive criminal law

In this book we will be exploring the criminal law of England and Wales. Many aspects of the criminal law feature in the news and debates in the media every day, which is useful and important because it reminds us about the vital role played by the criminal law in society. It makes the study of criminal law more interesting, and it can also highlight conflict and potential problems for the law. However, readers need to be aware that the focus of these debates and discussions is commonly very different from that involved in the study of substantive criminal law. The debates will often relate to sentencing, procedure, police investigation, and criminal justice matters generally. Our focus in this book is on *substantive* criminal law. It is about how offences like theft and murder are defined, not about who commits them or why (criminology), how they are investigated by the police (policing and criminal procedure), how they are prosecuted and proved in court (evidence), or how they are sentenced (sentencing). Take the following example:

> The defendant (D) kicks the victim (V) hard in the back. D commits an offence.

Our focus involves an analysis of what D did, what circumstances she did it in, and what effect it had on V. Did D do it while she was drunk or insane or acting in self-defence? Did V suffer serious injury or minor injury? Was V consenting (eg was it in a wrestling match)? Questions like these lead us to identify the correct category of possible offences (and any defence(s)). Having identified the category of offences that may have been committed, our task is then to explore the specific offences in detail, asking precisely what actions or omissions are criminal and comparing the offence requirements with the conduct of D.

Although our central study in this book is of the definitions of criminal offences and defences, in this introductory chapter it is important for us to set this in context. The following sections provide short descriptions of related matters that it is helpful for readers to be aware of in order to fully understand substantive criminal rules in context and to evaluate them effectively.

1.1.1 What should be criminalised?

When studying the substantive criminal law, it is natural to question the basis upon which certain conduct is criminalised and other conduct is not. We may ask *why* certain conduct has been made criminal (eg why is it an offence for D to kick V?);[1] we may ask why particular conduct *should* be criminal (eg why should it be an offence for D to kick V?).[2] Such questions and challenges are important and fruitful areas for research and study,[3] but they are questions that should be addressed by lawmakers and those interested in criminal law policy. Our focus in this book is not on what the criminal law should be and why, but on how current criminal offences are defined.

Questions about the legitimate targets for criminalisation, studies of moral and political philosophy, are perhaps inevitably imprecise. Traditionally, where theorists have attempted to explain and justify criminalisation, they have focused on the targeting of 'harm': conduct that infringes the autonomy of V (physically or otherwise), or causes

---

[1] This is referred to as a 'descriptive challenge': seeking an explanation for a current state.

[2] This is referred to as a 'normative challenge': questioning the rights or wrongs of a current state.

[3] Simester and Von Hirsch, *Crimes, Harms and Wrongs: On the Principles of Criminalisation* (2011).

serious offence.[4] Harm is a useful target because, unlike older theories based on *moral wrongs*, harm is at least relatively objective. However, although this approach is readily applicable to offences against the person such as murder, rape, or battery (eg D kicking V), it is much more difficult to present harm as the rationale for offences that are available to be charged before harm is caused (eg liability for attempting to commit a crime[5]) or the many regulatory offences (eg failing to have a valid road traffic licence for a vehicle). As a result, the advocates of a 'harms' or 'wrongs' approach are left with a difficult choice: maintain a narrow view of harm and fail to explain a large part of the criminal law that does not target such harm, or interpret harms and wrongs widely enough to encompass all offences (eg endangering public order) but in doing so risk the concept of harm becoming so broad that it is no longer useful.[6]

In order to address the perceived problem that a theory based on harms or wrongs may too readily justify creating too many criminal offences, Duff has recently outlined a useful distinction between what he terms 'private wrongs' (wrongs that are not legitimate targets for criminalisation) and 'public wrongs' (which are).[7] For example, if D finishes a relationship with V in an unkind manner, we can say that D has acted wrongfully and we may even say that she has harmed V. However, D's wrong is a private wrong: answerable to V, and perhaps to friends and family, but one where the state, and thus the criminal law, has no legitimate role. In contrast, where D kicks V, it may be that the damage done to V, and society's legitimate interest in protecting others, means that D's wrong is public and deserving of criminalisation. The problem here of course, recognised by Duff, is that the distinction between a private wrong and a public wrong is politically and morally subjective, and lacks clear criteria. However, although this is a problem for those who want to establish a clear separation of legitimate and illegitimate targets of the criminal law, it may be no more than an accurate description of the political process.[8]

Although theories of criminalisation are not directly relevant to our primary focus on identifying the current substantive criminal law, they will affect our discussion in a number of ways. We can highlight three obvious ones.

A) **When interpreting an imprecise offence:** Where an offence is imprecise, it is common for the courts to consider the intentions of the legislature in order to attempt to discover the precise definition of the crime. The aim is to identify the harm or wrong that the offence was designed to target, ensuring that it is interpreted in order to capture only that. Similarly, when you are answering a problem question (discussing the liability of a fictional defendant), you may have to engage in a similar process in order to predict the most likely legal outcome.

---

[4] For discussion and development of the 'harm principle', see Mill, *On Liberty* (1859); Feinberg, *Harm to Others* (1984).

[5] Criminal Attempts Act 1981.

[6] See Duff, *Answering for Crime* (2007) Ch6. For a modern defence of the harm principle, see Horder, 'Harmless Wrongdoing and the Anticipatory Perspective on Criminalisation' in Sullivan and Dennis (eds), *Seeking Security* (2012) 79; Horder, 'Bribery as a Form of Criminal Wrongdoing' (2011) 127 LQR 37.

[7] Duff, *Answering for Crime* (2007).

[8] For a more ambitious attempt to set limits on legitimate criminalisation, see Husak, *Overcriminalisation* (2008).

B) When we are evaluating the effectiveness of an offence: It may also be useful to consider the harm or wrong that the offence was designed to target when we are considering whether it is working well. We can then ask whether the definition of the offence has successfully targeted that wrong, and if it has, whether it has gone beyond that target to criminalise other conduct inappropriately. As we will see, the potential for overly broad criminalisation is a criticism that has been made of several recent statutes.[9]

C) When discussing the potential for a new offence: In several places in this book we discuss proposals for new criminal offences. When we do so, it is useful to consider the particular harms and wrongs that those new offences would be looking to target, and to consider whether they are adequately covered by existing law. For example, when discussing the offences against the person in **Chapter 7**, we consider the potential for specific offences relating to domestic violence and the transmission of HIV.

1.1.2 Why do people commit crime?

Exploring the reasons why people commit crimes, which types of people commit them, and whether certain groups are over-represented in criminal statistics, is a valuable pursuit.[10] For example, the reasons why a particular defendant assaulted or harassed a particular victim may help us to identify ways, whether legal or otherwise, to prevent such conduct in the future. However, this is the focus for studies in criminology, and will not be central to the discussions in this book.

Questions of why people make bad choices are not generally relevant to the substance of the law, unless those reasons are explicitly recognised as criminal defences. D may have a good reason (a good motive if you like) for committing an offence, but unless this is recognised within the legal rules, it is irrelevant to her criminal liability.[11]

1.1.3 How can we prove a crime has been committed?

When we consider how the criminal law is applied in practice, issues of procedure and evidence (eg how can we prove D kicked V, or that D intended to do so?) are extremely important.[12] Indeed, in order to practise in the area of criminal law, the study of criminal evidence is essential. However, again, criminal evidence is not directly relevant to the identification of legal rules governing the substantive criminal law—the definition of offences and defences.

Where issues of evidence can have a role, however, is in assessing how well criminal offences operate in practice. For example, if an offence requiring proof that D *intended* a particular result is too hard to prove, is it necessary to have a similar offence requiring proof of something short of intention? Similarly, evidential rules

---

[9] See eg our discussion of the Fraud Act 2006 in **Chapter 10**, and the Serious Crime Act 2007 in **Chapter 11**.

[10] Hale et al, *Criminology* (3rd edn, 2013).

[11] Although good reasons may provide mitigation affecting D's sentencing, this issue only arises *after* D has been found guilty for the relevant offence.

[12] Munday, *Evidence* (6th edn, 2011).

and their operation may be relevant in assessing whether it is better to focus on creating offences that capture D's conduct that leads up to, but does not result in a serious harm (eg focusing on offences of attempting to commit crimes or agreeing or arranging to do so)?

Assessment matters…

Where the facts of a problem question state what D is thinking, it is tempting to ask how this could be proved in real life. For example, if D kicks V in a game of football you may be told in the problem that D did so intentionally. You may then question how, in a game of football, the police and Crown Prosecution Service could ever know or prove that the kicking of V was intentional. However, this does not affect your application of the substantive criminal law. The method by which D's state of mind can be proved in court is a separate issue, and not one you need to deal with. Your task is to discuss and apply the definition of battery (the offence committed) on the facts you are given, and if you are told that D intended to kick V, then you should take this as a fact.

1.1.4 What are the punishments for committing crimes?

Where D is found guilty of a criminal offence (eg for battery when kicking V), D will be subject to a criminal sanction, most commonly a fine or prison sentence. Some basic understanding of punishment and sentencing is useful when discussing the substantive criminal law, although this is not usually part of a criminal law course and is not part of our study in this book.

What may be important in the course of your study of criminal law is to note the relative gravity of offences, by reference to their maximum sentence. For example, where D intentionally kicks V without V's consent, D will have committed the relatively minor offence of battery; if V suffers some harm (eg bruising) D commits the more serious offence of assault occasioning actual bodily harm;[13] and if V suffers serious harm (eg a broken back) D commits an even more serious offence of causing grievous bodily harm with intent.[14] The seriousness of these offences are graded on the basis of the maximum sentence available upon conviction. Therefore, although we are not concerned with theories of punishment, or even the precise methods employed by judges when setting a sentence in the individual case, it is important to appreciate the flexible nature of sentencing in order to understand the (logically prior) role of the substantive law in setting rules at the liability stage. For example, assault (maximum of six months' imprisonment) is less serious than causing grievous bodily harm (maximum of life imprisonment). This will help you to decide on the appropriate offence to discuss if a defendant's conduct amounted to the commission of many offences.

In practice, the criminal law is concerned with one question: is D guilty or not. If the elements of an offence are satisfied then D has committed the crime, if not, D has not. There is no grey area between these two final outcomes. However, if convicted, at the sentencing stage there is much greater flexibility. D's punishment will usually[15] vary depending upon the offence D has committed, with different offences allowing for

---

[13] Offences Against the Person Act 1861, s47.
[14] Offences Against the Person Act 1861, s18.
[15] Some offences specify a mandatory sentence.

different maximum sentences and the circumstances of its occurrence when setting the sentence below that maximum.[16]

1.1.5 What is the difference between criminal and civil law?

It may be helpful in some situations to distinguish a criminal offence from any civil law tort that is similar. For example, in harassment the criminal law offence and the tort of harassment share common definitions. This may also be relevant as certain offences are based on torts, as with false imprisonment.

However, although offences and torts may share definitions or common history, the civil and criminal laws are distinct systems. As with the criminal law, tort cases often centre on harms that one private party has done to another, as where D kicks V. In tort, the injured party is seeking monetary compensation from D, and if the court is satisfied that such compensation is appropriate, it will require D to make a payment to V in order to (in general terms) allow V to return to her pre-harmed position.[17] V must prove her case on the balance of probabilities (the civil standard of proof). Criminal cases in contrast, represent an action by the state (as prosecutor) against the defendant, with a successful prosecution leading to the *punishment* of D. The criminal law's focus on the wrongful conduct of D, as opposed to the compensation of V, provides an important context to our study of the substantive rules. Here, the state must prove its case against D beyond reasonable doubt (the criminal standard of proof). The criminal and civil law operate in parallel with one another, serving different priorities of justice.

1.1.6 What is the criminal law in other jurisdictions?

This book explores the substantive criminal law in England and Wales; it is not therefore directly concerned with the substantive criminal law in other jurisdictions.[18] However, this is not to say that some discussion and comparison with other jurisdictions will not aid our analysis of the law, and such comparison will arise regularly throughout this text. Where this is the case, comparison will generally be made with other common law jurisdictions such as those in the Republic of Ireland, the United States, Australia, New Zealand, and Canada. This is because with these jurisdictions employing similar systems of criminal law to our own, with a common tradition, comparisons are most easily drawn. Indeed, as the criminal law in these jurisdictions was previously administered by Britain, there are still a number of areas where offence definitions remain identical, or certainly very similar, to our own.

Our study of the substantive criminal law is aided by international comparison in two principal ways.

---

[16] Easton and Piper, *Sentencing and Punishment* (3rd edn, 2012).
[17] Deakin et al, *Markesinis and Deakin's Tort Law* (7th edn, 2012).
[18] Certain serious offences are extraterritorial in the sense that D can be convicted under English criminal law even where she has committed the criminal act in another jurisdiction. Here, however, we are discussing offences prosecuted under foreign law.

A) **When interpreting the law:** The substantive law in another jurisdiction has no bearing on the criminal law in this country. The criminal law in England and Wales, as discussed later, is established through a combination of statute (offences and defences defined in Parliament) and the decisions of the courts (*historically* common law offences and defences have been created and where the law is interpreted). However, the courts might find foreign law helpful when considering a problem that has arisen in that country and is now under scrutiny in the courts in England and Wales. What the foreign courts have decided does not have to be followed by the English courts, but it may be persuasive as to the best approach.[19]

B) **When evaluating the law:** In the years since other common law jurisdictions (eg those mentioned previously) have been independent from Britain, they have created and interpreted their own domestic criminal law. It is helpful to look to other countries with similar traditions of criminal law to examine how their laws are developing and to consider whether or not English law compares favourably. As a result, where we consider potential reform in this book, we will often consider the approaches of other common law jurisdictions.

> **Don't be confused...**
> When we compare the criminal law of different jurisdictions, we are not discussing international criminal law which is discussed separately later.[20] International criminal law is concerned with a distinct form of criminalisation that applies across multiple states (eg genocide) and is created through international agreement. Just as this text is focusing on the domestic criminal law of England and Wales, so our comparison here is focusing on the domestic criminal law of other national jurisdictions.

1.1.7 What is the process and procedure to obtain a criminal conviction?

Our final topic in this section relates to the administrative structure through which the substantive criminal law is interpreted and applied. For this, we are going to introduce the main actors within the criminal process and their roles (police, Crown Prosecution Service, defence, judge, and jury), and we will also introduce the court and appeals structure. The actors and the administrative structures within the criminal justice system rarely have a direct effect on the substance of criminal rules, but an awareness of both is essential in order to understand those rules in context.

1.1.7.1 The main actors within the criminal justice system

As we discuss the main actors within the criminal justice system, it is essential to remember that a criminal case is an action between the state (as prosecutor) and a private party (as defendant). The victim of the offence, where relevant, may be simply

---

[19] The reference to foreign case law is particularly common within smaller jurisdictions (eg the Republic of Ireland and Scotland) where the volume of cases, and therefore the body of previous case law nationally, is lower.

[20] See **1.2.5**.

a witness for the court.[21] This is why, unlike within civil law, the victim is not on our list of main actors.

A) The police: After an offence has been committed, the role of the police is to investigate that offence in order to obtain evidence for trial. Where D kicks V, the police will arrest and interview D; try to obtain CCTV footage of the incident; locate any witnesses; record the injuries to V; and so on.

B) The Crown Prosecution Service (CPS): The CPS act as prosecutors on behalf of the state.[22] The head of the CPS, the Director of Public Prosecutions (DPP), is accountable to the Attorney General (AG) who, in turn, is directly accountable to Parliament.

Pre-trial, the CPS have a duty to review the evidence gathered by the police in order to assess whether a prosecution is viable: whether there is sufficient evidence that D kicked V; whether this amounted to a particular offence; and whether it is in the public interest to prosecute.[23] At trial, the CPS present that evidence. In order to obtain a conviction, the CPS must demonstrate D's guilt 'beyond reasonable doubt' as to every element of the offence, the criminal standard of proof.

> **Don't be confused...**
> Civil law cases typically involve two private parties in opposition and are therefore referred to using both parties names (eg *Jones v Smith*). In contrast, criminal law cases typically include only one party name (eg *R v Smith*). This is because in criminal cases the action is between the state as prosecutor (Regina: R) versus a private defendant (party name).

C) The defence: The defendant (D) is the party alleged to have committed the offence. She will be represented in court by her own legal team.[24] As the prosecution have the burden of proving D's guilt 'beyond reasonable doubt', it is the aim of the defence to raise a 'reasonable doubt' within any essential element of the prosecution's case.

Where D wishes to raise a defence (eg D kicked V in self-defence) she must satisfy what is called an evidential burden: she must provide some evidence that could lead a jury to believe the defence is satisfied. However, this evidential burden is placed on the defendant principally for reasons of efficiency, to avoid wasting the court's time considering multiple defences that have no chance of success. This form of evidential burden should not be confused with the legal burden on the prosecution. It is for the prosecution to prove the elements of the offence beyond reasonable doubt: to prove (in our example) that D kicked V intentionally or having foreseen risk of making contact, and that V suffered some minor harm as a result. If D is able to present some evidence as to a defence (evidential burden), it is also for the prosecution to prove the absence of that defence beyond reasonable doubt (legal burden).

---

[21] As criminal justice reform moves towards a victim-focused system, the victim is included throughout the process. However, the main action remains between the state and D.

[22] There are many other agencies with prosecution powers (eg SFO, Defra, FCA, etc) but most trials are conducted by the CPS.

[23] Prosecution of Offences Act 1985, s10.

[24] Defence representation is paid for privately, or through state-assisted legal aid.

D) The jury: Only Crown Court trials involve a jury. The jury is made up of 12 people.[25] The role of the jury is to decide matters of fact (but not of law). For example, if the law makes it an offence for D to kick V, it is the jury's job to decide if D did in fact kick V. If the offence requires D to intend to injure V, the jury must decide whether D did so intend. The judge decides on matters of law. For example, it may be that D claims she kicked V as part of a wrestling match and she had V's consent. The judge would rule as a matter of law whether consent by V in wrestling was capable of providing D with a defence. The jury would decide whether, on the facts, V did consent, and whether it was a wrestling match.

E) The judge: The role of the judge is to decide matters of law (as opposed to fact). In the lower courts, therefore, the judge must adjudicate on any legal conflict between the opposing advocates relating to rules of evidence and admissibility, as well as the substantive elements of relevant offences and defences. The judge is also responsible for summing up the law in a direction for the jury before they retire to consider their verdict. Finally, in the Crown Court, if the jury find D guilty of an offence, the judge is responsible for setting the appropriate sentence.[26]

Decisions of higher courts (eg the Court of Appeal and the Supreme Court) are made by panels of judges and do not include a jury. In accordance with the doctrine of precedent, the legal interpretations and decisions of these courts then bind the future interpretations of the courts below them.

1.1.7.2 The burden of proof in criminal trials

The fact that it is for the prosecution to prove D's guilt (legal burden of proof) and that they must do so beyond reasonable doubt (criminal standard of proof) is designed to limit the risk of innocent people being wrongly convicted.[27] It also recognises the unequal resources of the two sides (ie the state's possession of investigatory powers and personnel). In line with the legal burden placed on the prosecution, the defendant is presumed innocent until proven guilty. A long established principle of English law,[28] this right is also codified in Article 6(2) of the European Convention on Human Rights (ECHR).

However, although the prosecution bearing the legal burden of proving D's liability may be considered fundamental to the criminal law, it is not an absolute rule. In certain instances, the legal burden is 'reversed' and D bears the burden of proving a particular element or defence. Reverse burdens of proof remain controversial within the law, not least for their effect on D's right to a fair trial (Art 6 ECHR). However, the use of reverse burdens has not diminished (eg where D claims to have been insane when kicking V, D must prove that she was insane).[29]

---

[25] Jury members are randomly selected from the voting register up to the age of 70. Only those who are mentally incapable, or those with specified (serious or recent) criminal convictions, are excluded: Criminal Justice Act 2003, s321.

[26] The role of the judge is usefully summarised in *Wang* [2005] UKHL 9, [3] and [8].

[27] This is a position neatly encapsulated in the ratio attributed to William Blackstone writing in the 1760s which maintains that 'it is better that ten guilty persons escape than that one innocent suffer'.

[28] *Woolmington v DPP* [1935] AC 462.

[29] See Dennis, 'Reverse Onuses and the Presumption of Innocence' [2005] Crim LR 901; Stumer, *The Presumption of Innocence, Evidential and Human Rights Perspectives* (2010).

To understand the role of reverse burdens of proof, two aspects require discussion. The first concerns the standard of proof. As highlighted previously, where the burden of proof is on the prosecution, they must prove D's liability 'beyond reasonable doubt'. However, where D holds a reverse burden, she need only prove the relevant element to the civil standard of proof: 'on the balance of probabilities'.[30]

Secondly, although reverse burdens arise in the law, this is usually in the context of defences as opposed to offences (eg insanity[31] and diminished responsibility[32]). This is important because defences only become relevant if the prosecution have already provided evidence that D has committed the elements of the offence. Asking D to prove some element of defence at this stage, once the Crown has already provided evidence of D's wrongdoing, is therefore not directly contrary to the presumption of innocence: the presumption only protects D 'until proven guilty'. In contrast, where reverse legal burdens impose an obligation on D to establish her innocence before the Crown have provided evidence of wrongdoing, the same logic cannot apply. In fact, in many cases where there appeared to be a reversed legal burden, even if this only applied to a single element within an offence, the courts have rejected it and interpreted it as an evidential burden instead to ensure compliance with Art 6 ECHR.[33] This arrangement provides some protection for D's Article 6 rights but remains problematic, particularly as the pivotal distinction between defences and offences lacks objective criteria. For example, the non-consent of V is an offence element in the context of sexual offences, but the consent of V is considered by some to be a defence in the context of other non-fatal offences against the person.[34]

The greatest effect of a reverse burden is as a matter of practice and procedure. However, it may also be directly relevant to the substantive definition of the offence. This is apparent in relation to certain wrongs that, although deserving of criminalisation, are particularly difficult for external agencies to prove. For example, as we will discuss in **Chapter 8**, this is true of sexual offences: although involving serious wrongs, it is difficult to prove offences that invariably take place in private, and often come down to dispute over D's and/or V's state of mind as to consent. The temptation to employ a reverse burden as to aspects of the offence (eg consent) is obvious: where we are discussing D's state of mind, surely D is in a better position to present evidence of this than the police or CPS. Indeed, within the Sexual Offences Act 2003, we already see a movement in this direction with the use of reversed rebuttable *evidential* burdens as to consent.[35] However, despite their potential practical utility, whether such reform would serve the interests of justice remains a separate question.[36]

---

[30] Proving simply that it is more likely than not.

[31] See the *M'Naghten* Rules (1843) 10 Cl & Fin 200, 210.

[32] Homicide Act 1957, s2(2).

[33] The courts do so using the interpretive powers within the Human Rights Act 1998, s3. See eg *Lambert* [2001] UKHL 37 relating to the possession of drugs.

[34] See **Chapters 7** and **8** respectively.

[35] Sexual Offences Act 2003, s75.

[36] Ashworth and Blake, 'The Presumption of Innocence in English Criminal Law' [1996] Crim LR 306.

1.1.7.3 The criminal court structure and appeals process

In this section we consider the structure of the criminal appeals system.[37] It is important to understand this structure as reference to the different stages of appeal will arise regularly in our discussion of the law. It is also necessary to understand this structure when considering the doctrine of precedent. Just as legislation is binding on all courts, the doctrine of precedent dictates that interpretations of the law made by higher courts will bind (must be applied by) lower courts in future cases. Essentially, the doctrine of precedent is a common law system to ensure consistency between courts and to make future interpretations of the law more predictable. It is on this basis that when looking to identify substantive rules of law we will often do so by discussing the interpretations of the Court of Appeal and the Supreme Court (formerly the House of Lords[38]) in particular. When doing so, it is necessary, albeit not always straightforward, to distinguish legal interpretations that were required by the court to reach their decision (referred to as the *ratio decidendi* of the case, and capable of creating binding precedent) and interpretations that were additionally made, but not necessary to reach the decision (referred to as *obiter dicta*, creating only a persuasive and non-binding precedent).

In **Table 1.1**, we set out the role of each court within the criminal appeals system. We also highlight the potential for appeal between the courts.

Table 1.1 Criminal courts and appeals process

Magistrates' court	The magistrates' courts are the lowest criminal courts in England and Wales. They are usually made up of volunteer magistrates who are not legally qualified, and who are intended to represent the community. They rely on a legal advisor for legal guidance. In some courts there are legally qualified magistrates who sit alone (District Judges). They tend to hear the more serious cases in the magistrates' courts. The sentencing power of the magistrates' court is limited to six months' imprisonment for each offence (12 months overall), and fines of up to £5,000.
	All summary offences (eg assault and battery) are tried in the magistrates' court. Other offences, known as triable either way offences (offences of which the seriousness can vary considerably on their facts, eg theft and criminal damage) are tried in the magistrates' court unless D elects to be tried in the Crown Court or the magistrates think the case deserves to be tried in the Crown Court. All the most serious cases (triable on indictment only) that are tried in the Crown Court also pass through the magistrates' court. In fact, over 95% of all criminal cases will be settled in the magistrates' court without appeal.

(Continued)

---

[37] See Spencer, 'Does Our Present Criminal Appeal System Make Sense?' [2006] Crim LR 667; Law Commission, *The High Court's Jurisdiction in Relation to Criminal Proceedings* (No 324, 2010).

[38] The Supreme Court replaced the Appellate Committee of the House of Lords as the highest court in the UK in October 2009.

Table 1.1 Continued

Appeal from magistrates' court	• *D may appeal her conviction to the Crown Court.* This route is available if D pleaded 'not guilty' in the magistrates' court, but was found guilty. This appeal will result in a rehearing of the case in the Crown Court.
	• *D may appeal the level of her sentence to the Crown Court.* Again, this will result in a rehearing.
	• *D and/or the Crown can appeal by 'way of case stated' to the High Court.* This appeal must contend that the magistrates made a mistake in law or acted in excess of their jurisdiction, but there can be no appeal on factual matters.
	• *D and/or the Crown can apply for judicial review to the High Court.* This application must contend that the magistrates acted beyond their power (*ultra vires*).
Crown Court	A Crown Court case will include both a professional judge (High Court Judge, Circuit Judge, or recorder) and a jury. In exceptional cases there is a credible risk of violence or intimidation in which case it can be tried by judge alone—there has only been one such case in 400 years.[39] As discussed earlier, the role of the judge is to decide matters of law, and the role of the jury is to decide matters of fact. The sentencing power of the Crown Court is only limited by the individually prescribed maximum sentence for each offence
	We discuss very few Crown Court cases in this text. This is partly because cases at this level are not always reported, and partly because of their limited precedent value when it comes to identifying the substantive law.
Appeal from Crown Court	• In long and complex cases D and/or the Crown can make an interlocutory appeal on the judge's rulings relating to the way the trial will be conducted. The appeal is made to the Court of Appeal before the Crown Court trial commences.[40]
	• The Crown can make an interlocutory appeal to the Court of Appeal on a point of law, if this is made before the trial judge (at Crown Court) begins summing up.[41] This route is only available to trials on indictment, and requires leave from the trial judge or Court of Appeal. If leave to appeal is refused, or the Court of Appeal accepts but upholds the trial judge's ruling on the disputed point of law, then D is acquitted. If the appeal is successful, then the point of law will be corrected and the case will resume at the Crown Court on those amended terms. Thus, this route entails significant risks for the Crown and is very rare.

[39] Criminal Justice Act 2003, ss43–44.
[40] Criminal Procedure and Investigation Act 1996, ss28–38. See also Part 9 of the Criminal Justice Act 2003.
[41] Criminal Justice Act 2003, Part 9.

- If D is convicted at a Crown Court trial she may appeal her conviction to the Court of Appeal. The court will examine the appeal having regard to all its circumstances – 'in the round'. If the Court of Appeal finds the conviction 'unsafe' they will allow the appeal,[42] quashing the conviction and ordering a retrial in the Crown Court as appropriate.[43]

- D may appeal the level of her sentence to the Court of Appeal. The court has the power to quash and substitute any sentence or order as appropriate, although they may not increase its severity if D appealed. The Court of Appeal will only make such a substitution if the sentence is manifestly excessive or wrong in principle, not justified in law, or where matters were improperly considered or ignored.

- D's conviction and or sentence can be referred to the Court of Appeal by the Criminal Cases Review Commission.[44] If D has had an appeal rejected (or leave for appeal refused), and the CCRC believe there has been a potential miscarriage of justice (relating to conviction or sentence), they can refer it to the Court of Appeal for consideration at any time

- The Crown may *not* appeal D's acquittal. Founded in the logic of double jeopardy (the principle that D should not face trial for the same crime twice), prosecutors cannot appeal an acquittal in the hope of convicting D. However, changes in the law relating to double jeopardy have created a narrow exception to this. If D was acquitted of a serious specified offence (eg murder or rape), and if new and compelling evidence is discovered making it more likely that D committed the offence, and if the DPP consents, the Court of Appeal may quash an acquittal and allow for new proceedings to be brought against D in the Crown Court.[45]

- If D is acquitted, the AG can refer a point of law to the Court of Appeal (AG's Reference cases).[46] As stated earlier, where D has been acquitted the Crown cannot appeal against this acquittal. However, if the Crown Court's decision to acquit was based on a potentially mistaken interpretation of law, the lack of an appeal risks further damage (other courts applying similar reasoning). Therefore, this process allows the AG to refer a point of law that emerged at trial. D's acquittal is not at issue, and will remain in place irrespective of the Court of Appeal's decision. However, the mistaken point of law (if there is one) can be corrected for future cases.

- The AG can appeal the level of sentence to the Court of Appeal.[47] Where D has been convicted and sentenced for certain offences identified by Parliament, the AG (on behalf of the prosecution) can refer the case to the Court of Appeal if the AG believes the sentence is unduly lenient. The court is empowered to quash the previous sentence or order and replace it as appropriate, including the potential for a more severe penalty.

(Continued)

[42] Criminal Appeal Act 1995, s2. If 'safe', the appeal will be rejected and the conviction will stand.
[43] Criminal Appeal Act 1968, s7(1).
[44] Criminal Appeal Act 1995, Part 2.
[45] Criminal Justice Act 2003, Part 10.
[46] Criminal Justice Act 1972, s36.
[47] Criminal Justice Act 1988, ss35–36.

Table 1.1 Continued

Court of Appeal (Criminal Division)	When the Court of Appeal sits to hear an appeal it is usually comprised of three judges presided over by a Lord Justice of Appeal (senior judge). Decisions of the Court of Appeal create precedent that binds the future interpretations of lower courts and, generally, future interpretations in the Court of Appeal as well.[48] Occasionally, however, where a case is taken before an expanded Court of Appeal panel of five judges the court is more open to departing from its own precedents
	The majority of the cases that we discuss in this book are Court of Appeal cases.
Appeal from Court of Appeal	• *D and/or the Crown may appeal to the Supreme Court.* Appeals to the Supreme Court will only be available where the disputed point of law is of 'general public importance'. Leave must be granted by the Court of Appeal or the Supreme Court. Where leave is granted, the Supreme Court may also, at its discretion, consider related issues of law that are not directly connected to the point appealed.
Supreme Court	The Supreme Court (formerly the House of Lords) is the highest court in the UK, presided over by 12 Justices of the Supreme Court. Decisions of the Supreme Court create binding precedent for all lower courts (including the Court of Appeal). The Supreme Court is not, however, bound by its own precedent.[49]
	Supreme Court (House of Lords) cases will be discussed throughout this text. Creating the strongest judicial precedent, these decisions form a central part of our identification of the substantive law.
Privy Council	At a number of points in this text we will consider decisions of the Judicial Committee of the Privy Council. The Privy Council is based in the Supreme Court building, with roughly the same set of judges sitting in both courts. However, the Privy Council is not part of the court structure for cases originating in England and Wales. Rather, the Privy Council is the court of final appeal for UK overseas territories and Crown dependencies, and for those Commonwealth countries that have retained the appeal to Her Majesty in Council or, in the case of republics, to the Judicial Committee.
	As the Privy Council is not directly applying the law of England and Wales, decisions of the Board have no binding effect on the courts within the structure outlined above. However, when interpreting areas of law that are identical or similar to that in this jurisdiction, bearing in mind that the judges in the Privy Council are usually also Supreme Court Justices, the Board's decisions can have a strongly persuasive effect.

---

[48] *Campbell* [1977] 1 Cr App R 199.
[49] *Practice Statement* [1996] 1 WLR 1234.

1.2 Sources of the substantive criminal law

Having spent some time setting the substantive criminal law in context, and distinguishing other approaches to the study of crime, it is now possible to narrow our focus to the substantive rules themselves. The first part of this involves a discussion about the sources of the criminal law. Before we begin to interpret and apply the substantive law, we must first learn how to identify it and its basis.

Recognising the sources of the criminal law is extremely important. For example, when D kicks V causing harm, D commits a public wrong that is deserving of criminalisation. However, the formal source that criminalises D's conduct is the Offences Against the Person Act 1861.

1.2.1 Statute

Most of the substantive criminal laws in England and Wales are now set out in statutory form, the principal binding source of criminal law. There are two main benefits to this. First, as the criminal law defines and controls such an important area of interaction between state and citizen, it is appropriate that these rules should be constructed by democratically accountable process. Secondly, statutes are accessible, at least by comparison with the common law discussed later. Particularly since the development and consolidation of online resources (eg www.legislation.gov.uk), it is now possible for citizens to have access to statutory rules quickly and easily. However, a degree of caution is needed on several matters.

A) **Quantity of legislation:** Although statutes are accessible, the sheer quantity of legislation makes it impossible for the legal practitioner, let alone the public, to be fully informed.[50] Problems can also be created where, as is very common, new statutes include multiple amending provisions that make patchwork changes to other legislation.

Beware...
When using older sources to identify the law, or even newer ones such as legislation.gov.uk, care must be taken to ensure that you are aware of any subsequent amendments that may affect the text (even the online resources can take a long time to update).

B) **Form and detail of legislation:** Although there are formal parliamentary procedures for the creation of legislation, there are very few rules defining its form. As a result, you will find that different statutes vary greatly from one another in their detail and presentation, leading to problems at both ends of the detail spectrum. For example, the law that criminalises D as a secondary party to an offence committed by another is set out in the Accessories and Abettors Act 1861. Section 8 states, simply:

Whoever shall aid, abet, counsel or procure the commission of any indictable offence...shall be liable to be tried, indicted, and punished as a principal offender.

---

[50] Chalmers and Leverick, 'Tracking the Creation of Criminal Offences' [2013] Crim LR 543.

As discussed in **Chapter 12**, although the simplicity of this provision may be superficially appealing, it quickly becomes clear that it is rather more unhelpful and misleading. With the provision leaving so many questions unanswered (eg what is it to aid, abet, counsel, or procure?), the true definition of the offence is left to the common law (see later). On the other hand, the modern trend in favour of very detailed provisions in statutes should be approached with equal caution. As we will explore in later chapters, although these statutes have been designed to pre-empt disputes and to clarify the law, some have had the opposite effect and have tended towards unnecessary complexity and impenetrability.[51]

C) **Type of legislation:** As long as a statute containing the offence in question is valid, then so are its provisions. In this book, we will not dwell on the types of legislation employed. However, it is worth highlighting two concerns in this area. First, criminal offences are often created in statutes that are not primarily concerned with the criminal law. This makes those offences more difficult to find and set in context. Secondly, and more worryingly, a great many criminal offences are created through subordinate or secondary legislation. Such legislation does not receive full parliamentary scrutiny, and therefore lacks some democratic legitimacy.[52]

1.2.2 Common law

The law in England and Wales, both civil and criminal, owes its ancient origins to societal customs and traditions. Some of these customs and traditions were formalised within codifying legislation. However, the greater part of these rules were not codified and relied on recognition and enforcement through the courts directly. Through the courts, and the system of precedent, these customs-turned-laws created a body of rules known as the 'common law'.[53] Even today, these common law rules still form the basis of the criminal law in England and Wales, as well as other 'common law jurisdictions': former British colonies that were administered using the same system. The common law system can be contrasted with the 'civil law' system that dominates most of Europe, a system that is based firmly on the creation and interpretation of legal codes (legislation that attempts to codify all areas of law) rather than law created and developed in the courts.

Importantly, despite the common law system in England and Wales, it is now firmly accepted (and has been for many years) that courts are no longer at liberty to create new offences or defences[54] or to abolish such rules.[55] This is uncontroversial. Although the development of new common law offences and defences served to create an essential body of rules, it is accepted that such rules are now more appropriately dictated by a democratically accountable Parliament. A further reason for preferring statutory law

---

[51] See eg discussion of the Serious Crime Act 2007 in **Chapter 11**. Spencer, 'The Drafting of Criminal Legislation, Need It Be So Impenetrable?' (2008) 67 CLJ 585.

[52] Criticised in Law Commission, *Criminal Liability in Regulatory Contexts* (Consultation 195, 2010) para 3.114.

[53] Holmes, *The Common Law* (2012).

[54] *Jones at al* [2006] UKHL 16.

[55] See *Goldstein and Rimmington* [2005] UKHL 63, where the House of Lords denied having power to abolish the offence of public nuisance.

is that court-made law can be criticised as retrospective: when first recognised by the court as an offence, D has had no warning as to the criminality of her action until after it has taken place and is considered by the court. Such retrospectively may allow the law to punish a wrong, but if that wrong was not yet recognised as a criminal wrong we cannot claim that D has *chosen* to break the law.

Although the common law no longer creates or abolishes new offences or defences, it remains the source for a significant part of the current criminal law. Thus, for example, when discussing offences such as murder and manslaughter, and defences such as duress, insanity, and necessity, the relevant rules are not all defined in statute. Rather, as with many other offences and defences, we have to look to the common law and individual leading cases. This is obviously a challenge for those studying the substantive criminal law within a common law jurisdiction, but it should not be overstated. Indeed, as highlighted earlier, even when offences and defences are codified in a statute, the courts still have an important role in interpreting such legislation in practice (whether the legislation is detailed or otherwise). The difference, it is submitted, is that legislation at least allows the democratic lawmakers to choose what discretion to leave to the courts, to control the framework of the law, and to promote consistency. With the common law, all such decisions are judge made.

Assessment matters...

In line with the previous discussion, if you are dealing with a statutory offence/defence then your identification of the substantive rules should *always* begin with the statute. From here, you then explore case law in order to resolve any ambiguities from the statute and to see how the rules are applied in practice: the courts 'put meat on the bone'. With a common law offence/defence you need to do exactly the same thing, but this time your only source is the case law.

1.2.3 European Convention on Human Rights

The UK ratified the ECHR in 1951, allowed individual petition to the European Court of Human Rights (ECtHR) in 1966 (essentially a rights-based appeal from UK courts), and further incorporated it into domestic law through the Human Rights Act 1998 (allowing the Convention to be applied in domestic courts). The effect of the ECHR on substantive criminal law, as elsewhere, has been extensive.[56] However, unlike the statute and common law sources discussed earlier, the ECHR does *not* create any new criminal offences or defences. Rather, it sets out a number of 'rights' that the UK is obliged to protect in the creation and application of the law.

The role of the Human Rights Act 1998 (HRA) in particular, has been to highlight and prioritise rights jurisprudence and the ECHR at every stage of the legal process. Section 1 of the HRA formally incorporates ECHR rights into domestic law. This ensures the ECHR's influence from the earliest stages: every new piece of legislation, including criminal law matters, require a government minister to make a statement to Parliament of compatibility between the proposed legislation and the ECHR.[57] Beyond this, and very importantly, there is also an obligation on domestic courts to take account

---

[56] Cooper and Colvin, *Human Rights in the Investigation and Prosecution of Crime* (2009).
[57] Human Rights Act 1998, s19.

of ECHR rights when interpreting and applying *all* areas of law (not simply relying on potential appeal to the ECtHR in Strasbourg). Thus, through section 3 of the HRA, domestic courts at all levels must *as far as is possible* interpret domestic legislation to give effect to ECHR rights. Under section 4, higher courts also have the power to make a 'declaration of incompatibility' where there is an inconsistency with ECHR rights and no obvious interpretive (s3-based) solution. This latter provision does not strike down or invalidate the incompatible domestic law, and has been exercised sparingly, but provides a strong incentive to maintain consistency.[58]

Thus, the main role of the ECHR with regard to the substantive criminal law, facilitated by the HRA, has been in terms of interpretation and evaluation. Below is a list of ECHR rights and some examples of their effect on the law. The specific influence of the ECHR within each area of criminal law will be discussed throughout this text.

- **Article 2:** The right to life. Article 2 has affected the definition of homicide offences (murder and manslaughter),[59] abortion, euthanasia,[60] as well as leading to conflict where D kills V in self-defence.[61]

- **Article 3:** The prohibition of torture and inhuman and degrading treatment. Article 3 has been relevant to offences relating to parental (and school-based) application of corporal punishment,[62] as well as the treatment of criminal suspects.

- **Article 4:** The prohibition of slavery and forced labour. Article 4 led to the creation of a slavery offence in 2009, and is particularly relevant to the discussion of human trafficking and sex workers.

- **Article 5:** The right to liberty and security. Article 5 has greatest effect on any defendant who has not yet been convicted (eg D's right to know charges, false imprisonment, and unfitness to plead), as well as D who is found not guilty by reason of insanity.[63] It might also affect the definition of offences such as false imprisonment.

- **Article 6:** The right to a fair trial. Article 6, including the presumption of innocence, is central to the debate concerning reverse burdens of proof introduced previously.[64]

- **Article 7:** The prohibition on criminal laws being applied retrospectively is found in Article 7. At its strongest, it applies if an offence is created and made to apply to conduct that was not criminal at the time the conduct was performed. In such a situation it would not be permissible to convict D for his conduct before the offence was created. Article 7 provides strong support for the codification of criminal law and the limitation of judicial discretion which (inevitably) is applied after the event.

- **Article 8:** The right to respect for private and family life. Article 8 is relevant, in particular, in offences that criminalise consensual sexual violence.[65]

---

[58] See *AG's Reference (No 4 of 2002)* [2004] UKHL 43, [28].
[59] See **Chapters 5** and **6**.
[60] See **Chapters 11** and **12**.
[61] See **Chapter 14**.
[62] See **7.3.1**.
[63] **Chapter 13**.
[64] See, in particular, **Chapters 13** and **14**.
[65] See **7.8.2**.

- **Article 9:** Freedom of thought, conscience, and religion. Article 9 provides a framework for religiously aggravated offences,[66] as well as potential public order offences involving public worship.
- **Article 10:** Freedom of expression. Article 10 is relevant to the application of several offences and defences where D's acts are expressing protest (eg criminal damage and public order offences).
- **Article 11:** Freedom of assembly and association. Article 11 is most obviously relevant to public order offences as they apply to assemblies.
- **Article 12:** The right to family life. Article 12 has affected debates about whether married couples should be liable for an offence if they conspire (agree to commit a crime) with one another.[67]
- **Article 13:** The right to an effective remedy for breaches of Convention rights. Article 13 is most relevant to the civil law, but will also have an impact on what is known as restorative justice.[68]
- **Article 14:** The right to non-discrimination under Convention rights. Article 14, as with Art 12, is also relevant to the debate about whether married couples should be treated differently in certain areas of criminal law.

Articles 2 and 3 are absolute (do not allow for discretion) in the negative obligations they provide.[69] However, many of the other rights listed above are subject to important qualification. This means that, even if there is an apparent breach of a Convention right, it can be justified by the state if it is: (a) prescribed by law; (b) necessary in the pursuit of a specified objective (eg public order, health or morals, or the freedom of others); and (c) proportionate to that objective. In view of the substantive criminal law, such qualifications are obviously essential. Substantive offences proscribe D from performing certain acts (inevitably restricting, eg, her Art 10 freedoms), as well as depriving or restricting her liberty (Art 5) where she breaks the law. Therefore, when discussing the impact of these rights on the substantive criminal law, such qualifications should always be considered.

1.2.4 European Union

As a member of the European Union (EU), an increasing proportion of law in the UK is generated either directly from the EU institution,[70] or indirectly through mutual recognition and cooperation. However, traditionally such provisions have not affected domestic criminal law. This is because, as the EU was originally conceived as a trade and economic union, criminal law was not within its competencies. As the EU has developed, however,

---

[66] See **7.9.2**.

[67] See **Chapter 11**.

[68] Restorative justice involves a novel approach to criminal processes and sentencing that focuses on the role of the victim and the community. As it is not directly relevant to the substantive criminal law, it is not considered further in this text.

[69] This is not the case where a claimant alleges a breach of a positive obligation, eg the potential right to assisted death under Art 2, *Pretty v UK* (2002) 35 EHRR 1.

[70] Secondary law from the EU takes the form of regulations, decisions, and directives. Art 288 Treaty on the Functioning of the European Union (TFEU).

particularly in relation to the protection of fundamental rights, its spheres of competence have now expanded well beyond their original trade-based limits.

> **Don't be confused...**
> Although all member states of the EU are signatories to the ECHR (and the EU will soon become a signatory in its own right), the EU is not the author of the Convention; this is the separate European body, the Council of Europe. Therefore, our discussion of ECHR rights in the previous section must be distinguished from our discussion of the EU.

The expansion of EU competencies has now begun to affect the domestic criminal law.[71] Importantly, criminal law remains primarily an issue for individual states, with the EU gaining only limited competence. However, with the increased flow of people across borders, and the ease of technology connecting people together, there is much that can be gained from linking (or at least coordinating) criminal jurisdictions that have traditionally remained separate and insular. Coordination through the EU has therefore targeted offences that commonly involve a cross-border element (eg terrorism, human trafficking, corruption, and other organised crimes), preventing criminal groups from taking advantage of the patchwork of legal inconsistencies across Europe.[72] Such coordination has made particular strides in relation to criminal evidence and procedure.[73]

Despite this expansion of EU competence, the vast majority of the substantive criminal law remains a preciously guarded area of national competence and sovereignty. Therefore, although we see an increased internationalisation of criminal offending in almost every area of the criminal law, the EU's competence remains relatively narrow and specific, with what we might call the more traditional offences (eg murder, offences against the person, etc) strictly excluded. As these more traditional offences are the subject of this book, we will largely set the influence of the EU to one side from this point forward.[74] However, it is important to recognise this growing area of influence within the criminal law, as well as to examine any EU developments as they arise.

1.2.5 International law

International law has had an effect on the substantive criminal law in England and Wales in two main ways. The first is the most direct influence, but the least relevant to our current study: through the creation of international crimes. Where such international offences have not been incorporated into national law, they can be problematic.[75] However, through Part 5 of the International Criminal Court Act

---

[71] Criminal law emerged as a third pillar (basis for intergovernmental cooperation) within the Maastricht Treaty. Following the Lisbon Treaty, specified criminal matters now come within the competence of the EU institutions. TFEU, Title V, Ch4.

[72] Art 83 TFEU.

[73] Art 82. Examples of this include measures on extradition and the European Arrest Warrant.

[74] For a wider discussion, see Baker, 'The European Union's Area of Freedom, Security and (Criminal) Justice 10 Years On' [2010] Crim LR 833; Mitsilegas, *EU Criminal Law* (2008).

[75] See *Jones* [2006] UKHL 16, where D *unsuccessfully* attempted to use the international crime of 'aggression' as part of his defence when damaging military property in the UK: claiming that he

2001, a number of international offences defined in the Rome Statute[76] have been incorporated into national law. The Rome Statute focuses on a relatively small core of internationally recognised war crimes such as genocide. These offences are therefore now part of the domestic criminal law. However, they are not discussed further in this book.[77]

The second area of influence arises from softer sources of international law: conventions arising from groups such as the United Nations (UN), EU, Council of Europe, and the Organisation for Economic Co-operation and Development (OECD), where the UK agrees to create criminal offences to tackle certain agreed wrongs.[78] In this manner, although several areas of substantive criminal law have been directly influenced or mandated by the signing of such conventions, their binding source remains the national statute (discussed earlier). Reference to such *origins* of national law, and an examination of their ambitions, can be useful when evaluating the domestic implementing offences. Such evaluation is similar to our earlier discussion of criminal wrongs: identifying the mischief which the offence is tackling in order to evaluate how effectively it has been criminalised.

1.2.6 The Law Commission and the Draft Criminal Code

As with the softer forms of international law, the work of the Law Commission and the Draft Criminal Code are not binding sources of criminal law. However, in different ways, its work provides a powerful and pervasive influence affecting both the reform of criminal offences and defences, as well as the interpretation of substantive rules within the courts. Both will be discussed throughout this text, and thus both require some introduction.

A) **The Law Commission of England and Wales:**[79] The Law Commission is a national law reform body, sponsored by the Ministry of Justice but independent from government. The Commission has been prolific, particularly in recent years, consulting on several areas of the substantive criminal law and producing reports, including draft legislation, that have directly led to several of the major reforms that will be discussed in later chapters. Where Law Commission projects have been successfully taken forward by government the Commission's papers can provide a useful background to this reform, explaining the rationale behind it and discussing examples of how it might be applied.[80] Even where the Commission's recommendations are not taken forward,

---

was acting to prevent the international offence. The crime of aggression is unlikely to be incorporated into national law until it is formally agreed by states in 2017.

[76] The Rome Statute 1998 is an international agreement, creating the International Criminal Court and defining core international criminal offences.

[77] Cassese and Gaeta, *Cassese's International Criminal Law* (2013).

[78] eg the new Bribery Act 2010 was conceived with explicit reference to several international obligations. Law Commission, *Reforming Bribery* (Consultation 185, 2007) Appendix A.

[79] Law Commissions Act 1965. Law Commission publications can be downloaded from http://lawcommission.justice.gov.uk. Although David Ormerod is the Criminal Law Commissioner nothing in this book should be taken to represent the views of the Commission unless expressly stated to do so.

[80] See most recently, eg, assisting and encouraging crime (**Chapter 11**), fraud (**Chapter 10**), and corporate manslaughter (**Chapter 6**).

these papers are also useful as summaries and evaluations of the current law, as well as providing alternative approaches that can be compared with the current position.[81] In either case, the accessible and authoritative nature of Law Commission material makes it a vital source for the study of criminal law.

B) The Draft Criminal Code: Criminal codes have become prevalent even among common law jurisdictions. Within a code, all the major criminal offences and defences can be brought together in a single document (referred to as the 'special part' of the code), as well as general provisions such as definitions of common language (referred to as the 'general part' of the code).[82] The most recent attempt to construct a criminal code for England and Wales was published by the Law Commission in 1989,[83] following earlier proposals from an academic team in 1985.[84] The 1989 Draft Code is an exceptional piece of work, and its detailed yet succinct definitions continue to influence debate. However, very importantly, despite support from successive Lord Chief Justices, the Draft Code has never been taken forward by government and adopted into law. The approach of the Commission in most recent years since 2009 has been focused on the reform and codification of individual areas of the law. This offers many potential benefits, but the lack of a criminal code remains regrettable.[85]

> **Beware...**
> The Draft Criminal Code, as with all Law Commission draft Bills, can provide a useful point of reference when evaluating the law or seeking alternatives to it. However, such material does not represent the law, and should never be represented as such: they are simply reform recommendations. Also, where a new statute is based on a prior Law Commission draft, be careful to look out for differences between the two.

1.3 The internal structure of offences and defences

Having discussed the sources of criminal offences and defences, it is useful to provide a brief introduction to the structures or forms which they might take. Strictly speaking there are very few rules that restrict how offences or defences should be framed and this is partly due to the lack of a criminal code. However, certain patterns and conventions have emerged, both within the common law and from statute, which can help to make sense of the law. These conceptual tools provide a framework for those drafting the law,

---

[81] See eg parties to crime (**Chapter 12**), attempts and conspiracy (**Chapter 11**), and intoxication (**Chapter 13**); and, most recently, Offences Against the Person Act 1861 and kidnapping.

[82] The language of 'general' and 'special' parts was coined by the criminal law academic Glanville Williams.

[83] Law Commission, *A Criminal Code for England and Wales*, 2 vols (No 177, 1989).

[84] Law Commission, *Codification of the Criminal Law: A Report to the Law Commission* (No 143, 1985).

[85] Dennis, 'RIP—The Criminal Code (1968–2008)' [2009] Crim LR 1. The potential benefits of a criminal code are set out in the Law Commission's Draft Code documents. See also de Búrca and Gardner, 'Codification of the Criminal Law' (1990) 10 OJLS 559.

for the courts applying the law, and for the academic evaluating it as well as for the student trying to do all three.

The most important structural devises for *offences*, discussed in the following chapters, are:

- **Actus reus (guilty act):** The actus reus of an offence describes the wrongful conduct and/or consequences required for liability in proscribed circumstances. For example, when D kicks V she may have committed the crime of battery, among other potential offences. This will depend on what conduct she performed, in what circumstances (eg was V consenting?), and with what consequences (ie what level of harm). The actus reus of battery describes what is prohibited: D must not make non-consensual contact with another (V).

- **Mens rea (guilty mind):** The mens rea of an offence describes the wrongful state of mind that D must have when completing the actus reus. In battery, for example, D must either intend to make contact without consent or at least foresee the risk that her conduct will result in non-consensual contact with V.

Defences, on the other hand, do not involve guilty acts or guilty minds (quite the opposite). Thus, in this context we simply speak of the 'elements' of a defence.

- **Defence elements:** A defence will be available where its elements (its requirements) are fulfilled. For example, if D kicks V to prevent V from attacking her, she may rely on the defence of self-defence. This defence requires two central 'elements': first, that D acted with an honest belief in the need for preventative force and, secondly, that the force used (the kick) was a reasonable response based on the facts as D believed them to be.[86]

In many ways, understanding the structures of the criminal law is the most important part of our study, particularly in the context of offences. There are now well in excess of 10,000 offences known to the law of England and Wales, only a handful of which can ever be included in a book of this kind. Therefore, as well as studying the offences in their own right, our focus (particularly in the early chapters) is to develop methods of analysis that can be used to understand any offence within the law. It should be remembered, however, that these methods and conceptual tools are not essential parts of the law, they are simply methods developed to analyse it. As a result, areas of inconsistency and uncertainty have emerged within the techniques as they have been applied to different offences.

As we discuss each new offence, we will employ the structures of analysis traditionally employed in relation to that offence. This usually involves the simple separation of actus reus, mens rea, and defences introduced previously, but this will not always be the case. It is important to reflect any different forms of analysis so that when you read court judgments and other academic material that are likely to use this style, you are familiar with them. However, in order to provide you with a *consistent* structure of analysis, we will also highlight how every offence could be analysed using an approach which we will call 'element analysis'. This approach will be explored fully over the following three chapters. Based on the separation of actus reus and mens rea, element analysis further

---

[86] Self-defence is discussed fully in **Chapter 14**.

subdivides an offence into conduct, circumstances, and results. It is an approach that can be set out using simple charts, as in **Table 1.2**.

Table 1.2 Offence elements chart (eg battery)

	Actus reus	**Mens rea**
Conduct element	Any physical acts or omissions required for the offence. For battery, D's act of kicking	Any mens rea required as to D's acts or omissions. For battery, that D's conduct was performed voluntarily by her
Circumstance element	Any factual circumstances required for the offence. For battery, V's lack of consent to the contact, and that V is a person	Any mens rea required as to those facts or circumstances. For battery, that D lacked belief that V consented, and that D knew V was a person
Result element	Any consequences of D's action/omission required for the offence. For battery, the physical contact with V	Any mens rea required as to those consequences. For battery, that D intended contact with V or foresaw a risk of that and took the risk unjustifiably

We have chosen to employ this analytical approach as our consistent tool for two main reasons. First, it allows us to explore in more detail the requirements of the offence rather than the traditional approach of analysing just actus reus and mens rea. Secondly, when we come to discuss the general inchoate offences (eg attempts and assisting and encouraging) in **Chapter 11**, as well as certain other areas,[87] the use of element analysis is essential in order to apply the law. Thus, becoming familiar with it from an early stage will be very useful.

1.4 The principles of the substantive criminal law

References to the 'principles' of criminal law, common in case law and academic debate, are drawing upon the idea that there are certain common ideals or aims underpinning the substantive rules. Led most recently by the work of Andrew Ashworth,[88] the identification and discussion of legal principles has become very important to the study of crime. Such principles are primarily employed as evaluative tools. For example, the principle of fair warning states that criminal offences should be clearly constructed and communicated in order to guide the actions of society. The ECHR (discussed earlier) provides certain checks to the quality of the law, particularly in relation to the presumption of innocence (Art 6) and in terms of basic clarity (Art 7).

---

[87] eg reform proposals in relation to the intoxication rules (**Chapter 13**) and complicity (**Chapter 12**).
[88] Ashworth and Horder, *Principles of Criminal Law* (7th edn, 2013).

However, academic discussion of the principles of criminalisation provides clearer guidance on the *ideal* qualities of the criminal law, providing points of reference that can be used to commend or criticise individual offences or defences as appropriate. As certain principles have become more widely accepted, it is clear that they also play a role in the interpretation of the law, with certain approaches preferred by judges over others in line with underpinning principles. Thus, there is a two-pronged effect on the immediate substance of the criminal law (through interpretation), and on the potential for reform (through evaluation). In the following sections we highlight a selection of the most important principles that are most closely connected to the substantive criminal law.

> **Don't be confused...**
> The principles of the criminal law are useful tools for evaluating the quality of an offence or defence. However, they do not affect its validity as law. As long as an offence or defence has originated from a binding source (statute or the common law), it is valid regardless of its quality in terms of legal principles and regardless of its format within element analysis or otherwise.

1.4.1 The principle of fair warning

This principle requires clear communication of the law to the public. As stated earlier, the criminal law aims to deter people from certain wrongful activities, and to punish those who *choose* to pursue wrongful ends in disregard of the law. However, to achieve either of these aims, there is an implicit assumption that the public are aware of the law in the first place: to be guided by it, or to deserve punishment for choosing to break it.

The principle of fair warning is used to discuss and evaluate how effectively offences are communicated to the public. It is a discussion that engages with several areas of debate. For example, the principle of fair warning is central to the contention that offences existing in the common law should be codified in statute, and ideally within a criminal code. In each case, public access to the law would be improved. Fair warning is also a principle that guides *how* offences should be codified. On the one hand, offences and statutory drafting must be sufficiently detailed to allow the public to know what exactly is being criminalised, and allow them to moderate their behaviour accordingly. For example, imagine an offence drafted in simple terms such as 'it is a crime to make unlawful contact with another'. Such an offence would inform D that kicking V *may* be criminal, but without a definition of 'unlawful' the only way D could moderate her behaviour to be sure to avoid liability would be to make no contact with others at all. Hardly an ideal message! On the other hand, however, offences and statutory drafting should avoid being overly complex. For example, as we will discuss in **Chapter 8**, several sexual offences (eg voyeurism) have been defined in an extremely complex manner. However, the complex nature of the statutory drafting does little to provide fair warning to the legal expert trying to predict the law, let alone the public.[89]

---

[89] **Chapter 8**.

> **Extra detail…**
> For those researching this area in greater depth, some exciting work has been done by the Ameri-
> can academic Paul Robinson. Robinson advocates the creation of multiple criminal codes, with
> 'rule articulation' (a code written in accessible language to tell the public what they cannot do),
> separated from other necessarily more complex codes that would focus on 'liability assessment'
> and 'grading'.[90]

1.4.2 The principle of fair labelling

The principle of fair labelling requires accurate correlation between the name of an offence and the conduct it criminalises.[91] The rationale for this principle can be linked with that of fair warning in the previous section. The knowledge most people have of substantive crimes will not go far beyond their awareness of offence names and the implications of those names (eg kidnapping, rape, etc). Therefore, the fairness of the label dictates the fairness of the warning. However, the principle is perhaps more important when it is applied to someone after they have been convicted. This is because, as well as sentencing D as is appropriate (fines, prison, etc), the name of D's offence labels her in the eyes of the public. D is not simply sent to prison for a certain duration, she is labelled as a murderer, a thief, a robber, etc.

The role of criminal labelling is not straightforward; it has both positive and negative aspects. Labels can be very useful in terms of the clear stigma and message created: allowing the state to condemn the accused in language that the public, on whose behalf the state acts, can understand. However, labelling and stigmatisation are difficult to control and quantify, relying on changeable social constructions and attitudes. Thus, in terms of the additional punishments they provide, they cannot be objectively prescribed.

What can be controlled, however, returning us to our central focus, is that we can ensure the label given to D's offence is at least accurate, and in *this* sense fair. It is here that the principle engages most directly with the substantive law. First, it demonstrates the importance of separating different wrongs into different offences with different labels. For example, if D1 steals V1's car, and D2 sets V2's car on fire, both Ds have caused the loss of a car. However, the wrongs committed by D1 and D2 are different and their conduct should be separately labelled: D1 has committed theft, D2 arson. This debate arises in later chapters, for example when we consider the creation of new offences that would relabel conduct already criminalised elsewhere (eg whether *domestic* violence should be a separate offence[92]). The aim of fair labelling also has a direct effect on the content of offences and defences whose names are well known to the public, eg rape and attempt. This is because, as well-known labels can communicate more clearly to the public, there is often a desire that they should be maintained, even when the substantive content of the offence is changed. This

---

[90] Robinson, 'A Functional Analysis of Criminal Law' (1994) 88 Nw U L Rev 857; Robinson *Structure and Function in Criminal Law* (1997).

[91] Chalmers and Leverick, 'Fair Labelling and Criminal Law' (2008) 71 MLR 217; Williams, 'Convictions and Fair Labelling' (1983) 42 CLJ 85.

[92] See **7.10.1**.

is partly why, for example, there has been debate about whether the offence 'rape' should be extended to include non-consensual anal or oral penetration.[93] The concern here is that if such labels are used inappropriately, not only is D unfairly labelled if convicted, but because D's conduct does not fit with the general understanding of the label there is a risk that a jury might acquit a defendant who fulfils the elements of the offence, and who should, therefore, be found guilty. We see this rationale, for example, behind changes in Canadian criminal law where the label of 'rape' has been removed from the sexual offences entirely.[94]

1.4.3 The principle of autonomy

Where we discuss the principle of individual autonomy, we are usually referring to the autonomy of a potential offender. Again, it is a principle that can arise in various contexts. In simple terms, it can be used as a principle of minimum criminalisation. To have autonomy is to be free to act and pursue our goals unrestrained. The criminal law, by design, restricts our options by criminalising certain conduct. Indeed, in the context of criminalising failures to act, the law is limiting *all* of our options and requiring a certain course of conduct.[95] Therefore, if we see autonomy as something that should be preserved and maximised, criminal offences, particularly those involving omissions liability, that limit our autonomy should be kept to a minimum.[96]

The principle of autonomy is also the primary vehicle for the promotion of 'choice' as an essential ingredient of both moral and legal blame. The impact of this can be seen in two main areas. First, we should not criminalise conduct that D cannot avoid. The most basic implications of this would rule out the criminalisation of, for example, belonging to a certain race, of breathing, or of sleeping, where we have no choice at all. More interestingly, it may also affect debate on the fairness of criminalising unrealistic choices. For example, the defence of duress applies where D commits an offence to avoid threatened serious violence. However, even if we recognise that a reasonable person would have acted as D did, and therefore D's choice was in some sense a reasonably unavoidable one, duress is never allowed as a defence to murder. Thus, where D kills V whilst acting under severe duress and is convicted of murder, we may question the law's respect for her autonomy.[97]

Secondly, autonomy and choice are also central to debates about mens rea. At minimum, this can be seen in the contention that all offences should involve voluntary or intentional action: if D kicks V involuntarily, for example whilst having an epileptic fit or when tripping over, there should be no offence. Taken more widely, we could similarly contend that every element of an actus reus should require a corresponding mens rea. For example, if D kicks V and V dies, should D only be liable for an offence related to that death if D intended or at least foresaw, in some sense chose, that

[93] **Chapter 8**.
[94] Criminal Code of Canada, Part VIII.
[95] Williams, 'Criminal Omissions—The Conventional View' (1991) 107 LQR 86.
[96] Husak, *Overcriminalisation* (2008).
[97] Interestingly, the Law Commission raise the principle of autonomy to support their recommendation that duress *should* be a defence to murder. This is discussed in **Chapter 14**.

level of harm? Alternatively, is it enough that D intended to kick V, with this intentional conduct enough to link D with the death even if it was not foreseen? This latter debate is central to much of the discussion of mens rea in **Chapter 3**, and the distinction between what is termed subjective (choice-based) and objective (results-based) approaches to the law.

1.4.4 The principle of welfare

The principle of welfare promotes the role of the law in protecting society from harm. From a potential victim's perspective the welfare principle is therefore in line with the autonomy principle discussed previously: for an individual to be autonomous and free to pursue her goals, she must be protected from others who would unfairly interfere with her, physically or otherwise. However, the protection of V requires the restriction of D. Thus, from this latter perspective, the welfare principle provides a counterbalance to that of autonomy, and one that could justify a highly restrictive criminal law. For example, as discussed in the previous section, if D kicks V during an epileptic attack the principle of autonomy would point towards there being no liability, D has not chosen to cause harm to V. However, D's kick has still interfered with the welfare of V. Therefore, if D is prone to such attacks, and particularly if they regularly result in the injury of others, the welfare principle could be used to favour criminalisation.

The challenge for the criminal law is to find balance to promote maximum autonomy and welfare by creating the conditions, through minimum criminalisation, that allow and support people in the pursuit of legitimate social goals.[98] How effectively the law finds this balance within individual offences and defences is a something that will emerge in several later chapters. A number of these points were highlighted in our earlier discussion of autonomy, including the criminalisation of unrealistic choices (eg affecting the defence of duress), criminalising involuntary harms (affecting the requirement of voluntary movement) as well as unforeseen harms or circumstances (affecting mens rea more generally). In each case, balancing the welfare principle reminds us to consider the objective result of D's conduct as well as what D intended or foresaw. Where the result is serious harm to V, it may be that criminalisation is justified even where D has not chosen every aspect of the offence.

A final example that demonstrates the difficulty of finding balance is the defence of insanity. As discussed in **Chapter 14**, this defence allows D to escape liability where a disease of the mind leads her to commit an offence. However, as such defects are often more than temporary, and as D may therefore pose a continuing danger to others, a successful insanity defence will not result in simple acquittal. Rather, D is 'not guilty by reason of insanity', and a range of disposal orders, including involuntary detention in hospital, become available to the court. D is not guilty because her 'insanity' means that she did not choose to offend; but she may still have her autonomy sacrificed in the name of societal welfare.

---

[98] Lacey, 'Community in Legal Theory: Idea, Ideal or Ideology?' (1996) 15 Studies in Law, Politics and Society 105.

1.5 The subjects of the substantive criminal law

As well as considering the content of the criminal law, it is also important to remember who it is aimed at: whose behaviour it seeks to regulate, and who is subject to punishment for breaking the law. The typical subject of the criminal law is a natural person. However, as we discuss briefly in the following sections, the criminal law will also apply to legal persons (ie corporations), and will not apply, or at least not in the same way, to natural persons in certain circumstances (ie minors and those unfit to plead).

1.5.1 Corporations

Where a natural person commits an offence in the course of acting on behalf of a corporation or other legal entity, they will be liable directly for that offence.[99] However, additionally, and sometimes even in the absence of individual liability, the corporation itself (which the law deems to be a legal person) may also be liable for an offence in its own right. This is referred to as corporate criminal liability.

> *Extra detail ...*
> Beyond corporate criminal liability (targeting public limited companies (plc), private limited companies (Ltd), and limited liability partnerships (LLP)), the criminal law can also target unincorporated associations. However, in the absence of a legal personality to identify and target, the rules governing such liability are often unclear.[100]

Most criminal offences with the exception of murder[101] and a few others are capable of being committed by legal as well as natural persons.[102] Indeed, in many cases, the legal *and moral* case in favour of convicting the corporation may be considerably stronger than any individual involved. An example of this would be where the negligence of a particular employee leads to harm, corporate liability may be more appropriate when that negligence is set in the context of a company that encourages risk taking and dangerous practices on a wider scale.[103] However, corporate criminal liability also raises several unique challenges for the law. First, in the absence of a physical entity, where do we look for the actions and mental states of the company? And, secondly, where we find liability how can we punish the company in an effective manner? In the following section, in line with the focus of this book, we focus on the first of these concerns.[104]

---

[99] See generally Law Commission, *Criminal Liability in Regulatory Contexts* (Consultation 195, 2010).

[100] See discussion in *L* [2008] EWCA Crim 1970.

[101] Murder cannot be committed by a corporation because it carries a mandatory life sentence, a sentence that cannot apply to a corporate entity.

[102] The term 'person' must be interpreted in this manner, unless the contrary is specified. Interpretation Act 1978, s5 and Sch 1.

[103] Gobert, 'A Corporate Criminality: New Crimes for New Times' [1994] Crim LR 722.

[104] On the problem of effective punishment, see Jefferson, 'Corporate Criminal Liability: The Problem of Sanctions' (2001) 65 J Crim L 235.

1.5.1.1 Vicarious criminal liability of corporations

Vicarious liability, common in the context of tortious claims for damages, allows the liability of an employee acting in the course of their duties to be attributed to the corporation they are working for. In the context of the civil law, the doctrine serves a crucial role to enable victims to be adequately compensated for their losses, with the corporation being considerably more likely than the employee to be able to bear the costs.

> **Don't be confused…**
> Vicarious liability does not require the corporation to have assisted, encouraged, or contributed to the actions of the employee. In this way, vicarious corporate liability should not be confused with complicity (discussed in **Chapter 12**).

In the context of the criminal law, where the primary aim is to punish/deter D rather than to compensate V, vicarious liability makes little sense. Where D (the corporation) has acted in a criminally blameworthy fashion then it should be targeted directly as discussed in the following section, and where it has not, the use of vicarious liability is surely unfair. However, the law does allow for the vicarious criminal liability of corporations in relation to a number of offences,[105] mainly of a regulatory nature.

1.5.1.2 Direct criminal liability of corporations

There are three primary routes to the direct criminal liability of corporations: (a) specific corporate offences; (b) the identification doctrine; and (c) liability for a failure to prevent.[106]

A) **Specific corporate offences:** Arguably the most efficient way to regulate corporations by criminal law is through the specific criminalisation of certain conduct. Thus, rather than attempting to reinterpret legislation drafted with natural persons in mind, corporate offences can be tailored, by removing mens rea requirements, by including due diligence defences, and so on. Such offences are often preferred, for example when criminalising failure to meet certain health and safety standards. The disadvantages of such offences are that they can be perceived as purely regulatory, and thus not 'true' crimes, which can undermine the stigmatising effect of the law.

B) **Identification doctrine:** The identification doctrine is a mechanism created at common law to attribute criminal liability to corporation where such liability includes both actus reus and mens rea requirements. Essentially, the doctrine provides that a corporation can be liable for a crime of mens rea if that mens rea was possessed by an officer in the corporation of sufficient seniority to be a 'controlling mind'—someone whose actions and mens rea can fairly be said to represent that of the corporation as a whole.[107]

---

[105] *Tesco Stores Ltd v Brent LBC* [1993] 2 All ER 718.

[106] See generally Cavanagh, 'Corporate Criminal Liability: An Assessment of the Models of Fault' (2011) 75 J Crim L 414.

[107] Developed and discussed in *Bolton* [1956] 3 All ER 624; *Tesco v Nattrass* [1972] AC 153; *Re Supply of Ready Mixed Concrete (No 2)* [1995] 1 AC 456; *X Ltd* [2013] EWCA Crim 818.

The major disadvantage of this doctrine, however, is that identifying a 'controlling officer' who had mens rea can be very difficult, particularly where the corporation is large and complex such that the 'controlling officers' are unlikely to be involved with those working at lower levels.

C) **Failure to prevent:** Partly as a reaction to the perceived inadequacies of the identification doctrine, modern statutes have begun to develop a form of corporate liability based around a failure to prevent. Modelled on the tort of negligence, this doctrine does not seek to blame the corporation criminally for something it has done or thought via the identification doctrine, but rather for its failure to provide adequate procedures and mechanisms to prevent the harms caused by those throughout the corporation. We can see variations of this model in place with the new offences of corporate manslaughter discussed in **Chapter 6**,[108] for bribery,[109] and depending upon its success, it is an approach that has the potential to be expanded across almost all criminal offences.[110]

1.5.2 Minors

Section 50 of the Children and Young Persons Act 1933 creates a *conclusive* presumption that children under the age of 10 years cannot commit a criminal offence. Therefore, in substance, no criminal prosecution can apply to this group. This will be the case regardless of the circumstances, eg even where D (under 10) has acted intentionally and caused serious harm or death. Those under 10 years require protection and support, and this can be gained through the civil law. They do not deserve, at this young age, the punishment and stigma of criminalisation.

Once D reaches the age of 10, the criminal law will apply regardless of her lack of maturity.[111] Prior to 1998,[112] a common law doctrine (*doli incapax*) created a rebuttable presumption that those between 10 and 13 years were not capable of forming a criminal mens rea: rebutted only where the prosecution could prove that D knew that her acts were 'seriously wrong' as opposed to merely naughty. The abolition of the common law doctrine, combined with the comparatively low age of criminal responsibility, has led to cogent criticism of the over-criminalisation of children within this jurisdiction.[113]

1.5.3 Defendants who are unfit to plead

D is 'unfit to plead' or unfit to be tried if, because of a disability, she is incapable of being tried within the normal criminal court process. The conditions for competence were set out in *M*,[114] and require D to have sufficient ability to:

(a) understand the charges;

(b) understand the plea;

---

[108] See **6.4.1**.
[109] The Bribery Act 2010, s7.
[110] Law Commission, *Criminal Liability in Regulatory Contexts* (Consultation 195, 2010).
[111] *T v UK* [2000] Crim LR 187: criminally punishing a 10-year-old is not contrary to Art 3 ECHR.
[112] Crime and Disorder Act 1998, s34.
[113] Keating, 'The Responsibility of Children in the Criminal Law' (2007) 19 CFLQ 183.
[114] [2003] EWCA Crim 3452.

(c) challenge jurors;

(d) instruct counsel and her solicitor;

(e) understand the course of the trial; and

(f) give evidence (if she chooses to do so).

To establish D's unfit state, the onus of proof is on the party raising the issue: if it is raised by the defence, then they must prove D's unfitness on the balance of probabilities; if it is raised by the prosecution, then they must prove it beyond a reasonable doubt.[115] The matter is decided by a judge alone. Where D is found unfit to plead (because, *at the time of trial*, one or more of the conditions in *M* is not satisfied[116]), she is removed from the standard criminal process. This is the case regardless of the evidence against D: even if there is overwhelming evidence that D committed the relevant offence and was competent at the time of the offence, her lack of competence at the time of trial means that a standard criminal trial would be unfair and illegitimate.

Where D is found unfit, instead of a standard criminal trial, the case will be decided through a 'trial on the facts'. This procedure is set out in sections 4 and 4A of the Criminal Procedure (Insanity) Act 1964, as amended. Essentially, a trial of the facts is a trial before a jury to determine whether D committed the acts or omissions required for the offence charged. In other words, the court will explore the actus reus of the offence, but *not* the mens rea. If it is found that D did not commit the actus reus, she will be acquitted in the normal manner. However, where D is found to have committed the actus reus, although she is not liable for the full offence, a range of disposal options become open to the court. These include a hospital order, with or without a restriction order, a supervision order, or an absolute discharge.[117]

As the number of people pleading unfitness continues to rise, so the inadequacies of the current law become more apparent.[118] Chief among these has been the difficulty of finding a principled and consistent separation of acts and omissions, relevant to a trial on the facts, from mens rea considerations that are not relevant to a trial on the facts. The case of *B* provides a useful example of this where, on a charge of voyeurism, the court struggled to decide whether the relevant acts amounted to the simple conduct of viewing, or whether they included a motivation of doing so for sexual gratification.[119] Despite the issue of motivation seeming to go beyond an analysis of acts, the Court of Appeal held that D's sexual motivation was so essential to the 'act' of voyeurism, that it remained essential even for a trial on the facts. Similar problems have also emerged in relation to potential defences.[120]

---

[115] *Podola* [1959] 3 All ER 418.

[116] Where D is competent at trial, but was suffering from a defect of reason caused by a disease of the mind when committing the criminal act, the insanity rules should be applied. **Chapters 13 and 14**.

[117] Criminal Procedure (Insanity) Act 1964, s5.

[118] Mitchell and Howe, 'A Continued Upturn in Unfitness to Plead—More Disability in Relation to the Trial under the 1991 Act' [2007] Crim LR 530.

[119] [2012] EWCA Crim 770.

[120] *Antoine* [2000] UKHL 20.

The Law Commission is shortly to produce recommendations for reform [121] and a draft Bill.

1.6 Reform

In the penultimate section of every chapter we will have a separate discussion about legal reform. This is not to say that we will *only* discuss reform in such sections. However, where possible, we will look to separate the discussion in this way to avoid common confusions between the current law and reform recommendations. The main aim of these sections is to help you to engage critically with the current law: moving beyond an investigation of the rules themselves, to the evaluation of those rules and the consideration of alternatives. Such material is most directly relevant to essay-type questions, where you are expected to discuss and engage with your topic. However, it will also be useful for problem questions where you are asked to comment on the law as you apply it. More generally, considering the reform of offences and defences is also often the best way to gain a deeper understanding of the rules themselves.

When discussing reform proposals, it is obviously important that you understand what the proposal is attempting to do. Just as your understanding of the current law requires you to be able to identify and describe the rules, the same is true for your discussion of a reform proposal. In addition, discussion of reform requires you to engage with and to evaluate the law, and this will be a major theme of these sections. Thus, you will need to consider the law on four separate levels.

- **Describe the current law:** You cannot hope to discuss the reform of law that you do not understand.
- **Evaluate the current law:** You need to be able to identify the problems with the current law that have led to the reform proposals, evaluating the seriousness of such problems.
- **Describe the reform proposal:** You need to know how the reform proposal is seeking to remedy the problems identified with the current law.
- **Evaluate the reform proposal:** To what extent would the proposal succeed in remedying the identified problems with the current law? Would the reform create any new problems?

Our discussion of reform proposals will, of course, differ with each chapter. However, the tools for evaluation (both of the current law and of reform proposals) do not change, and have been introduced in this chapter. We might ask, for example, how accurately the current law or the reform proposal targets the mischiefs that it is attempting to criminalise; how similar reforms have worked out in other common law jurisdictions; whether they conform to ECHR rights, etc. In each case, we can also apply the principles of criminalisation discussed in the previous section, asking whether the current law or

---

[121] Law Commission, *Unfitness to Plead* (Consultation 197, 2010); *Issues Paper* (2014).

reform proposal fairly warns and labels, whether it respects autonomy, and whether it protects welfare.

The substantive criminal law should not be thought of as a static body of rules to be committed to memory. Rather, it is dynamic and changing, through judicial interpretation as well as through statutory reform. Thus, you should consider the evaluative tools discussed in this chapter as an armoury, equipping you to grapple with the substantive law. The criminal law is clearest and most interesting and rewarding when you cannot only identify and apply the rules as they stand, but do so with an understanding of how those rules have developed and how they are likely to change.

1.7 Eye on assessment

The final section of every chapter will provide an 'eye on assessment'. The idea of these sections is to discuss the *application* of the current law, particularly in the context of problem questions. Having discussed the substantive rules themselves, and having discussed potential reform, this section aims to help you to structure an answer that will demonstrate that knowledge.

Without any particular offences in mind, set out below is a generic guide to structuring a *problem question* that we will return to throughout this text. Although our approach may vary from this model when discussing particular offences and defences, it remains a useful structure around which these variations can be discussed and justified.

INTRODUCTION

The introduction to a problem question should be brief. It can be useful to identify the offences and defences relevant to the question in order to show your examiner you understand, and to say how you are going to answer the question (eg chronologically, defendant by defendant, crime by crime, etc). However, be sure to get into the body of the answer as quickly as possible.

STEP 1 Identify the potential criminal event in the facts

This is unlikely to take more than a sentence, but it is essential to tell your reader where in the facts you are focusing (eg 'The first potential offence is committed when D kicks V'). If you go straight into an analysis of the law without highlighting the event in the facts then it is very difficult for a reader to follow your answer.

STEP 2 Identify the potential offence

Having identified the facts (eg D kicking V), you must now identify the offence you are going to apply. Usually, this means identifying the most serious offence that D might have committed. As an example: 'When kicking and seriously injuring V, D may have committed a grievous bodily harm offence contrary to section 18 of the Offences Against the Person Act 1861'.

STEP 3 Applying the offence to the facts

Actus reus: What does the offence require? Did D do it?

Mens rea: What does the offence require? Did D possess it?

Remember, to be liable for the offence every element of the actus reus and mens rea must be satisfied. Thus, every element should be discussed even where it is easily satisfied and little discussion is necessary. Where there is doubt, in law or in fact, highlight and discuss areas of likely dispute between prosecution and defence. Also, if the question asks you to critically engage with the law as you apply it, take particular care to include evaluation of the law.

STEP 4 Consider defences

The word 'consider' here is important, as you should not discuss every defence for every question. Rather, think whether there are any defences that *could* potentially apply. If there are, discuss those only.

STEP 5 Conclude

This is usually a single sentence either saying that it is likely that D has committed the offence, or saying that it is not likely because an offence element is not satisfied or because a defence is likely to apply. It is not often that you will be able to say categorically whether D has committed the offence or not, so it is usually best to conclude in terms of what is more 'likely'.

STEP 6 Loop

Go back up to Step 1, identifying the next potential criminal event. Continue until you have discussed all the relevant potentially criminal events.

CONCLUSION

It is good practice to complete your problem question answer with a brief conclusion. This is usually no more than a few sentences highlighting where you believe offences have been committed and where they have not.

 ONLINE RESOURCE CENTRE

www.oxfordtextbooks.co.uk/orc/smithandhogan/

This chapter is accompanied by a selection of online resources to help you with this topic, including:

- **Multiple choice questions**
- **Chapter summary sheet**

- Two **sample examination questions** with answer guidance
- **Further reading**

Also available on the Online Resource Centre are:

- A selection of **videos** from the authors explaining key topics and principles
- **Legal updates**
- Useful **weblinks**

2

Actus reus

2.1 Introduction

The term 'actus reus' is loosely translated as 'guilty act', although probably the most helpful term to describe what we are discussing is the 'external elements' of an offence. This reminds us that an actus reus is not simply about the movements of D; that is, her conduct. Rather, as we will see, the actus reus of an offence includes any offence requirement that is external from the mind of D: anything that is not 'mens rea'. This will include D's acts or omissions, but also the surrounding circumstances such as the ownership of property in theft and criminal damage. It will also include the required results of the offence such as death in homicide offences. And in addition, proof of necessary links between elements: for example, that the results must be caused by D's conduct. So, taking the simple case of battery by kicking, the actus reus involves D's kick (conduct), to a person without their consent (circumstances), making contact with V (result).

It should be remembered that 'actus reus' and 'mens rea' are terms of art. We separate actus reus and mens rea in our analysis because breaking down offences into their elements helps us to understand them. But we must not lose sight of the fact that no matter what methods are used to distinguish the elements of an offence, D's liability depends upon the satisfaction of *all* of them as a whole. To be liable for an offence, it must be proved beyond reasonable doubt that D satisfied *all* the requirements of *both* the actus reus and the mens rea, and D must lack a defence. This is illustrated in **Figure 2.1.**

Figure 2.1   Structure of liability

The separate analysis of actus reus elements, which is the focus of this chapter, has several advantages. Most importantly, it is the physical conduct of D that identifies in time and in location[1] when the offence has taken place. This is why the analysis of a potential offence should always begin with actus reus, as it is only after this that we can then ask if D had the requisite mens rea *at that point.* The actus reus is also the only universal feature of a criminal offence: although offences have been created in the absence of mens rea,[2] there is no liability in the absence of actus reus, there is no 'thought crime'.[3]

Although all offences require some basic ingredient of actus reus, this does not mean that the actus reus is necessarily the most important part of an offence, or even that it must be independently wrongful. In fact, the wrongs targeted by almost all offences can only be clearly demonstrated when actus reus and mens rea elements are brought together. For example, picking up a friend's bag that has been left behind in class will satisfy the actus reus of theft. However, if this is done with the intention of returning the bag it is certainly not wrongful. The wrongs targeted by theft are only established if this conduct is accompanied with an intention to keep the bag, and a dishonest action which is the mens rea of theft.[4] Equally, we may not approve of D if we learned that she was planning to take V's bag in this way with a dishonest intent, but without actually acting on that intention by taking the bag in fact; D again falls short of perpetrating wrongs targeted by the offence.

---

[1] Where the offence takes place is important in relation to jurisdictional issues. Jurisdictional discussion will arise in certain chapters, but is generally not a focus of this book.

[2] See **Chapter 3** and discussion of the voluntary act requirement in particular.

[3] Duff, *Answering for Crime* (2009) Ch5.

[4] Theft Act 1968, s1.

2.2 Separating actus reus and mens rea

Before we explore the elements that form the actus reus, we must first learn to sepa-rate them from mens rea elements. For many offences this is relatively straightforward. Whether you are analysing a statutory or common law offence the task is to separate any offence requirement that is external from D's state of mind (actus reus elements) from anything that is internal to D's mind, *or* concerned with such fault (mens rea elements). For example, case law tells us that the common law offence of murder is committed when D unlawfully causes the death of a person under the Queen's peace with the inten-tion to kill or the intention to cause grievous (very serious) bodily harm.[5] Here, the only part of the offence that is concerned with D's state of mind or fault is her intention to kill or cause grievous bodily harm; this is therefore the mens rea. D's actions and their results—acting to cause the unlawful death of a person—are all matters other than to do with D's state of mind or fault, and therefore represent the actus reus.

However, although these simple rules of separation are capable of consistent applica-tion, this is made more difficult when dealing with terms that appear to include both fault and external requirements.[6] Examples include 'appropriates',[7] 'cultivates',[8] 'aban-dons',[9] etc.[10] Where this is the case, we have two options: separate the fault and external aspects through the use of alternative terminology; or accept that actus reus elements occasionally include aspects that are about the fault or state of mind of D. It is contended that the former approach (separation) should always be preferred. However, this is not the consistent approach of the courts. Below are two examples of terms that could, *and should,* be separated into actus reus and mens rea elements, but are popularly analysed as only one or the other.

- 'Sexual': An actus reus requirement for sexual assault,[11] as well as a number of other sexual offences,[12] is that D's conduct must be 'sexual'. Section 78 of the Sexual Offences Act 2003 states that D's conduct can be sexual (a) 'because of its nature', in the sense that a reasonable observer would describe it as sexual or (b) if its nature may be sexual (external) and the 'circumstances' (external) or 'purpose' of D (fault or internal state of mind) make it sexual. Thus, in the latter case, it seems that the sexual requirement can be spread across actus reus and mens rea elements. However, again, it is more commonly presented as an actus reus element alone.[13]

- 'Dishonesty': One of the main elements of theft[14] and fraud[15] (and many other offences) is the requirement that D acted 'dishonestly', an element that is almost universally

---

[5] *Cunningham* [1982] AC 566. See further *Smith and Hogan's Criminal Law* (14th edn, 2015), Ch4.

[6] Lynch, 'The Mental Element in the Actus Reus' (1982) 98 LQR 109.

[7] **Chapter 9.**

[8] *Champ* [1982] Crim LR 108 and commentary.

[9] *Hunt and Duckering* [1993] Crim LR 678.

[10] Robinson and Grall, 'Element Analysis in Defining Criminal Liability: The Model Penal Code and Beyond' (1983) 35 Stan L Rev 681.

[11] Sexual Offences Act 2003, s3.

[12] **Chapter 8.**

[13] Sullivan, 'Bad Thoughts and Bad Acts' [1990] Crim LR 559.

[14] Theft Act 1968, s1.

[15] Fraud Act 2006, s1.

referred to as a mens rea requirement.[16] However, despite this, the common law definition of dishonesty set out in *Ghosh*[17] contains both external and internal elements: D
acts dishonestly if her conduct would be considered dishonest by the standards of honest and reasonable people (external) and she realises that it would be considered dishonest by those standards (internal).

This kind of imperfect separation of actus reus and mens rea will arise within several of the offences discussed in later chapters. It is far from ideal, and has caused
considerable confusion. However, without a criminal code or some other codified
source setting out the definitions of actus reus and mens rea elements[18] such inconsistency is largely inevitable. It is also, for the most part, an inconsistency that does
not damage the application of the law: D is only liable when every element of actus
reus and mens rea is proved beyond reasonable doubt whether we call them one
thing or the other.

2.3 Actus reus elements

Within the broad category of 'actus reus', it is useful to further subdivide elements into
acts, circumstances, and results.[19]

- **Conduct:** D's physical acts or omissions required for liability.
- **Circumstances:** Facts surrounding D's conduct required for liability.
- **Results:** The effects of D's acts required for liability.

As with the actus reus/mens rea distinction, the further separation of acts, circumstances, and results within the actus reus can be useful when setting out the detail of an
offence. It is also useful to employ this terminology when singling out a particular part
of the actus reus for criticism or comment. As an illustration of how this subdivision
works, consider the offence of criminal damage. The actus reus requires D to have completed certain acts or omissions (conduct element) that cause damage (result element) to
property belonging to another (circumstance element).

2.3.1 The conduct element

The conduct element of the actus reus is concerned with the physical movement of D's
body. The conduct element, therefore, focuses only on the external movement (or, as we
will see, lack of movement) of D's body. This is illustrated in **Table 2.1**.

All criminal offences require a conduct element of some description as it is this element that locates where and when the offence happened. This is also the element that
provides a nexus between D and the other elements required for liability. For example,

---

[16] Discussed in **Chapter 3**.
[17] [1982] 1 WLR 409.
[18] See eg definitions in the US Model Penal Code 1962, §2.02.
[19] Robinson and Grall, 'Element Analysis in Defining Criminal Liability: The Model Penal Code
and Beyond' (1983) 35 Stan L Rev 681.

Table 2.1 Actus reus of the conduct element

	Actus reus	Mens rea
Conduct element	D's physical acts or omissions required for liability	*
Circumstance element	*	*
Result element	*	*

we will soon ask whether the results were *caused by D's conduct element*, and whether D has a certain mens rea *at the time of the conduct element*. Therefore, when assessing potential liability within a problem question, for example, you should always begin by identifying the conduct element of the actus reus: what did D do or fail to do in breach of duty?. All analysis flows from here.

The conduct required for different offences will vary considerably. For example, certain offences require quite specific acts such as penile penetration,[20] or driving.[21] However, it is also common to leave the conduct element unspecified. This is often the case when an offence is seeking to criminalise a certain harmful result no matter how it is caused by D. For example, the actus reus of murder includes *any* conduct that causes the unlawful death of a person; it does not matter if this is hitting, or shooting, or stabbing, etc. The conduct element is still essential to D's liability, it is still the element that links D to the death, but D's method of killing is unspecified within the offence.[22]

Where a conduct element is satisfied in this way by D's positive movements then applying the conduct element is relatively straightforward. However, certain offences are defined in such a way that liability can arise even in the absence, or apparent absence, of[23] movement. There are three main examples.

A) **Omissions liability:** The major exception to any requirement of positive action is liability based on D's omission to act. Offences of this kind are extremely common in the law and in many cases largely uncontroversial.[24] For example, there will be liability for an omission where someone (whether a human or a company) fails to comply with some requirement to register or file documents with the state (eg tax or licences);[25] where a motorist fails to report an accident that she was involved in;[26] or where a

[20] Sexual Offences Act 2003, s1.
[21] In the context of driving offences.
[22] Although the type of conduct may affect the sentence imposed, it will not affect D's substantive liability.
[23] Most examples of liability in the absence of 'action' can be reconciled within a suitably framed definition of the 'action'. See Moore, *Act and Crime* (1993).
[24] This is a problem for those who, like Moore, would prefer to represent omissions liability as a rare and mistaken option for the law: Moore, *Act and Crime* (1993) 22.
[25] See eg Companies Act 1985, s444 (Secretary of State's power to demand documents).
[26] Road Traffic Act 1988, s170(4).

motorist fails to provide police with a specimen of breath when properly instructed to do so.[27] These cases are easy to deal with because the statutory offence tells us what must be done and also that if it is not done a specific crime is committed. However, more controversially, outside these *specific* omissions-based offences many offences can be committed either by movement or omission. For example, the offence of murder is committed where D unlawfully shoots V (movement) with the intention to kill or cause grievous bodily harm; it is also committed where D starves their child (omission of care) with the intention to kill.[28] Where liability is based on an omission, three ingredients must be satisfied:

(a) *Recognised offence*: the offence charged must be recognised in law as one that is capable of being committed by omission.

(b) *Duty to act*: there must be a legally recognised duty requiring D to act in a certain manner.

(c) *Breach of duty*: D's failure to act must fall below the standard expected in the performance of the duty.

More will be said about omissions liability, and we continue this discussion in a separate section later.

B) **Possession offences:** Numerous offences are defined to criminalise the possession of certain dangerous material such as offensive weapons[29] or offensive material such as child pornography.[30] Possession can be reconciled with the language of acts or omissions: D may have acted to gain possession, and the state of possession can be presented as D's omission to dispense of the item possessed.[31] However, it is perhaps more natural to describe 'possession' as a state of affairs where the movement (or non-movement) of D's body is not the crucial factor.[32] Thus, when discussing such offences it is perfectly acceptable to describe the conduct element as a state of possession.

C) **State of affairs offences:** Another category of offences that do not require positive action are called state of affairs or 'situational'[33] offences. Such offences should be treated with caution and can be the hallmark of tyrannical regimes that may attach criminal liability to membership of a certain political party,[34] or even race or religion. However, even within England and Wales, state of affairs offences can be identified. For example, it is an offence under section 11 of the Terrorism Act 2000 to be a member, or profess to be a member, of a terrorist organisation. Other examples include offences of 'being found' in a particular situation, for example the case of *Winzar* and being found drunk in a highway contrary to section 12 of the Licensing Act 1872.

---

[27] Road Traffic Act 1988, s6.
[28] *Gibbins and Proctor* (1918) 13 Cr App R 134.
[29] Prevention of Crime Act 1953, s1.
[30] Protection of Children Act 1978, s1.
[31] Moore, *Act and Crime* (1993) 20–22.
[32] Duff, *Criminal Attempts* (1996) Chs9–11; Husak, 'Does Criminal Liability Require an Act?' in Duff (ed) *Philosophy and the Criminal Law* (1998) 60.
[33] Cohen, 'The Actus Reus and Offences of Situation' (1972) 7 Is LR 186.
[34] *Scales v US*, 327 US 203 (1961) regarding communist party membership.

> **Winzar v Chief Constable of Kent** (1983) The Times, 28 March
>
> D was taken to hospital on a stretcher, but was found to be drunk and told to leave. The police took D to their car on the highway outside the hospital. When on the highway, D was charged with being 'found drunk' in the highway.
> - Divisional Court: guilty of section 12 offence.

In *Winzar*, and other similar cases,[35] it is particularly difficult to represent the conduct element of D's offence as a physical action. As with possession offences mentioned previously, we could focus on D's action (if there was one) in creating the state of affairs, or her omission in failing to remove herself from that state. Indeed, when criticising liability in cases such as *Winzar* reference to actions or omissions may help to highlight a significant problem with the case: the lack of voluntariness in the form of mens rea as to the conduct element.[36] However, again, it seems more natural to describe D's part in the offence without reference to bodily movement. Therefore, it is acceptable to describe the conduct element of these offences in terms of a state of affairs.

> *Terminology...*
> **Note:** In line with the Law Commission and others, we employ the term 'conduct element' to describe the part of the offence that deals with D's physical movements or omissions. However, several statutes (as we will see) prefer the term 'act', even where that term is intended to include omissions liability. Take care with this when reading and interpreting statutes.

2.3.2 The circumstance element

Whatever D's conduct, it will be surrounded by a multitude of external circumstances: surrounding facts that are not performed by D and not caused by D's action. For example, circumstances may include that V is female; V is under 18 years old; a reasonable person would be offended by D's act; V has a heart condition; V is a police officer; etc. Depending on the terms of the offence, these circumstances might be crucial to determining liability, but it should *not* be assumed that all surrounding circumstances are part of the offence. Look at the definition of the offence and identify which circumstances specified within an offence, whether by statute or at common law, are required to be proved to exist at the time of D's potentially criminal act. This is illustrated in **Table 2.2**.

Every criminal offence will include some manner of circumstance element used to focus in on the wrong targeted by the offence. For example, the actus reus of murder is not satisfied simply by conduct causing death unlawfully, D's conduct must cause the death *of a person*; the actus reus of criminal damage not simply conduct causing damage

---

[35] See *Larsonneur* (1933) 24 Cr App R 74 (D was brought into the UK against her will by police, and then charged with landing in the UK illegally contrary to the Aliens Order 1920). See Lanham, '*Larsonneur* Revisited' [1976] Crim LR 276; with response from Smith [1999] Crim LR 100, and Lanham, Letter [1999] Crim LR 683.

[36] Smart, 'Criminal Responsibility for Failing to Do the Impossible' (1987) 103 LQR 532.

Table 2.2 Actus reus of the circumstance element

	Actus reus	**Mens rea**
Conduct element	D's physical acts or omissions required for liability	*
Circumstance element	Surrounding facts that must exist for liability	*
Result element	*	*

without lawful excuse but conduct causing damage *to property belonging to another.* Indeed, every offence will contain certain core circumstance elements: that D is a person, and that D is over the age of criminal responsibility (10 years old).

The above are examples where the relevant circumstances are physical ones such as that property belongs to another. Beyond these examples of physical circumstances it is also possible for offences to require mental circumstances to exist. For example, sexual offences such as rape require D to penetrate V with his penis (conduct) without V's consent (circumstance). In this example, V's mental state is the circumstance element.

Circumstance elements will, of course, vary between offences. For example, despite the central role of consent within many sexual offences, it is irrelevant to murder. V's consent to being unlawfully killed may be a circumstance of D's conduct, but it is not a circumstance element of the offence of murder and thus it has no bearing on D's liability. As we explore offences in later chapters, an important task is to identify from statute and/or common law what circumstances are required because they come within the circumstance element of each offence.

> *Point to remember…*
> **Note:** Sexual offences such as rape provide a useful example of how important circumstances can be to the targeting of a criminal wrong. Sexual penetration in the absence of consent is a serious criminal wrong; yet when the same conduct is done with consent, it is a social good.[37]

2.3.3 The result element

Just as D's conduct will take place in the context of certain circumstances, that conduct is also likely to cause a number of results. For example, when I move my fingers on the keyboard, this results in words appearing on the computer; when I throw a stone at your window, this results in damage to your window; and so on. However, as with the circumstance element in the previous section, when we refer to the result element of an offence we are not referring to every result of D's conduct. Rather, the result element of an offence is only concerned with certain results of D's conduct (and/or exceptionally the conduct of another[38]) that are required for liability, as illustrated in **Table 2.3**. For example, the result

---

[37] The 'moral magic' performed by consent will be discussed in **Chapter 8**.
[38] This is the case, eg, in the context of vicarious liability or secondary liability. See **Chapter 12**.

element of the actus reus of murder is 'death' (D's conduct must cause the death of V): if, in causing V's death, D's conduct also unlawfully harms a bystander and perhaps damages property, these other results are irrelevant to the charge of murder. Such results may give rise to additional criminal charges in their own right but these will be separate from the issue of murder.

Table 2.3 Actus reus of the result element

	Actus reus	Mens rea
Conduct element	D's physical acts or omissions required for liability	*
Circumstance element	Surrounding facts that must exist for liability	*
Result element	Things caused by D's acts required for liability	*

Not all offences require a result element. For example, the offence of perjury applies where D lies in court when giving evidence.[39] In such a case, D's offence includes a conduct element (speaking) and a circumstance element (what she says is a lie; she is giving evidence in court), but nothing needs to result from D's acts. Whether the court is misled, for example, is irrelevant: it is not a requirement of the offence. Other offences of this kind with no result element include the general inchoate offences of attempt, conspiracy, and assisting and encouraging.[40] D is liable for these offences as soon as she gets beyond mere preparation in trying to commit a crime (attempt), agrees with another to commit a crime (conspiracy), or assists or encourages another to commit a crime (assisting and encouraging). In each case, whether the offence tried/agreed/promoted results, or is caused, is irrelevant, D's actus reus focuses on actions and circumstances only.

Some of the most prominent offences in the criminal law, however, will require a result element. For example, murder requires D's conduct to *cause death*; offences against the person are structured around D's conduct *causing various levels of bodily harm*; criminal damage requires D's conduct to *cause damage*; and so on. It should be stressed that, where this is the case, we are not simply asking whether these results came about. Rather, as well as showing that they came about, the result element requires proof that they have been *caused* by D's conduct.

Therefore, whenever an offence includes a result element, this includes the requirement that the result must be causally connected to the conduct of D. There are two stages that must be satisfied to establish causation.

- **Causation in fact:** There must be a logical connection in fact. Thus, if the result would have come about in the same manner regardless of D's conduct, there is no factual causation.

---

[39] Perjury Act 1911, s1.
[40] **Chapter 11**.

- **Causation in law:** A variety of legal principles have developed to limit a finding of causation to conduct that had a substantial affect; was blameworthy; and was not superseded by the subsequent events thereby breaking the chain of causation.

Causation between D's conduct and results will only be found where *both* stages of this test are satisfied. There is considerably more to say about how causation rules operate and this will be continued in a separate section later.

> *Beware...*
> It is common for students to think of causation as a separate issue from the actus reus. This is not correct. Causation is an essential part of the actus reus of any offence that includes a result element. It is the essential link between conduct element and result element.

2.3.4 Separating conduct, circumstances, and results

Although the separation of acts, circumstances, and results provides a useful structure through which to view and discuss the law, it remains controversial. The main problem is that adopting precise and consistent separation of elements is often very difficult.[41]

In the absence of a criminal code or some other codified source setting out the definitions of offence elements,[42] such inconsistency is again largely inevitable. It may be, however, that a lack of consistency can be tolerated. As we discussed in relation to the problems with the actus reus/mens rea distinction, it is important to remember that D's liability requires proof of *every* element of an offence. Therefore, in practice, the criminal law will be unaffected whether we label an offence requirement as act, circumstance, or result; it must still be proved in the same way. The criminal courts rarely engage in this type of analysis, although it is helpful when learning the law and analysing offences. As a device for discussing the law, it is only useful if it represents a reasonably common language: the more difference between interpretations, the less useful the technique becomes.

Below we highlight two areas where the separation of elements has proven to be particularly problematic:

A) **Expanding the conduct element:** In this book, when we refer to the conduct element we will be focusing on the physical movement of, or omission to move, D's body.[43] This is criticised by those who prefer to view action in its social context (eg D's conduct is shooting; not simply moving a finger).[44] However, if we expand the definition of the conduct element beyond a focus on D's body, it is very difficult to know where to stop, for example D's conduct is shooting a person, not simply shooting. Such expansion would undermine the separation of actus reus elements.

---

[41] Buxton, 'The Working Paper on Inchoate Offences: (1) Incitement and Attempt' [1973] Crim LR 656; Buxton, 'Circumstances, Consequences and Attempted Rape' [1984] Crim LR 25; and Duff, *Criminal Attempts* (1996) 12–14.

[42] See eg definitions in the US Model Penal Code 1962, §2.02.

[43] In line with Robinson and Grall, 'Element Analysis in Defining Criminal Liability: The Model Penal Code and Beyond' (1983) 35 Stan L Rev 681.

[44] Duff, *Criminal Attempts* (1996) Ch9.

B) **Expanding the result element:** In this book, when we refer to the result element, we will be focusing only on events *caused* by D's acts. However, there is always a temptation to include circumstances within a discussion of the result element. For example, the academic Moore would include a basic 'moral criterion' that would add further detail (eg the result of sexual assault is not simply sexual contact, but sexual contact with a person).[45] Williams would also add to the result element based on what is 'customarily regarded' within elements.[46] Both approaches lack the necessary precision for maintaining the separation of actus reus elements.

> **Don't be confused...**
> When applying the general inchoate offences (**Chapter 11**) it is essential to use the terminology of acts, circumstances, and result. However, when discussing offences outside this you should only use it if it is useful. For example, if you wish to make a particular point about one part of an offence, then the subdivision can be helpful to identify the part of the offence you mean. However, when making more general points about the law, or summarising the requirements of an offence, it will often be easier and less cumbersome to talk of actus reus and mens rea only.

2.4 Categories of offences

The actus reus of an offence is made up of a combination of actus reus elements: the conduct element; circumstance element; and result element. However, as we have already noted, although all offences will include acts (broadly defined) and circumstances, not all offences will include a result element. Whether an offence includes a result element or not has been used to distinguish two categories of offences.

2.4.1 Conduct crimes

Conduct crimes are so called because they do not include a result element. Examples include perjury, and the general inchoate offences, etc. The actus reus of these offences are complete as soon as D performs certain conduct in certain proscribed circumstances. As there is no result element, there is also no need to apply the rules of causation: D's conduct does not need to cause anything to satisfy the requirements of the offence.

2.4.2 Result crimes

Result crimes, unsurprisingly, are so called because they do include a result element. Examples include murder and criminal damage. The actus reus of these offences is complete when D performs conduct in certain proscribed circumstances, with that action causing a certain proscribed result. As the result must be caused by D's actions, the rules of causation must be applied to these cases. It is common for result crimes to specify certain circumstances and results, but to leave the conduct element unspecified. For

---

[45] Moore, *Act and Crime* (1993) 208.
[46] Williams, 'The Problem of Reckless Attempts' [1983] Crim LR 365, 369.

example, the offence of murder requires the unlawful killing (result) of a person (circumstance), but it does not specify D's act: it must be conduct of D that has caused the result, but it does not matter what this was (eg shooting, stabbing, omitting to feed, etc) as long as the killing was unlawful.

Assessment matters…

All result crimes require D's conduct to have caused the result element. However, your discussion of causation does not need to be equally detailed in every case. For example, in a case where D wounds V by cutting her with a knife, there is no space between conduct and resulting wound. As there is no space in time or proximity between conduct and result, there is little room for doubting the causal connection between the two, and so discussion of causation can be brief. In contrast, where D attacks V and V dies some time later, the gap between D's conduct and the result (death) means that a more extended discussion of causation is required.

2.5 Summary

In the previous discussion we have provided an overview of actus reus (external) elements: acts, circumstances, and results. In later chapters, a significant part of our study will be to identify the actus reus requirements of various offences both from statute and from the common law and to learn how they are/should be applied in practice. Understanding the elements of the actus reus in general terms will help us with both.

The next two sections of this chapter revisit two areas discussed earlier: omissions and causation. It is important to remember the role that these play in the context of the previous discussion. However, as each of them raise a number of important issues, and have attracted significant judicial and academic attention, they require some additional examination.

2.6 Omissions liability

When looking to identify the conduct element of an offence it is always preferable to focus on D's movement as opposed to her omission to move. This is because, aside from a small number of omission-specific offences,[47] D's positive movement will *always* satisfy the conduct element of an offence, with the full offence being completed if the other elements are also satisfied. In contrast, there is reluctance from both courts and the legislature to impose liability for omissions. A common illustration of this reluctance, and one that provides a useful starting point for the discussion of omissions liability, is that *without more* there will be no liability in English law if D watches a child drown in a shallow pool, even if D could easily save the child, and even if D omits to help because she intends the child to die.[48] Of course, if the child had died as a result of D's

---

[47] eg a motorist failing to provide police with a specimen of breath when properly instructed to do so, contrary to the Road Traffic Act 1988, s6.

[48] Ashworth, 'The Scope of Liability for Omissions' (1989) 105 LQR 424.

positive action in these circumstances, D would be straightforwardly liable for murder. However, in the absence of a positive action, D's omission will not satisfy the conduct element of murder and therefore the crime will not be complete.

There are several justifications for this reluctance when it comes to omissions liability.[49] Although we might see D's failure to save the drowning child as morally blameworthy, nevertheless, with limited criminal law resources we may see the conduct of the other party who pushed the child as a more pressing target. Also, whereas a positive action makes it easy to identify the particular defendant who may be liable, D's omission to save is logically one that is shared with everyone else in the world, and so it is difficult to construct laws to isolate particular *criminal* omissions: it creates problems for fair warning, certainty, and coherence. Perhaps the most important reason for reluctance relates to respect for D's autonomy in the sense of her right to peruse person goals without undue interference from the law.[50] Let us imagine that, at any one time, D has 100,000 options when it comes to her movements (go left; right; sit; go to the shops; to work; and so on). When a criminal offence imposes liability for a positive action, D now has 99,999 options: she can act as she wishes, as long as she does not act in the proscribed manner. In contrast, when a criminal offence imposes liability for an omission to act, D has only one option: she must act in the manner required by the offence to avoid liability.[51] Thus, although D's omission may be morally wrongful, the question of criminalisation must weigh D's wrongful omission (favouring criminalisation) against issues of practicality and respect for D's autonomy (weighing against criminalisation). This is illustrated in **Figure 2.2.**

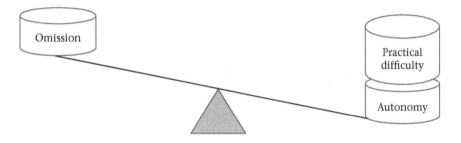

Figure 2.2 Weighing up omissions liability

Therefore, in contrast to liability based on movement, D's omission alone will not be enough to satisfy the conduct element of an offence. However, this is not to say that there is no liability for omissions, it is simply to highlight that for omissions liability to be found further ingredients are required to tip the balance. These include:

(a) D's offence must be capable of commission by omission;

(b) D must have a legally recognised duty to act; and

(c) D must have unreasonably failed to act on that duty.

---

[49] Williams, 'Criminal Omissions—The Conventional View' (1991) 107 LQR 86.

[50] See the discussion of the principle of autonomy at **1.4.3**.

[51] There are, of course, a number of problems with this illustration. However, it serves to highlight (in general terms at least) the core of the autonomy argument.

This is illustrated in **Figure 2.3**.

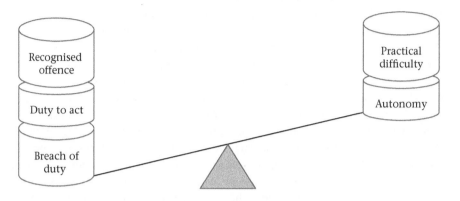

Figure 2.3 Where omissions liability is justified

Therefore, for D's omission to satisfy the conduct element of an offence each of these three requirements must be found. Following this, as long as the other offence elements are also satisfied, D will be liable for the offence.

2.6.1 Offences capable of commission by omission

In certain cases it will be clear from the wording of a statute that an offence can be committed by omission. A clear example is of a motorist failing to provide police with a specimen of breath when properly instructed to do so,[52] etc. However, for the majority of offences including all those discussed in this book, the question of whether an offence can be committed by omission will be a matter of statutory interpretation and case law precedent.

The approach of the courts has not been entirely consistent, and it is difficult to draw definite conclusions. For example, in the case of *Ahmad*,[53] D, who was V's landlord, omitted to undertake essential work that left V's home uninhabitable, with D intending to force V to leave. D was charged with 'doing acts calculated to interfere with [V's] peace and comfort',[54] but found not guilty: 'doing acts' could not be satisfied by omission. However, in relation to other offences, the term 'act' within a statute has not prevented liability for omissions. For example, where D remains motionless in response to sexual touching from a child, it has been held that he commits a sexual offence even where that offence is drafted in terms of D's actions.[55]

In the absence of general rules relating to statutory terms such as 'act', it is now clear that each offence must be assessed individually. This will be done in detail in later chapters but a few illustrations may be useful.

- **Homicide (murder and manslaughter offences)**: It has long been recognised that homicide offences can be committed by omission. For example, in *Gibbins and*

---

[52] Road Traffic Act 1988, s6.
[53] (1986) 84 Cr App R 64.
[54] Protection from Eviction Act 1977.
[55] *Speck* [1977] 2 All ER 859. See **Chapter 8**.

Proctor,[56] a man and woman were convicted of murder on the basis of their omission to feed the man's child (V). They had a duty to feed the child, they breached that duty, and they acted with the intention to cause serious harm thereby satisfying the mens rea of murder.

- **Non-fatal offences against the person:** Employing terms such as 'assault', 'wound', and 'battery', there has been a reluctance to find omissions liability in relation to non-fatal offences.[57] However, liability has been found. For example, in *Santana Bermudez*,[58] D was liable when a police officer, V, was pricked by a needle when searching D who had told the officer that he did not have any needles. This approach is surely correct. With reference to *Gibbins* above, for example, it would be absurd if D was liable for causing death by omission, but would avoid any liability if the police had intervened before V's death at a stage when V would still have been seriously harmed.

- **Property offences:** Again, despite some doubt,[59] omissions liability has been found in relation to certain property offences. For example, in *Miller*,[60] D was convicted of arson when, having inadvertently started a fire, he did not act to try and put out the fire or call for assistance.

As with the previous offences, there appears to be a trend towards accepting omissions liability for an ever greater range of offences. However, this expansion remains controversial.[61] It is also far from complete (eg there is still no liability for offences *attempted* by omission[62]). As such, when applying omissions liability within a problem question, some consideration of whether the offence is capable of commission by omission remains essential.

2.6.2 Duties to act

Having established that the offence charged is one that is capable of commission by omission, the next requirement is that D must have a legally recognised duty to act.[63] It is this duty that narrows the law's focus from *all* those who failed to act (which could be everyone in the world), to isolate those few whose omission can be described as criminal. In this regard, duties are not simply imposed on those who are in a position to help such as those who know about the danger and are able to provide assistance: that approach may seem appealing in order to catch D who watches the child drown for example, but it would also catch anyone who watches an aid appeal on television and chooses not to donate in the knowledge that lives could be saved. Rather, the law will only impose a duty to act in very narrow categories. These include offence-specific duties; contractual duties; familial duties; duties based on the assumption of care; and duties created through endangerment.

---

[56] (1918) 13 Cr App R 134.
[57] **Chapter 7.**
[58] [2004] Crim LR 471.
[59] The Draft Criminal Code, eg, would not have allowed omissions liability for property offences.
[60] [1983] 2 AC 161.
[61] See criticism from Williams in 'Letter to the Editor' [1982] Crim LR 773.
[62] See **Chapter 11.**
[63] See Alexander, 'Criminal Liability for Omissions: An Inventory of Issues' in Shute and Simester (eds) *Criminal Law Theory* (2002) 121.

Unfortunately, despite the importance of these categories, their development within the common law means that outside a few core examples where duties to act have been found within particular cases, considerable uncertainty remains.

> **Beware...**
> A 'duty to act' sounds like, and is often confused with, a 'duty of care'. A duty of care is a tort law concept essential to the tort of negligence, and identifies all those we must take care to avoid harming by our acts and omissions when conducting our lives. Indeed, we will discuss duties of care when we analyse the crime of gross negligence manslaughter in **Chapter 6**, a crime that borrows heavily from the tort of negligence. In contrast, duties to act identify a considerably narrower set of duties where D's liability can be based on an omission. Where a duty to act is found there will always be a duty of care; however, a duty of care will not always indicate a duty to act. Therefore, whenever D's liability is omission-based, a duty to act must be identified.

2.6.2.1 Offence-specific duties to act

Where an offence is specifically drafted to allow for omissions liability, it is straight-forward to identify the duty to act that is created. Statutory examples include section 170(4) of the Road Traffic Act 1988, which makes it an offence to fail (i.e. omit) to report a motor accident in which D is involved. If an accident is not reported, we can say that everyone has omitted to report it. However, the statute creates a special duty on those involved in the accident: only their omission to report is singled out as a potentially criminal omission which will satisfy the conduct element of the offence. There are also examples, albeit rare ones, in the common law. For example, the case of *Dytham* and the common law offence of misconduct in public office.[64]

> **Dytham** [1979] 3 All ER 614
>
> D, a police officer, was charged with misconduct in public office after he failed to intervene in an incident in which V was kicked to death by a nightclub bouncer 30 yards away.
> - Crown Court: guilty of misconduct in public office.
> - Court of Appeal: conviction upheld on appeal.

Offence-specific duties of this kind are unproblematic, but they are also rather nar-row: they apply only in the context of the individual offence that creates them. This contrasts with the duties to act such as familial duties discussed later that can be applied as part of the conduct element in numerous offences.

It is arguable that an offence-specific duty such as those mentioned earlier could be employed to form the conduct element of other offences. For example, what if Dytham omitted to intervene because he desired V to be hurt? In this case we could say that D's duty to act and breach created by the misconduct offence could form the conduct element of an offence against the person, with the additional elements of that offence (showing that D had the required mens rea and that D's omission

---

[64] See also, *AG's Reference (No 3 of 2003)* [2004] 3 WLR 451.

caused the harm) constructed upon it. However, this route has not yet been taken, and it may be that other duties such as contractual duties to act may be more appropriate.

2.6.2.2 Contractual duties to act

Where D has a contractual duty to act, such a duty is also capable of being recognised in criminal law as the basis for omissions liability. Contracts can give rise to duties between the parties where D is contracted to protect V or her property, as well as third parties such as carers and health professionals. Most commonly, as in *Pittwood*, this will involve contracts of employment.

> **Pittwood** (1902) 19 TLR 37
>
> D, a railway crossing gate-keeper, opened the gate to let a cart cross the lines and then went to lunch forgetting to close it again. As a result, a subsequent cart collided with a train, killing the train driver. D was charged with manslaughter on the basis of his omission (contractual duty to close the gate).
> - Crown Court: guilty of gross negligence manslaughter.

Such duties to act, particularly in relation to the caring professions, are now firmly established. However, outside these core examples, uncertainty remains. For example, how strictly will a court adhere to the terms of a contract? If a lifeguard is contracted until 5 pm, for example, is there a duty to act if she spots someone drowning at 5.05 pm as she leaves her shift?

2.6.2.3 Familial duties to act

Core examples where a duty to act has been found between family members include a parent's duty to care for their child (eg *Gibbins and Proctor*,[65] discussed earlier), and between a married couple (eg *Hood*).

> **Hood** [2004] 1 Cr App R 431
>
> D omitted to summon help for three weeks after his wife fell and suffered broken bones. She died as a result. D was charged with manslaughter on the basis of his omission and his familial duty to assist.
> - Crown Court: guilty of gross negligence manslaughter.
> - Court of Appeal: conviction upheld on appeal.

Outside these core examples, however, a lack of case law has (again) led to considerable uncertainty. First, although duties have been recognised between parent and child and between a married couple, it is difficult to predict what other relationships will also give rise to similar duties. For example, if the duty is family-based, will it extend to siblings[66] or extended family? On the other hand, if the duty is based on dependence, which is arguably a more justifiable route,[67] will it extend to unmarried couples or even

---

[65] (1918) 13 Cr App R 134.
[66] There is some indication of this in *Stone and Dobinson* [1977] QB 354.
[67] Fletcher, *Rethinking Criminal Law* (1978) 613.

cohabiting friends?[68] A second layer of uncertainty relates to the boundaries of a duty within a recognised relationship. For example, will a parent still owe a duty to a fully emancipated child over the age of 18,[69] or a wife to her husband if they have been separated although perhaps not yet divorced? Again, it may be better to focus on dependence as opposed to formal relationships, but this simply leads to another question: how much dependence?

2.6.2.4 Duties to act based on an assumption of care

Assumption of care duties will arise when D has voluntarily undertaken to care for V whatever the formal relationship between D and V, in circumstances where V becomes dependent upon that care.[70] A duty to act will arise where the promise of care is explicit, as in *Nicholls*.

Nicholls (1874) 13 Cox CC 75

D, V's grandmother, agreed to take care of V after the death of V's mother. V was neglected by D and died. D was charged with gross negligence manslaughter based on the duty arising from assumption of care.

• Crown Court: guilty of gross negligence manslaughter.

A similar duty will also arise where the promise of care is implicit, as in *Instan*.

Instan [1893] 1 QB 450

D, V's niece, moved into V's house. V became extremely unwell with a gangrenous leg and was unable to look after herself. However, although D continued to live in the house and eat V's food, etc, she did not care for V or summon help. V died and D was charged with gross negligence manslaughter based on the duty arising from an implicit assumption of care.

• Crown Court: guilty of gross negligence manslaughter.

Although the imposition of a duty to act in these cases seems broadly just, assumption of care duties can be problematic. Most importantly, it remains unclear exactly what D must do (or how little) before a duty will arise. For example, cases such as *Ruffell*[71] in which D briefly and unsuccessfully attempted to revive a fellow drug user after an overdose suggest that a duty can arise after a relatively short period of attempted assistance.[72] Equally, *Stone and Dobinson*[73] in which D, of low intelligence, tried ineffectually to assist V before her death suggests that an assumption of care can arise even where D's initial attempts to help V are relatively minor and of little affect. Aside from issues about when this kind of duty will arise, there is also the related problem of when

---

[68] There is some indication of this in *Sinclair, Johnson and Smith* (1998) 21 August, CA.
[69] *Sheppard* (1862) Le & Ca 147 suggests not.
[70] Mead, 'Contracting into Crime: A Theory of Criminal Omissions' (1991) 11 OJLS 147.
[71] [2003] EWCA Crim 122.
[72] This conclusion is muddied by the fact that the court also stresses the close friendship between D and V.
[73] [1977] 2 All ER 341.

it will end. It may be supposed, for example, that D could fulfil the duty by inform-ing the authorities that she will no longer be caring for V, or perhaps if V expressly releases D from the duty.[74] However, without clarifying case law these propositions are far from clear.

Finally, it should be highlighted that a duty to act arising from an assumption of care gives rise to an uncomfortable contrast. D who tries to help V will create a duty to continue acting that can lead to serious criminal liability if breached. Whereas D who does not try to help will not create a duty and will not therefore risk liability. The legal message, it could be said, is not to try.[75]

2.6.2.5 Duties to act based on endangerment

A duty to act will arise where D's previous conduct has created a dangerous situation, as in *Miller*. Having created the danger whether inadvertently or otherwise D must act to try to prevent the harm coming about. Where D fails to act and breaches her duty, the conduct element of the actus reus will be satisfied.

◻ *Miller* [1983] 2 AC 161

D, a squatter in V's house, went to sleep holding a lit cigarette. He awoke to find the mattress smoul-dering, but did nothing save move to an adjoining room. The fire caused extensive damage, and D was charged with criminal damage based on his omission to tackle the smouldering mattress or alert the authorities. The duty arose from his inadvertent creation of a dangerous situation.

- Crown Court: guilty of criminal damage.
- Court of Appeal: conviction upheld on appeal.
- House of Lords: conviction upheld on appeal.

Not only does *Miller* establish a duty to act based on endangerment, but it is also a useful reminder that omissions liability is not restricted to cases of murder and manslaughter. Such offences are over-represented in the case law on omissions simply because the seri-ous level of harm encourages courts to find duties to act, and thereby impose liability, when they may not otherwise have done so. However, it should be remembered that omissions liability is not offence-specific and may satisfy the conduct element of any offence that is capable of being committed by omission.

The *Miller* principle has been extended by the more recent case of *Evans*.

◻ *Evans* [2009] EWCA Crim 650

D, V's half-sister, supplied her with heroin which she self-administered. Realising V showed symptoms of an overdose, D stayed with V but did not alert the authorities for fear of personal liability for sup-plying the drugs. V died and D was charged with gross negligence manslaughter on the basis of her omission to aid V. The duty arose from her creation of a dangerous situation when supplying the drugs.

---

[74] There is some indication of this in *Smith* [1979] Crim LR 251.

[75] If this is the message, it is not indefensible. Eg when D begins to aid V, it may be that others stop helping in view of D's presence and/or that V stops asking for help. Thus, if D's assistance is then stopped, V may be worse off as a result.

- Crown Court: guilty of gross negligence manslaughter.
- Court of Appeal: conviction upheld on appeal.

Although *Evans* is broadly similar to *Miller* with D's duty arising from her creation of a dangerous situation, in *Miller* D's duty to act only arose at the point he became personally aware (subjectively) of the danger he had created. In contrast, within *Evans*, the court stated that the duty would arise when D realises *or should have realised* that the danger was created. Thus, this allows for possible omissions liability even where D did not realise the danger she had created if a reasonable (objective) person would have done.[76] In *Lewin v CPS*,[77] a case that preceded *Evans*, a challenge to the CPS's decision not to prosecute D failed where D had left a heavily intoxicated friend (V) in his car in extremely hot conditions abroad leading to V's death. The court held that D did not owe a duty to V after he had parked his car. However, employing *Evans*, it could now be argued that leaving V in the car created a dangerous situation that D *should have realised*, creating a duty to act and potential liability.

> *Assessment matters . . .*
>
> Within several cases mentioned previously, the courts have discussed more than one possible duty to act. For example, in the case of *Evans* there is discussion of potential duties based on relationship (D was V's half-sister), assumption of care (when D begins to look after V), as well as a duty arising from endangerment. Indeed, in certain cases it is unclear upon which basis the duty has been found (or whether it is found from the combination of possible duties). With this in mind, when answering a problem question, try to highlight all possible duties to act that may give rise to D's liability. Additionally, as these are common law duties, remember the list is not exhaustive: if you cannot find a recognised duty but you think liability should be found, you may wish to highlight the possibility that one of the existing duties may be extended, or the (admittedly rather remote) possibility that a new duty may be recognised.

2.6.3 Breach of duty to act

After it has been established that D's offence was capable of commission by omission, and that D had a recognised duty to act, the next requirement is that D breached that duty. This requirement is useful to focus our minds on an obvious (but easily confused) point about omissions liability: D does not satisfy the conduct element because at the relevant moment she was perfectly still (it is very likely that D will have been moving her body in one way or another); she omits in law because she fails to do what the duty to act requires of her. Thus, to test whether D has breached her duty to act, we must question what the particular duty to act required her to do.

In general terms, the omissions duty obliges D to do what is *reasonable*. What is reasonable is a question for the jury. Thus, for example, in the case of *Miller* it was required that D should attempt to put out the smouldering mattress or contact the fire brigade if this was not possible; in *Evans* to contact the emergency services; in *Dytham* to intervene

---

[76] See Williams, 'Gross Negligence Manslaughter and Duty of Care in "Drugs" Cases: *R v Evans*' [2009] Crim LR 631.

[77] [2002] EWCA 1049.

in the bouncer's attack on V or at least call on other officers for backup. Importantly, the duty to act does not require *more* than is reasonable. For example, if Miller awoke to a roaring inferno, he would not have a duty to charge into the fire and put it out single-handedly. In such a case, there would be a duty to act, but this would probably be simply to call for help. Thus, even where harm is caused, this will not necessarily mean that D has breached her duty to act and the question of breach must always be discussed.

Some confusion, however, should be highlighted. This is illustrated through the case of *Stone and Dobinson*.

> ### *Stone and Dobinson* [1977] 2 All ER 341
>
> D1 (a man of low IQ) and D2 (described as 'ineffectual and inadequate') took in D1's sister (V) to live with them. V suffered from anorexia nervosa which led her to avoid food, eventually being confined to her bed. D1 and D2 made some effort to feed and clean V, and contact a doctor, but eventually stopped. V later died in appalling conditions. D1 and D2 were charged with gross negligence manslaughter on the basis of their omission. The duty was created by voluntary assumption of care.
>
> • Crown Court: guilty of gross negligence manslaughter.
> • Court of Appeal: conviction upheld on appeal.

This case is important because the extremely low functioning of D1 and D2 made it difficult for them to look after themselves, let alone care for V. Therefore, even after a duty to act is found on these facts, it is surely questionable whether D1 and D2 were bound to act given their lack of capacity. If the test is whether they acted reasonably *based on their impaired ability to act*, then it may be that there is no clear breach. However, the little attention given to this question by the court may suggest that the test was rather: did they do what is reasonable based on the standards of reasonable competent people? If the current law is represented by this latter test (the judgment was not clear), then there is potential for considerable injustice. Just as we should not require Miller to act beyond the capabilities of the reasonable man by putting out a house fire single-handedly, surely it is equally unfair to demand things from Stone and Dobinson that are beyond their abilities.

> *Assessment matters...*
> If a scenario akin to *Stone and Dobinson* were to arise in a problem question where D's acts fall below the standards of a reasonable person, but potentially not below a standard reasonable for them, you should apply *Stone and Dobinson* (a reasonable person standard) as the most closely applicable case. However, it would also be useful to highlight in your application that this issue was not directly addressed by the court and that the unfairness it entails may well lead a future court to adopt a different approach at least allowing the reasonable standard to take account of D's physical and mental limitations.

2.6.4 Causation by omission

If it is established that D's offence is capable of commission by omission; that D had a recognised duty to act; and that D breached that duty; then D's omission will fulfil the requirements of the conduct element. Where D's offence is a conduct crime such as a failing to report-type offence, the question then becomes whether D's omission is accompanied by the circumstances and mens rea required for the offence to be complete. However, where D's offence is a result crime such as a homicide offence, it must also be demonstrated that a certain result came about, and that it was *caused* by the conduct element. We discuss causation in detail later. However, it is worth highlighting here the unique issues that arise where D's causing conduct element is an omission.

It is arguable that an omission to act can never cause a result element. The point here is that although D's omission may allow for the result to happen it has not materially contributed to the result any more than D's omission has contributed to every other event that takes place at that point in time.[78] This is not, however, the approach taken by the law and it is clear that an omission can be found to have caused a result element. Although D's omission may not be the only cause and may not even be the most significant cause we will see later that this is not definitive. Further, there is no concern that finding causation here means that D will be liable for failing to prevent and thereby causing all other events taking place at any one time: the restrictive nature of duties to act will have already narrowed D's potential liability to only those events where the law requires D to act.[79]

Therefore, for D to commit a result crime by omission, the causation rules (set out later) must be applied. It should be remembered that although the law has accepted that omissions can cause results, this is not an empty requirement: the Crown must show that it is because D had not acted in line with her duty to act that the result came about and that if she had acted in line with her duty it would not or might not have done. For example, if the duty in *Evans* was for D to call an ambulance as soon as it became obvious that V was suffering a drugs overdose, it must be demonstrated by the prosecution that had she done so V would/may not have died. If, *hypothetically,* V died immediately after self-injecting the drug, then it is highly unlikely that D could have been liable for causing death: even if she had acted in line with her duty (calling for help), V would still have died.

> *Assessment matters...*
> Having established a conduct element through D's omission (relevant offence; duty to act; breach of duty), it is common for students to forget to discuss a requirement of causation. Remember, even if D has omitted in breach of her duty, unless that omission has causally contributed to the result there can be no liability for a result crime.

2.6.5 Distinguishing acts and omissions

In the majority of cases it will be obvious whether D has acted or omitted to act and it will be a case of assessing her liability on that basis. However, there is a grey area between the legal understanding of act and omission that is capable of causing problems. For example, if D and V are playing tug-of-war and D lets go of the rope (causing V to fall and hurt herself), has D acted (letting go) or omitted (stopped pulling)? If a doctor (D) turns off a life-support machine, has she acted (turning off) or omitted (stopped treatment)? And so on.[80]

---

[78] Hogan, 'Omissions and the Duty Myth' in Smith (ed) *Criminal Law: Essays in Honour of JC Smith* (1987) 85. Moore, *Act and Crime* (1993) 267.

[79] Leavens, 'A Causation Approach to Criminal Omissions' (1988) 76 Cal LR 547.

[80] Kennedy, 'Switching Off Life Support Machines: The Legal Implications' [1977] Crim LR 443.

This grey area between acts and omissions is capable of causing problems for the law. It is obviously crucial where the offence charged cannot be committed by omission (eg attempts). However, even where the offence (as is increasingly the case) can be committed by act or omission, it is important to remember that omissions liability is still more restrictive. For example, if D acts by movements to kill V then the conduct element of murder is satisfied immediately. However, if D kills V by omission, the conduct element requires further ingredients: a duty to act and a breach of that duty. Where there is no duty to act, D will avoid liability in the second (omissions-based) example where she would have been potentially liable in the first.

Without a rule of interpretation to guide courts in this area, it seems that the decision whether to classify D's conduct as an act or omission is one that is made on a case-by-case basis. This gives rise to inconsistency. For example, in *Fagan*[81] where D accidentally drove onto a police officer's foot and then rested the car there intentionally D's conduct was interpreted as an action: driving on and staying on the foot rather than an omission to move off the foot. This allowed for straightforward liability without consideration of duties to act. However, where D's behaviour is such that the courts will have a more sympathetic attitude, courts are much more likely to interpret their conduct as an omission. For example, in termination of medical care cases such as *Bland*[82] (doctor's decision to terminate care) and *Re B (A Minor)*[83] (parents' decision to terminate care), it has been held that stopping treatment will be an omission even if it involves acts such as turning off machines, and that such omissions might not breach D's duty where V's best interests are not served by further treatment. The issue here is not whether these cases reached the correct outcomes, but the unprincipled basis upon which those outcomes were reached.[84]

> **Assessment matters...**
> If you are faced with conduct in a problem question that could be interpreted as an act or an omission it will usually be necessary, at least briefly, to consider both options. First, explain that the conduct element could be satisfied if we interpret D's conduct as an act. Then consider the omissions alternative, highlighting whether it is likely that D had a duty to act and breached that duty. Finally, discuss which approach you believe the court is likely to take (considering, eg, the different approaches taken by the court in relation to different classes of defendant).

2.7 Causation

When assessing liability for conduct crimes such as perjury, attempts liability, etc there is no result element and therefore no requirement that it should be *caused* by D's conduct element. In contrast, when assessing liability for a result crime such as homicide offences, criminal damage, etc a result element must be found, and so it is also essential to demonstrate a causal link between D's conduct element and that result.

[81] [1969] 1 QB 439. Discussed further in **Chapter 4**.
[82] *National Health Service Trust v Bland* [1993] 1 All ER 821.
[83] [1981] 1 WLR 1421.
[84] Keown, 'Restoring Moral and Intellectual Shape to the Law after *Bland*' (1997) 113 LQR 481.

If D's conduct element (movement- or omission-based) did not cause the result element, there will be no liability for a result crime.

It is often quite straightforward to demonstrate that D's acts caused a particular result. For example, if D throws a stone at V's window and it breaks there seems to be little dispute: the damage was caused by D's act. In such cases, the judge will direct the jury to simply apply their common understanding of causation. However, in real life (*and particularly in problem questions*), examples may not be this straightforward. For example, what if the window was only broken because the glass was unusually thin? What if D was not aiming for the window, but the stone was caught by a strong gust of wind? What if another stone, thrown by X, would have smashed the glass a split second later, or even made contact at the same time? In such cases, the issue of causation (did D's conduct cause the result?) is likely to be disputed between prosecution and defence. This time, although the judge will again direct the jury to apply their common understanding of causation, the judge will also guide the jury's deliberation with a number of legal principles.[85]

> *Assessment matters...*
>
> The approach of the court should be mirrored in your approach to problem questions. If you are discussing a result crime then causation is essential for liability. However, if causation is straightforwardly satisfied either because D's offence entails no gap between conduct and result[86] or because there are no complicating factors hinted at then there is no need to discuss the full detail of the causation rules. A full discussion of the causation rules, the legal principles developed to assist with difficult cases, are only required where there are (or may be) problems identifying causation.

Legal principles have developed in the common law to assist juries where a common-sense understanding of causation does not provide a clear answer. In doing so, application of the causation rules has become a two-part process:

- **Causation in fact:** Did the result come about because of D's conduct?
- **Causation in law:** Was D's conduct a substantial; blameworthy; and operating cause?

Importantly, the answer to *both* these questions must be 'yes' in order to find causation. We will discuss each in turn.

2.7.1 Causation in fact

Factual causation is always the starting point for a discussion of the causation rules, asking generally whether the result came about because of D's contributory act or her failure (omission) to prevent the result. Another way to express this is through the commonly used 'but for' test:[87] it must be proved that, *but for* D's conduct element, the result would not have come about.[88]

If D's conduct is not a factual cause, as in *White*, there can be no causation.

---

[85] *Pagett* (1983) 76 Cr App R 279. See also *Smith and Hogan's Criminal Law* (14th edn, 2014), Ch4.

[86] See **2.4.2**.

[87] Also referred to as a '*sine qua non*' cause.

[88] The only exception to this rule is where D1 and D2 act simultaneously to cause a result, where either act alone would have been sufficient (eg D1 and D2 both shoot V in the head at the same time). Here, even though we cannot say that either is a 'but for' cause of V's death, factual causation would still be found.

White [1910] 2 KB 124

D put poison in his mother's (V's) drink intending to kill her. V drank some of the poison and died. However, medical evidence demonstrated that V died due to an unrelated heart condition, not because of the poison.

- Crown Court: D was not guilty of murder (result crime requiring causation), but was guilty of attempted murder (conduct crime not requiring causation).
- Court of Criminal Appeal: conviction upheld on appeal.

In *White*, D had completed acts capable of causing death (conduct element of murder), and death came about (result element of murder), but liability for murder failed because of the lack of causation linking D's conduct with the result. The death would have come about in exactly the same way whether D had acted or not: he was not the factual cause. Drawing on our previous stone-throwing example, this would also rule out liability where a stone from X hits and smashes the window a split second before the stone thrown by D. Since the window is already broken and D's conduct has caused no further damage, her conduct has not in fact caused criminal damage.

Although the test of factual causation will rule out liability in these cases, the class of conduct that will satisfy the test is still extremely wide. This is particularly clear in two regards.

- **Accelerating the result:** As long as D's conduct caused the result to come about when it did, she is the factual cause; it is irrelevant if it would have come about later without D's involvement. For example, if V had died as a result of the poison in *White* or D's stone had hit before X's in our criminal damage example, factual causation would be established: the results may have occurred just seconds later without D's involvement, but D is still the factual cause of the result that did come about.[89] This rule holds certain logic, particularly in homicide cases: as we will all die at some point, D can never do more than speed up this process.
- **More than one cause:** Again, as long as the result would not have happened but for D's conduct, it is not necessary to show that D was the only cause. This is illustrated in the case of *Benge*.

 Benge (1846) 2 Car & Kir 230

D, a railways foreman, misread a train timetable when taking up sections of track. A train arrived when the track was up and V was killed. D contended that death could have been avoided if his 'flagmen' (stationed along the track to warn unexpected trains) had placed themselves at the proper distance from the worksite, and also if the train driver had kept a proper lookout.

- Court: D was guilty of gross negligence manslaughter.

In *Benge* it may be that other actors were also 'but for' causes of V's death, and may have been independently liable for it, but this does not undermine the fact that D was a

89 *Dyson* [1908] 2 KB 454.

'but for' cause as well. Unlike the civil law, criminal liability does not seek to apportion blame or look for principal causes: it simply asks whether each defendant individually facing the prospect of liability was a factual cause. In relation to our criminal damage example, this would be the case where D, a 12 year old, is allowed to throw the stone by her father (D2): both D (by her act) and D2 (by his omission to stop D) are factual causes of the damage.

> **Don't be confused…**
> The possibility of multiple causes is particularly important in relation to omissions liability. In such cases, it will often be another party who begins the course of events that will lead to the result, and so there is often at least one other obvious cause. However, this is irrelevant (even if the other cause is V herself[90]). As long as D's omission satisfies the requirements of the conduct element, it is a factual cause if D would have prevented the result by acting in line with her duty to act (the result would not have come about 'but for' her omission).

2.7.2 Causation in law

Although the basic test for factual causation will filter out defendants in cases such as *White*, it must be supplemented with a test for legal causation to avoid an overly broad catchment. For example, where D throws a stone and breaks V's window, she is the factual (but for) cause of the damage. However, we could also say that V is a factual cause if but for V's action in annoying D, D would not have sought revenge and thrown the stone. Similarly, we could say the glass manufacturer is a but for cause: but for their creation of the glass, it would not be there to be damaged and even D's parents might be a factual cause: but for their decision to have children, there would be no D; and so on. The test for legal causation seeks to narrow causation to only those acts that can be *fairly* called a cause in law.

The role and ambition of legal causation is unproblematic. However, unlike the relative objectivism of 'but for' factual causation, any test that is formulated with reference to abstract notions such as 'fairness' is always likely to be controversial. And so it has proved.[91] Through common law case-by-case development, several principles of legal causation have been established. However, such is the inconsistency of their interpretation and application that several commentators have concluded that talk of established principles is misguided, with the so-called principles being used by courts to reach a *desired* conclusion and not as an objective test to find a conclusion.[92] We discuss these principles in the following sections.

2.7.2.1 Legal cause must be 'substantial'

Probably the least controversial principle of legal causation is that D's conduct element must have made a substantial contribution to the result. The term 'substantial' should not, however, imply that D must be the main cause. In fact, as long as D's role is not

---

[90] *Swindall and Osborne* (1846) 2 Car & Kir 230.
[91] Hart and Honoré, *Causation in the Law* (1985).
[92] Williams, eg, describes legal causation as a 'moral reaction': Williams, *Textbook of Criminal Law* (2nd edn, 1983) 381.

de minimis it will satisfy this requirement: D's role must be more than 'slight or trifling',[93] 'negligible',[94] or 'insubstantial or insignificant'.[95]

Having been established as a factual cause of the result, it will be rare that D's conduct will not also be at least more than a *de minimis* cause. However, the fact that D's conduct element is a factual cause will not *automatically* satisfy this requirement. For example, if D pricked V with a pin seconds before he was stabbed to death by X, it is possible to describe D's conduct as a 'but for' cause of death: where V dies of blood loss, D's conduct has caused a slight loss of blood that will have marginally speeded up the time of death. V may have died without D intervention only a split second later, but (as discussed previously) this does not prevent D's conduct being described as a factual cause of the death *at the time it did happen*.[96] It would be similar if D telephoned V, only for V to be startled by the ring and drop a vase:[97] D may not play a major role in the damage, but she remains a factual cause. In each case, we may assume that legal causation will not be found because the role played by D was negligible (*de minimis*).

2.7.2.2 Legal cause must be 'blameworthy'

As well as 'substantial', it has also been held that D's conduct that caused the result must be the 'blameworthy' conduct. This requirement is rarely discussed in case law and often confused by students (*so take care*). When a result crime is created, it is usually attempting to target certain wrongful or blameworthy conduct that leads to a harmful result. For example, criminal damage criminalises D's conduct performed whilst foreseeing the risk of harming another's property (blameworthy) which does so as a result. Gross negligence manslaughter criminalises D's conduct performed in a grossly negligent manner (blameworthy) which causes a death as a result. In each case, as with almost all result crimes, the wrong of the offence (the target for liability) is established by a link not simply between conduct and result, but between blameworthy conduct and result. Thus, it is essential to identify the conduct that has caused the result, and then ask if that conduct was the blameworthy conduct that is the target of the criminal law.

However, in certain cases,[98] it is possible for D to carry out blameworthy conduct which seems to be caught by the definition of an offence ,and to cause a certain result, but for the *blameworthiness* of D's conduct to play no role in bringing the result about. This is illustrated in *Dalloway*.

Dalloway (1847) 2 Cox CC 273

D was driving a horse and cart on a highway, whilst negligently allowing the reins to lie on the horse's back rather than keeping control of them. A small child (V) ran into the road a few yards ahead of the cart and was killed. Even if D had control of the reins, he could not have stopped in time to save V.

• Court: D was not guilty of gross negligence manslaughter.

---

[93] *Kimsey* [1996] Crim LR 35.

[94] *L* [2010] EWCA Crim 1249.

[95] *Cato* [1976] 1 All ER 260.

[96] Perkins and Boyce, *Criminal Law* (1982) 779.

[97] Based on an example from Hall, *General Principles of Criminal Law* (1960).

[98] This can only arise in offences where D does not require subjective mens rea as to the result element. See **Chapter 3**.

In *Dalloway* D was negligent in his driving and, in that sense, his conduct was blame-worthy. He was also the factual cause of V's death. However, his *blameworthy conduct* was not the cause of the death: V would have died even if D was not driving negligently. The crime (gross negligence manslaughter) is seeking to criminalise deaths that are brought about because of grossly negligent behaviour; it is not intended to target deaths (as in *Dalloway*) where D's negligence has no causal effect. Thus, D was not guilty of gross negligence manslaughter. Another example could be the offence of causing death by dangerous driving.[99] Here, again, it is possible for the requirements of 'dangerous driving' and 'causing death' to be satisfied separately but without liability. For example, whilst D is driving dangerously, V jumps from a bridge to commit suicide and lands on D's car. Liability should not arise: as with gross negligence manslaughter, it must be shown that D's dangerous driving (blameworthy act) caused the death, not simply that they both occurred. The cause must be a blameworthy cause.

Although rarely at issue, some debate has recently emerged with regard to offences such as causing death by driving without insurance or without a licence.[100] For example, in *Williams*[101] and *H*,[102] the Court of Appeal found liability for this offence even where the death caused could not have been avoided by D (was not caused by blameworthy conduct). Criticising the court, academics have pointed out that the precedent from *Dalloway* should have been applied to avoid liability.[103] The law has now been clarified by the Supreme Court in *Hughes*, re-endorsing a requirement of blameworthiness.

> ### *Hughes* [2013] UKSC 56
>
> D (driving without insurance and a full licence) was involved in a fatal collision with V. V was entirely responsible for the accident, veering onto the wrong side of the road whilst under the influence of drugs. D was charged with causing death when uninsured and without a full driving licence contrary to s3ZB of the Road Traffic Act 1988.
>
> - Crown Court: D did not cause death.
> - Court of Appeal: appeal allowed, finding liability under s3ZB. The offence is one of strict liability, requiring no mens rea or blameworthiness as to the causing of death.
> - Supreme Court: appeal allowed, restoring the Crown Court decision. Offence requires some more than minimal fault/blameworthiness causing the result.

> *Assessment matters...*
> It should be remembered that for the vast majority of cases, if all offence elements are satisfied, it will be very obvious that the cause was a blameworthy cause. In such cases, you need only highlight that this requirement is satisfied. Only discuss this requirement where the result (although factually caused by D) was in some sense unavoidable, and could/would have happened if D was acting innocently.

---

[99] Road Traffic Act 1988, s1.

[100] Road Traffic Act 1988, s3ZB. Discussed at **6.4.2.4**.

[101] [2010] EWCA Crim 2552.

[102] [2011] EWCA Crim 1508.

[103] Sullivan and Simester, 'Causation Without Limits: Causing Death While Driving Without a Licence, While Disqualified, or Without Insurance' [2012] Crim LR 753.

2.7.2.3 Legal cause must be 'operative'

As well as being substantial (more than *de minimis*) and blameworthy, D's conduct must also be the operative cause of the result. The term 'operative' means that D's conduct must still be a significant cause of the result at the time it comes about; the chain of causation between conduct and result elements must not be broken. For example, where D supplies V with a dangerous drug and V self-injects causing death, D is not the legal cause of the death.[104] D is the factual cause (but for the supply of the drug V would not have died); plays a substantial role (obtaining the drug is a major step on the way to death); and her conduct is clearly a blameworthy cause (she is likely to know that the drug is dangerous); but the conduct of V breaks the chain of causation between D's conduct and the result. It is V's free and voluntary choice to self-inject the drug, and by making that choice V has taken control of the causal chain. This is illustrated in **Figure 2.4**.

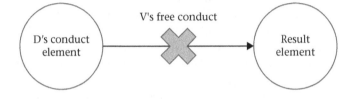

Figure 2.4 Breaking the chain of causation

Breaks in the chain of causation (*novus actus interveniens*) can arise as a result of the subsequent actions of D; natural events; the actions of V; or the actions/omissions of a third party. Each will be discussed.

Lord Hoffmann highlighted in *Empress Cars*,[105] that 'it is of course the causal significance of acts of third parties…or natural forces that gives rise to almost all the problems about the notion of "causing" and drives judges to take refuge in metaphor [eg causal chains] or Latin [*novus actus*].' It is a quotation that highlights two important issues. The first is that cases of this kind arise often in the courts, and certainly more than cases questioning the 'substantial' or 'blameworthiness' of causes. The second is that judges have found these cases particularly difficult. We will see this in our discussion later, with legal principles often applied inconsistently or developed in open contradiction with one another.

Intervention from defendant

It will be very rare for D's own subsequent conduct to break the chain of causation. For example, where D stabs V and then shoots V within the same attack, the second act will certainly not break the chain: all of D's acts will be grouped as a single transaction causing death. The exceptional situation where a break may be found is where D's subsequent acts are part of a separate transaction. For example, D, having wounded V, visits her in hospital and accidentally infects her with smallpox from which she dies.[106]

---

104 *Kennedy (No 2)* [2007] UKHL 38.
105 [1999] AC 22.
106 See *Le Brun* (1991) 94 Cr App R 101, on quite different facts, citing *Smith and Hogan's Criminal Law*.

Here, D's original conduct (wounding) is effectively superseded by the primary cause of death (infection). D remains liable for a wounding offence, but that initial conduct is not the legal cause of the death. We could focus on D's subsequent conduct (infecting) as an alternative conduct element, and this would solve our problems of causation. However, as a new conduct element we would have to find the other elements of the offence (including any mens rea) existing at this new time. In the example given, this may be problematic.

Where rare cases of this kind have arise, it is therefore important to identify the limits of a transaction (a grouping of acts within a single event). This is discussed in more detail in **Chapter 4**.

Intervention from naturally occurring events
Naturally occurring events (or 'acts of God') will only break the chain of causation if they are unforeseen by D and unforeseeable to the reasonable person. For example, if D assaults V and then leaves her on the beach at low tide it is foreseeable that the tide will come in and that V may drown. The natural event (tide) will not break the chain of causation: D's original conduct (assault) is the legal cause of V's death.[107] Equally, if D attacks V (act) and leaves her in a coma, making V more vulnerable to potential infection, any subsequent infection (natural event) that kills V will not break the chain. D's original conduct (attack) is the legal cause of death.[108]

However, where D attacks V and then leaves her in an apparently safe environment, only for V to be killed when struck by lightning, or a falling tree, or caught in a freak earthquake, the unforeseen and unforeseeable event *will* break the causal chain.[109] Here, D remains liable for what he has caused (namely the harm from the initial attack), but cannot be liable in relation to the death. D's original conduct (attack) is not the legal cause of V's death.

Intervention from victim
As with our drugs supply example at the beginning of this section, it is clear that the acts of V can break the chain of causation between D's conduct and the result. Three main principles have emerged from judgments dealing with these cases, they focus on: (A) the foreseeability of V's acts; (B) the voluntariness of V's acts; and (C) the unique vulnerabilities of V. We will discuss each, as well as (D) the apparent inconsistency between them.

A) **Foreseeability:** As with natural events, the foreseeability of the intervention (this time the actions of V) is key to whether that intervention will break the causal chain. For example, if D jumps out and scares V who is perched on a window ledge, and V falls from the window and dies, D is the legal cause of death: V's response in fright leading to a loss of balance is foreseeable. However, if D jumps out and scares V who is sitting on the sofa in her living room, and V then jumps, runs up some stairs to find a window, and then jumps out, it is likely that D's conduct will not be the legal cause of death: V's response was unforeseeable and, to use the language of various cases, 'daft'. The key then, when applying this rule to problem facts, is to identify the tipping point

---

[107] Example from *Perkins* (1946) 36 J Cr L & Cr 393.
[108] *Gowans* [2003] EWCA Crim 3935.
[109] Examples from *Perkins* and Hart and Honoré, *Causation in the Law* (1985).

between reactions of V that are foreseeable which do not lead to a break in the causal chain, and those that are daft that will break the chain. As *Roberts* illustrates, it is clear that courts will rarely interpret V's conduct as daft.

Roberts (1971) 56 Cr App R 95

D, driving V home after a party, began making unwanted sexual advances towards her, threatening her, and touching her coat. V jumped out of the moving car and suffered actual bodily harm. D was charged with assault occasioning actual bodily harm, contrary to section 47 of the Offences Against the Person Act 1861.

• Crown Court: guilty of section 47 offence.

• Court of Appeal: conviction upheld on appeal.

D's conviction in *Roberts* demonstrates the broad interpretation that courts apply to the test of foreseeability. It is also clear that the test will vary in line with V's age, mental capacity, and other circumstances. For example, where V is intoxicated, the court will ask if V's response was within the range of foreseeable responses of an intoxicated person.[110]

B) **Voluntariness:** A principle has emerged (primarily from drugs-related cases) that where, following D's conduct, the result comes about because of V's free, voluntary, and informed act, the chain of causation *will* be broken. D is not the legal cause of the result. For example, if D supplies V with a hammer, and V then uses the hammer to commit criminal damage, D is not the legal cause of the damage: the chain of causation is broken by V's free, voluntary, and informed choice to cause damage. However, at the other end of the spectrum, where D gives V a poisoned apple and V eats it being unaware of the poison, D will remain the legal cause of death: the chain of causation is not broken because, although V acted freely and in some sense voluntarily, when choosing to eat the apple, her actions were not informed. As previously, and as we see in *Kennedy (No 2)*, problems emerge when cases fall between these extremes.

Assessment matters...

Problems emerge for the courts when cases fall between extremes, but these are exactly the cases that help us the most: they indicate the borderline between acts that break the chain of causation and those that do not.

Kennedy (No 2) [2007] UKHL 38

D supplied V with a prepared syringe of heroin. V self-injected the drug and died as a result. D was charged with manslaughter on the basis that his unlawful conduct (drug supply) caused V's death.

• Crown Court: guilty of constructive manslaughter.

• Court of Appeal: conviction upheld on appeal.

• House of Lords: quashing D's conviction on appeal—D was not guilty because he was not the legal cause of V's death.

[110] *Corbett* [1996] Crim LR 594.

Terminology...
Take care when discussing *Kennedy (No 2)*. The precedent that an informed and voluntary act will break the chain of causation is *Kennedy (No 2)*—NOT *Kennedy*.[111]

In *Kennedy (No 2)* D's conduct was not the legal cause of death because V's free, voluntary and informed choice to self-inject the drug broke the chain of causation.[112] This case overruled a number of previous cases that had found liability in these circumstances,[113] and demonstrates a relatively broad interpretation of what is free, voluntary and informed: V's acts were seen as free and voluntary despite his addiction to the drug supplied. For liability to be found in these circumstances post-*Kennedy (No 2)*, it would have to be shown that D participated in the administration of the drug (if the drug is jointly administered then it is not solely the conduct of V and will not break the causal chain),[114] or to focus on D's behaviour after the self-administering to locate an alternative conduct element.[115]

C) **Vulnerabilities:** It is a long-established principle in criminal law, as in civil law, that D must 'take his victim as he finds him'. Where D punches V in such a way that would ordinarily cause no more than minor bruising, but V's 'egg-shell skull' means that V suffers much greater harm and even death, D will be the legal cause of that greater harm: V's unique vulnerability will not break the chain of causation even if unknown to D. The same principle will apply (drawing on our criminal damage example) where D's stone only smashes the window because the glass is unusually thin: D remains the legal cause of the damage. Where, as with these examples, V's vulnerabilities are physical, there is little problem. However, as we see in *Blaue*, the principle is capable of wider application.

Blaue [1975] 3 All ER 446

D stabbed V. V required a blood transfusion to save her life, but refused on religious grounds (being a Jehovah's Witness). V died and D was charged with her manslaughter.

- Crown Court: guilty of manslaughter.
- Court of Appeal: conviction upheld on appeal—V's refusal did not break the chain of causation.

In *Blaue*, following *Holland*,[116] V's refusal of medical care was interpreted as part of her character rather than a separate, potentially intervening, event. Thus, as D must take V

---

[111] In *Kennedy* [1999] Crim LR 65, the Court of Appeal held that D *had caused* V to take the noxious substance despite free and informed consent. *Kennedy (No 2)* arose following intervention from the Criminal Cases Review Commission.

[112] Ormerod and Fortson, 'Drug Suppliers as Manslaughterers (Again)' [2005] Crim LR 819. For an alternative view (supporting liability), see Jones, 'Causation, Homicide and the Supply of Drugs' (2006) 26 LS 139.

[113] Including *Rogers* [2003] Cr App R 10; *Finlay* [2003] EWCA Crim 3868.

[114] *Burgess* [2008] EWCA Crim 516.

[115] eg an omission to assist where D has a duty to do so. See the previous omissions discussion (and *Evans* in particular).

[116] (1841) 2 Mood & R 351. In *Holland*, the state of medical safety at that date made the refusal of treatment potentially reasonable. In *Blaue*, the court clarified that reasonableness is irrelevant.

as she is found, V's refusal could not be a break in the causal chain: D remained the legal cause of death. The question becomes, if V's religious convictions are part of V, what else can be similarly considered? For example, what if V simply did not like doctors, was afraid of needles, or even refused treatment in order to increase D's liability? The *Blaue* precedent opens the *possibility* that V's refusal in such circumstances will not break the causal chain.

D) **Unprincipled:** Having set out these three principles, it should be highlighted that there is a certain tension between them. For example, in *Roberts* we can accept that V jumping from a car is foreseeable. But it also seems to be voluntary (breaking the causal chain as per *Kennedy (No 2)*). It may be that V's act was not voluntary (she was under threat from D), but is this any less voluntary than the consumption of drugs by an addict? Equally, in *Blaue* we could say that V's refusal of a blood transfusion was both unforeseeable (breaking the causal chain as per *Roberts*) and voluntary (breaking the causal chain as per *Kennedy (No 2)*). Perhaps the difference is that V's refusal in *Blaue* was an omission, but this is not clear. The issue here is whether the courts are using the principles to make a decision in line with the rule of law, or choosing between principles in order to justify a prior moral decision about D's culpability.[117]

A useful illustration of this concern is the courts' response to cases where V commits suicide following an attack from D.[118] On the one hand, we have a set of cases where D injures V and then V acts to exacerbate that injury and cause death. For example, in *Dear*,[119] D's conviction for murder was upheld where V intentionally aggravated his wounds that had been inflicted by D. In such cases, V's acts appear voluntary, and they are certainly unforeseeable, but may *perhaps* be justified as an extension of *Blaue*: V is acting (rather than omitting), but D's acts would have caused death anyway if untreated. However, on the other hand, the Court of Appeal has also left open the possibility of finding legal causation where D's acts would not have caused death, with death only resulting due to V's act in committing suicide.[120] Here, V's acts may be described as unforeseeable and voluntary, and do not appear to come within the *Blaue* principle either: it is hard to describe V's future actions as 'part of' V. This is not to say that liability for causing death in such cases would be unfair, where V commits suicide after prolonged abuse (physical or mental) from D there is a strong moral case that D has caused V's death. Rather, the problem is one for the rule of law: are the courts guided by legal principles, or simply by their (subjective) moral intuitions?

Intervention from third parties

We have already discussed the possibility of multiple causes. For example, where D, aged 12, smashes V's window and X (D's parent) allows this to happen in breach of their duty to control D, it may be that both D and X have caused the damage. Where this is the case, both D and X can be independently liable for criminal damage. However, there will also be cases where following D's conduct the result element only comes about because of the conduct of X. In such cases, the acts of X take on responsibility

---

[117] See generally Hart and Honoré, *Causation in the Law* (1985).
[118] Horder and McGowan, 'Manslaughter by Causing Another's Suicide' [2006] Crim LR 1035.
[119] [1996] Crim LR 595.
[120] *D* [2006] EWCA Crim 1139.

for what results and break the chain of causation between D and the result element.[121] For example, where D supplies X with poison, and X then poisons and kills V, D will not be the legal cause of V's death: the causal chain is broken by the acts of X. As in the previous section, the principles of (A) foreseeability and (B) voluntariness play an obvious role in the case law. However, more controversially, (C) the status of X and (D) the type of offence charged also seems to be important considerations.

> **Don't be confused...**
> When discussing the potential intervention of third parties it is important to remember that we are not discussing the liability of X. Rather, we are only discussing the liability of D: if X's acts break the chain of causation, D is not liable; if they do not then D remains the cause and may be liable. The only reason you are discussing X is to ascertain the liability of D. You are not addressing X's liability, but simply whether X's conduct breaks the chain of causation between D and the result.
> Having discussed the liability of D, we may then go on to separately discuss the potential liability of X. The liability of one will have no bearing on the liability of the other.

A) **Foreseeability:** As with the intervention of V, to break the chain of causation the acts of X must be unforeseen by D and unforeseeable to the reasonable person.

B) **Voluntariness:** To break the chain of causation, the acts of X must also be free, voluntary and informed. For example, if D asks X to deliver a cake to V and the cake contains a secret bomb, if X does so, D is the legal cause of V's death: X has not acted in a free, voluntary and *informed* manner. This was illustrated in the case of *Michael*.[122] D, the mother of V sought to kill V by providing X who was V's nurse, with a large dose of poison and telling her that it was medicine for V. The 'medicine' was eventually administered to V by Y, a small child living at the house. Again, despite the acts of both X and Y following from D, there was no break in the chain of causation: the third party acts were not free, voluntary and informed—they did not know it was poison.

C) **Status of X:** When applying these principles, it is clear that the courts will apply different standards depending upon the status of X, the potentially intervening party. This is most obvious where X is a doctor, treating V as a result of D's previous attack. In such circumstances, negligent treatment from X that leads to greater harm will only break the chain of causation if the court considers it 'palpably wrong', and that the injuries inflicted by D are largely healed, as in *Jordan*.

Jordan (1956) 40 Cr App R 152

D stabbed V. At hospital, at a stage when V's wound was largely healed, X (a doctor) administered a large quantity of a drug to which V had shown he was intolerant. The treatment was described as palpably wrong. D was charged with murder.

- Crown Court: guilty of murder.
- Court of Criminal Appeal: allowing the appeal and quashing D's conviction—X's acts broke the chain of causation such that D was not the legal cause of death.

---

[121] *Latif* [1996] 2 Cr App R 92.
[122] (1840) 9 C & P 356.

Jordan demonstrates that the conduct of doctors *can* break the chain of causation, but its potential was narrowed considerably in two later cases of *Smith* and *Cheshire*.

Smith [1959] 2 QB 35

D stabbed V in a fight between soldiers from different regiments. When carrying V to the medical reception, X dropped him twice. Y (a doctor) failed to note that the wound had pierced a lung and provided treatment later described as 'thoroughly bad'. D was charged with manslaughter.
- Crown Court: guilty of constructive manslaughter.
- Court of Criminal Appeal: upholding D's conviction—D remained a legal cause of V's death.

In *Smith*, despite similarly poor treatment from two third parties, D remained a legal cause. The distinction here is that, unlike *Jordan*, the wounds inflicted by D were not largely healed and remained a significant and operative cause of death. Thus, as long as the injury inflicted by D is still ongoing and not 'merely part of the history' leading to injurious acts from X or Y, D will remain a legal cause.

Cheshire [1991] 3 All ER 670

D shot V. In hospital, V was treated and the wounds ceased to be life threatening. However, following a negligently performed tracheotomy by a doctor (X), V's windpipe narrowed and he died. D was charged with murder.
- Crown Court: guilty of murder.
- Court of Appeal: upholding D's conviction—D was still a legal cause of V's death.

In *Cheshire*, unlike *Smith* (but in common with *Jordan*) V's wounds had largely healed at the point of X's negligent intervention. However, despite this, X's acts did not break the chain of causation. The court clarified that the test was not about X's mens rea, but rather whether X's act was 'so independent of [D's] acts, and in itself so potent in causing death, that [the jury] regard the contribution made by [D's] acts as insignificant.' Exactly how 'so independent' and 'so potent' should be interpreted is unclear. However, although the possibility of doctors breaking the chain of causation, as demonstrated in *Jordan*, remains open, it seems that *Cheshire* has further narrowed the already rather narrow circumstances in which it may be found.

To claim that such cases involve foreseeable and involuntary acts on the part of doctors is only possible if those principles are stretched to insignificance. Rather, the courts appear to be acting on the *understandable* basis of policy: D's acts led to V requiring care and so D should take the full consequences if things go wrong.[123] As we see in *Pagett*, it is a policy that may not be isolated to doctors.

---

[123] Although understandable, it may be argued that attempt liability may be more appropriate: punishing D for what she was trying to do rather than maintaining the fiction that her acts achieved that end.

Pagett (1983) 76 Cr App R 279

D, to resist lawful arrest, held V in front of him as a human shield and shot at police (X). X returned fire and killed V. D was charged with the manslaughter of V.

• Crown Court: guilty of constructive manslaughter.
• Court of Appeal: upholding D's conviction—D was still a legal cause of V's death.

In *Pagett*, as with previous cases, we can understand why on policy grounds the courts would not want to say that X's act broke the chain of causation as this would prevent D being liable for a homicide offence. However, in order to achieve this end, the legal principles of causation are compromised. For example, in *Pagett* the court accepted that X's instinctive reaction to return fire was in some sense 'involuntary', as well as holding more generally that acts done in line with a duty to prevent crime would never break the chain of causation.

D) Type of offence: It has become apparent that, as well as special categories of X distorting the principles of causation, there may be a similar issue with certain types of offence.[124] We see this in *Empress Cars* in relation to pollution offences.

Empress Car Co Ltd [1999] 2 AC 22

D, a company, allowed oil to be stored on its site and failed to take precautions to prevent the foreseeable danger that someone would release it into the river. X (an unidentified stranger) released the oil. D was charged with offences related to the pollution of the river.

• Crown Court: guilty of pollution offences.
• Court of Appeal: conviction upheld on appeal.
• House of Lords: upholding conviction—D remained a legal cause.

In *Empress Cars*, despite the presumably free and voluntary act of a third party, the chain of causation was not broken. The House of Lords in *Kennedy (No 2)* has since clarified that the *Empress Cars* precedent is isolated to pollution cases alone. However, in allowing the exception at all, it demonstrates a further erosion of the principles of causation in this area.

Summary

It is important to remember the basic structure of the legal question: is there a break in causation between D's conduct and the results, see **Figure 2.4**.

In order to answer this question, we must then consider the circumstances of the potential break. This is illustrated in **Table 2.4**.

Although these principles should be applied, it is equally important to discuss any potential conflict between principles. In some cases, with reference to academic discussion, it may be useful to think about the outcome you think the court would on policy grounds prefer and then discuss whether the principles of causation will allow for that outcome.

---

124 Padfield, 'Clean Water and Muddy Causation: Is Causation a Question of Law or Fact, or Just a Way of Allocating Blame?' [1995] Crim LR 683.

Table 2.4 Varieties of intervening acts

Type of intervention	Principles
Intervention from D	(1) Will only break the chain if it is part of a new transaction
Intervention from naturally occurring events	(1) Will only break the chain if it is unforeseen by D and unforeseeable by a reasonable person
Intervention from victim	(1) Will break the chain if it is unforeseen by D and unforeseeable by a reasonable person; and (2) will break the chain if it is free, voluntary and informed; (3) but, D must take the victim as he finds him
Intervention from third party	(1) Will break the chain if it is unforeseen by D and unforeseeable by a reasonable person; and (2) will break the chain if it is free, voluntary and informed; (3) but, special categories of third parties and offences will apply different rules

2.8 Reform

With essay-type questions in mind, it is useful to pick up on three major debates that have arisen during the chapter. These include (a) the availability of omissions liability; (b) the role of results within offences; and (c) the extent of the courts' discretion when applying legal causation. We provide a brief overview of each, highlighting potential options for reform.

2.8.1 Omissions

The central debate with regard to omissions is to what extent the law should recognise a duty to act. It will be remembered from the earlier discussion that, unlike acts that will always satisfy the conduct element of an offence,[125] omissions will only do so if: (a) the offence is capable of commission by omission; (b) D has a recognised duty to act; and (c) D has breached that duty. Thus, famously, if D stands and watches a small child drown in a shallow pool she will not be liable for any offence in relation to the death—even if she could easily save the child, and even if she chose not to act because she wanted the child to die. D will only be liable if she comes within a narrow legal category creating a duty to act as, for example, where she is V's parent.

Examples of this kind have led several academics to contend that the narrow categories of duty should be expanded. At its broadest, the extension could include a new

---

[125] The only exception being where the offence can only be committed by omission.

omissions-based 'easy rescue' (so-called 'bad Samaritan') offence of the type seen in several other jurisdictions.[126] This makes it an offence to fail to avert serious harm where such harm could be easily and safely prevented.[127] It would also include a new category of duty to act based in 'citizenship'. In circumstances where we would expect a citizen to act to prevent harm to another (potentially well beyond the easy rescue offence), someone who fails to do so will satisfy the conduct element and may be liable for a number of offences depending upon the harm caused and her mens rea at the time; for example, for murder if she fails to save the drowning child with the intention that it should die.

The case for expanding omissions liability in this manner is put most convincingly by Ashworth.[128] For Ashworth, the current approach to omissions, which he terms the 'conventional view', falls into two main errors. First, it assumes a moral difference between acts and omissions that is not there. In certain cases an omission may be more culpable than an act. For example, consider V1 who is caught in a house fire when D1 then fails to press a button to set off a sprinkler system that would save V1; and contrast that with D2 who, seeing that V2 will die in considerable pain, and with no way to rescue, shoots V. Who is more culpable? In many cases it will be difficult to determine if D has acted or omitted as where D releases his grip of the tug-of-war rope: is that acting to let go or omitting to hold on?[129] Secondly, Ashworth contends that the autonomy argument against omissions liability is misconceived. Although omissions liability restricts the options of D more than act-based liability,[130] bearing in mind that a duty will only arise in exceptional circumstances where V is in considerable danger, and bearing in mind the low expectation of D, overall autonomy is respected: not to rescue will severely restrict V's autonomy (through injury) and D will also benefit from the potential for similar assistance in the future. He terms this the 'social responsibility view'. Alongside these points, drawing on our earlier discussion of duties to act, there may also be a benefit in terms of fair warning.[131] Under the current law there are a number of duties to act, but in each case the law is very unclear as to the boundaries of when the duty arises. As a result, D has to wait until after the event to find out if the court will identify a duty or not. It could be argued that a more general citizenship duty would be fairer,[132] clearer and simpler: warning that omissions liability is possible whenever D unreasonably fails to act.

The arguments against such an expansion, effectively supporting the status quo, are numerous. They are also usefully summarised by Glanville Williams who in response to Ashworth, defends the conventional view.[133] Central again is the autonomy

---

[126] Including France and a number of US states: Ashworth and Steiner, 'Criminal Omissions and Public Duties: The French Experience' (1990) 10 LS 152.

[127] The specified level of potential harm to V and the ease of D's potential acts both vary between jurisdictions.

[128] Ashworth, 'The Scope of Criminal Liability for Omissions' (1989) 105 LQR 424.

[129] See **2.6.5**.

[130] See discussion of this at **2.6**.

[131] See **1.4.1**.

[132] Cobb, 'Compulsory Care Giving: Some Thoughts on Relational Feminism, the Ethics of Care and Omissions Liability' (2008) 39 Cam LR 11.

[133] Williams, 'Criminal Omissions—The Conventional View' (1991) 107 LQR 86.

argument: whereas act-based liability stops D pursuing one course of action, omissions liability stops her pursuing *all* courses of action that are not the action required to avoid liability. Beyond this, there are also a number of other concerns. First, despite the occasional counter-example, it is contended that omissions are less culpable than actions: D is not making the world worse; she is *merely* failing to make it better. Secondly, and following from this, if the criminal law has limited resources (both in detection and punishment) it should focus on acts as the most blameworthy conduct. Thirdly, Williams contends that a citizenship duty', or specific offence of failure to rescue, would be too uncertain with no common standard of social responsibility to provide fair warning of when people may become liable for their omissions.

2.8.2 Results

One of the most interesting tensions within the criminal law is found between subjectivism (focusing on D's individual culpability) and objectivism (focusing on the harms caused by D's conduct).[134] When discussing the result elements, this tension is readily apparent. On one side, results are central to liability because they usually represent the harm caused by D (objectivism); but on the other side, they are almost redundant because they are not fully controlled by D and are therefore an imperfect reflection of her culpability (subjectivism). The current law represents an *often uncomfortable* compromise between the two.

Starting with the subjectivist approach, the logic of this position is simple. Let us imagine that D1 shoots at V1 with the intention to kill. Meanwhile, D2 shoots at V2 with the intention to kill. If D1 kills V1, but D2 does not manage to kill V2 (because, eg, she is saved by doctors), the difference between D1 and D2 is simply a matter of luck. And, as luck is not a reflection of D's culpability, both D1 and D2 are equally culpable and should be punished in the same way.[135] Indeed, on this basis, *all* result crimes could be remodelled into 'acting with intent' conduct crimes: focusing liability on what D controls (ie her acts and her mens rea) and not being distorted by luck.[136] The subjectivist position can be seen in several areas of the law. For example, where D attempts to commit an offence intending to commit it, but not completing the result element the same maximum sentence will generally[137] apply to the attempt as to the principal offence attempted.[138]

An objectivist approach, in contrast, contends that *results matter.*[139] Although D1 and D2 in our example have performed the same acts, our reaction to them will be very

---

[134] See **1.4.**

[135] Ashworth, 'Belief, Intent and Criminal Liability' in Eekelaar and Bell (eds) *Oxford Essays in Jurisprudence* (1989); Ashworth, 'Taking the Consequences' in Shute, Gardner, and Horder (eds) *Action and Value in Criminal Law* (1993); Ashworth, 'Defining Offences Without Harm' in Smith (ed) *Criminal Law: Essays in Honour of JC Smith* (1987). See also Alexander and Kessler, *Crime and Culpability* (2009).

[136] Although this is the logical conclusion of a subjectivist approach, few academics would support this extreme.

[137] The only exception is attempted murder, where there is a discretionary (as opposed to mandatory) life sentence.

[138] Criminal Attempts Act 1981, s4.

[139] Moore, *Placing Blame: A General Theory of the Criminal Law* (1997); Moore, *Causation and Responsibility* (2009).

different: we condemn D1 for her acts *and* for causing the death of V; we condemn D2 for her acts, but we are relieved that death did not result.[140] Results are therefore perceived as an additional wrong for which D is responsible. It is also contended that holding D1 responsible for the additional wrong is not punishing her on the basis of luck. As Duff makes clear, 'if I [behave in a particular way] with the intention of bringing X about…I have control over X's occurrence in that it depends to a significant degree on me and on what I do; X will not ensue if I do not [behave in that particular way].'[141] The objectivist position can also be seen in several areas of the law. For example, when we discuss the non-fatal offences against the person in **Chapter 7**, it will be seen that a ladder of offences is used to label and punish D principally with reference to the seriousness of the harm inflicted upon V. An objectivist approach can also be seen in the absence in this jurisdiction of any general offence of reckless endangerment.[142] If D acts with the intent to cause harm she may be liable for attempt; but if she acts merely foreseeing the risk of harm even where this is sufficient mens rea for the principal 'result-based' offence she will not be liable for a general endangerment offence where the result does not come about.[143]

2.8.3 Causation

The causation rules dictate the required connection between the conduct and result elements of a result crime: D's conduct must cause the result in fact (but for test) *and* in law (significant, blameworthy, and operative). As we have seen earlier, the development and application of causation rules within the common law has been and remains highly problematic. In response, several alternative approaches have been advanced.

Hart and Honoré, for example, suggest an alternative based on a distinction between what they term 'normal' causal conditions such as environmental factors (not legal causes) and 'abnormal' causal conditions such as voluntary intervention which will constitute legal causes, and may also break the chain of causation if performed by another.[144] There is much to commend this approach, but it may be that the central distinction remains too vague and subjective to perform the objectifying role intended. Another alternative can be taken from a 2002 Law Commission Criminal Team working paper on causation. The Commission set out its proposals in the form of a draft Bill.

(1) Subject to subsections (2) to (5), a defendant causes a result which is an element of an offence when—

    (a) he does an act which makes a substantial and operative contribution to its occurrence; or

    (b) he omits to do an act, which he is under a duty to do according to the law relating to the offence, and the failure to do the act makes a substantial and operative contribution to its occurrence.

---

[140] Duff, *Criminal Attempts* (1996) Ch4.
[141] Duff, *Answering for Crime* (2007) 63.
[142] Duff, 'Criminalising Endangerment' in Duff and Green (eds) *Defining Crimes* (2005).
[143] The English law contains several specific endangerment offences (eg speeding offences), but no general offence (eg attempt) to catch reckless endangerment beyond these.
[144] Hart and Honoré, *Causation in the Law* (1985).

(2) (a) The finders of fact may conclude that a defendant's act or omission did not make a substantial and operative contribution to the occurrence of a result if compared with the voluntary intervention of another person, unless:

    (i) the defendant is subject to a legal duty to guard against the very harm that the intervention or event causes; and

    (ii) the intervention was not so extraordinary as to be unforeseeable to a reasonable person in the defendant's position; and

    (iii) it would have been practicable for the defendant to have taken steps to prevent the intervention.

  (b) The intervention of another person is not voluntary unless it is:

    (i) free, deliberate and informed; and

    (ii) performed or undertaken without any physical participation from the defendant.

(3) (a) The finders of fact may conclude that a defendant's act or omission did not make a substantial and operative contribution to the occurrence of a result if compared with an unforeseeable natural event;

  (b) A natural event is not unforeseeable unless:

    (i) the defendant did not foresee it; and

    (ii) it could not have been foreseen by any reasonable person in the defendant's position.

The substance of the Commission's proposals is largely a reflection of the current law, and so it would do little to resolve many of the uncertainties discussed earlier. However, it may be that codification of the basic structure of causation would have advantages: creating a settled base for the law and, equally importantly, a settled terminology. However, as the Commission has not taken these proposals forward, reform of this kind is unlikely in the near future.

> **Beware...**
> This is the first time (of many) that we have quoted a draft Bill from the Law Commission. Remember that these do not represent the current law and you should not apply them as if they do. Rather, they are reform suggestions and should be discussed only in this context.

2.9 Eye on assessment

This section sketches a structure for analysing the actus reus of an offence when applying the law in a problem-type question. Drawing on the structure outlined at the end of **Chapter 1**, we are focusing on the first part of 'Step 3'.

> **STEP 1 Identify the potential criminal event in the facts**
>
> This should be simply stated (eg 'The first potential criminal event arises where D kicks V). The role of this stage is to highlight which part of the question you are answering before you begin to apply the law.

> **STEP 2 Identify the potential offence**
>
> Again, state this simply (eg 'When breaking the vase, D may be liable for criminal damage'). The role of this stage is to highlight which offence you are going to apply.

> **STEP 3 Applying the offence to the facts**
>
> Having highlighted a possible offence, Step 3 requires you to both identify the actus reus and mens rea of that offence, *and* apply them to the facts.

Step 3 will probably require most analysis within a problem question (although Steps 1 and 2 should not be forgotten). It includes the identification and application of both actus reus elements and mens rea elements. This should always begin with the actus reus: the actus reus of an offence locates it in time and space and provides a base from which to ask if D had the required mens rea *at that point*. Our analysis of actus reus requires us to answer two (deceptively) simple questions.

(1) What is the actus reus of the potential offence?

(2) Did D complete the actus reus (did she do it)?

The answer to these questions will vary between offences (question 1) and between factual scenarios (question 2). The answer to the first question will be discussed in relation to each offence covered in this book: gleaned from a combination of statutory and common law sources. However, the structure of application (question 2) is common between offences and can be usefully introduced at this point through **Table 2.5** which shows the stages of analysis.

Table 2.5 Applying the actus reus to problem facts

Actus reus	
A) Conduct element: what did D physically do?	Although there is some flexibility in stages B and C, application of the actus reus should always begin with the conduct element. This is because you need a conduct element before you can ask if the required circumstances were present *when D acted* or omitted, and whether *D's acts* or omissions caused the result. Your analysis of the conduct element will vary between conduct and result crimes.
	Conduct crime: conduct crimes (offences not including a result element) will usually specify a particular act or omission that D must have done. The question is therefore simple: did D do it?
	Result crime: result crimes are a little trickier because you are usually looking for any (non-specific) conduct that caused the result. Where D performs several acts and omissions, you may have a choice of potential conduct elements. When choosing between them, *always* look for an action of D as opposed to an omission. This is because, if you focus on an omission, you must show the additional requirements (relevant offence; duty to act; breach of duty).

	Only focus on D's omission if: D has not acted (eg *Gibbins and Proctor*), D acted but there is an obvious problem with mens rea at that point (eg *Miller*), or D acted but there is an obvious problem with causation from that conduct (eg *Evans*). If you are forced to move on to consider omissions liability in this manner, always tell your reader the reason you are forced to do so. If there is no problem with finding liability based on D's acts, there is no need to consider her omissions as well (eg if D shoots V intentionally, then fails to get medical help and V dies—there is no need to consider D's omission to get help).
B) Circumstance element: were the required circumstances present?	All offences (conduct and result crimes) include circumstance elements (eg that D does not own the property damaged for criminal damage). Remember, when asking if these requirements are satisfied, the question is whether the circumstance is present *at the time of the conduct element*.
C) Result element: did D's conduct element cause the required result?	This will only be required, of course, for result crimes. This part of your analysis has two parts. First, you have to ask if the result (whatever is specified in the offence) actually happened. Secondly, you must ask if it was caused by D. Having identified the conduct element (act- or omission-based) that is most likely to have caused the result, you must now apply the causation rules (factual and legal causation) in relation to that conduct element. Thus, if D has acted but you have chosen to focus on her omission (eg because the act was involuntary), your question is whether her omission caused the result.

To illustrate this structure, take the facts of *Miller*:[145] D fell asleep with a lit cigarette, awoke to find it smouldering on the mattress, but simply left the fire to spread rather than attempt to put it out or summon help. The potential criminal event here relates to the damage to the property (Step 1) and the most likely offence is arson (Step 2). Arson is discussed in **Chapter 9**, but the actus reus essentially requires D to damage another person's property by fire.[146]

When applying this, our first task is to identify the conduct element. As D has set fire to the mattress we should begin here. However, it is apparent that this act is not a suitable conduct element: although it causes the damage, it is done when D is asleep and is not accompanied by mens rea. Therefore, we must look for an alternative conduct element. In this case, the alternative arises when having realised the danger when he wakes up D fails to try and prevent further damage. At this point D is most likely to have the mens rea for the offence. Focusing on this point, D's conduct element is an omission. As an omission, liability will require D's conduct to satisfy additional requirements: arson must be capable of commission by omission (*Miller* shows that it is), D must have a duty to act (D has created a dangerous situation and therefore has a duty to try an mitigate that danger), and D must have breached that duty (a reasonable person would be

---

145 Discussed at **2.6.2**.
146 Criminal Damage Act 1971, s1.

expected to try and put out the fire or summon help; by doing neither, D breaches his duty). D therefore satisfies the conduct element of criminal damage.

Having identified the conduct element, the next question is whether D's omission caused damage (result) to the property of another by fire (circumstance). It is clear from the facts that the fire does damage the property of another, so our focus turns to the causal relationship between this damage and the omission of D. Applying the causation rules, it is evident that D's omission is a factual cause of the damage: but for D's omission to take reasonable steps, the fire would not have spread and caused such extensive damage. D's omission was a blameworthy cause (he chose not to act despite foreseeing the danger), it was a substantial cause (certainly more than *de minimis*), and it was an operative cause (there were no events or other actors that could have broken the chain of causation). Therefore, the actus reus of arson is satisfied.

Assessment matters...

In this example, the bulk of our discussion related to the conduct element of the actus reus. This is because the facts of *Miller* present a challenge when locating a suitable conduct element, but are quite straightforward when it comes to circumstances, results, and causation. In another example, the conduct element may be straightforward and there may be more discussion of other elements. It is important in your answer not to miss out any stages in the analysis, but you need only discuss issues in detail where there is some uncertainty.

ONLINE RESOURCE CENTRE

www.oxfordtextbooks.co.uk/orc/smithandhogan/

This chapter is accompanied by a selection of online resources to help you with this topic, including:

- **Multiple choice questions**
- **Chapter summary sheet**
- Two **sample examination questions** with answer guidance
- **Further reading**

Also available on the Online Resource Centre are:

- A selection of **videos** from the authors explaining key topics and principles
- **Legal updates**
- Useful **weblinks**

3

Mens rea

3.1 Introduction

The Latin term 'mens rea' is loosely translated as 'guilty mind'. Where the actus reus of an offence focuses on D's conduct, the results of that conduct and the circumstances in which it takes place (external elements), the mens rea focuses on what is going on in D's mind (internal elements): did she *intend* to do it; *believe* it would happen; *foresee a risk* it might happen; did she know of the circumstances; what did she believe the circumstances were and so on. Other fault terms such as negligence are also included within this category.

As with our discussion of actus reus, it should be remembered from the outset that these terms (actus reus and mens rea) are terms of art. The ambition of the criminal law is to define *offences* which are combinations of actus reus and mens rea elements that criminalise wrongful events.[1] However, the separation of actus reus and mens rea elements is helpful when discussing and applying the criminal law, and is almost universally adopted by the courts as well as within academic writing. The liability of D will always require the ingredients set out in **Figure 3.1**.

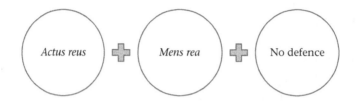

Figure 3.1 Elements of criminal liability

3.1.1 Identifying mens rea elements

If the actus reus/mens rea distinction were strictly applied, then the identification of mens rea within a statutory or common law offence would be straightforward: any requirement external to D's state of mind or fault would be an actus reus requirement, and anything internal to D's state of mind or fault would be a mens rea requirement. This remains a useful rule of thumb. For example, the common law offence of murder criminalises D who unlawfully causes the death of a person under the Queen's peace (external actus reus requirements), with the *intention* to kill or cause serious bodily harm to a person (internal fault based mens rea requirements).

However, as we have already discussed in the context of the actus reus, the precise labelling of external requirements as actus reus and internal requirements as mens rea is not always as consistent as we might hope. There are certain offence requirements that are *internal* to the mind of D and yet are traditionally referred to as part of the actus reus; as well as requirements that are *external* to the mind of D and yet are traditionally referred to as part of the mens rea.[2]

A useful terminology has developed to make sense of this distinction.

- **Subjective mens rea:** The term 'subjective' is used to indicate a mens rea requirement that is looking to the mind of the individual D: something that is internal. For example, criminal damage requires a mens rea of recklessness as to the causing of damage.[3] To satisfy this mens rea, the prosecution must prove that D personally foresaw a risk of damage: it is not enough to show that she should have done, or that a reasonable person would have done. Our focus is the mind of D. That is a subjective mens rea requirement.

---

[1] See discussion at **1.1.1**.
[2] See discussion in **2.2**.
[3] Criminal Damage Act 1971, s1.

- **Objective mens rea:** The term 'objective' is used to indicate a requirement that is *not* looking within the mind of D; it is looking externally, but is still concerned with D's state of mind in general terms, and is still analysed as part of the mens rea. For example, certain offences require proof that D was 'negligent'. Although a state of negligence is commonly referred to as a mens rea state, it does not focus on D's mind. Rather, to prove negligence the prosecution must show that D's conduct dropped below the standards expected of a reasonable person in her position. To have acted in this manner it is likely that D's personal state of mind is in some manner blameworthy, but this need not be demonstrated in order to prove negligence.

> *Don't be confused...*
>
> Looking within the mind of D is, of course, impossible for a jury considering subjective mens rea requirements. A jury can also only speculate as to what a reasonable person would do in a case of objective fault. Therefore, the jury are likely to consider objective factors when they apply either type of mens rea (eg asking themselves whether they would have foreseen the risk if they were in D's shoes). However, there is still an important difference between the two. This difference becomes clear in cases where the jury believe that D's state of mind was or may have been different from that expected of a reasonable person. For example, let us consider the foresight of damage where the jury believe a risk of damage would have been obvious to a reasonable person.
>
> - Objective test: the fact that it was obvious to a reasonable person is definitive. D satisfies the offence requirement without needing to consider whether she actually foresaw it or not.
>
> - Subjective test: the fact that the jury think it would have been obvious to a reasonable person is evidence that may encourage the jury to think that D also foresaw it. However, if they believe D that (for whatever reason) she did not foresee it at the time, or they have a reasonable doubt on the issue, the offence requirement will not be satisfied.

Identifying the mens rea of an offence is not, therefore, a case of surgically separating internal from external requirements. Rather, it is a case of identifying those offence requirements that are focusing, in general terms, on D's state of mind or fault, whether these are subjective or objective requirements.[4] In more practical terms it is also about learning the vocabulary of mens rea terms that have developed in the common law (eg 'intention'; 'recklessness'; 'malice'; 'knowing'; 'belief'; etc), and looking to pick them out from the definition of an offence.

A final point to remember, when identifying and applying mens rea elements, is that your task is not a moral one. The term mens rea may imply some kind of moral evaluation in terms of *guilty* mind and the law *is* seeking to criminalise wrongful or guilty behaviour. However, the absence of moral fault should not affect how you identify and apply the law in practice: if D's behaviour is within the definition of the law's requirements for mens rea D is caught by the offence and her conduct is still criminal. Discussion, if any, of the morality of her action is relevant only to a critique of the law.

---

[4] An alternative terminology that seeks to make a similar distinction has been to label subjective mens rea as 'mens rea', and objective mens rea as 'fault'. Unfortunately, this approach is not consistently applied by courts or academics, with 'mens rea' and 'fault' often used interchangeably to mean the same thing. Therefore, it is not employed in this chapter. Eg the Law Commission consistently employs the term 'fault element' as a simple substitute for 'mens rea'.

For example, where D kills V at V's request, and in order to relieve V from some manner of incurable illness or painful condition, it is popularly referred to as a 'mercy killing'. For many people, the actions of D in these circumstances by causing the death of V, with her mental state of intending to kill would not be considered wrongful or guilty. However, since she has satisfied the actus reus of murder by acting unlawfully to cause death and she does so with the mens rea of murder, intending to kill or cause grievous bodily harm, and she has no legal defence, she has committed the offence of murder. We may criticise the law and say that the offence should not apply in these circumstances (this is a reform discussion), but this will not affect the application of the *current* law: the elements of the offence are satisfied.[5]

> **Extra detail...**
> The same logic underpins the classical maxim that 'ignorance of the law is no excuse'. If D satisfies the actus reus and mens rea and has no defence she has committed the offence: it is irrelevant to her liability if she or anyone else considers what she did to be morally justifiable (as with mercy killers) and it is irrelevant whether she knew what she was doing was a crime.

3.1.2 The role of mens rea elements

When offences are created in an attempt to criminalise wrongful behaviour, if the offence focused only on the conduct of the accused it would be a rather blunt weapon. Actus reus elements can define harmful conduct and/or consequences, such as causing death, causing damage, taking another's property, etc, but such wrongs or harms alone will not necessarily justify punishing D and labelling her as a criminal. Rather, before we can fully blame D for what she has done, it is often necessary to know whether she meant to do it; knew the risk it would happen; should have known the risk; and so on. This is the role of the mens rea of an offence. Compare the following examples in which D shoots and kills V:

(a) D1 shoots V1 intending to cause death;

(b) D2 shoots at a shooting range target. V2 is (unknown to D) hiding behind the target.

In both examples, D1 and D2 have completed the actus reus of a homicide offence: their action has unlawfully caused the death of a person. However, the difference between their states of mind (D1 intending to kill; D2 knowing nothing of V2) means that our reaction to the two events is likely to be very different. D1 has killed intentionally and we therefore blame her for the death, we want her to be punished and to prevent her from acting in this manner again. D2, on the other hand, has simply shot at a target, with the death of V2 following as a terrible accident. Here, rather than blame D2 we are more likely to feel sorry for her, as someone having to live with the consequences of the accident, and we are much less likely to want to stop her doing the same thing again. her conduct was not blameworthy: there is nothing wrong with shooting at a target on a gun range.

---

[5] See *Kingston* [1994] 3 WLR 519: liability was found despite D only committing the offence due to the wrongful actions of others.

The way the law distinguishes these events is through mens rea requirements. D1 has committed the offence of murder, she has unlawfully killed a person *with the intention to kill or cause serious harm.*[6] D2, in contrast, is unlikely to have committed any offence: a terrible result may have occurred (the death of V2), which is the same result caused by D1, but D2 lacks the mens rea for a homicide offence.

Extra detail…

If we think back to the principles of criminalisation discussed at **1.4**, these would (predominantly) support the current law in criminalising D1 and not D2.

- Fair warning: a warning not to kill by accident could only be heeded by stopping doing anything potentially dangerous. As such activities are common and often beneficial (eg driving), this would not be a useful message. A warning not to kill intentionally avoids such problems.

- Fair labelling: our different moral reactions to the conduct of D1 and D2 means that they should not be labelled in the same way.

- Autonomy: criminalising D2 where she does not choose to kill, or even to risk the death of V, would not respect her autonomy.

- Welfare: a focus on welfare may encourage us to look at the objective results (death in both cases) ahead of mens rea. Thus, such an approach may favour the criminalisation of D1 and D2.

When thinking about the role of mens rea, and the construction of offences, we should not fall into the trap of seeing mens rea in terms that are too simplistic. The difference between D1 who intended to kill and D2 who had no knowledge of V2 is quite straightforward; and we can appreciate the role of mens rea to catch D1 within an offence and to exclude D2. However, these examples are at the very clear ends of what is otherwise a rather murky spectrum. For example, what if, when D shot V:

- D did not want to kill V, but recognised that she was virtually certain to do so, for example because she saw V standing behind the target;

- D did not want to kill V, but recognised that there was a risk she might do so, for example because of her bad aim?

- D did not know V was behind the target, but only because she failed to check the target as the gun range staff had informed her to do?

In these examples, D does not intend to kill or cause serious bodily harm to V in the conventional sense because she was not shooting in order to bring that result about.[7] However, we may still want to find liability for murder, or some other homicide offence. Thus, the mens rea of an offence must define which states of mind within the spectrum will be enough to satisfy the particular offence and which will not. To do so, the common law has developed a rich language of mens rea terms including 'intention', 'knowledge', 'belief', 'recklessness', 'negligence', 'dishonesty', and many more. Much of this chapter will be spent discussing what each of these terms mean so that you can understand their legal meaning when they are used within an offence and apply them to problem facts.

---

[6] *Cunningham* [1982] AC 566.
[7] See discussion of intention at **3.4.1**.

3.2 Mens rea in context

Although most of this chapter will be spent discussing the legal meaning of the central mens rea terms (eg 'intention'; 'recklessness'; etc), it is first important to introduce how these terms work in the context of a whole offence. The actus reus of an offence can be viewed independently: we can ask whether D unlawfully caused death; damaged another's property; had non-consensual intercourse; and so on. However, this is not the case with mens rea terms. Although we will, following our discussion later, understand what each mens rea term means, and will be able to spot them in the definition of an offence, on their own the terms are useless. For example, if you heard that a friend, D, had hurt one of your other friends, V, it would be natural to ask D what she was thinking. If D answered simply 'intention' or 'recklessness', this would be entirely unhelpful: even understanding the terms, they need context to provide any assistance. It makes no sense for D to intend, for example, in the abstract. However, if D were to explain that she 'intended to hurt V' or 'meant to' or realised her actions 'might hurt V' then this tells us a lot.

The same is true with the mens rea of an offence. Mens rea terms carry the same meaning across different offences: 'intention' in relation to murder means the same as 'intention' in relation to theft.[8] However, what must be intended in each case will be very different: in murder D must intend to kill or cause GBH; in theft D must intend to deprive V permanently of the property. The mens rea relates to the elements of the actus reus for the offence in question.[9] Take the offence of simple criminal damage set out in **Table 3.1**.[10]

Table 3.1 Criminal damage

	Actus reus	**Mens rea**
Conduct element	Any act (or omission) that causes the result	Voluntary
Circumstance element	The property damaged belongs to another	Intention or recklessness
Result element	Damage or destruction	Intention or recklessness

If we were to state the mens rea of criminal damage it would not be accurate to say that D must 'intend or be reckless': these words alone tell us nothing. Rather, we should say that D must 'intend or be reckless as to causing damage to another's property'. Or, if it was necessary to be more precise, we could state the mens rea required in relation to each element or the actus reus (as set out in the table).

As with criminal damage, most offences require some mens rea to correspond with each element of the actus reus. In such cases, as long as you know what the mens rea

---

[8] There are, however, unhelpful exceptions to this within certain offences: Stark, 'It's Only Words: On Meaning and Mens Rea' (2013) 72 CLJ 155.

[9] See also the discussion of the correspondence principle in **Chapter 4**.

[10] Criminal Damage Act 1971, s1.

terms mean (discussed later), and as long as you know which element of the actus reus they correspond with, then you will understand the mens rea of the offence. However, there are two exceptions to this rule: two categories of offences where mens rea will not correspond with every element of the actus reus. Each requires some introduction.

3.2.1 Strict liability: actus reus with no corresponding mens rea

Certain offences are constructed to require actus reus elements with no corresponding mens rea. This can arise in two different ways, each of which will be discussed in **Chapter 4**.

A) **Strict or 'absolute' liability 'offences':** There are some offences in which the only fault element is that D's acts must be voluntary, but beyond this no mens rea is required as to any other element of the offence. Offences of this kind are usually dealing with regulatory matters and attract limited punishments to reflect the lack of mens rea. An example would be D selling defective products or failing to observe regulatory formalities in her business, etc.[11] Since these offences punish D for things that happen (actus reus) without regard to D's choices in bringing those things about (D's state of mind), they are criticised as lacking respect for the principle of autonomy.[12] These are commonly called absolute offences.

B) **Strict liability elements:** Much more common are offences which require mens rea as to certain actus reus elements but not to all. Where mens rea is not required as to an element of the actus reus, it is said that liability for that element is 'strict'. Offences of this kind are generally less controversial than absolute offences where no mens rea is required as to circumstances *and* results. Nevertheless, strict liability remains problematic: liability is still possible in the absence of choice as to an essential part of what D is being blamed for.

3.2.1.1 The presumption in favour of mens rea

Although strict liability is common within many criminal offences, its controversial nature means that it must be obvious in the drafting of an offence if that is what was intended by Parliament. Where an offence sets out a certain actus reus and is simply silent as to mens rea, there is a *presumption* that mens rea will required as to that element. As stated in the House of Lords:

> the test is not whether it is a reasonable implication that the statute rules out mens rea as a constituent part of the crime—the test is whether it is a *necessary* implication.[13]

In the case of K,[14] D was charged and convicted of the (now repealed) offence of indecent assault,[15] an offence that criminalised sexual touching with victims under 16 years old.

---

[11] Baldwin, 'The New Punitive Regulation' (2004) 67 MLR 351. See also Law Commission, *Criminal Liability in Regulatory Contexts* (Consultation 195, 2010).

[12] See **1.4.3**.

[13] *B (A Minor) v DPP* [2000] 2 AC 428.

[14] [2002] 1 AC 462.

[15] Sexual Offences Act 1956, s14 (repealed).

One element of the actus reus was that V was under 16. The offence did not state that D had to 'know' or 'intend' or be 'reckless' about that element of V's age. The statute was silent. The lower courts interpreted that element as strict: if V was under 16 it did not matter what D's state of mind about V's age was. However, the House of Lords held that the presumption of mens rea should be applied. It was for the prosecution to prove that D lacked mens rea as to V's age even where the terms of the offence in the statute were silent as to its requirement.

If statutory offences were carefully drafted explicitly to set out every actus reus and mens rea requirement then the presumption of mens rea would be unnecessary. Unfortunately, as we will discuss in later chapters, this has never been the case with criminal legislation where political compromise, or simple oversight, will often result in ambiguous and incomplete definitions. Therefore, a presumption of mens rea is useful to ensure such oversight does not result in overly broad legislation that criminalises D without due respect for the principle of autonomy. However, the presumption can be problematic. For example, despite the sweeping language of the House of Lords in *B* and *K*, the courts have not always been consistent in their application of the presumption.[16] Further, although it is generally accepted that the presumption will require a mens rea of at least recklessness,[17] this *rather important detail* is rarely made explicit in the case law.[18]

3.2.2 Ulterior mens rea: mens rea with no corresponding actus reus

Ulterior mens rea, which is more commonly termed 'ulterior intention', describes a mens rea requirement that does not correspond to an act, circumstance, or result element of the actus reus. For example, to be liable for the offence of theft, D must appropriate the property of another (actus reus) dishonestly and with the intention to permanently deprive V of that property (mens rea).[19] Here, the requirement that D must 'intend to permanently deprive V' is an ulterior mens rea requirement: D must intend something (permanent deprivation) that does not have to actually happen for the offence to be committed, something that is not part of the actus reus of the offence.

Where we see ulterior mens rea within offences, the mens rea standard that is invariably required is intention (hence the common use of the term 'ulterior intention'). However, this is not always the case. For example, section 1(2) of the Criminal Damage Act 1971 criminalises D who destroys or damages property (actus reus) intending or being reckless as to whether any property would be destroyed or damaged, *and* intending or being reckless as to whether the life of another would be thereby endangered (mens rea). The second part of this mens rea, that D must be reckless as to the

---

[16] Horder, 'How Culpability Can, and Cannot, Be Denied in Under-Age Sex Crimes' [2001] Crim LR 15. See also, *Brown (Northern Ireland)* [2013] UKSC 43.

[17] *G* [2008] UKHL 37. This is also the level of mens rea preferred within the Law Commission's 1989 Draft Criminal Code, cl20.

[18] See eg *Tolson* (1889) 23 QBD 168, which talks ambiguously of states of mind that can make wicked acts into innocent ones.

[19] Theft Act 1968, s1.

endangerment of the life of another constitutes ulterior mens rea even though intention is not required. D must be at least reckless as to the endangerment of the life of another, but it is irrelevant whether another's life is endangered in fact as endangerment is not part of the actus reus of the offence. The requirement that D must be recklessness is a mens rea standard (as we will see later) that is clearly different from intention.[20]

3.2.3 Conclusions from mens rea in context

In **Chapter 2** we concluded that, when identifying the actus reus of an offence, it can be useful to identify the separate elements of which it is made up: the conduct element, the circumstance element, and for result crimes the result element. In general terms, the same approach should be taken when identifying the mens rea of an offence. Thus, in most cases the mens rea can be discussed broadly (eg the mens rea for murder is the intention to kill or cause grievous bodily harm). However, where necessary, the mens rea of an offence can also be discussed more precisely as it relates or corresponds to each element of the actus reus, as set out in **Table 3.2**.

Table 3.2 Elements of an offence

	Actus reus	**Mens rea**
Conduct element	Any physical acts or omissions required for the offence	Any mens rea required as to D's acts or omissions
Circumstance element	Any factual circumstances required to exist for the offence	Any mens rea required as to those facts or circumstances
Result element	Any consequences of D's action/omission required for the offence	Any mens rea required as to those consequences
Ulterior mens rea element	*	Any mens rea required as to something that is not part of the actus reus

3.3 Voluntary act requirement

When identifying the mens rea of an offence, we are generally looking to find which mens rea term (eg 'intention', 'recklessness', 'negligence', and so on) is required of D in relation to each element of the actus reus. For example, the offence of battery is committed by D who makes non-consensual contact with V (actus reus). Corresponding to the actus reus requirement of 'contact' is that D must (mens rea) have intended or been

[20] Child, 'The Structure, Coherence and Limits of Inchoate Liability: The New *Ulterior* Element' (2014) 34 LS 537.

reckless as to contact. The same pattern is repeated when discussing potential mens rea as to circumstances, results, and ulterior mens rea.

However, this is not the case with the conduct element. Whether we are discussing D's movement or omission to move her body, it is not intuitive to think of D desiring to move; believing she is moving; foreseeing a risk of moving; etc. In short, the standard mens rea terms defined and discussed later are inappropriate. Rather, for the conduct element of the actus reus, it is more common to inquire as to the 'voluntariness' of D's movement or omission to move.[21] Just as *all* offences, whether conduct or result crimes, include a conduct element within their actus reus,[22] so in (almost) all cases must this conduct be voluntary.

> **Don't be confused...**
>
> As the standard mens rea terms are inappropriate to describe the mens rea that corresponds with the conduct element of the actus reus, and because of the near universal nature of the voluntariness requirement, this requirement is often in fact described as part of the actus reus as opposed to the mens rea.[23] However, this is not the approach preferred within this book. Just as we attempt to separate internal and external offence requirements in relation to circumstances and results, the same approach can also be useful with the conduct element (for reasons of consistency if nothing else). The only difference with regard to the conduct element (as opposed to circumstances and results) is that we only ever have to apply a single mens rea term: voluntariness.

3.3.1 The test for voluntariness

This is the mens rea requirement for the conduct element of every offence. There is a great deal of philosophical and neurological debate as to the meaning of 'voluntary action'.[24] However, although this debate will influence and inform a legal definition, where possible the courts prefer to use terms in their 'natural' or 'everyday' meaning, and this is certainly easier when directing a jury. The test of voluntariness, then, is simply whether D had control over her movement, or omission, at the time of acting.

In a majority of cases it will be obvious that D's movement or omission to move—what we can conveniently call D's conduct element—was voluntary. This will be the case where D has considered her options before acting, as well as cases where D acts instinctively in a fight, for example. In fact it is so unlikely that D will not have control of her body that within the criminal law there is an established presumption that she is acting voluntarily. Rather than the prosecution having to prove that D's conduct was voluntary in every case, it will be *presumed* that D's conduct was voluntary unless D can produce evidence to suggest that it was not. It is only when D has discharged this evidential burden of proof that the prosecution will then have to prove beyond reasonable doubt (the criminal standard of proof) that D's acts were in fact voluntary.[25]

---

21 Some courts and academic writers refer to an 'intention' to move. Where this is the case, they mean simply the same as voluntary movement.

22 See **2.3.1**.

23 See **2.3.1**. See, for support of the actus reus approach, Patient, 'Some Remarks About the Element of Voluntariness in Offences of Absolute Liability' [1968] Crim LR 23.

24 Moore, *Act and Crime* (1993), and references therein.

25 See **1.1.6.1**.

A claim, by the defence, that D's conduct was involuntary can take several forms. Most obviously, this will be the case where D was unconscious or semi-conscious as, for example where D broke an object whilst sleepwalking. However, this need not be the case. For example, if D moves her arm—for example, to stab V—because X is pushing D's arm, then D's conduct will not be voluntary and she will not be liable for an offence. The same is true where D omits to move, for example by failing to save her child because she is physically restrained from doing so by X. Equally, if while driving D acts on reflex because she is attacked by a 'swarm of bees' or a 'malevolent passenger',[26] her driving will not be voluntary. Similarly, if D strikes V while suffering from a 'spasm' or 'convulsion',[27] again, liability will fail because D has not acted voluntarily. The only exception to this is that D cannot claim to have acted involuntarily if the reason for her lack of control was self-induced as, for example, where D voluntarily became intoxicated or through her own fault as where she was driving when tired and fell asleep.

> **Don't be confused…**
> Where D claims to have acted involuntarily, she is attempting to avoid liability by denying an element of the offence (mens rea as to the conduct element). However, because the presumption of voluntary movement places an evidential burden on D to provide some evidence of involuntariness, claims of this kind are more commonly referred to as defences: the defences of automatism and insanity. Therefore, we will discuss this issue (including the exception where D's lack of control is self-induced) in more detail in **Chapter 13**.

3.3.2 The role of voluntariness

When discussing the actus reus we explained that the conduct element represented a basic ingredient of every crime: we can only blame D for harmful results because they were caused by her act, and for circumstances because they were present when she acted. Thus, with all responsibility and liability flowing from D's actions, the requirement that this action should be at least voluntary is fundamental to the law's respect for D's autonomy. Even where the offence charged is a strict liability offence where no mens rea as to circumstances and results is required, we can at least say that the basic ingredient of action was one that D must have chosen. As stated by Hart, 'unless a man has the capacity and fair opportunity to adjust his behaviour to the law, its penalties ought not to be applied to him.'[28]

What makes people object so strongly to the few 'absolute' offences which do not even require voluntary action is that they conflict with the fundamental role played by voluntariness within the principle of autonomy. For example, it was an offence under the Aliens Order 1920 for D to be found in the UK when leave to land in the UK had been refused. This was the charge in *Larsonneur*.

---

[26] Examples from *Bell* [1984] 3 All ER 842.
[27] Examples from *Bratty v AG for NI* [1961] 3 All ER 523.
[28] Hart, *Punishment and Responsibility* (1968) 181.

> **Larsonneur** (1933) 24 Cr App R 74
>
> D was ordered to depart from the UK and travelled to the Irish Free State. However, she was then arrested and brought back to the UK against her will. Having been brought back to the UK, she was then charged with the offence of being found in the UK contrary to the Aliens Order.
>
> • Court: guilty of the offence. The offence does not require D's presence to be voluntary.

Larsonneur is already slightly exceptional because it involves one of the few offences where D's conduct is not straightforwardly based on movement or an omission, but rather on a status (being found).[29] However, the real problem with liability in this case is not the actus reus, but rather the lack of a voluntariness requirement attached to it: D is liable for being found in the UK even though her presence is not voluntary. Despite extensive criticism of the case and the offence, however,[30] *Larsonneur* was followed by the more recent case of *Winzar v Chief Constable of Kent*,[31] and there is nothing in principle to prevent Parliament creating other offences of this kind in the future.

Despite this discussion, however, it is probably better to see exceptional offences of this kind, which do not include a voluntariness requirement, as unwelcome anomalies within the law. They should not be allowed to distort or distract our more general analysis. The requirement that D's conduct element must be performed voluntarily is all but universal within the criminal law, and certainly common between *all* of the offences discussed in the later chapters of this book.

Thus, although the actus reus of the conduct element will vary in detail between different offences, the mens rea for this element will always be the same. This is illustrated in **Table 3.3**.

Table 3.3 Mens rea of the conduct element

	Actus reus	**Mens rea**
Conduct element	Any physical acts or omissions required for the offence	Voluntariness

Assessment matters...
As D's acts are presumed in law to be voluntary, unless D provides some evidence to rebut this presumption, the issue of voluntariness will not be discussed by the court. Likewise, when you are applying the law to problems facts, you do not need to consider the issue of voluntariness unless there is some indication that D's acts or omissions may be involuntary. If you are told, for example, that D hates V and runs over and stabs her, it would be unnecessary (and rather odd) to begin a discussion about whether D's motion to stab might have been a reflex or spasm. In contrast, if you are told (for example) that the stabbing happened whilst D was suffering from some kind of fit, then a discussion of this kind would be important.

---

[29] See **2.3.1**.
[30] See eg Horder, *Excusing Crime* (2004) 251.
[31] (1983) The Times, 28 March.

3.4 Mens rea terms

Although there is only a single mens rea term to apply for the conduct element (voluntariness), the standard of mens rea required for other elements will vary greatly between offences. These include, but are not limited to, 'intention', 'knowledge', 'belief', 'recklessness', 'negligence', and 'dishonesty'. The relationship between elements is set out in **Table 3.4**.

Table 3.4 Mens rea of the other offence elements

	Actus reus	Mens rea
Circumstance element	Any factual circumstances required to exist for the offence	Any mens rea required as to those facts or circumstances
Result element	Any consequences of D's action/omission required for the offence	Any mens rea required as to those consequences
Ulterior mens rea element	*	Any mens rea required as to something that is not part of the actus reus

To understand the mens rea of an offence, it is therefore necessary to identify: (a) which mens rea terms (eg intention, etc) are used within the definition of the offence; (b) which part of the actus reus they are referring to (eg D must intend a result); and (c) what that mens rea term means. The first two of these tasks were previously discussed generally, and will be discussed in relation to various offences in the later chapters. The third task will be undertaken in the following sections.

The criminal law has developed a rich and varied vocabulary of mens rea terms. In the sections that follow, we will set out the most important of these terms and discuss their meaning. Our aim is to clarify these terms so that when they arise in later chapters you will be able to understand them, and then to apply them in context. However, before we begin this discussion, there are three important points that should be borne in mind.

A) **Mens rea terms are interpreted consistently between offences:** Despite the occasional *and regrettable* exception,[32] the general rule is that each mens rea terms can be defined independently of the offence in which it arises. There is one definition of intention and one of knowledge, etc and every time any offence uses those terms that same definition is the one to apply. The meaning of the mens rea terms does not change depending upon the offence context.

B) **The criminal law is concerned with the legal definition of mens rea terms:** Although this sounds obvious, it is very easy to allow our common non-legal understanding of terms such as 'intention' and 'recklessness' to cloud our reading and understanding of their legal definitions. As we will discuss later, there is a consistent effort

---

[32] Stark, 'It's Only Words: On Meaning and Mens Rea' (2013) 72 CLJ 155.

to align legal and non-legal definitions, particularly with the needs of jurors' understanding in mind. However, whereas it is acceptable for vague definitions to be used in everyday discourse, in the legal context the definitions need to be precise and consistently applied: the definitions distinguish criminal from non-criminal conduct and hence make the difference in serious offences between prison or liberty. In an effort to provide this rigidity, legal definitions depart from non-legal understandings in several areas. Remember, to understand and apply the law you must learn and apply only these legal definitions.

C) **Mens rea terms are (for better and for worse) defined by the common law:** Where mens rea terms are codified within a criminal code or other statute, there is an opportunity to set out a limited number of terms within a clear and defined hierarchy. We see this in the US Model Penal Code 1962, for example,[33] as well as within the 1989 Draft Criminal Code for England and Wales.[34] However, the current law in England and Wales in this area remains uncodified, with mens rea terms defined almost exclusively within the common law. There are two main consequences of this. First, the definition of mens rea terms is not fixed, but rather a matter of precedent between courts. In relation to each term, we will see that definitions have changed over time, and are not necessarily settled in their present state. Secondly, we do not have a fixed list of mens rea terms. Here, we will discuss the most commonly used mens rea terms, but in later chapters we will occasionally encounter other mens rea terms that have been developed by the courts.

3.4.1 Intention

Intention is the most serious standard of mens rea, demonstrating the greatest culpability and the greatest blameworthiness.[35] It can be satisfied in either of two rather different ways:

- **Direct intention:** D intends something in law if she acts with a *purpose* or *aim* towards it. So, if the actus reus requirement is a circumstance element (eg, that property belongs to another), D intends it 'directly' where she acts with the purpose or aim that it should be present. Where the actus reus requirement is a result element, D acts with direct intention towards it if her purpose or aim is that it should be caused by her action. Importantly, for direct intention, whether she thinks it is likely or not is irrelevant. The leading case defining direct intention is *Moloney*.[36]

- **Oblique intention:** D intends an actus reus requirement (whether circumstance or result) 'obliquely' where it is (i) virtually certain to arise; (ii) she recognises that it is virtually certain; and (iii) the jury find that this recognition amounts to an intention. The leading case defining oblique intention is *Woollin*.[37]

Despite their differences, it is important to remember that both direct intention and oblique intention are simply alternative definitions of the same mens rea term: intention.

---

[33] US Model Penal Code 1962, §2.02.

[34] Law Commission, *A Criminal Code for England and Wales: Report and Draft Criminal Code Bill* (No 177, 1989) cl18. See also *Smith and Hogan's Criminal Law* (14th edn, 2014) Ch5.

[35] See generally Lacey, 'A Clear Concept of Intention: Elusive or Illusory?' (1993) 56 MLR 621.

[36] [1985] AC 905.

[37] [1999] AC 82.

Where an offence has a mens rea of intention, this requirement can be satisfied by *either* direct or oblique intention.

> **Don't be confused...**
> The mens rea for most serious offences can be satisfied by intention or recklessness. One of the few exceptions to this is murder where D must act with the intention to kill or cause serious harm (reck-lessness is not enough). As a result, you will notice that most of the cases defining intention tend to be murder cases: as only intention will suffice for this offence, it is particularly important to know where its definition starts and ends. Remember, however, that the definition of intention derived from these cases is not isolated to murder and will apply wherever the term is used.

3.4.1.1 Direct intention

Direct intention is relatively uncontroversial. In line with common understanding, it holds that D intends something if it forms part of her purpose when acting (a purely internal, subjective requirement). Such intention does not require premeditation or planning, but it must be present at the time of action. For example, D smashes V's vase in retaliation for V scratching her car. Here, D commits criminal damage with intention as to both circumstance and result elements:

- D directly intends the result element of the offence (damage) because she acts in order to cause damage;
- D directly intends the circumstance element of the offence (that the property belongs to another) because she hopes that the property belongs to V.

An alternative way of expressing direct intention, promoted by Duff,[38] is to think about success and failure. Employing this approach, we can say that D directly intends the damage because her enterprise would be a failure if the vase was not damaged. Equally, she directly intends that the vase should belong to V because, if it did not, her enterprise would be a failure.

In most cases, as with the vase example, direct intention is also synonymous with 'desire'; that is, D intends to damage the vase if she desires to damage the vase. However, this is not always true. In certain cases D may directly intend an offence element as a *means to an end* even though she does not specifically desire it. For example, if D kills her mother in order to obtain her inheritance we can say that she acts with the direct intention to cause death. D may not desire the death of her mother, she may be very sad afterwards, but the death is an essential means to her desired ends: the inheritance. Using Duff's language, D directly intends to kill her mother because she will only succeed (her actions will only lead to the gaining of inheritance) if she causes death: if she does not cause death, her enterprise has failed. The same would be true, for example, where D burns down V's house in order to see her reaction. D directly intends to cause damage by fire, thereby satisfying the mens rea for arson, because even if she does not desire the fire in its own right, she intends it as a necessary means to a desired end: seeing V's reaction to the burning house. This interpretation of intention is confirmed in *Hyam v DPP*,[39] where Lord Hailsham states that intention clearly includes 'the means as well as the end'.

---

[38] Duff, *Intention, Agency and Criminal Responsibility* (1990).
[39] [1975] AC 55.

Very importantly, *unlike oblique intention discussed in the following section*, direct intention is not affected by the foreseen likelihood of success. For example, in law we would say that D, a hopeless darts player, throws a dart *intending* to hit a treble 20 even though D knows that she is very likely to fail; it is still her direct intention. This will also apply to our examples earlier. Thus, if D throws V's vase in order to damage it, it is her direct intention to cause damage even if she knows that the vase is very solid and is unlikely to be broken. Where D thinks that the vase may be hers, and not belong to V at all, she still directly intends that it belongs to another if she hopes that it belongs to V. Equally, if D tries to gain inheritance by shooting her mother, but knows that she is a bad shot or that V may be out of range, or that the gun may not fire, etc, she still directly intends to kill as a means to an end.

3.4.1.2 Oblique intention

When the courts are dealing with offences that require a mens rea of intention (eg murder), the 'golden rule' for directing a jury is to avoid any elaboration on the meaning of the term unless it is truly necessary.[40] Thus, the jury are left to apply their common understanding of 'intention' that is likely to be broadly in line with the definition of direct intention given earlier. However, where a finding of direct intention is unlikely, it will (exceptionally[41]) be necessary to direct the jury so that they can apply a legal definition of intention that includes oblique (or indirect) intention.

> *Assessment matters...*
> This is the same approach you should take when discussing a requirement of intention in a problem question. Always start with direct intention. If D directly intends the offence element then there is no need to consider oblique intention. Only consider oblique intention if there is some doubt as to D's direct intent.

By the oblique intention approach D can intend an offence element even where it is not her purpose or aim, and even where it is not a means to a separate purpose or aim. Oblique intention involves assessing three questions which are similar whether intent relates to results or circumstances:

- D has obliquely intended a *result* element (eg death or GBH for murder) if that result: (a) was a virtually certain consequence of her act; (b) she realised that it was a virtually certain consequence of her act; and (c) the jury find that her realisation amounted to an intention;
- D has obliquely intended a *circumstance* element (eg V's ownership of property for theft) if: (a) the circumstance was virtually certain to be present at the time she acted; (b) she realised that it was virtually certain to be present at that time; and (c) the jury find that her realisation amounted to an intention.

The potential for oblique intention is very useful in practice. For example, let us imagine that D placed a bomb on a passenger plane, her intention being to blow up the plane and thereby to destroy certain insured items in the plane's hold. If the bomb explodes and kills the pilot and passengers, has D acted with the intention to kill? Her

---

[40] *Moloney* [1985] AC 905, 926.
[41] *Allen* [2005] EWCA Crim 1344, [63].

direct intention is to gain insurance money, not to cause death. That result is what she acted in order to bring about. If, miraculously, the insured items were destroyed but the people on board were saved, her enterprise would not have failed. D does not have a direct intent to kill in the conventional sense. Equally, she does not directly intend death as a means to an end. The deaths of those on board are not *essential* means to her end; if they all parachuted to safety she would still succeed in getting the insurance for the packages on board. The destruction of the insured items could be described as an intended means to an end (the end being the insurance claim), but not the deaths. Thus, she does not directly intend to kill in either manner. However, the fact that deaths were a virtually certain consequence of her conduct, and the fact that she realised this and continued anyway, makes her state of mind look very much like an intention to kill. It is the three-part test for oblique intention that allows us to say that D intended to kill.[42]

The leading case, confirming the three-part test for oblique intention, is *Woollin*.

Woollin [1998] 4 All ER 103

D killed his child by throwing it against a hard surface. D did not desire to kill the child. D was charged with murder, requiring a mens rea of intention to kill or cause serious bodily harm.

- Crown Court: guilty of murder—judge's direction to the jury that they could find intention if they were satisfied that D realised that his actions posed a 'substantial risk' of causing death or serious injury.
- Court of Appeal: conviction upheld on appeal—direction as to intention was acceptable.
- House of Lords: allowing D's appeal. A direction in relation to 'substantial risk' is not appropriate. Oblique intention requires the result: (a) to be virtually certain; (b) to be foreseen by D as virtually certain; and (c) for the jury to find intention.

Before we provide a little more detail on the three steps of the *Woollin* test, it is important first to understand the term 'virtual certainty'.

'Virtual certainty'

The first two parts of the three-part test use the concept of a 'virtual certainty': to be intended, the actus reus element (a) must be virtually certain to arise and (b) must be foreseen by D as a virtual certainty. The level of foresight set by this term is vitally important. It is not intended to cover cases where D foresees a future event as simply likely, very likely, or even probable: these are (as we will discuss later) states of belief or recklessness, but not intention. Rather, the standard of virtual certainty is designed to catch *only* those cases where D sees the circumstance or result as *nearly* inevitable. The word *virtually* is used largely because it is impossible to be completely certain about something that happens in the future. For example, when D puts her bomb on the plane set to detonate in flight she is likely to be virtually certain that deaths will result from an explosion because she can see no reason to doubt this, but she could legitimately claim that without the ability to look into the future she was not and could not be completely certain.

---

[42] Pedain, 'Intention and the Terrorist Example' [2003] Crim LR 579.

The high threshold set by 'virtual certainty' is essential to provide a clear definition of intention (separate from belief and recklessness). This is because as soon as we start equating intention with high levels of foresight short of a virtual certainty, it is very difficult to know where to draw the line and what language to use to do it. However, despite this importance, the common law has struggled to maintain a consistent definition. This can be illustrated in the chain of murder appeal cases in **Table 3.5**, the issue in each being whether D *intended* to kill or cause serious harm to V.

Table 3.5 History of the meaning of intention

Case reference	Case facts	Level of foresight
Hyam v DPP [1975] AC 55	D put blazing newspaper through the letterbox of her rival (X) causing a house fire. D's intention was to scare X, but in fact caused the deaths of X's children (V).	House of Lords upheld a conviction where oblique intention was defined in terms of foresight of a 'high probability'.
Moloney [1985] AC 905	D shot his stepfather V (whom he loved) in a drunken contest that involved the quick-drawing of loaded shotguns. D's gun was directed point blank at V's head.	House of Lords quashed D's conviction because it was based on an incorrect direction that D foreseeing a mere 'probability' could amount to an intention. Despite this, however, in summing up Lord Bridge talked loosely of foresight of a 'natural consequence' being sufficient.
Hancock & Shankland [1986] AC 455	D (who were striking miners) pushed a concrete block from a motorway bridge intending to scare those travelling (crossing the picket line) below. The block hit a car and killed V.	The trial court convicted D of murder, following Lord Bridge's 'natural consequence' formulation. However, the conviction was quashed on appeal. The concern of both the Court of Appeal and the House of Lords was that foresight of a 'natural consequence' may go beyond foresight of something that is certain (or at least virtually certain). However, again, some of the language used by the Lords implied that some lower threshold may be acceptable (eg Lord Scarman's statement that 'the greater the probability of a consequence the more likely it is that the consequence was foreseen and that if that consequence was foreseen the greater the probability is that the consequence was also intended...').

Nedrick [1986] 1 WLR 1025	D poured paraffin through the letterbox of X's house and set it alight. A child (V) died in the house fire.	The trial court convicted D of murder, following a direction from the judge that intention could be found where D foresaw death or injury as 'highly probable'. The Court of Appeal quashed D's conviction and clarified (Lord Lane CJ) that the jury 'are not entitled to infer the necessary intention, unless they feel sure that death or serious bodily harm was a *virtual certainty* (barring some unforeseen intervention) as a result of the defendant's actions and that the defendant appreciated that such was the case'.
Woollin [1998] 4 All ER 103	D killed his child by throwing it against a hard surface. D did not desire to kill the child.	The court convicted D of murder, following a direction that intention could be found where D foresaw a 'substantial risk' of death or injury. The House of Lords allowed D's appeal, substituting a manslaughter conviction, and endorsed the standard of 'virtual certainty' set out by the Court of Appeal in *Nedrick*, adding it is for the jury to find whether D intended in this oblique sense.

Despite this historical inconsistency, the current law (following *Woollin*) is clear that if D's foresight of a result is less than of it being a virtual certainty, that will not be sufficient: such foresight may amount to a belief and/or recklessness, but not to an intention.

Objective part: (a) the offence element must be a virtual certainty
The first part of the test for oblique intention, it will be remembered, is that the offence element must be virtually certain in fact. This is an example of an objective mens rea requirement: it is not looking to the mind of D, but rather to the objective external world.

This first part is consistently referenced in the case law and is relatively straightforward to apply. However, it has the potential to cause problems, and we may question if it is useful within the definition. For example, using the plane bomber example again, let us imagine that unknown to D the hold of the plane was lined with special bomb-proof material such that the destruction of the plane was not inevitable. Where death results despite this protective material, can we still say that D obliquely intended to kill? She may have foreseen death as a virtual certainty (part (b)), but since the protective material *may* have protected those on board, we cannot say that death was virtual certain in fact (part (a)). Thus, despite the internal part of the *Woollin* test being satisfied (part (b)), a finding of intention is undermined by an objective and external requirement (part (a)). In effect, objective facts that are not known to D (in this case the materials of the plane) are partly defining the law's view of D's state of mind.

Whilst odd, it should be noted that the first part of the *Woollin* test will rarely cause problems in practice. This is because, where part (b) is satisfied (ie D foresees a virtual certainty), this will usually be because the element is a virtual certainty in fact. However, the example in the previous paragraph at least demonstrates the potential for a problem to arise.

Extra detail...
Although the full three-stage test has been endorsed by later cases,[43] it will be interesting to see if it is followed by a case such as the plane bomber example (where D is virtually certain of an element, but it is not virtually certain in fact). It may be that the first part of the *Woollin* test will be removed as a requirement of oblique intention, and recognised instead as evidence relevant to the second question (evidence to help the jury decide whether D foresaw the element as a virtual certainty). If an example of this kind were to arise in a problem question, if would be useful to acknowledge this possibility.

Subjective part: (b) D must foresee the offence element as virtually certain

The requirement that D must foresee the offence element as a virtual certainty is clear and relatively uncontroversial. It should be remember that this is a subjective question that looks to the mind of D. Thus, if the jury believe that D *honestly* did not foresee or might not have foreseen the offence element as a virtual certainty, even if it was virtually certain in fact (part (a)) and even if it would have been obvious to a reasonable person, this part of the *Woollin* test will not be satisfied and the jury are not entitled to find oblique intention.[44]

Jury part: (c) the jury may find intention

The final part of the *Woollin* test is that (*only* when the first two parts are satisfied) the jury are entitled to find that D intended the offence element. It is also the most controversial. It is controversial because the fact that the jury are 'entitled' to find, or 'may' find, means that even where the first two parts of the test are satisfied, the jury are not *obliged* to find intention. Further, although this third part creates a separate and independent question from the other two, the case law does not provide criteria to guide the jury in their decision. Having found that the offence element was virtually certain and that it was foreseen as a virtual certainty by D, the jury are then left with the question 'is that intention': they may equate this with intention if they wish, or they may not.

Extra detail...
There has been considerable academic debate about whether satisfaction of the first two parts should oblige the jury to find intention, and thus to remove discretion from this third part.[45] This arose most recently where the court in *Woollin* described the jury as 'finding' intention rather than 'inferring' it as they had in *Nedrick*: the implication being that to 'find' intention seems to contain less discretion than to 'infer' it. However, the dominant interpretation remains that this third part is not simply a rubber stamping of the first two: satisfaction of parts (a) and (b) do not equate to intention, they merely provide the basis from which the jury may (or may not) find intention.[46]

The discretion afforded to the jury within this third part (whether or not to find intention) has both positive and negative aspects. On the positive side, allowing the jury to

---

[43] eg *Matthews* [2003] EWCA Crim 192.

[44] In *DPP v Smith* [1961] AC 290 the House of Lords had opened the possibility for an objective definition of intention. However, post-Criminal Justice Act 1967, s8 and *Woollin*, it is clear that this objective route has been foreclosed.

[45] Norrie, 'After *Woollin*' [1999] Crim LR 532; Williams, 'Oblique Intention' (1987) 46 CLJ 417.

[46] *Matthews* [2003] EWCA Crim 192.

find that D did not intend an offence element despite it being a foreseen virtual certainty, can provide useful 'moral elbow room' within difficult cases.[47]

In the civil law case of *Gillick v West Norfolk*,[48] for example, the House of Lords ruled that it was not unlawful for a doctor (D) to prescribe the contraceptive pill to a girl under the age of 16 (X). The issue is that assisting or encouraging underage sex (which providing the proscription arguably does), if done with an intention to assist or encourage, constitutes an offence.[49] The question therefore becomes, did D intend to encourage such conduct? Applying the first two parts of the *Woollin* test, we may conclude that he did: it is virtually certain that X's boyfriend will be encouraged to have sex with X if he knows she is not going to become pregnant, and it is likely that the doctor will have foreseen this encouragement as virtually certain to follow from his prescribing X the pill. In the case itself, the House of Lords avoided this conclusion by saying that an intention to act in a patient's medical interests cannot amount to a criminal intention.[50] However, this line of reasoning is clearly unacceptable: if D (a doctor) honestly believed that it was in the best interests of a patient to die, for example, we would not say that this negated the intention to kill. Rather, a better approach may be to rely upon the third part of the *Woollin* test, accepting that the result (encouragement of X and her boyfriend) is virtually certain; accepting that D foresees it as virtually certain; but in light of D's intention to protect his patient, allow the jury to find that D did not intend to encourage such unlawful conduct. Indeed, in an analogous case of *Re A*,[51] a similar approach could have been adopted. This case involved the medical separation of conjoined twins where it was virtually certain that the operation would kill one of the twins, and the doctors (D) recognised it as such. Again, when asking if D intended to kill, it is possible that the third part of the *Woollin* test could be used to avoid this conclusion.

The main advantage of this approach, therefore, is the discretion that it allows the jury. The first two parts of the *Woollin* test cannot separate the plane bomber in the earlier example from D in *Gillick* or *Re A*: in each case the result is a virtually certain consequence of D's conduct (part (a)); and D will be aware that it is a virtual certainty consequence (part (b)). It is through the discretion in this third part that the jury may find that the plane bomber intended to kill, and that D in *Gillick* and *Re A* did not intend the relevant results.

Unfortunately, for two reasons, this same discretion (or moral elbow room) is also highly problematic. First, it is unpredictable: without criteria to guide a jury, different juries may come to different conclusions when assessing the same or similar facts. This is objectionable from a rule of law perspective since we cannot tell in advance whether conduct will be criminal, and it is also unreliable as a method of distinguishing cases such as those described previously. We may predict (or at least *hope*) that a jury will find intention in relation to the plane bomber, and no intention in relation to *Gillick* and *Re A*, but there are no guarantees of this. It is little wonder, for example, that the court and

[47] Horder, 'Intention in the Criminal Law—A Rejoinder' (1995) 58 MLR 678, 688.
[48] [1985] 3 All ER 402.
[49] **Chapter 12**.
[50] Lord Scarman (at 19) states that the 'bona fide exercise by a doctor of his clinical judgement must be a complete negation of the guilty mind'.
[51] [2001] 2 WLR 480.

medical profession would rather rely on a defence of necessity in cases such as *Re A* than they would rely on the unfettered discretion of a jury on whether to find intention.[52]

Secondly, the third part of the *Woollin* test has also been criticised for allowing the jury to, in effect, decide the law. As discussed at **1.1.6.2**, the role of the jury is meant to be isolated to issues of fact. The law as interpreted by the court tells us the elements of a crime, the law defines those elements, and it is then for the jury to decide whether or not D completed those elements in fact. However, leaving the third part of the *Woollin* test completely in the hands of the jury by not providing a legal definition to guide them, means that the jury are not only being asked to apply a legal rule, they are being asked to define it. This problem is limited, of course, because the discretion will only arise where the first two parts of the *Woollin* test are satisfied, so the jury do not have complete freedom to define any state of mind they wish as an intention, but it is still apparent.

> **Assessment matters...**
>
> When applying the *Woollin* test to problem facts, the third part provides particular difficulty. You may conclude from the facts that an offence element (eg death in murder) was a virtual certainty and that D foresaw it as such, but (like the jury) you have no criteria to apply in order to answer the third part. The best approach is to highlight this problem (as a criticism of the current law) and then to say what you think the jury are most likely to decide based on an assessment of the facts as a whole. For example, it is likely that a jury will have little sympathy for the plane bomber and are therefore likely to find an intention to kill.

3.4.1.3 Conditional intention

Unlike direct and oblique intention, 'conditional' intention does *not* provide an alternative definition of intention.[53] Rather, it is discussed simply to confirm that in the context of ulterior mens rea,[54] D's direct or oblique intention may be conditional without undermining the fact that she is intending.[55] For example, the (ulterior) mens rea of theft requires D to intend to permanently deprive V of the property she has appropriated. Where D takes V's property, her intention to keep it is likely to contain a multitude of conditions: for example, to give it back if it is no longer useful; if the police find out and ask her to; if her conscience catches up with her; etc. However, as long as these conditions do not fully undermine D's intention so that they amount to a position where she knows she will definitely give it back, then she is still intending to permanently deprive in law. This is because, in effect, all mens rea of this kind that relates to future results is likely to be conditional.

Conditional intention is not relevant in the context of circumstances or results that have come about within the actus reus of the offence. This is because, where D has acted in certain circumstances and/or causing certain results she has made a definite (non-conditional) decision to do so. For example, D may conditionally intend to kill V tomorrow if the weather is good: her future action being conditional on the weather. However, where D has acted to kill V, the decision to act is no longer conditional it has been made.

---

[52] Necessity is discussed in **Chapter 14**.

[53] Williams, 'Intents in the Alternative' (1991) 50 CLJ 120.

[54] That is mens rea as to an element that does not need to come about, is not part of the actus reus. See **3.2.2**.

[55] *O'Hadhmaill* [1996] Crim LR 509.

We can ask whether it was D's purpose to kill (direct intent) or whether it was a foreseen virtual certainty (oblique intent), but talk of conditions is illogical.

> **Point to remember...**
> The basic rule is that a conditional ulterior intention is still an intention. This rule is relevant to all offences that contain a requirement of ulterior mens rea, from single requirements (as with theft, where there is a single ulterior mens rea requirement) to more substantial requirements (as with general inchoate offences, where D's ulterior mens rea relates to a full future offence).

3.4.2 Knowledge

The mens rea of 'knowledge' is generally seen as equivalent to 'intention' in terms of culpability. D has knowledge of an offence element if (a) she believes that it is the case and (b) she is correct in that belief.[56] This interpretation was confirmed in two cases in the House of Lords. In *Montila*:[57]

> A person cannot know something is A when in fact it is B. The proposition that a person knows that something is A is based on the premise that it is true that it is A. The fact that the property is A provides the starting point. Then there is the question whether the person knows that the property is A.

And in *Saik*:[58]

> the word 'know' should be interpreted strictly and not watered down. In this context, knowledge means true belief....If D1 and D2 agree they will...exchange money that comes into their bureau de change, they cannot be said to be agreeing to launder money which they *know* to be from a criminal source if they merely see a risk that it might be from a criminal source.

In this manner, a mens rea of 'knowledge' includes both subjective and objective parts.

The subjective part (a) focuses on D's state of mind: she must believe that the offence element is the case. For example, D must believe that the property belongs to another in theft; or that V is a person for murder; etc. As stated in the quotation from *Saik*, belief that something 'is the case' is not satisfied by a belief that it '*may be* the case' although this could be 'recklessness', as discussed later. However, it also seems that something short of virtual certainty may be acceptable. For example, in *Hall*[59] it was accepted that D could *know* goods were stolen if she was informed by someone with first-hand experience, and in *Griffiths*,[60] it was held to be enough if D has no serious doubts. In each case, we are focusing on what D actually believed (subjective mens rea), not on what she should have believed or what a reasonable person in her position would have believed (objective mens rea).

---

56 Shute, 'Knowledge and Belief in the Criminal Law' and Sullivan, 'Knowledge, Belief and Culpability' in Shute and Simester (eds), *Criminal Law Theory* (2007) Chs8 and 9.
57 [2004] 1 WLR 3141, [27].
58 [2006] UKHL 18, [26].
59 (1985) 81 Cr App R 260.
60 (1974) 60 Cr App R 14.

The objective part (b) focuses on the objective reality: what D believes must be true in fact before we can say that she has knowledge of it. For example, if D takes property that she believes belongs to another, but in fact belongs to her, she does not *know* that the property belongs to another. This part of the legal definition is very important, and explains why the mens rea of knowledge is, *generally*,[61] only used in the context of circumstance elements. It should be remembered that D's mens rea must be identified at the time she acts.[62] As the result element of a crime relates to things *caused* by D's conduct (eg death for murder), such results will always come after D has acted, even if this is just a fraction of a second. Because of this, it is logically impossible for D to have knowledge as to a result element: at the point of acting (relevant point for mens rea) we do not know if D's belief about the future is correct or not, the objective part of the definition cannot be satisfied. In contrast, circumstance elements relate to facts that must be present at the time of D's conduct (eg that V is a person for murder). Therefore, it is possible for both parts of the 'knowledge' definition to be applied.

> **Don't be confused...**
> It is common for offences to specifically require a mens rea of knowledge as to a circumstance element. However, as knowledge is considered to be equivalent to intention, even where an offence specifies a mens rea of intention as to a circumstance element, knowledge will suffice.[63]

3.4.2.1 Wilful blindness

A state of knowledge can alternatively be found where D: (a) foresees the possibility of a certain circumstance; (b) it would be easy for D to discover the truth; (c) D deliberately avoids finding out; and (d) the circumstance is in fact present. Where this is the case, D's decision to 'shut her eyes' to the facts, or 'bury her head in the sand', is described as wilful blindness. The status of wilful blindness as sufficient to amount to knowledge was confirmed in the House of Lords in *Westminster CC v Croyalgrange Ltd*.[64]

Although there has been relatively little case law discussing the meaning of wilful blindness,[65] and not a great deal of academic scholarship,[66] it remains a useful concept. For example, let us imagine that D receives a state-of-the-art stolen television from her friend P for only a few pounds. For D to commit the offence of handling stolen goods, she must *know* or believe that the property (the television) is stolen.[67] However, even where D knows that P is a burglar, and even where she suspects that the property is stolen, she may still remain unsure as to its origins: she may lack belief. In such cases, because the route to finding out (simply asking P) is straightforward and available to her, the law translates her wilful blindness into a form of knowledge that will satisfy the offence mens rea.

There are problems with the law here, some of which are obvious from the previous example. First, in the absence of case law, there is a lack of clarity as to how the stages of

---

[61] A notable exception emerges in the context of accomplice liability, **Chapter 12**.
[62] Discussed further in **Chapter 4**.
[63] Discussed further in the context of the general inchoate offences, **Chapter 11**.
[64] (1986) 83 Cr App R 155.
[65] See, most usefully, *Roper v Taylor Garages* [1951] 2 TLR 284.
[66] Wasik and Thompson, 'Turning a Blind Eye as Constituting Mens Rea' (1981) 32 NILQ 324.
[67] Theft Act 1968, s22.

the definition should be applied. For example, it is unclear how much foresight D must have to satisfy (a); how easy it must be for her to discover the truth within (b); as well as how consciously (as opposed to absent-mindedly) D must have avoided finding out within (c). Secondly, there may be cases where wilful blindness does not appear blameworthy. For example, what if D in the previous example avoided asking her friend about the television because she had promised to trust her in the future. Imagine also a parent who does not inquire about the activities of their child because they want to encourage independence and respect privacy.

> *Assessment matters…*
> When applying lesser developed terms such as wilful blindness to problem questions, it is important to highlight areas of doubt. You should still apply the criteria that are available from the case law. However, where there is a lack of clarity (eg the question for (b) of how easy must it be for D to discover the truth), it is best to highlight this lack of clarity and then to predict in general terms whether (and why) you think that the court will find that D satisfied the requirement or not.

3.4.3 Belief

'Belief' is a mens rea term that is not as culpable as 'intention' or 'knowledge'. D has belief that a circumstance exists, or that a result will be caused, where she foresees it as highly likely. This is identical to the first subjective limb of the definition of knowledge. The difference for 'belief' is that there is no objective second limb requiring D's belief to be correct in fact. Thus, where D believes a fact and she is correct, we can say that she had knowledge or belief of it. However, where D believes a fact and she is not correct, we can only say that she had belief.[68] Although, unlike knowledge, it is possible to believe that a future event will come about and thus belief logically can correspond to results and ulterior mens rea. It arises most commonly in relation to circumstance elements.

3.4.4 Recklessness

Below 'intention' and 'knowledge', and also below 'belief', 'recklessness' represents the next most culpable mens rea term. It is also one of the most important, arising in the majority of the offences discussed in this book. To satisfy a mens rea of recklessness, it must be demonstrated that D (a) foresaw a risk of the relevant element of the actus reus and (b) unreasonably continued to run that risk. This interpretation was confirmed by the House of Lords in *G*.[69]

Again, this general definition should be expressed and applied slightly differently depending upon the element of the actus reus at issue. For example:

- D is reckless as to a circumstance element, such as the property belonging to another for criminal damage, when she (a) foresees a risk that the circumstance is present and (b) unreasonably continues to run that risk;

---

[68] Shute, 'Knowledge and Belief in the Criminal Law' and Sullivan, 'Knowledge, Belief and Culpability' in Shute and Simester (eds), *Criminal Law Theory* (2007) Chs8 and 9.

[69] [2003] UKHL 50. The definition provided by the court is taken from the Law Commission's 1989 Draft Criminal Code, s18.

- D is reckless as to a result element, such as property damage for criminal damage, when she (a) foresees a risk that the result will be caused by her action and (b) unreasonably continues to act and run that risk.

In this manner, the test includes a subjective part (a) and a minor *but necessary* objective part (b). We will discuss each in turn.

Beware...

We highlighted earlier the importance of understanding and applying the legal definition of mens rea terms and not being distracted by their (often different) common non-legal meanings. The term 'recklessness' is one that students often confuse in this way. In common use, the term recklessness is often used to describe a person's dangerous behaviour (eg she flailed her arms recklessly). Indeed, the criminal law will occasionally use 'reckless' in this manner as an actus reus term (eg in the context of dangerous and reckless driving). However, where 'recklessness' is used as a mens rea term it is not concerned with D's physical behaviour. The test is simply: (a) did D foresee a risk of the offence element? And (b) did D continue unreasonably to run that risk? If the answer to both questions is 'yes', then a mens rea of recklessness is satisfied.

Subjective part: (a) D must have foreseen a risk of the offence element being satisfied

The first part of the 'recklessness' test focuses on D's state of mind: at the time of acting D must have foreseen a risk of the relevant circumstance or result. To illustrate the detail of this first part, we may consider the offence of criminal damage. The actus reus of criminal damage requires (a) property, (b) belonging to another (c) to be destroyed or damaged by D's conduct. The mens rea of recklessness is sufficient as to all three elements, but later we focus on the last of these (the damage) only.[70] Let us take the example of D who, before the days of mobile phones, tries to rouse her friend by throwing small stones at her bedroom window. Four important points should be noted when applying this part of the test to this, and any other, set of facts.

A) **D must foresee the risk of damage to the window:** It must be remembered that this part of the 'recklessness' test is purely subjective: our focus is on D's state of mind alone. Thus, for example, if the jury believe that D did *not* foresee or might not have foreseen a risk of damaging the window with the stone then the test will not be satisfied even where the risk would have been obvious to a reasonable person in D's position. This is illustrated in *Stephenson*.

▢ *Stephenson* [1979] QB 695

D, who suffered from schizophrenia, sheltered in a haystack and made a fire for warmth. Inevitably, the fire spread and caused damage. D was charged with criminal damage, the mens rea of which requires D to be reckless as to causing damage. Medical evidence indicated that D may not have been aware of the risk of damage as a result of his condition.

- Crown Court: guilty of the offence. The trial judge directed the jury in terms of risks that would have been obvious to them.
- Court of Appeal: appeal allowed against conviction. The test is purely subjective: it was a misdirection to question the obviousness of the risk; the only question is whether D foresaw a risk.

---

[70] Criminal Damage Act 1971, s1.

B) **The size of the risk foreseen by D is irrelevant:** For oblique intention, D must foresee the actus reus element (in this case damage) as virtually certain; for belief, it must be foreseen as highly likely. However, for recklessness there is no such restriction. Whether D foresees the risk as virtually certain, highly likely, likely, unlikely, etc, as long as *a* risk is fores een, it will be sufficient. Thus, where D throws the stone at V's window foreseeing only a small chance of causing damage, it will still be enough to satisfy this part of the test. This is illustrated in *Brady*.

▢ *Brady* [2006] EWCA Crim 2413

D was drunk in a nightclub. He climbed onto a railing and then fell to the dance floor beneath, causing serious injury to V. D was charged with an offence against the person that included a mens rea of recklessness as to causing harm.[71]

- Crown Court: guilty of the offence against the person.
- Court of Appeal: conviction upheld on appeal. D had appealed on the basis that the test of recklessness required D to foresee 'an obvious and significant' risk. This was rejected: foresight of any risk is sufficient.

C) **How carefully D considers the presence of the risk is irrelevant:** Before throwing the stone at V's window, D may have carefully considered the chances of causing damage. She may have selected a smaller stone and thrown it with less force. Alternatively, she may have only considered it in the fleeting moment as she began to throw the stone. However, in each case D's state of mind will be sufficient for this part of the recklessness test: some foresight of the risk is all that is required, however fleeting or superficial that is. This is a sensible rule, and it avoids the court becoming bogged down in trying to distinguish between D's degrees of thought or focus. However, the basic line between foreseeing and not foreseeing can still be problematic. In certain cases, at the very edges of subjective foresight, the courts have even been willing to accept that a risk was foreseen when it was 'suppressed', or 'driven out', or where D 'closed his mind' to it. In cases such as *Parker*, the test is satisfied therefore on the *somewhat artificial* basis that the risk was foreseen by D in the back of her mind.

▢ *Parker* [1977] 1 WLR 600

After a very bad day, D lost his temper when he found a public telephone out of order and proceeded to 'smash down' the receiver into the dialling box. This caused minor damage. D was charged with criminal damage, the mens rea of which requires D to be reckless as to causing damage. D claimed that, in the heat of the moment, he was not aware of this risk.

- Crown Court: guilty of criminal damage.
- Court of Appeal: conviction upheld on appeal—although D's awareness of the risk of damage was suppressed by his anger, the risk still must have entered his mind.

---

[71] **Chapter 7.** For discussion of the implications of D's intoxication, see **Chapter 13**.

D) What D thinks about the risk is irrelevant: Having foreseen the risk of damaging V's window, D may worry and hope that no damage will be caused. She may dislike V and not mind the idea of the window breaking. She may not care either way. However, in each case D's state of mind will be sufficient for this part of the recklessness test: some foresight of the risk is all that is required however indifferently D may view it. This question used to arise in the context of rape and other sexual offences, before the definition of those offences changed, where D performed sexual acts and 'could not care less' whether V consented or not.[72] In such cases, it has been consistently held that D's state of mind will satisfy the test for recklessness: D may not attach any weight to the risk, but it is still foreseen.[73]

A more difficult case is where D claims that she had so little regard for her potential victims that she did not even consider the possible risks of her actions. This is problematic because unlike earlier examples, despite D's obvious culpability, she is claiming that she did not foresee the risk before choosing to ignore it. There is some support for the proposition that D's state of mind would still be sufficient to satisfy a mens rea of recklessness: Lord Goff in *Reid*, for example, suggested that D could be recklessly indifferent to a risk without being aware of it.[74] However, the better view, in light of *G* and other subsequent case law, is that D would not be reckless in these circumstances. The basic subjective ingredient of this mens rea term is that D must have foreseen the risk.

Objective part: (b) D must have unreasonably continued to run the risk
Having established (a) that D foresaw a risk of the circumstance or result element, it must also be demonstrated (b) that D *unreasonably* chose to run that risk. This second part of the test is objective: it does not matter whether D thought it was reasonable to run the risk, the question is whether the court think it was reasonable based on the standards of reasonable people acting in D's circumstances. For example, D may believe that it is reasonable to throw stones at her friend's window, because she wants to get her friend's attention, even though she foresees a risk of damage. The question for the court, however, is whether such conduct would be considered reasonable by others in her position. In this case, unless she has the permission of V, or she is trying to rouse V whose house is on fire, the answer is likely to be 'no': meaning that recklessness would be found.[75]

In many cases, it will be obviously unreasonable to run the risk of causing damage or injury, and this part of the test will be easily satisfied. However, this will not always be the case. For example, when D drives she may foresee a risk of someone jumping out in front of her and being injured; when a doctor performs an operation they may foresee a chance that the patient will die; etc. However, the law does not want to discourage socially useful activities such as driving and performing operations. In such cases, D will not have a mens rea of recklessness: she foresees a risk (a), but it is not unreasonable to run that risk (b).

---

[72] The issue no longer arises in such cases because the mens rea of these offences no longer requires recklessness. See discussion in **Chapter 8**.

[73] *Satnam and Kewal Singh* (1984) 78 Cr App R 149.

[74] (1992) 95 Cr App R 391. See Leigh, 'Recklessness after *Reid*' (1993) 56 MLR 208.

[75] Consent would also raise the possibility of a statutory defence. See discussion in **Chapter 14**.

> **Point to remember…**
>
> In this discussion we have focused on the result element of causing damage, but the same care needs to be taken to applying recklessness to circumstance elements (in the case of criminal damage that would be (a) property, (b) belonging to another).

3.4.4.1 Historical background: the rise and fall of objective recklessness

In order to understand the current definition of recklessness set out earlier, it is useful to bear in mind the common law journey that has been taken to get there.[76] This is set out in **Table 3.6**.

Table 3.6 History of the meaning of recklessness

Case reference	Case facts	Definition of 'recklessness'
Cunningham [1957] 2 QB 396	D tore a gas meter from the wall in order to steal money from it. Gas escaped into his neighbour's house and was inhaled by V. D was convicted of an offence against the person, including a mens rea of malice (which is the same as recklessness) as to the endangerment of life.[77] This was quashed on appeal.	*Subjective beginnings* The Court of Criminal Appeal quashed D's conviction because the trial judge had defined the offence term 'malicious' (meaning the same as 'reckless', see **3.5.4.1**) as synonymous with 'wicked'. The court set out a test for recklessness that is similar to the current law: D must foresee the risk. This is why the current subjective test for recklessness is often referred to as *Cunningham* recklessness.
Caldwell [1982] AC 341	D, who had been drinking heavily, started a fire in a hotel as part of an ongoing dispute. D was convicted of aggravated criminal damage, including a mens rea of recklessness as to the endangerment of life.[78] The House of Lords upheld this conviction.	*Objective recklessness* With Lords Wilberforce and Edmund-Davies dissenting, the House of Lords expanded the *Cunningham* definition of recklessness to include what is referred to as 'objective recklessness'. Under this new test, set out by Lord Diplock, D would be reckless where: (a) she foresees a risk (in line with *Cunningham*); or (b) she failed to foresee a risk that would have been obvious to the reasonable person.

(Continued)

---

[76] Davies, 'Lawmakers, Law Lords and Legal Fault' (2004) 68 J Crim L 130; Crosby, 'Recklessness—The Continuing Search for a Definition' (2008) 72 J Crim L 313.

[77] Offences Against the Person Act 1861, s23. See **7.9.4**.

[78] Criminal Damage Act 1971, s1(2). See **Chapter 9**.

Table 3.6 Continued

		The second possibility here is objective because it does not look to the mind of D: it asks if the reasonable person would have foreseen the risk and allows the court to find recklessness on this basis. This is often referred to as *Caldwell* recklessness.
Lawrence [1982] AC 510	This case involved reckless driving, including a mens rea of recklessness as to that danger.	*Expanding objective recklessness* Lord Diplock reiterated his objective definition of recklessness, adding that the obvious risk must also be serious. Its use in this case demonstrated its general application outside criminal damage cases.
Elliott [1983] 1 WLR 939	D (a 14-year-old girl with learning difficulties) started a fire in a garden shed. The fire spread and caused damage. D was charged with criminal damage, including a mens rea of recklessness as to the damage. D claimed that she did not foresee the damage.	*Unfairness of objective recklessness* D was liable for criminal damage in this case because although she did not foresee damage (she was not subjectively reckless), because the damage would have been obvious to a reasonable person, recklessness was found using the *Caldwell* test. D was liable despite not foreseeing the risk of damage, and despite her age and learning difficulties making it impossible for her to appreciate the foresight of the objective reasonable person.
G [2003] UKHL 50	D (children aged 11 and 12) set fire to some newspapers under a wheelie bin. They left the fire and it spread to surrounding buildings. They were convicted of criminal damage of the building, on the basis of their mens rea of recklessness as to the damage. They had not foreseen the chance of the fire spreading and damage being caused although that was obvious to a reasonable person.	*Full circle: overruling* Caldwell *and back to* Cunningham The House of Lords allowed the appeal and quashed the convictions. Following the extensive criticism of *Caldwell*, the House of Lords took the opportunity to overrule it and to restate the subjective recklessness test set out in *Cunningham*.
AG's Reference (No 3 of 2003)	The case involved the offences of manslaughter	*Expanding* Cunningham; G; *subjective recklessness*

[2004] EWCA Crim 868	and misconduct in public office. The latter including an element of recklessness.	This case is useful because it confirms 'general principles' laid down in G: that 'recklessness' should be interpreted in a subjective manner for all offences where the term is used.

In this manner, the common law definition of recklessness has completed a full circle: from subjective to objective to subjective. Importantly, you should be clear that objective (*Caldwell*) recklessness has been overruled in *G*: it is no longer a definition of recklessness used in English law.

3.4.4.2 Maliciously and wilfully

The mens rea term 'maliciously' arises in several offences against the person.[79] The mens rea term 'wilful' also arises in a host of offences, including wilfully obstructing a police officer[80] and misconduct in public office.[81] Where such terms are applied to circumstance or result elements, it is now settled that their meaning is the same as 'recklessness'.[82] The fact that different mens rea terms are used to mean the same thing is obviously not ideal, and has the potential to cause confusion. However, aligning their meanings with recklessness in this manner at least reduces the complex variety of mens rea definitions that are present in the common law.

3.4.4.3 Intoxication mens rea

Voluntary intoxication through drink or other drugs can cause problems for the definition of recklessness. The problem arises where D is charged with an offence requiring proof of recklessness as to an element, but failed to foresee the risk *due* to her intoxicated state. If we apply the definition of recklessness mentioned previously then D is not reckless (she did not foresee a risk), and she has not committed an offence. However, the law understandably looks further than this by examining the cause of the intoxicated state. If D was *in*voluntarily intoxicated, for example because she had her drinks laced then she will not be liable: she did not foresee the risk and she was not at fault in bringing about that failure to see the risk. If, however, D's lack of foresight was in some manner her own fault, brought about by her decision to become intoxicated, the situation becomes more complicated. Indeed, in certain cases the law is willing to accept that D's intoxication is equivalent to a mens rea of recklessness. Therefore, in these cases D can be convicted of an offence that requires a mens rea of recklessness, not because she satisfies the test for recklessness set out earlier, but simply on the basis of her intoxicated state.[83] The intoxication rules will be fully discussed in **Chapter 13**.

3.4.5 Summary of mens rea terms

As we have discussed, despite their general focus on the mind of D, mens rea terms will often include objective as well as subjective parts within their definition. For example,

---

[79] **Chapter 7.**
[80] Police Act 1996, s89.
[81] *AG's Reference (No 3 of 2003)* [2004] EWCA Crim 868.
[82] For 'maliciously' see *Cunningham* [1957] 2 QB 396. For 'wilfully' see *D* [2008] EWCA Crim 2360.
[83] *Heard* [2007] EWCA Crim 125.

'oblique intention' requires that the offence element was not only foreseen as a virtual certainty, but that (objectively) it was a virtual certainty; 'knowledge' requires belief in a circumstance, and also that (objectively) the belief is true; 'recklessness' requires foresight of a risk, and also (objectively) a consideration of reasonableness. However, despite these objective considerations, the core of each term still focuses on the subjective mind of D. In each case, the prosecution must prove that D brought the relevant circumstance or result to mind in some manner before mens rea can be established.

These subjective requirements within the definition of mens rea terms arise in two distinct forms:

- **Where D acts in order to bring about a certain result, or a certain circumstance:** Where D acts with this state of mind, she is 'intending'. Intention, and this definition of (direct) intention in particular, is the most culpable form of mens rea. Importantly, in contrast to other subjective mens rea terms, it is irrelevant whether D foresees the offence element as likely or unlikely.

- **Where D acts foreseeing the causation of a result, or the presence of a circumstance:** Where D acts with this state of mind, she may be intending (in the oblique sense); knowing; believing; and/or being reckless. The mens rea demonstrated will depend on how likely D foresees the offence element to be: the more likely it is foreseen, the more serious the level of mens rea. This can be set out through simple spectrums of foresight.

Although mens rea terms are usefully presented as a hierarchy, with intention and knowledge at the top and recklessness at the bottom, this does not exclude overlap between them (set out in the following tables). The finding of one mens rea term will also include those below it in the hierarchy. For example, if you are applying an offence that requires recklessness as to a certain result, and you are told in the problem facts that D intends or believes that result, then you can be sure that recklessness will also be satisfied. Whether D intends the result in the sense of foreseeing it as a virtual certainty, or believes it is very likely, in both cases she has also *logically* foreseen a risk of it. This is set out in **Tables 3.7** (results) and **3.8** (circumstances).

Table 3.7 Mens rea as to the result element

D's foresight that conduct will cause a certain result	Mens rea term
Virtually certain	Intention; belief; recklessness
Very likely	Belief; recklessness
Likely	Recklessness
Possible	Recklessness
Unlikely (but still a risk)	Recklessness
Not foreseen	None

Table 3.8 Mens rea as to the circumstance element

D's foresight that circumstance will be present	Mens rea term
Virtually certain	Intention; knowledge (if true); belief; recklessness
Very likely	Knowledge (if true); belief; recklessness
Likely	Recklessness
Possible	Recklessness
Unlikely (but still a risk)	Recklessness
Not foreseen	None

Don't be confused…

Despite the overlap of mens rea terms, many offences (needlessly and incompletely) list more than one mens rea term that will satisfy the offence. For example, offences will often specify a mens rea of intention or recklessness. Here, as D cannot intend without being reckless as well, it is advised that you focus on the minimum requirement (recklessness) only. It is a bit like a sign on the beach saying 'no swimming' and also 'no swimming breaststroke': they are both accurate, but the second is unnecessary because the prohibition is covered by the first.

3.5 Objectifying 'subjective' mens rea terms

Since 2003 and the decision in *G* bringing about the demise of objective recklessness, each of the core mens rea terms ('intention', 'knowledge', 'belief', and 'recklessness') are now defined to require some degree of subjective mens rea. In each case, the mens rea term will only be satisfied if D herself possessed a certain purpose or certain foresight. However, although this positively serves the principle of autonomy,[84] it also makes the finding of mens rea more difficult: proving that D possessed a certain state of mind at the relevant time, not simply that a reasonable person in her position would have done so.

The greater difficulty of proving a subjective mens rea may be acceptable in view of the serious consequences of criminal prosecution, and the need for certainty that D is deserving of those consequences. However, for certain offences, where proving subjective mens rea has been particularly difficult,[85] or where Parliament simply deems it necessary, the construction and context of mens rea terms can be adapted to reduce (or even to

---

[84] See **1.4.3**.
[85] eg sexual offences or terrorism offences.

eliminate) their subjective parts. These offence constructions are not claiming to redefine the mens rea term more generally, and will not affect its definition when used in other offences, but they do affect the way it should be applied within that particular offence.

As the process of objectifying mens rea terms does not affect their general definitions, we will not discuss them in detail here. Rather, this will be done as they arise in relation to particular offences in later chapters. However, by way of introduction, such constructions will usually take one of two forms:

- **Objectifying the subjective part:** Where this construction is used, the subjective part of the mens rea term (eg D's required foresight) can alternatively be satisfied by a finding that a reasonable person in D's position would have had that mens rea. For example, harassment offences require D to know that her behaviour will cause harassment, or that she *ought to have* known that.[86] Thus, the second alternative allows for a purely objective mens rea: it does not matter what D actually believed as long as she should have believed because a reasonable person would have.

- **A lack of positive belief:** An even stricter mens rea construction is to require D to have a positive and reasonable belief. For example, to commit rape D must have penetrated the vagina, anus, or mouth of V with his penis and without V's consent.[87] Mens rea as to V's non-consent is satisfied where D 'does not reasonably believe that [V] consents'. There are two aspects to this. First, there is a positive obligation on D to have held a belief in consent: if D did not believe that V consented because he did not care, for example, D will satisfy the mens rea.[88] Secondly, even where D did believe that V was consenting, that belief must be reasonably (objectively) held: unless a reasonable person in D's position would have so believed, D will satisfy the mens rea.

Point to remember...

The use of objective constructions is not uncommon in the law. Therefore, when identifying the mens rea of an offence, as well as looking to spot mens rea terms, it is equally important to consider their context: are they being used in the standard manner or are they adapted or objectified in some manner?

3.6 Non-conventional mens rea terms

In this section we discuss the terms 'dishonesty' and 'negligence'. Although both are often described as mens rea terms, they are importantly different from the more common mens rea terms discussed previously. This is because unlike intention and recklessness, for example, they do not correspond to separate requirements within the actus reus of an offence. Rather, they include both external and internal requirements: they correspond with themselves. For example, if D intends to kill; believes her acts will kill; foresees a risk that her acts will kill, D's mens rea (intention, belief, or recklessness) is corresponding to a separate actus reus requirement (causing death). In contrast, D

---

[86] Protection from Harassment Act 1997.
[87] Sexual Offences Act 2003, s1.
[88] This will be the case even if a reasonable person would have believed that V was consenting.

cannot 'dishonest to kill' or 'negligent to kill'. Rather, 'dishonesty' and 'negligence' are free-standing and separate offence requirements. D may be dishonest *and* kill, or be negligent *leading to* death, but in both cases we are dealing with more than D's state of mind alone. In this manner, it would be better, *in an ideal world*, to separate aspects of dishonesty and negligence between actus reus and mens rea. However, as they are traditionally referred to as mens rea terms, they are discussed here.

> **Don't be confused...**
> The analysis of these terms as mens rea is an inconsistency within the common law, but it is not one that causes too many problems: whether we call an offence requirement actus reus or mens rea, it must be satisfied in the same way for liability to be found. However, we are discussing them separately as 'non-conventional' mens rea terms to avoid confusion with the mens rea terms mentioned earlier. For the previous terms, we have to think about the corresponding actus reus to make sense of D's mens rea (what she is intending, etc). However, this is not the case for dishonesty and negligence.

3.6.1 Dishonesty

A mens rea requirement of dishonesty appears regularly in the context of property offences (**Chapter 9**), and much of its detail can be left for consideration until this later stage. However, it is useful to provide a brief introduction.

The definition of dishonesty is now settled within the common law, set out in *Ghosh*.[89] The jury must consider two questions.

(a) Was what was done dishonest according to the ordinary standards of reasonable and honest people? If no, D is not dishonest. If yes:

(b) Did the defendant realise that reasonable and honest people regard what she did as dishonest? If yes, she is dishonest; if no, she is not.

Although it is not often necessary to set out the full test when directing a jury,[90] it is clear that both parts of the test must be satisfied for dishonesty to be found. The two parts combine both objective and subjective considerations.

A) **Objective part (a):** The first question is purely objective, asking the jury to assess the dishonesty of D's conduct in relation to the standards of reasonable people. Indeed, it may be more accurate to describe this part of the test as an actus reus requirement: the jury are assessing D's physical conduct (eg taking property without permission) and comparing it with common standards, a process that does not focus on D's state of mind. This part of the test has been criticised because it assumes that there is an objective standard of dishonesty against which D's conduct can be measured. If this is not the case, there is a risk of inconsistency, with different juries deciding similar cases differently.[91]

B) **Subjective part (b):** The second question is subjective, and focuses on the mind of D. When applying this test, the question is *not* whether D believed or recognised that her conduct was dishonest. Rather, the question is whether D realised that *others* would consider her conduct as dishonest. This is an important distinction. For example, if D is

---

[89] [1982] QB 1053.

[90] *Roberts* (1985) 84 Cr App R 177.

[91] Griew, 'Dishonesty—The Objections to *Feely and Ghosh*' [1985] Crim LR 341.

struggling financially and has a rather loose moral code, she may well convince herself that taking property from her workplace is not dishonest. However, it would be much harder for her to maintain, and for a jury to believe, her claim that she did not think that reasonable honest people would consider that such taking is dishonest.[92]

3.6.2 Negligence

The test for 'negligence', even more than 'dishonesty', is not concerned with D's state of mind. Rather, negligence is used to describe a certain type of *behaviour* from D that drops below the standards that we expect from reasonable people. A requirement of negligence most commonly arises in relation to regulatory and driving offences.[93] In these cases, D is performing a lawful act (eg driving) that entails obvious risks to others. Rather than focusing on D's state of mind (eg did she foresee the risk?), a negligence requirement assumes that D must be aware of the risks and will apply if D does not correctly modify her behaviour in relation to them if she does not act safely.

The test for negligence in the criminal law is similarly constructed to the tort of negligence. Thus, a negligence requirement entails the following questions.

(a) What was D's duty of care?

(b) Did D breach that duty of care?

Both of these questions are objective, focusing on external standards and conduct.

A) **What was D's duty of care?** This question encourages us to consider who D has a duty to care for, and also, what standard of care is required. Certain statutory negligence offences will specify this within the offence, but this will not always be the case. Where it is unspecified in the offence, the first part of this (the 'who') is interpreted very widely in line with civil law, and it is clear that D has a general duty to consider how her conduct may affect others: *remember: this is not the same as the 'duty to act' required for omissions liability, a duty to act is interpreted very narrowly.* The more difficult question is to assess the standard of care required. Here, the general rule is that D must act *reasonably* or in the manner that would be expected of the reasonable person. Importantly, where D is performing a skilled activity or holds specialised knowledge, she will be judged against the standard of a reasonable person with that knowledge. For example, negligent driving is measured against the standard of a 'competent and careful driver', and so D can be held to have driven negligently even if a reasonable non-driver could not have performed better.[94] Likewise, a surgeon must perform an operation to the standard of a reasonable surgeon, not to the standard of a reasonable layperson handed the scalpel.

Although the standard of reasonableness increases to take account of D's specialised knowledge, the same will not be true in the other direction. Therefore, when assessing the standard of the reasonable person, the jury may not take account of characteristics that may lead to D's inability to meet that standard through no fault of D. For example, it would be no defence to a charge of careless driving for D to say she was a learner driver and therefore unable at that moment to achieve the standard of the 'competent and careful driver'. Equally, if D walks into something and causes damage or injury,

---

[92] Campbell contends that this second limb is superfluous: Campbell, 'The Test for Dishonesty in *Ghosh*' (1994) 43 CLJ 349.

[93] eg the offence of driving without due care and attention: Road Traffic Act 1988, s3.

[94] *McCrone v Riding* [1938] 1 All ER 721.

it will be no excuse to a negligence-based offence for D to point out that she is blind. The strict application of the reasonable person standard in such cases has attracted criticism,[95] and there is some indication that it may be softening to allow for the age of D to be considered,[96] but the basic position remains largely unchanged.

B) Did D breach that duty of care? Negligence also requires D to have breached the duty of care discussed and quantified by the previous question. A breach requires the prosecution to prove that D's conduct was performed below the reasonable standard required of her. When applying this question to problem facts, some harm or injury resulting from D's conduct is an indication that D has breached their duty of care, but it is not definitive. For example, if a car (V) brakes suddenly in front of D and she crashes into it, this is an indication that she may have been driving negligently by driving too fast or being too close to V's vehicle. However, it is also possible that she was driving competently, and that the crash could not have been avoided or, at least, a reasonable driver may have had the same accident.[97]

Assessment matters...
When applying a negligence-based offence to problem facts, it can be easy to equate resulting harm with a breach of duty. Take care: this is not always the case. Always discuss whether D's conduct fell below (or is likely to have fallen below) the standard of the reasonable person.

3.6.2.1 Gross negligence

Gross negligence has no equivalent in the civil law and arises in the criminal law in relation to one offence only: gross negligence manslaughter.[98] To satisfy 'gross negligence', D must fulfil the conditions of negligence discussed earlier, and D's negligence must be sufficiently extreme to be considered by the jury as 'gross'. This definition was set out in the House of Lords in the leading case *Adomako*.[99]

Simple lack of care such as will constitute [standard civil negligence] is not enough. For the purposes of the criminal law there are degrees of negligence, and a very high degree of negligence is required to be proved before [gross negligence] is established.

It is therefore up to the jury to consider whether D's negligence is sufficiently serious to be considered 'gross'.

Judge and jury...
This is another area where the law is criticised for asking the jury to decide issues of law as well as issues of fact. In this respect it is like the final part of the *Woollin* test for intention. This is because, when deciding if D's negligence is 'gross', the jury are given no definition of grossness to apply. If the jury believe that D's behaviour is really bad (if they want her to be criminalised) then they will call it gross; and if they think that it does not deserve criminalisation then they will say that it is not gross. In this manner, the jury are deciding (not applying) the boundaries of the offence.

[95] Simester, Spencer, Sullivan, and Virgo, *Criminal Law Theory and Doctrine* (4th edn, 2010) 155.
[96] *R (RSPCA) v C* [2006] EWHC 1069 (Admin). See also *obiter* statements in *Hudson* [1966] 1 QB 448.
[97] Discussed in *Simpson v Peat* [1952] 2 QB 24, 28.
[98] **Chapter 6**.
[99] [1995] 1 AC 171.

3.7 Reform

With essay-type questions in mind, it is useful to pick up on two issues in particular that have arisen within this chapter. The first is the potential benefit of codifying mens rea terms and thereby removing their core definitions from the common law. The second is to look in slightly more detail at the relative merits of subjective mens rea requirements on the one hand, and objective mens rea requirements on the other.

3.7.1 Codifying mens rea terms

Although most criminal law academics favour general codification, there is always a balancing of benefits (eg consistency and clarity) against the loss of flexibility within the common law. However, when it comes to the codification of mens rea terms, there are few if any who would oppose having statutory definitions: that would have avoided the continuously changing definitions that have dogged the criminal over the past 50 years. As highlighted at various points in this chapter, these changes have come in a range of forms. Some have been subtle changes, and others full redefinitions. Some have been the product of careful consideration, and some simply from an imprecise choice of words. However, in each case the general application of mens rea terms which potentially apply to many hundreds of offences magnifies and exacerbates problems in the law.[100]

The codification of mens rea, in a manner seen in other jurisdictions,[101] remains a long way off in England and Wales. Despite notable attempts by the Law Commission within the 1989 Draft Criminal Code,[102] and later when suggesting reforms to the offences against the person,[103] the Commission's recommendations have not been taken forward into law.[104] Probably the three main reasons in favour of codification are: (A) creating a set mens rea vocabulary; (B) creating settled core definitions; and (C) creating the clarity of definition necessary to improve the law. We will look briefly at each.

A) A settled vocabulary: One of the main advantages of the US Model Penal Code, for example, is that it reduced the amount of mens rea terminology to four key terms: intention, knowledge, recklessness, and negligence.[105] By this simple act, the host of terms that were rarely used within the law, and not well understood, were removed. The terms that remained were defined to recognise a spectrum of mens rea, but also to provide a useful core set of well understood definitions.

B) A settled definition: Codification of mens rea terms does not eliminate all discretion for the court, and there remains room for disagreement through

---

[100] For a discussion of the problems caused by a lack of codification in this area, see Law Commission, *Report on the Mental Element in Crime* (No 89, 1978).

[101] See eg Australian Model Criminal Code (1992) Div 5; US Model Penal Code 1962, §2.02; Gainer, 'The Culpability Provisions of the Model Penal Code' (1987) 19 Rut LJ 575.

[102] Draft Criminal Code Bill 1989, cl18.

[103] Law Commission, *Offences Against the Person and General Principles* (No 218, 1993) cl1.

[104] The most recent move has been a 1998 Home Office Consultation Paper. See Smith, 'Offences Against the Person: The Home Office Consultation Paper' [1998] Crim LR 317.

[105] Gainer, 'The Culpability Provisions of the Model Penal Code' (1987) 19 Rut LJ 575.

interpretation.[106] However, a statutory definition can at least provide a core definition that will be protected from change within the common law. Thus, although we might still disagree on the exact level of foresight required for belief, for example, we would not have (as we have had with recklessness over the last 30 years) the dramatic redefinition of core terms between subjective, to objective, to subjective.[107]

Settled core definitions are important to protect defendants from retrospective lawmaking: where D's state of mind fulfils the mens rea only due to its redefinition.[108] Also, they provide Parliament with the assurance that if it creates offences with a certain mens rea in mind and use a certain mens rea term, that that mens rea term will continue to have the same meaning when the offence is applied. Indeed, this was one of the central criticisms of the *Caldwell*[109] objective redefinition of recklessness, as Parliament had created the Criminal Damage Act 1971 on the basis of the then subjective definition of recklessness.[110]

C) **A clear definition:** One of the main problems with common law definitions is that it is easy for precise meanings to be lost within a judicial judgment, and even easier if a definition is gleaned from a combination of several judgments across multiple cases. This has been problematic, for example, in the context of oblique intention and the meaning of 'virtual certainty'.[111] Codification, in contrast, has the potential to make a definition considerably clearer. In turn, this should make it easier to spot problems within the law and to correct them.

A useful example of this can again be seen in the context of oblique intention, where D obliquely intends a result element (eg unlawful killing for murder). It will be remembered that the *Woollin* definition of oblique intention requires: (a) that the result be a virtual certain consequence of D's act; (b) that D realises it is a virtually certain consequence of her act; and (c) that the jury choose to find intention. In line with this, the Law Commission defined intention within the 1989 Draft Criminal Code as:

act[ing] in order to bring [the result] about or being aware that it would occur in the ordinary course of events.

Set out in these terms, the definition is much easier to analyse and evaluate. One problem that was noted was that although it is clear that the result must be virtually certain and foreseen as a virtual certainty in order for parts (a) and (b) to be satisfied, it is not clear of what virtually certain consequence the result must be. The most obvious answer, and that implied in the *Nedrick* and *Woollin* directions, is that the result must be a virtually certain consequence of D's act. However, this can be problematic. To go back to our plane bomber examples, what if D sets a bomb in order to destroy insured property on

---

[106] See, on the US Model Penal Code, Simons, 'Should the Model Penal Code's Mens Rea Provisions be Amended?' (2003) 1 Ohio JCL 179.

[107] Davies, 'Lawmakers, Law Lords and Legal Fault' (2004) 68 JCL 130.

[108] Contrary to the principle of fair warning, see **1.4.1**.

[109] [1982] AC 341.

[110] McEwan and Robilliard, 'Recklessness: The House of Lords and the Criminal Law' (1981) 1 LS 267.

[111] See **3.4.1.2**.

a plane, but thinks there is a 50 per cent chance that the bomb will malfunction and fail to explode? If the question is whether it is virtually certain that death will arise from D's *conduct* (planting the bomb), and whether it is foreseen as a virtual certainty, then the answer is 'no': there is only a 50 per cent chance that the bomb will explode. However, D's purpose in acting (direct intent) is for the bomb to explode and the property to be destroyed, and if this happens then it is virtually certain (and foreseen as virtually certain) that death will result. Therefore, the Law Commission's definition of intention was adapted in their later report,[112] applying where:

(a) It is [D's] purpose to cause [the result]; or

(b) although it is not [D's] purpose to cause it, he knows that it would occur in the ordinary course of events if he were to succeed in his purpose of causing some other result.

Under the new definition, D in the previous example would satisfy an intention to kill. It is not D's purpose to kill, but she knows that death will occur in the ordinary course of events, in other words be virtually certain, if she succeeds in her purpose (blowing up the items).

Assessment matters…

If an example of this kind were to arise in problem facts, it is not clear whether the courts would interpret the *Woollin* definition in line with the Law Commission's adapted approach. However, highlighting this possibility would be very impressive.

3.7.2 Subjective vs objective mens rea

As we have seen, a subjective approach to mens rea requires the prosecution to prove that D had a particular purpose or foresight at the time of acting. In contrast, an objective approach to mens rea focuses on reasonableness, asking whether a reasonable person in D's shoes would have foreseen a particular risk, and finding fault with D on that basis. As mens rea terms have developed within the common law, there has often been an apparent conflict between these two approaches. When discussing mens rea in this manner, it is important to remember that both approaches have their own advantages and disadvantages. Equally, the ideal test may well be one that incorporates elements of both.[113]

A convenient way to set out and compare the relative merits of subjective and objective approaches is to look back to our discussion of 'recklessness'.[114] It will be remembered that, following its subjective beginnings, the case of *Caldwell*[115] (and Lord Diplock in particular) redefined recklessness in an objective manner: applying where D foresaw a risk (subjective) but also where she unreasonably failed to do so (objective).

---

[112] Law Commission, *Offences Against the Person and General Principles* (No 218, 1993) cl1.

[113] Tur, 'Subjectivism and Objectivism: Towards Synthesis' in Shute, Gardner, and Horder (eds), *Action and Value in Criminal Law* (1993) 213.

[114] See **3.4.4**.

[115] [1982] AC 341.

Caldwell attracted considerable criticism because of the apparent judicial lawmaking involved, but also simply on the basis that it employed an objective approach. Sir John Smith, for example, wrote that 'the decision sets back the law concerning the mental element in criminal damage in theory to before 1861'.[116] The concern was, *and remains*, that before we are ready to convict D of a serious offence, we should be sure she has chosen to commit, or at least chosen to risk committing, that offence.[117] However, D will be reckless under *Caldwell* even where she has not made such a choice because she has not foreseen the risk of the offence element (in this case, the risk of causing damage), it will be enough that she *should have done so*. The objection is made considerably stronger when we realise that D will be reckless under this definition even in cases where it would be impossible for her to have lived up to that reasonable standard. For example, if a blind D were to walk into and damage another's property, she will be (objectively) reckless as to that damage as long as a reasonable (sighted) person would have foreseen the risk of causing damage.[118] Thus, D is liable for a criminal offence despite not choosing to commit it; not choosing to risk it; on the basis of a reasonableness standard that was impossible for her to meet.

Criticism of *Caldwell* and the objective test led directly to it being overruled by the House of Lords in *G*,[119] with the law reverting to the old subjective test: D will only be reckless when she has foreseen the risk (in this case, of damage). However, the obvious problems with the purely objective test should not imply that a purely subjective one is necessarily the perfect answer. For example, what about D who damages the property of another and does not foresee the risk of damage because she could not care less about the risk to others, or because she was angry? In such cases, D may not have consciously chosen to risk the offence, but the reason for this lack of choice is in great measure D's own fault.[120] These criticisms are further strengthened by recognition that in *some* circumstances, the current law will find recklessness despite D not foreseeing the risk in the conventional sense, as for example when D is intoxicated, or when the court says D must have foreseen the risk 'in the back of her mind'.[121] If these exceptions are allowed, why not also allow recklessness where D failed to foresee a risk because of her selfishness and lack of concern for others?

Much of the current academic work in this area is not promoting complete subjectivism or complete objectivism, but rather looking for compromise approaches between them. For example, allowing recklessness to be found in cases where D has not foreseen a risk, but only if this lack of foresight was D's fault. In this manner, the blind D who causes damage will not be measured against the standard of the reasonable sighted person. However, on the other hand, D who does not care about others will not be able to rely on her callous attitude to avoid liability either.[122]

---

[116] Smith, 'Comment on *Caldwell*' [1981] Crim LR 393.

[117] For discussion of the principle of autonomy, see **1.4.3**.

[118] See *Elliott* [1983] 1 WLR 939, at **3.4.4.1**.

[119] [2003] UKHL 50.

[120] Even on the facts of *G*, the majority of the general public would support liability being found. Keating, 'Reckless Children' [2006] Crim LR 546.

[121] See **3.4.4**.

[122] See eg Duff, *Intention, Agency and the Criminal Law* (1990); Tadros, 'Recklessness and the Duty to Take Care' in Shute and Simester (eds), *Criminal Law Theory* (2002) 248.

3.8 Eye on assessment

This section sketches a structure for analysing the mens rea of an offence when applying the law in a problem-type question. Drawing on the structure outlined at the end of **Chapter 1**, we are focusing on the second part of 'Step 3'.

> **STEP 1 Identify the potential criminal event in the facts**
>
> This should be simply stated (eg 'The first potential criminal event arises where D kicks V). The role of this stage is to highlight which part of the question you are answering before you begin to apply the law.

> **STEP 2 Identify the potential offence**
>
> Again, state this simply (eg 'When breaking the vase, D may be liable for criminal damage'). The role of this stage is to highlight which offence you are going to apply.

> **STEP 3 Applying the offence to the facts**
>
> Having highlighted a possible offence, Step 3 requires you to both identify the actus reus and mens rea of that offence, *and* apply them to the facts.

Step 3 is where the bulk of your analysis will take place within a problem question (although Steps 1 and 2 should not be forgotten).

Step 3 includes the identification and application of both actus reus elements and mens rea elements. As we discussed in **Chapter 2**, this should always begin with the actus reus elements, ensuring that your analysis answers two core questions.

(1) What is the actus reus of the potential offence?

(2) Did D complete the actus reus (did she do it)?

If you conclude that D has *not* completed the actus reus of the offence, there is no need to continue to discuss mens rea elements (if there is no actus reus then there is no crime). However, if you conclude that D has completed the actus reus, or (*as is more likely in a problem question*) if you conclude that D may or is likely to satisfy the actus reus elements, then it is correct to move on to discuss the mens rea. Again, your analysis should focus on two core questions.

(1) What is the mens rea of the potential offence?

(2) Did D have that mens rea at the point in time of her relevant conduct?

The answer to these questions will vary between offences (question 1) and between factual scenarios (question 2). The answer to the first question will be discussed in relation to each offence covered in this book: gleaned from a combination of statutory and common law sources. However, the structure of application (question 2) is common between offences and can be usefully introduced at this point. It involves the stages of analysis set out in **Table 3.9**.

Table 3.9 Applying mens rea to problem facts

Mens rea	
A) Mens rea as to the conduct element?	As we discussed earlier (*almost*) all offences require D's acts to be voluntary.[123] Thus, you must always consider whether, at the point of acting, D was in control of her movements or lack of movements. Although this must be considered, you do not always have to discuss it in your answer. As we discussed previously, there is a common law presumption that D's acts are voluntary. Thus, although voluntariness is a requirement for liability, and although you should always consider this (keep it in mind) when applying the law, you do not need to discuss it in your answer unless there is some indication in the facts that D's acts were not voluntary. Where this is the case, you will discuss it through the defence of automatism.
B) Mens rea as to the circumstance element?	All offences (conduct and result crimes) include circumstance elements (eg that the property belongs to another for criminal damage). Examine the offence to see if these requirements must be intended; be known; believed; foreseen; or if any mens rea is required. If mens rea is required then you need to discuss the facts of the problem question to see if that mens rea is likely (on the known facts) to be satisfied. If the mens rea is obviously satisfied then do not dwell on it, simply say that it is likely to be present and move on. For example, if D stabs and kills V, it is unlikely that you need a lengthy discussion about whether D *knew* V was a person. However, if the issue is not straightforward, discuss it.
C) Mens rea as to the result element?	Only result crimes will include a result element (eg that D's acts must cause death for murder). Where such an element of the actus reus is present, examine the offence to see if it must be intended; be known; believed; foreseen; or if any mens rea is required. If mens rea is required then you need to discuss the facts of the problem question to see if that mens rea is likely (on the known facts) to be satisfied. Again, you should focus your discussion on areas that are unclear or contentious from the facts. However, as with mens rea for circumstances, mens rea here is not assumed and so all requirements must be discussed at least briefly.
D) Ulterior mens rea?	Only certain offences will include an ulterior mens rea requirement (eg the intention to permanently deprive for theft). As above, make sure you clearly identify what mens rea term is required (intention, etc), and then apply it to the facts.

Although we have set out the table using element analysis (separating acts, circumstances, and results), this is not necessary within your answer. For example, when discussing murder, it is more common to talk generally of a mens rea of 'intention to kill or

---

[123] See **3.3**.

cause serious harm to a person' than it is to separate mens rea as to the unlawful killing (result) from mens rea as to the circumstance (that V is a person). Discussing mens rea in such general terms is perfectly acceptable (*and often more straightforward*), but you must still remember to cover every mens rea requirement within the offence: D only commits the offence if every element is satisfied. With this in mind, it can be useful to employ the language of element analysis to pinpoint certain elements for particular comment (eg if D intended to kill but did not think she was unlawfully killing a person), and it can also be useful to have it in the back of your mind as a checklist to make sure you have not left anything out.

Three final points should be noted:

- **Liability requires D to complete every element of the offence:** As with actus reus elements, if *any* element of the mens rea is or may be missing then D has not committed the offence. You may then consider if D has committed an alternative (lesser) offence.

- **Don't be afraid of the unknown:** Problem question facts are often incomplete. Thus, particularly when applying the mens rea terms, you will often find that you are unsure if D satisfies the term or not. A common mistake students make is to pretend they are sure—stating that intention, for example, is clearly satisfied or clearly absent. In such a case, where it is not clear, this is wrong. It is much better to talk of likelihoods, particularly when predicting if a jury will find mens rea or not. Thus, unless you are very sure (eg the facts say that D intends or does not intend) then discuss whether mens rea will be proved in terms of what you think is more likely and why. Of course, you must be certain about which mens rea test is being applied and what the legal definition of that mens rea test means.

- **Intention (again):** This is a repetition from the discussion of intention, but it relates to a common mistake and so it is worth repeating. If the mens rea of an offence requires D to intend, always begin your discussion with direct intention (ie was it D's purpose or desire). Only if this is not found should you then consider oblique intention (ie was it foreseen as a virtual certainty) as a backup alternative definition.

ONLINE RESOURCE CENTRE

www.oxfordtextbooks.co.uk/orc/smithandhogan/

This chapter is accompanied by a selection of online resources to help you with this topic, including:

- **Multiple choice questions**
- **Chapter summary sheet**
- Two **sample examination questions** with answer guidance
- **Further reading**

Also available on the Online Resource Centre are:

- A selection of **videos** from the authors explaining key topics and principles
- **Legal updates**
- Useful **weblinks**

4

Interaction of actus reus
and mens rea

4.1 Introduction

In **Chapters 2** and **3** we discussed actus reus (the conduct/external requirements) and mens rea (the mental/internal requirements) as largely separate concerns. However, although it is useful to discuss the law in these terms, it is important to remember that criminal liability can only be found when these two concepts are proved together in relation to the same offence. This is illustrated in **Figure 4.1**.

Figure 4.1 Elements of criminal liability

In this chapter, our aim is to provide some more detail about this structure, bringing together the interaction of actus reus and mens rea.

The interaction of actus reus and mens rea elements arises in two separate contexts. First, it is important to understand how actus reus and mens rea elements relate to one another within the structure of an offence. We introduced this issue at the start of **Chapter 2**, but some more detail will be useful. Secondly, interaction issues also emerge when applying offence requirements to a set of facts. In this second context, we focus in particular on cases where actus reus and mens rea elements appear to be satisfied, but they do not take place at the same time or are not focused on the same target. We discuss each in turn.

4.2 Interaction within the structure of an offence

When identifying actus reus and mens rea elements within an offence, it is useful to remember how these elements interact with one another. This interaction is called the 'correspondence principle'.

The correspondence principle is the name given to the basic idea that each element within the actus reus of an offence should have a mens rea element that corresponds/couples with it. For example, the offence of criminal damage requires D to cause damage (actus reus) and intend or be reckless as to causing damage (mens rea).[1] From the actus reus point of view, the corresponding mens rea (intention or recklessness) provides a justification for holding D responsible for the damage: she has not only caused damage, but has chosen to do so or at least to risk unjustifiably doing so. Equally, such correspondence is also essential to our understanding of mens rea. As highlighted in **Chapter 3**, it is nonsense to inquire if D intends or is reckless in the abstract; we need to know the corresponding element of the actus reus. Our question is not 'is D intending or reckless', but '*is D intending or reckless as to causing damage to property belonging to another*'.[2]

When discussing an offence, it is therefore useful to think about the required correspondence of actus reus and mens rea within each offence element. For example, criminal damage is set out in **Table 4.1**.

Table 4.1 Corresponding offence elements (eg criminal damage)

	Actus reus	**Mens rea**
Conduct element	Any act (or omission) that causes the result	Voluntary
Circumstance element	The property damaged belongs to another	Intention or recklessness
Result element	Damage	Intention or recklessness

As we can see, for this offence every element (conduct, circumstance, and result) includes an actus reus requirement and a corresponding mens rea requirement.

---

[1] Criminal Damage Act 1971, s1.

[2] See **3.2**.

4.2.1 Exceptions to the correspondence principle

The correspondence principle does not represent an absolute rule of offence construction. Exceptions arise in two forms. First, an offence may contain actus reus elements without corresponding mens rea elements. These are called strict liability elements, arising most commonly within strict liability offences and constructive liability offences. Secondly, an offence may contain mens rea elements without corresponding actus reus elements. These elements are called ulterior mens rea elements. Both are common within the current law, but remain controversial.

4.2.1.1 Actus reus without corresponding mens rea: strict liability

We discussed strict liability[3] in **Chapter 3** to mean, simply, an absence of mens rea.[4] Thus, where an offence contains elements of strict liability—that is, where there are actus reus elements without corresponding mens rea—that offence can be seen as contrary to the correspondence principle. Strict liability is a label that you will find used in three main contexts. First, where an offence requires no mens rea beyond voluntary movement, it is referred to as a 'strict liability offence'. Secondly, where an offence requires mens rea for each element apart from one, this element (where no mens rea is required) is referred to as a 'strict liability element'. Thirdly, in the context of 'constructive offences', offences that include a basic offence with full actus reus and corresponding mens rea, but also include an additional actus reus element alone which is *constructed* on the basic offence to make a more serious crime.

Strict liability offences

Strict liability offences require no mens rea beyond voluntariness as to the conduct element. An example is the offence of driving when over the prescribed alcohol limit, set out in **Table 4.2**.[5]

Table 4.2 Strict liability offences (eg Road Traffic Act 1988, s5)

	Actus reus	**Mens rea**
Conduct element	Movement required to drive, attempt to drive or be in charge of vehicle	Voluntary
Circumstance element	Being in a 'motor vehicle'; being on a road or in a public place; being over the prescribed alcohol limit	None

Strict liability offences are controversial because they criminalise D for acting in circumstances (and sometimes causing results) that have not been proved to have been chosen by D in the sense of being intended, foreseen, or even negligently missed. For example, D would commit the driving offence in the previous paragraph even if she

---

[3] See generally Simester (ed), *Appraising Strict Liability* (2005).
[4] See **3.2.1**.
[5] Road Traffic Act 1988, s5.

did not realise that she was over the alcohol limit when driving, and even if she was not negligent as, for example, where her drink was spiked. As long as her actions satisfy the actus reus, and as long as she satisfies the basic mens rea of being voluntary in her movements, she has committed the offence.

Strict liability elements

Many more offences will require mens rea as to certain elements, or specific requirements within an element, but not to others. Where no mens rea is required to a certain element, this is commonly referred to as a strict liability element. An example is the offence of causing a child (V) to watch a sexual act, set out in **Table 4.3**.[6]

Table 4.3 Strict liability elements (eg Sexual Offences Act 2003, s12)

	Actus reus	**Mens rea**
Conduct element	Any act (or omission) that causes the result	Voluntary
Circumstance element	D is over 18 *and*	None
	(V is under 16	Lack of reasonable belief V is over 16
	or V is under 13)	None
Result element	Causing V to watch a third person engaging in a sexual activity *or* an image of sexual activity	Intention
Ulterior mens rea	*	Intention to gain sexual gratification

This offence provides a useful example because it includes several mens rea requirements: D's acts must be *voluntary*; she must *intend* the result element—to cause V to view sexual activity; and she must intend an ulterior mens rea requirement—to gain sexual gratification. Indeed, if V is between 13 and 16, D must also have mens rea as to this circumstance element. However, if V is under 13, the statute is clear that mens rea as to this element is strict: it is irrelevant if D intended V to be under 13; foresaw it as a risk; should have foreseen it; or had no way of knowing.

Offences of this kind where liability is strict as to one element are generally less controversial than strict liability offences, where no mens rea is required as to circumstances *and* results) but they remain problematic. Liability is still possible in the absence of proof of D's choice as to an essential part of what D is being blamed for.

Constructive liability offences

Constructive liability offences have an interesting and unique offence structure. At their base is a full offence that includes both actus reus and corresponding mens rea elements.

---

[6] Sexual Offences Act 2003, s12.

At this stage there is no exception to the correspondence principle. However, in addition to this base offence, constructive crimes also include additional actus reus elements, usually in the form of result elements, that construct upon the base offence to make a more serious crime. These additional constructing elements have no corresponding mens rea, they are strict liability elements. Thus, if D satisfies the elements of the base offence, and the additional actus reus element, she becomes liable for the constructive and more serious offence.

Probably the most famous constructive crime is murder.[7] D can be guilty of murder having intentionally caused serious injury (base offence) if that then results in the death of another person (additional actus reus) even though D has no intention or other mens rea as to that additional actus reus (death being caused). This is set out in **Table 4.4**.

Table 4.4 Murder and constructive liability

	Actus reus	**Mens rea**
Conduct element	Any act (or omission) that causes the result	Voluntary
Circumstance element	V is a person under the Queen's peace	Knowledge
Result element	**Death of V**	Intention to cause death *or* **intention to cause** grievous bodily harm

The *minimum* mens rea required of D relates to her voluntarily and intentionally causing grievous bodily harm to a person. If D acted in line with this intention (intentionally causing grievous bodily harm) she would commit a serious offence against the person.[8] Constructing upon this base offence of intentionally causing grievous bodily harm, the offence of murder also requires an additional actus reus element: that D caused death. However, this additional actus reus element does not require any additional corresponding mens rea. In effect, the grievous bodily harm offence (actus reus and mens rea) + death (additional actus reus) = murder.

> **Beware...**
> Although many offences include elements of strict liability, make sure that you check the case law for a particular offence to ensure that it has been interpreted in this manner. As discussed at **3.2.1.1**, the presumption of mens rea means that several offences that appear to lack mens rea requirements have been interpreted by the courts as requiring mens rea.

---

[7] See **Chapter 6**.
[8] Offences Against the Person Act, s18.

4.2.1.2 Mens rea without corresponding actus reus: ulterior mens rea

In contrast to strict or constructive liability where an offence contains actus reus elements without corresponding mens rea, ulterior mens rea[9] describes the opposite phenomenon; mens rea elements that lack corresponding actus reus. Of course, for mens rea to make sense it must still relate to something (eg we cannot understand an intention requirement without knowing *what* D must intend). However, the object of D's mens rea, what she must intend, does not form part of the actus reus and thus does not need to come about for the crime to be completed.

For example, to be liable for the offence of theft, D must appropriate the property of another (actus reus) dishonestly and with the intention to permanently deprive V of that property (mens rea).[10] Here, the requirement that D must 'intend to permanently deprive V' is an ulterior mens rea requirement. This is illustrated in **Table 4.5**.

Table 4.5 Theft and ulterior mens rea

	Actus reus	**Mens rea**
Conduct element	Any act (or omission) causing the result	Voluntary
Circumstance element	What is appropriated is property	Knowledge
	What is appropriated belongs to another (ie not exclusively to D)	Knowledge
	D's appropriation is objectively dishonest	Knowledge of dishonesty
Result element	Appropriation of V's property	Intention
Ulterior mens rea element	*	**Intention to permanently deprive V of the property**

The offence requirement that D must 'intend to permanently deprive V' is an ulterior mens rea element because it lacks a corresponding actus reus element: D must *intend* to permanently deprive, but whether D actually permanently deprives V of her property is irrelevant.

Ulterior mens rea requirements are relatively common in the criminal law. They provide a useful option for the legislator in a variety of ways.[11]

A) **Where corresponding actus reus would be impractical:** In cases such as theft it is obviously impractical to include an actus reus requirement that D must 'permanently deprive' V of her property: the offence could never be complete unless the property was

---

[9] See Horder, 'Crimes of Ulterior Intent' in Simester and Smith (eds), *Harm and Culpability* (1996) 153.

[10] Theft Act 1968, s1.

[11] Horder, 'Crimes of Ulterior Intent' in Simester and Smith (eds), *Harm and Culpability* (1996) 153.

destroyed because D would always have the option to return it thereby negativing the actus reus. However, without the mens rea requirement of an intention to permanently deprive the offence would be too wide, criminalising non-consensual borrowing.

B) **Where we wish to intervene to prevent harm:** Many offences, such as the general inchoate offences of attempt, conspiracy, and assisting and encouraging, seek to criminalise D for taking steps towards committing a future offence (trying to commit it; agreeing to commit it; assisting or encouraging another to commit it) with the intention, or in some cases recklessness, that the future offence will be completed. In such cases, we do not want to wait for the future offence to be completed before we can act to criminalise D, so such offences punish D for taking steps towards the future offence (actus reus) and her ulterior mens rea as to it coming about.[12]

C) **Where D has already committed a certain offence, but she does so with the intention to commit another:** Where this is the case, certain offences have been drafted to criminalise D for a more serious offence that takes account of her ulterior intention. For example, section 62 of the Sexual Offences Act 2003 criminalises D who commits an offence with the (ulterior) intention to commit a sexual offence. Again, this future sexual offence does not need to come about in fact, so it is not part of the actus reus, it must simply be intended.

Terminology...
It is important for you to understand the terminology of strict and constructive liability, and of ulterior mens rea. However, this is simply to highlight them as exceptions to the correspondence principle. Although common within the law, you will see that offences that have been constructed in these forms are often some of the most controversial.

4.3 Interaction within the application of an offence

Having explored the different ways actus reus and mens rea elements can interact within the structure of an offence, this second part of the chapter explores their interaction when applying an offence to problem facts. With problem facts, we are looking to identify a criminal event, an event in which D completes all of the actus reus and mens rea elements of the offence.

In most cases, as long as you understand the offence requirements, and as long as the facts are clear, the application stage can be quite straightforward. Your task is to work through the offence elements: if they are all satisfied then D has committed the offence; if one or more of them is missing then she has not committed the offence.

In a minority of cases, however, additional problems relating to the interaction of actus reus and mens rea will emerge. In these cases, although D completes all the actus reus and mens rea elements, the two halves do not mesh with one another. There are two main examples of this. First is the case where D's actus reus is directed at one object (eg D hits V), but her mens rea is directed at another (eg she intended to hit X). Here, the question is whether we can we use D's mens rea directed at X as sufficient mens rea for an offence against V. Can we bring the elements together to create a single *whole* offence? The second set of cases is

---

[12] **Chapter 11.**

where D completes the actus reus and mens rea elements of an offence, but they do not appear to coincide with one another, they come about at different times. As highlighted in **Chapters 2** and **3**, D's mens rea must correspond with, or must be apparent at the same time as, the conduct element of the actus reus. However, in a case where D has possessed that mens rea, either before or after her act, is there any way we can find liability?

4.3.1 Actus reus and mens rea at different objects: transferred malice

When D completes the actus reus of an offence (eg causing damage or injury) for which mens rea is required, that mens rea must correspond with the actus reus elements (eg D must intend to cause that damage or injury). In some cases, D's mens rea will be indiscriminate. For example, D may detonate a bomb intending to kill *anyone nearby*, or set a fire intending to *cause general damage*. Where D's mens rea is indiscriminate in this way, it is straightforward to find that D's mens rea corresponds with the actus reus and satisfies the offence. If D's bomb kill's V, for example, we can say that D intended to kill V because V was within the group ('anyone nearby') that D intended to kill. Equally, if V survived and V2 was killed, we can say that D intended to kill V2 as well (V2 is within the same group).

Problems can emerge, however, where D acts with a specific target in mind. For example, D may detonate a bomb intending to kill V in particular, or start a fire intending to damage specific property. Where D has such an intention, and succeeds in her plan, then liability is also straightforward. For example, D intends to kill V in particular and does so: actus reus and mens rea elements are directed at the same target. However, where D explodes the bomb intending to kill V in particular but also kills V2, or misses V and only kills V2, then we have a problem. Equally, if D's fire spreads in an unexpected way and damages property other than that intended, we have the same problem. In these cases, we have actus reus (death and damage), and we have mens rea (intention to cause death and damage), but the targets of the two are different: D intends to kill or damage one target, but actually kills or damages another. Is D liable for an offence?

Where D's actus reus and mens rea target different objects in this manner liability is found through the doctrine of 'transferred malice' or more accurately 'transferred mens rea'. Essentially, D's targeted mens rea (eg D's intention to kill a particular person or intention to damage particular property) is *transferred* to the object that was the victim of D's actus reus (eg the actual person killed or property damaged). This was discussed in *Latimer*.

Latimer (1886) 17 QBD 359

D swung a belt at V attempting to hit him. V was only lightly hit by the belt. However, a woman (V2), who was standing by V, was also hit by the belt and severely injured. D had clearly committed an offence against V. However, D was charged with a more serious offence against the person in relation to V2's injuries.[13]

• Court: guilty of offence. D's malice (mens rea) directed at V could be transferred to V2, satisfying the mens rea of the offence in relation to V2.

---

[13] Offences Against the Person Act 1861, s20. See **7.5**.

In the absence of transferred malice, D would not escape liability altogether: he would still be liable, for example, for his attempt to seriously injure V. However, attempt liability alone in these circumstances would seem odd. After all, D not only tried to cause serious injury, but he did so, albeit to an unforeseen victim. It is this intuition that D deserves liability for the full offence that has given rise to the legal fiction that is transferred malice, with the court manipulating D's mens rea towards one object into a men rea towards another. With both actus reus and mens rea now focused on the same target, liability for, what was in this case an offence against the person, can be found. This is illustrated in **Figure 4.2**.

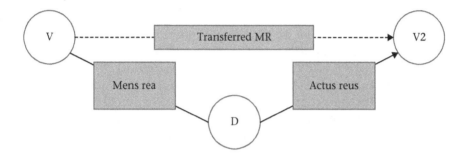

Figure 4.2 Transferred mens rea

The transfer of mens rea is therefore able to ensure liability by linking actus reus and mens rea elements that would otherwise lack for coincidence on a single object. This will apply for assault cases such as *Latimer*, homicide cases where D kills an unintended target,[14] as well as a host of other offences such as criminal damage where D may cause damage to an unintended target, for example. In each case, as made clear in *Latimer*, it is not necessary for D to have foreseen harm to V2, or even for D to have been negligent in failing to foresee it. Rather, it is D's mens rea towards V that is simply transferred to bring together the elements of liability.

4.3.1.1 Limitations to the doctrine of transferred malice

There are two important limitations to the doctrine of transferred malice. First, D's mens rea can only be transferred where it relates to the *same* crime as her actus reus. For example, D throws a stone at V, a person, but misses and causes property damage. In this case, although D's intention to cause harm to V is hardly to her credit, an intention to hurt a person is categorically different from intention or recklessness as to property damage, and transfer of mens rea is therefore prevented.[15] Equally, if D shoots at a dog (property) in an attempt to kill it, but misses and hits its owner, V, no transfer will be possible. D has acted with the intention to destroy the dog, so his mens rea is an intent to cause criminal damage, but his actus reus is the killing of a person; D's mens rea cannot be transferred from the damage to the dog to find D liable for V's death as a murder. This is illustrated in **Figure 4.3**.

---

[14] *Mitchell* [1983] QB 741. See also *Smith and Hogan's Criminal Law* (14th edn, 2014), Ch5.
[15] *Pembliton* (1847) LR 2 CCR 119.

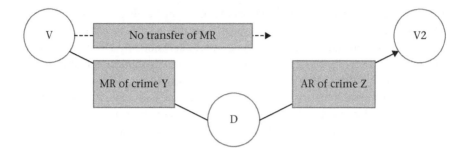

Figure 4.3 No transferred mens rea between different crimes

The second limitation to the doctrine is where liability would require a *double transfer of malice*. In *AG's Reference (No 3 of 1994)*,[16] D stabbed his pregnant girl-friend, V, several times with the intention required for murder. As a result of this, V gave birth prematurely and her baby, V2, later died. The House of Lords rejected D's liability for the murder of V2 [17] because such liability would require a double transfer of mens rea: from the mother, V, to her foetus, X, and then from the foetus to its changed status as a person at birth,V2. This is illustrated in **Figure 4.4**.

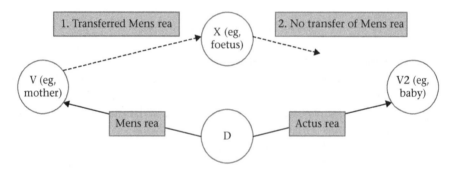

Figure 4.4 No double transfer of mens rea

Despite these two limitations, the doctrine of transferred malice remains controversial. For some, the doctrine remains too open and should be limited further. For example, Horder has criticised the doctrine for allowing a transfer of mens rea even where the victim of the harm (V2) was unintended *and* the circumstances of the harm were unanticipated as, for example, where D shoots a gun at V; V2, who is hiding in the bushes nearby, is startled by the noise and dies of a heart attack. Horder recommends the introduction of a 'remoteness' limitation.[18] Beyond this, others have questioned whether given that the doctrine is a legal fiction, it is necessary at all. In most cases involving transferred mens rea, it would be possible without the need for transfer to find attempt liability in relation to D's intended target, and possibly a reckless- or negligence-based offence in relation to the actual harm caused.[19]

16 [1996] 1 Cr App R 351.
17 Although liability for manslaughter was upheld, D's conviction for unlawful act manslaughter did not rely on a transfer of malice. See **Chapter 5**.
18 Horder, 'Transferred Malice and the Remoteness of Unexpected Outcomes from Intentions' [2006] Crim LR 383. See also Eldar, 'The Limits of Transferred Malice' (2012) 32 OJLS 633.
19 Ashworth, 'Transferred Malice and Punishment for Unforeseen Consequences' in Glazebrook (ed), *Reshaping the Criminal Law* (1978) 77.

4.3.2 Actus reus and mens rea at different times: coincidence principle

When discussing transferred malice, we highlighted the need for mens rea and actus reus to coincide, or come together, in relation to the same object (V). Beyond this, it is also essential that they should coincide at the same point in *time*; this is traditionally referred to as the coincidence principle. For example, D forms the intention to kill her husband (V) by poisoning his food. However, when D is driving home from work someone runs in front of her car and is killed, it is V. D has not committed murder. Although D has caused V's death, which is the actus reus of murder, and she intends in general terms to kill him, she lacks the mens rea in the form of intention to kill *by this act* and *at this point in time*.

This need for temporal coincidence is the reason why our application of criminal law to problem facts should always begin with the actus reus. Once it is established that the actus reus of an offence has been completed we can then inquire whether D possessed the mens rea for the offence *at the point in time* that she completed the *conduct element of the actus reus*. Whether or not she possessed the mens rea at some other point in time is irrelevant; liability demands that she must have possessed it at that particular time for liability to be established. It is worth stressing here that we are talking about coincidence between mens rea and the *conduct element* of the actus reus (D's act or omission within the actus reus) rather than with the actus reus more generally. For example, if D laces V's food with poison with the intention to kill, and does in fact do so, she has committed murder even if she changes her mind before the poison takes effect and kills V. Indeed, she may even change her mind the split second after lacing V's food, well in advance of V even ingesting the poison. As long as V's conduct is the cause of V's death, and as long as D had the required mens rea when completing that conduct, there will be coincidence and the offence will be committed.

In **Figure 4.5** the point of coincidence is represented by the vertical dotted line.

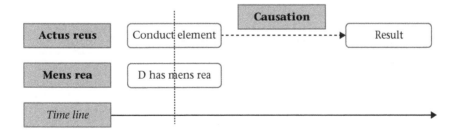

Figure 4.5 Coincidence of actus reus and mens rea

Coincidence is an absolute rule of law to which there are *no exceptions*: a lack of coincidence will mean a lack of liability.

However, in the rare cases where an apparent lack of coincidence is at issue it can be very difficult to accept this conclusion. After all, D has the mens rea for the crime, at some point in time and has completed the actus reus at some point in time and so it can be very appealing to try to find ways around the rule. Indeed, this is what we have seen in several cases; *not* exceptions to the coincidence principle, but the courts finding often ingenious ways to identify coincidence where it looks like there is none. Such cases can be split into two categories: where actus reus seems to precede mens rea, and where mens rea seems to precede actus reus.

4.3.2.1 Actus reus and then mens rea

The first example of a potential lack of coincidence is where D's acts causing the result (actus reus) precede the point in time at which D holds the requisite mens rea. This is illustrated in **Figure 4.6**.

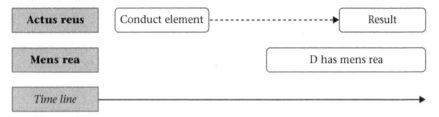

Figure 4.6 Lack of coincidence—actus reus then mens rea

Where this problem has emerged, the courts have developed two possible methods of finding coincidence.

The first, the *continuing act* approach, is exemplified in *Fagan* (see **Figure 4.7**).

> **Fagan** [1969] 1 QB 439
>
> D accidentally drove his car onto a policeman's (V's) foot and, when he became aware of this, intentionally took his time moving the car in order to cause further pain. When discussing Fagan's potential liability for an offence against the person, the problem became apparent: when performing acts within the actus reus (driving onto the foot) D lacked mens rea; but when he gained mens rea (intentionally causing pain) these acts were already complete.
>
> • Divisional Court: guilty of offence against the person. D's 'act' did not stop when driving onto the foot, but continued when on the foot. Thus, D's act did coincide with a time when he possessed the required mens rea.

Figure 4.7 Understanding the approach in *Fagan*

By extending and expanding the conduct element, coincidence between actus rea and mens rea can be found. The courts are not creating an exception to the coincidence principle, but they are manipulating the definition of the conduct element in order to find it.

However, although the continuing act approach reaches the desired conclusion, its operation can be criticised as rather artificial. With this in mind, perhaps a better approach to the problem, as outlined in more recent case law, is to abandon a focus on D's initial acts, and to focus instead on her later omission.

The second, the *omissions approach*, is exemplified in *Miller* (see **Figure 4.8**).

 Miller [1983] 2 AC 161

D, a squatter in V's house, went to sleep holding a lit cigarette. He awoke to find the mattress smouldering, but did nothing other than move to an adjoining room. The fire caused extensive damage, and D was charged with criminal damage[20] based on his omission to tackle the smouldering mattress or alert the authorities (a duty arising from his inadvertent creation of a dangerous situation).

- Court: guilty of criminal damage.
- Court of Appeal: conviction upheld on appeal.
- House of Lords: conviction upheld on appeal.

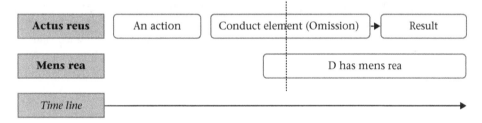

Figure 4.8 Understanding the approach in *Miller*

In this case, the fire was caused by D's positive act by dropping the cigarette. However, if the court were to focus on this act then the same coincidence problem emerges: when D acted to cause the fire he lacked mens rea as he was asleep, and when he had the mens rea by foreseeing the possibility of damage his action was complete. Rather than trying to reinterpret and lengthen D's acts as in *Fagan*, the House of Lords instead focused on D's omission to act having become aware of the danger. As discussed in **Chapter 2**, omissions liability is only applicable where D has a duty to act. However, in this case, having created the dangerous situation and become aware of that danger, D has a clear duty to act by taking reasonable steps to prevent the harm. In failing to do so and thereby breaching that duty, he has completed an omission that satisfies the actus reus of the offence, and has done so at a time that he possesses the requisite mens rea. Again, we have coincidence, and so we have liability.

Beware...
As the continuing act approach (*Fagan*) and the omissions approach (*Miller*) both provide answers to the same problem, it is tempting to think of them interchangeably. However, you should be careful not to do so. As set out previously, they are *alternatives*. It is often good to acknowledge both options, but remember that they are not the same.

---

[20] Criminal Damage Act 1971, s1(1) and (3).

4.3.2.2 Mens rea and then actus reus

The second example of a potential lack of coincidence is where D acts with the requisite mens rea for the offence, but it is her later action without mens rea that forms the actus reus of the offence. This is illustrated in **Figure 4.9**.

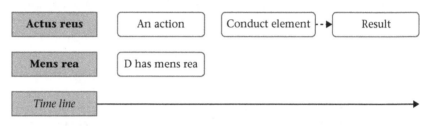

Figure 4.9   Lack of coincidence—mens rea then actus reus

Where this problem has emerged, the courts have sought to find coincidence using the *single transaction* approach. An early example of this is the Privy Council case *Thabo Meli* (see **Figure 4.10**).

Thabo Meli [1954] 1 All ER 373

D and others hit V over the head and then as they had planned attempted to disguise their crime by pushing his corpse over a cliff. However, it was later discovered that V had not died from the initial blows, but rather from exposure at the bottom of the cliff. Thus, D had the mens rea for murder when striking the initial blows that did not cause death, but when completing the later act that did cause death he lacked mens rea. There was no further intention to kill because D thought V was already dead.

- Court: guilty of murder.
- Privy Council: conviction upheld on appeal. Rather than looking at each individual action separately, D's actions were better analysed as part of a general plan to cause death and to hide the body: a series of acts that could be linked within one logical transaction. Analysed in this way, since D possessed the mens rea for murder at one point during this single transaction, coincidence was found.

Figure 4.10   Understanding the approach in *Thabo Meli*

Within this small class of cases where D believes she has killed with mens rea, but actually kills with a later act, the transaction approach has become firmly established.

There is an appealing logic about this approach, and there is little doubt that D is deserving of liability, but there is also some uncertainty. Chiefly, this uncertainty relates to the basis upon which the courts link D's acts within the transaction. A series of cases in **Table 4.6** set out how the courts have approached this task.

Table 4.6 Developing cases on single actus reus transactions

Case reference	Case facts	Basis for linking acts
Thabo Meli [1954] 1 All ER 373	D hit V with the intention to kill (mens rea for murder). D thought V was dead and pushed him off a cliff to make it look like an accident. D died from exposure following the fall. A single transaction links D's initial attack (with mens rea) to pushing V off the cliff (actus reus causing death).	Hitting D over the head (act 1) and pushing him off the cliff (act 2) were both part of D's single plan. Thus, they can be linked as a single transaction.
Church [1966] 1 QB 59	D fought and began to strangle V until she passed out (with mens rea for manslaughter). D thought V was dead and threw her body into a river to hide the body (no mens rea as he thought she was dead). V drowned; D was convicted of manslaughter on the basis of linking his first act (with mens rea) to his second act (causing death) to find coincidence.	There was no 'plan' linking D's first act (attacking V) and second act (throwing her in the river). However, the Court of Criminal Appeal still found that they could be linked within a single transaction. It did not explain why.
Le Brun [1992] QB 61	D hit his wife (V) causing unconsciousness (with the mens rea for manslaughter). D realised that V was not dead. D dragged V home to try and cover up his offence, but dropped her accidentally and caused further head injuries from which she died. D was convicted of manslaughter on the basis of linking his first act (with mens rea) to his second act (causing death) to find coincidence.	There was no 'plan' linking D's first act (hitting V) and second act (dropping V). Also, unlike the previous cases, D did not believe V was dead. However, the Court of Appeal still found that D's acts could be linked as a single transaction on the basis that D's acts were of the same type. Thus, if D had dropped V trying to take her to a doctor, this act may not be linked with the former. However, as he was trying to conceal his crime, it could.

In light of these cases, it seems that the courts have a wide discretion when deciding whether D's acts can be linked within a single transaction or not. If they deem that D's acts remain of the same type, which they seem to regard in general terms as meaning that they remain 'bad', then they are likely to link D's acts in order to allow for coincidence. It is only if D accidentally causes harm when later trying to help as, for example, by dropping V when taking her to a hospital, that the courts are unlikely to link D's acts.

Extra detail...

An alternative approach to this second problem of coincidence may be to focus solely on D's initial acts and simply establish a chain of causation from these acts. For example, in *Le Brun* 'but for' D's initial attack, D would not have dragged her and she would not have died when dropped, and a generous view of legal causation may allow that this original attack was also a significant and ongoing cause of death. The appeal of this approach is that we can ignore D's second act and we do not have to link it with the first. Rather, through the causation rules, we can say that the first act is an alternative actus reus that caused the death, and find coincidence with mens rea at this point.

This approach was discussed in *Le Brun*, but the court preferred the single transaction approach. However, were a similar case to arise in problem facts, it would be useful to highlight this as an alternative approach.[21]

4.4 Reform

In many ways, the correspondence principle remains the ideal of criminalisation: offences should consist of harmful actions (actus reus) that D has chosen to bring, or risk bringing about (mens rea).[22] However, to the extent that this is true, the topics discussed earlier represent at least partial failures to meet that ideal:

- Through offence definitions:
  - ▷ strict and constructive liability—offences containing actus reus elements without corresponding mens rea;
  - ▷ ulterior mens rea—offences containing mens rea elements without corresponding actus reus.

- Through the application of offences:
  - ▷ transferred malice—finding liability even though D's actus reus and mens rea were targeted at different objects;
  - ▷ coincidence—finding liability even though D's actus reus and mens rea (analysed standardly) occurred at different times.

With this in mind, it is unsurprising that each of these areas has given rise to considerable debate, a debate that is often picked up in essay questions. Such debates have already been highlighted within our previous discussion of the law, and we do not propose to repeat them. However, when thinking about potential reform in this area it is useful to structure your thinking, and possibly your essay, by separating two importantly distinct questions.

- **Do we want liability in these circumstances at all?**

This is what we might call a threshold question. If we agree that offences *should only* be committed where D demonstrates both guilty mind and guilty act, and that these

---

[21] Arenson, '*Thabo Meli* Revisited: The Pernicious Effects of Result-Driven Decisions' (2013) 77 J Crim L 41.

[22] Horder, 'A Critique of the Correspondence Principle' [1995] Crim LR 759; Mitchell, 'In Defence of a Principle of Correspondence' [1999] Crim LR 195.

should focus on the same object and occur at the same time, are we willing to tolerate any exceptions? For example, in the context of constructive liability, if D's acts cause an additional harm, for example death, should we define offences to punish D for this even if she only foresaw causing a lesser harm?[23] In the context of transferred malice, where D hits V2 when intending to hit V1, should we allow a rule that artificially transfers the mens rea from V1 to V2, or should we reject it? In this latter example, such rejection seems even more appealing when we could still charge D with an attempt offence in relation to V1, and possibly a reckless- or negligence-based offence in relation to V2.[24]

- If we do want liability in these circumstances, what is the least objectionable way to secure it?

This question is based on an acceptance that (in certain cases) constructive and strict liability, ulterior mens rea, transferred malice, or the stretching of coincidence can be acceptable. In the context of strict liability, constructive crimes, and ulterior mens rea, the debate then becomes how *widely* the practice should be available. Are such offences acceptable generally, or are they only acceptable in certain exceptional circumstances, for example to combat particularly serious harms,[25] or only where finding mens rea is particularly difficult.[26] In the context of transferred malice and coincidence, the same question arises: if these techniques can be used, where should we place the limits, for example by the additional restrictions to transferred malice suggested by Horder?[27] However, in addition to this, transferred malice and coincidence also raise issues of *method*: how are we to make sense of mens rea transfers, and how can we find coincidence when it appears to be absent? This second issue is also discussed earlier, and particularly in the context of coincidence where the common law seems to have developed multiple and alternative methods for addressing the same problem. Again, here, your job is to discuss these methods and comment on which, if any you believe is the most appropriate.

4.5 Eye on assessment

This section focuses on problem-type questions, and how the topics discussed previously should be structured into your answers. To do so we need to distinguish, again, between those topics relating to the elements of an offence (strict, constructive liability, and ulterior mens rea), and those relating to the application of an offence (transferred malice and coincidence).

---

[23] Several jurisdictions have sought to eliminate offences of constructive liability. Eg in the Republic of Ireland we see this in the reform of the offences against the person: Non-Fatal Offences Against the Person Act 1997.

[24] Ashworth, 'Transferred Malice and Punishment for Unforeseen Consequences' in Glazebrook (ed), *Reshaping the Criminal Law* (1978) 77.

[25] This is often a justification for punishing ulterior harmful intentions before any corresponding action is completed. See **Chapter 11**.

[26] This is often the justification for regulatory offences (especially those targeting companies) being strict. See **Chapter 3**.

[27] See **4.3.1.1**.

4.5.1 Offence content

The content of an offence provides you with the offence elements of actus reus and mens rea that you must apply in a problem question. Whether the offence is one that contains elements of strict liability or ulterior mens rea may therefore be useful to highlight in order to explain why it is not necessary to identify certain corresponding mens rea in the context of strict liability, or actus reus in the context of ulterior mens rea. However, unless the question specifically asks you to evaluate or discuss the law as you apply it, then there is no need to enter a debate about the rights and wrongs of the offence. In most cases, you are asked to 'discuss potential liability', not to 'discuss the merits of the law'.

4.5.2 Offence application

The rules relating to coincidence of actus reus and mens rea, that is coincidence on the same object and at the same time, are essential to the application of the law. They are therefore essential considerations within all problem questions. However, although essential, it is relatively rare that a problem question, *and very rare that a real case* will involve problems in this area. The ideal approach to a problem question will therefore be to ensure coincidence, but not to waste unnecessary time discussing it unless such discussion is required.

As with **Chapters 2** and **3**, we are focusing on the third step of the problem question structure introduced in **Chapter 1**.

STEP 1 Identify the potential criminal event in the facts

This should be simply stated (eg 'The first potential criminal event arises where D kicks V'). The role of this stage is to highlight which part of the question you are answering before you begin to apply the law.

STEP 2 Identify the potential offence

Again, state this simply (eg 'When breaking the vase, D may be liable for criminal damage'). The role of this stage is to highlight which offence you are going to apply.

STEP 3 Applying the offence to the facts

Having highlighted a possible offence, Step 3 requires you to both identify the actus reus and mens rea of that offence, *and* apply them to the facts.

As discussed in **Chapter 2**, your analysis within Step 3 should always begin with the actus reus elements of the offence. Identify the act/omission that D has completed, the relevant circumstances, and where necessary the unlawful results of those acts. Remember, where the actus reus does specify results, you must also show that D's acts *caused* those results.

Having examined the actus reus of the offence, you now know the point in time that D completed the relevant acts/omissions. Thus, when moving to mens rea (discussed in

Chapter 3) you can now ask more precisely whether D satisfies the mens rea at the *time* she completes the conduct element and *directed* at the relevant object.

The issues discussed in this chapter should be considered when applying the mens rea elements. There are two possibilities.

- **If D satisfies the mens rea at that time and directed at that object:** Then there is no problem with coincidence. You do not need to say more on the topic: by explicitly identifying the mens rea at that relevant time and directed at that relevant object you have already demonstrated that coincidence is present.

- **If D does not satisfy the mens rea at that time and directed at that object:** Then there is a problem with coincidence. You can now highlight the problem; moving on to a full discussion of transferred malice and/or the reinterpretation of acts in order to see if coincidence can be found.

ONLINE RESOURCE CENTRE

www.oxfordtextbooks.co.uk/orc/smithandhogan/

This chapter is accompanied by a selection of online resources to help you with this topic, including:

- **Multiple choice questions**
- **Chapter summary sheet**
- Two **sample examination questions** with answer guidance
- **Further reading**

Also available on the Online Resource Centre are:

- A selection of **videos** from the authors explaining key topics and principles
- **Legal updates**
- Useful **weblinks**

5

Murder

5.1 Introduction

From this point in the book our focus narrows from the general principles and structures of criminal law, to explore particular offences and defences. We begin with a category of crimes known as homicide offences in general (offences which involve the killing of a person), and with the offence of murder in particular.

> *Terminology...*
> When we refer to categories of offences such as 'homicide offences', we are not referring to an offence with a distinct actus reus and mens rea. Rather, we are simply referring to a label that describes a group of offences that share certain characteristics (other categories include, eg, sexual offences; property offences; etc). It is not accurate to say D is liable for homicide as such, but rather she is liable for a homicide offence such as murder or manslaughter.

D commits murder where she, as a person,[1] unlawfully causes the death of V who is also a human being, with the intention to kill or cause serious bodily harm—called grievous bodily harm or GBH. Murder is generally considered the most serious crime. The harm involved does not simply affect the interests of V, but undermines V's potential to experience any future 'worldly' interests of any kind. Even within the law's class of 'homicide' offences murder is distinguished as most serious by the requirement of proof of intent: D has not simply killed V, she has done so *intending* to kill or cause GBH. It is because of its gravity as an offence that murder was until relatively recently punished with the death penalty,[2] and currently attracts a *mandatory* life sentence.

> **Don't be confused...**
>
> A mandatory life sentence will rarely equate to a lifetime in prison. Rather, a life sentence is made up of a tariff period; that is, a minimum period in prison reflecting the circumstances of the killing, followed by a release on licence during which time D is released from prison but is monitored and may be restricted in various ways.[3] The sentence is a 'life sentence' because the licence-period restrictions continue for the life of D. The typical tariff period for a single murder in unexceptional circumstances is 15 years' imprisonment.

Despite the perceived position of murder at the apex of criminal law, however, it remains a problematic and controversial offence. Indeed, the Law Commission has described it as a 'rickety structure set upon shaky foundations'.[4] This is both a criticism of the offence itself, which will be discussed later, as well as a criticism of its position and definition in the context of the other homicide offences (discussed in **Chapter 6**).

5.2 Defining murder

The Homicide Act 1957 and, more recently, the Corporate Manslaughter and Corporate Homicide Act 2007, have codified several offences and defences within the wider group of homicide offences. However, crucially, the offence of murder remains a common law and uncodified offence.

The definition of murder still quoted widely by the courts derives from a seventeenth-century book by Coke:[5]

> Murder is when a man of sound memory, and of the age of discretion, unlawfully killeth within any country of the realm any reasonable creature *in rerum natura* under the king's peace, with malice aforethought, either expressed by the party or implied by law, so as the party wounded, or hurt, etc die of that wound or hurt, etc within a year and a day after the same.

---

[1] Murder cannot be committed by a corporation or other organisation. See **Chapter 6** for the possibility of corporate manslaughter.

[2] Homicide Act 1957 marked the end of a mandatory death sentence for all convicted murderers.

[3] Criminal Justice Act 2003, Sch 21. See Padfield, 'Tariffs in Murder' [2002] Crim LR 192.

[4] Law Commission, *A New Homicide Act for England and Wales* (Consultation 177, 2005) para 1.4.

[5] 3 Inst 47. See also *Smith and Hogan's Criminal Law* (14th edn, 2015), Ch14.

Despite its continued application, the archaic and increasingly inaccurate definition contained in this quotation should not be applied straightforwardly in a modern context. Rather, although it establishes authority for the offence of murder, a contemporary translation and clarification of the offence elements is essential.

In modern language, the offence of murder requires D to unlawfully kill another person under the Queen's peace, and to do so intending to kill or cause GBH (serious bodily harm). The elements of murder are set out in **Table 5.1**.

Table 5.1 Murder

	Actus reus	**Mens rea**
Conduct element	Any conduct that causes the result	Voluntary
Circumstance element	V must be a person;	Knowledge
	under the Queen's peace;	Knowledge
	killing must be unlawful	Lack of belief in lawfulness
Result element	Death of V	Intention to kill or cause GBH

This represents the current definition of murder: modernising the language from Coke's definition and also recognising important changes within the law. For example, contrary to Coke, the modern definition of murder does not include a requirement for V's death to follow 'within a year and a day' of D's conduct. This requirement made some sense historically where a delay of this kind would make it almost impossible to demonstrate a causal link from V's death back to D's original conduct. However, with the advancement of medical science, not only has demonstrating such a causal link become easier, but the likelihood of delay before death has also increased through the use of life-support machines, etc. The rule was abolished by the Law Reform (Year and a Day Rule) Act 1996.[6] As a result, as long as causation can be established, D may now be liable for murder regardless of the delay between her original conduct and the death of V. The only remaining restriction is that where there is considerable delay (over three years) or where D has already been prosecuted for a non-fatal offence relating to the same incident the Attorney General must consent to the murder prosecution.[7]

Despite the seriousness of murder as a crime, it is important to recognise that cases caught within the definition will not always be morally straightforward. As with other offences, where D satisfies the actus reus and mens rea elements she is liable irrespective of her motive.[8] Thus, murder is committed where D kills due to hatred or spite, but it is also committed in more morally ambiguous cases such as so-called 'mercy killings' where D intentionally kills, often with V's consent, in order to relieve pain or suffering. The moral diversity of these cases is useful to keep in mind when discussing the precise

---

[6] Yale, 'A Year and a Day in Homicide' (1989) 48 CLJ 202.
[7] Law Reform (Year and a Day Rule) Act 1996, s2.
[8] The only exception is where D's reasons/motives satisfy the elements of a criminal defence.

requirements of the offence. It is also something that we will return to when we consider potential reforms in this area, not least the continued application of a mandatory life sentence to all murder cases.[9]

5.3 Actus reus of murder

The actus reus of murder is satisfied where D unlawfully kills another person under the Queen's peace. We discuss each element in turn.

5.3.1 Acts and omissions

As with other result crimes[10] murder does not specify a certain act that D must complete (eg shooting, stabbing, etc), but rather proscribes *any* conduct that causes the result—any conduct causing death. Thus, it is necessary to identify some conduct by D, but, as long as it causes the result, the type of conduct is irrelevant. D may also commit murder by omission, as in *Gibbins and Proctor*, as long as the requirements of omissions liability are satisfied.[11]

> **Gibbins and Proctor** (1918) 13 Cr App R 134
>
> D1 (Gibbins) and his lover D2 (Proctor) failed to feed D1's 7-year-old child (V), resulting in V's death.
>
> • Crown Court: D1 and D2 convicted for murder.
> • Court of Criminal Appeal: conviction upheld on appeal. D1 liable for his omission to feed based on a familial duty owed to V; D2 based on her assumption of a duty (she was in charge of buying food).

5.3.2 Necessary circumstances

There are several circumstances that must be present for D to satisfy the actus reus. In most cases these will be clear and very little discussion will be required. However, problem cases can arise.

5.3.2.1 Under the Queen's peace

Where soldiers kill alien enemies 'in the heat of war, and in actual exercise thereof',[12] the killing is not under the Queen's peace and is not, therefore, murder. This exception is important, particularly as section 9 of the Offences Against the Person Act 1861 makes any murder or manslaughter committed by a British citizen, *committed on any land outside the UK*, an offence that can be tried and punished in England. It is, however, a narrow exception. Where a soldier kills another, even an alien enemy, in a war zone

---

[9] See **5.6.1**.
[10] For discussion of 'result crimes', see **2.4.2**.
[11] See **2.6**.
[12] Hale, *The History of the Pleas of the Crown* (1736), vol I, 443.

and it is not done in the heat of battle, this will be considered as having been committed under the Queen's peace and D will satisfy the actus reus of murder.[13]

5.3.2.2 Unlawful killing

To say that the killing must be 'unlawful' is simply to stress that it must satisfy all actus reus and mens rea elements, and be done without lawful defence. Thus, for example, where D kills in self-defence, she is not liable for murder.[14]

> *Point to remember...*
> As we will see in **Chapter 14**, some defences do not apply to murder (eg duress and duress of circumstance).

5.3.2.3 V must be a person

For murder, as with other homicide offences; offences against the person; etc, the victim must be a human being. This sounds straightforward, and in the vast majority of cases it will be. However, particularly in relation to homicide offences, the status of the victim as a person will occasionally require discussion. This discussion focuses on two questions: when does V begin to be a person and, secondly, when does this status end?

A) **When does V begin to be a person:** An unborn child (foetus) is not a person within the criminal law. Thus, where D kills an unborn child she may commit an offence of child destruction or procuring a miscarriage,[15] but she cannot commit murder. V only becomes a person in law when she is 'fully expelled from the womb' and alive.[16] Whether the umbilical cord and/or afterbirth have been expelled is irrelevant, as long as the whole of the baby's body is removed.[17] This position may be criticised in purely biological terms, the difference between a late-term foetus and a neonate is only (as Simester and Sullivan put it) a matter of location.[18] However, it is a divide that has rarely troubled the courts,[19] and the exclusion of murder from prenatal deaths is also useful to allow for specific offences that can be more easily tailored to the unique issues that arise in this area, and thereby avoid any conflict with legal abortive procedures. Despite Article 2 ECHR protecting the right to life, the ECtHR has left the issue of when life begins to member states as within the margin of appreciation.[20]

The focus on birth gives rise to a notable issue: prenatal harms that cause postnatal death. Where D harms a foetus that is subsequently born alive, but later dies as a result of those injuries, D has caused the death of a person at the time he or she dies. The courts have long accepted that such cases satisfy the actus reus of murder[21]

---

[13] Hirst, 'Murder Under the Queen's Peace' [2008] Crim LR 541; Rowe, 'The Criminal Liability of a British Soldier Merely for Participating in the Iraq War' [2010] Crim LR 752.

[14] See **5.5**.

[15] Infant Life (Preservation) Act 1929, s1 or Offences Against the Person Act 1861, s58.

[16] *Poulton* (1832) 5 C & P 329.

[17] *Reeves* (1839) 9 C & P 25.

[18] Simester, Spencer, Sullivan, and Virgo, *Simester and Sullivan's Criminal Law* (5th edn, 2013) 373.

[19] The Criminal Law Revision Committee identified the last case where this was directly relevant to have been in 1874: *Handley* (1874) 13 Cox CC 79.

[20] *Vo v France* [2004] 2 FCR 577; O'Donovan, 'Taking a Neutral Stance on the Protection of the Foetus' (2006) 14 Med L Rev 115.

[21] *Senior* (1832) 1 Mood CC 346.

although, interestingly, this has not been applied to cases where D injures her own foetus through neglect.[22]

> **Don't be confused...**
> Where prenatal harm causes postnatal death, the actus reus of murder is satisfied. However, mens rea will often be problematic. This is because, where D acts with the intent to seriously injure or kill the foetus this is not the mens rea for murder (not an intent to seriously injure or kill a person); and where D intends to seriously injure or kill the mother then a transfer of malice to the baby is ruled out by the double transaction (from the mother to the foetus to the baby).[23] Murder, as opposed to manslaughter, is only available in these cases where D intends the foetus to be killed or seriously injured after being born alive.

B) When does V stop being a person: As a result of medical advances, the stage where V stops being a person because she dies can also be problematic. There is no authoritative definition of death within the criminal law, but courts will often refer to medical definitions to assist them. In this regard, it is clear that death should not always be assumed where V stops breathing or even where V's heart stops, as such occurrences can, if treated in good time, often be reversed. However, the problem becomes acute where V's body can be kept 'alive' by medical means despite little or even no chance of recovery. In such cases, V will be considered *medically* dead at the point of 'brain death' (complete and irreversible non-functioning of the brain stem), and this status has been accepted by the House of Lords in *Bland*.[24] Where V's condition falls short of brain death, for example a persistent vegetative state; a profound and permanent coma; etc, V will not be considered dead and therefore remains a 'person' capable of being murdered.

5.3.3 Causing death

To complete the actus reus of murder, D's act or omission must *cause* V's death. This requires application of the general rules of factual and legal causation discussed at **2.7**, where many of the cases analysed were murder cases. There is no need to repeat that discussion here.

One issue that should be highlighted, however, is that 'causing death' will include any 'acceleration of death'. For example, the killing of a terminally ill patient or someone who, for whatever reason, has only a short time to live will still satisfy the actus reus of murder. As death will come to us all at some point, the act of 'causing death' must be logically synonymous with 'accelerating death'. Thus, where a doctor or family member or anyone else intentionally ends the life of V in order to relieve pain or suffering, knowing that V would not have lived long anyway, D still commits murder. This may be perceived as a problem if we believe that 'mercy killing' should be permissible, and this will lead to a discussion of reform, but the current law offers no exception of this kind.[25]

---

[22] *Knights* (1860) 2 F & F 46.
[23] See discussion of transferred malice and *AG's Reference (No 3 of 1994)* [1997] 3 All ER 936 at **4.3.1.1**.
[24] [1993] 1 AC 789.
[25] *Inglis* [2010] EWCA Crim 2637.

5.4 Mens rea of murder

Coke's definition describes the mens rea of murder as 'malice aforethought', and this term is still often used. However, malice aforethought is now simply a term of art, with its modern interpretation bearing little resemblance to the original words. For example, it is now clear that D's mens rea need not be malicious: that is, need not demonstrate some manner of evil character.[26] Similarly, it need not involve aforethought: as long as D has the mens rea at the moment of action, there is no requirement of pre-planning.[27] Rather, at the time of acting or omitting to act causing death, the current law requires D to have an intention to kill or cause GBH (serious bodily harm).[28]

The meaning of the term 'intention' was discussed at **3.4.1**, and this definition applies to murder as it does to other offences requiring intention. We will not repeat the detail of that discussion here. D intends to kill or cause GBH where her conduct is carried out in order to bring about a certain result (direct intent); and/or where her conduct is virtually certain to cause that result, she foresees it as a virtual certainty, and the jury choose to find intention (oblique intent). At one time, the House of Lords expanded the definition of oblique intention in murder to include cases where D did not foresee a virtual certainty but a reasonable person in D's position would have done so, creating a form of objective intention.[29] However, this is no longer good law. The current law defining intention will require *subjective* purpose or *subjective* foresight of a virtual certainty in every case.[30]

> **Don't be confused...**
> As we will see in later chapters, most serious offences require a mens rea of intention or recklessness as to a certain result. For such offences, the divide between intention and recklessness is unproblematic: either will suffice for liability. As murder is only satisfied by an intention to kill or cause GBH (recklessness is insufficient) the divide between these mens rea terms becomes very important. This is why most of the cases discussed at **3.4.1**, attempting to define intention, were murder cases.

The fact that the mens rea for murder can be satisfied by an intention to cause GBH as an alternative to an intention to kill is very important. D acts or omits to act with the intention to cause GBH if she intends, directly or obliquely, to cause serious bodily harm: 'grievous' being given its ordinary meaning of 'serious' or 'really serious'.[31] For example, an intention to break a major bone or severely wound V would amount to an intention to cause GBH.[32] The jury must assess what D was thinking: they are asking how much harm D intended to cause V and that is a question of D's subjective state of mind. The jury must then assess that amount of harm, as D subjectively intended, to decide for themselves as reasonable people whether they consider that would be an

---

[26] eg so-called 'mercy' killing will still constitute murder.
[27] Mitchell, 'Thinking about Murder' (1992) 56 J Crim L 78.
[28] *Cunningham* [1982] AC 566; *Moloney* [1985] AC 905.
[29] *DPP v Smith* [1961] AC 290.
[30] *Woollin* [1999] AC 82, [1998] 4 All ER 103, [1998] Crim LR 890.
[31] *Bollom* [2003] EWCA Crim 2846.
[32] We discuss this further at **7.6** in relation to offences of causing GBH with intent.

intention to cause GBH. Thus, D cannot avoid liability by claiming that *she* would not consider the harm she intended to cause as serious harm.

Allowing liability for murder where D acts with the intention to cause GBH means that murder is a constructive offence. Where D acts with intention to kill, as in **Table 5.2**, there is uncontroversial correspondence between actus reus (causing death) and mens rea (intending to do so).

Table 5.2 Murder and intention to kill

	Actus reus	**Mens rea**
Result element	Death of V	Intention to kill

However, where D acts with the intention to cause GBH, her intended act of causing GBH is constructed upon by the additional actus reus element (V's death) to create the more serious offence of murder. As with other constructive crimes, this additional element constructs greater liability despite a lack of corresponding mens rea.[33] This is illustrated in **Table 5.3**.

Table 5.3 Murder and intention to cause GBH

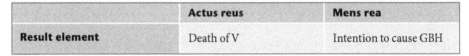

	Actus reus	**Mens rea**
Result element	Death of V	Intention to cause GBH

The possibility for constructive liability in murder where D merely intends to cause GBH has attracted severe criticism from academics[34] and appeal court judges[35] alike. Such criticism arises because in these cases D does not choose to kill or perhaps even to risk killing, and therefore arguably lacks the culpability to deserve liability for murder. For example, consider the case of D, a paramilitary, who shoots V in the knee as a punishment for V's disloyalty. D intends to cause GBH but definitely does not want V to die: D wants V to be a walking deterrent to disloyal members. D is liable for a serious offence against the person.[36] However, where V, for whatever reason, whether it be lack of treatment; infection; etc, dies as a result of the shot, D's liability increases to murder and the mandatory life sentence is applied.[37] In this manner, under the current law D satisfies the mens rea for murder even if she has no anticipation that her conduct risks

---

[33] Constructive liability is discussed at **4.2.1.1**.

[34] Mitchell, 'In Defence of the Correspondence Principle' [1999] Crim LR 195; cf Horder, 'A Critique of the Correspondence Principle in Criminal Law' [1995] Crim LR 795.

[35] *Hyam* [1975] AC 55, see the reasoning of Lord Diplock.

[36] See **7.6**.

[37] In theory, if D simply intends to prick V with a pin and V is a haemophiliac, this could lead to liability for murder (whatever D's impression, a reasonable jury are likely to see the intended pinprick as an intention to cause serious harm to someone with this condition).

killing V. All that is required is that D intends a certain level of harm and the jury inter-pret it as an intention to cause GBH. This will be discussed further in the reform sec-tion later, along with the counter-argument which is common to constructive liability, that as soon as D intends any harm her normative position changes and she should be responsible for *all* the consequences that follow.[38]

5.4.1 Other mens rea requirements

As will be noted from **Table 5.1** setting out the offence, the mens rea of murder includes elements beyond an intention to kill or cause GBH. Most importantly, as with all other criminal offences, D can only commit murder if her act or omission causing death was performed voluntarily. Additionally, she must intend or know that what she is killing is a person under the Queen's peace.

> *Assessment matters...*
> In most cases, and most problem questions, it will be straightforwardly apparent that D acts voluntar-ily and she is aware that V is a person, and in these cases discussion of mens rea need not go beyond the required intention to kill or cause GBH. However, where there is uncertainty (eg where a spasm in D's finger causes her to pull the trigger of a gun; or where D shoots at a figure unsure if it is a person; etc) then these elements will require specific discussion.

5.5 Defences to murder

If the actus reus and mens rea elements of murder are satisfied, the next step is to explore the possibility of a defence.

5.5.1 General defences

Most of the *general* defences (so called because of their application across multiple offences) will potentially apply to murder, with the notable exception of duress. These are fully discussed later in two separate chapters. In **Chapter 13** we discuss denials of mental responsibility: D contends that he lacks responsibility for the offence due to some form of mental abnormality, age, or intoxication. In **Chapter 14** we discuss the general defences of self-defence and necessity: D contends that her actions were justi-fied or should be excused because she lacked a *viable* choice not to offend. Satisfying the elements of one of these defences will lead to a complete acquittal.[39]

5.5.2 Doctors and the treatment of terminally ill patients

Over a number of years, with the increased use of powerful pain-relieving medication in hospitals, a category of cases has emerged that has put a strain on the boundaries of the law of murder. These cases involve the prescription of pain-relieving drugs to

---

[38] See **5.6.2**.

[39] The only exception being the insanity defence, which leads to the special verdict of 'not guilty by reason of insanity'. This is discussed in **Chapter 13**.

terminally ill patients, where doctors are aware that as a side effect the patient's life expectancy will be reduced. Such practices are very common and relatively uncontroversial in their medical context. However, to the extent that they satisfy the definition of murder, it seems that the avoidance of liability is now best explained as a form of specific defence for medical professionals.

It is important first to understand how the elements of murder will be satisfied in these cases. The doctor completes the actus reus of murder because of her conduct in prescribing drugs in a manner that accelerates the patient's death.[40] In terms of mens rea, although she does not *directly* intend to kill or cause GBH because she does not act in order to bring about that result, the shortening of life is a virtually certain consequence of her act and her knowledge of this is likely to amount to an *oblique* intention to kill.[41] Thus, the elements of murder are satisfied.

This problem arose in *Adams*, although the solution offered by the court did not rely on criminal defences.

Adams [1957] Crim LR 365

D, a doctor, was charged with murder having 'eased the passing' of several patients including V with strong pain-relieving drugs.

- Crown Court: not guilty. Devlin J directed the jury that there was no special defence for doctors, but that 'he is entitled to do all that is proper and necessary to relieve pain and suffering even if measures he takes may incidentally shorten life'.

The principle applied in this case is sometimes referred to as the doctrine of double effect, which holds that intentionally causing a harmful result (eg death) can be morally defensible where it is a side effect of promoting a good end (eg pain relief). Crucial to this is Devlin J's focus on the *incidental* shortening of life, as the same act completed by another party for example to hasten the collection of inheritance, or by a doctor where the shortening of life was the main purpose, would lead to conviction.[42] However, the direction and the principle are problematic: it is unclear whether it is actus reus (causation) or mens rea (intention) that is being undermined. It also unclear how it is being undermined: what exactly does it mean to 'incidentally shorten life'?

In line with the result of *Adams*, but moving away from the reasoning of Devlin J, it is now best to see this exception as a special common law defence. In *Bland*,[43] Lord Goff referred, *obiter*, to:

the established rule that a doctor may, when caring for a patient who is, for example, dying of cancer, lawfully administer painkilling drugs, despite the fact he knows that an incidental effect of that application will be to abbreviate the patient's life.

---

[40] As discussed at **5.3.3**, causing death includes doing an act that accelerates death.

[41] *Woollin* [1998] 4 All ER 103. We may hope that despite D's foresight the jury will choose not to 'find' intention, but this is not certain: see **3.4.1.2**. Cf *Moors* discussed in [1999] Crim LR.

[42] See eg *Cox* (1992) 12 BLMR 38, where the 'defence' did not apply to a doctor who prescribed non-therapeutic drugs with the principal intention of causing death.

[43] [1993] 1 AC 789.

Constructed as a defence, the rule may still lack some clarity, but it is able to provide specific protection for doctors within this category of cases. It is also able to do so without distorting the general rules of causation, or relying upon the vagaries of oblique intention.

5.5.3 Partial defences

As well as the complete defences discussed earlier (defences that, if satisfied, will lead to D's acquittal), the law of murder also includes three partial defences. If one of these partial defences is satisfied then D's liability for murder will be downgraded to voluntary manslaughter, an offence which still carries a maximum life sentence, but at the discretion of the court rather than as a mandatory sentence. These partial defences are *not* general defences, and apply only to the offence of murder.

The three partial defences to murder are:

- **Loss of self-control:** D kills while out of control owing to fear of serious violence or by seriously grave circumstances giving her a justifiable sense of being seriously wronged.[44]

- **Diminished responsibility:** D's recognised medical condition led to an abnormality of mind and substantially impaired her capacity, causing her to kill.[45]

- **Suicide pact:** D kills V in pursuance of an agreement that they will both die together.[46]

Each of the partial defences will be discussed in detail in **Chapter 6**, as their satisfaction will lead to liability for manslaughter.

> *Beware...*
> When considering defences to murder, students often skip straight to discussion of the partial defences. However, remember that these defences will still lead to liability for manslaughter. Therefore, you should always consider the complete defences first. Only if D lacks a complete defence would she want to consider the partial defences.

5.6 Reform

Despite sustained criticism of several aspects of the offence of murder, and despite numerous reform recommendations, the law has remained largely unchanged over the past 50 years.[47] In this section, we provide some additional discussion of the two main areas of criticism identified earlier, and sketch some of the recommendations for reform that have been offered. These relate to the maintenance of the mandatory life sentence and, secondly, the scope of the mens rea for murder.

---

[44] Coroners and Justice Act 2009, s54.
[45] Homicide Act 1957, s2 (as amended by the Coroners and Justice Act 2009, s52).
[46] Homicide Act 1957, s4.
[47] See generally Horder, *Homicide and the Politics of Law Reform* (2012).

5.6.1 Reforming the mandatory life sentence

In order to achieve the partial removal[48] and subsequent abolition[49] of the death penalty, the substitution of a mandatory life sentence[50] of imprisonment provided the necessary political compromise. The death penalty could be removed, but there was, and remains, maintenance of the idea that murder as the ultimate crime should be punished with some comparable level of 'ultimate' punishment.

In the majority of cases the mandatory life sentence does not lead to imprisonment for the rest of the offender's life. However, its terms remain uniquely draconian. Depending upon the circumstances of the murder, the minimum period of imprisonment will be set by the court at between 15 years and a full-life term: this is known as the tariff period.[51] Importantly, and unlike standard sentences, the tariff period must be served in full before D's release is considered by a parole board. At the end of the tariff, a parole board will then decide whether D should stay in prison because she represents a continued risk to particular persons or to the public, or be released into the community. Even where D is released, this is only a release on a life-long licence: allowing administrative (not judicial) action to call D back into prison where necessary.

Despite the original utility of the mandatory life sentence as a compromise in the abolition of the death penalty, arguments against preservation of the mandatory sentence are overwhelming. Central to this, highlighted from the outset of this chapter, is that the law of murder does not target a single specific 'ultimate' wrong but is, rather, broad enough to catch conduct across a wide moral spectrum: from cold-blooded serial killers or sexual killers, to the morally ambiguous mercy killing. This is common of most criminal offences, for example there is similar disparity between D who carelessly breaks another's pen and D who intentionally smashes another's computer, and yet both are liable for the same offence of criminal damage.[52] The difference, of course, is that a judge can reflect the moral disparity in criminal damage cases within the courts sentencing discretion from discharge to ten years' imprisonment, or potentially life imprisonment where there are aggravating factors,[53] whereas for murder, such discretion is removed. Over time, reflecting such criticisms, attitudes towards the mandatory life sentence have hardened academically,[54] judicially,[55] within Parliament,[56] and even within the general public.[57]

---

[48] Homicide Act 1957, s5: singling out certain types of murder that continued to attract the death penalty.

[49] Murder (Abolition of the Death Penalty) Act 1965.

[50] Wasik, 'Sentencing in Homicide' in Ashworth and Mitchell (eds), *Rethinking English Homicide Law* (2000) 167.

[51] Criminal Justice Act 2003, s269 and Sch 21.

[52] Criminal Damage Act 1971, s1. Discussed at **Chapter 9**.

[53] Criminal Damage Act 1971, s4.

[54] Mitchell, *Murder and Penal Policy* (1990).

[55] See eg *Howe* [1987] 1 All ER 771, 781.

[56] House of Lords, Select Committee on Murder and Life Imprisonment (1989) HL Paper 78, para 108-18: recommending the removal of the mandatory sentence.

[57] Law Commission, *A New Homicide Act for England and Wales?* (Consultation 177, 2005) Appendix A (Mitchell); Mitchell and Roberts, *Public Opinion and Sentencing for Murder* (2010): empirical work finding majority public support for removing the mandatory sentence.

However, despite hardening attitudes against the mandatory life sentence, the current political reality is that the sentence is unlikely to be reformed.[58] We have seen this most recently, for example, in the Law Commission's terms of reference relating to their review of murder in 2005 and 2006 where the mandatory sentence was not open for the Commission to consider.[59] In light of this reality, focus has turned to the reform of murder itself and the rules relating to it, the aim being to remove behaviour from the offence that does not warrant the mandatory sentence. Three areas are of particular interest.

- **Narrowing the definition of murder:** This possibility is discussed in the next section.

- **Reforming the partial defences:** Satisfying a partial defence allows D's liability to be mitigated from murder to manslaughter and thereby avoids the mandatory life sentence. Recent reform in relation to these defences is discussed in the next chapter.

- **Extenuating circumstances mitigation:** The idea of 'extenuating circumstances' has been introduced in other jurisdictions in exceptional circumstances to allow the mandatory life sentence not to apply for certain murder cases.[60] However, despite a similar proposal (outlined by John Spencer) being advocated in this country, and even put forward as an amendment to a Bill in the House of Lords in 2009, it has not been adopted.[61] Indeed, this option seems unlikely to gain political traction, as it is perceived as an erosion of the mandatory sentence.

5.6.2 Reforming the mens rea of murder

Debates about the appropriate boundaries of murder have generally focused on mens rea elements: adapting the mens rea in order to target more effectively those seen as deserving of the label of murderer and, of course, in view of the mandatory life sentence. Two examples provide useful illustration.

A) **Lord Goff:** In a wide-ranging article published in 1988, Lord Goff recommends reforming the mens rea of murder in a manner that would at once (a) narrow the current law by removing liability where D intends GBH, as opposed to death, and by narrowing an intention to kill to direct intention only, and also (b) widen it by allowing liability where D is 'wickedly reckless' as to death.[62] Goff would narrow the law, excluding those who intend to cause GBH, chiefly because he believes such defendants are inappropriately labelled as murderers.[63] As Goff comments, 'it seems very strange that a man should be called a murderer even though not only did he not intend to kill the victim, but he may even [in certain cases] have intended that he should not die.'[64] Conversely, Goff would find liability where D is wickedly reckless as to death which is a concept

---

[58] Horder, *Homicide and the Politics of Law Reform* (2012).

[59] Law Commission, *Murder, Manslaughter and Infanticide* (No 304, 2006) para 1.1.

[60] eg in Israel and the French Penal Code, art 345.

[61] Hansard, HL, 26 October 2009, cols 1008–9.

[62] Goff, 'The Mental Element in the Crime of Murder' (1988) 104 LQR 30.

[63] See also Wilson, 'Murder and the Structure of Homicide' in Mitchell and Ashworth (eds), *Rethinking English Homicide Law* (2000).

[64] Goff, 'The Mental Element in the Crime of Murder' (1988) 104 LQR 30, 48.

borrowed from Scottish criminal law. This would apply where D did not necessarily act with the purpose of killing V, but her actions demonstrated a callous or careless disregard for V's life. To understand these proposals, it is useful to also see the meticulous rebuttal of Goff's approach in the reply article of Glanville Williams.[65]

B) The Law Commission: The most recent and most comprehensive review of murder has come from the Law Commission.[66] In its 2005 Consultation Paper, the Commission sets out proposals for a new ladder of homicide offences including first degree murder (punished with a mandatory life sentence); a new offence of second degree murder (punished with a discretionary life sentence); and manslaughter (punished with a discretionary life sentence). The separation of first and second degree murder allows the Commission to narrow the offence of first degree murder and, thereby the mandatory sentence, so that it would only catch those who kill with the intention to kill. Those intending to cause serious harm would be liable for the lesser offence of second degree murder.[67]

In the Commission's 2006 Report, although it retains the three-offence structure, it make significant amendments. Most importantly, it recommends that first degree murder should include both cases where D kills with the intention to kill, and where D kills with the intention to cause a serious injury where she is aware that such injury carries a serious risk of causing death. This approach widens the category of first degree murder beyond those intending death (its consultation proposal), but would still be significantly more restrictive than the current law: D who intends to cause GBH but does not foresee a serious risk of death will not be caught within the Commission's definition.[68] Despite the merits of these recommendations, they have yet to be acted upon by the government and (at the time of writing) appear unlikely to be acted upon.

> **Beware...**
> When and if you discuss Law Commission (or any other) recommendations in an essay, remember that they are just that: recommendations. It is very easy to refer to such policies inaccurately as if they represent the current law. Do not fall into this trap.

5.7 Eye on assessment

The offence of murder is one of the most commonly used offences within problem scenarios. This is because, not only is the offence important and interesting in its own right, but it is also a useful vehicle through which to focus discussion on several matters. Murder is one of the few offences that is only satisfied by a mens rea of intention as opposed to recklessness; it gives rise to the most difficult issues of

[65] Williams, 'The Mens Rea of Murder: Leave It Alone' (1989) 105 LQR 387.
[66] Law Commission, *A New Homicide Act for England and Wales?* (Consultation 177, 2005); Law Commission, *Murder, Manslaughter and Infanticide* (No 304, 2006).
[67] For comment on the Consultation's proposals, see Wilson, 'The Structure of Criminal Homicide' [2006] Crim LR 471; Rogers, 'The Law Commission's Proposed Restructuring of Homicide' (2006) 70 J Crim L 223.
[68] For comment on the Report's recommendations, see, Ashworth, 'Principles, Pragmatism and the Law Commission's Recommendations on Homicide Law Reform' [2007] Crim LR 333.

causation with most reported causation cases involving murder. It also has more complex defences: with the partial and general defences, murder scenarios can involve a wide variety of defences.

Despite the range of potential issues, however, as with all problem questions it is important to work through the problem/offence methodically in order to discuss liability. With this in mind, we can work through the step-by-step approach outlined in previous chapters to see how this applies to a murder scenario.

STEP 1 Identify the potential criminal event in the facts

This is unlikely to take more than a sentence, but it is essential to tell your reader where in the facts you are focusing.

In the context of murder, or other potential homicide offences, Step 1 simply requires you to point out a death in the facts that may be connected with D. For example, 'We will first examine the potential liability of Lucy for the death of Tom'.

STEP 2 Identify the potential offence

Having identified the facts (eg D potentially killing V), you must now identify the offence you are going to apply. Usually, this means identifying the most serious offence that D might have committed.

Whenever there is a death in a problem question that may have been caused by D, you should *always* begin with a consideration of murder even if it is reasonably clear that an element within the offence will not be satisfied.[69] If the offence is satisfied, you can then move to a discussion of defences, both full and partial. If not, depending upon which elements of murder are missing this will lead you to the consideration of an alternative offence.

STEP 3 Applying the offence to the facts

Actus reus: What does the offence require? Did D do it?

Mens rea: What does the offence require? Did D possess it?

Remember, to be liable for the offence, every element of the actus reus and mens rea must be satisfied. Thus, every element should be discussed even where it is easily satisfied and little discussion is necessary. Where there is doubt, in law or in fact, highlight and discuss areas of likely dispute between prosecution and defence. Also, if the question asks you to critically engage with the law as you apply it, take particular care to include evaluation of the law.

A) **Actus reus:** When discussing the actus reus of murder you are looking for an act or omission that has caused V's death. This will involve the standard rules of causation and, where necessary, omissions liability discussed at **Chapter 2**.

---

[69] The only exception being where the problem question tells you to *only* discuss some other offence.

If D does not satisfy every element of the actus reus she will not be liable for murder or any other homicide offence. If the question only asks you to consider liability for murder or homicide offences, then this is the end of the story: no liability for murder. However, if the question asks you to consider D's liability more generally, having concluded that she did not cause death, your next question will be whether she has criminally contributed to the death. For example, has she assisted, encouraged, or caused another person to kill V (leading to potential liability as a secondary party: **Chapter 12**); or has she assisted or encouraged V to kill herself (leading to potential liability for assisting or encouraging suicide: **Chapter 11**)? However, if D does satisfy the actus reus of murder, continue to discuss mens rea.

B) **Mens rea:** The mens rea of murder is only satisfied where D acts or omits to act with the intention (direct or oblique) that her conduct will cause death or GBH (serious bodily harm). It is useful to think of this as a tick-box exercise, with any one of four states of mind sufficient. This is illustrated in **Table 5.4**.

Table 5.4 Mens rea for murder

Intention...	to cause death...	or to cause GBH
Direct	1	2
Oblique	3	4

When applying the mens rea for murder to problem facts, it is also useful to follow this ordering. If you find that D has acted with the direct intention to cause death (1), then there is no need to discuss the GBH rule in any detail and certainly no need to discuss the complex rules of oblique intention.[70] If it is necessary to discuss oblique intention as, for example, where D does not want to harm V at all, but recognises that her actions are extremely likely to do so, it is good practice to lead your reader to that point: tell the reader (drawing on the facts of the problem) why you think a court would be unlikely to find a direct intention.

If D lacks mens rea when performing the conduct element of the actus reus then she will not be liable for murder. If the question only asks you to consider liability for murder then this is the end of the story: no liability. However, where the question is more general and asks you to consider liability for homicide offences, or all potential offences, then, assuming the actus reus was satisfied, you will now move to consider potential liability of an offence of involuntary manslaughter. These offences (discussed at **Chapter 6**) require the same actus reus as murder (an act or omission causing death), but are much less restrictive in terms of mens rea. However, if D does satisfy the mens rea for murder, continue to discuss defences.

---

[70] This approach, only discussing oblique intention where necessary, is also taken by the courts. An approach described by Lord Bridge as a 'golden rule' in *Moloney* [1985] AC 905, 926.

> **STEP 4 Consider defences**
>
> The word 'consider' here is important, as you should not discuss every defence for every question. Rather, think whether there are any defences that *could* potentially apply. If there are, discuss those only.

When discussing defences always begin with the complete defences (**Chapters 13** and **14**) as these usually lead to a complete acquittal. Remember that the defence of duress does not apply to murder. If none of the complete defences apply or there is some doubt over their application also continue to discuss the partial defences (**Chapter 6**).

> **STEP 5 Conclude**
>
> This is usually a single sentence either saying that it is likely that D has committed the offence, or saying that it is not likely because an offence element is not satisfied or because a defence is likely to apply. It is not often that you will be able to say categorically whether D has committed the offence or not, so it is usually best to conclude in terms of what is more 'likely'.

> **STEP 6 Loop**
>
> Go back up to Step 1, identifying the next potential criminal event. Continue until you have discussed all the relevant potentially criminal events.

ONLINE RESOURCE CENTRE

www.oxfordtextbooks.co.uk/orc/smithandhogan/

This chapter is accompanied by a selection of online resources to help you with this topic, including:

- **Multiple choice questions**
- **Chapter summary sheet**
- Two **sample examination questions** with answer guidance
- **Further reading**

Also available on the Online Resource Centre are:

- A selection of **videos** from the authors explaining key topics and principles
- **Legal updates**
- Useful **weblinks**

6

Manslaughter

6.1 Introduction

As with murder, manslaughter is a common law homicide offence: an offence with an actus reus of unlawful conduct causing the death of a person. However, the spectrum of conduct and mens rea attracting liability for manslaughter is considerably wider than that for murder, covering all unlawful killings that fall short of murder. The sentencing options for manslaughter are also considerably wider than those for murder: with murder, the judge must pass a 'mandatory' life sentence; with manslaughter, the judge has discretion up to a maximum of life imprisonment.[1] As the types of conduct and mens rea caught within the

---

[1] Consistency in such sentencing discretion is managed through sentencing guidelines.

offence of manslaughter can differ greatly in terms of blameworthiness, sentencing discretion allows the court to reflect those differences at the sentencing stage.

Although manslaughter is a single offence at common law, one of its complexities lies in the fact that it does not consist of a single set of offence elements. Rather, the same offence (manslaughter) can be committed in a variety of ways. Within this chapter we will explore and discuss each of these alternative forms of liability for manslaughter.

The different forms of manslaughter are separated into two distinct categories. In the first category (known as *voluntary* manslaughter), D satisfies both the actus reus and the mens rea of murder, but also satisfies the elements of a partial defence that reduces her liability to manslaughter. In the second category (known as *involuntary* manslaughter), D does not satisfy the mens rea for murder, but becomes liable for manslaughter because her conduct and mens rea satisfy the elements of a lesser involuntary manslaughter offence. Thus, voluntary manslaughter involves a *partial defence* to murder, whereas involuntary manslaughter involves a separate *offence*.

Assessment matters...

When applying the law to a problem question, it is useful to begin by considering liability for murder. Whether the elements of murder are satisfied or not will then lead to a discussion of the appropriate category of manslaughter.[2]

The structure of homicide offences is illustrated in **Figure 6.1**.

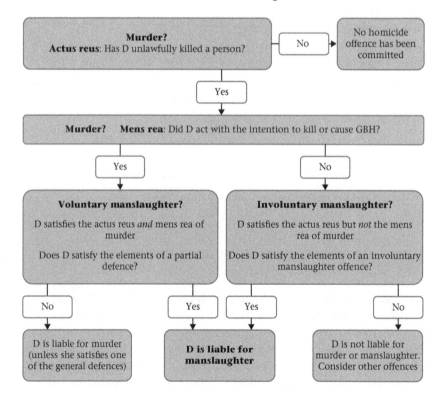

Figure 6.1 Locating homicide liability

2 See **6.6**.

> *Terminology...*
> The categories of voluntary and involuntary manslaughter mark an important distinction between the two routes to liability for manslaughter. However, the terminology ('voluntary' and 'involuntary') can be misleading: the distinction between the two categories has nothing to do with the voluntariness or otherwise of D's conduct. Indeed, as we discussed at **3.3**, all offences require voluntary conduct, and so-called involuntary manslaughter is no different.

Although murder and manslaughter are the only homicide offences at common law, a number of statutory homicide offences have been created, particularly in recent years, to address perceived weaknesses with the common law. Some of these have employed the term manslaughter (eg corporate manslaughter[3]), whereas others have avoided it (eg causing death by dangerous driving[4]). There is also a number of offences that apply to the killing of a foetus as opposed to a legal 'person' (eg child destruction[5]). Each of these offences exists outside the common law definitions of murder and manslaughter. We will discuss these bespoke offences at **6.4**. However, we begin with a discussion of the core common law offence of manslaughter, and the categories of voluntary and involuntary manslaughter.

6.2 Voluntary manslaughter

The first category of manslaughter (voluntary manslaughter) can only arise where D satisfies *both* the actus reus and the mens rea of murder. After this is established, and assuming that D does not have a complete defence (eg self-defence[6]), it then becomes relevant to discuss the possibility for a partial defence: a defence that may reduce D's liability from murder to voluntary manslaughter. There are three partial defences:

- **Loss of self-control:** D kills while having lost her self-control owing to fear of *serious* violence or because of her justifiable sense of being seriously wronged.[7]

- **Diminished responsibility:** D's recognised medical condition led to an abnormality of mind which substantially impaired her capacity and caused her to kill.[8]

- **Suicide pact:** D kills V in pursuance of an agreement that they will both die together.[9]

We will discuss each of these partial defences in turn.

---

[3] Corporate Manslaughter and Corporate Homicide Act 2007, s1.
[4] Road Traffic Act 1988, s1 (as substituted by the Road Traffic Act 1991, s1).
[5] Infant Life (Preservation) Act 1929, s1.
[6] These defences are discussed at **Chapters 13** and **14**.
[7] Coroners and Justice Act 2009, s54.
[8] Homicide Act 1957, s2 (as amended by the Coroners and Justice Act 2009, s52).
[9] Homicide Act 1957, s4.

> **Beware...**
> The partial defences are *only* defences to murder and should not therefore be discussed or applied in the context of any other crime. In practical terms, it can be useful to think of them as mechanisms for avoiding the mandatory sentence for murder because if the defence is satisfied it will mitigate D's offence to manslaughter and thereby allow the court discretion in sentencing.

6.2.1 Loss of self-control

The partial defence to murder of 'loss of self-control' (LOC) is defined in sections 54 and 55 of the Coroners and Justice Act 2009.[10] The statutory defence represents a codification and substantial reform of the previous common law partial defence of provocation (repealed by section 56 of the 2009 Act).[11]

The basic rationale of the partial defence is that where D kills with the intention required for murder, D's level of culpability is lower when she does so in circumstances of exceptional antagonism and is (in some sense) overwhelmed by a violent passion likely to have similarly affected others in her position. Paradigm examples of the latter, where the defence is intended to apply, would include cases where D kills V upon discovering V abusing D's child; or where D reacts to personal bullying or abuse by killing, using force so excessive that it would not provide her with a defence of self-defence.

Despite relative clarity within core examples, the development of the defence of provocation at common law (pre-2009 Act) was characterised by uncertainty and perceived unfairness. The uncertainty was often compounded by inconsistent interpretations within the appellate courts.[12] The most important areas of confusion in the law (pre-2009 Act) are set out in **Table 6.1**.

Table 6.1 Questions relating to the old offence of provocation

What types of conduct could have qualified as provocation under the old law?	Although the defence was traditionally restricted to provocative acts of violence, this was later expanded to include *anything* 'said or done'. The problem then emerged with Ds who claimed to have been provoked by something that we would not want to form the basis of a defence (eg a crying baby[13]). Under the pre-2009 Act law, all such cases would have to be put to the jury.[14]

---

[10] Norrie, 'The Coroners and Justice Act 2009—Partial Defences to Murder (1) Loss of Control' [2010] Crim LR 275. See also, *Smith and Hogan's Criminal Law* (14th edn, 2015), Ch15.

[11] For a detailed discussion of the old common law defence of provocation, see Ormerod, *Smith and Hogan's Criminal Law* (12th edn, 2008) Ch15. See also Horder, *Provocation and Responsibility* (1992).

[12] For a useful summary of these problems, see Law Commission, *Partial Defences to Murder* (Consultation 173, 2003) Part 4.

[13] *Doughty* (1986) 83 Cr App R 319: involving the persistent crying of a two-week-old baby, and D's reaction of killing it.

[14] The prosecution must then prove, beyond reasonable doubt, that D was either not provoked to lose control, or that a reasonable person would not have been.

What characteristics of D could have been taken into account when deciding if her reaction should qualify for the old defence?	The defence was never open to D as a reward for bad character: for her tendency to overreact violently to even minor provocation. Rather, it had to be shown that a reasonable person would similarly have been caused to lose their control. However, where D's characteristics (eg, young age; mental disability; etc) made her more susceptible to a loss of control, the courts struggled to define whether these characteristics could be taken into account (ie is the question whether a reasonable person would have lost their control, or whether a reasonable person sharing D's characteristics would have lost their control?). This culminated in an inconsistent approach between the House of Lords in *Smith (Morgan)*,[15] where the court held that *all* of D's characteristics could be taken into account, and the de facto overruling of *Smith (Morgan)* by the Privy Council in *Holley*,[16] holding that only sex and age could be taken into account.
Was the defence gender biased in its operation?	A powerful influence towards reform was the contention that the old law operated in a discriminatory fashion. The elements of the old defence, applying where D was offended or angered into a sudden outburst of uncontrolled violence, were much more likely to be found in masculine (as opposed to feminine) reactions. This perception gained standing over the years with the inability of abused women to satisfy the elements of the defence where they reacted by killing their abusers. In such cases, the female defendants would rarely kill in the heat of the moment (not least because of the typical physical disparity between D and V), and may have done so in fear of future abuse rather than having been provoked by previous abuse.[17]
Was the defence designed as a partial justification (D acted wrongly, but as others would have) or as a partial excuse (D's weakness makes her action less blameworthy)?[18]	This is a fundamental question about the rationale of the partial defence (at the heart of why we think it should be a defence at all), and so the uncertainty here demonstrates the depth of the problems with the pre-2009 law.[19] The answer to this question is, in many ways, a necessary precursor to consistently answering any of the more specific questions above.

---

[15] [2001] AC 146.

[16] *AG for Jersey v Holley* [2005] UKPC 23.

[17] Dressler, 'Battered women who kill their sleeping tormentors' and Horder, 'Killing the Passive Abuser: A Theoretical Defence' in Shute and Simester (eds), *Criminal Law Theory* (2002).

[18] We discuss the difference between justifications and excuses further at **Chapters 13** and **14**.

[19] Dressler, 'Provocation: Partial Justification or Partial Excuse?' (1988) 51 MLR 467.

The old defence of provocation at common law, despite statutory supplementation,[20] struggled to find a satisfactory (or consistent) answer to these questions. Therefore, following a number of Law Commission papers and recommendations,[21] the new partial defence of LOC was created.

> **Extra detail…**
> As we will discuss in the reform section later in the chapter, although many of the Law Commission's recommendations were followed within the 2009 Act, there are also substantial differences in approach. Thus, Law Commission material is useful as an accessible summary of problems with the pre-2009 law; and also as a way of evaluating the current law to see if the Commission's approach (as a complete package) may have been preferable; but it should not be used as a guide to what the current law requires.

The current LOC partial defence is defined, principally, within section 54 of the Coroners and Justice Act 2009.

(1) Where a person ('D') kills or is a party to the killing of another ('V'), D is not to be convicted of murder if—

    (a) D's acts and omissions in doing or being a party to the killing resulted from D's loss of self-control,

    (b) the loss of self-control had a qualifying trigger, and

    (c) a person of D's sex and age, with a normal degree of tolerance and self-restraint and in the circumstances of D, might have reacted in the same or in a similar way to D…

(7) A person who, but for this section, would be liable to be convicted of murder is liable instead to be convicted of manslaughter.

In line with section 54(1), the LOC partial defence is made up of three elements, set out in **Table 6.2**. All three must be satisfied for the defence to apply.

Table 6.2 Partial defence of LOC

A) D's role in the killing must have resulted from a loss of self-control

B) D's loss of self-control must have been caused by a qualifying trigger:
   i) a fear of serious violence from V against D or another, *or*
   ii) a thing or things done or said (or both) which constituted circumstances of an extremely grave character, *and* caused D to have a justifiable sense of being seriously wronged

C) A hypothetical person, of D's age and sex, might have reacted in the same way

---

[20] The common law was supplemented by statutory clarification in the Homicide Act 1957, s3. This was also repealed by the 2009 Act, s56.

[21] Law Commission, *Partial Defences to Murder* (Consultation 173, 2003); *Partial Defences to Murder* (No 290, 2004); *A New Homicide Act for England and Wales* (Consultation 177, 2005); *Murder, Manslaughter and Infanticide* (No 304, 2006).

Where an issue of LOC arises,[22] the legal burden is on the prosecution to prove beyond a reasonable doubt that one or more of these elements is absent. If the prosecution are unable to disprove the defence, then D will be liable for manslaughter and not for murder.

> **Terminology…**
> Although we are again speaking of 'elements', the terms actus reus and mens rea are not applicable to defences. This is because, when discussing the elements of a defence (as opposed to the elements of an offence), we are focusing on factors that makes D's conduct less blameworthy.

We will explore each element of the partial defence in turn. However, first we consider an important qualifier to the defence: D's conduct must not be motivated by a desire for revenge.

6.2.1.1 D must not act in a considered desire for revenge

Section 54(4) excludes the defence where D acts in a considered desire for revenge. In many cases, such a 'considered' desire will be evidence that D did not lose her self-control and so D will also lack a vital element of the defence. However, crucially, even if D satisfies the elements of the defence, it will still be excluded if this section applies. For example, if D kills V following a verbal attack by V giving D a justifiable sense of being seriously wronged, even where D is out of control at the moment of causing death, D will still be excluded from the defence if the attack was 'thought about and considered'.[23] This exclusion has been seen as vital to prevent the defence being used inappropriately by revenge killers, but is likely to present a difficult hurdle for abused women who kill because these are cases where there is usually an element of planning.

> **Point to remember…**
> It is useful to begin a discussion of the LOC defence with this exclusion because, when it applies, there is no need to move on to a discussion of the defence elements.

6.2.1.2 D must have lost self-control

The first element of the partial defence, and perhaps its central feature, is the requirement that D's conduct (which caused V's death) must have resulted from a lack of self-control. This is a *subjective* requirement: we ask whether D herself lost self-control; it is irrelevant (for this element) whether a reasonable person in D's position would have done so or not.

There is a problem, however, in knowing exactly what the law means by 'a loss of self-control', and the term is not defined in the 2009 Act. It is clear that loss of self-control should not be interpreted too strictly by isolating it to cases where D fully lacks control over her physical bodily movement: such cases are already catered for within the complete defence of insanity, or a claim of automatism.[24] Rather, the term should be

---

22 The defence will only be put to the jury (become a live issue) where the judge is satisfied that there is sufficient evidence that a reasonable jury may find the defence elements satisfied. Coroners and Justice Act 2009, s54(6).

23 See *Evans* [2012] EWCA Crim 2.

24 See **Chapters 13** and **14**. Recognised and discussed in *Richens* [1993] 4 All ER 877.

interpreted to require extreme emotion and/or a loss of rationality, but not more than this. This was accepted by the Court of Appeal in *Jewell*.[25] The court, adopting the wording of the 13th edition of *Smith and Hogan's Criminal Law*, defined loss of self-control as the 'loss of the ability to act in accordance with considered judgment or a loss of normal powers of reasoning.'[26] In this manner, a loss of self-control is not a claim that D lacked the mens rea for murder, but rather, it is an explanation why she had it.

One important difference between the old law of provocation and the new LOC defence is that it is no longer necessary that D's loss of self-control is 'sudden and temporary'. The old requirement of a sudden and temporary loss of self-control was heavily criticised for its perceived gender bias: whilst men are more likely to react immediately to provocation, women, although similarly affected, may react later after a slow-burn period. This was discussed in *Ahluwalia*.

Ahluwalia [1992] 4 All ER 889 (pre-2009 case)

D killed her abusive husband (V) following years of violence. She poured petrol over V whilst he was asleep and set fire to it; V died from the burns. D admitted murder, but claimed a defence of provocation.

- Crown Court: guilty of murder.
- D appealed, questioning the trial judge's direction that D's loss of control must be sudden and temporary to qualify for the defence.
- Court of Appeal: quashed D's conviction (and ordered a retrial) on the basis that D's depression may give rise to an alternative defence of diminished responsibility (later accepted on retrial). *But* confirmed that the court was correct in finding that provocation required a 'sudden and temporary' loss of control.

Ahluwalia is a useful case to illustrate the problems with the pre-2009 Act law. The court allowed the defence of provocation to go to the jury on the basis that (despite the time delay between V's provocation and D's reaction) D's loss of self-control may still have been sudden and temporary. However, for a jury applying a test framed in these terms, the defence was always likely to fail.[27] By removing the 'sudden and temporary' requirement, the potential now is that defendants such as Ahluwalia, i.e the victims of abuse who react after a period of time, will be *more* likely to satisfy the test. However, it remains uncertain whether this will be the case. This is because, although the words 'sudden and temporary' have been removed, it is difficult to make sense of the loss of self-control requirement in the way that it has been understood (a 'rush of blood', or 'emotional surge'), without taking account of the time delay between provocation and reaction: a long delay implies that the trigger has not caused a loss of self-control.[28] Indeed, we see this to a certain extent in the recent case of *Jewell*.

---

[25] [2014] EWCA Crim 414.

[26] Per Rafferty LJ at [23].

[27] For a discussion of the law after *Ahluwalia*, but pre-2009, see Wells, 'Battered Women Syndrome and Defences to Homicide: Where Now?' (1994) 14 LS 266.

[28] This is recognised in the 2009 Act's Explanatory Notes, para 337 and in parliamentary debates prior to reform.

> **Jewell** [2014] EWCA Crim 414
>
> D killed V, a workmate, after an extended period of perceived intimidation by V. D gave evidence that he was unable to sleep in the preceding days, and was gradually 'shutting down' before he acted to kill, describing his final acts as having been done in a dream-like state. D was charged with murder.
>
> - Crown Court: guilty of murder. LOC was not left to the jury, with the judge finding no basis for the defence.
> - Court of Appeal: conviction upheld on appeal. The planning that preceded the killing undermined a claim of loss of self-control.

The approach taken in *Jewell* confirms that the requirement of loss of self-control will remain a significant hurdle for those wishing to make use of the defence, particularly in the most difficult cases such as those involving abused women. For example, if D kills her partner following domestic abuse, she may not have done so in a manic/rush of blood-type manner, but she may have felt, as a result of the abuse, that she lacked control in the sense of seeing no alternative options to end the abuse. Expanding the definition of loss of self-control in this manner has an obvious appeal in the context of people who kill their abusers, and even perhaps for so-called mercy killers who are driven to kill their loved ones believing it is the only way they can assist them.[29] However, as we see in *Jewell*, it is unlikely that such an expansion will gain traction within the current law.

6.2.1.3 There must be a qualifying trigger

D's loss of self-control must have been caused by a 'qualifying trigger'. Where D loses self-control and kills in the absence of such a trigger, the LOC defence will not apply. Section 55 of the 2009 Act, sets out two qualifying triggers for the defence: a fear of serious violence, and/or a sense of being seriously wronged by things said or done. Although each trigger provides a separate, alternative route into the defence, many cases will involve a combination of the two.[30]

A) **Fear of serious violence from V (s55(3)):** The first qualifying trigger arises where D loses self-control in fear of serious violence against herself or another identified person (eg against her child, etc). This is a *subjective* requirement: D must react to a genuine fear, and it must be a fear of *serious* violence, but this fear need not be based on a correct assessment of the facts (there does not need to be an actual threat) and D's fear need not be reasonable; a reasonable person in D's position may have realised there was no need to fear. This trigger, new to the 2009 Act, is partly designed to remove gender bias from the defence. It extends qualifying triggers from classically masculine responses to verbal or physical affronts, to include reactions to fear of serious violence. This trigger is intended to be employed, for example, in the context of abused women who kill their abusers in fear of future violence.

It is useful to consider how this trigger and the LOC *partial* defence will operate alongside the *complete* defence of self-defence, a defence discussed at **Chapter 14**.

---

[29] *Serrano* [2006] EWCA Crim 3182 (pre-2009): a tragic case in which D's caution when killing his terminally ill wife demonstrated that he was not out of control, and thus outside the provocation defence.

[30] Coroners and Justice Act, s55(5); *Dawes* [2013] EWCA Crim 322, [56].

Of course, in cases where D might raise self-defence then this will be her priority: successfully pleading self-defence will result in acquittal. However, where D kills in fear of serious violence and self-defence is not available (eg because the threat to D from V was not imminent; or because the force used was unreasonably excessive; etc[31]) then the partial defence of LOC may provide a useful safety net, reducing D's liability to manslaughter.

> **Extra detail...**
> Whether D fears violence is a subjective question that does not rely on reasonableness. However, where that belief is unreasonable and only arises as a result of voluntary intoxication, it is unclear whether this would qualify as a trigger under the current law. Similarly subjective requirements in self-defence, for example, apply an exception in relation to beliefs formed from voluntary intoxication.[32] However, in line with the old common law of provocation,[33] it is contended that even intoxicated beliefs should be sufficient (should not be excluded) in the context of the LOC defence.
>
> However, even where such beliefs are not excluded, D's intoxication may still undermine the third element of the defence—the claim that a reasonable (sober) person might have reacted similarly.[34]

D's fear of serious violence will not be a sufficient trigger where D has consciously caused the conditions of her own defence: where D has incited V to act (causing D to fear) in order to have an excuse to use violence against V.[35] For example, where D taunts or provokes V to punch her, and D is acting in that way so that she may then kill V and seek to rely on the partial defence. In that case D may not rely on this trigger and, thus, may not rely on a LOC defence. This is an important restriction, but will only apply where D has consciously manipulated the circumstances. Where D acts in a manner that is likely to provoke violence, but is not doing so consciously in order to gain an excuse to react violently, then the defence may still operate. This interpretation was confirmed in *Dawes and Ors*.

> **Dawes and Ors** [2013] EWCA Crim 322
>
> D discovered his estranged wife asleep with another man (V), and stabbed V with a kitchen knife, causing death. D was charged with murder, and raised the defence of self-defence.
>
> - Crown Court: guilty of murder. The jury did not accept the defence of self-defence, and the judge refused to allow the partial LOC defence to go to the jury because: (a) if D did kill in reaction to an attack from V, then this only happened because D had provoked the attack; and (b) there was no evidence of a loss of self-control; he was acting in an angry but controlled manner.
> - Court of Appeal: as part of a combined appeal with two other cases, Dawes's conviction was upheld. Importantly, the court confirmed that the Crown Court had been wrong on point (a): although D may have provoked the attack from V, this will only undermine a LOC defence where it is done consciously in order to provide a defence for retaliatory violence. That was not the case here. However, the Crown Court was still correct not to leave LOC to the jury on the basis of point (b).

---

[31] See discussion of self-defence at **Chapter 14**.
[32] Ibid.
[33] *Letenock* (1917) 12 Cr App R 221.
[34] *Asmelash* [2013] EWCA Crim 157.
[35] Coroners and Justice Act, s55(6)(a).

B) A sense of being seriously wronged by things said or done (s55(4)): The second qualifying trigger arises where D loses self-control as a result of a 'justifiable sense of being seriously wronged' by 'things said or done' (not necessarily by V[36]) that were of an 'extremely grave character'. In common with the pre-2009 Act defence, this trigger requires D to identify specific actions or comments which caused the loss of self-control, with mere circumstances (eg losing money on the stock market, or a farmer losing her crops to flood) being insufficient.[37] This trigger is partly *subjective* (D must personally feel seriously wronged) and partly *objective* (the feeling of wrong must be objectively justifiable, and the circumstances must be objectively grave).

The inclusion of objective requirements within this trigger is new to the 2009 Act. It is designed to prevent the defence being used (or even raised[38]) in circumstances where D is provoked by trivial events (eg a crying baby[39] or a poorly cooked steak[40]) or by events that are only grave for D because of something objectionable about her character (eg a white supremacist provoked by a lack of deference from V, a black man[41]). In such cases, it is clear that a trivial event is not one of an 'extremely grave character', and a racist perception can never result in a '*justifiable* sense of being seriously wronged'. There is a useful discussion of this in *Dawes and Ors*, concerning the linked appeal of Barry Bowyer.

> **Dawes and Ors** [2013] EWCA Crim 322
>
> D and V were both romantically involved with the same woman (X). D broke into V's house in order to steal items to sell, but when V returned home D beat and killed him. D was charged with murder.
>
> - Crown Court: guilty of murder. The trial judge allowed the LOC defence to go to the jury, but they did not accept it.
> - Court of Appeal: as part of a combined appeal with two other cases, Bowyer's conviction was upheld. The court confirmed the accuracy of the trial judge's direction on LOC, but also stated that the judge should not have left the defence to the jury at all. On the issue of the qualifying trigger, the court stated that 'it is absurd to suggest that the entirely understandable response of the deceased to finding a burglar in his home [ie attacking and insulting D] provided the appellant with the remotest beginnings of a basis for suggesting that he had a justifiable sense of being wronged, let alone seriously wronged' [66].

Although the use of language of the section to inject objectivity can be generally welcomed in order to exclude clear cases of this kind, the terms used ('extremely grave'; 'justifiable sense'; 'seriously wronged') are regrettably vague for such an important defence element. This results in considerable discretion for juries when applying the law, and through this, the potential for inconsistency.[42]

---

[36] eg *Davies* [1975] QB 691 (pre-2009): D killed his wife after being provoked by her lover.

[37] *Acott* [1997] 2 Cr App R 94 (pre-2009).

[38] A judge will not allow the defence to go to the jury unless there is sufficient evidence upon which it might be accepted. Section 54(6).

[39] *Doughty* (1986) 83 Cr App R 319 (pre-2009).

[40] Example from Law Commission, *Murder, Manslaughter and Infanticide* (No 304, 2006) para 1.47.

[41] The Commission, and government, were similarly keen to exclude so-called honour killings: where D kills his daughter because she has had a sexual relationship before marriage. *Mohammed* [2005] EWCA Crim 1880 (pre-2009).

[42] Withey, 'Loss of Control, Loss of Opportunity?' [2011] Crim LR 263, 271–274.

Two exclusions apply to this trigger. First, as with the fear of serious violence trigger, D cannot rely on things said or done where she has incited them in order to use violence in response.[43] For example, if D encourages V to shout abuse at her so that she (D) has an excuse to react violently, the defence will not be available.

Additionally, section 55(6)(c) specifically excludes things said or done constituting 'sexual infidelity'. This exclusion was added by the government to send a clear message that killing in response to sexual infidelity should never ground a defence to murder, as it had in a number of pre-2009 Act provocation cases.[44] However, the exclusion has been highly controversial.[45] Criticism of the exclusion has focused on the principle itself: why should sexual infidelity be singled out for exclusion in cases where all other elements of the defence are satisfied, particularly as LOC is only a partial defence? More damagingly, criticism has also focused on the coherence of the exclusion: the lack of a definition of 'sexual infidelity' (eg does fidelity assume a certain status of relationship between D and V?); the potential for mixed issues (eg where D discovers her husband sexually abusing their daughter); the ambiguous drafting of things said or done that 'constituted' sexual infidelity (eg would this include V telling D that she planned to be unfaithful in the future?); and so on. These problems were discussed by the Court of Appeal in *Clinton*.

Clinton [2012] EWCA Crim 2

D killed his wife following an argument in which she informed him that she was having an affair; that she had had sexual intercourse with a number of other men during their marriage; and she taunted him about his previous failed attempts to commit suicide. D accepted that he had completed the elements of murder, but claimed a LOC defence.

- Crown Court: guilty of murder. LOC was withdrawn from the jury because it was excluded by the sexual infidelity exclusion.
- Court of Appeal: appeal allowed, and retrial ordered. Where sexual infidelity is not the sole trigger said or done (as here), it should be allowed to go to the jury alongside all other factors.

In a well-reasoned judgment, the court in *Clinton* exposed the poor drafting of the exclusion, and revealed that for coherence it could not apply in the manner that many had expected.[46] Where the sole trigger relied on by D is something said or done which amounts to sexual infidelity, then that is not something to which the jury should have regard in considering the defence. However, whenever there are other potential triggers, as will invariably be the case in complex real-world relationships, then sexual infidelity will not be excluded from those other factors when they are considered by the jury. Therefore, in most cases involving sexual infidelity, the courts are likely to focus more on the general objective standards for exclusion rather than the specific terms of section 55(6)(c).

---

[43] Coroners and Justice Act, s55(6)(b); *Dawes* [2013] EWCA Crim 322, [56].

[44] Hansard, HC, 9 November 2009, col 82.

[45] Reed and Wake, 'Sexual Infidelity Killings' in Reed and Bohlander (eds), *Loss of Control and Diminished Responsibility: Domestic, Comparative and International Perspectives* (2011) 117.

[46] Morgan, 'Loss of Self-Control: Back to the Good Old Days' (2013) 77 J Crim L 119.

Extra detail...

Although D must have been provoked or caused to fear by another party, there is no requirement that this party was V. For example, D may be taunted by X about the behaviour of her daughter V, causing D to lose control and kill V. Equally, if D loses control and attempts to kill X, but misses and kills V, D's defence may transfer to the killing of V in a manner similar to transferred malice.[47]

6.2.1.4 A person of normal tolerance and self-restraint might have reacted similarly

The third and final element within the LOC partial defence is that D's reaction to the qualifying trigger must have been *objectively* understandable in the sense that 'a person of D's age and sex, with a normal degree of tolerance and self-restraint, and in the circumstances of D, might have reacted in the same or in a similar way to D.'[48] As with provocation in the pre-2009 Act, this element is core to the rationale of the LOC defence: it is not simply that D has a good reason for losing self-control and killing, it is also that she was provoked, or caused to fear serious violence, to such an extent that anybody might have reacted as she did. In this manner, this element is necessary to show that D's offence was, at least partially, not a reflection of an evil character. We are not saying that D acted correctly, but we can sympathise, and partially excuse, on the basis that, as the old adage goes, 'there but for the grace of God go I'.

Despite being at the core of the defence, the equivalent objective element under the old law of provocation caused considerable problems for the courts. This is because, when identifying the objective standard, it is necessary to decide if there is a single, fixed standard (eg that of a 'normal' human), or whether we can take account of certain characteristics of D that might affect what is a 'normal' degree of self-restraint for her (eg her age; any mental conditions; intoxication; etc: with different fixed levels required for each). On this issue, the pre-2009 Act case law diverged into two streams: one identifying the standard through a strict test of a 'normal' person of D's age and sex;[49] and the other applying a much more liberal test that allowed almost any of D's characteristics to be taken into account when identifying a 'normal' expected standard for that defendant.[50] This divergence came to an end in the case of *Holley*,[51] where a specially convened nine-member Board of the Privy Council concluded that the narrower approach (considering age and sex only) was to be preferred.[52] The academic debate surrounding this conflict provides a useful background for an evaluation of the current law.[53]

---

[47] *Gross* (1913) 23 Cox CC 445 (pre-2009): D was provoked by her husband X, shot at him, but missed and hit V. D could use the partial defence in relation to the killing of V. Transferred malice was discussed at **4.3.1**.

[48] Coroners and Justice Act, s54(1)(c).

[49] Exemplified by *Camplin* [1978] AC 705 (pre-2009).

[50] Exemplified by *Smith (Morgan)* [2001] AC 146.

[51] *AG for Jersey v Holley* [2005] UKPC 23 (pre-2009).

[52] Despite its status as a Privy Council decision, the Court of Appeal in *James and Karimi* [2006] EWCA Crim 14 took the radical approach of endorsing the decision in *Holley* in preference to the House of Lords case of *Smith (Morgan)*.

[53] The debate here is broadly the same as that under the pre-2009 law between *Smith (Morgan)* (liberal approach) and *Holley* (restrictive approach). See Macklem and Gardner, 'Compassion Without Respect: Nine Fallacies in *R v Smith*' [2001] Crim LR 623; cf Mitchell, Mackay, and Brookbanks, 'Pleading for Provoked Killers: In Defence of *Morgan Smith*' (2008) 124 LQR 675.

The 2009 Act does not seek to codify either of the competing positions under the old common law, but rather seeks something of a compromise position between them. In line with the old law, age and sex remain relevant considerations: the jury must consider the likely reaction of a reasonable person of D's age and sex.

> **Extra detail…**
> Taking account of 'age' seems sensible: it is logical that we might expect a higher degree of tolerance and self-restraint from an older person than, for example, a child. And, conversely, to hold a child to an adult standard would seem unfair.[54] However, the inclusion of 'sex' seems to be an odd legacy from the case law: there is no evidence that men and women have different levels of 'normal' tolerance or self-restraint.

The novelty of the current law is that, beyond age and sex, section 54(1)(c) also makes reference to 'the circumstances of D'. This implies a reversal of *Holley* and suggests that all of D's circumstances will be relevant (eg mental condition, intoxication, etc). However, opening this element to *all* of D's circumstances would take us back to the criticised position that preceded *Holley*, and was one of the major catalysts for reform of the defence. To avoid this, section 54(3) provides a vital qualification, stating that 'the circumstances of D' should be interpreted to mean:

> all of D's circumstances other than those whose only relevance to D's conduct is that they bear on D's general capacity for tolerance and self-restraint.

In this manner, the current law is considerably wider than the approach in *Holley*; recognising that a fair reasonable person test should take account of certain of D's characteristics beyond age and sex. However, at the same time, the test remains objective: D's characteristics will only be taken into account where they genuinely affected her appreciation of and reaction to the specific trigger, not simply because the characteristic makes her generally more short-tempered, for example.

The ambition of this compromised position seems sensible, but the drafting is unfortunately vague. There is useful clarity at the extremes. Thus, we know that where D's circumstances have a bearing *only* on her ability to control herself they will be excluded. This was confirmed in *Asmelash* in the context of voluntary intoxication.

> **Asmelash** [2013] EWCA Crim 157
>
> D and V spent the day drinking and arguing, culminating in D stabbing V twice and killing him. D was charged with murder.
> - Crown Court: guilty of murder. Directing the jury as to LOC, the judge explained that they should ask whether a reasonable person sharing D's characteristics, *but not intoxicated*, might have acted in the same way.
> - Court of Appeal: conviction upheld on appeal. Voluntary intoxication was only relevant to D's general capacity of self-control and was therefore rightly excluded.

At the other end of the spectrum, it is clear that where D's characteristics also have an explicit bearing on the relevant trigger they will be taken into account. For example, if D

---

[54] *Camplin* [1978] AC 705 (pre-2009): recognising this in a case where D (a 15-year-old boy) killed V after being raped and then mocked by his rapist.

is insulted for being a drug addict, her status as an addict may affect both the gravity of the provocation and D's ability to control herself.[55] However, it is the grey area between these extremes that is likely to cause problems. For example, where D has a psychiatric illness, this may not be expressly linked to the trigger, but may still be interpreted as affecting D beyond her general capacity for self-control because of, for example, its effect on her ability to understand and evaluate the trigger. In view of the troubled history of this element of the defence under the old law, it is likely to be interpreted narrowly and rarely to allow more than age and sex to be considered. Given the well-known troubled history of the old law, the ambiguity of the drafting is very disappointing.

> *Point to remember…*
> The last part of the test 'might have reacted in the same or in a similar way' should not be forgotten. Two points are important. First, it is not necessary that a normal person 'would' have reacted in a similar way, only that one might have (lowering the standard). Secondly, even if a normal person might have lost control and killed as D did, you must still look at the 'way' it was done. For example, if D lost control and killed V in a particularly brutal or prolonged attack, in a manner in which a normal person would never do, then she may fall outside the defence.[56]

6.2.2 Diminished responsibility

As with the LOC defence, diminished responsibility (DR) is a partial defence to murder (and *only* to murder[57]) that reduces D's liability from murder to 'voluntary' manslaughter, thereby avoiding the mandatory life sentence.[58] For the LOC defence, as we have seen, D claims that she should be partially excused for the killing on the basis that a 'normal' person might have reacted as she did. For DR, in contrast, D is claiming a partial excuse on the basis that she should not be held to the standard of a 'normal' person because of her medical condition.[59] Where D's medical condition creates a defect of reason that *completely* undermines her ability to understand the nature or quality of her acts, or to know if they are wrong, then she will have a *complete* defence of insanity—even when the offence is murder.[60] DR is different: where D's medical condition causes her an abnormality of mind that *substantially* impairs her abilities, she will be liable only for manslaughter.

The elements of the DR defence, contained in section 2 of the Homicide Act 1957, have been amended significantly by section 52 of the Coroners and Justice Act 2009. The pre-2009 DR defence was defined broadly and imprecisely to apply where D's 'abnormality of mind' substantially impaired her 'mental responsibility'. This was welcomed in certain cases, allowing for flexibility and legal equity, essentially allowing courts and juries to interpret and apply the law as they wished to find a 'fair' result. However, as discussed by the Law Commission, flexibility also resulted in 'chaotic' use of the defence, with it being

---

[55] Also confirmed in *Asmelash* [2013] EWCA Crim 157.

[56] *Van Dongen* [2005] Crim LR 971 (pre-2009): D's acts demonstrated abnormal savagery and fell outside the defence.

[57] *Campbell* [1997] Crim LR 495: will not apply to attempted murder.

[58] The maximum sentence for manslaughter is life imprisonment, but (unlike for murder) this sentence is not mandatory.

[59] Horder, *Excusing Crime* (2004) Ch1.

[60] *M'Naghten* (1843) 10 Cl & Fin 200, 8 Eng Rep 718. See **Chapter 14**. Although the verdict will be the 'special' one of 'Not Guilty by Reason of Insanity'.

'grossly abused' in certain cases, resulting in a 'lottery' between cases.[61] In view of these problems, the Commission made recommendations for reform,[62] many of which were adopted within the 2009 Act.

The current (post-2009[63]) DR defence is set out (as amended) in section 2 of the Homicide Act 1957:[64]

(1) A person ('D') who kills or is a party to the killing of another is not to be convicted of murder if D was suffering from an abnormality of mental functioning which—

    (a) arose from a recognised medical condition,

    (b) substantially impaired D's ability to do one or more of the things mentioned in subsection (1A), and

    (c) provides an explanation for D's acts and omissions in doing or being a party to the killing.

(1A) Those things are—

    (a) to understand the nature of D's conduct;

    (b) to form a rational judgement;

    (c) to exercise self-control.

Don't be confused...

Both LOC and DR defences have been reformed by the 2009 Act. For LOC, as the old provocation defence (replaced by LOC) existed at common law, the new defence is located in the 2009 Act itself. In contrast, as the old DR defence was already fully codified within the Homicide Act 1957, the 2009 Act simply amended that statute. Therefore, when referring to the current DR defence, you should still refer to section 2 of the 1957 Act.

DR can be separated into four elements, set out in **Table 6.3**. All four must be satisfied for the defence to apply.

Table 6.3 Partial defence of diminished responsibility

A) D must demonstrate an abnormality of mental functioning
B) The abnormality must have arisen from a recognised medical condition

C) The abnormality must have substantially impaired D's ability to:
   i) understand the nature of her conduct; *or*
   ii) form a rational judgement; *or*
   iii) exercise self-control

D) The abnormality must provide an explanation (or cause) of the killing

---

[61] Law Commission, *Partial Defences to Murder* (No 290, 2004) Part 5.

[62] Law Commission, *Murder, Manslaughter and Infanticide* (No 304, 2006).

[63] In force since October 2010.

[64] See generally Mackay, 'The New Diminished Responsibility Plea' [2010] Crim LR 290.

In common with the insanity defence, but in contrast to LOC, the burden of proving these elements is on the defendant and not the prosecution.[65] As we have discussed,[66] where the burden of proof is reversed in this manner, the defence only have to prove their case to the civil standard: on the balance of probabilities.[67] They must prove every element of the DR defence, and only then will D's liable be reduced from murder to 'voluntary' manslaughter. We will explore each element in turn.

6.2.2.1 D must have had an abnormality of mental functioning

The term 'abnormality of mental functioning' is not defined in the statute and remains somewhat vague. In line with the old law, the element is designed to require a link between D's medical condition and some impact on her mind.

The language of 'mental functioning' (as opposed to 'abnormality of mind' under the pre-2009 law) demonstrates a move towards medical/psychiatric definitions that are likely to standardise the potential application of the element. For example, in *Byrne*[68] Lord Parker CJ described the pre-2009 test as 'a state of mind so different from that of ordinary human beings that the reasonable man would term it abnormal.'[69] The defence always required medical evidence to succeed, but since the 2009 Act, with the move to more medicalised elements, that has become more transparent.[70]

6.2.2.2 The abnormality must have arisen from a recognised medical condition

The required link between D's abnormal mental functioning and a recognised medical condition is one of the most important and clearly medicalising elements of the reformed partial defence. Therefore, although the ultimate question remains a legal one for the court, discussion of a 'recognised' medical condition will inevitably make use of medical glossaries such as the World Health Organization's *International Statistical Classification of Diseases and Related Health Problems* (ICD 10) and the American Medical Association's *Diagnostic and Statistical Manual* (SSM). Additionally, it will also be open for the court to recognise medical conditions that are not on these lists, but are supported by a reliable body of expert opinion. In both cases, it is clear that psychiatric and purely physical conditions are capable of satisfying this element, although of course purely physical conditions are less likely to satisfy the other defence elements.

Extra detail...

Although D must have a recognised medical condition, there is no requirement of seriousness. Thus, as long as the other defence elements are satisfied, even mild depression would be sufficient.

The rationale for linking this element of DR to medical definitions is to ensure that the legal test is not left behind by developments in medical science. However, as medical

---

[65] Homicide Act 1957, s2(2).
[66] See **1.1.7.2**.
[67] The reverse burden for DR has been found to be compatible with the Art 6 ECHR right to a fair trial: *Lambert* [2001] 1 Cr App R 205; *Foye* [2013] EWCA Crim 475.
[68] [1960] 2 QB 396 (pre-2009 version of the defence).
[69] Ibid, 403.
[70] See *Bunch* [2013] EWCA Crim 2498.

definitions are not specifically designed to assist the criminal law, problems are likely to emerge about which conditions are included and excluded by this coupling.

A) Included: Popular lists of medically recognised conditions include some diagnoses which the law would not want to qualify within the DR defence (eg Hughes LJ lists references in the *Dictionary of Scientific Medicine* including 'unhappiness', 'anger', and 'paedophilia'[71]). It is now clear, therefore, that the fact D suffers from a condition that is 'recognised' by the medical profession is necessary but is not sufficient for it to found the defence: it must also be one that the courts are prepared to 'recognise' in law. This was discussed in the *Dowds* case.

Dowds [2012] EWCA Crim 281

D killed his partner whilst heavily intoxicated, inflicting 60 stab wounds. D attempted to use the DR defence, relying on his 'acute intoxication' (extreme drunkenness) which is a medical condition recognised by the World Health Organization.

- Crown Court: guilty of murder. The judge refused to allow DR.
- Court of Appeal: conviction upheld on appeal. Although acute intoxication was a medically recognised condition, it will not qualify as such within the DR defence.

B) Excluded: Whereas before 2009 the defence could be used flexibly, there has been a fear that the new formulation of the defence, with its requirement of a recognised medical condition, will exclude defendants such as abused women who kill and so-called mercy killers.[72] However, this problem may have been exaggerated. First, most defendants in such cases *will* be suffering from a recognised anxiety- or depression-related condition. Further, where there is no such condition, there are strong grounds to maintain that D's case should not come within the defence: the rationale of the defence is to provide a partial excuse for those acting as a result of their medical affliction; not as a method for courts to engage with a debate on euthanasia or other defences they might want to create (in the guise of DR) in the absence of governmental will.[73]

More troubling is the potential exclusion of developmental immaturity, particularly with young defendants: this will sometimes coincide with a recognised condition (eg autism), but will not always do so. The Law Commission recommended that developmental immaturity should be explicitly included as an alternative to a recognised medical condition.[74] This was rejected by the government as unnecessary, who stressed the general overlap with recognised conditions. Despite this, the omission is unfortunate, and may lead to unfairness. As has been noted, a 40–year-old with a mental age of 10 can use the defence; a 10-year-old with a mental age of 10 cannot.

---

[71] *Dowds* [2012] EWCA Crim 281.
[72] Kennefick, 'Introducing a New Diminished Responsibility Defence for England and Wales' (2011) 74 MLR 750; evidence of 'Dignity in Dying' to the Joint Committee on Human Rights, 8th Report, 2008–9, para 1.150.
[73] A point made by Ashworth and Horder, *Principles of Criminal Law* (7th edn, 2013) 270–271.
[74] Law Commission, *Murder, Manslaughter and Infanticide* (No 304, 2006) paras 5.125–5.137.

6.2.2.3 The abnormality must have substantially impaired D's mental ability to…

Although the defence is still called 'diminished responsibility', the pre-2009 requirement of a 'substantially impaired mental responsibility' has been replaced with an element that makes no reference to 'responsibility' at all. Rather, D's 'substantial' impairment must be shown to relate to one of three rather more precise abilities (each capable of medical assessment). We will explore each in turn.

Terminology…

The term 'substantial' is not defined in the statute. Recent cases are in disagreement over the definition of this term. The latest view of the Court of Appeal is that it means not just 'more than trivial', but something having a greater impact.[75] The term is important in the context of DR because it ensures the defence is not too widely available (D's condition must have had a significant impact to warrant the partial excuse), but also that DR does not require total destruction of capacity and blame (intruding on the complete defence of insanity).[76]

…understand the nature of D's conduct

This first possibility carries an obvious echo of the insanity defence: which also refers to an inability to understand the nature of one's own conduct.[77] However, unlike insanity, where there must be a complete inability, DR is satisfied by a substantial impairment. An example, adapted from the Law Commission, is a child with a mental illness who obsessively plays violent video games and then kills in the belief that the victim will regenerate as they do in her games.[78] Here, D may understand the physical dynamics of her action, but she does not understand its impact on V.

…form a rational judgement

The second possibility is where D's abnormality substantially impairs her ability to form a rational judgement. As the Law Commission highlights,[79] this is the most likely route within DR for an abused person who kills their abuser, or for a so-called mercy killer: in each case the pressure of the circumstances may substantially impair D's ability to make rational choices.[80]

…exercise control

The final possibility within this element, where D's ability to exercise control is substantially impaired, has the potential to be interpreted very widely. The availability of this option makes it possible to restrict the LOC defence to cases where a person of 'normal' self-restraint might have reacted similarly. Where D is incapable of living up to the standard of 'normal' self-restraint, her defence (if she satisfies all the elements) should be DR.

---

[75] *R* [2010] EWCA Crim 194 (applying pre-2009 law).
[76] Discussed in *Golds* [2014] EWCA Crim 748.
[77] **Chapter 14**.
[78] Law Commission, *Murder, Manslaughter and Infanticide* (No 304, 2006) para 5.21.
[79] Ibid, para 5.121.
[80] The issue is really about whether D was able rationally to make a choice rather than whether the choice made was a rational one.

6.2.2.4 The abnormality must provide an explanation
(or cause) of the killing

The final element of the DR partial defence requires a causal link between D's abnormality and the killing. Although section 2(1)(c) only states that the abnormality must provide an 'explanation' for the killing, section 2(1B) clarifies that an 'explanation' will be found 'if it causes, or is a significant contributory factor in causing, D to carry out the conduct.' In this manner, the DR defence does not partially excuse D simply because of her abnormality of mental functioning and/or her recognised medical condition. It is rather because these elements combine to have affected her conduct to cause her to kill.

Demonstrating a causal link of this kind, however, is far from straightforward. Causation in criminal law, as we have discussed in **Chapter 2**, usually focuses on the external causal effect of D's acts or omissions on a particular result. This is often difficult, but causation in the context of DR requires something even more challenging: assessment of the causal effect of an abnormality *within* the mind of D upon her choice of conduct. Even with the help of medical experts, this is far from an exact science.[81]

Another difficulty when applying this element is the chance, which is not uncommon, of multiple causes/motivations (eg D kills as a result of her abnormality and her anger at losing her job). When applying the law to such facts, it is clear that D's abnormality can be a substantial cause, satisfying this element of the defence, without being the sole cause. However, it will be necessary for D to demonstrate, on the balance of probabilities, that her condition was not merely incidental. There is a useful discussion of this in the (pre-2009 Act) case of *Dietschmann*.[82]

> *Dietschmann* [2003] 1 AC 1209 (pre-2009)
>
> D became heavily intoxicated and killed V. D was also suffering an mental abnormality, a form of depression following the death of his aunt to whom he was very close. D raised the DR defence.
> - Crown Court: guilty of murder.
> - Court of Appeal: conviction upheld on appeal.
> - House of Lords: appeal allowed (D liable for voluntary manslaughter only). It was clarified that although D's killing may have been partly caused by circumstances other than D's abnormality (in this case, voluntary intoxication) it is still open to a jury to find DR as long as D's abnormality remained a substantial aspect. Ignoring the other circumstance, the DR elements were nevertheless satisfied.

Where, as in *Dietschmann*, one of the causes of D's killing is intoxication, three situations should be carefully separated when applying the defence.

(a) First, as confirmed in *Dowds* (discussed earlier), acute intoxication is not a *legally* recognised condition for the purposes of DR, and so intoxication alone cannot provide a basis for the DR defence.

---

[81] Miles, 'A Dog's Breakfast of Homicide Reform' [2009] 6 Arch News 6.
[82] Confirmed in *Dowds* [2012] EWCA Crim 281.

(b) Secondly, where D is intoxicated and has a separate recognised condition (as in *Dietschmann*), the jury should ask whether D's recognised condition caused the killing and, as far as possible, exclude the intoxication from their consideration.

(c) Thirdly, where D has a recognised condition that caused the intoxication (eg drug or alcohol dependency), the jury may take account of *both* the condition and the intoxication related to that condition when considering causation.[83]

6.2.3 Suicide pact partial defence

The third partial defence to murder arises where D kills V pursuant to an agreement that they will die together (a suicide pact). Section 4 of the Homicide Act 1957 states:

(1) It shall be manslaughter, and shall not be murder, for a person acting in pursuance of a suicide pact between him and another to kill the other or be a party to the other... being killed by a third person...

(2) For the purposes of this section 'suicide pact' means a common agreement between two or more persons having for its object the death of all of them, whether or not each is to take his own life, but nothing done by a person who enters into a suicide pact shall be treated as done by him in pursuance of the pact unless it is done while he has the settled intention of dying in pursuance of the pact.

There are two main elements to this defence, set out in **Table 6.4**. Both must be satisfied for D's liability to be reduced from murder to voluntary manslaughter.

Table 6.4 Partial defence of suicide pact

A) D must have agreed with V that they will die together
B) D must intend, at the point of killing V, to die herself in line with the agreement

As with the DR defence, the burden of proof is on D to establish the elements of the defence on the balance of probabilities.[84]

Assessment matters...
When applying the law to apparent suicides, take care to identify the correct offences. Where D kills V, then you are right to apply homicide offences and (where relevant) the partial defence of suicide pacts. However, where D assists or encourages V to kill herself, D will not have committed a homicide offence (she has not caused death). Rather, you should apply the offence of assisting or encouraging suicide.[85] The act of suicide or attempted suicide is not an offence.

---

[83] The pre-2009 Act approach is likely to be followed here: *Wood* [2008] EWCA Crim 1305.

[84] Homicide Act 1957, s4(2). This is compatible with D's right to a fair trial under Art 6 ECHR: *AG's Reference (No 1 of 2004)* [2004] 1 WLR 2111.

[85] Discussed at **Chapter 11**.

6.3 Involuntary manslaughter

Involuntary manslaughter has nothing to do with 'involuntariness'. Rather, the label 'involuntary' is used to differentiate this second form of manslaughter liability from the first (voluntary manslaughter) discussed previously. Crucially, whereas voluntary manslaughter arises where D commits murder and then relies on a partial *defence*, involuntary manslaughter arises where D does not satisfy the mens rea of murder, so does not commit murder, but becomes liable for a manslaughter *offence*.[86] As with all homicide offences, involuntary manslaughter offences require the actus reus of murder to have been fulfilled (the unlawful killing of a person). However, the mens rea requirements of involuntary manslaughter offences do not require an intention to kill or cause GBH which is the mens rea of murder.

Three main involuntary manslaughter offences will be discussed in this section. All exist at common law.

• **Unlawful act manslaughter:** D commits a criminal act in dangerous circumstances, and this causes the death of V.

• **Gross negligence manslaughter:** D causes V's death through criminal negligence.

• **Reckless manslaughter:** D causes V's death, being reckless as to causing death or GBH.

> *Don't be confused...*
> A fourth involuntary manslaughter offence is that of corporate manslaughter. However, as this offence requires a different actus reus from other manslaughter offences, it will be discussed separately at **6.4**.

The main point of contention within these offences, as we will discuss, has been breadth of the forms of mens rea capable of giving rise to liability. Although courts have a wide sentencing discretion from absolute discharge to life imprisonment, it remains questionable whether all of the conduct currently captured within these offences deserves the label manslaughter. Indeed, the Law Commission has cautioned against this category becoming a 'residual, amorphous, "catch-all" homicide offence'.[87]

6.3.1 Unlawful act manslaughter

Unlawful act manslaughter (UAM) is also (interchangeably) referred to as 'unlawful and dangerous act manslaughter' or 'constructive manslaughter'. In each case, it refers to an involuntary manslaughter offence in which, by her acts, D commits a criminal offence (the base offence), the base offence carries an objective risk of harm to V, and V dies as a result. The current state of the law is presented in **Table 6.5**.

---

[86] See flowchart at **6.1**.

[87] Law Commission, *Murder, Manslaughter and Infanticide* (No 304, 2006) para 2.9.

Table 6.5 Unlawful act manslaughter

	Actus reus	**Mens rea**
Conduct element	Any acts causing the results	Voluntary
Circumstance element	Any circumstances required for the base offence	As required for the base offence
	A reasonable person in D's position would recognise a risk of some harm to V	None
Result element	Any results required for the base offence	As required for the base offence
	Death of V	None

The elements of UAM can be alternatively, and more simply, presented as the combination of three core requirements (illustrated in **Figure 6.2**). The presentation and analysis of UAM in this three-part structure (as opposed to a more traditional discussion of actus reus and mens rea) is the most common approach taken by courts and academics.

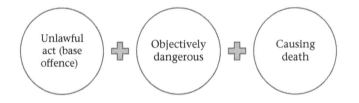

Figure 6.2 Unlawful act manslaughter

From the outset of our discussion, the potential breadth of UAM should be highlighted. At its most serious, UAM applies to cases falling just short of liability for murder. For example, as we have seen, where D kills V while accurately foreseeing death or GBH as a virtual certainty, then a jury may find liability for murder.[88] Where D kills V foreseeing death or GBH as a high probability (short of a virtual certainty) it is likely that UAM will be applied. However, UAM can also arise where D completes a relatively minor offence without foreseeing such fatal risks, where as a matter of 'bad luck' death results.[89] For example, UAM will apply where D commits a battery (eg hits V) and V falls, hits her head, and dies.[90] As **Table 6.5** makes clear, liability for UAM does not require D to have any mens rea as to the dangerousness of her act, or as to the resulting death: UAM is a constructive liability offence, with dangerousness and the death constructing upon the

---

[88] See **5.4**.
[89] Mitchell, 'More Thoughts About Unlawful and Dangerous Act Manslaughter and the One Punch Killer' [2009] Crim LR 502.
[90] *Mallett* [1972] Crim LR 260.

base offence to increase liability to UAM.[91] The appropriateness of this construction will be discussed further in the 'reform' section (see **6.5**).

6.3.1.1 The unlawful act (base offence)

We must first identify the charge that D would have faced if no one died. We call this the base offence. Historically, this base offence was interpreted very widely to include all criminal offences, and even civil wrongs.[92] However, under the current law, it is clear that only criminal offences will be sufficient.[93]

The most common base offences within UAM are offences against the person (eg D physically attacks and kills V without the mens rea for murder, but with the mens rea for an offence against the person).[94] However, other criminal offences will also qualify. For example, UAM convictions have been based upon criminal damage (eg *Goodfellow*:[95] where D set fire to his council house, causing death); and burglary (eg *Watson*:[96] where an elderly homeowner had a heart attack during a burglary). However, there are two important restrictions on the types of base offence that will satisfy this element.

A) **The base offence must be one requiring subjective mens rea:** In the case of *Andrews v DPP*,[97] at trial, a charge of UAM was constructed upon a negligence-based dangerous driving offence (D having killed a pedestrian whilst overtaking another car). But the House of Lords in that case stated that a base offence for UAM required an intrinsically criminal offence, not satisfied by 'a lawful act with a degree of negligence that the legislature makes criminal.' The original meaning of this dictum is ambiguous and troublesome. However, it has been interpreted to mean that offences satisfied by a mens rea of negligence (eg dangerous driving),[98] or those requiring no mens rea at all (ie strict liability offences),[99] will not qualify as potential base offences for UAM. Thus, where D acts negligently to cause death, the appropriate course will be to consider liability for gross negligence manslaughter (discussed in the following section).

B) **The base offence must have been completed by an act rather than an omission:** Until this issue is revisited in the courts (when we anticipate it will be reversed) it is currently the case that the base offence within UAM must have been completed by an action as opposed to an omission.[100] In *Lowe*,[101] the Court of Appeal held that D was not guilty of UAM where his base offence was one of *omitting* to care for his child (a base offence under section 1(1) of the Children and Young Persons Act 1933). Liability in this case should have been rejected on the basis that D's base offence was negligence based (see point (A)). However, the court instead focused on the requirement of

---

[91] Constructive crimes are introduced at **4.2.1.1**.
[92] eg *Fenton* (1830) 1 Lew CC 179: involving civil trespass; Buxton, 'By Any Unlawful Act' (1966) 82 LQR 174.
[93] *Kennedy (No 2)* [2007] UKHL 38.
[94] For discussion of the non-fatal offences against the person, see **Chapter 7**.
[95] (1986) 83 Cr App R 23.
[96] [1989] Crim LR 730.
[97] [1937] AC 576.
[98] *Lamb* [1967] 2 QB 981.
[99] There is no direct authority on this point, but it is generally accepted and must surely follow from the exclusion of negligence-based offences. See the commentary to *Andrews* [2003] Crim LR 477.
[100] Dennis, 'Manslaughter by Omission' (1980) 33 CLP 255.
[101] [1973] QB 702.

a physical act by D. With respect, the use of the act/omission distinction in this context lacks any coherent basis: if the criminal law outside UAM places harm caused by omission where there is a duty to act alongside harm caused by action, why should it be different in this context?[102] Indeed, as we have discussed,[103] the distinction between acts and omissions is often difficult to define, and so the use of the distinction here simply adds unnecessary complexity to the law.

> *Assessment matters…*
>
> Most omissions cases can be dealt with under the alternative involuntary manslaughter offence of gross negligence manslaughter where liability can be found for omissions. However, criticism of the act/omission rule has been included above because, if applying UAM to omissions within a problem question, it would be sensible to highlight the criticism of the rule and the potential that it may not survive future appellate decisions.

Having identified a potential qualifying base offence (a criminal offence, requiring subjective mens rea, and which is committed by D's acts), it remains essential that every element of that base offence is satisfied by D, and that she does not have a valid defence to the base offence. Although this sounds self-evident, an 'unlawful act' is only *unlawful* if all criminal elements are completed, it is easily neglected even by the highest courts.[104] The requirement is illustrated in *Lamb*.[105]

> **◰** *Lamb* [1967] 2 QB 981
>
> D pointed a loaded revolver at V as a joke. Neither D nor V understood how a revolver worked, and so when D pulled the trigger neither realised that the barrel of the gun would revolve and the bullet would be fired. It did, and V was killed.
>
> - Crown Court: guilty of unlawful act manslaughter.
> - Court of Criminal Appeal: appeal allowed. The base offence (assault or battery) was not complete because D lacked mens rea, he did not intend or foresee a risk of harm to V or a risk of causing V to apprehend harm.

When identifying the relevant base offence upon which to construct UAM liability, it should be remembered that general doctrines of criminal law will still apply to the base offence. For example, where D commits a base offence requiring a mens rea of recklessness, whilst in a state of voluntary intoxication, the intoxication rules will apply to construct any missing mens rea (eg D attacks and kills V whilst hallucinating due to illegal drugs, D will be liable for UAM).[106] The same is true where D lacks mens rea due to self-induced automatism (D's actions are involuntary).[107]

---

[102] Ashworth, 'Editorial' [1976] Crim LR 529.

[103] See **2.6.5**.

[104] *DPP v Newbury* [1977] AC 500: where the House of Lords fail to specify the offence at the base of the UAM conviction.

[105] See also *Arobieke* [1988] Crim LR 314: D caused V's death, but not through a completed base offence; there was no liability for UAM.

[106] *Lipman* [1970] 1 QB 152. See **Chapter 13**.

[107] See **Chapter 13**.

The other side of this, of course, is that potential defences to the base offence should also be considered: if D has a defence to the base offence then there is no unlawful act upon which to construct liability.[108] This requires consideration of the general defences.[109] As many UAM cases involve base crimes of offences against the person, this will also often involve consideration of the defence of self-defence or of the defence of consent as it applies to these offences.[110] In *Slingsby*, for example, there was no battery, and therefore no UAM, where V *consented* to acts of sexual touching, even though those acts resulted in an unexpected injury and infection from which V died.[111] However, in cases where the defence of self defence or consent is not established, D becomes liable for the base offence and potential liability for UAM where V dies as a result. For example, in the case of *A*, D threw V into a river as part of a post-exam celebration, and V drowned. D claimed that V was consenting, but the Crown established that V was not consenting on the facts and D was liable for UAM.[112]

6.3.1.2 The base offence must be dangerous to V

The second element of dangerousness is important, but easily misunderstood. It is not simply a requirement that D's actions be dangerous in fact: as they have caused death, such a requirement would be self-evident and unnecessary. Rather, it is the requirement that a sober and reasonable person in D's position would have foreseen that her acts carried a risk of harm to V at the time D acted. This is an objective requirement: there is no need to show that D herself foresaw any such risks unless that is a requirement of the mens rea of the base offence.

The focus on V here is important. Despite some inconsistent authorities,[113] it is now clear that the first element of UAM (the base offence) does not need to be directed or targeted at V. For example, in *Watson*,[114] D's base offence of burglary was not directed at the elderly homeowner (V), but nevertheless D was liable for UAM when V died from a stress-induced heart attack. In contrast, it is contended that the second element (dangerousness) should be applied with reference to V: the element should not be satisfied if danger to another is foreseeable, but not danger to V. For example, if the frail householder in *Watson* had died from a heart attack having watched footage of a violent crime perpetrated by D on the television news, D should not be liable for UAM unless at the time of D's acts there was a foreseeable risk of harm to V, and not just a risk to the more immediate victim of her violent attack. There is support for this approach in *Carey*.[115]

---

108 *Scarlett* (1994) 98 Cr App R 290.
109 **Chapters 13 and 14.**
110 See **7.3.2–7.3.3** and **7.8.2–7.8.3.**
111 *Slingsby* [1995] Crim LR 570.
112 *A* (2005) 69 J Crim L 394.
113 *Dalby* [1982] 1 All ER 916.
114 [1989] Crim LR 730.
115 [2006] EWCA Crim 17: an affray (involving danger/harm to others) was not foreseeably dangerous to V.

The full test of dangerousness is usefully set out by Edmund Davies J in *Church*:[116]

> the unlawful act must be such that all sober and reasonable people would inevitably recognise that it must subject the other person to, at least, the risk of some harm resulting therefrom, albeit not serious harm.

It is important to understand and apply this test of foresight/recognition carefully. In particular, three core questions should be borne in mind.

A) **What type of foresight?** As the quotation from *Church* makes clear, the requirement is that a sober and reasonable person would have foreseen danger to V, *not* whether D herself foresaw it. The test is objective, and not a question of D's mens rea (not about D's perception). Rather, this is a strict liability element.[117] In *Watson*, for example,[118] where D burgled V's house and V died of a stress-induced heart attack, the focus is on the foreseeability of danger to V, an elderly homeowner, from a reasonable person's perspective. In this case, the risk of harm was foreseeable. The only exception to this is where D has 'special knowledge' of V that may not be obviously apparent to a reasonable person, but means that D is aware of a risk of harm. For example, if the victim in *Watson* had been apparently young and healthy then the risk of harm from a non-violent burglary may not have been foreseeable to the sober and reasonable individual. However, if D had known (special knowledge) that the apparently healthy victim had a fragile heart condition, then this could be taken into account within the test: and that would be likely to make the harm foreseeable in the *Church* sense.

Although a risk of harm will often be foreseeable (it usually is where death has resulted!), this will not always be the case. This is illustrated in *Dawson*.[119]

⬛ *Dawson* (1985) 81 Cr App R 150

D and others attempted to rob a petrol station using an imitation gun. V, who died of a heart attack, was not elderly, was in apparent good health, and protected behind bullet-proof glass. D was charged with UAM.

- Crown Court: guilty of UAM. Jury directed to consider the risk of danger from the perspective of a reasonable person knowing what they knew (including that V was, in fact, suffering from a heart condition).
- Court of Appeal: appeal allowed. Direction was wrong to include facts that were known to the jury, but would not have been apparent to a reasonable person in D's shoes at the time of the acts.

In cases of this kind, D has clearly completed a relevant base offence (attempted robbery); and caused death. However, as harm to V was not objectively foreseeable, this element was not satisfied and there could be no liability for UAM.

B) **What degree of foresight?** The *Church* test speaks of '*all* sober and reasonable people...*inevitably*' recognising a risk to V. From this, it is clear that the potential for risk/danger should not be interpreted too widely to include a mere possibility of harm

---

[116] [1996] 1 QB 59, 70.

[117] See **4.2.1.1**.

[118] [1989] Crim LR 730.

[119] See also *Carey* [2006] EWCA Crim 17: death of an apparently healthy young woman when fleeing from an affray. No foreseeable risk of danger to V: no UAM.

(where harm is possible, but unlikely). The risk must be one that a reasonable person *would* have foreseen rather than *may* have foreseen.

    C) **Foresight of what?** We have so far spoken loosely of foresight of a risk of harm or danger. However, precisely what must be foreseen is crucial. Starting again with the quotation from *Church*, we are told that D must foresee 'the risk of some harm…albeit not serious harm.' *Church* is therefore important authority that the foreseeable risk of harm need not be serious, and certainly need not be a risk of life-threatening harm. For example, if D hits V where a reasonable person would foresee the risk of some minor bruising only, this element would be satisfied. Importantly, as long as some harm is objectively foreseeable, the circumstances that make that harm life-threatening need not be foreseeable.[120]

    Although there is no requirement for a foreseeable risk of *serious* harm from D's base crime, a foreseeable risk of a legally recognised harm is essential. In this regard, a foreseeable risk of unlawful physical contact with V (potentially causing various levels of bodily injury) will obviously qualify. Equally, it is clear from the case law that a base crime can be foreseeably dangerous even if no physical contact with V is anticipated, where, for example, bodily harm is nevertheless foreseeable (eg from heart attack).[121] Although there is no UAM case to settle this point, it is likely that a foreseeable risk of psychiatric harms would also be sufficient: psychiatric harms (recognised psychiatric conditions) have been accepted as bodily harms in the context of the offences against the person, so there is no reason why they would be excluded here.[122] However, a foreseeable risk of psychological or emotional harms short of psychiatric injury (eg fear or distress) will not be sufficient.[123]

> *Extra detail…*
>
> Proving that sober and reasonable people would inevitably foresee a risk of D's acts causing a psychiatric disorder will always be extremely difficult. In practice, when courts are looking for potential dangerousness, we will almost always be talking about objective foresight of a risk of unlawful contact, or shock/distress causing physical injury (eg heart attack). Further, even in extreme cases where a risk of psychiatric injury is objectively foreseeable (eg potentially following prolonged domestic abuse), the element of causing death will also be a major hurdle.

6.3.1.3 The base offence must cause the death of V

The third and final element of UAM is the requirement that D's base offence, as well as foreseeably endangering V, should *cause* V's death. As with the requirement of dangerousness, this is a strict liability element: D's base offence must cause death, but there is no requirement for D to have intended; known; foreseen; or had any mens rea at all as to this result. This is the core of this offence as a 'constructive crime': constructing liability for UAM by the accumulation of the two strict liability elements upon the base offence. This was at issue in *AG's Reference (No 3 of 1994)*.

---

120 *JM* [2012] EWCA Crim 2293: UAM possible where minor physical harm was foreseeable from a nightclub fight, but the heart condition that caused death was not foreseeable.

121 *Watson* [1989] Crim LR 730.

122 *Ireland and Burstow* [1998] AC 147. See **7.4.1**.

123 *Dhaliwal* [2006] EWCA Crim 1139, [32]: no UAM liability in case involving psychological abuse causing distress (short of a recognised psychiatric disorder) and ultimately suicide.

> **AG's Reference (No 3 of 1994)** [1998] AC 245
>
> D stabbed his girlfriend (M), with the intention required for murder and knowing that she was pregnant. Although M survived, the attack later caused her to enter premature labour. The baby (V) was born, but only survived for four months in intensive care before it died. D was charged with the murder of V.
>
> - Crown Court: no liability for murder or UAM. As D was acquitted, the AG appealed the point of law.
> - Court of Appeal: D should have been liable for murder using transferred malice—transferring D's intent to kill M to V.
> - House of Lords: D should not have been liable for murder as there can be no double transfer of malice.[124] However, D should have been liable for UAM.

Extra detail...
Liability for murder was not possible in *AG's Reference (No 3 of 1994)* because of the difficulty of demonstrating mens rea as to the death of V. However, UAM should have been found because no such mens rea is required: D need only complete a base offence (here, the assault of M); for that offence to be objectively dangerous to V (here, clearly satisfied); and for that base offence to cause the death V (here, when the baby dies it is a person, it is not still in the womb).

The causation element of the offence simply requires us to apply the standard causation rules discussed at **2.7**: D's act must be the cause of death in fact (the 'but for' cause); and the cause of death in law (proximate; substantial; and operating). As with other result crimes, the possible time delay between D's act (here, D's base offence) and the result (here, death) is irrelevant as long as a causal link can be demonstrated. For example, if D attacks and harms V without the intention of killing, for example by committing an offence against the person, D's liability for manslaughter would be constructed from that base offence against the person if V died of her injuries much later—again, as long as the causal link can be demonstrated.[125]

Within the general rules of causation, there are three areas of particular interest for UAM.

A) **Fright and flight:** V flees from the scene of a crime (base offence) committed by D, and dies when in flight, for example from a heart attack brought on from the exertion; by tripping and hitting her head; by running in front of a car; etc. These cases are particularly relevant for UAM because D will often not have intended or foreseen V's death or serious injury: D will lack mens rea for murder, but as we have discussed, mens rea as to death is not required for UAM. When applying UAM, however, there are two main barriers to liability. First, where D appears healthy and there are no obvious physical hazards, it may be difficult to demonstrate an objectively foreseeable risk of harm in flight.[126] Secondly, it must be shown that V's own conduct in taking flight has not broken the chain of causation between D's base offence and V's death: V's response must not be 'wholly disproportionate' or 'daft'.[127] Thus, where V ran into a road to escape an

---

[124] See **4.3.1.1**.
[125] *AG's Reference (No 3 of 1994)* [1998] AC 245: Lord Hope stated that UAM would be committed even if the death was 'many hours, days or even months' after the base offence.
[126] *Carey* [2006] EWCA Crim 17.
[127] *Lewis* [2010] EWCA Crim 151.

ongoing assault from D, and was killed by a car, there was no break in causation and D was liable for UAM: V's response in running was not daft and it was foreseeable.[128] In contrast, if V had managed to escape the immediate danger of the assault, and had clear safe options for further flight, her choice to nevertheless run into a busy road may well have passed beyond the foreseeable into the daft, and thus broken the causal chain.

B) **Drug supply:** V voluntarily takes prohibited drugs supplied by D (base offence), and dies from their effects. Following several years of confusion, the case of *Kennedy (No 2)* has now clarified that there can be no liability for UAM in these cases.

Kennedy (No 2) [2007] UKHL 38

D supplied V with a prepared syringe of heroin. V self-injected the drug and died as a result. D was charged with UAM on the basis that his unlawful conduct (drug supply) caused V's death.

- Crown Court: guilty of UAM.
- Court of Appeal: conviction upheld on appeal.
- House of Lords: quashing D's conviction on appeal—D was not guilty because he was not the legal cause of V's death.

In such cases, V's free and voluntary act in self-administering the drug will break the chain of causation between D's base offence (supply) and V's death. It is also debatable whether the act of drug supply alone can give rise to an objectively foreseeable risk of bodily harm.[129] Therefore, to find liability for UAM in these cases it will be necessary to show that D administered the drug directly to V: this base offence[130] is foreseeably dangerous, and does not require the voluntary acts of V to cause death.

C) **Suicide:** V is distressed by D's base offence (eg physical abuse) to such an extent that this causes her to commit suicide. Two categories of cases should be distinguished. The first is where D's base offence causes physical injury to V, and V either fails to treat or exacerbates that injury in some manner to cause death. In these cases, causation (and thus liability for UAM) has been found on the basis that D's original offence remains a significant and operating cause of death; V has no duty to limit the harm caused by D; and D must take her victim as she found her.[131] The second category is where D's base offence causes psychiatric harm or where D's injuries are healed at the point of suicide. In these cases, it will be much more difficult to demonstrate that V's suicide was not a free and voluntary act that breaks the chain of causation. However, the possibility of causation in these circumstances, particularly where a history of abuse can be shown to have undermined the voluntariness of V's choice, has been left open within the case law.[132]

128 Ibid.
129 Wilson, 'Dealing with Drug Induced Homicide' in Clarkson and Cunningham (eds), *Criminal Liability for Non-Aggressive Deaths* (2008).
130 Offences Against the Person Act 1861, s23.
131 *Blaue* (1975) 61 Cr App R 271: refusal of medical treatment on religious grounds. *Dear* [1996] Crim LR 595: reopening of wounds caused by D. There is some tension here with the foreseeability principle in causation (see **2.7.2**).
132 *D* [2006] EWCA Crim 1139; Horder and McGowan, 'Manslaughter by Causing Another's Suicide' [2006] Crim LR 1035.

When exploring such details, it is important to remember the basic structure of the offence, as illustrated in **Figure 6.3**.

Figure 6.3 Unlawful act manslaughter

> *Extra detail…*
>
> Within the structure for UAM, it is worth highlighting that the objectively foreseeable danger to V does not need to be the ultimate cause of her death. For example, in *JM and SM*,[133] V (a doorman) died after a fight with D. The fight carried an objectively foreseeable risk of harm: standard risks from fighting. However, V did not die as a result of this danger, he died due to a heart attack resulting from a rush of blood during the fight combined with an (undiagnosed) heart condition. D was liable for UAM.

6.3.2 Gross negligence manslaughter

Generally, liability for serious offences will be imposed only where D has taken the *choice* to harm or *chosen* to risk harm: punishing D for the harms caused, but also for her blameworthy *choice* in bringing them about. This approach respects the principle of autonomy: we should only be blamed for advertent wrongdoing.[134] This general approach has meant that there are not many serious offences in English law based on negligence (other than those in a regulatory context).[135] However, gross negligence manslaughter (GNM) stands as an extreme exception, punishable with a maximum of life imprisonment.

GNM provides an offence designed to catch cases where, despite the lack of a conscious choice to risk harms, D's conduct is seriously negligent (unreasonably careless or inattentive), and where that negligence causes death: the most serious harm. For example, if D decided to test her new gun in a busy park, failing to foresee any potential harm to others because she did not care about and therefore did not consider the safety of others, she is likely to be liable for GNM. Such liability has been recognised for many years.[136]

Despite its long-term recognition, however, GNM has developed inconsistently at common law. For example, during the 1970s and particularly the 1980s, GNM and reckless manslaughter became confused by the use of the *Caldwell*[137] test to define

---

[133] [2012] EWCA Crim 2293.
[134] See **1.4.3**.
[135] See **3.6.2**.
[136] *Finney* (1874) 12 Cox CC 625; *Bateman* (1925) 94 LJKB 791.
[137] See **3.4.4**.

recklessness.[138] However, the current law can be stated with some confidence, having been clarified in the leading case of *Adomako* in the House of Lords.

> **Adomako** [1994] 3 All ER 79
>
> D (an anaesthetist) failed to notice that a tube supplying oxygen to his patient (V) had become detached. As a result, V died. D was charged with GNM on the basis that his conduct fell dramatically below the standards expected of a reasonable anaesthetist.
>
> • Crown Court: convicted of GNM—negligent test applied without reference to objective recklessness.
> • Court of Appeal: conviction upheld on appeal.
> • House of Lords: appeal dismissed—correct test requires a duty of care between D and V; a breach of that duty; that D's acts caused death; and that D's acts were 'gross' in their negligence. The court clarified that objective recklessness is not part of the test.

The elements of GNM can be set out to separate actus reus and mens rea, as in **Table 6.6**.

Table 6.6 Gross negligence manslaughter

	Actus reus	**Mens rea**
Conduct element	Any conduct causing the results	Voluntary
Circumstance element	There must be a duty of care between D and V	None
	D's breach of duty must be 'grossly negligent': must pose a risk of death	None
Result element	D must breach her duty of care	None
	Death of V	None

Setting out GNM in this manner highlights the lack of mens rea required as to any circumstance or result elements. However, partly because of this lack of mens rea and partly because of its links with the civil law concept of negligence, GNM is more commonly presented and applied (as in *Adomako*) as the four core elements in **Figure 6.4**.

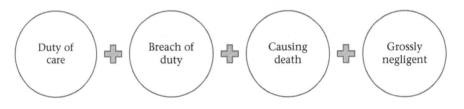

Figure 6.4 Gross negligence manslaughter

---

[138] *Stone and Dobinson* [1977] QB 354; *Seymour* [1983] 1 AC 624; *Kong Cheuk Kwan* (1986) 82 Cr App R 18.

We will discuss each of these elements in turn.

6.3.2.1 Duty of care

The first element of GNM requires the prosecution to prove that, at the time of acting to cause death, D owed V a duty of care. Core examples of duties of care include doctors to patients;[139] transport carriers to passengers;[140] employers to employees;[141] etc. However, duties will be recognised far beyond these examples. With the definition of a 'duty of care' taken largely from the civil law, it has been interpreted broadly to apply wherever D's conduct caries a foreseeable risk to those around her.[142]

The criminal law is not, however, bound to follow the civil definition of 'duty of care'. As illustrated in *Wacker*, the criminal law has taken a more expansive approach to recognising duties.

Wacker [2003] QB 1203

D was engaged in smuggling 60 illegal immigrants into the UK. D shut the air vent to the container carrying the immigrants, and 58 of them suffocated as a result. D was charged with GNM.

- Crown Court: convicted of GNM.
- Court of Appeal: conviction upheld on appeal. Although the joint criminal venture between D and the victims would undermine any duty of care in civil law, this was not the case in criminal law.

The ability of the criminal law to recognise duties of care outside those recognised in civil law is important because it allows criminal courts (as in *Wacker*) to avoid complex civil rules/exclusions that do not serve the interests of the criminal law. The aims of the two bodies of law are different: civil law is structured around private compensation between individuals and the consent of both parties to a risky activity or crime may, therefore, undermine a civil claim; whereas the criminal law is structured more generally around the prevention and punishment of wrongs, the blame is coming from the state, rather than in the form of compensation to another non-innocent party.[143]

Judge and jury

Whether a relationship is capable of giving rise to a duty of care is a legal question for the judge. The jury will be directed that a duty exists if they find certain facts to be present and (where there is dispute on facts) to not find a duty if they find other facts to be present.[144]

Unlike UAM, GNM can be committed by act or *omission*. Where D's positive acts cause death (eg negligent mistreatment by a doctor), then it is only necessary to demonstrate a duty of care as discussed earlier. However, where D's omissions cause death (eg negligent lack of treatment by a doctor), then the standard rules of omissions liability will also

---

[139] *Adomako* [1994] 3 All ER 79.

[140] *Barker* [2003] 2 Cr App R 110.

[141] *Dean* [2002] EWCA Crim 2410.

[142] *Evans* [2009] EWCA Crim 650; Herring and Palser, 'The Duty of Care in Gross Negligence Manslaughter' [2007] Crim LR 24.

[143] See also *Willoughby* [2005] Crim LR 389: death of V when helping D to commit arson, leading to UAM liability.

[144] *Evans* [2009] EWCA Crim 650, [45].

apply.[145] This means that as well as a duty of *care*, the court must also identify a duty from the much narrower categories of duties to *act*. We have already discussed the limited duties to act recognised in law: contractual; relationship-based; where D assumes a duty by caring for V; where D has created or contributed to a dangerous situation.[146] Although *both* a duty to act and a duty of care will be required for omission-based GNM, the duties within the narrower category of duties to act will always also satisfy a duty of care. Thus, in practice, it is only necessary to identify a duty to act, which will then double as a duty of care as well.

A leading case in relation to omission-based GNM is *Evans*.

Evans [2009] EWCA Crim 650

D, V's half-sister, supplied her with heroin which she self-administered. Seeing symptoms of an over-dose, D stayed with V but did not alert the authorities for fear of personal liability for supplying the drugs. V died and D was charged with GNM on the basis of her omission to aid V (duty arising from her creation of a dangerous situation when supplying the drugs).

- Crown Court: guilty of gross negligence manslaughter.
- Court of Appeal: conviction upheld on appeal.

Evans is an important case for two main reasons.[147] First, it demonstrates a novel way in which GNM can be used to find liability in a drug supply and overdose case. As we discussed earlier, UAM cannot operate in these cases as V's voluntary self-injection will break the chain of causation. However, by focusing on D's negligent omission *after* the self-injection, there is the potential for a causal link between this 'conduct' and V's death. This is illustrated by **Figure 6.5**, with the cross representing V's self-injection (the break in the causal chain).

Figure 6.5 Breaking the chain of causation

Evans is also important because it demonstrates the willingness of the courts to expand the definition of a duty to act in certain cases. *Evans* had a duty as per the *Miller*[148] principle: D has a duty to make reasonable efforts to avoid a danger that she has created and then becomes aware of. In *Evans*, in order to find liability it was held that D need not have *created* the danger as long as she *contributed* to its creation: D did not cause the danger in *Evans* because V's self-injection breaks the causal chain. Equally, the court

---

[145] See **2.6**.

[146] See **2.6.2**.

[147] Williams, 'Gross Negligence Manslaughter and Duty of Care in "Drugs" Cases: *R v Evans*' [2009] Crim LR 631.

[148] [1983] 2 AC 161.

made clear that D need not become subjectively aware of the danger to which she contributed, as long as a reasonable person would have done so. Both represent significant expansions of the offence.

> **Point to remember...**
> The approach to a duty to act in *Evans* makes it much easier to find liability where D supplies V with a drug, V self-administers, and V dies. However, remember that the duty to act still requires a reasonable person in D's position to have foreseen life-threatening harm. This may be possible where D is present to observe V's overdose or reaction, but is very unlikely where D simply supplies the drug and leaves.

6.3.2.2 Breach of duty of care

The second element of GNM is the requirement that D breaches her duty of care, and duty to act in the context of omission-based GNM. Again, this requirement mirrors negligence in the civil law, and similar principles apply. The question is whether D's conduct has fallen below that expected of a reasonable person in her position. For action-based GNM, we ask whether a reasonable person would have refrained from the acts carried out by D and/or whether a reasonable person would have acted differently. For omission-based GNM, we ask whether a reasonable person in D's position would have acted. As with the civil law, where D purports to exercise a certain skill, the standard against which D is measured is the reasonable person with that skill. Thus, D in *Adomako* was measured against the standard of a reasonable anaesthetist.

> **Don't be confused...**
> The consent of V to D's conduct is not relevant to the issue of breach (although it may be relevant to the final element of 'grossness' discussed later). For example, the victims in *Wacker* discussed in the previous section consented to the obviously dangerous venture of attempting to be smuggled in a lorry container. Their consent did not undermine the fact that D's conduct, including the shutting of the vent which led to their deaths, was a breach of his duty to them.

6.3.2.3 Causing death

After it is established that D owed V a duty of care (ie a duty to act in omission cases), and that D breached that duty, it must be proved that D's breach caused V's death. For example, where a doctor, D, breaches a duty of care to her patient with negligent treatment, and V dies, it must still be shown that V would not have died in the same way if she had been treated reasonably. For omission-based GNM, this requires us to ask what a reasonable person in D's position would have done, and whether that action would have prevented her dying in the manner she did. For example, if the victim in *Evans* had died very quickly from her reaction to the heroin, rather than over a course of hours, D may not have been able to prevent her death even if she had acted reasonably by calling an ambulance, etc. In such a case, where (as in *Evans*) D has failed to act reasonably, even though we may disapprove morally of her omission to try and help V in this short period, we would not be able to say that her omission caused death.

In this manner, the causation element of GNM simply requires us to apply the standard causation rules discussed at **2.7**: D's conduct must be the cause of death in fact (the 'but for' cause); and the cause of death in law (proximate; substantial; and operating). As we have discussed previously (regarding *Evans*), GNM can provide a useful mechanism for avoiding breaks in the chain of causation by focusing on negligent omissions after V shows signs of being in danger (ie after the potential break in the chain).

6.3.2.4 Grossly negligent

The final element of GNM requires D's negligence to be sufficiently 'gross' (ie sufficiently bad) to be deserving of criminal as opposed to simply civil liability. This is a question for the jury. Lord Mackay sets out the question in *Adomako* as follows:

> having regard to the risk of death involved, [was] the conduct of the defendant...so bad in all the circumstances as to amount to a criminal act or omission?

Lord Mackay's question, as stated, needs qualification. After all, D's negligent conduct may satisfy a negligence-based criminal offence such as careless or dangerous driving, and yet still not be sufficiently gross for such a serious offence as GNM. Therefore, the grossness element is not simply about distinguishing non-criminal conduct; instead, it asks the jury if D's behaviour warrants liability for manslaughter.

The term 'gross' is rather ambiguous as an offence element, and so it is useful to consider what factors a jury should take into account when applying it to the facts of a case. The first factor will be whether D foresaw the risk of injury or death to V at the time of acting. Crucially, it has been consistently held that such foresight is not a necessary element of GNM, thus D *requires* no mens rea as to the causing of death.[149] However, foresight of this kind will be taken into account by the jury when assessing the grossness (badness) of D's negligence, and will make that finding more likely.

Although *subjective* foresight of death or injury is not required, the case law requires *objective* foresight of *death*: a reasonable person in D's position would have foreseen the risk that the conduct might cause death; if the reasonable person would have foreseen only injury or serious injury that is not sufficient. As part of the grossness test, this is implied by the reference to 'the risk of death' in the quote from *Adomako* at the beginning of this section. It was also supported in the later case of *Gurphal Singh*,[150] and has been confirmed more recently in *Misra*.[151]

Objective foresight of death is therefore a necessary factor within the grossness test, but not automatically sufficient. Rather, the jury must look at all the surrounding circumstances in order to make their assessment; eg what were D's motives; was she acting maliciously; how did she explain her conduct; and so on. The discretion given to the jury here can be useful to ensure only those deserving, all things considered, of GNM liability are brought within the offence. However, the absence of clear criteria makes it difficult to predict the outcome of cases, and has given rise to powerful criticism about the potential for inconsistency[152] with different juries applying the test differently, and about the role of the jury more generally.

---

[149] *AG's Reference (No 2 of 1999)* [2000] QB 796; *Misra* [2004] EWCA Crim 2375.
[150] [1999] Crim LR 582.
[151] [2004] EWCA Crim 2375.
[152] Such inconsistency can also be reflected in decisions to prosecute. Quick, 'Prosecuting "Gross" Medical Negligence: Manslaughter, Discretion and the Crown Prosecution Service' (2006) 33 JLS 421.

The latter criticism, about the role of the jury, focuses on whether the grossness element is asking the jury to establish facts, which is the correct role of the jury, or whether it is asking them to establish matters of law, which is the correct role of the judge.[153] When applying elements of a crime, the jury should be given the legal definition of that element by the judge and then decide whether, on the facts as they believe them to be, that element is satisfied. With regard to the grossness element, it can appear as if this division of expertise has broken down: the jury are told to find the grossness element as having been satisfied if they find the facts to be criminal in nature, and to find the facts criminal if they find them gross. This test is circular and, in effect, it is asking the jury to define the offence (the law) as they apply it. However, despite the apparent circularity, the test has survived challenges on human rights grounds and remains valid.[154]

6.3.3 Reckless manslaughter

Reckless manslaughter is the last of the three common law involuntary manslaughter offences. D will come within this offence where she causes V's death by act or omission and is at least reckless as to causing death or GBH. The elements are set out in **Table 6.7.**

Table 6.7 Reckless manslaughter

	Actus reus	**Mens rea**
Conduct element	Any act or omission causing the result	Voluntary
Circumstance element	V is a person	Knowledge
Result element	Death of V	Recklessness as to a risk of death or GBH

The offence of reckless manslaughter is rarely prosecuted, and so there are few appeal cases discussing its interpretation.[155] This is because cases coming within this offence will almost always also satisfy the elements of either UAM or GNM and, as these two latter offences do not require subjective mens rea as to death or serious harm, they will usually be easier to prosecute. Interestingly, Mitchell and Mackay have found that reckless manslaughter is occasionally charged where the facts of a case involve culpability just short of murder where it is clear that D foresaw a high risk of causing death or GBH, but it would be difficult to demonstrate that it was foreseen as a virtual certainty. In this regard, the sentences received for reckless

---

[153] See **1.1.7.1.**
[154] See Lord Justice Judge's attempt to explain the test in a non-circular way in *Misra* [2004] EWCA Crim 2375, [62]–[63].
[155] One of the few exceptions is *Lidar* [2000] 4 Arch News 3.

manslaughter are often higher than those for UAM or GNM.[156] Additionally, reckless manslaughter is necessary to criminalise D who kills by omission (thus no UAM), and where D's omission does not pose an objectively foreseeable risk of death (thus no GNM).

6.4 Statutory offences of unlawful killing

This chapter has focused on the traditional manslaughter conviction: voluntary manslaughter resulting from a partial defence to murder, and involuntary manslaughter resulting from a common law manslaughter offence. However, the criminal law also recognises a number of other offences of unlawful killing, some of which employ the label manslaughter. These offences are discussed briefly in this section, and their differences from the traditional forms will be highlighted.

6.4.1 Corporate manslaughter

Under standard rules of corporate liability,[157] it has been possible for a corporation to commit homicide offences: most commonly GNM. However, with the Corporate Manslaughter and Corporate Homicide Act 2007 (CMA 2007),[158] a new route to corporate liability has been created and GNM for companies has been abolished.[159] The new offence is commonly presented as a form of involuntary manslaughter alongside the traditional common law offences of UAM, GNM, and reckless manslaughter. However, we have separated it in our discussion because unlike the traditional involuntary manslaughter offences, corporate manslaughter does require the actus reus of murder to have been committed (the killing of a person, by a person), but can be satisfied where a variety of acts or omissions within the corporation, potentially from many different individuals, combine to cause death.

The CMA 2007 is based indirectly on preceding Law Commission recommendations.[160] The Commission and others were critical of the way the common law had failed to find GNM in relation to companies. This was because, particularly with respect to large and complex companies, it would often be impossible to identify a 'controlling mind' (ie very senior figure) within the company who was individually[161] responsible in GNM for V's death. In the absence of such a figure, even if a general culture of negligence was found within large parts of the corporation, and these were found to have caused V's death, the common law identification doctrine could not link liability to

---

[156] Mitchell and Mackay, 'Investigating Manslaughter: An Empirical Study of 127 Cases' (2011) 31 OJLS 165. The maximum sentence for reckless manslaughter, as with UAM and GNM, is life imprisonment.

[157] See **1.5.1**.

[158] Ormerod and Taylor, 'The Corporate Manslaughter and Corporate Homicide Act 2007' [2008] Crim LR 589.

[159] CMA 2007, s20.

[160] Law Commission, *Involuntary Manslaughter* (No 237, 1996).

[161] The old law would not allow the acts of employees to be aggregated together and viewed as the acts of the corporation: *AG's Reference (No 2 of 1999)* [2000] QB 796.

the corporation.[162] As we discuss later, the CMA 2007 seeks to address these problems within the new offence. However, it is noteworthy that the few successful prosecutions under the new offence have also (so far) focused on smaller corporations.[163]

> **Extra detail…**
>
> Directors and other individuals within a corporation cannot be charged with the corporate manslaughter offence, and cannot be a secondary party to a corporate manslaughter offence. However, they can still be individually liable under one of the standard common law involuntary manslaughter offences or for health and safety offences.[164]

The corporate manslaughter offence is set out in section 1(1) of the CMA 2007. Where D (a corporation) is found liable under this section, it will face an unlimited fine,[165] potentially combined with a remedial order and/or a publicity order.[166]

(1) An organisation to which this section applies is guilty of an offence if the way in which its activities are managed or organised—

(a) causes a person's death, and

(b) amounts to a gross breach of a relevant duty of care owed by the organisation to the deceased.

The structure of this offence is similar to GNM, and its analysis and application should be approached in a similar manner. The elements are set out in **Figure 6.6**.

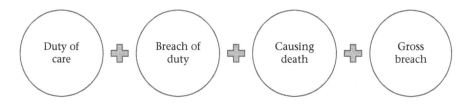

Figure 6.6 Corporate manslaughter

Before discussing these elements, it is necessary first to identify which organisations are capable of committing the offence. This is set out in section 1(2) to include most corporations, police forces, partnerships, trade unions, or employers' associations, as well as various government departments.

6.4.1.1 Duty of care

D (the relevant organisation) must owe a duty of care to V (the person killed). As with GNM, the duty requirement will be interpreted in line with established civil law duties. As set out in section 2, the most relevant duties will be to employees; visitors on

---

162 Wells, 'Corporate Manslaughter: Why Does Reform Matter?' (2006) 123 SALJ 646.

163 *Cotswold Geological Holdings Ltd* [2011] EWCA Crim 1337; Dobson, 'Shifting Sands: Multiple Counts in Prosecutions for Corporate Manslaughter' [2012] Crim LR 200.

164 Antrobus, 'The Criminal Liability of Directors for Health and Safety Breaches and Manslaughter' [2013] Crim LR 309.

165 CMA 2007, s1(6).

166 CMA 2007, ss9–10.

premises; customers; etc. As with GNM, it is for the judge to decide as a matter of law what is capable of giving rise to a duty of care.[167]

The scope of this element and therefore the offence is severely limited by a number of exceptions where a duty of care will not be found. For example, section 3 excludes public policy decisions. This will exclude a number of cases, including where government departments make potentially negligent decisions to remove funding from projects (eg the funding of certain medical drugs) and people die as a result. Section 4 excludes military activities; section 5 excludes certain police activities; section 6 excludes certain activities of the emergency services; and section 7 has a similar role for child protection and probation services. In each case, these provisions are unnecessarily complex in their construction, and are likely to lead to appeals.

6.4.1.2 Breach of duty of care

This element requires D (the relevant organisation) to have breached its duty to V by failing to perform in a reasonable manner (to the standard of a relevant reasonable organisation). Importantly, and in contrast to the old identification doctrine approach discussed earlier, this breach does not need to be identified in the conduct of a single representative of the organisation, but can be found through an aggregation of the organisation's activities as a whole.

The crucial restricting qualification to this is that a 'substantial element' of the breach must be traceable to 'the way in which [D's] activities are managed or organised by its senior management.'[168] This is not as restrictive as the old identification doctrine: 'senior management' is interpreted more broadly than those who would have qualified as controlling minds;[169] 'senior management' allows aggregation across those in that class; and their impact only needs to be 'substantial' as opposed to sole or even dominant. However, any restrictions of this kind relating to senior figures will inevitably make the prosecution of larger and more complex organisations more difficult.

6.4.1.3 Causing death

As with GNM, the standard rules of causation will apply.[170]

6.4.1.4 Gross breach of duty

Finally, it must be established that D's (the relevant organisation's) breach of duty was 'gross'. As with GNM, this is a question for the jury. However, unlike with GNM, the CMA 2007 provides significant guidance for the jury in their assessment. Section 1(4)(b) states that:

> a breach of a duty of care by an organisation is a 'gross' breach if the conduct alleged to amount to a breach of that duty falls far below what can reasonably be expected of the organisation in the circumstances.

---

[167] CMA 2007, s2(5).
[168] CMA 2007, s1(3).
[169] CMA 2007, s14(c) defines 'senior management' as those having significant roles in managing significant activities or parts of the organisation.
[170] See **2.7**.

Section 8 then goes on to provide factors for the jury to consider, including the seriousness of D's failure and how foreseeable the risk of death was that was created. Additional factors listed in section 8 also include an assessment of the culture towards risk within the organisation, as well as any breaches of health and safety law.[171]

6.4.2 Driving causing death

There are now also many statutory offences involving causing death by driving. Where D kills V with her car, there is nothing to stop her being charged with murder or manslaughter at common law, provided the relevant elements of the offence—including any mens rea—can be proved. However, for reasons of fair labelling, and in order to tailor offences to secure convictions for road-based homicides, a series of bespoke offences have been created.[172]

6.4.2.1 Causing death by dangerous driving

Section 1 of the Road Traffic Act 1988 (RTA 1988)[173] makes it an offence to cause death by driving a 'mechanically propelled vehicle dangerously on a road or other public place'.[174] The elements are set out in **Table 6.8**.

Table 6.8 RTA 1988, s1

	Actus reus	**Mens rea**
Conduct element	Causing the result by driving	Voluntary
Circumstance element	D's driving of a vehicle in public is dangerous	None
Result element	Death of V	None

As the table demonstrates, causing death by dangerous driving is a negligence-based offence. All that is required is that D's driving caused V's death, employing the standard rules of causation,[175] and that D's driving, at the relevant time, was objectively dangerous.

D's driving will qualify as 'dangerous' where 'the way he drives falls far below what would be expected of a competent and careful driver, *and* it would be obvious to a competent driver that driving in that way would be dangerous' (ie would risk injury or serious property damage).[176] This also includes cases where the mechanical state of the car makes

---

[171] Wright, 'Criminal Liability of Directors and Senior Managers for Deaths at Work' [2007] Crim LR 949.

[172] Cunningham, 'The Reality of Vehicular Homicides: Convictions for Murder, Manslaughter and Causing Death by Dangerous Driving' [2001] Crim LR 679.

[173] As amended by the Road Traffic Act 1991.

[174] The Legal Aid, Sentencing and Punishment of Offenders Act 2012, s143 has inserted a new offence within the RTA 1988, s1A of causing GBH by dangerous driving. Applying similar terms to s1, this offence applies where D causes serious harm which falls short of death.

[175] See **2.7**.

[176] RTA 1988, s2A (emphasis added).

driving dangerous, and this would have been obvious to a reasonable driver.[177] As with other negligence-based offences, D's knowledge of the factors making her driving dangerous are irrelevant to her liability if they would have been obvious to a reasonable person.[178] The only exception is one working against D: where she has special knowledge of potential danger beyond that of a reasonable driver, as for example where she is a mechanic and recognises signs of danger, her driving may be found to be dangerous on that basis.

6.4.2.2 Causing death by careless driving

Section 2B of the RTA 1988 makes it an offence to cause death by driving a 'mechanically propelled vehicle on a road or other public place without due care and attention, or without reasonable consideration for other persons using the road or place.'[179] The elements are set out in **Table 6.9**.

Table 6.9 RTA 1988, s2B

	Actus reus	**Mens rea**
Conduct element	Causing the result by driving	Voluntary
Circumstance element	D's driving of a vehicle in public is without due care and attention, Or without reasonable consideration for others	None
Result element	Death of V	None

Filling the perceived gap below the section 1 offence, here D's driving does not need to carry an obvious objective risk of causing harm to the person or property. Rather, it is enough that D was driving in a careless manner,[180] and that she caused death.

6.4.2.3 Causing death by careless driving when under the influence of drink or drugs

Section 3A of the RTA 1988 makes it an offence to cause death by driving a 'mechanically propelled vehicle on a road or other public place without due care and attention, or without reasonable consideration for other persons using the road or place, and he is, at the time when he is driving, unfit to drive through drink or drugs, *or* he has consumed so much alcohol that the proportion of it in his breath, blood or urine at that time exceeds the prescribed limit, *or* he is…required to provide a specimen…but without reasonable excuse fails to provide it, *or* he is required by a constable to give his permission for a laboratory test of a specimen of blood taken from him…but without reasonable excuse fails to do so.' The elements are set out in **Table 6.10**.

---

177 RTA 1988, s2A(2) and (3); *Strong* [1995] Crim LR 428.
178 *Roberts and George* [1997] Crim LR 209.
179 Created by the Road Safety Act 2006, s30.
180 Defined at RTA 1988, s3ZA.

Table 6.10 RTA 1988, s3A

	Actus reus	**Mens rea**
Conduct element	Causing the result by driving	Voluntary
Circumstance element	D's driving of a vehicle in public is without due care and attention, *or* without reasonable consideration for others And Is unfit to drive through drink or drugs; or she exceeds the alcohol limit; or she fails to provide a specimen; or she does not give permission for a specimen to be tested	None None
Result element	Death of V	None

This offence constructs upon the section 2B offence, leading to more serious liability where one of the aggravating factors is present.

6.4.2.4 Causing death while driving unlawfully

Section 3ZB of the RTA 1988[181] makes it an offence to cause death whilst driving without a valid driving licence, whilst disqualified from driving, or whilst uninsured. The elements are set out in **Table 6.11**.

Table 6.11 RTA 1988, s3ZB

	Actus reus	**Mens rea**
Conduct element	Causing the result by driving	Voluntary
Circumstance element	D is driving a vehicle in public; and D has no licence; or D is disqualified; or D is uninsured	None
Result element	Death of V	None

This offence has been controversial because, read literally, it appears to criminalise D for causing death even where she is not a blameworthy cause: her driving is competent. Indeed, this is how the offence was originally applied.[182] However, following academic

---

[181] Created by the Road Safety Act 2006, s21.
[182] *Williams* [2010] EWCA Crim 2552.

criticism,[183] the Supreme Court has now confirmed that D's driving must have caused death through some fault on her part.[184] This confirms the general principle of causation that all causes must be blameworthy.[185]

6.4.3 Infanticide

The infanticide rules apply to cases in which D (a mother) kills V (her child) within the first year of its life where, at the time of killing, D's mind was disturbed due to the birth or due to her lactation as a result of the birth.[186] These rules are specifically designed to distinguish killings of this type from traditional homicide offences. To this end, infanticide can operate either as an offence in its own right, *or* as a partial defence to murder or manslaughter. The law is set out in section 1 of the Infanticide Act 1938.[187]

6.4.3.1 The offence of infanticide

Section 1(1) of the 1938 Act makes it an offence:

> Where a woman by any wilful act or omission causes the death of her child being a child under the age of twelve months, but at the time of the act or omission the balance of her mind was disturbed by reason of her not having fully recovered from the effect of giving birth to the child or by reason of the effect of lactation consequent upon the birth of the child, then…she shall be guilty of…infanticide, and may for such offence be dealt with and punished as if she had been guilty of the offence of manslaughter of the child.

The elements of infanticide are set out in **Table 6.12**.

Table 6.12 Infanticide

	Actus reus	**Mens rea**
Conduct element	Act or omission causing the result	Voluntary
Circumstance element	D is the mother of V; and V is under 12 months old; and D's mind was disturbed by the effects of giving birth, or her lactation from giving birth	None
Result element	Death of V	None

---

[183] See commentary at [2011] Crim LR 473, and Sullivan and Simester, 'Causation Without Limits: Causing Death Whilst Driving Without a Licence, While Disqualified, or Without Insurance' [2012] Crim LR 754.

[184] *Hughes* [2013] UKSC 56.

[185] See **2.7.2.2**.

[186] Mackay, 'The Consequences of Killing Very Young Children' [1993] Crim LR 21; Wilczynski and Morris, 'Parents Who Kill Their Children' [1993] Crim LR 31; Brennan, 'Beyond the Medical Model: A Rationale for Infanticide Legislation' (2007) 58 NILQ 505.

[187] As amended by the Coroners and Justice Act 2009, s57.

Where D satisfies these elements, she will be liable for infanticide regardless of whether she satisfies the elements of any other homicide offence (the *offence* of infanticide is free-standing and independent of other offences).[188] The offence will often be charged where D kills V when suffering from postnatal depression, and sentences are usually relatively mild.[189] It should be noted that the rather artificial link to the physical birth of the child or D's lactation has been criticised, but it seems that the courts will interpret these requirements broadly to allow appropriate cases to come within the offence.[190]

6.4.3.2 The partial defence of infanticide

Section 1(2) of the 1938 Act states that:

> Where upon the trial of a woman for the murder of her child, being a child under the age of twelve months, the jury are of opinion that she by any wilful act or omission caused its death, but that at the time of the act or omission the balance of her mind was disturbed by reason of her not having fully recovered from the effect of giving birth to the child or by reason of the effect of lactation consequent upon the birth of the child, then the jury may, notwithstanding that the circumstances were such that but for the provisions of this Act they might have returned a verdict of murder, return in lieu thereof a verdict of infanticide.

The effect of this section is that even where D is charged with and satisfies the elements of murder or manslaughter, if the jury find the elements of infanticide to be satisfied as well, they should find liability for infanticide only. D has an evidential burden to raise the defence, and it is then for the prosecution (if they so choose) to disprove the elements beyond a reasonable doubt.

> *Point to remember...*
> The infanticide rules only apply to biological mothers within the first year of birth. Outside this (eg fathers who kill), D will be potentially liable for the traditional homicide offences, and will have to rely on defences such as diminished responsibility.

6.4.4 The killing of a foetus

The unlawful killing of a foetus does not represent a homicide offence because a foetus is not a person in law until it is fully independent of its mother by being fully expelled from the womb.[191] Indeed, the abortion of a foetus within 24 weeks of conception in certain conditions, or after this point in more exceptional conditions, has been a legal practice for some time.[192] However, outside this regulated procedure, the killing of a foetus is likely to constitute an offence under one of two headings.

---

[188] *Gore* [2008] Crim LR 388: clarifying that infanticide does not require mens rea as to death.
[189] The maximum sentence is life imprisonment, but most cases result in probation orders.
[190] *Kai-Whitewind* [2006] Crim LR 348.
[191] See **5.3.2.3**.
[192] The Abortion Act 1967, s1.

A) **Section 1 of the Infant Life (Preservation) Act 1929:** This section creates the offence of 'child destruction': the intentional killing of a foetus capable of being born alive. A foetus is capable of being born alive where it would be capable of independent breathing, at around 26 weeks.[193] The offence is punishable with a maximum of life imprisonment.

B) **Section 58 of the Offences Against the Person Act 1861:** This section creates the offence of attempting to procure a miscarriage: where D (whether the mother of V or any other person) intentionally attempts to cause a miscarriage at any stage by means of ingestion of a noxious thing (eg poisons) or other means. The offence may be committed even where the 'mother' is not in fact pregnant, where D (any person other than the 'mother') acts with the intent to cause a miscarriage.

> **Point to remember...**
> As discussed earlier,[194] although the killing of a foetus will not amount to a homicide offence, liability for a homicide offence may be possible where the foetus is injured by D when in the womb and dies later after birth. As long as the foetus is born alive before it dies, it becomes a 'person' within the meaning of the law.

6.5 Reform

In this section we will highlight a number of ongoing debates in relation to manslaughter and the potential for further reform. We begin with debates focused on the core defences leading to voluntary manslaughter and offences leading to involuntary manslaughter, we then consider the overall structure of manslaughter within the law.

6.5.1 Reforming voluntary manslaughter

Despite the extensive reform of loss of control and diminished responsibility within the Coroners and Justice Act 2009, considerable debate remains about the role and construction of these partial defences. To some extent this is inevitable, particularly where academics and/or courts identify categories of defendant that should, morally, fall outside the scope of murder and the mandatory life sentence, and where the partial defences seem to be the only method of achieving this end.[195]

Beginning with the partial defence of loss of control, it is useful to look back (see **Table 6.13**) on the controversial points identified in relation to the pre-2009 law and see whether they remain a concern for the current law.

---

[193] *Rance v Mid-Downs Health Authority* [1991] 1 QB 587; Foster, 'Forty Years On' (2007) 157 NLJ 1517.

[194] See **6.3.1.2**, discussing *AG's Reference (No 3 of 1994)* [1998] AC 245.

[195] Such inevitability, while we retain the mandatory life sentence for murder, is recognised by the Law Commission in *Partial Defences to Murder* (No 290, 2004) para 2.68.

Table 6.13 Evaluating the current partial defence of LOC

What types of conduct can qualify as provocation (or, under the current law, as 'triggers')?	The 2009 Act defines 'qualifying triggers': narrowing the trigger based on the acts or omissions of another to cases where there is a justifiable sense of being seriously wronged; and expanding to a new category of trigger caused by a fear of serious violence. These general categories, although rather vague, have been generally welcomed.[196] However, the specific exclusion of sexual infidelity has not been successful.[197]
What characteristics of D can be taken into account when deciding if her reaction should qualify for the defence?	This question was problematic under the old law, but the 2009 Act seems to resolve it in a compromise between the two options debated within the old law. However, the slightly ambiguous reference in the statute to 'in the circumstances of D' may have the unfortunate consequence of reopening this debate.[198] Indeed, some believe that it should be reopened in order to allow the offence to have a wider application.[199]
Is the defence gender biased in its operation?	Significant efforts have been made to make the defence more gender neutral, including the new trigger of 'fear of serious violence' and the removal of the 'sudden and temporary' requirement for D's loss of control. However, the government's choice to retain the requirement that D should have lost control in fact (contrary to the Law Commission's recommendations) maintains a significant hurdle for female defendants who are much less likely to react through a loss of control (particularly in the context of abused women).[200]
Is the defence designed as a partial justification (D acted wrongly, but as others would have) or as a partial excuse (D's weakness makes her action less blameworthy)?	Arguably, this fundamental question remains unanswered within the current law. The Law Commission's scheme created a defence based on D acting in a manner in which other reasonable people might have acted (semi-justificatory). However, the government's maintenance of 'loss of control' as an essential element looks more like a weakness of D's character (semi-excusatory).[201]

For diminished responsibility, it is useful to start with the general scope and aim of the defence. This is because the medicalisation of the elements of DR will almost inevitably restrict its use as a flexible (undefined) tool of legal equity: a tool for avoiding murder and the mandatory life sentence in 'deserving' cases. In this regard, we may think the

---

[196] See **6.2.1.3**.

[197] For a useful discussion of specific and general exclusions, see Crofts and Loughnan, 'Provocation, NSW Style: Reform of the Defence of Provocation in NSW' [2014] Crim LR 109.

[198] See **6.2.1.4**.

[199] Mitchell, Mackay, and Brookbanks, 'Pleading for Provoked Killers: In Defence of *Morgan Smith*' (2008) 124 LQR 675.

[200] See **6.2.1.2**.

[201] Norrie, 'The Coroners and Justice Act 2009—Partial Defences to Murder (1) Loss of Control' [2010] Crim LR 275.

law should have remained broadly defined thereby allowing flexibility to deal more sensitively with women who kill their abusers; and even so-called mercy killers). On the other hand, we may think the law should be strictly defined so that Parliament should be responsible for creating defences for these classes of defendants where necessary. One's view of the new defence, and the appropriateness of future reform, will chiefly depend upon which side of this debate is preferred.

Accepting that the current law has adopted a relatively precise definition of DR, there is also room to question that detail. Two areas stand out. First, there remains a concern that developmentally immature defendants without an associated learning disability will fall outside the defence. The Law Commission's recommendations extended the defence to the developmentally immature and it is concerning that they have been omitted from the final reform.[202] Secondly, having established the first three limbs of the defence (abnormality of mental functioning; caused by a recognised condition; substantially impairing D's ability to control or understand her actions), it is arguable that the further requirement of a causal link between D's abnormality and the killing is both medically incapable of being proved and morally unnecessary.[203]

6.5.2 Reforming involuntary manslaughter

The common law offences of UAM and GNM are some of the most controversial in the criminal law. In both cases, the offences label and punish D for manslaughter without requiring her to have foreseen the possibility that her acts will cause death: they both include elements of strict liability.[204]

For UAM, this led the Law Commission at one time to recommend abolition of the offence without replacement.[205] However, more recently, the Commission has made recommendations that reduce the constructive nature of the offence by requiring *some* mens rea as to death or injury, but leaving its basic structure largely intact.[206] For those opposed to constructive liability, this remains inadequate.[207]

Similar criticisms can be made of GNM. Indeed, as GNM does not require D to have committed a base offence with necessary mens rea, it is capable of criminalising D for manslaughter where she has not chosen to commit, or risk committing, any offence at all. Rather, it will be enough that her behaviour is classified by a jury as falling grossly below the level expected. The Law Commission has consistently recommended the maintenance of GNM, although they would like it to be codified in legislation, and to make D's ability to appreciate the risk of death (capacity) an express element.[208]

6.5.3 Reforming the structure of manslaughter offences

The Law Commission has recommended a restructuring of murder and manslaughter into three tiers (a ladder) of offences.[209] This was introduced in the context of murder in

---

[202] See **6.2.2.2**.

[203] Mackay, 'The New Diminished Responsibility Plea' [2010] Crim LR 299.

[204] See generally Clarkson and Cunningham (eds), *Criminal Liability for Non-Aggressive Death* (2008).

[205] Law Commission, *Involuntary Manslaughter* (Consultation 135, 1994).

[206] Law Commission, *Murder, Manslaughter and Infanticide* (No 304, 2006) para 2.163.

[207] Keating, 'The Restoration of a Serious Crime' [1996] Crim LR 535.

[208] Law Commission, *Murder, Manslaughter and Infanticide* (No 304, 2006) para 3.60.

[209] Law Commission, *Murder, Manslaughter and Infanticide* (No 304, 2006); Ashworth, 'Principles, Pragmatism and the Law Commission's Recommendations on Homicide Law Reform' [2007] Crim LR 333.

the previous chapter, where we acknowledged the unlikelihood of this structure being adopted into legislation.[210] However, the recommendations provide a useful insight into how that law might be rationalised. The structure recommended by the Commission is as follows:

...first degree murder should encompass:

(1) intentional killings, and

(2) killings with the intent to cause serious injury where the killer was aware that his or her conduct involved a serious risk of causing death.[211]

> **Extra detail...**
> First degree murder is expanded beyond intentional killing to include a killing with the intention to cause serious harm (as with the current law). However, the requirement that D must foresee a serious risk of death would (if enacted) reduce the scope of the offence as where D stabs V in the leg causing GBH, but V dies following an unforeseen medical complication.
>   The mandatory life sentence would apply to first degree murder.

...second degree murder should encompass:

(1) killings intended to cause serious injury; or

(2) killings intended to cause injury or fear or risk of injury where the killer was aware that his or her conduct involved a serious risk of causing death; or

(3) killings intended to kill or to cause serious injury where the killer was aware that his or her conduct involved a serious risk of causing death but successfully pleads provocation, diminished responsibility or that he or she killed pursuant to a suicide pact.[212]

> **Extra detail...**
> The new offence of second degree murder would carry a maximum (non-mandatory) life sentence. This offence would encompass certain cases currently dealt with as murder (1), but also the more serious cases currently dealt with as manslaughter (2 and 3).

...manslaughter should encompass:

(1) killing another person through gross negligence ('gross negligence manslaughter'); or

(2) killing another person:

  (a) through the commission of a criminal act intended by the defendant to cause injury, or

  (b) through the commission of a criminal act that the defendant was aware involved a serious risk of causing some injury ('criminal act manslaughter').[213]

> **Extra detail...**
> The least culpable form of homicide would retain the label of manslaughter, with a maximum (non-mandatory) life sentence. This would cover reformed versions of the current involuntary manslaughter offences.

---

[210] See **5.6.2**.
[211] Law Commission, *Murder, Manslaughter and Infanticide* (No 304, 2006) para 9.5.
[212] Ibid, para 9.6.
[213] Ibid, para 9.9.

6.6 Eye on assessment

In this section we discuss the potential application of manslaughter within a problem question. The same structure of analysis should be employed as we have discussed in previous chapters.

> **STEP 1 Identify the potential criminal event in the facts**
>
> This is unlikely to take more than a sentence, but it is essential to tell your reader where in the facts you are focusing. For homicide offences, this involves pointing out where a person has died (eg 'The first potential criminal event arises where Mary shoots at Vicky and Vicky dies').

> **STEP 2 Identify the potential offence**
>
> Having identified the facts (eg D potentially killing V), you must now identify the offence you are going to apply. Usually, this means identifying the most serious offence that D might have committed.

When applying Step 2, it is useful to keep in mind the flowchart with which we began the chapter, repeated in **Figure 6.7**.

Figure 6.7 Locating homicide liability

In line with the flowchart, unless the question isolates a specific offence for discussion (eg 'Discuss Mary's potential liability for unlawful act manslaughter'),[214] you should begin with the most serious potential offence: murder.

> ### STEP 3 Applying the offence to the facts
>
> Actus reus: What does the offence require? Did D do it?
> Mens rea: What does the offence require? Did D possess it?

6.6.1 Where the elements of murder are satisfied

Where the elements of murder are satisfied, you should move on to discuss potential defences.

> ### STEP 4 Consider defences
>
> The word 'consider' here is important, as you should not discuss every defence for every question. Rather, think whether there are any defences that *could* potentially apply. If there are, discuss those only.

When discussing defences, always begin with the complete defences (**Chapters 13** and **14**) as these usually lead to a complete acquittal. Remember that the defence of duress does not apply to murder. If none of the complete defences apply or there is some doubt over their application, continue to discuss the partial defences to murder.

When discussing the partial defences, it is usually appropriate to discuss loss of control first and then go on to consider diminished responsibility (this reflects the preference of most defendants, partly because LOC does not entail a reversal of the burden of proof). As both of these defences are statute-based, your discussion should be structured around the elements of the defences as stated in the statute. Cases that post-date the statute are most useful to identify how the courts apply the defence elements in practice. Cases pre-dating the statute may also be useful as an indication of how the statute is likely to be applied particularly where the statute appears to be the codification of rules taken from an old case, but remember that such cases are not binding precedent and should not be presented as such.

When applying the partial defences, take care to acknowledge areas of uncertainty. Particularly in relation to diminished responsibility, many of the questions for the jury are likely to be led by expert medical evidence. If you are not told medical details about D within the problem facts (eg that she is suffering from clinical depression, etc), then you should highlight this omission of essential information. You can still apply the law on the facts that you are given, and you can still predict *likely* outcomes based on those facts, but your answer should be expressly qualified (eg 'on the facts available it seems likely that . . . ').

---

[214] Where a specific offence is isolated by the question, the elements of this offence (and potential defences to it) are all that should be discussed.

> ### STEP 5 Conclude
>
> This is usually a single sentence either saying that it is likely that D has committed the offence, or saying that it is not likely, either because an offence element is not satisfied, or because a defence is likely to apply. It is not often that you will be able to say categorically whether D has committed the offence or not, so it is usually best to conclude in terms of what is more 'likely'.

> ### STEP 6 Loop
>
> Go back up to Step 1, identifying the next potential criminal event. Continue until you have discussed all the relevant potentially criminal events.

6.6.2 Where the elements of murder are not satisfied

Where the actus reus of murder is not satisfied, then you need to look for other potential offences outside homicide. Where the actus reus of murder is satisfied, but the mens rea is lacking, you should apply the involuntary manslaughter offences.

> *Beware...*
> Remember that the three common law involuntary manslaughter offences are separate and should not be confused. Apply them to the facts one at a time.

When selecting which offence to apply first, the following distinction is useful.

A) **D lacks mens rea for murder, but she clearly foresaw the risk of death or GBH:** Where D's mens rea is just short of that required for murder, it is logical to step down to the offence of reckless manslaughter. This is because reckless manslaughter shares a similar structure to murder, with the only difference being that D need not intend to cause death or GBH (recklessness being sufficient). Thus, there is no need to demonstrate a base offence (required for UAM), or duty of care and grossly negligent conduct (required for GNM). Rather, you can simply refer back to your discussion of several elements of murder (particularly the actus reus), and then apply the recklessness-based test for mens rea to demonstrate liability.

B) **D lacks mens rea for murder, and it is unclear if she foresaw a risk of death or GBH:** In many cases, the simple step down to an obviously satisfied offence of reckless manslaughter will not be possible. In these cases, reflecting the approach generally taken in the courts, it is good practice to apply UAM first, and then to apply GNM where UAM is not satisfied. In certain cases you can skip over UAM very briefly (eg where D's conduct is an omission, or there is clearly no base offence).

Where you do not find liability for any offence then move to Step 5. Where you find a likelihood of liability, move to Step 4.

STEP 4 Consider defences

The word 'consider' here is important, as you should not discuss every defence for every question. Rather, think whether there are any defences that *could* potentially apply. If there are, discuss those only.

Remember that the partial defences cannot apply here—they can only potentially apply where D commits murder.

STEP 5 Conclude

This is usually a single sentence either saying that it is likely that D has committed the offence, or saying that it is not likely, either because an offence element is not satisfied, or because a defence is likely to apply. It is not often that you will be able to say categorically whether D has committed the offence or not, so it is usually best to conclude in terms of what is more 'likely'.

STEP 6 Loop

Go back up to Step 1, identifying the next potential criminal event. Continue until you have discussed all the relevant potentially criminal events.

ONLINE RESOURCE CENTRE

www.oxfordtextbooks.co.uk/orc/smithandhogan/

This chapter is accompanied by a selection of online resources to help you with this topic, including:

- **Multiple choice questions**
- **Chapter summary sheet**
- Two **sample examination questions** with answer guidance
- **Further reading**

Also available on the Online Resource Centre are:

- A selection of **videos** from the authors explaining key topics and principles
- **Legal updates**
- Useful **weblinks**

7

Non-fatal offences against the person

7.1 Introduction

One of the central values upon which the criminal law is constructed is that of bodily autonomy: the right not to be physically interfered with against your will.[1] We have already discussed the role of this value in the context of murder (**Chapter 5**) and manslaughter (**Chapter 6**) where D's conduct results in the ultimate loss of V's bodily autonomy through death. However, the criminal law's protection of bodily autonomy extends to conduct well short of that causing death. Grouped within the 'non-fatal offences against the person', a variety of offences have been designed to criminalise behaviour that ranges from the infliction of serious (non-fatal) injuries, through to the potential targeting of any non-consensual contact.

Although the detailed content of these offences can vary considerably, it is possible to identify patterns in the law to aid understanding. It is useful, for example, to separate the various non-fatal offences into two separate categories, result-focused and conduct-focused.

The offences in the first category, and the main focus of this chapter, are 'result-focused' and are defined largely in relation to the *degree* of harm suffered by V. These offences can be presented as an imperfect 'ladder', with the most serious at the top and the least serious at the bottom.

(a) Wounding with intent to cause GBH, or causing grievous bodily harm with intent.

(b) Maliciously wounding or inflicting grievous bodily harm.

(c) Assault occasioning actual bodily harm.

(d) Assault and battery.

We discuss this category of offences first, beginning at the bottom of the ladder and working up.

The second category of non-fatal offences is 'conduct-focused'. Although offences in this category are still concerned with D causing harm, they are equally concerned with the *manner* in which that harm is inflicted. This can be illustrated, for example, with harassment and poisoning offences. In each case, the conduct targeted could alternatively be charged within the first category of offences, focusing on the degree of

---

[1] Respect for bodily autonomy is enshrined in Art 8 ECHR (respect for private life). For more serious infringements the protection lies in Art 3 (freedom from torture, inhuman and degrading treatment) and Art 5 (freedom from unlawful deprivation of liberty). See **1.1.1** and **1.4** for a more general discussion of the values protected by the criminal law. See also Wilson, *Central Issues in Criminal Theory* (2002) Ch 1.

harm suffered by V. However, to do so would be to ignore the special circumstances of D's offending. By employing the more specific offences of harassment and poisoning, offences which can be defined and labelled to highlight the particularly harmful methods D has employed, the law can send a clear message to both the individual offender as well as society more generally.

As will become clear, unlike the first category of non-fatal offences, the second category does not attempt to target a particular spectrum of resulting harms. Rather, offences in this second category have been developed in an ad hoc manner, arising to fill gaps found within the first category as well as reflecting social and political priorities. It is within this second category that we might also locate the sexual offences, a series of offences that are defined independently to reflect the uniquely serious manner of their commission. However, due to the importance and complexity of these offences, they will be discussed separately in **Chapter 8**.

> *Terminology...*
> Only a natural 'person' can be a victim of an offence against the person. The meaning of 'person' has already been discussed in relation to murder and manslaughter, and these rules apply equally to the non-fatal offences (eg an unborn foetus or someone who is legally dead cannot be the victim of an offence in this chapter).
>
> Although we use the language of 'victim' in relation to the person offended against, the implications of this label can appear inappropriate in the context of certain non-fatal offences. For example, as we will discuss later, it is possible for D to commit an offence even when the 'victim' has consented to, and even gained pleasure from, D's actions. Think about this when evaluating the offences. If the label 'victim' seems inappropriate, does this mean you think the law is in need of reform? If not, who is the law protecting?

7.2 Assault and battery

Within the first category of non-fatal offences, and at the bottom of the imaginary ladder introduced in the previous section, are the offences of assault and battery. Many of the offences in this first category are defined in the Offences Against the Person Act (OAPA) 1861. However, the offences of assault and battery are not defined in statute. The power to charge them now derives from section 39 of the Criminal Justice Act 1988.[2] This has given rise to a technical dispute as to whether these offences should be *referred to* as statutory or common law offences. Whichever is preferred, the *definitions* of these offences are found in the common law.[3]

7.2.1 Assault

An assault involves any conduct by D that, intentionally or recklessly, causes V to *apprehend* imminent unlawful personal violence. In contrast, a battery (discussed in the following section) is any conduct by which D, intentionally or recklessly, *inflicts* unlawful personal violence upon V. The elements of assault are set out in **Table 7.1**.

---

[2] 'Common assault and battery shall be summary offences and a person guilty of either of them shall be liable to a fine ..., to imprisonment for a term not exceeding six months, or to both.'

[3] Assault and battery are also torts. As a result, the definition of these offences has been partly derived from civil law cases, and some of these cases are discussed later.

Table 7.1 Assault

	Actus reus	Mens rea
Conduct element	Any conduct causing the result	Voluntary
Circumstance element	V is a person	Knowledge
Result element	V apprehends an imminent threat of unlawful force	Intention or recklessness

7.2.1.1 Actus reus of assault

In contrast to the everyday/non-legal meaning of 'assault', the legal definition does *not* require D to make any physical contact with V. Such contact is only required for the distinct offence of 'battery'. The actus reus of assault is satisfied as soon as D causes V to apprehend or believe that V is about to suffer some personal violence.

The actus reus of assault is therefore less concerned with the conduct of D, and rather more concerned with the impact of that conduct on V. For example, if D acts in a manner that would usually cause another to apprehend unlawful violence as, for example, where she drives at V or motions to strike V, but V does not apprehend imminent violence, perhaps because V is asleep or knows D is bluffing, then no assault is committed. To understand the actus reus fully, several questions must be considered:

A) **What do we mean by 'unlawful personal violence'?** The language of 'unlawful personal violence' is now well established.[4] As with battery, 'unlawful personal violence' includes any non-consensual contact. Thus, although the apprehension of some such contact is required, V need not believe that the 'violence' would be serious or cause injury. Care should also be taken, however, not to interpret this requirement too widely. It is not sufficient, for example, that D causes V to fear in a general sense by, say, watching a scary film: V must specifically be caused to apprehend the imminent application of force.

B) **How imminent must V believe the violence will be?** V must be caused to fear immediate or imminent unlawful personal violence. Thus, threats of violence at some non-imminent point in the future (eg 'I will beat you up next month'), however serious, will not constitute an assault. The distinction between imminent violence, which does satisfy the actus reus, and non-imminent violence, which does not, is therefore central to liability. The courts have applied a part subjective and part objective approach.

- Subjective: in order to establish the nature of the threat from D, the law focuses on the facts as V believes or is caused to believe them to be.

For example, if D points an unloaded or imitation gun at V, causing V to believe that she is about to be shot, then D has completed the actus reus of assault. In reality, under any definition of 'imminence', there is no imminent threat of V being shot by a gun

---

[4] *Ireland* [1998] AC 147. See also *Smith and Hogan's Criminal Law* (14th edn, 2014) Ch5.

that cannot be fired. However, based on the facts that V is caused to believe, a finding of imminence is possible.[5]

- Objective: although the facts are established from what V is caused to believe, the question of whether this belief amounts to an apprehension of *imminent* violence remains an objective one for the court.

For example, if V is caused to believe she will be shot in one hour, whether this is imminent will be a question for the court. The tendency of the court has been to interpret the requirement of imminence very broadly, allowing for liability even where V knows that the threat will inevitably involve some delay.[6] This approach has been adopted consistently by the courts,[7] as illustrated by the case of *Constanza*.

Constanza [1997] Crim LR 576

D harassed V over a period of 20 months, sending threatening letters, writing on her front door, and taking items from her washing. V suffered clinical depression as a result. D was charged with assault causing actual bodily harm, which as we will see is an offence that requires an assault to have been committed.[8] D claimed that the letters could not have caused V to anticipate an *immediate* threat.

- Crown Court: guilty of assault, and thus assault causing actual bodily harm.
- Court of Appeal: conviction upheld on appeal. The court found assault on the basis that V was caused to apprehend violence 'at some point not excluding the immediate future.'

Assessment matters...

When applying cases such as *Constanza* to problem facts, a very wide definition of 'imminence' should be employed. However, take care not to fall into the trap which the courts arguably have, by confusing an imminent anticipation of violence at some point in the future (not enough to satisfy the actus reus) from an anticipation of imminent violence (which will satisfy the actus reus). It is not disputed that the cases discussed earlier displayed the former, but it is debatable whether they should have been held to include the latter.

C) Can the result be caused indirectly? Most assaults will involve a threat of, or incomplete, battery as where D threatens to punch V in the face. However, although D must cause V to apprehend imminent unlawful violence it is not necessary that such apprehension should involve violence *from D*. Thus, where D threatens V with a dog,[9] or even presumably with attack from another person, the actus reus of assault will be satisfied by D's conduct.

D) Can the conduct element be satisfied by words alone, or by omission? As assault is based on causing another to apprehend violence (as opposed to the infliction

---

[5] *Logdon v DPP* [1976] Crim LR 121, DC.

[6] See Virgo, 'Offences Against the Person—Do-It-Yourself Law Reform' (1997) 56 CLJ 251.

[7] *Logdon v DPP* [1976] Crim LR 121: D showed V a pistol in a draw, saying he would keep her hostage; *Smith v Chief Superintendent of Woking Police Station* (1983) 76 Cr App R 234: D seen looking through a window at V; *Ireland* [1998] AC 147: D made phone calls to V.

[8] Discussed at **7.4**.

[9] *Dume*, The Times, 16 October 1986.

of violence), it is clear that D's conduct may be words alone. It is irrelevant whether such words are communicated orally or in any written format.[10] It is also likely that assault can be committed by omission. For example, where D *inadvertently* causes V to apprehend imminent violence, as where D is checking the sights on his gun when V walks into the room and then *intentionally* omits to withdraw the threat by lowering the gun, an assault is likely to be found.[11]

E) **Can the threat be implied or conditional?** Implied or conditional threats are most likely in the context of a verbal assault as, for example, where D says to V 'if the coin toss lands on heads then I will hit you'. As before, provided D's threat causes V to apprehend imminent violence, the actus reus of assault will be satisfied.[12] The only exception to this is where the communicated condition undermines *any chance* of the threat being carried out. For example, if D shouts at V 'I would hit you if you weren't already ugly', he has not committed an assault even if his actions alone might seem otherwise threatening: D's words make it clear that there will be no imminent attack.[13]

7.2.1.2 Mens rea of assault

The mens rea for assault, and as we will see the mens rea for battery, requires D to intend *or* be reckless as to causing the result. Thus, for assault, D must intend or foresee the possibility that his act will cause V to apprehend imminent unlawful violence. This was established in *Venna*.[14] Although this case involved a battery that caused actual bodily harm, it remains good authority for the mens rea of, both assault and battery.

As well as mens rea as to the result, D must also have the appropriate mens rea as to the other offence elements. Thus, as with all offences, D must have performed the relevant conduct voluntarily.[15] D must also be aware that his victim, V, is a person.

> *Assessment matters...*
> Although D's mens rea as to the result of causing V to apprehend imminent violence should always be discussed in a problem answer, this is not true of the other mens rea requirements. It will usually be self-evident that D acted voluntarily and is aware that V is a person, for example, and so these requirements need only be explicitly discussed if there is some room for doubt. This is equally true of the other offences discussed later.

7.2.2 Battery

A battery is any conduct by which D, intentionally or recklessly, inflicts unlawful personal violence upon V.[16] The elements of battery are set out in **Table 7.2**.

---

[10] As in *Constanza*.
[11] Omissions liability requires a duty to act: here, D has a duty to act to remedy his inadvertent creation of a dangerous situation: *Miller* [1983] AC 161. See **2.6**.
[12] See Williams, 'Assault and Words' [1957] Crim LR 219.
[13] See *Tuberville v Savage* (1669) 1 Mood Rep 3. D's potential assault (putting hand on sword) was undermined by the accompanying statement: 'if it were not assize time I would not take such language'.
[14] [1976] QB 421.
[15] See **3.3**.
[16] *Rolfe* (1952) 36 Cr App R 4.

Table 7.2 Battery

	Actus reus	Mens rea
Conduct element	Any conduct causing the result	Voluntary
Circumstance element	V is a person	Knowledge
Result element	Unlawful physical contact with V	Intention or recklessness

7.2.2.1 Actus reus of battery

The actus reus of battery consists of the infliction of unlawful personal violence. Again, the term 'violence' in this context will encompass *any* unlawful contact with another. As Blackstone explained:

> The law cannot draw the line between different degrees of violence, and therefore prohibits the first and lowest stage of it; every man's person being sacred, and no other having a right to meddle with it, in even the slightest manner.[17]

In line with this approach, the courts have interpreted the actus reus of battery very broadly. The following questions have emerged.

A) Does the result require physical contact? Unlike assault, where D can cause V to apprehend violence through any means, including words, battery will *always* require physical contact with V. This is a fundamental difference between the two offences. However, although some force must be applied, the requirement has been interpreted widely. For example, it will be satisfied even if V is unaware of the touching as where V is asleep, and will include touching V's clothes, as illustrated in *Thomas*.

> **Thomas** (1985) 81 Cr App R 331
>
> D (a school caretaker) touched the hem of a 12-year-old pupil's skirt. He was charged with the (now repealed) sexual offence of indecent assault which, like battery, required a touching.
>
> • Court: guilty of indecent assault.
> • Court of Appeal: appeal allowed on the basis that the touching was not indecent. However, it was confirmed that there was a touching: 'There could be no dispute that if you touch a person's clothes while he is wearing them that is equivalent to touching him.'[18]

Despite this wide interpretation, the requirement of contact can be problematic. For example, where D causes bodily harm in the form of psychiatric injury, this may be inflicted without any physical impact on V's body. In such a case, because there is no physical force, there will be no battery.[19]

---

[17] *Commentaries*, iii, 120, cited in *Collins v Wilcock* [1984] 3 All ER 374, 378.
[18] At 334.
[19] Ormerod and Gunn, 'In Defence of *Ireland*' [1996] 3 Web JCLI.

B) **Can the result be caused indirectly?** Although battery will always require physical contact with V, it is not essential that this contact should be *directly* inflicted by D. Standard cases will involve direct contact as where D hits V with his fist, with an instrument, or by throwing things at V or spitting at V, etc. However, battery will also be found where contact is caused indirectly as where D punches X causing her to drop her baby (V), in which case D has committed a battery on V.[20] Several cases confirm this point. In *DPP v K*,[21] for example, D committed battery when he poured acid into a toilet hand-dryer, causing the next user to be sprayed. Equally, in *Martin*[22] it was agreed that battery could be found where D digs a pit for V to fall into, or causes injury through the placing of an obstruction. Other cases will involve battery where D sets his dog[23] or other animal[24] on V.

C) **Can the conduct element be satisfied by an omission?** Battery will invariably involve an act, and it has been generally assumed that acts are required for liability.[25] However, as with assault (discussed in the previous section), it is likely that the courts will find battery can be committed by omission. Support for this can be found in *Santana-Bermudez*.

> 🔲 *Santana-Bermudez v DPP* [2004] Crim LR 471
>
> D assured V, who was a policewoman, that he was not carrying any 'sharps' (hypodermic needles) before she searched him. He was, and V was injured. D was charged with battery occasioning actual bodily harm,[26] an offence where battery must be demonstrated.
>
> - Magistrates' court: guilty of battery occasioning actual bodily harm.
> - Crown Court: not guilty—no actus reus.
> - High Court: although no retrial was ordered, the court confirmed that D's omission was capable of giving rise to a battery.

For omissions liability, it is of course necessary to demonstrate a duty to act and a breach of that duty. In *Santana-Bermudez*, this is established by D's creation of a dangerous situation: having sharp objects in his pocket and assuring V that he did not.[27]

7.2.2.2 Mens rea of battery

The mens rea of battery requires that D intended or was subjectively reckless as to causing the result: the application of unlawful force to the body of V. This was established in *Venna*.[28] D must also perform her conduct voluntarily, and know that V is a 'person'.

---

[20] *Haystead v Chief Constable of Derbyshire* (2000) 164 JP 396. Liability could *alternatively* be found through transferred malice.

[21] [1990] 1 All ER 331, overruled on *other* grounds by *Spratt* [1991] 2 All ER 210.

[22] (1881) 8 QBD 54.

[23] *Murgatroyd v Chief Constable of West Yorkshire* [2000] All ER 1742.

[24] eg where D causes a horse to bolt: *Gibbon v Pepper* (1695) 2 Salk 637 (*obiter*).

[25] *Innes v Wylie* (1844) 1 Car & Kir 257.

[26] See **7.4**.

[27] *Miller* [1983] AC 161.

[28] [1976] QB 421.

7.2.3 Hostility as an element of assault or battery?

It is generally accepted that hostility is *not* an element of assault or battery. Lord Lane CJ has described battery as:

> an intentional touching of another person without the consent of that person and without lawful excuse. It need not necessarily be hostile, or rude, or aggressive, as some of the cases seem to indicate.[29]

Although some doubt has been raised by the House of Lords in *Brown*,[30] where the majority indicated that hostility *is* required, this interpretation is unlikely to be followed. This is because the facts of *Brown* involved sadomasochistic acts that were consented to for the mutual satisfaction of those involved, and such acts could not, in plain English, be described as hostile. In order to find hostility in this case, the House of Lords effectively emptied the word of its meaning: saying the acts were hostile because they were unlawful.[31] Under this approach, hostility does not seem like an offence element at all, but rather a description of events that have been found to be criminal on other grounds.

7.2.4 The relationship between assault and battery

Assault and battery are two separate offences. However, this was not always the case, and they are still often referred to interchangeably, inconsistently, and/or cumulatively in cases, academic discussion and statute. The main reason for this continued problem is because, without an acceptable verb to correspond with the noun of 'battery', the term 'assaulted' is used to describe D who commits both assault and/or battery. As a result, great care should be taken to ensure that you are not misled about what a particular author is attempting to communicate.

7.3 Defences to assault and battery

Where D has satisfied the offence elements of assault or battery, she will nevertheless avoid liability if she has a specific defence of 'lawful chastisement', 'consent', or 'belief in consent'. These will be discussed in the following sections.

> *Assessment matters...*
> When considering defences, it is usually good practice to begin with specific defences. However, if these do not apply, remember that D can also avoid liability if she satisfies one of the general defences that apply across a greater part of the criminal law. See **Chapter 13**, where we discuss denials of mental responsibility, and **Chapter 14**, where we discuss the general defences.

---

[29] *Faulkner v Talbot* [1981] 3 All ER 468, 471.
[30] [1994] AC 212.
[31] Per Lord Jauncey.

7.3.1 Lawful chastisement of children

A lawful chastisement or 'corporal punishment' defence has traditionally applied at common law to allow parents and teachers to use physical force to discipline children.[32] However, the definition of this defence at common law was uncertain, and the subject of challenges in the ECtHR.[33] As a result, the defence was codified within section 58 of the Children Act 2004 and was considerably restricted in scope. Importantly, the defence will not apply to any offence against the person that is more serious than assault or battery. Further, even in the context of assault or battery, the force used must be both reasonable and proportionate in the circumstances, and involve no cruelty.

Under section 549(4) of the Education Act 1996, a member of school staff now has no defence merely by virtue of her position as a teacher, to any offence against the person committed on a pupil by way of punishment. This includes assault or battery. However, the Act does make clear that reasonable force can be used to restrain violent pupils (s550A), those who are endangering themselves and/or property (s548(5)), or to search for a weapon (s550AA).

7.3.2 Consent to assault and battery

The defence of consent is vitally important in relation to non-fatal offences against the person.[34] Where D makes *consensual* contact with V, such as by shaking V's hand, or *consensually* causes V to apprehend contact by D motioning towards shaking V's hand, we would not want to find liability for assault or battery. Indeed, such examples are so obviously outside that intended to be criminalised that there are strong grounds for contending that consent should not be analysed as a defence at all, but rather that 'non-consent' should be analysed as part of each offence. In practice, little turns on which interpretation is preferred—in both cases V's valid consent will undermine D's potential liability. Examples of both presentations can be found in the courts and surrounding commentaries. We discuss this in the 'reform' section later (**7.10.3**). In what follows, for the sake of consistency, and in line with a slight predominance in the case law,[35] we analyse consent as a defence.

The structure of the defence of consent, as it applies to assault or battery, is set out in **Table 7.3**.

---

[32] Keating, 'Protecting or Punishing Children: Physical Punishment, Human Rights and English Law Reform' (2006) 26 LS 394; Barton, 'Hitting Your Children: Common Assault or Common Sense?' (2008) 38 Fam L 65.

[33] *A v UK* [1998] TLR 578; Phillips, 'The Case for Corporal Punishment in the UK—Beaten into Submission in Europe' (1994) 43 ICLQ 153.

[34] There is a vast literature on this subject. See Law Commission, *Consent and Offences against the Person* (Consultation 134, 1994), on which see Ormerod, 'Consent and Offences Against the Person: LCCP No 134' (1994) 57 MLR 928; and Law Commission, *Consent in Criminal Law* (Consultation 139, 1995), on which see Ormerod and Gunn, 'Consent—A Second Bash' [1996] Crim LR 694. See also Elliott and de Than, 'The Case for a Rational Reconstruction of Consent in Criminal Law' (2007) 70 MLR 225.

[35] This was the approach preferred by the bare majority in *Brown* [1994] AC 212.

Table 7.3 Defence of consent

A) V's consent must be expressed or implied to D in a legally recognised manner
B) V's consent must be effective: V must have the capacity, freedom, and information required to make a choice

As we go on to discuss the more serious offences against the person later, a third element to the consent defence emerges: the context of V's consensual harm must come within an accepted category (eg surgery).[36] However, in the context of assault and battery, due to the low levels of harm involved, no such additional limitations apply. Thus, as long as V's consent is effective, D will not be liable for assault or battery whether we perceive his conduct as socially acceptable or not as, for example, where D and V agree to have a fight that does not result in bodily harm.

7.3.2.1 Expressed and/or implied consent

The most straightforward cases involving consent are those in which V expressly consents to contact with D. However, particularly in the context of assault or battery, implied consent is very common.

The notion of implied consent is particularly important to prevent the liability for touching which, although not explicitly consented to, is part of everyday life.[37] The logic behind this is that, by voluntarily moving in society, we agree to be exposed to the foreseeable contact that social life entails. It is therefore not assault or battery, for example, if one is jostled in a busy street or when entering a crowded train; or even if one is embraced, within reason, as the clock strikes for the New Year. There are, of course, limits to implied consent. For example, as demonstrated in *Wood v DPP*, contact must be genuinely within the realms of everyday activity.

Wood v DPP [2008] EWHC 1056 (Admin)

D was restrained by V, a police officer, as he left a public house. Importantly, V was not in the process of arresting D, but merely restraining him in order to establish his identity. D resisted, and was charged with assaulting the police officer.

- Magistrates' court: D is guilty of assault.
- Crown Court: conviction upheld.
- High Court: appeal allowed, and D acquitted. V is not entitled to restrain D in this manner outside a lawful arrest (no implied consent). Thus, as V was assaulting D, D's resistance was lawful.

A further limit on implied consent, clarified in *H v CPS*,[38] is that, just because assault or battery might be foreseeable, does not mean it is impliedly consented to. This case

---

[36] See **7.8.2.1**.
[37] *Collins v Wilcock* [1984] 3 All ER 374.
[38] [2010] All ER 56.

involved a teacher in a special needs school (V) who was assaulted by a student. V was well aware of the risk of assault within the school, but the court rejected the submission that such awareness should be equated with implied consent.

7.3.2.2 Effective consent

For consent to be valid in law, it must be effective. For example, if V is unaware of exactly what D is planning to do, or is mentally unable to understand what D is going to do, then it is highly questionable whether V's apparent acquiescence should absolve D of liability. The principal questions are the following:

- What *mental capacity* is required for V to be capable of effective consent?
- What degree of *knowledge* is required for V to be capable of effective consent?
- Can *fraud* from D undermine the effectiveness of consent?
- Can *duress* or pressure from D or another undermine the effectiveness of consent?

These questions will be considered in turn.

> *Extra detail...*
>
> Although central to all other cases, effective consent is not relevant where V has implicitly consented in the manner discussed earlier. Where consent is implied as to assault or battery (eg light contact between people on a busy train), such consent is assumed to also be effective. This assumption is clearly artificial, particularly where V is unable to understand the implied consent she is providing through age or mental deficiency, for example. However, despite the artificiality, bearing in mind the type of conduct involved, it is unlikely to lead to substantial problems.[39]

Capacity

V may lack the capacity[40] to consent for a variety of reasons, for example mental disorder or learning difficulties, infancy, or more temporary conditions such as intoxication. In each case, the issue of capacity should be considered. However, it should be remembered that degrees of capacity are likely to vary between individuals, over time, and in relation to the particular issue. For example, V may lack capacity in relation to certain complex decisions, but not in relation to others. This makes the assessment of capacity very difficult.

Where the courts have been tempted to take the easier option of simply equating a certain status with a lack of capacity, the result has been some rather questionable judgments. An example of this is *Burrell v Harmer*.

> **Burrell v Harmer** [1967] Crim LR 169
>
> D was charged with battery causing actual bodily harm, an offence which required proof of a battery after tattooing the arms of boys aged 12 and 13. D's defence was that the boys had consented, having actively instigated the tattooing.

---

[39] In *F v West Berkshire Health Authority* [1990] 2 AC 1, Lord Goff criticised the current approach as 'artificial', and recommended an alternative modelled on the defence of necessity.

[40] See Law Commission, *Consent in Criminal Law* (Consultation 139, 1995) Part 5; Law Commission, *Mental Capacity* (No 231, 1995).

> • Crown Court: guilty of the offence. The boys, as minors, were not capable of understanding the nature of the act of tattooing (ie they lacked capacity) and therefore there was no effective consent.

How can this be right? With the court taking little time to explain and discuss exactly what knowledge the boys lacked, this case demonstrates the rather superficial approach too often taken to the assessment of capacity.

A more nuanced approach to capacity has been set out in the Mental Capacity Act 2005. The Act states that 'a person lacks capacity in relation to a matter if at the material time he is unable to make a decision for himself in relation to the matter because of a temporary or permanent impairment of, or a disturbance in the functioning of, the mind or brain.' Stressing the importance of individual assessment, the Act also cautions that a lack of capacity should not be equated from '(a) a person's age or appearance, or (b) a condition of his, or an aspect of his behaviour, which might lead others to make unjustified assumptions about his capacity.' The criminal courts are not bound by this Act in relation to the offences against the person. However, it is likely to influence courts to look more carefully at the circumstances of each individual case and victim.[41]

> *Assessment matters...*
> Where problem facts state that V suffers from a certain mental condition, is a minor, or is intoxicated, it is tempting to assume that she lacks capacity to consent. This should certainly be discussed, but the best answers will also consider the possibility that she might have sufficient capacity despite her status. A conclusion should then be provided with an opinion of what is most likely based on the facts that have been provided.

Informed consent

Although V may have the *capacity* to consent to a particular action, she must also, logically, be told what that action entails before she can exercise her capacity and make a decision. Again, the level of information required is not easy to measure and will depend on the degree of harm that V is potentially consenting to: the more harm, the greater the knowledge required for the consent to be informed and valid. It should therefore be of little surprise that most of the cases discussed here involve more serious offences than simple assault or battery. However, as the same general rules apply to assault and battery (just with a lighter touch), it is still useful to have the discussion at this stage.

How informed consent should be applied in the context of the non-fatal offences was considered in the important case of *Konzani*.

Konzani [2005] EWCA Crim 706

D engaged in consensual unprotected sexual intercourse with three complainants. As a result of this, each contracted HIV, a condition that D was aware he had but of which he had not informed the complainants.

• Crown Court: guilty of maliciously inflicting grievous bodily harm.[42]

---

[41] See *Re S and another (Protected Persons)* [2010] 1 WLR 1082, [53].
[42] See **7.5.**

- Court of Appeal: conviction upheld on appeal. The victims had consented to sexual intercourse, but, because of the lack of information made known to them, they had not consented to the risk of contracting HIV.

The court explained the role of informed consent in the following terms:

If an individual who knows that he is suffering from the HIV virus conceals this stark fact from his sexual partner, the principle of her personal autonomy is not enhanced if he is exculpated when he recklessly transmits the HIV virus to her through consensual sexual intercourse. On any view, the concealment of this fact from her almost inevitably means that she is deceived. Her consent is not properly informed, and she cannot give an informed consent to something of which she is igno-rant.... Silence [from D] in these circumstances is incongruous with honesty, or with a genuine belief that there is an informed consent. Accordingly, in such circumstances the issue either of informed consent or honest belief in it will only rarely arise: in reality, in most cases, the contention would be wholly artificial.[43]

Most important within this decision is the court's clear distinction between (a) being informed as to the nature of the sexual intercourse (to which there *was* effective consent), and (b) being informed as to the risk of HIV infection (to which there was *no* effective consent). This distinction is critical because if it is not made, then there is either consent to both and thus no liability at all, or there is no consent to both and thus D has also committed rape. The clear distinction between (a) and (b) therefore allows us to focus only on the aspect of D's conduct that V was not informed about—focusing liability for an offence against the person and not a sexual offence.[44]

In this manner, *Konzani* provides a clear precedent that, where D alone is aware of a significant risk of harm in relation to a particular activity, such as sexual inter-course, if V is not informed of it then V's apparent consent to that additional risk will not be effective and thus legally invalid. However, importantly, the same will not follow where D is not fully aware of the risk he poses. Thus, for example, it was accepted in *Konzani* that if D lacked knowledge of his HIV status at the time of intercourse, his failure to disclose information he did not possess could not under-mine V's consent. On these facts, although V does not have the information about D's HIV status, because D is not *responsible* for that lack of information, the law will treat V's consent as effective. V was, after all, informed of the relevant risks *known* to D.

Point to remember...

Informed consent can be summarised as follows:

- D is aware of a risk associated with a certain action—D must inform V for V's consent to be effective;
- D is unaware of the risk—V's consent will be effective despite lack of knowledge.

---

43 At [23] per Judge LJ.
44 For critical commentary, see Weait, 'Knowledge, Autonomy and Consent: *R v Konzani*' [2006] Crim LR 763; Munro, 'On Responsible Relationships and Irresponsible Sex' [2007] CFLQ 112.

Consent procured by fraud

Fraud has the potential to undermine V's apparent consent in two main areas: fraud as to the identity of D; and fraud as to the nature of the act consented to.[45] Unfortunately, the current law has become complex and confused.

A) **Fraud as to the identity of D:** The basic rule is easy to apply. If D gains V's consent to being touched by impersonating X, V's consent to that touching (battery) is not legally effective. V's consent is given to X in relation to X's acts, not the impersonating D.

Problems emerge where D is not impersonating another person but, rather, D is lying about certain characteristics or qualifications. In these cases, it is much less clear if D is being fraudulent about her *identity*. The courts have generally interpreted 'identity' narrowly in such cases, as seen in *Richardson*.

> **Richardson** [1998] 2 Cr App R 200
>
> D was suspended from practising dentistry, but continued to treat patients. D was charged with assault occasioning actual bodily harm in relation to her treatment of patients during this time. The patients were clear that they would not have consented to treatment if they had known that D was suspended.
>
> • Crown Court: guilty of assault occasioning actual bodily harm. Fraud as to identity (presenting as a licensed dentist) undermined the patients' apparent consent.
>
> • Court of Appeal: appeal allowed. No fraud as to identity: D did not lie about who she was, but rather simply about the holding of a licence.

In cases such as *Richardson*, it is arguable that D's lack of qualifications were more important to V's consent than whether D claimed to be someone else. However, the law has maintained a narrow test of 'identity' focusing only on the latter.

B) **Fraud as to the nature of D's conduct:** Fraud as to the nature of D's conduct is capable of undermining otherwise effective consent as, for example, where D tells V that it is customary to greet someone by punching them in the face. However, where V is not deceived as to the core nature of the act, but simply as to a collateral issue, this will not generally undermine consent. The courts have consistently interpreted the 'nature' of conduct very narrowly. For example, in *Mobilio*,[46] where V consented to D inserting an instrument into her vagina for diagnostic purposes, but D was secretly acting only for his sexual gratification, the court held that consent was effective: the fraud was not as to the *nature* of the act.

This issue has also arisen in relation to consensual sexual intercourse where D does not inform her sexual partner of a known sexually transmitted infection. This was considered in *Dica*,[47] where D infected two sexual partners with HIV. As with the more recent case of *Konzani* (discussed earlier in relation to informed consent), the Court of Appeal in *Dica* made the crucial distinction between: (i) consent as to sexual intercourse, which was both informed and non-fraudulent, and (ii) consent as to the risk of

---

[45] See Law Commission, *Consent in Criminal Law* (Consultation 139, 1995) Part 6.
[46] [1991] 1 VR 339. Ormerod, 'A Victim's Mistaken Consent in Rape' (1992) 56 J Crim L 407.
[47] [2004] EWCA Crim 1103.

infection, which was uninformed and gained through fraud.[48] Although V was not misled as to the *nature* of the sexual act, and thus D had not committed rape, V was misled as to the *nature* of the associated risk of infection (the risk of bodily harm). D was guilty of inflicting grievous bodily harm.

Consent procured through duress

V's apparent consent will not be effective if it is gained by threats (duress). For example, if D submits to a light beating only amounting to a battery in order to avoid a greater one, the threat of the greater beating is likely to undermine her consent. Similar results have emerged even where D's threats were non-criminal (eg submit to this beating or be dismissed from employment[49] or bringing a prosecution[50]). Indeed, duress may even be implied from a relationship, such as that between teacher and young pupil.[51]

Despite these examples, however, the exact test for duress in this context remains unclear. It must be demonstrated that V's apparent consent was *caused* by D's threat as opposed to other factors, and so it is important to balance the gravity of the threat against the act consented to. However, it remains unclear whether this balancing is a purely objective procedure (asking if a person of reasonable firmness would have submitted to the violence), or whether it includes a subjective dimension (eg where D knew V was particularly vulnerable through mental abnormality or alcoholism, etc).

> *Assessment matters...*
>
> In order to assess whether consent is effective, it is necessary to consider each of the topics discussed in this section: capacity, level of knowledge, fraud, and duress. However, applying these to problem facts is not a tick-box exercise. Therefore, again, you should fully explore and discuss where there is an element of doubt (eg D is a minor or is tricked in some way), but this may not be necessary if there is no such doubt.

7.3.3 Belief in consent to assault and battery

In addition to the consent defence, where D claims that V provided valid consent in fact D may also avoid liability on the basis that she *believed* that V had provided valid consent. Thus, even if V is not consenting, D will avoid liability if she *genuinely* believes that consent is present. As seen in *Jones*, this will be the case even where D's belief is unreasonable.

> *Jones* [1987] Crim LR 123
>
> The defendant schoolboys threw V into the air with the intention of catching him as part of a joke. However, they missed and V suffered severe injuries. They sought to rely on the consent of V.
>
> - Crown Court: guilty of an offence causing grievous bodily harm. The judge did not allow the defence of consent to be put to the jury.

---

[48] The court in *Dica* disapplied the earlier case of *Clarence* (1888) 22 QBD 23, where the court had held that V's consent to sexual intercourse amounted to an implied consent to the risk of infection.

[49] *McCoy* 1953 (2) SA 4.

[50] *State v Volschenk* 1968 (2) PH H283, here the threat did *not* undermine consent.

[51] *Nichol* (1807) Russ & Ry 130.

- Court of Appeal: appeal allowed. Consent should have been left to the jury. Consent could have been a valid defence if V had consented, *or* if D genuinely (even if unreasonably) believed that V consented.

This defence is rarely pursued in court. D must raise enough evidence that she genuinely believed that V provided valid consent (ie express or implied, and effective).

7.4 OAPA 1861, s47: assault occasioning actual bodily harm

Section 47 is satisfied where D commits an assault or battery that causes V to suffer actual bodily harm (ABH).

47. Whosoever shall be convicted on indictment of any assault occasioning actual bodily harm shall be liable to imprisonment for not more than five years.

The elements of the section 47 offence are set out in **Table 7.4**.

Table 7.4 OAPA 1861, s47

	Actus reus	**Mens rea**
Conduct element	Any conduct causing the results	Voluntary
Circumstance element	V is a person	Knowledge
Result elements	(1)(a) V apprehends an imminent threat of physical contact	Intention or recklessness
	Or	
	(b) Physical contact is applied And	Intention or recklessness
	(2) V suffers actual bodily harm	None

An alternative illustration of section 47 is provided in **Figure 7.1**.

Figure 7.1 OAPA 1861, s47

7.4.1 Actus reus of s47

The actus reus of the section 47 offence requires D to commit the actus reus of assault or battery, with the additional result that V suffers ABH.

7.4.1.1 Assault or battery

The term 'assault' in section 47 should be read as 'assault or battery'. The actus reus elements of these base offences have been discussed earlier. Most cases will involve a battery that occasions ABH. However, a base offence of assault is also possible as, for example, where D causes V to apprehend imminent violence (assault) and V hurts herself when attempting to escape (ABH).[52]

7.4.1.2 Occasioning

Having demonstrated an assault or battery, the prosecution must prove that this assault or battery *occasioned* ABH. 'Occasioning', in this context, has been interpreted to mean nothing more than 'causing'.[53] Thus, in addition to the requirement of causation within the base offence of assault or battery which proves that D's conduct caused the apprehension or actual touching required in those offences, it must also be shown that D's conduct caused V to suffer ABH.

7.4.1.3 The result element of bodily harm

'Actual bodily harm' is not defined in the OAPA, and thus the courts have attempted to interpret it in line with its common meaning, influenced also by the maximum five-year sentence.[54] Distinct from mere battery, it is clear that ABH will not be found where V's injury is merely 'transient and trifling'.[55] However, ABH has been described in expansive terms to include 'any hurt or injury that is calculated to interfere with the health or comfort' of V.[56] Examples of ABH include:

- scratches, grazes, and abrasions;
- bruising and swelling;
- temporary loss of consciousness;[57]
- cutting a substantial amount of hair;[58]
- psychiatric injury; etc.[59]

The recognition of psychiatric injury within ABH represents a significant judicial extension of section 47. However, as in the case of *Ireland*, ABH will only extend to

---

[52] *Roberts* (1972) 56 Cr App R 95.
[53] Ibid. This interpretation is challenged in Gardner, 'Rationality and the Rule of Law in Offences Against the Person' (1994) 53 CLJ 502, 509.
[54] *DPP v Smith* [1961] AC 290 at 334 describe the term as requiring 'no explanation'.
[55] *T v DPP* [2003] Crim LR 622.
[56] *Miller* [1954] 2 QB 282.
[57] *T v DPP* [2003] Crim LR 622.
[58] *DPP v Smith* [2006] EWHC 94 (Admin).
[59] CPS Charging Standards: www.cps.gov.uk/legal/l_to_o/offences_against_the_person.

psychiatric injury where that injury is an identified or recognised psychiatric condition. 'Injury' that is not a recognised psychiatric condition, such as fear and anxiety, cannot amount to ABH.

◻ *Ireland and Burstow* [1998] AC 147

These cases were combined in the House of Lords. Ireland was charged with a section 47 offence having made a series of silent telephone calls which caused V to suffer psychiatric harm. Burstow was charged with an offence of causing grievous bodily harm, having harassed a different V including making silent calls and causing her to suffer severe depression.

- Crown Court: both found guilty of the offences charged.
- Court of Appeal: both convictions upheld on appeal.
- House of Lords: appeals dismissed. Psychiatric injury is capable of amounting to actual and/or grievous bodily harm.

7.4.2 Mens rea of s47

The only mens rea requirements for section 47 are those relating to the base offence of assault or battery. Thus, D must intend to cause or be reckless as to causing V to apprehend imminent violence (assault) *or* intend to make or be reckless as to making contact with V (battery). There is no additional mens rea required in relation to the result of ABH. (Assault or battery + ABH = s47.)

The lack of a mens rea requirement as to causing ABH was established in *Roberts*.

◻ *Roberts* (1971) 56 Cr App R 95

D made unwanted sexual advances towards V when driving her in his car. D tried to take off V's coat (a battery), and this led to V jumping out of the moving car and sustaining grazes and concussion (ABH). D was charged with a section 47 offence.

- Crown Court: guilty of section 47 offence.
- Court of Appeal: conviction upheld on appeal. Liability does not require D to foresee the chance that his acts will cause ABH.

The rule in *Roberts* was later thrown into doubt following a remarkable series of cases.[60] However, it has now been confirmed by the House of Lords in *Savage* and *Parmenter*.[61]

---

[60] *Spratt* [1991] 2 All ER 220 (without reference to *Roberts*) held that recklessness was required as to the ABH. However, on the same day, *Savage* [1991] 2 All ER 210 (without reference to *Roberts*) held that no mens rea was required. Later, confronted with this conflict (but, again, without reference to *Roberts*), *Parmenter* [1992] 1 AC 699 preferred *Spratt*.

[61] Reversing *Parmenter* and overruling *Spratt* on this point.

Savage* and *Parmenter [1992] 1 AC 699

Cases combined in the House of Lords. Savage involved D who intended to throw merely the contents of her beer glass over V but slipped and threw the glass as well causing a wound. Parmenter involved D who handled a baby (V) in such a way that caused serious injury. In both cases, the defendants claimed that they did not intend or foresee a risk of causing harm.

- Crown Court: both found guilty of offences involving grievous bodily harm.
- Court of Appeal: appeals allowed—there was a lack of mens rea for the GBH offences. However, in *Savage* liability for GBH was replaced with section 47. In *Parmenter* section 47 was not applied, as the court found that mens rea was needed as to causing ABH.
- House of Lords: *Parmenter* appeal allowed. *Savage* appeal dismissed. Both liable for a section 47 offence: this offence requires no mens rea as to the causing of ABH.

Section 47 is, therefore, an example of a constructive liability offence: the additional result caused by D (ABH) leads to increased liability even though she may not have foreseen it, and therefore could not be said to have *chosen* to bring it about.[62]

7.5 OAPA 1861, s20: wounding or inflicting grievous bodily harm

Section 20 criminalises malicious wounding *and/or* inflicting GBH, with at least foresight of some bodily harm.

20. Whosoever shall unlawfully and maliciously wound or inflict any grievous bodily harm upon any other person, either with or without any weapon or instrument shall be guilty of [an offence triable either way] and being convicted thereof shall be liable to imprisonment for five years.

The elements of the section 20 offence are set out in **Table 7.5**.

Table 7.5 OAPA 1861, s20

	Actus reus	**Mens rea**
Conduct element	Any conduct causing the results	Voluntary
Circumstance element	V is a person	Knowledge
Result element	V is wounded Or V suffers GBH	Recklessness as to *some* bodily injury Recklessness as to *some* bodily injury

---

[62] Discussed at **7.10.2**.

7.5.1 Actus reus of s20

The two ways of completing the actus reus of section 20 are through wounding and/or inflicting GBH.

7.5.1.1 Wounding

In order to constitute a wound, V's skin must be broken by, for example, stabbing.[63] The standard case will involve V's outer skin but wounding will also be found where D breaks internal membranes that are similar to the outer skin as, for example, where D punches V and splits the inside of her cheek or lip.[64] There are limits, however. First, the whole skin (every layer) must be broken. For example, a scratch that breaks the 'surface of the skin' but not every layer will not amount to a wound.[65] Secondly, wounding cannot be *purely* internal. In *Wood*,[66] for example, despite causing V's broken collarbone, as the skin remained intact, there was no wound.

Doubt remains as to whether wounding can be caused by omission. However, although rare, it is likely that omissions liability is possible. For example, D omits to put sharp knives in a safe place having foreseen the possibility that V—a young child—might injure herself with them. Breaching a duty to remove the danger created, D is likely to commit the section 20 offence by omission if injury results.

7.5.1.2 Inflicting grievous bodily harm

In the absence of a statutory definition, GBH has been defined by the House of Lords to mean 'serious bodily harm'.[67] Thus, V's injuries must be more serious than ABH: 'bodily harm'. However, this should not be overstated, and it is clear that GBH does not require injury to be permanent or life-threatening,[68] with even brief unconsciousness being potentially sufficient.[69] Classic examples include broken bones and disfigurement. It is also clear that *serious* psychiatric injuries may amount to GBH, as discussed previously in *Ireland*.[70] However, as with ABH, such injury must amount to a recognised psychiatric condition; simple fear or distress is insufficient.

> *Extra detail…*
> As with section 47, when deciding on the degree of harm caused, the court will consider the totality of V's injuries. Thus, it is not necessary to demonstrate that V suffered ABH or GBH as a result of a single act (eg punch), provided that the harm was sustained from one attack or relevant period.[71]

As the section 20 offence requires D to 'inflict' GBH as opposed to simply 'cause' it,[72] there has been some disagreement about whether the two words require different tests. For example, it has been contended that 'inflict' implies that D must cause injury

---

[63] *Moriarty v Brooks* (1834) 6 C & P 684.
[64] *Waltham* (1849) 3 Cox CC 442.
[65] *Morris* [2005] EWCA Crim 609.
[66] (1830) 1 Mood CC 278.
[67] *Smith* [1961] AC 290.
[68] *Bollom* [2004] 2 Cr App R 50.
[69] *Hicks* [2007] EWCA Crim 1500.
[70] See **7.4.1.3**.
[71] *Brown* [2005] EWCA Crim 359: case involving abuse over several days.
[72] In contrast with the s18 offence discussed later.

through an assault or battery as with section 47.[73] However, it is now settled law that 'inflict' should be interpreted in exactly the same way as 'cause'. Thus, D's conduct must be shown to have caused the harm to V applying the standard rules of causation, and there is *no* extra requirement of assault or battery.

> *Assessment matters...*
>
> There are two distinct ways to bring about the actus reus of section 20: by wounding or by inflicting GBH. It should be remembered that although these will often overlap (eg D stabs V in the stomach), this will not always be the case. Where D breaks one of V's bones, for example, but does not break the skin, this is GBH and not a wound.[74] Conversely, a minor wound (eg injection from a needle) will amount to a wound but not GBH. With this in mind, when applying section 20 to problem facts, it is good practice to identify which (if not both) are caused by D.

7.5.2 Mens rea of s20

Whether the allegation is of wounding or causing GBH or both, section 20 specifies a mens rea that D must be acting 'maliciously'. This has been interpreted to mean 'intentionally or recklessly'.[75] However, although intent or recklessness is required, section 20 does *not* require D to intend or foresee the full extent of the harms caused (ie wounding or GBH). Rather, liability merely requires D to intend or foresee that *some* bodily harm might be caused, not necessarily amounting to a wounding or GBH. As Diplock LJ explained in *Mowatt*:[76]

> the word 'maliciously' does import upon the part of the person who unlawfully inflicts the wound or other grievous bodily harm an awareness that his act may have the consequence of causing some physical harm to some other person. ... It is quite unnecessary that the accused should have foreseen that his unlawful act might cause physical harm of the gravity described in [s20], ie, a wound or serious physical injury. It is enough that he should have foreseen that some physical harm to some person, albeit of a minor character, might result.

It should be remembered, however, that intent or foresight of some harm is still necessary for liability. Thus, for example, D will not commit a section 20 offence if her intention is simply to frighten V and she does not foresee the possibility of V suffering injury as a result.

7.5.3 Coexistence of s20 and s47

As the section 47 and section 20 offences are punishable with the same maximum of five years' imprisonment, it is arguable that their coexistence is unnecessary.[77] However, as section 20 will *usually* involve greater harms,[78] and also includes a higher requirement

---

[73] *Wilson* [1984] AC 242, clarifying that assault and battery are *not* required for s20 liability.

[74] *Wood* (1830) 1 Mood CC 278 (broken collarbone).

[75] *Savage* and *Parmenter* [1991] 4 All ER 698, 721.

[76] [1968] 1 QB 421, 426. Reiterated in *C* [2007] EWCA Crim 1068.

[77] Gardner, 'Rationality and the Rule of Law in Offences Against the Person' (1994) 53 CLJ 520.

[78] This will not always be the case. See reform discussion at **7.10.1.1**.

of mens rea, section 20 is regarded in practice as the more serious offence. In this manner, conviction for section 20 will usually result in a higher sentence than for section 47.

As we have highlighted earlier, one of the aims of this first category of non-fatal offences is the creation of a ladder that provides appropriate offences and sentences in relation to different levels of harm. The lack of clarity in the current distinction between section 47 and section 20, and its reliance on prosecutors and the courts to create that distinction in practice, reflects poorly on the current law. This is discussed in the context of possible reforms later in the chapter.[79]

7.6 OAPA 1861, s18: wounding, or causing grievous bodily harm with intent

Section 18 criminalises malicious wounding *and/or* the causing of GBH, with intention to cause GBH or resist apprehension etc.

> 18. Whosoever shall unlawfully and maliciously by any means whatsoever wound or cause any grievous bodily harm to any person with intent to do some grievous bodily harm to any person or with intent to resist or prevent the lawful apprehension or detainer of any person, shall be guilty of [an offence triable only on indictment], and being convicted thereof shall be liable to imprisonment for life.

The elements of the section 18 offence are set out in **Table 7.6**.

Table 7.6 OAPA 1861, s18

	Actus reus	**Mens rea**
Conduct element	Any conduct causing the results	Voluntary
Circumstance element	V is a person	Knowledge
Result element	V is wounded Or V suffers GBH	Intention to cause GBH *or* intention to resist apprehension etc and reckless as to GBH Intention to cause GBH *or* intention to resist apprehension etc and reckless as to GBH

7.6.1 Actus reus of s18

The actus reus of the section 18 offence is identical to that of section 20: D's conduct must have caused V to suffer either a wound and/or GBH. There is no need to demonstrate that the elements of assault or battery are also present.

---

[79] See **7.10.1.1**.

7.6.2 Mens rea of s18

The mens rea as to section 18 is the same regardless of whether D has wounded V or caused GBH. In either case, D must have acted with the intention to cause GBH to any person *or* with intent to resist or prevent the lawful apprehension or detention of any person.

The standard case of section 18 will involve causing GBH with malice and an intention to cause GBH. However, the various alternative results and intentions discussed earlier mean that section 18 can have a variety of constructions:

- wounding with malice and intent to cause GBH;
- wounding with malice and intent to resist lawful apprehension;
- wounding with malice and intent to prevent lawful apprehension;
- wounding with malice and intent to resist lawful detainer;
- wounding with malice and intent to prevent lawful detainer;
- GBH with malice and intent to resist lawful apprehension;
- GBH with malice and intent to prevent lawful apprehension;
- GBH with malice and intent to resist lawful detainer; and
- GBH with malice and intent to prevent lawful detainer.

Amongst these variations, two important details should not be missed. First, unlike other offences against the person, the mens rea of section 18 is only satisfied by an *intention* (recklessness is not sufficient). Therefore, the meaning of 'intention' as distinct from recklessness becomes crucial. As discussed in relation to murder, D intends when she either (a) acts with the purpose/desire of bringing about the result, or, if it was not her purpose, (b) acts with foresight that the result is a virtually certain consequence of her action, the result is in fact a virtually certain result, and the jury choose to find that she intended it.

Secondly, as held in *Taylor*, an intention to wound is *not* sufficient mens rea for section 18.

 Taylor [2009] EWCA Crim 544

D stabbed V in the back during an altercation. There was no evidence that D intended to cause GBH.

- Crown Court: guilty of a section 18 offence. The court defined the mens rea of section 18 as an intent to wound or to cause GBH.
- Court of Appeal: appeal allowed, and liability for section 20 substituted. Section 18 requires intention to cause GBH (not simply to wound), and there was insufficient evidence of such intention in this case.

7.6.2.1 Malice

'Malice' has already been discussed in relation to section 20. It requires, broadly, for D to intend or foresee the possibility of causing V bodily harm. For the section 18 offence, the role played by the malice requirement is therefore very different between cases where D intends GBH and cases where she does not.

A) Where D intends to cause GBH: In this, the most common construction of the section 18 offence, the word 'maliciously' adds nothing at all. By intending to cause GBH, D already satisfies the requirement of malice: intention or foresight of bodily harm.[80]

B) Where D's mens rea is based on intention to prevent apprehension etc: Here, the 'maliciously' requirement becomes central to liability. This is because it could appear that in these cases D requires no intention or foresight of any violence at all. However, the 'maliciously' requirement means that D must foresee at least some bodily harm and although there is no direct authority, probably also requires the foresight of GBH.[81] Thus, where D intends to prevent apprehension, etc, 'maliciously' should be interpreted to require him to *also* foresee the possibility of GBH before section 18 liability is established.

7.7 Sections 47, 20, and 18: alternative verdicts

Consistent with the 'laddering' of these offences, it has been held that a charge relating to a more serious offence against the person will include the less serious offences as alternatives. Thus, if D is charged under section 18, GBH with intent, a jury may alternatively find liability under section 20 or section 47 if they believe that the essential elements of liability for section 18 are unproven.[82] In this manner, analysis of liability will generally focus on the most serious potential offence before working down the ladder if necessary.[83]

Despite the utility of this approach, research suggests that it has also led to unfortunate consequences. Particularly, because of the availability of the lesser alternatives, it seems that many juries will shy away from reaching guilty verdicts for the most serious section 18 offence even where the elements of this offence appear to be satisfied.[84] Such research demonstrates a flaw to the laddering of offences.

7.8 Defences to sections 47, 20, and 18

Where D satisfies the elements of section 47, 20, or 18, she will nevertheless avoid liability if she has a specific defence of 'consent' or 'belief in consent'. Additionally, D may also avoid liability by relying on one of the general defences discussed in **Chapter 13** (denials of mental responsibility) and **Chapter 14** (general defences). However, our focus in this section will be the specific defences.

It should be noted that although the defences of 'consent' and 'belief in consent' are available in relation to sections 47, 20, and 18, these defences are *not* constructed in the same way as they were in relation to assault and battery discussed previously. To apply to the more serious offences, V's consent, or D's belief in consent, will require additional elements before being legally effective.

---

[80] *Brown* [2005] EWCA Crim 359, [17].

[81] This is assumed in *Morrison* (1989) 89 Cr App R 17.

[82] *Mandair* (1994) 99 Cr App R 250.

[83] This is also the model form of analysis for answering problem questions, see **7.11**.

[84] Genders, 'Reform of the Offences Against the Person Act: Lessons from the Law in Action' [1999] Crim LR 689.

7.8.1 Defences to the base offence for s47

The defences to assault and battery discussed earlier (including lawful chastisement, consent, and belief in consent) will not ordinarily prevent liability for a section 47, 20, or 18 offence. However, the unique construction of section 47, requiring a base offence of assault or battery that causes ABH, opens the possibility that one of these defences might apply to undermine liability for the base offence. With the base offence removed, the construction of section 47 liability would then become impossible (assault or battery + ABH = s47). Thus, in effect, a defence to simple assault or battery could act as a defence to section 47 liability.

Where D has caused the level of harm necessary for a section 47 offence, the courts have been reluctant to allow a defence to simple assault or battery (the base offence) to undermine liability. Therefore, a line of authority has developed in relation to these cases that can prevent D from raising a defence to the base offence, depending upon her foresight of causing ABH. Where D is prevented from raising a defence to the base offence, she will be restricted to those defences that are available for the more serious offences (discussed later). Although the courts have struggled for consistency, their general approach can be summarised as follows.

A) **D causes ABH, she intended or foresaw the possibility of causing ABH:**

Example…
D and V agree to practise shadow boxing, intending no contact or only very light contact. D knows that she lacks really tight control of her punches and foresees she might hit V causing ABH. D does so.

V may have given informed and effective consent to assault or battery, but D's foresight that she might cause ABH means that such consent will *not* prevent section 47 liability. Rather, D will only avoid liability if she satisfies the elements of the more restrictive consent defences discussed later. This is confirmed in *Donovan*.[85]

B) **D causes ABH, she did not intend or foresee the ABH:**

Example…
D and V play a game trying to push each other over. V falls and accidentally hits her head causing ABH.

In this case, as D does not foresee the chance of causing ABH or greater, V's informed and effective consent to assault or battery *will* prevent section 47 liability. V has consented to the assault or battery, and there is no reason (no further fault from D) that justifies not legally recognising that consent. This has been confirmed in *Meachen*.[86]

C) **D causes ABH. She did not intend or foresee the ABH, although she *should* have foreseen it:**

Example…
D and V play a game trying to push each other over. V falls and accidentally hits her head causing ABH. V hit her head on an obvious rock that was directly behind her.

---

[85] [1934] 2 KB 498.
[86] [2006] EWCA Crim 2414.

This final example is the most problematic: D's defences to simple assault or battery are not obviously undermined by a foresight of ABH, but she has been negligent in not foreseeing that risk. There are conflicting cases, but following *Boyea*,[87] it is likely that D will be liable: V's informed and effective consent to assault or battery being sufficient to prevent liability for section 47 given that D was negligent as to causing harm. Rather, D will only avoid liability if the elements of the more restrictive consent defences discussed later are satisfied.

> **Don't be confused...**
> The cases discussed in this section are rare: where D commits a section 47 offence and V was consenting to assault or battery. However, the approach of the courts, focusing on D's foresight of ABH, is interesting. It should be remembered that D need not foresee the chance of causing ABH to be liable for section 47, as it is a constructive liability offence. However, such foresight becomes a primary concern when deciding which defences are available.

7.8.2 Consent to the more serious offences against the person

Consent can be a valid defence to offences under section 47, 20, or 18. However, in addition to the defence elements required for consent as to assault or battery, consent to the more serious offences will only be available where D's conduct comes within an excepted category. For example, D cannot avoid liability for GBH if she demonstrates that V asked to be shot. However, a doctor can avoid such liability by showing that V consented to a surgical operation that was duly performed. The elements of the defence are set out in **Table 7.7**.

Table 7.7 Defence of consent to serious offences against the person

A) V's consent must be expressed or implied to D in a legally recognised manner
B) V's consent must be effective: V must have the capacity, freedom, and information to make a choice
C) The conduct and harms consented to must come within a recognised category

We have discussed the first two elements of the defence in the context of assault and battery earlier,[88] and the same rules apply here. Therefore, our focus here will be on the additional element, identifying the categories of conduct (where D commits a sections 47, 20, or 18 offence) that can be validly consented to.

---

[87] (1992) 156 JP 505.
[88] See **7.3.2**.

The third element of the defence was established in what remains the leading case, *Brown*.

> ▢ **Brown** [1994] AC 212
>
> D and others were involved in sadomasochistic homosexual groupings. Within the group, the men filmed various acts causing both ABH and wounding for their mutual sexual pleasure. They were charged with offences under sections 47 and 20.
>
> - Crown Court: guilty of section 47 and 20 offences.
> - Court of Appeal: convictions upheld on appeal.
> - House of Lords: appeal dismissed. The court set out the additional requirement for consent in relation to sections 47, 20, and 18. They then concluded that sadomasochism did not qualify within one of the special categories.

The recognised categories, or accepted activities where V's consent will be legally effective, have not been designed in accordance with particular legal principles or with regard to any legal or medical notions of acceptable harm.[89] Rather, as Lord Woolf rather candidly admitted in *Barnes*,[90] they have evolved as a matter of 'public policy'. This policy-based approach allows the courts flexibility to reach what they consider to be socially desirable results. However, in their attempts to do so, the list of accepted activities has developed inconsistently and, as many would now accept, incoherently. The categories that have so far been acknowledged by the courts include:

- surgery;
- body modification;
- religious flagellation;
- sports;
- horseplay; and
- sexual pleasure.

We will discuss each in turn.

7.8.2.1 Surgery

Surgery is a straightforward example where V can provide valid consent to what might otherwise constitute a serious offence against the person.[91] This includes both essential and non-essential (cosmetic) treatment.[92]

---

[89] See Tolmie, 'Consent to Harmful Assaults: The Case for Moving Away from Category Based Decision Making' [2012] Crim LR 656; Kell, 'Social Disutility and Consent' (1994) 14 OJLS 121; Giles, 'Consensual Harm and the Public Interest' (1994) 57 MLR 101.

[90] [2005] Crim LR 381.

[91] Law Commission, *Consent in Criminal Law* (Consultation 139, 1995) Part 8; Skegg, 'Medical Procedures and the Crime of Battery' [1974] Crim LR 693 and (1973) 36 MLR 370.

[92] *Corbett v Corbett* [1971] P 83: sex-change operation.

7.8.2.2 Body modification

There are several common forms of body modification—involving bodily harm—that may be validly consented to (eg hair cutting, piercing, tattooing, etc).[93] There are, however, borderline cases. This can be illustrated in the comparison of *Wilson* and *Brown*.

> **Wilson** [1996] Crim LR 573
>
> At his wife's (V's) request, D consensually branded his initials onto V's bottom with a hot knife. D was charged with a section 47 offence.
>
> • Crown Court: guilty of section 47 offence.
> • Court of Appeal: appeal allowed. D's conduct was akin to tattooing and other body modification and V's consent was therefore valid.

The outcome of *Wilson* was decided by the Court of Appeal in a manner that gave short shrift to the prosecution, making clear that this was not a place for criminal liability. This would suggest that *Wilson* was a clear case on its facts where V's consent was valid. However, although some of the acts in *Brown* could equally have been treated as analogous to acceptable forms of body modification (eg genital piercing), the court in *Brown* found consent to be invalid.

Body modification is also common in a religious context (eg circumcision of Jewish and Muslim males).[94] Religious body modification gains some protection from Article 9 ECHR which respects religious freedom. However, certain foreign cultural practices have not been accepted within this exception, for example cheek incision.[95] Such distinctions appear incoherent.

7.8.2.3 Religious flagellation

Although rarely practised, religious flagellation (methodical beating or whipping) is also likely to constitute an exception where V may validly consent to bodily harm.[96] This was recognised by Lord Mustill in *Brown*.

7.8.2.4 Sports

Various sports, provide a clear social utility despite the high risk of bodily injury involved in them, for example rugby, roller derby, etc.[97] However, although the

---

[93] Law Commission, *Consent in Criminal Law* (Consultation 139, 1995) Part 9; Elliott 'Body Dismorphic Disorder, Radical Surgery and the Limits of Consent' (2009) 17 Med L Rev 149.

[94] Gilbert, 'Time to Reconsider the Lawfulness of Ritual Male Circumcision' [2007] EHRLR 279; Vickers, 'Circumcision—The Unkindest Cut of All?' (2000) 150 NLJ 1694. See also Regional Court judgment in Cologne, Germany (June 2012) where male circumcision was held unlawful (Docket No Az 151 Ns 169/11, Landgericht Köln). Female circumcision is an offence (Female Genital Mutilation Act 2003).

[95] *Adesanya* (1974) The Times, 16 July; Poulter, 'Foreign Customs and the English Criminal Law' (1975) 24 ICLQ 136.

[96] Law Commission, *Consent in Criminal Law* (Consultation 139, 1995) paras 10.2–10.7.

[97] Law Commission, *Consent in Criminal Law* (Consultation 139, 1995), Part 12; Cutcheon, 'Sports, Violence and the Criminal Law' (1994) 45 NILQ 267; Livings, 'A Different Ball Game' (2007) 71 J Crim L 534.

law seeks to allow valid consent in these cases, it must take care not to exempt acts of violence carried out under the guise of sport. A number of principles have developed.

First, we must examine the rules of the sport. This is because, generally, the law will recognise V's consent to any conduct that comes within those rules: consent that will be implied from V's agreement to play. However, this will not *always* be the case, and the criminal law is not dictated by the rules of sporting bodies. So, if the Football Association (FA) decided that footballers could hit each other with bats, this would not automatically mean that consent to such hitting would be legally recognised. Despite this potential however, with sports like boxing allowing participants to intentionally inflict GBH, and the courts recognising this as lawful, it is clear that organised sport represents a powerful exception.[98]

Secondly, we must question the extent to which V's consent and the law's recognition of that consent is interpreted to include conduct *outside* the rules of the sport. In this regard, human imperfection dictates that for sport to be played at all, consent must be recognised in relation to certain forms of inadvertent or reckless behaviour, such as a late tackle in football or a legitimate bouncer in cricket.[99] The task, then, is to distinguish *legitimate* foul play in the shape of conduct breaching the rules (that is impliedly and validly consented to) from *illegitimate* foul play (conduct that is not validly consented to). This was discussed in *Barnes*.[100]

🔒 *Barnes* [2005] 1 WLR 910

D was playing in an amateur football match. D mistimed a sliding tackle against V, and caused serious injury. D was charged with a section 20 offence.

- Crown Court: guilty of section 20 offence.
- Court of Appeal: appeal allowed. D's conduct can be outside the rules of the game (within a margin of appreciation) and still be validly consented to.

Where the risk is impliedly consented to by those involved, even though it is outside the rules of the game, the Court of Appeal set out a number of factors that should be considered: the type of sport, the level at which it is being played, the nature of the act, the degree of force, the extent of the risk of injury, and D's state of mind.[101] With sporting sanctions and/or civil remedies often readily available, criminal prosecutions are rare and usually reserved for only the gravest conduct.

The test in *Barnes* may be usefully imagined as a target board, as set out in **Figure 7.2.**

---

[98] Gunn and Ormerod, 'The Legality of Boxing' (1995) 15 LS 181; Anderson, *The Legality of Boxing: A Punch Drunk Love?* (2007).

[99] *Moore* (1898) 14 TLR 229.

[100] Anderson, 'No Licence for Thuggery: Violence, Sport and the Criminal Law' [2008] Crim LR 751.

[101] Supported by the Law Commission, *Consent and Offences against the Person* (Consultation 134, 1994). See Gardiner, 'Should More Matches End in Court?' (2005) 155 NLJ 998.

According to *Barnes*:
- Inner circle (rules of the game): V provides valid implied consent to any non-intentional injury occurring within the rules of the game.
- Middle circle (just outside the rules of the game): V provides valid implied consent to any non-intentional injury occurring just outside the rules of the game, but within a margin of appreciation.
- Outer circle (outside the margin of appreciation): V's implied consent to the risk of harm does not include conduct that breaks the rules of the game and is outside the margin of appreciation.

Figure 7.2 Consent and sport

Picking up on the last of the factors highlighted in *Barnes*, D's state of mind requires some special attention. This is because, with the exception of boxing and certain martial arts, playing sport should not involve D *intentionally* causing V bodily harm. Thus, although in sports such as hockey or cricket V's implicit consent will extend to the risk of D causing bodily harm, V has not consented to D *intentionally* causing such injury. Where D does cause injury with intent, there is, therefore, no consent: *Bradshaw*.[102]

7.8.2.5 Horseplay

Focusing predominantly on children, the horseplay exception goes beyond sport to recognise consent in relation to general undisciplined play. Although such conduct carries a risk of injury, it is felt that as long as the *genuinely* non-consenting individual remains protected by the law,[103] V's consent should be recognised even to the risk of GBH. Not recognising this exception would criminalise thousands of acts in playgrounds across the country and also, perhaps, deny a valuable part of growing up.[104]

The horseplay exception has been interpreted widely. For example, 'robust games' in *Aitken*[105] saw celebrating RAF officers setting fire to one another's fire-resistant clothing, eventually leading to V suffering severe burns. It was held that if V consented, such consent could be recognised within the exception.

7.8.2.6 Sexual pleasure?

Where V's consent derives from a context of sexual pleasure as opposed to the pleasure of sport or other non-sexual play, the courts have struggled to maintain a clear or coherent approach.

Risk of sexually transmitted infection

It is now clear from *Dica*[106] that V may validly consent to the *risk* of even potentially lethal infection in the context of a sexual encounter, such as unprotected sex with a

---

[102] (1878) Cox CC 83.
[103] *A* [2005] All ER 38: V was clearly not consenting.
[104] *Jones* (1986) 83 Cr App R 375.
[105] [1992] 1 WLR 1006.
[106] [2004] EWCA Crim 1103.

person with HIV. For such consent to be valid, V must be fully informed of the risk.[107] This will not, of course, include consent where either party is *intending* that the infection should be spread.

Unlike many recognised exceptions (discussed earlier), consent to even the risk of infection is not socially desirable. However, it was found in *Dica* that not recognising this exception would involve an 'impracticality of enforcement', as well as invading a part of life that remains 'pre-eminently private'.

Harm and sexual pleasure: sadomasochism

Sadomasochism (giving and receiving targeted pain for sexual pleasure) is always likely to be problematic for the law in this area.[108] An analogy could be drawn with the risk of sexual infection discussed previously, allowing consent in recognition of the impracticality of enforcement and the privacy of sexual relationships. However, unlike the risk of sexual infection and most sport, and horseplay, D is not simply risking bodily harm. Rather, the intentional infliction of bodily harm is essential to what both D and V are consenting to. This should not automatically disqualify V's consent as invalid. Within the recognised categories, D intends to inflict bodily harm in the context of body modification, religious flagellations, and sports such as boxing and martial arts. However, it has emboldened the court to look more deeply into the perceived social utility of the practice. In doing so, the law has become confused, inconsistent, and indefensible.

The following cases provide an overview of the current legal position:

- *Brown:*[109] the leading case in this area, involving sadomasochistic homosexual encounters between a group of men resulting in prosecutions under sections 47 and 20. A majority in the House of Lords (3:2) upheld the convictions, reasoning that despite the consent of those involved, the actions were not 'sexual' but 'violent': reflecting a cult of violence that endangered and corrupted those involved.

- *Donovan:*[110] this early case reflects many of the same public policy concerns that led to the decision in *Brown*. In this case, D beat a consenting 17-year-old girl with a cane for purposes of sexual gratification. D was convicted of both indecent assault and common assault. As D was only charged with common assault it is even more astounding that a conviction resulted: as discussed earlier, valid consent for these cases should not require D's conduct to come within the recognised categories. Although such a result is unlikely to be repeated, the policy aims discussed in this case (referred to in *Brown*) remain relevant to the current law.

- *Wilson:*[111] here, D's conviction under section 47, following the consensual branding of his wife's bottom, was overturned on appeal. The Court of Appeal considered the activity to be akin to tattooing, and made clear that they did not believe

---

[107] *Konzani* [2005] EWCA Crim 706.
[108] Law Commission, *Consent in Criminal Law* (Consultation 139, 1995) Part 10; Bamforth, 'Sadomasochism and Consent' [1994] Crim LR 661; Leigh, 'Sado-Masochism, Consent and the Reform of the Criminal Law' (1976) 39 MLR 130.
[109] [1994] AC 212.
[110] [1934] 2 KB 498.
[111] [1996] Crim LR 573.

that this is an area in which the criminal law should interfere: 'consensual activity between husband and wife, in the privacy of the matrimonial home, is not, in our judgment, normally a proper matter for criminal investigation, let alone criminal prosecution.'

Recognising the apparent conflict between *Brown* and *Wilson* in particular, subsequent cases have attempted find a sensible distinction. Unfortunately, however, courts have tended to do so by focusing on the degree or nature of the harms involved.[112] This is unfortunate because, as both cases involved ABH, it is hard to identify the measurement by which the harms in *Brown* can be characterised as worse. This is particularly evident when we consider that it was only in *Wilson* that hospital treatment was required.

Despite a number of appeal cases, it therefore remains unclear whether sexual gratification constitutes a recognised category through which V may provide valid consent to bodily harm in excess of simple assault or battery. This may be possible where the activity can be likened to other accepted practices such as tattooing, and more controversially those appeal cases may also suggest that it is more acceptable in the context of heterosexual married couples. However, the courts' willingness to label certain practices as 'violent' as opposed to 'sexual', or to conclude that they involve a different 'degree' or 'nature' of harm, makes the law in this area unpredictable.

7.8.3 Belief in consent to the more serious offences against the person

As well as the consent defence, D may also avoid liability on the basis that she believed that V had provided valid consent to conduct recognised as within an accepted category. Thus, even if V is not consenting, D will avoid liability if she *genuinely* believes that consent is present.[113] This defence is rarely pursued in court. The defence is that D genuinely believed that V provided valid consent: that it was expressly or impliedly given, effective, and that it was in relation to a recognised category,

7.9 Conduct-focused offences against the person

The first category of non-fatal offences discussed earlier was primarily concerned with the *degree* of harm caused by D: creating a ladder of offences in order to label and punish the degree of harm caused most appropriately. However, in this section we move to discuss a new category of offences. These offences, although still concerned with degrees of harm, are no longer attempting to form part of the ladder explored in the first category. Rather, this second group of offences are conduct-focused: created

---

[112] *Laskey v UK* (1997) 24 EHRR 39: claiming the injuries were not 'comparable in seriousness'; *Emmett* (1999) The Times, 15 October: V's consent to ABH was invalid because D's conduct went 'beyond that which was established in *Wilson*'.

[113] *Jones* [1987] Crim LR 123.

independently in order to recognise certain specifically harmful circumstances or motives, in order to fill perceived gaps in the law, and/or to reflect political and social priorities.

There are many offences that fall within this second category. In the following sections we explore a sample of these, including harassment and stalking, racially or religiously aggravating elements, torture and slavery, and administering poison.

7.9.1 Harassment and stalking

The criminalisation of harassment and stalking has for many years been, and remains, a challenge for the criminal law.[114] This is because, unlike standard offences against the person, harassing conduct can take almost any form, including apparent acts of kindness such as the repeated sending of flowers. Also, whereas other offences will focus on a single attack from D, the harms associated with harassment are usually cumulative: perhaps minor in their own right, but severely debilitating in combination. With this in mind, despite the broadening of the OAPA offences to include purely verbal assaults and psychological injuries,[115] specific offences have been required to combat the full range of potentially harassing behaviour.[116] These are provided within the Protection from Harassment Act 1997 (PHA).

7.9.1.1 PHA 1997, s2: offence of harassment

Section 2 makes it an offence to cause harassment, to pursue a course of conduct in breach of section 1(1) or 1(1A) (see **Table 7.8**):[117]

(1) A person must not pursue a course of conduct—

    (a) which amounts to harassment of another, and

    (b) which he knows or ought to know amounts to harassment of the other.

(1A) A person must not pursue a course of conduct—

    (a) which involves harassment of two or more persons, and

    (b) which he knows or ought to know involves harassment of those persons, and

    (c) by which he intends to persuade any person (whether or not one of those mentioned above)—

        (i) not to do something that he is entitled or required to do, or

        (ii) to do something that he is not under any obligation to do.

---

[114] Babcock, 'The Psychology of Stalking' in Infield and Platford (eds), *The Law of Harassment and Stalking* (2000); Addison and Lawson-Cruttenden, *Harassment Law and Practice* (1998); Finch, 'Stalking the Perfect Stalking Law: An Evaluation of the Efficacy of the Protection from Harassment Act 1997' [2002] Crim LR 702.

[115] *Ireland* [1998] AC 147.

[116] See Home Office, *Stalking the Solutions* (1996).

[117] Section 1A was added by the Serious Organised Crime and Police Act 2005, s125.

Table 7.8 PHA 1997, s2

Section 2	Actus reus	Mens rea
Conduct element	Any course of conduct that causes the result	Voluntary
Circumstance element	V is a person	Knowledge
Result element	(s1(1)) Harassment of V Or (s1A) Harassment of V and others	Know *or* ought to have known Know *or* ought to have known
Ulterior mens rea element	*	(s1A) Intention to persuade V not to do something she is entitled to do, *or* to do something she is not obliged to do.

Actus reus of s2

The actus reus of section 2 proscribes a course of conduct that results in V, or V and others, being harassed. The terms 'harassment' and 'course of conduct' are crucial.

A) **Harassment** is not fully defined in the PHA and leaves considerable discretion to the court to interpret the term as it is commonly understood.[118] We are told in section 7(2) that harassment includes 'the causing of alarm or distress'. However, as we are only told that harassment *includes* causing alarm or distress, it is possible that harassment can also be found without proof of either.[119] Equally, alarm and distress can be caused without harassment. In *Curtis*,[120] for example, D undoubtedly caused alarm and distress to V through a number of minor assaults and other dangerous behaviour. However, although D's actions were 'oppressive, unreasonable and unacceptable', the Court of Appeal quashed his conviction for harassment, finding that the relevant six incidents spread out over a nine-month relationship between D and V, involving violence on both sides, did not amount to harassment.

Assessment matters...
The lack of a clear definition should encourage you to discuss the law when applying it to problem facts. Look for the causing of alarm or distress, but remember that this is not conclusive.

B) **A course of conduct** must be shown to have *caused* the harassment. The main point here is the need for persistence from D, with a course of conduct requiring at least two separate incidents. In this regard, as established in *James v CPS*, D's active role in these incidents will not necessarily undermine liability.

[118] *Thomas v News Group Newspapers Ltd* [2001] EWCA Civ 1233.
[119] *DPP v Ramsdale* (2001) The Independent, 19 March.
[120] [2010] EWCA Crim 123.

James v CPS [2009] EWHC 2925 (Admin)

V, the manager of a social services team, had a duty to return the calls of D (a receiver of care) despite D's persistent abuse on such calls.

- Magistrates' court: guilty of section 2 offence.
- Crown Court: conviction upheld on appeal.
- High Court: conviction upheld on appeal. V's self-exposure to the harassment was irrelevant.

When identifying the incidents within D's course of conduct, it is important to distinguish between cases involving a single victim, and cases involving multiple victims. The rules are set out in section 7:

(3) A 'course of conduct' must involve—

(a) in the case of conduct in relation to a single person (see section 1(1)), conduct on at least two occasions in relation to that person, or

(b) in the case of conduct in relation to two or more persons (see section 1(1A)), conduct on at least one occasion in relation to each of those persons.

In standard cases involving a single V under section 7(3)(a), a course of conduct will require D to repeat certain conduct on at least two occasions to that V. Although relatively simple to state, the test can cause problems, particularly where it is difficult to identify or divide incidents. For example, in *Kelly v DPP*,[121] D made three calls to V's mobile between 2.57 am and 3.02 am, leaving abusive voicemail messages on each occasion. Listening to these messages later, and without pause between messages, V was caused severe distress. *Is this more than one incident?*[122] Similarly, in an effort to find multiple incidents, the courts have also been willing, whether rightly or wrongly, to accept indirect acts or harassment. For example, in *DPP v Williams*[123] D put his hand through a bathroom window startling X who was in the room showering, and causing V (X's flatmate who was later *told* of the incident) to also be fearful. Later, D looked into a bedroom window, this time frightening V directly. The court held that, as V was caused distress by both incidents, the offence was made out even though the first was indirect.[124]

In cases involving multiple victims, a course of conduct will require only a single harassing act in relation to at least two victims. In this manner, V's multiple acts of harassment are not excused from liability simply because they are not aimed at the same V. This provision is particularly useful in the context of protesters who harass those connected with animal breeding and testing.[125] Where D's course of conduct is

---

[121] [2003] Crim LR 43, DC.

[122] See also *DPP v Hardy* [2008] All ER (D) 315: 95 phone calls within a 90-minute period held to constitute a course of conduct rather than a single incident.

[123] *DPP v Williams* (DC, 27 July 1998, Rose LJ and Bell J).

[124] Section 7(3A) provides the additional possibility that where D aids and abets an act of harassment that is carried out by another, the law will also treat the act has having been completed by D.

[125] Home Office, *Animal Welfare: Human Rights—Protecting People from Animal Rights Extremists* (2004).

based on section 7(3)(b), however, it must be remembered that the additional element of ulterior mens rea will be required.[126]

Alongside evidence of multiple acts, in order to establish a 'course of conduct' in either guise, it must also be demonstrated that those acts were in some way connected. In many cases, such as repeated telephone calls within a short period of time, this will be relatively easy to establish. However, what if the acts are separated by a considerable period of time, say, two birthday cards, or are of a very different nature? This was discussed in *Lau v DPP*.

> **Lau v DPP** [2000] Crim LR 580
>
> The first incident involved D slapping V (his then girlfriend) on the face. The second, four months later, involved D threatening V's new partner with a brick. D was charged with a section 2 offence.
>
> - Magistrates' court: guilty of section 2 offence.
> - Crown Court: appeal allowed. Although a course of conduct could be found despite a lengthy gap, even up to a year, the incidents must have a logical connection. An example given was of racial harassment outside a synagogue on the Day of Atonement. In this case, however, there was insufficient evidence of that connection or nexus.

It is clear from *Lau* that each case will turn on its facts. The question for the court is a general one: are the incidents logically connected as a single course of conduct? To fulfil the actus reus of section 2, this must be answered in the affirmative.

Mens rea of s2

Applying the mens rea for section 2 again requires a distinction to be made between cases where D harasses a single V on multiple occasions (s1(1)) and cases where D harasses multiple Vs (s1(1A)). This is because it is only in the latter that there is an additional ulterior mens rea requirement.

A) **Mens rea required for s 1 and s 1A:** At the time of acting, D must know, or ought to have known, that her course of conduct would result in harassment. In this manner, the mens rea of section 2 can be satisfied both subjectively by D's actual knowledge or objectively by the fact that a reasonable person would have known.

The objective approach is illustrated in *Colohan*.[127]

> **Colohan** [2001] EWCA Crim 1251
>
> D, who suffered from schizophrenia, sent a number of letters to his local MP (V). The letters were threatening in places and caused V substantial distress. D was charged with a section 2 offence.
>
> - Crown Court: guilty of section 2 offence.
> - Court of Appeal: conviction upheld on appeal. Although D may not have known that his letters would cause alarm or distress, a reasonable person not suffering such an illness would have done. Therefore, the mens rea is satisfied.

---

[126] Section 7(3A) provides the additional possibility that, where D aids and abets an act of harassment that is carried out by another, the law will also treat that act as having been completed by D.

[127] [2001] EWCA Crim 1251.

Although, within the objective standard, D's lack of appreciation, or inability to appreciate, the effects of her conduct will not be taken into account, any additional information that D possesses will. This is important where D is aware of particular circumstances that make her otherwise innocuous conduct more likely to be harassing (eg D knows that V has consistently rejected her advances, and yet continues to send gifts).

B) **Mens rea only required where D harasses multiple Vs (s1(1A))**: D must intend her course of conduct to persuade the Vs to refrain from something they are entitled to do, or to do something they are not (eg for an animal breeder to stop trading with a biological research lab). In the more common section 2 case, where D harasses a single victim (s1(1)), this additional intention is *not* required.

Defences for s2
With such a broadly defined offence it is important to consider any defences that D might have to avoid liability.[128] A specific defence is provided by section 1(3), specifying three cases where no course of conduct will be found:

(3) Subsection (1) or (1A) does not apply to a course of conduct if the person who pursued it shows—

  (a) that it was pursued for the purpose of preventing or detecting crime,

  (b) that it was pursued under any enactment or rule of law or to comply with any condition or requirement imposed by any person under any enactment, or

  (c) that in the particular circumstances the pursuit of the course of conduct was reasonable.

A) **Defence 1(3)(a)**: This defence seems tolerably clear. Although the defence is predominantly intended to protect the police and other law enforcement agencies, it can also be used by others, such as investigative journalists, and even members of the public. However, particularly where the defence is raised by non-officials, the court will closely scrutinise whether such conduct was required.[129]

B) **Defence 1(3)(b)**: This defence is also relatively uncontroversial, protecting free speech and expression, for example through public demonstrations.[130]

C) **Defence 1(3)(c)**: This defence is more problematic, and more difficult to define.[131] The defence requires D to prove (on the balance of probabilities) that her harassing course of conduct was *reasonable* for her to pursue in the circumstances. For the court, particularly in protest-related cases, this will mean difficult policy decisions regarding the reasonableness of protest that causes others alarm or distress.[132]

Alongside these specific defences, the *general defences* must also be considered. We discuss these in **Chapters 13** and **14**.

---

[128] Discussed in *Hayes v Willoughby* [2013] UKSC 17.
[129] *Howlett v Holding* (2006) The Times, 8 February: D conducted a campaign against V, a local councillor, by flying banners from his aircraft referring to her in abusive terms.
[130] *Huntingdon Life Sciences v Curtin* (1997) The Times, 11 December.
[131] *Baron v DPP* (13 June 2000).
[132] *Debnath* [2006] 2 Cr App R 25.

7.9.1.2 PHA 1997, s4: causing fear of violence

Section 4 criminalises D's course of conduct that not only causes harassment to a particular V, but *also* leads to a fear that violence will be used against V (see **Table 7.9**):

(1) A person whose course of conduct causes another to fear, on at least two occasions, that violence will be used against him is guilty of an offence if he knows or ought to know that his course of conduct will cause the other so to fear on each of those occasions.

(2) For the purposes of this section, the person whose course of conduct is in question ought to know that it will cause another to fear that violence will be used against him on any occasion if a reasonable person in possession of the same information would think the course of conduct would cause the other so to fear on that occasion.

Table 7.9 PHA 1977, s4

Section 4	Actus reus	Mens rea
Conduct element	Any course of conduct that causes the result	Voluntary
Circumstance element	V is a person	Knowledge
Result element	Harassment of V	Know or ought to have known
	V fears violence will be used against him	Know or ought to have known

Actus reus of s4

Section 4 shares many of the same actus reus elements as section 2, with the addition that D must cause V to fear that violence will be used against her. Section 4 is the more serious offence and carries the higher maximum sentence: five years' imprisonment on indictment, as opposed to six months for a summary conviction under section 2.

The requirement that D causes V to fear that violence will be used against her is therefore central to the more serious section 4 offence. In many ways, this is a similar requirement to the one explored earlier in relation to assault. Thus, although 'violence' is not defined in the PHA, it is clear that V must anticipate that she personally will come to harm, and it is not sufficient if V *only* anticipates violence to another.[133] It will be sufficient, though, where D's threats made to another lead V to indirectly fear for her own safety.[134] However, it is important to note that, unlike the required anticipation of *imminent* violence for assault, no such imminence is required for section 4.

---

[133] *Henley* [2000] Crim LR 582: D harassed V and his family, including threats to kill. The trial judge wrongly failed to direct the jury that V must fear violence to himself and that foreseeing violence to others *only* is insufficient for s4.

[134] Ibid. See also *Caurti v DPP* [2002] Crim LR 131 and commentaries.

The requirement of 'harassment' (defined earlier) is not explicit in the text of section 4 and many have argued that, with section 4 requiring D to cause a fear of violence, it is unnecessary. However, a series of decisions have made clear that harassment *is* an essential result element within section 4.[135] This means that harassment must be considered.[136] However, as causing a fear of violence will also *generally* cause alarm or distress (harassment), the addition of the harassment requirement is unlikely to cause significant problems/narrowing.

Finally, and also in common with section 2, it must be demonstrated that both of these result elements were caused by D's 'course of conduct' (defined earlier). An isolated event, no matter how serious, will not be sufficient. Rather, a course of conduct requires the causing of harassment and the fear of violence on at least two occasions. It should be noted that, unlike the section 2 offence, a course of conduct under section 4 will only be satisfied where it is focused on a single V. Thus, multiple acts directed at different Vs (caught within section 2 through section 1(1A)), will not be sufficient for section 4.

Mens rea of s4

As with the section 2 offence, D is not required to intend or even to foresee a possibility that her course of conduct will cause harassment and a fear of violence. Rather, it is sufficient mens rea if a reasonable person, imbued with any special knowledge D has, would have known that the course of conduct would cause those results.

Defences for s4

As with section 2, there are a set of specific defences set out within the PHA that apply to section 4:

> (3) It is a defence for a person charged with an offence under this section to show that—
>
> > (a) his course of conduct was pursued for the purpose of preventing or detecting crime,
> >
> > (b) his course of conduct was pursued under any enactment or rule of law or to comply with any condition or requirement imposed by any person under any enactment, or
> >
> > (c) the pursuit of his course of conduct was reasonable for the protection of himself or another or for the protection of his or another's property.

The defences in section 4(3)(a) and (b) largely mirror those already discussed in relation to section 2: where D is attempting to prevent/detect crime, and where D is acting in accordance with a rule of law. However, the third specific defence in section 4(3)(c) contains an important difference. Although the corresponding defence to section 2 allows *any* reasonable excuse to act as a defence, in relation to section 4, D's reasonable conduct will only be a defence where it is directed at protecting herself or another or for the protection of property. This represents a significant narrowing of the defence in light of the more harmful conduct that D has completed to come within section 4.

Alongside these specific defences, the general defences must also be considered. We discuss these in **Chapters 13** and **14.**

---

135 eg *Curtis* [2010] EWCA Crim 123.
136 *Widdows* [2011] EWCA Crim 1500: D's conviction for s4 quashed because the trial judge failed to make clear in summing up that harassment was required. However, see *Haque* [2011] EWCA Crim 1871: D's conviction was safe despite a similar failure.

7.9.1.3 New stalking offences

Although the harassment offences in section 2 and section 4 of the PHA have been employed to tackle stalking, following a media campaign that led to an Independent Parliamentary Inquiry into Stalking Law Reform,[137] new specific stalking offences have been created.[138] The report concluded that since sections 2 and 4 had been interpreted so widely by the courts to include, for example, neighbourhood disputes, they were no longer fit for purpose in relation to stalking. The new offences are therefore designed to build upon the current section 2 and 4 offences, but to include additional offence elements that expose the full extent of the harm associated with stalking as opposed to simple harassment.

The new offences, sections 2A and 4A of the PHA, came into force from November 2012.[139] The new offences do not replace sections 2 and 4. Rather, where D commits an offence under section 2 or 4, and D's course of conduct includes acts or omissions 'associated with stalking', D may now be alternatively liable under one of the new offences. Despite the additional circumstance element, the maximum sentences for the two new offences will be the same as those under sections 2 and 4.

An exact definition of the additional element is not provided within the statute. However, section 2A(3) does provide a number of illustrative examples intended to aid the court's interpretation:

> (3) The following are examples of acts or omissions which, in particular circumstances, are ones associated with stalking—
>
> (a) following a person,
>
> (b) contacting, or attempting to contact, a person by any means,
>
> (c) publishing any statement or other material—
>
>   (i) relating or purporting to relate to a person, or
>
>   (ii) purporting to originate from a person,
>
> (d) monitoring the use by a person of the internet, email or any other form of electronic communication,
>
> (e) loitering in any place (whether public or private),
>
> (f) interfering with any property in the possession of a person,
>
> (g) watching or spying on a person.

Interestingly, the PHA does not specify any corresponding mens rea element in relation to this requirement. Thus, as long as D's course of conduct includes acts or omissions that are associated with stalking, there is no requirement for D to have realised that this was the case.

The structure of the new section 2A offence is set out in **Figure 7.3**.

---

[137] Justice Unions' Parliamentary Group, 'Independent Parliamentary Inquiry into Stalking Law Reform: Main Findings and Recommendations', February 2012.

[138] Gowland, 'Protection from Harassment Act 1997: The "New" Stalking Offences' (2013) 77 JCrimL 387.

[139] The amendments to the PHA were included in the Protection of Freedoms Act 2012, ss111–112.

Figure 7.3 PHA 1997, s2A

The structure of the new s4A offence is set out in Figure 7.4.

Figure 7.4 PHA 1997, s4A

Due to a late parliamentary amendment, the section 4A offence (but *not* the section 2A offence) can *also* be committed through an alternative construction. Thus, although most of the elements of section 4 are also required for section 4A, the requirement that V must fear violence has been broadened considerably. This is set out in section 4A(1)(b):

(b) either—

    (i) causes another ('B') to fear, on at least two occasions, that violence will be used against B, or

    (ii) causes B serious alarm or distress which has a substantial adverse effect on B's usual day-to-day activities.

This extension was felt necessary because using section 4 as the base offence was believed to be overly restrictive: it would not have allowed for a stalking conviction under section 4A where V did not anticipate physical attack but was nevertheless caused substantial distress.

The statute does not provide a definition of what constitutes 'serious alarm or distress' or a 'substantial adverse effect on B's usual day-to-day activities'. This will be left to the courts, with the potential to be interpreted very widely indeed. As for mens rea, as with a charge based on V fearing violence, it is clear that D's mens rea as to section 4A(1)(b)(ii) is also satisfied by knowledge that such results will be caused, or by the fact that a reasonable person, imbued with any special knowledge D may have, would have known.[140]

This alternative structure for section 4A is set out in **Figure 7.5**.

---

140 PHA, s4A(3).

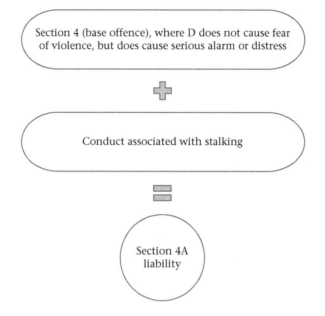

Figure 7.5 Alternative route to PHA 1997, s4A

Defences for s2A and s4A

As we have already observed, the section 2A and 4A offences are very similar to the section 2 and 4 offences discussed previously, the major difference being that the new stalking offences also require D's course of conduct to include conduct associated with stalking. Consistent with this observation, the specific defences discussed earlier in relation to the section 2 and 4 offences are also capable of negating liability for the section 2A and 4A offences. Thus, for section 2A (as with section 2), if D acts with one of the intentions listed in section 1(3) then this will negate her liability for the course of conduct. Equally, for section 4A (as with section 4), if D acts with one of the intentions listed in section 4(3)[141] she will also avoid liability.

Alongside these specific defences, the general defences must also be considered. We discuss these in **Chapters 13** and **14**.

7.9.2 Racially or religiously aggravating elements

Where D's violence has been motivated by hatred towards a particular racial or religious group, it has always been open to the court to reflect this aggravating factor at the sentencing stage.[142] However, first the Crime and Disorder Act 1998 (in relation to race) and then the Anti-Terrorism Crime and Security Act 2001 (amending the Crime and Disorder Act in relation to religion) have adapted these aggravating factors and

---

141 This time the defences that are also explicitly repeated in s4A(4).
142 Walters, 'Conceptualizing "Hostility" for Hate Crime Law: Minding "the Minutiae" When Interpreting Section 28(1)(a) of the Crime and Disorder Act 1998' (2014) 34 OJLS 47; Burney, 'Using the Law of Racially Aggravated Offences' [2003] Crim LR 28; Malik, 'Racist Crime: Racially Aggravated Offences in the Crime and Disorder Act 1998' (1999) 62 MLR 409.

made them elements of a new species of offences. Although somewhat controversial,[143] these offences are now a fully established part of the law. Indeed, the Law Commission has recently recommended expanding the categories to include aggravation based on disability, sexual orientation, and transgender.[144]

D commits one of these 'aggravated offences' when she perpetrates one of the offences discussed earlier (assault and battery; section 47 OAPA; section 20 OAPA; or harassment or stalking[145]), *and* she satisfies one of the additional racially or religiously aggravating elements. Thus, for example, what would be a conviction for assault or harassment becomes a conviction for racially aggravated assault or religiously aggravated harassment. In each case involving offences against the person, the aggravated version of the relevant base offence has a maximum sentence that is increased by between one and two years.

The offences are stated in sections 29[146] and 32[147] of the Crime and Disorder Act 1998. However, it is section 28 that sets out the requirements for racial or religious aggravation:

(1) An offence is racially or religiously aggravated for the purposes of sections 29 to 32 below if—

    (a) at the time of committing the offence, or immediately before or after doing so, the offender demonstrates towards the victim of the offence hostility based on the victim's membership (or presumed membership) of a racial or religious group; or

    (b) the offence is motivated (wholly or partly) by hostility towards members of a racial or religious group based on their membership of that group.

Section 28 thereby creates two separate forms of aggravating element: actus reus-based (s28(1)(a)), and mens rea-based (s28(1)(b)). D's base offence need only satisfy *one* of these to become an aggravated offence.

7.9.2.1 Aggravated through actus reus

The first species of aggravating element is where, *regardless of D's mens rea*, her actions at the time of committing the base offence (eg assault) objectively demonstrate hostility towards a racial or religious group. In this manner, even where D's base offence is not motivated by racial or religious hostility as, for example, where D is angry after V took her parking space, if D acts so as to display such hostility in the course of her offence then she is caught by the aggravated form of liability. The question in each case will be whether D's demonstration of hostility is linked to her base offence. This was discussed in *Babbs*.

---

[143] We may question, eg, why 'race' and 'religion' should be singled out from other deplorable motives that continue to be taken into account at sentencing only (eg hostility towards sexual orientation and disability, Criminal Justice Act 2003, s146). Sir John Smith, commenting on *Pal* [2000] Crim LR 757, went so far as to say 'it is deplorable that the government is able to find time for ill-considered, "politically correct" legislation of this kind.'

[144] Law Commission, *Hate Crime: Should the Current Offences be Extended?* (No 348, 2014).

[145] There is no need for aggravation for s18 which carries the maximum life sentence.

[146] In relation to assault and battery, s47 and s20 OAPA.

[147] In relation to harassment and stalking.

Babbs [2007] EWCA Crim 2737

D racially abused V in a takeaway restaurant, and a scuffle broke out. Some minutes later, after D had received his food, he then headbutted V. D was charged with racially aggravated assault relating to the headbutt.

- Crown Court: guilty of aggravated assault.
- Court of Appeal: conviction upheld on appeal. Despite the delay between the racial abuse and the assault, there was sufficient proximity for the prosecution to stand.[148]

This form of aggravating element is very broad in its reach, attaching increased liability where a base offence is simply accompanied by, rather than inspired by, hostile comment or action. This was intended by its drafters who feared that proving racial or religious hatred as a sole motive would be too difficult for the prosecution. However, it has also drawn criticism, particularly when other forms of hate will have no such effect, for example where D assaults V whilst calling him a 'fat bastard'.[149] As the statute matures it will be interesting to see if it has the effect of deterring people from racist language or whether (as has been feared) it may harden the racist attitudes of those convicted.[150]

The structure of the offence is set out in **Figure 7.6**.

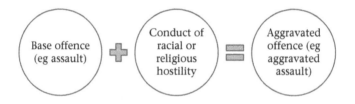

Figure 7.6 Aggravated liability (AR)

7.9.2.2 Aggravated through mens rea

The second species of aggravating element is based on D's mens rea. Set out in section 28(1)(b), D is liable for the more serious offence if her commission of the base offence (eg assault) was *motivated* by racial or religious hostility. This second aggravating element is much narrower and less controversial than that in section 28(1)(a).

Although D must be motivated by racial or religious hostility to come within this form of aggravation, as in *Kendall v DPP*, such hostility need not be her sole motivation.

---

[148] Note, however, *Parry v DPP* [2004] EWHC 3112 (Admin), where a 20-minute delay was held to be too long.

[149] Noted by Maurice Kay J.

[150] Burney and Rose, 'Racially Aggravated Offences: How is the Law Working?' [2002] HORS 244.

Kendall v DPP [2008] EWHC 1848 (Admin)

D attached posters in public places with photos of illegal immigrants who had recently been found guilty of murder, with the heading 'Illegal Immigrant Murder Scum'. The posters also advertised the British National Party. D was charged with a public order offence, including racial aggravation under section 28(1)(b).

- Magistrates' court: guilty of aggravated offence.
- High Court: conviction upheld on appeal. As long as D was partially motivated by racial hostility, it does not matter that he may have had other motives as well.

Racial or religious hostility must, however, form *part* of D's motivation. In *DPP v Howard*[151] D was charged using section 28(1)(b) after chanting 'I'd rather be a Paki than a cop' at his neighbours who were white police officers. Despite D's abusive language, it was held that he could not be liable using section 28(1)(b): there was no evidence to demonstrate that D's words were *motivated* by hostility towards people from Pakistan, and rather more to suggest that his sole motivation was the personal dislike of his neighbours.[152]

The structure of the aggravated offence is set out in **Figure 7.7**.

Figure 7.7 Aggravated liability (MR)

7.9.2.3 Defining terms

The terms 'race' and 'religion' are core to both species of aggravating element. However, neither is defined with any detail within the Crime and Disorder Act.[153]

A) 'Race' and racial group have been interpreted by the courts in an extremely broad and non-technical manner. It will include nationality (including citizenship), ethnic origin and colour.[154] Race will also include non-inclusive expressions, so D will have demonstrated racial hostility if she refers to V as 'foreign' or 'non-white'.[155]

---

[151] [2008] EWHC 608 (Admin).

[152] Moses LJ cautioned: 'Prosecutors should be careful not to deploy [s28(1)(b)] where offensive words have been used, but in themselves have not in any way been the motivation for the particular offence with which a defendant is charged. It diminishes the gravity of this offence to use it in circumstances where it is unnecessary to do so and where plainly it cannot be proved', [12].

[153] Partial definitions are provided. The Crime and Disorder Act 1998, s28(4) and (5).

[154] This can create problems for the court, eg *White* [2001] Crim LR 576.

[155] *Rogers* [2007] UKHL 8.

B) 'Religious group' is defined in the Act simply as a group of persons defined by reference to religious belief or lack of religious belief. As with the interpretation of 'race', and that employed in relation to Article 9 ECHR, it is likely that 'religion' will be interpreted widely. Non-inclusive terms such as 'unbeliever' will also qualify as religious hostility.[156]

In cases of racial and religious hostility the accuracy of D's assumptions about V's racial or religious status is irrelevant. So, where D calls V a 'Paki' when V is from India, the element of the offence is committed.[157] Equally, racial and religious hostility can be evident even where D and V are of the same racial or religious group. And, finally, it has been held that such hostility does not require V to be aware of D's actions, or even be present at the time.[158]

7.9.2.4 Defences to the aggravated offences

There are no *specific* defences that apply solely to these aggravated offences. However, as each of these offences will include a base offence (eg assault), any specific defences that apply to those base offences (discussed earlier) will also undermine liability for the aggravated offence. The general defences should also be considered. We discuss these in **Chapters 13** and **14**.

7.9.3 Torture and slavery

Conduct constituting torture and/or slavery is already criminalised without reference to the specific offences. Where D causes bodily harm, for example, we could employ one of the non-fatal offences from the first category discussed earlier. Equally, where V is not harmed beyond subjection to non-consensual captivity, we have the offence of false imprisonment.[159] However, specific offences of torture and slavery have been created. This is because, as with other overlapping offences, specific offences enable defendants to be labelled more appropriately, to provide a clear social message that such conduct represents a serious wrong, as well as demonstrating compatibility with ECHR rights.

7.9.3.1 Torture

A specific torture offence was created by section 134 of the Criminal Justice Act 1988, carrying a maximum sentence of life imprisonment (see **Table 7.10**). The offence is designed in accordance with Article 3 ECHR.

134. A public official or person acting in an official capacity, whatever his nationality, commits the offence of torture if in the United Kingdom or elsewhere he intentionally inflicts severe pain or suffering on another in the performance or purported performance of his official duties.

---

[156] *DPP v M* [2004] EWHC 1453 (Admin).
[157] *Rogers* [2007] UKHL 8.
[158] *Dykes v DPP* [2008] EWHC 2775 (Admin).
[159] *Pearson-Gaballonie* [2007] EWCA Crim 3504.

Table 7.10 Criminal Justice Act 1988, s134

Section 134	Actus reus	Mens rea
Conduct element	Any conduct causing the result	Voluntary
Circumstance element	V is a person	Knowledge
	D is acting, or purporting to act, in an official capacity	Intention
Result element	V suffers severe pain or suffering	Intention

7.9.3.2 Slavery

A specific slavery offence was created by section 71 of the Coroners and Justice Act 2009, carrying a maximum sentence of 14 years' imprisonment (see **Table 7.11**). The offence is designed in accordance with Article 4 ECHR.

(1) A person (D) commits an offence if—

    (a) D holds another person in slavery or servitude and the circumstances are such that D knows or ought to know that the person is so held, or

    (b) D requires another person to perform forced or compulsory labour and the circumstances are such that D knows or ought to know that the person is being required to perform such labour.

(2) In subsection (1) the references to holding a person in slavery or servitude or requiring a person to perform forced or compulsory labour are to be construed in accordance with Article 4 of the Human Rights Convention (which prohibits a person from being held in slavery or servitude or being required to perform forced or compulsory labour).

Table 7.11 Coroners and Justice Act 2009, s71

Section 71	Actus reus	Mens rea
Conduct element	Any conduct causing the result	Voluntary
Circumstance element	V is a person	Knowledge
Result element	V is held in slavery or servitude	Knew *or* ought to have known
	Or	
	V performs forced or compulsory labour (in line with Art 4 ECHR)	Knew *or* ought to have known

7.9.3.3 Defences to torture and slavery

There are no *specific* defences to either of these offences. The general defences should be considered, particularly if D lacks capacity. However, these are also unlikely to apply. We discuss the general defences in **Chapters 13** and **14**.

7.9.4 Administering poison

Sections 23 and 24 of the OAPA 1861 create two specific poisoning offences. In addition to more specific labelling, these offences are designed to close a potential gap in the law: as poisoning is often non-violent, D's conduct will, for example, lack the assault or battery essential to section 47 of the OAPA.[160]

7.9.4.1 OAPA 1861, s23: administering poison so as to endanger life or cause GBH

Section 23 represents the more serious poisoning offence, punishable with a maximum of ten years' imprisonment (see **Table 7.12**):

> 23. Whosoever shall unlawfully and maliciously administer to or cause to be administered to or taken by any other person any poison or other destructive or noxious thing, so as thereby to endanger the life of such person, or so as thereby to inflict upon such person any grievous bodily harm, shall be guilty of [an offence] and being convicted thereof shall be liable...to [imprisonment] for any term not exceeding ten years...

Table 7.12 OAPA 1861, s23

Section 23	Actus reus	Mens rea
Conduct element	Any conduct causing the result	Voluntary
Circumstance element	V is a person	Knowledge
Result element	V takes or is administered a noxious thing	Reckless
	V's life is endangered or V suffers GBH	None beyond recklessness as to some minor harm

Actus reus of s23

Two areas within the actus reus of section 23 require clarification: the alternative *methods of poisoning*; and the definition of a *noxious thing*.

A) **Method of poisoning:** Section 23 criminalises D where she acts in one of three possible ways.[161] It should be remembered, however, that nothing substantively turns on which method is employed; they all result in liability for section 23.

---

160 *Hanson* (1849) 2 Car & Kir 912.
161 For a useful overview, see *Kennedy (No 2)* [2007] UKHL 38.

(a) *D administers the noxious thing to V directly*: this is the most straightforward method, including cases where D injects V with a noxious thing, sprays it into her face, etc.[162]

(b) *D causes an innocent third party to administer the noxious thing to V*: this will cover cases where, for example, D asks X to inject V with the noxious thing (X believing that the syringe contains non-harmful medicine).

(c) *D causes V to take the noxious thing herself*: this final method has caused considerable difficulty for the courts in relation to causation: if V acts voluntarily when taking the noxious thing, when is this caused by D and when will it break the chain of causation? For the answer, our focus shifts to V's knowledge, or lack of knowledge at the time of the taking.

    (i) If V is *not* aware that the thing she is taking is noxious as, for example, where she believes she is drinking tea, then, despite V's voluntariness, the law will treat D as having *caused* the taking.[163] Thus, (c) will be satisfied.

    (ii) If V *is* aware that the thing is noxious, and makes a free and informed decision to take it, this will break the chain of causation from D and point (c) will not be satisfied. This point was finally settled by the House of Lords in *Kennedy (No 2)*.[164] In this case, D was charged with constructive act manslaughter (based on section 23 poisoning), having handed a syringe containing heroin to V who self-injected causing death. D was not liable under section 23, and therefore not liable for manslaughter, because he had not *caused* V to take the heroin.

  B) **Noxious thing:** When defining a noxious thing, some distinction should be drawn between substances that are noxious per se, such as arsenic and other materials that will commonly lead to death, and those that are potentially noxious when administered in certain circumstances, such as when taken in large quantities.

(a) Where a substance is noxious *per se*, this requirement will be satisfied irrespective of whether D has administered a sufficient quantity to risk harm to V (eg not enough arsenic in the tea), and irrespective of whether V may have some resistance that makes the substance less harmful (eg having built up a resistance from regular use).[165]

(b) *Potentially* noxious substances have been interpreted widely. The court in *Marcus*,[166] for example, stated that '"noxious" mean[s] something different in quality from and of less importance than poison or other destructive things', going on to quote the *Shorter Oxford Dictionary* definition that includes the terms 'injurious, hurtful, harmful, unwholesome'. The court also made it clear that, although a substance may be harmless in small quantities, it will be held as noxious if it is administered in sufficient quantities to endanger life or cause GBH, or to injure, aggrieve, or annoy in the context of section 24.

With this expansive definition in mind, where the substance administered has caused V's life to be endangered or GBH (or injury, grievance, or annoyance in the context of section 24), it is difficult to see how the court could not also conclude that it was noxious.

---

[162] *Gillard* (1988) 87 Cr App R 189: spraying into V's face.

[163] *Harley* (1830) 4 C & P 369; *Dale* (1852) 6 Cox CC 14.

[164] [2007] UKHL 38. See **2.7.2.3**.

[165] *Kennedy (No 2)* [2007] UKHL 38: heroin was considered noxious despite the tolerance built up through addiction.

[166] [1981] 1 WLR 774.

Mens rea of s23

Mens rea for the result element consists of two requirements, both arising from the term 'maliciously'. First, D must intend or be reckless as to the method used. D must foresee a risk that her actions will cause the administration/taking of the noxious thing and go on unreasonably to take the risk. Secondly, as before, maliciously has been interpreted to require D to foresee some risk of bodily harm.[167] However, no fault is required as to V's suffering of life endangerment or GBH.[168] This contrasts with the section 24 offence where D must act with 'intent to' bring about the harms suffered by V.[169]

7.9.4.2 OAPA 1861, s24: administering poison intending to injure, aggrieve, or annoy

Section 24 represents the less serious poisoning offence, punishable with a maximum of five years' imprisonment (see **Table 7.13**).

24. Whosoever shall unlawfully and maliciously administer to or cause to be administered to or taken by any other person any poison or other destructive or noxious thing, with intent to injure, aggrieve, or annoy such person, shall be guilty of a misdemeanor, and being…convicted thereof shall be liable to be kept in penal servitude…

Table 7.13 OAPA 1861, s24

Section 24	Actus reus	Mens rea
Conduct element	Any conduct causing the result	Voluntary
Circumstance element	V is a person	Knowledge
Result element	V takes or is administered a noxious thing	Reckless
Ulterior mens rea element		Intention to injure, aggrieve, or annoy

Actus reus of s24

D must again expose V to a noxious thing. This has already been discussed in relation to section 23. However, there is no requirement that this exposure should lead to life endangerment or GBH, or indeed to any harm at all.[170]

---

[167] *Cunningham* [1957] 2 QB 396: D damaged a gas meter, causing gas to seep into the neighbouring houses and endangering life.

[168] *Cato* [1976] 1 WLR 110.

[169] This is extraordinary: a less culpable state of mind is required for the more serious offence (s23) than the less serious (s24).

[170] Ashworth, 'Defining Criminal Offences without Harm' in Smith (ed), *Criminal Law Essays in Honour of JC Smith* (1987), 13.

Mens rea of s24

Alongside mens rea elements already discussed in relation to section 23, section 24 also requires ulterior intention to 'injure, aggrieve, or annoy'. It will be remembered that *ulterior* intention is mens rea that does not correspond to an element in the actus reus—thus D must intend it, but whether it is caused is irrelevant to her liability. In this manner, D's *motives* become central. For example, if a paedophile administers drugs to a child in order to facilitate sexual offences, then she has intent to injure and satisfies the ulterior mens rea. However, if a parent administers a drug to their child in order to keep them awake to see fireworks or to stay up for the other parent to return from work then, although we may question D's conduct, the ulterior mens rea will not be satisfied.[171]

7.9.4.3 Defences to s23 and s24

As with several of the offences against the person, there will be a specific defence where V provided valid consent or D believed that V provided valid consent. As the issue of consent here relates to substances that have the potential to cause bodily harm, the precedent from *Brown* must be applied. Thus, to be legally valid, V's consent must be *both* effective[172] and come within one of the recognised categories.[173] It is difficult to envisage how many of the recognised categories could apply in the context of poisoning.[174] However, it is certainly possible in relation to medicine, so there will be no poisoning offence where a doctor consensually administers an anaesthetic for surgery, even where V reacts to the anaesthetic and suffers serious harm. The general defences should also be considered. We discuss these in **Chapters 13** and **14**.

7.10 Reform

With much of the law in this area still governed by the OAPA of *1861*, it is perhaps unsurprising that there have been several calls for reform going beyond piecemeal amendments.[175] The Law Commission, for example, has described the law as 'defective on grounds both of effectiveness and of justice'.[176]

The following discussion aims to provide a brief overview of some of the most pressing areas of potential reform. These include:

- the case for modernisation and re-codification;

---

[171] Examples from *Hill* (1986) 83 Cr App R 386. For a borderline case, see, *Weatherall* [1968] Crim LR 115: D put a sleeping tablet in V's drink to enable him to search her handbag for proof of adultery. Held: there was insufficient evidence of intent to injure, aggrieve, or annoy.

[172] See **7.3.2.2**.

[173] See **7.8.2**.

[174] It has even been suggested that poisoning can *never* come within one of these exceptions (*Cato* [1976] 1 WLR 110).

[175] Genders, 'Reform of the Offences against the Person Act: Lessons from the Law in Action' [1999] Crim LR 689.

[176] Law Commission, *Legislating the Criminal Code: Offences Against the Person and General Principles* (Consultation 122, 1992).

- the controversial status of constructive liability; and
- the meaning and role of consent.

> *Assessment matters...*
> Try to think about these topics as they could relate to essay-type questions. Think about which posi-
> tions/ideas you agree with and, more importantly, why you think they are the more convincing. It is
> this second part in particular that your examiners want you to discuss.

7.10.1 Modernisation and re-codification

With regard to modernisation and re-codification, it is useful to separate our discussion of the first category of non-fatal offences (result-focused) and the second category
(conduct-focused).

7.10.1.1 Result-focused offences (ladder of harms)

Several attempts at re-codification and rationalisation have been made in this area,
including within both the 1985 and 1989 Draft Criminal Codes.[177] The Home Office,
Consultation Paper on Violence,[178] outlined a structured hierarchy (ladder) of offences
which the Law Commission has recently reconsidered in its scoping consultation
paper[179] follows:

1 (1) A person is guilty of an offence if he intentionally causes serious injury to another.

   (2) A person is guilty of an offence if he omits to do an act which he has a duty to do at common
       law, the omission results in serious injury to another, and he intends the omission to have
       that result...

   (3) A person guilty of an offence under this section is liable on conviction on indictment to
       imprisonment for life.

2 (1) A person is guilty of an offence if he recklessly causes serious injury to another . . .

   (2) A person guilty of an offence under this section is liable—

       (a) on conviction on indictment, to imprisonment for a term not exceeding 7 years;

3 (1) A person is guilty of an offence if he intentionally or recklessly causes injury to another....

   (2) A person guilty of an offence under this section is liable—

       (a) on conviction on indictment, to imprisonment for a term not exceeding 5 years;

4 (1) A person is guilty of an offence if—

       (a) he intentionally or recklessly applies force to or causes an impact on the body of
           another, or

---

177 Law Commission, *Codification of the Criminal Law: A Report to the Law Commission* (No 143,
    1985); Law Commission, *A Criminal Code for England and Wales* (2 vols) (No 177, 1989). See also
    Law Commission, *Legislating the Criminal Code: Offences Against the Person and General Prin-
    ciples* (Consultation 122, 1992); Law Commission, *Offences Against the Person and General
    Principles* (No 218, 1993).
178 (1998). See Smith, 'Offences Against The Person: The Home Office Consultation Paper' [1998]
    Crim LR 317.
179 No 217 (2014).

    (b) he intentionally or recklessly causes the other to believe that any such force or impact is imminent.

  (2) No such offence is committed if the force or impact, not being intended or likely to cause injury, is in the circumstances such as is generally acceptable in the ordinary conduct of daily life and the defendant does not know or believe that it is in fact unacceptable to the other person.

  (3) A person guilty of an offence under this section is liable on summary conviction to imprisonment for a term not exceeding 6 months or a fine not exceeding level 5 on the standard scale or both.

15 (1) In this Act 'injury' means—

    (a) physical injury, or

    (b) mental injury.

Several benefits within the proposed scheme can help to remind us of problems in the current law, as well as the relatively easy manner in which many could be resolved.

A) **Clear/modern language:** Unlike the current law where the courts are required to interpret and translate terms such as 'maliciously', 'inflict', and 'grievous', the language proposed in this scheme is simple and comprehensible. This provides clarity not only for the court but also for the public whose behaviour is intended to be guided by the law. It has been argued that reform should go even further in this regard, specifying types of harm, such as disables, disfigures, or dismembers in order to provide a clearer message and label.[180] The proposals also explicitly cater for mental injury (s15).

B) **Clear hierarchy/ladder in punishments:** It is a common criticism of the OAPA that offences under sections 47 and 20 have the same maximum sentence despite section 20 involving a more serious actus reus (GBH as opposed to ABH) and a more serious mens rea (recklessness as to some harm as opposed to simple assault or battery). The proposed scheme, from the most serious section 1 offence to the least serious section 4 offence, creates a clear sentence divide between each step on the ladder.

C) **Clear hierarchy/ladder in harms:** The current law attempts to create a ladder of harms, with different offences applicable depending on the level of harm caused. However, as we highlighted, this breaks down to some extent in relation to wounding: even the prick of a small needle may count as a wound and therefore classify D's conduct alongside GBH. This was more understandable in 1861, where any wound may have risked infection and death, but it is clearly out of step with the medical realities of the modern world. The proposed scheme deals with this by talking only of 'serious injury', 'injury', and application or anticipation of 'force'.

D) **Use of constructive liability:** The proposed scheme, unlike the current law, does not employ constructive liability offences: offences where parts of D's actus reus do not require any corresponding mens rea. The controversial status of constructive liability is discussed in more detail later.

E) **Problems with section 47:** As we have discussed, there is a problem with the current law, that in order to commit an offence under section 47, D must be shown to have committed an assault or battery. This seems strange: if D *has caused* bodily harm, why condition liability on demonstrating physical contact or a fear of such contact? The equivalent offence under clause 3 in the 1998 Bill does not contain such a requirement.

---

180 Horder, 'Rethinking Non-Fatal Offences Against the Person' (1994) 14 OJLS 335.

7.10.1.2 Conduct-focused offences

In relation to conduct-focused offences against the person, debate has centred on areas where new specific offences against the person could/should be created.

One prominent example relates to the potential for a specific offence of 'domestic violence'.[181] The idea is that a new offence could better label the distinctive wrongs involved in domestic abuse (its systematic nature, the destruction of trust, etc), as well as provide a clearer social message highlighting the issue, as well as informing the public and police attitudes. However, finding a balance between the inclusion of the various species of domestic abuse on the one hand, whilst keeping the offence sufficiently focused on the distinctive wrong on the other, would be very difficult.

Another possibility, and one that has attracted considerable debate, is the potential for a specific offence targeting the reckless sexual transmission of HIV.[182] This is partly driven by perceived problems within the current law, and partly by a seeming reluctance on the part of prosecutors to charge standard non-fatal offences in such cases.[183] However, as debate in this area focuses more on HIV alone, as opposed to all sexually transmitted infections, or simply all transmission of infections, then we must also question the basis upon which the focus is justified, as well as the potential stigmatising effects that an offence of this kind may produce. The Law Commission has also included this in its latest consultation exercise.

> *Assessment matters…*
> When writing about the potential for a new offence, it is a useful exercise to try and draft the actus reus and mens rea to consider what it might look like. In doing so, think about what form of behaviour you are trying to criminalise and why.

7.10.2 Constructive liability

Constructive liability describes an offence where D must cause a particular result, but there is no requirement for corresponding mens rea. For example, section 47 requires D's acts to cause an assault or battery, and to cause V bodily harm (all actus reus). However, in terms of mens rea, D need only have fault in relation to the assault or battery. It may be that D did not intend the bodily harm element, she may not have even foreseen it as a possibility, and it may not even be that a reasonable person would have foreseen it—but her mens rea as to this element is irrelevant. Rather, the simple fact that she caused it (actus reus) is *constructed* upon her liability for assault or battery and makes her liable for the more serious section 47 offence. We see a similar construction in a number of

---

[181] Tadros, 'The Distinctiveness of Domestic Abuse: a Freedom Based Account' in Duff and Green (eds), *Defining Crimes* (2005), 119.

[182] Ormerod, 'Criminalizing HIV Transmission—Still No Effective Solutions' (2001) 30 CLWR 135; Bennett, 'Should we Criminalise HIV Transmission' in Erin and Ost (eds), *The Criminal Justice System and Health Care* (2007) 225; Weait, *Intimacy and Responsibility: The Criminalisation of HIV Transmission* (2007); Matthiesson, 'Should the Law Deal with Reckless HIV Infection as a Criminal Offence or as a Matter of Public Health?' (2010) 21 KLJ 123 (responding to *Weait*); Cherkassky, 'Being Informed: The Complexities of Knowledge, Deception and Consent when Transmitting HIV' (2010) 74 J Crim L 242.

[183] *Dica* [2004] EWCA Crim 1103; Weait, 'Criminal Law and the Transmission of HIV: *R v Dica*' (2005) 68 MLR 121; Spencer, 'Retrial for Reckless Infection' (2004) 154 NLJ 762.

the offences against the person (discussed earlier), in unlawful act manslaughter (**6.3.1**), as well as in murder (**5.4** and **5.6.2**). An extreme version of constructive liability can be seen with strict liability offences: D does not require mens rea as to any elements of the actus reus beyond the voluntariness of his acts/omissions.[184]

Constructive liability is controversial for a number of reasons, principally relating to D's lack of choice. As we discussed in **Chapter 1**, justifications for criminal law are often tied to the notion of autonomy: people should be free to act as they wish as long as they do not choose to break the law. The problem with constructive liability is that it ignores the issue of choice. Thus, for example, if D assaults or batters V and causes bodily harm, she will be liable under section 47 whether or not she chose to cause or risk the bodily harm. Not only does this conflict with the criminal law's general disposition towards subjectivism (requiring choice), but it also increases the role of luck. For example, D1 and D2 both intentionally push V1 and V2, each foreseeing no more harm than involved in simple contact. In the case of V1 this is all that results: D1 is liable for a minor battery offence. However, in the case of V2 he falls and sustains an injury: D2 is now liable for a section 47 offence. Or worse, V2 dies: D2 is now liable for unlawful act manslaughter. The liability of D1 and D2 is very different, and yet their intentions and *choices* (ie their culpability) were the same. *Is this just?*[185]

For some, of course, the answer is 'yes'. Although D2 may not have chosen to cause bodily injury or to kill, as in the example above, that is what her actions have caused. Indeed, although we may not wish to criminalise accidents, by choosing to commit the battery on V (the push), D has chosen to break the criminal law and there is a persuasive argument that D has therefore changed her normative position: she has chosen to break the law and so must accept *all* of the consequences of her actions, even unforeseen/unforeseeable ones.[186]

Whether or not we accept this argument in support of constructive liability offences will play a central role in future re-codification of the offences against the person. Currently it seems that the dominant view is that constructive liability should be avoided: this is illustrated in the reform proposals outlined previously, and can also be illustrated in other jurisdictions such as the Irish Non-Fatal Offences Against the Person Act 1997.[187] However, the debate remains open.

7.10.3 Consent

V's consent, or D's belief in consent, will undermine liability for most of the non-fatal offences. However, it is also an area that has caused the court significant problems. By way of summary, the central problems identified include the following.

A) **Consent as a defence, or non-consent as an offence element:** In our earlier discussion, we have treated V's consent as a *defence*. However, the OAPA leaves open the

---

[184] Simester, *Appraising Strict Liability* (2005).

[185] Ashworth, 'The Problem of Luck' in Shute, Gardner, and Horder (eds), *Action and Value in Criminal Law* (1993) 107.

[186] Simons, 'Strict Liability in the Grading of Offences: Forfeiture, Change of Normative Position, or Moral Luck?' (2012) 32 OJLS 445; Ashworth, 'A Change of Normative Position: Determining the Contours of Culpability in Criminal Law' [2008] New Crim LR 232.

[187] This Irish statute replaces and/or codifies common law assault, as well as most of the OAPA offences formally applying in the Republic of Ireland. See Charleton, McDermott, and Bolger, *Criminal Law* (1999) paras 9.77–9.185.

possibility that non-consent could be analysed as an offence element, and this alternative has been preferred by several courts and commentators.[188] Indeed, in the leading case of *Brown*, only a bare majority of the Lords preferred to analyse consent as a defence.[189]

When the Supreme Court is next called to consider offences within the OAPA, it would be highly desirable for this point to be clarified. It is contended that analysis of non-consent as an *offence* element represents the better view. The cumulative role of offence elements is to set out a specific harmful and/or wrongful event that the criminal law wishes to prevent and punish. D may be able to rely on a defence to excuse or justify her conduct, or to excuse her from liability, but the criminal event is still regrettable. In relation to V's non-consent, we believe that this requirement is an essential part to the *wrong* within the offences against the person. If V provides valid consent (eg in the context of contact sports), D is not committing a wrong that relies on a defence to justify or excuse it. Equally, when we come into consensual contact with others in our daily life, we are not committing wrongs that require justification. Rather, we believe that such conduct is only wrongful in the absence of consent and, thus, V's non-consent must form part of the offence elements rather than a defence.[190]

> *The two options for interpretation...*
>
> • *Offence*: requires (a) non-consent in fact and (b) a lack of belief in consent.
>
> • *Defence*: satisfied by (a) consent in fact or (b) belief in consent.
>
> On either interpretation, D's liability will always require that V does not consent and that D does not believe that consent is present.

B) **Effective consent:** Considerable work has been done to understand and define consent in relation to sexual offences.[191] However, in the context of the offences in this chapter, the meaning of consent remains elusive, ill-defined, and too often susceptible to overly broad rules.

C) **Degree of harm that can be legally consented to:** This problem arises where V is of full capacity, is informed, and has not been misled as to the anticipated harm: at what stage (if at all) should the law nevertheless say that V's consent is invalid?[192] This discussion raises difficult moral questions, and taken to its natural conclusion, will also lead to consideration of euthanasia. Whatever moral view is preferred, the approach of the current law is clearly unacceptable—particularly when we begin to explore the inconsistently applied recognised categories where valid consent is recognised, such as sports, horseplay, and sexual gratification. Particularly in relation to the latter example, people need to know the law in order to guide and model their behaviour. The fact that the current law (in cases like *Brown*) fails to provide that guidance demonstrates a clear need for reform.

---

[188] eg Lord Woolf stated in relation to assault that 'it is a requirement of the offence that the conduct itself should be unlawful': *Barnes* [2005] EWCA Crim 3246, [16].

[189] Although Lord Jauncey, Lord Lowry, and Lord Templeman analysed consent as a defence, Lord Mustill and Lord Slynn considered non-consent as part of the offence. See Shute, 'Something Old, Something New, Something Borrowed: Three Aspects of the Project' [1996] Crim LR 684.

[190] Williams, 'Consent and Public Policy' [1962] Crim LR 74.

[191] **Chapter 8.**

[192] Feinberg, *The Moral Limits of the Criminal Law, Vol 1: Harm to Others* (1984).

7.11 Eye on assessment

In this section we discuss the potential application of the offences against the person within a problem question. The same structure of analysis should be employed, as we have discussed in previous chapters.

STEP 1 Identify the potential criminal event in the facts

This is unlikely to take more than a sentence, but it is essential to tell your reader which facts of the case you are focusing on. For offences against the person, this involves pointing out where a person has been hurt (eg 'The first potential criminal event arises where Mary kicks Vicky').

STEP 2 Identify the potential offence

Having identified the facts (eg D potentially injuring V), you must now identify the offence you are going to apply.

When applying Step 2, it should be remembered that the main non-fatal offences can be viewed as a ladder, with the least serious offences (assault and battery) at the bottom and the most serious (s18 GBH) at the top. When *learning* these offences it is helpful to start at the bottom of this ladder and work up, and this approach has previously been adopted in this chapter. However, when *applying* these offences to a problem scenario, the opposite approach should be taken.

If we apply these offences to a problem in the same order we learnt them (bottom up), then we end up with rather peculiar results:

> Take the example of D who breaks V's arm by hitting her with a bat. Here, it is likely that D will have committed assault if V saw her coming, as V is likely to have apprehended non-consensual imminent violence; D will also have committed battery, as she intentionally comes into non-consensual contact with V; D will also have committed a section 47 offence, as D's assault and battery have caused harm; D will also have committed a section 20 offence, as D has caused GBH and intends to cause harm; and D will also have committed a section 18 offence, as GBH is intentionally caused.

In this manner, D satisfies the elements of each of the offences. However, as she does so through a single act (hitting V with a bat), it is inappropriate to find liability for more than one offence. Therefore, much like Russian dolls, more serious offences subsume less serious ones committed by the same action: leaving D in our example liable for a section 18 offence only. The problem with starting our discussion at the bottom of the offence ladder, therefore is that, having discussed the elements of several offences, the only one that is relevant is the last. (*A particularly serious problem if you run out of time and miss it off!*)

With this in mind, when applying the offences against the person to a problem scenario, it is advised that you should begin by exploring the most serious *potential* offence first. The word potential here is important. Just as it is bad practice to discuss less serious offences when a more serious one has been committed, it is also important not to spend a long time discussing more serious offences if V has only suffered minor harm. Our recommended approach is set out in the simple flowchart at **Figure 7.8**.

Assessment matters...

Although it is useful to keep in mind the types of harm that are commonly charged, such as ABH or GBH, their broad definitions make some overlap inevitable. Further, it should be remembered that V's characteristics will also play a role—what is GBH to a child, for example, might not be for an adult. Therefore, if in doubt, for example, tell your reader what the result would be 'if the court find the level of harm to be GBH' or 'if the court finds the level of harm to be ABH'.

Figure 7.8 Problem question flowchart for offences against the person

Having highlighted the potential criminal event (Step 1), you should assess the level of harm caused to V in order to identify the relevant entry point to the flowchart in **Figure 7.8** (A, B, or C). Having identified the relevant entry point, this tells you the most serious potential offence that D may have committed (Step 2) (eg section 18 in relation to GBH, section 47 for bodily harm, etc). In line with the flowchart, the next step is to assess D's liability for that offence.

> **STEP 3 Applying the offence to the facts**
>
> Actus reus: What does the offence require? Did D do it?
> Mens rea: What does the offence require? Did D possess it?

If D does not satisfy the elements of the most serious potential offence (eg lacks mens rea for section 18), then you should go on to consider the next possible offence down the ladder. Continue this until you find an offence that D satisfies, or you conclude that D has not committed one of these offences. Where you find an offence that D satisfies, move to consider potential defences (both specific and general defences).

> **STEP 4 Consider defences**
>
> The word 'consider' here is important, as you should not discuss every defence for every question. Rather, think whether there are any defences (eg consent) that *could* potentially be relevant to the facts. If there are any, discuss those only.

> **STEP 5 Conclude**
>
> This is usually a single sentence either saying that it is likely that D has committed the offence, or saying that it is not likely either because an offence element is not satisfied or because a defence is likely to apply. It is not often that you will be able to say categorically whether D has committed the offence or not, so it is usually best to conclude in terms of what is more 'likely'.

> **STEP 6 Loop**
>
> Go back up to Step 1, identifying the next potential criminal event. Continue until you have discussed all the relevant potentially criminal events.

 ONLINE RESOURCE CENTRE

www.oxfordtextbooks.co.uk/orc/smithandhogan/

This chapter is accompanied by a selection of online resources to help you with this topic, including:

- **Multiple choice questions**
- **Chapter summary sheet**

- Two **sample examination questions** with answer guidance
- **Further reading**

Also available on the Online Resource Centre are:

- A selection of **videos** from the authors explaining key topics and principles
- **Legal updates**
- Useful **weblinks**

8

Sexual offences

8.1 Introduction

In common with the non-fatal offences against the person (**Chapter 7**), the core sexual offences focus predominantly on non-consensual contact. However, the additional sexual dimension within these offences makes the underlying wrongs targeted by the criminal law rather different. Within other offences against the person although all non-consensual contact is potentially criminal as at least a battery, more serious offences require that contact to have caused physical injury or a recognised psychiatric injury.[1] In contrast, even the most serious sexual offence of rape does not require injury beyond simple unlawful contact (in the case of rape that is penile penetration[2]). Rather than physical or psychiatric injury, sexual offences focus on D's invasion of V's sexual, as opposed to simply physical, autonomy. It is the intimate nature of this invasion, qualified by its nature and degree, which provides the focus for offences in this area.

Sexual offences are now almost[3] entirely codified within a single modern statute: the Sexual Offences Act 2003 (SOA 2003).[4] With previous legislation variously described as 'cumbersome and inadequate'[5] and 'archaic, incoherent and discriminatory',[6] the SOA 2003 has consolidated the law, modernised it in line with changing social attitudes,[7] as well as created a host of new offences.[8] Two aspects of this reform are particularly interesting, and usefully introduced at this point.

The first relates to the detail of the legislation. In contrast to the relative simplicity of the Fraud Act 2006, offences within the SOA 2003 are highly, some would say *excessively,*[9] detailed. As a result, focusing on the wording of the statute itself and unpacking its meaning will provide much greater assistance to understand the offences. Case law will not be as important to fill in gaps within the legislation, but it will be essential in order to interpret the language of that statute and to understand how it should be applied.

Secondly, and most importantly, there is also a trend within the substance of these offences that seems somewhat out of step with other offences against the person. As we will see later, offences within the SOA 2003 are notable for their use of very wide actus reus elements as well as the use of objective, as opposed to subjective, mens rea requirements and even strict liability.[10] For example, the mens rea for rape does not require D to intend or know that V lacks consent to sexual penetration or even foresee a risk of this non-consent or even negligently fail to foresee a risk of it. Rather, the mens rea

---

[1] See also **Chapter 7** and *Smith and Hogan's Criminal Law* (14th edn, 2015), Ch18.

[2] See **8.2**.

[3] Certain sexual offences remain outside the Sexual Offences Act 2003 (eg those relating to prostitution and indecent photographs).

[4] For background, see Home Office Papers, *Setting the Boundaries: Reforming the Law on Sexual Offences* (2000) and *Protecting the Public: Strengthening Protection Against Sex Offenders and Reforming the Law on Sexual Offences* (2002).

[5] Temkin, 'Getting it Right: Sexual Offences Law Reform' (2000) 150 NLJ 1169.

[6] Lord Falconer in HL, vol 644, col 771.

[7] Both in terms of the boundaries of criminalisation, as well as the language used to construct them.

[8] For a critique of the SOA 2003, see Rodwell, 'Problems with the Sexual Offences Act 2003' [2005] Crim LR 290.

[9] See discussion at **8.9**.

[10] Arenson, 'Rape in Victoria as a Crime of Absolute Liability' (2012) 76 J Crim L 399.

is satisfied unless D holds an objectively reasonable belief in consent.[11] The inconsistency here with other offences against the person as well as most other serious offences which typically require a minimum mens rea of subjective intention or recklessness is marked.[12] There are several possible explanations.

- It could be that this is a trend within modern legislation. However, it will be remembered that 2003 was also the year in which the House of Lords (in the case of G[13]) were championing the integral role of *subjective* mens rea within serious offences.

- It may be a reaction to the high offending rates and allegedly low conviction rates for sexual offences.[14] As sexual offences invariably take place in private, it is particularly difficult to prove to the criminal standard that D held a certain subjective mens rea state at the time of offending. However, this is also true of many offences against the person, particularly in the context of domestic abuse involving repetitive minor injuries. Also, it is arguable that procedural and evidential changes may be a more appropriate way of tackling the low conviction rate.[15]

- Another possible explanation may be the unique nature of *sexual* offending in the context of wider gender inequality. In this manner, by structuring offences using objective mens rea, the law is attempting to correct, or at least acknowledge, that inequality by punishing Ds for a failure to consider the harmful consequences of his actions. Again, the extent to which this represents a contrast to other offences against the person remains debatable.

As we go on to discuss the offences in this chapter, it is useful to keep these differences in mind. If you are convinced that sexual offending is fundamentally different from other offences against the person for one of the reasons above or for some other reason, then you should consider if these differences are accurately reflected in the law. If you are not convinced of this difference, however, then you should consider how the current inconsistency should be resolved. Should the offences against the person be structured in a more objective manner? Or, should the sexual offences be more subjective requiring proof of D's awareness of harm to find liability? This returns us to one of the fundamental debates between autonomy and welfare in criminal law introduced in **Chapter 1**.[16]

With over 143 statutory sections, and 7 schedules, the SOA 2003 contains well in excess of 50 offences focusing on several different areas (eg child sex offending; abuse of trust relationships; human trafficking; and so on). It is not practical, therefore, to discuss every one of these offences within this chapter. Our main focus will be on the first four offences within the statute: rape; assault by penetration; sexual assault; and causing a person to engage in sexual activity without consent. The central feature

---

[11] The objective requirement is softened slightly to take account of D's characteristics, but remains very wide. See **8.2.2**.

[12] Bohlander, 'Mistaken Consent to Sex, Political Correctness and Correct Policy' (2007) 71 J Crim L 412.

[13] [2003] UKHL 50.

[14] Home Office, *Setting the Boundaries* (2000) paras 2.3 and 2.8.5. For up-to-date statistics, see: www.gov.uk/government/uploads/system/uploads/attachment_data/file/214970/sexual-offending-overview-jan-2013.pdf.

[15] Lacey, 'Beset by Boundaries' [2001] Crim LR 3.

[16] See **1.4**.

within these offences is that V does not consent to the sexual activity. Following this, we will also briefly discuss three other categories of offences: offences against children under 13 (where consent is irrelevant); offences against young people under 16 (where consent is again irrelevant, but some awareness of age is required); and status and relationship-based offences (where D is abusing a position of trust). Apart from exceptional offences involving penile penetration, these offences are gender neutral: both men and women can commit and be victims.

8.2 SOA 2003, s1: rape

The offence of rape,[17] set out in section 1 of the SOA 2003, carries one of the most recognised and stigmatising labels within the criminal law.[18] The maximum sentence is life imprisonment.[19]

(1) A person (D) commits an offence if —

    (a) he intentionally penetrates the vagina, anus or mouth of another person (V) with his penis,

    (b) V does not consent to the penetration, and

    (c) D does not reasonably believe that V consents.

The elements of rape are set out in **Table 8.1**.

Table 8.1 SOA 2003, s1

	Actus reus	**Mens rea**
Conduct element	Penile penetration of V's vagina, anus or mouth	Intention
Circumstance element	V does not consent	D lacks a reasonable belief in consent
Result element	None	None

Terminology...
The offence of rape is commonly described as a conduct crime. However, if we isolate the conduct element of all crimes to bodily movement alone, it is alternatively possible to describe rape as a result crime: D's bodily movement (conduct) causing penetration (result). In this chapter, we adopt the standard description of rape as a conduct crime.

---

[17] For a comparative review of rape legislation in a range of jurisdictions, see McGlynn and Munro (eds), *Rethinking Rape Law* (2010).
[18] Discussed at **8.9**.
[19] SOA 2003, s1(4).

8.2.1 Actus reus of s1

The actus reus of rape requires the prosecution to prove that D penetrated the vagina, anus, or mouth of V with his penis, and without V's consent.

8.2.1.1 'Penile' penetration

Rape can only be committed where D penetrates V with his penis. If D uses anything other than his penis to penetrate V, he does not commit rape: although he is likely to commit an offence under section 2. The government review that led to the SOA—Sexual Offences Review—considered removing this requirement to achieve gender equality, but decided that the limitation should remain.[20] This conclusion was based on the additional risks associated with penile penetration including pregnancy; disease transmission; etc, as well as the interests of fair labelling[21] because rape is commonly understood to require penile penetration.

As a result of this requirement rape can only be committed as a principal offender by a man. Under section 79(3), a 'penis' will include a surgically constructed penis: allowing conviction where D is a post-operative transsexual. Women can be accessories to rape where they assist or encourage a man to commit rape, leading to their liability for rape, but they cannot commit the offence as a principal offender.[22]

8.2.1.2 Penetration of the vagina, anus, or mouth

As the historical wrongs of rape used to focus on the protection of virginity, the actus reus was only completed with penetration of the vagina. However, as the law has developed to protect sexual autonomy more generally, this element of the offence has expanded to include anal penetration,[23] and most recently, oral penetration.[24] Additionally, section 79(3) clarifies that 'vagina' includes a surgically constructed vagina following gender reassignment surgery. As a result of these expansions, it is now possible for a man to be the victim of rape—anally or orally.

The requirement of 'penetration' has been interpreted broadly. It is clear, for example, that penetration need not be substantial or repetitive. In the context of vaginal penetration, this requirement will be satisfied even where D's penis has only penetrated the vulva (outer part of the vagina).[25] It has also been confirmed that D's act of penetration 'is a continuing act from entry to withdrawal'.[26] This is potentially important where D penetrates V's vagina, anus, or mouth with her consent, but fails to withdraw his penis after that consent is removed.[27] A narrow interpretation of penetration (entry only) would cause a coincidence problem: at the point of penetration there is consent (no coincidence), at the time that consent is removed the penetration is complete (no coincidence). Interpreting penetration as a continuing act resolves this problem, extending

---

[20] Home Office, *Setting the Boundaries* (2000) para 2.8.4.
[21] See **1.4.2**.
[22] *Ram* (1893) 17 Cox CC 609. See **Chapter 12**.
[23] Criminal Justice and Public Order Act 1994, s142.
[24] SOA 2003, s1. *K* [2008] EWCA Crim 1923: charge does not have to specify which.
[25] SOA 2003, s79(9).
[26] SOA 2003, s79(2).
[27] *Leaver* [2006] EWCA Crim 2988. This may include where D intentionally fails to withdraw (despite having agreed to) prior to ejaculation, *F* [2013] EWHC 945 (Admin).

the conduct element to allow for the coincidence of offence elements at any time between entry and withdrawal.

8.2.1.3 Age and/or status restrictions?

Under the old law the age and/or status of D and V used to affect whether rape could be committed. This is no longer the case. As long as D is over the age of 10 (the age of criminal responsibility) he is capable of committing the offence on V of any age. Additionally, the relationship between D and V is also irrelevant; it does not matter that they are strangers, married, on a date, etc. To the shame of the criminal law, marital rape was only confirmed as rape as recently as 1991, and only through the courts.[28] However, the offence of rape post-SOA 2003 is no longer affected by these issues.

8.2.1.4 Without V's consent

Central to the offence of rape, as well as offences under sections 2, 3, and 4, is the requirement that V did not consent. For example, for rape the requirement is for proof that V has not consented to penile penetration of the vagina, anus, or mouth. The role consent plays within these offences is a fascinating area of law, and certainly a very important one, but it can also be rather challenging. It is particularly important because of its vital role within the wrongs of the offence: non-consensual penetration of this kind is one of the most serious offences within the criminal law, and yet sexual penetration *with* consent is generally considered a social good, and a positive aspect of social life.[29] In this manner, V's consent or non-consent exercises a legal and moral magic, marking the difference between extreme responses to behaviour.[30] It is partly because of its central role that the concept of consent is also challenging. When applying the requirement of non-consent within sexual offences, the law requires a robust concept that can provide clear guidance for the jury: clear guidance to make a binary decision between finding a lack of consent or not. However, as we discussed in the context of the offences against the person in **Chapter 7**, finding whether V consented or not is rarely straightforward, and will involve the weighing of a variety of factors.

> **Don't be confused...**
> In this section we are discussing the actus reus requirement of V's non-consent (ie did V freely agree to penetration?). We are not discussing D's mens rea as to that non-consent (ie did D reasonably believe that V consented?). These are separate offence elements and you should take care not to confuse them. As with all criminal offences, we will analyse actus reus elements first and then mens rea elements.

In order to analyse whether V lacked consent, satisfying this element of the actus reus, our focus is on the subjective mind of V. At the time of penetration, whatever the external indications, was V a willing participant to the sexual contact? The case of *McFall*, although decided pre-SOA 2003, illustrates this point well.[31]

---

[28] *R* [1991] 4 All ER 481. Confirmed by the ECtHR in *CR v UK* [1996] 1 FLR 434. Giles, 'Judicial Law-Making in the Criminal Courts: The Case of Marital Rape' [1992] Crim LR 407.

[29] For an alternative and extreme view, contending that all sexual penetration *is prima facie* wrongful, see Dempsey and Herring, 'Why Sexual Penetration Requires Justification' (2007) 27 OJLS 467.

[30] Hurd, 'The Moral Magic of Consent' (1996) 2 LT 168.

[31] See also *Doyle* [2010] EWCA Crim 119.

> **McFall** [1994] Crim LR 226
>
> D kidnapped V, a woman with whom he had been cohabiting. D indicated that he wanted to have sexual intercourse with V and she accepted, fearing for her safety if she refused. V pretended to consent during the act and faked enjoyment. D was charged with rape.
>
> • Crown Court: guilty of rape—despite the outwards signs, V was not subjectively consenting.
>
> • Court of Appeal: conviction upheld on appeal.

Having identified that in addressing consent we look to *the mind of V*, we still need to know how consent is defined. Pre-SOA 2003, there was no codified definition of consent and the issue was left to the common law. The approach of the courts, in line with the approach to 'consent' in the context of the offences against the person, was largely to leave the definition of consent to the common understanding of the jury,[32] and to provide some additional guidance only where issues of capacity or deception were involved. However, this approach attracted considerable criticism, with Glanville Williams highlighting the 'deplorable tendency of the criminal courts to leave important questions of legal policy to the jury':[33] the jury are not being asked to apply the facts to a legal rule with a definition of consent, they are being asked to define it as well. As a result of this, the reformers working towards the SOA 2003 made a clear and robust definition of consent one of their primary ambitions.[34]

Despite this ambition, however, the challenge of providing a precise definition of consent proved to be a near impossible one. Although a rigid definition would provide greater guidance for juries, there was too great a risk that such rigidity would lead to unfairness: the great variety and complexity of human sexual interactions mean that some discretion was essential for the jury to assess individual cases on their merits. However, there are certain cases where such discretion is not beneficial, and the law is better served by providing clear guidance to a jury that certain facts will indicate a lack of consent. With this in mind, the definition of consent within the SOA 2003 is spread across three sections:

• **Section 76:** A set of 'conclusive presumptions' about consent: sets of facts which, if proved, will be enough to establish non-consent.

• **Section 75:** A set of 'evidential presumptions' about consent: sets of facts which, if proved, require D to provide some counter evidence to prevent a finding of non-consent.

• **Section 74:** A general, less precise, definition of consent.

Alongside the general definition of consent, sections 76 and 75 are intended to provide a clear message that consent will not be present in certain circumstances, and also to remove or reduce the juries' discretion in these cases to speed up trials and help to ensure appropriate convictions. Any facts falling outside these presumptions will be dealt with using the general definition in section 74.

---

[32] *Olugboja* [1981] 3 All ER 443.

[33] Williams, *Textbook of Criminal Law* (1978) 551.

[34] Home Office, *Setting the Boundaries* (2000) Part 2.

Assessment matters...
When applying the requirement of non-consent to problem facts, always begin with the presumptions of non-consent. If your facts come within the conclusive presumptions then non-consent can be found without further discussion. If they come within the evidential presumptions then you can say a finding of non-consent is likely unless D provides some evidence to the contrary. Only go on to discuss the general definition of consent if the presumptions do not apply or where an evidential presumption is likely to be rebutted.

Conclusive presumptions of non-consent: s76

If the facts of a case come within the conclusive presumptions then the actus reus requirement of non-consent will be established without any need to consider the general definition of consent (s74). The conclusive presumptions will only apply in two circumstances:

76. (2) The circumstances are that—

    (a) the defendant intentionally deceived the complainant as to the nature or purpose of the relevant act;

    (b) the defendant intentionally induced the complainant to consent to the relevant act by impersonating a person known personally to the complainant.

Point to remember...
The 'relevant act' will differ between offences (for rape, it is the penile penetration of V's vagina, anus or mouth, for the offence under section 2 it is penetration, for section 3 it is sexual touching, etc). This is set out in section 77.

Point to remember...
Within (a) and (b), D's acts must be intentional. Thus, for example, if V was inadvertently misled as to the nature or purpose of the act or as to D's identity without D's knowledge, then the conclusive presumptions will not be engaged, and the general definition of consent will be applied.

The circumstances outlined in section 76 have emerged as a result of pre-SOA 2003 case law. Thus, to illustrate how the section is likely to be applied, some of the older case law remains a useful supplement to the growing number cases decided after the statute.

    A) **Deception as to the nature or purpose of the act:** In general terms, V is deceived as to the 'nature' of the act where she is misled as to the physical mechanics of that act; she is deceived as to the 'purpose' of the act where she is misled as to why it should happen. In certain cases, as in *Williams*, such deception will be straightforwardly apparent.

Williams [1923] 1 KB 340

In a case under the old law pre-SOA 2003, D who was a singing teacher convinced V (a 16-year-old student) to let him do something to improve her singing voice. He was, in fact, having sexual intercourse with her. D was charged with rape.

• Crown Court: guilty of rape. D's deception as to the nature and quality of the act undermined V's apparent consent.

• Court of Criminal Appeal: conviction upheld on appeal.

As D did not understand the dynamics of sexual intercourse, the court was able to find deception as to the *nature* of the act.[35] However, even if V had understood the act as sexual intercourse, she was also deceived as to the purpose of the act: it was done for D's sexual gratification and not to improve V's singing voice.[36] Thus, in either case, if decided today the conclusive presumptions in section 76 would oblige a jury to find there was no consent.

Beyond straightforward cases of this kind, however, it is important to recognise the limits of the presumptions within section 76. This is particularly important because, although the presumptions in this section are conclusive in establishing a lack of consent, the terms used within the section (ie 'nature' and 'purpose') are rather ambiguous in their application. Thus, the legal interpretations of these terms, and the limits of those interpretations, become very important.

With regard to 'nature', for example, it is now clear that if V understands the basic dynamics of the sexual act, deception as to associated risks will not be sufficient to engage the conclusive presumptions. This has arisen chiefly in relation to the risk of sexual infection, as in *Dica*.

⬚ *Dica* [2004] EWCA Crim 1103

D, knowing he was HIV-positive, had unprotected sexual intercourse with two victims, infecting both with the disease. It was clear that neither of the victims would have consented to intercourse if they had known about D's infected status.

- Crown Court: guilty of an offence against the person (not guilty of rape).
- Court of Appeal: allowed D's appeal and ordered a retrial as the issue of consent had been wrongly withdrawn from the jury. However, the court clarified that a lack of knowledge about D's infection did not amount to deception as to the 'nature' of the act. There was no rape.

As we discussed in the previous chapter,[37] *Dica* established the important principle that consent to sexual intercourse does not include consent to a risk of infection where D knew of the infection and did not inform V. This allows D to be liable for an offence against the person despite V's consent as to intercourse.[38] Following similar logic, the court *could* also have found that D's act of intercourse while knowingly infected was of a different 'nature' to that consented to by V, namely intercourse with someone not knowingly infected. This would have engaged the conclusive presumption of non-consent and made V's apparent consent ineffective: resulting in liability for rape. However, importantly, the court did *not* take this step. The issue of D's infection and his choice not to inform V may be relevant when considering consent

---

[35] See also *Flattery* (1877) 2 QBD 410, where D deceived V into thinking that the sexual penetration was a medical operation.

[36] See also *Green* [2002] EWCA Crim 1505, where D induced men to masturbate while connected to monitors as part of a bogus medical experiment. They understood the nature of the act, but were deceived as to purpose.

[37] See **7.3.2.2**.

[38] Overruling *Clarence* (1889) 22 QB 23.

under the general definition (s74),[39] but it does not affect the nature of the act: V was not deceived as to the basic physical acts of sexual intercourse—she knew that D was going to put his penis in her vagina—and so the conclusive presumptions were not engaged.

The limits of the term 'purpose' have also been addressed by the courts. For example, it is clear from *Linekar* that deception as to the purpose of the sexual act does not include deception as to V's purpose.[40]

> ### *Linekar* [1995] 2 Cr App R 49
>
> In a case under the old law pre-SOA 2003, D had sexual intercourse with V, a prostitute, having promised to pay her £25. D never intended to pay. D was charged with rape on the basis that V would not have consented if she had known D had no intention to pay.
>
> • Crown Court: guilty of rape—V's apparent consent was not effective due to D's deception.
> • Court of Appeal: appeal allowed, consent was not undermined by D's deception.

The Court of Appeal recognised that V would not have consented without the promise of payment, but held that her consent remained effective: she was not deceived as to the nature of the act (she knew he was going to penetrate her vagina with his penis) or the purpose of D doing so (for him to derive sexual gratification). Thus, when interpreting the conclusive presumptions under section 76, it is likely that deception as to the purpose of the act will only include deception as to D's and not V's purpose.

However, even accepting this clarification, the interpretation of deception as to 'D's purpose' remains ambiguous. Individual cases have brought pockets of clarity. We know, for example, that V will be deceived as to the purpose of an act if she is led to believe that it is being done for non-sexual reasons.[41] However, other cases have added to the confusion. For example, the case of *Devonauld* seems to suggest that V *is* deceived as to purpose if (despite understanding the sexual context) V is deceived as to D's motives.

> ### *Devonauld* [2008] EWCA Crim 527
>
> V (a 16-year-old boy) was involved in a relationship with V's daughter. The relationship ended and D, believing V had treated his daughter badly, sought revenge. D posed as a young woman on the internet, formed a link with V, and persuaded V to masturbate in front of a webcam. D was planning to use the video to humiliate V. D was charged with an offence under section 4 of the SOA 2003.
>
> • Crown Court: guilty of sexual offence. Section 76 presumption applied: V was deceived as to D's purpose in relation to the sexual act.
> • Court of Appeal: conviction upheld on appeal.

---

[39] *B* [2006] EWCA Crim 2945 suggests that D's status may not even be relevant to the general definition of consent. However, it is submitted that this goes too far.

[40] Reed, 'Analysis of Fraud Vitiating Consent in Rape Cases' [1995] Crim LR 310.

[41] *Green* [2002] EWCA Crim 1505.

V's apparent consent was based on the understanding that he was masturbating for the sexual gratification of a young woman. D's deception in this regard undermined the effectiveness of that consent. However, it is arguable that this result should have been achieved through the general definition of consent (s74) rather than applying the conclusive presumptions (s76). V was not deceived as to D's intention to induce sexual behaviour, he was only deceived as to D's intended sexual enjoyment of it. If this is now caught within section 76, as the case suggests, what about D who has sex with V pretending that it is an expression of love when he simply sees it as a one-night stand, or as a route to promotion?

> *Extra detail...*
>
> *Devonauld* could be seen as a case where D has mixed purposes: to induce sexual behaviour and to gain material to humiliate V. D is honest about the first, but deceives V in relation to the latter.
>
> Few cases of this kind have come before the court, but they are likely to cause problems for the application of the section 76 presumptions. For example, what if in *Green* (see **n 36**) D was genuinely performing a medical experiment (as he told the men involved), but he was also acting for personal sexual gratification (as he did not tell them)? Would the court apply the section 76 presumption (as they did in *Devonauld*)? Would they ask what D's dominant purpose was? These questions remain unanswered.

B) **Deception as to the identity of D:** The second scenario in which the conclusive presumption of non-consent will apply is where D intentionally deceives V as to his identity. The presumption will *not* apply where D pretends to have certain attributes such as a well-paid job, or even where he pretends to be someone that is not known personally to the victim (eg a celebrity). Such cases will be decided under the general definition of consent in section 74. Rather, the conclusive presumption will only apply where D intentionally and actively pretends (it is not enough that V simply got the wrong idea[42]) to be someone who V knows personally such as her husband; boyfriend; friend; etc. In this manner, the presumption has been defined narrowly to catch only the clearest cases of wrongful impersonation.

Despite the narrow construction, two problem areas remain. First, as the statute does not expressly deal with deception as to personal attributes, we must assume in line with current case law[43] that this will never constitute deception as to identity. This may be acceptable in cases where D lies about his employment or prospects in order to induce intercourse; such cases will usually require the discretion of the general definition. However, where D fraudulently claims to be medically qualified, for example, and acting in line with that employment, it may be that a conclusive presumption of non-consent would have been appropriate.[44] Equally, of course, this also prevents any use of the presumption where D deceives V as to the risk of a sexual infection: such infection would be an attribute of D and not part of his identity.[45]

---

[42] *Elbekkay* [1995] Crim LR 163.

[43] *Richardson* [1998] 2 Cr App R 200.

[44] For discussion, see Law Commission, *Consent in Sex Offences*, submitted to the Home Office, *Sex Offences Review* (2000) para 5.25.

[45] *B* [2006] EWCA Crim 2945.

Secondly, the requirement that D's impersonation must be of someone 'known personally' to V is also problematic. It is clearly intended to avoid the conclusive presumptions applying where D impersonates a celebrity, for example. However, exactly who is known personally to V may be difficult to discern. Does it include everyone who V has ever met, however briefly? Does it include relationships formed on the internet where V may not have met the person at all?[46] Such questions have not yet arisen in the courts, but have the potential to cause real problems. It may also be questioned why the SOA 2003 limited the presumption in this manner: is it less serious for V to be deceived as to the identity of D if he pretends to be her favourite musician whom she does not know personally rather than her boyfriend?

Assessment matters...

Our discussion of section 76 has given rise to several areas of uncertainty. As we have discussed before, when learning and discussing the law, care must be taken not to avoid uncertainty. If the answer to a set of facts is uncertain on the basis of the current law then this should always be acknowledged. Your task is to analyse the statute, analyse the case law, and to see if you can find general rules or trends that will help you to predict how the courts are likely to deal with the issue.

Rebuttable presumptions of non-consent: s75

If the facts of a case do not come within the conclusive presumptions (s76), the next stage of analysis is whether they come within the rebuttable presumptions (s75). Unlike section 76, the rebuttable presumptions do not establish a lack of consent. Rather, as their name suggests, if the facts of a case come within the rebuttable presumptions, then the jury will find a lack of consent *unless D provides evidence to rebut (challenge) the presumption.* In this manner, section 75 creates a limited reverse evidential burden.[47]

For the presumption to apply it must be established that certain facts arose (discussed later), and also that D had knowledge of those facts. For example, the first rebuttable presumption will arise where violence has been used against V at the time or immediately before the relevant act (taking the offence of rape as an example, 'the act' would be penile penetration). Thus, if V were to suffer violence from another, without D's knowledge, the presumption will not arise. V may still lack consent under the general definition (s74), but section 75 will be irrelevant.

Point to remember...

The presumptions will arise if the facts exist and D is aware of those facts. Importantly, the prosecution do not need to demonstrate that those facts caused V's lack of consent. For example, if violence was knowingly used at the time of penile penetration, a rebuttable presumption of non-consent will arise without discussion of whether V would have consented or not if the violence was not used.

Once a presumption of this kind has arisen because the facts mirror one of the scenarios in s75 and D has knowledge of this, the burden is then on D to provide some evidence to rebut that presumption. This rebuttal does not necessarily require D to deny the facts themselves (eg deny that violence was used), it is enough for D to deny the implication

---

[46] *McNally* [2013] EWCA Crim 1051: D pretended to be male online and maintained the pretence when later making sexual contact with V.

[47] See **1.1.7.2**.

that such facts demonstrate a lack of consent. For example, in the context of violence, D could contend that he was engaged in a sadomasochistic sexual encounter with V and that V was consenting to both the violence and the penile penetration. Such evidence, however convincing or otherwise, will rebut the presumption. The burden of proof is then on the prosecution to demonstrate that there was a lack of consent despite D's explanation.[48]

> **Point to remember...**
>
> As the last paragraph demonstrates, evidential presumptions are not the most potent weapon for prosecutors. They are certainly less so than the conclusive presumptions under section 76. However, by placing even a weak burden on D to explain his behaviour, they allow the prosecution to engage with that explanation in order to establish their case. As sexual offences often take place in private with no witnesses, tools of this kind can be very useful.

Section 75(2) provides six scenarios in which a rebuttable presumption of non-consent will arise. We will explore each in turn.

(a) *any person was, at the time of the relevant act or immediately before it began, using violence against the complainant or causing the complainant to fear that immediate violence would be used against him.*

As stated earlier, the potential for consenting sadomasochistic relationships makes it sensible that violence creates a rebuttable (as opposed to conclusive) presumption of non-consent. The width of the presumption is also to be welcomed, going beyond violence to include threats of violence,[49] as well as violence and threats from others provided D is aware of them. The requirement that D's threat be of 'immediate violence' is more troubling: why not include cases where D threatens future violence unless V submits to sexual acts? One may also question the limitation of the presumption to threats of *violence*. Prior to the SOA 2003, there was an offence based on procuring sexual intercourse by threats: this covered threats of all kinds, including damage to property; threats of dismissal from employment; threats of arrest; or any other threat that induced V to submit to intercourse. Under the current law, a lack of consent may still be found in these cases applying the general definition of non-consent under s74, but they will not give rise to a presumption under section 75.

(b) *any person was, at the time of the relevant act or immediately before it began, causing the complainant to fear that violence was being used, or that immediate violence would be used, against another person.*

The presumption is usefully expanded to include cases where D or another inflicts violence or threatens to inflict violence on another. For example, if D threatens to harm V's child unless she submits to intercourse, then the presumption will apply. The presumption is limited in the same manner as (a) with regard to 'immediacy' and 'violence'. It may also be overly broad at times: read literally, if V watches a news report about a

---

[48] *White* [2010] EWCA Crim 1929.

[49] See *Dagnall* [2003] EWCA Crim 2441: where D dragged V from the road promising to rape her. V responded that he could 'do what he liked as long as he did not harm her'. V was clearly not consenting.

violent crime and then consents to intercourse, it will be presumed that she does not consent! In this example, it will be straightforward for the presumption to be rebutted, but the fact that it applies suggests defective drafting.

(c) *the complainant was, and the defendant was not, unlawfully detained at the time of the relevant act.*

This presumption is relatively uncontroversial, and rather difficult for D to rebut. It applies where V submits to sexual acts whilst the hostage of D or others.[50]

(d) *the complainant was asleep or otherwise unconscious at the time of the relevant act.*

There will be relationships in which sexual contact while the other party is asleep, for example, is done with that party's consent. However, this will not often be the case and a rebuttable presumption of non-consent is appropriate. Indeed, under the old common law, unconsciousness would have been enough to find non-consent irrespective of D's explanations.[51] It should be noted that this presumption will only apply where V is fully unconscious, and D is aware of this: where V is intoxicated, for example, but short of unconsciousness, this presumption will not apply.

(e) *because of the complainant's physical disability, the complainant would not have been able at the time of the relevant act to communicate to the defendant whether the complainant consented.*

Although V may be able to communicate with others or on other occasions (eg through sign-language), if a physical disability prevents her communicating her consent on this occasion and with this D, there will be a presumption of non-consent. This presumption reinforces the idea from the general definition of consent (discussed further later) that consent should be seen as an active expression of willingness from V rather than a lack of active opposition. However, the fact the presumption is limited to physical disability will prevent it being used, for example, where V is too intoxicated to communicate.

(f) *any person had administered to or caused to be taken by the complainant, without the complainant's consent, a substance which, having regard to when it was administered or taken, was capable of causing or enabling the complainant to be stupefied or overpowered at the time of the relevant act.*

The final scenario within section 75 covers cases of so-called drug-date rape, where D or another causes V to consume unwanted stupefying substances by, for example, spiking her drink with alcohol or other drugs such as Rohypnol.[52] Importantly, the presumption will only apply where the substance is added without V's consent. Thus, if V becomes voluntarily intoxicated, even if she is encouraged to do so by D, the presumption will not arise.

General definition of non-consent: s74

Many of the clearest cases of non-consent will be dealt with under the previous presumptions (ss76 and 75). With this in mind, it is easy to fall into the trap of thinking that

---

[50] *David T* [2005] EWCA Crim 2668.
[51] *Larter and Castleton* [1995] Crim LR 75.
[52] See Finch and Munro, 'Intoxicated Consent and the Boundaries of Drug Assisted Rape' [2003] Crim LR 773, and revisited [2004] Crim LR 789.

if the presumptions do not apply then V's apparent consent must be effective. This is not the case. Rather, where the presumptions do not apply at all, or where a presumption under s75 is rebutted by D, it is still vital to apply the general definition of consent under section 74. Indeed, certain cases will fall outside the presumptions and yet it will be very clear that V's apparent consent is not effective, as was the true in *Jheeta*. Whether V lacks consent under section 74 will be a question for the jury.

Jheeta [2007] EWCA Crim 1699

D sent V anonymous text messages over several years, purporting to be from the police, telling her to continue having a sexual relationship with D in order to avoid fines for causing distress. D was charged with rape.

- Crown Court: guilty of rape: D's deception undermined V's apparent consent.
- Court of Appeal: conviction upheld on appeal.

In this case, although D has deceived V, he has not deceived her as to the nature (physical dynamics of sexual intercourse) or the purpose (his sexual gratification) of the sexual act. Thus, the conclusive presumptions of non-consent do not apply. Equally, the facts do not fall within the rebuttable presumptions either. However, employing the general definition of consent under section 74, it is nevertheless a clear case in which V's apparent consent is ineffective.[53]

> 74. For the purposes of this Part, a person [V] consents if he agrees by choice, and has the freedom and capacity to make that choice.

The general definition is designed to afford the jury some discretion in cases falling outside the presumptions. However, it does provide two important clarifications.

First, the construction 'agrees by choice' is a clear indication that consent should be viewed as a *positive* sign of willingness, as opposed to the absence of an objection. The distinction here may be subtle, but it is vital as a move away from a historical view of rape as a necessarily violent encounter. As a matter of substantive law, the question of consent does not rely on V's objections or whether she physically resisted penetration, although this will be useful evidence of non-consent,[54] the absence of consent is the absence of a freely made choice to participate.

Secondly, the definition also highlights two major factors (although it does not define them) that should be considered when deciding if any apparent consent from V should be viewed as legally effective. Mirroring the similar considerations of effective consent in the context of the offences against the person, these factors are 'freedom' and 'capacity'.

A) **Capacity:** To make a valid choice to consent, V must be able to understand that choice: she must have sufficient mental capacity. When assessing capacity, the test is specific to the individual V on the specific occasion, so it is not status-based. Thus, for example, the simple fact that V is very young[55] or old, or that V has a mental

---

[53] See similarly *B* [2013] EWCA Crim 823.

[54] *Malone* [1998] All ER 176.

[55] Very young children are, however, protected by specific offences for which consent is irrelevant. See **8.6** and **8.7**.

disorder,[56] will not automatically undermine her ability to consent.[57] This interpretation was confirmed in the leading case of *C*, a case that also sets out a test for the level of capacity required for consent to be effective. *C* focused on section 30 of the SOA 2003 (sexual activity with a person with a mental disorder impeding choice[58]), but the discussion of capacity is equally applicable to capacity in the context of consent more generally.

> *C* [2009] 1 WLR 1786
>
> V had a history of mental disorders manifesting in manic episodes and delusions involving irrational fears for her safety. D befriended V, gave her crack cocaine, and made her perform acts of oral sex on him and another. V claimed that she only consented out of fear for her safety.
>
> - Crown Court: guilty of the section 30 offence. Capacity undermined by fears originating from mental illness.
> - Court of Appeal: allowing D's appeal. Capacity not undermined by condition of this kind.
> - House of Lords: Court of Appeal was wrong, capacity can be undermined where V understands the nature of the act but a mental condition prevents her making a real choice.

Speaking in the House of Lords, Baroness Hale made several telling contributions to the jurisprudence in this area. For example, discussing a non-status-based approach to consent, she commented:

> it is difficult to think of an activity which is more person and situation specific than sexual relations. One does not consent to sex in general. One consents to this act of sex with this person at this time and in this place.[59]

In the absence of a status-based approach to capacity (ie one where the courts would hold that if V suffered certain mental disorders that would automatically mean that V was not consenting), a different test is required. For the House of Lords, the law on capacity recognises that to make a valid decision:

> a) a person must be able to understand the information relevant to making it, and
> b) must be able to weigh that information in the balance to arrive at a choice.[60]

Thus, in *C*, although V was able to understand the sexual acts (passing stage one), her inability to weigh that information to make a choice (due to her mental disorder) meant that she could not pass the second stage. Thus, she lacked capacity to consent and, therefore, there was no consent.

---

[56] As with children, mentally ill victims are also protected by specific offences for which consent is irrelevant. See **8.8.3**.

[57] Elliott and De Than, 'The Case for a Rational Reconstruction of Consent in Criminal Law' (2007) 70 MLR 225.

[58] See **8.8.3**.

[59] At [27].

[60] At [24].

B) Freedom: As well as the capacity to choose, V must have sufficient freedom. 'Freedom' is not defined in the SOA 2003 and has little precedent within the common law. It therefore provides a great deal of flexibility and discretion for the court and the jury to interpret the term as they deem appropriate. The negative consequence of this breadth being the potential for inconsistent interpretations. Generally, when we think of 'freedom', we think of freedom from external constraints. The following represents two possibilities.

First, V must have freedom from threats and deception from D. Certain categories of deception will be caught by section 76 and lead to a conclusive presumption of non-consent. Equally, certain threats of violence will lead to a rebuttable presumption under section 75. However, there will be many examples of threats or deceptions that, whilst not falling within the presumptions, may nevertheless undermine V's apparent consent under section 74. For example, where D threatens to injure V at some point in the future, but not immediately, unless she submits to a sexual act. Identifying the threshold at which deception and/or violence undermines consent within section 74 is very challenging. For example, on the one hand we have cases stating that non-disclosure of HIV will not undermine consent and judges stating that deception as to 'wealth', for example, will 'obviously not be sufficient to vitiate consent'.[62] However, on the other hand, we have had a recent flurry of cases where deception (outside the conclusive presumptions) has been enough to undermine consent under section 74, such as *Assange* (deception as to the use of a condom),[63] *F v DPP* (deception as to intentional internal ejaculation),[64] and *McNally* (deception as to gender).[65]

Secondly, we may also want to consider freedom from circumstances not caused by D. In certain cases D will not be the cause of V's lack of freedom, but he may take advantage of it in order to induce V to submit to a sexual act. This is a difficult area because V is likely to be under many pressures in everyday life, including financial pressure; pressures from wanting to maintain a relationship; wanting to start a family; etc, and these pressures may well cause her to accept a sexual act that she would

---

[61] *Bree* [2007] EWCA Crim 804.
[62] *McNally* [2013] EWCA Crim 1051, per Leveson LJ.
[63] [2011] EWHC 2849 (Admin).
[64] [2013] EWHC 945 (Admin).
[65] [2013] EWCA Crim 1051.
[66] Laird, 'Rapist or Rogue? Deception, Consent and the Sexual Offences Act 2003' [2014] Crim LR 492.

not otherwise have chosen. This will not, ordinarily, undermine consent. However, there are extreme examples where such pressures will undermine V's freedom of choice and thus her consent. For example, in *Kirk*,[67] a homeless teenager, V, agreed to sex with D in exchange for £3.25 to buy food. The Court of Appeal held that V was not consenting.

The general definition of consent set out in section 74, and the factors of 'freedom' and 'capacity', therefore provide *some* codified guidance for juries. However, considerable discretion remains.

> *Extra detail...*
> When discussing non-consent across sections 74, 75, and 76, voluntary intoxication has emerged as a particularly problematic area (where it does not come within the presumptions). We discuss this further in the 'reform' section later in the chapter.[68]

8.2.2 Mens rea of s1

The requirement of mens rea in rape reflects the criminal law's focus on D's wrongdoing as opposed to the compensation of V which is the focus of the civil law. If the actus reus is completed, V has suffered a serious wrong. If the mens rea is satisfied, then the law will attribute that wrong to D and the offence of rape is committed.

8.2.2.1 Mens rea as to penetration

D does not commit rape unless, at the time of penetration, he intends to penetrate V's vagina, anus, or mouth. Whether he penetrates the orifice intended is irrelevant as, for example, where D penetrates the anus, but intended to penetrate the vagina.

This requirement will rarely cause problems for the prosecution: it is difficult to imagine unintentional penetration of this kind. However, bearing in mind the minor depth required for penetration to be found, it could potentially be at issue where D and V embrace when naked and D's penis makes contact with V's vulva. Equally, intention would also be a central consideration were the acts to occur while D was asleep.

8.2.2.2 Mens rea as to V's non-consent

To be liable for rape or the other sexual offences requiring non-consent, D must have mens rea as to that non-consent. Again, it is important to remember that D's appreciation of V's non-consent (mens rea) is a separate requirement from non-consent in fact (actus reus). Here, we are only concerned with D's mens rea.

Prior to the SOA 2003, this aspect of the offence was heavily criticised. At this time, D would only be liable where he foresaw a risk of non-consent or did not care less about the issue.[69] Thus, where D believed that V consented he could avoid liability even if that belief was unreasonable. Criticisms of this approach often focused on the case of *Morgan*.

---

[67] [2008] EWCA Crim 434.
[68] See **8.9**.
[69] *Taylor* (1984) 80 Cr App R 327.

Morgan [1976] AC 182

In a pre SOA 2003 case, D and others had sex with V after being told by her husband that they should do so, and that her apparent resistance would only be done to increase her enjoyment. Each was charged with rape. They claimed that they honestly (though unreasonably) believed V consented.

- Crown Court: guilty of rape. D's belief in consent must be *reasonable*.

- House of Lords: appeal dismissed. Consent does not have to be reasonable (as long as it is honest), but no jury could have found their belief to be honest.

Although liability was found in *Morgan*, the possibility that an unreasonable belief of this kind could have led to an acquittal (if honestly held) was heavily criticised. Commentators contended that some objectivity (reasonableness) was required: recognising the seriousness of sexual offences as well as the ease through which D inquires with V as to her consent.[70]

The response within the SOA 2003, whilst short of the purely objective test mooted at the time,[71] nevertheless incorporates a considerable objective dimension. As with the actus reus of non-consent, the mens rea is dealt with over multiple sections.

Presumptions of mens rea as to non-consent

Just as sections 76 and 75 create presumptions of non-consent in the context of the actus reus, the same sections also create mens rea presumptions. Thus, where the facts of the case come within section 76 (discussed earlier) this is enough to establish that D satisfies the mens rea as to V's non-consent; where the facts come within section 75 (discussed later) there will be a rebuttable presumption that D satisfies the mens rea.

Assessment matters…

The presumption of non-consent within sections 76 and 75 also apply to mens rea. Thus, if your discussion of actus reus finds that one of the presumptions is engaged, the same presumption will also apply to your discussion of mens rea.

General approach to mens rea as to non-consent

Where the presumptions do not apply at all (or, in the context of section 75, are rebutted) we must consider the general approach. This is set out separately within each of the non-consent-based offences, but the same form of words is used in each. Mens rea will be satisfied where:

[D] does not reasonably believe that [V] consents.[72]

The requirement of a 'reasonable belief' in consent, added within the SOA 2003, represents a largely objective approach to mens rea. D will satisfy this aspect of the mens rea where he:

- intends V to lack consent;

- knows V lacks consent;

---

[70] Wells, 'Swatting the Subjectivist Bug' [1982] Crim LR 209.
[71] Early versions of the Bill even included a reversed burden of proof. See **1.1.7.2**.
[72] SOA 2003, s1(1)(c).

- is reckless as to consent;
- does not consider consent; and even
- honestly but unreasonably believes that V consents.

Where the last of these arises, the jury must consider whether a reasonable person in D's position would have believed (as he did) that V was consenting. Where the answer is 'no', as it would have been if *Morgan* was decided under the current law, mens rea will be satisfied.

The test is not, however, purely objective. This is because, for each offence, the reasonable belief requirement is qualified with subjective considerations.

> Whether a belief is reasonable is to be determined having regard to all the circumstances, including any steps [D] has taken to ascertain whether [V] consents.[73]

The question for the jury is not 'would a reasonable person have believed that V consented' but, rather, 'would a reasonable person sharing D's characteristics have believed that V consented'. The difference is not intended to weaken the objective (reasonableness-based) approach, but it will allow the jury to consider characteristics that genuinely affect D's ability to appreciate V's non-consent, such as D's age, sexual experience, learning disabilities,[74] or other factors of this kind. Voluntary intoxication will never be a relevant characteristic.[75] The law is imposing a duty on D to take reasonable steps to ensure that V is consenting, it is not expecting D to take steps that he is not physically or mentally equipped to take.

> **Assessment matters...**
>
> Although the mens rea is attempting to soften the objective approach with subjective considerations,[76] it will inevitably lead to uncertainty about which characteristics can be taken into account and which cannot. For example, if D lacks respect for women, is this a characteristic that means even the barest inquiry as to consent will be reasonable for him? This is (of course) unlikely, but it illustrates how difficult the line will be to draw.
>
> Where such cases arise in problem facts, it would be useful to discuss this problem before predicting whether you think the 'characteristic' in question is one that will be accepted by the court. For example, in *B*,[77] the Court of Appeal have stated that a 'delusional belief' in consent caused by a mental disorder would not amount to a reasonable belief.

8.3 SOA 2003, s2: assault by penetration

Section 2 of the SOA 2003 introduced a new offence of assault by penetration, carrying a maximum sentence of life imprisonment.[78]

---

[73] SOA 2003, s1(2).
[74] *TS* [2008] EWCA Crim 6.
[75] See discussion of the intoxication rules at **13.2**.
[76] See discussion of this at **3.7.2**.
[77] [2013] EWCA Crim 3. Child and Sullivan, 'When does the insanity defence apply? Some recent cases' (2014) Crim LR 788.
[78] SOA 2003, s2(4).

(1) A person (D) commits an offence if—

    (a) he intentionally penetrates the vagina or anus of another person (V) with a part of his body or anything else,

    (b) the penetration is sexual,

    (c) V does not consent to the penetration, and

    (d) D does not reasonably believe that V consents.

The elements of assault by penetration are set out in **Table 8.2**.

Table 8.2 SOA 2003, s2

	Actus reus	**Mens rea**
Conduct element	Penetration of V's vagina or anus	Intention
Circumstance element	V does not consent	D lacks a reasonable belief in consent
	Penetration is sexual	No mens rea
Result element	None	None

8.3.1 Actus reus of s2

The actus reus of section 2 overlaps with the actus reus of rape considerably. As with rape, D must perform an act that penetrates the vagina or anus of V without V's consent. These requirements are defined in exactly the same way as they are for rape, discussed previously. Thus, when discussing the element of non-consent, you should consider the following.

- Do the facts come within the conclusive presumptions of non-consent (s76)?
- Do the facts come within the rebuttable presumptions of non-consent (s75)?
- If not, or if a section 75 presumption is rebutted, the general definition of consent (s74) should be applied.

There are, however, notable differences between the actus reus of rape and the section 2 offence. Most importantly, for section 2, D's act of penetration does not need to be completed with his penis. D (male or female) will be liable where they penetrate V (male or female) with *any* body part (eg fingers, tongue, etc) or with 'anything else' (eg bottle, knife, etc). Not only does this offence recognise the seriousness of non-penile penetration,[79] but it will also be useful in cases where V is unsure whether she was penetrated with D's penis or another object, or lacks the capacity to tell.[80] The offence covers penetration of V's vagina or anus. Non-penile penetration of V's mouth will not be caught within this section, although it may constitute a sexual assault under section 3.

---

[79] The new offence separates acts of this kind from the more general offence of sexual assault, discussed at **8.4**.

[80] See *Minshull* [2004] EWCA Crim 2673, where V was severely disabled.

> *Terminology...*
> The broad definitions of 'penetration' and 'vagina', discussed in relation to rape, will have even more of an impact in relation to section 2. For example, where D performs non-consensual oral sex upon V's vagina this will be caught within the section 2 offence because D's tongue will have penetrated the vulva.

8.3.1.1 Penetration must be sexual

The other notable difference between the actus reus of rape and the section 2 offence is that, for section 2, the prosecution must prove that D's act is 'sexual'. Penile penetration, as required for rape, is self-evidently sexual and so this extra element is not required. However, there may be examples of non-penile penetration of the vagina or anus that are not self-evidently sexual, for example medical examinations. Where V is penetrated without her consent and the sexual element is present, it is correct to apply sexual offences. Where it is not present, the non-sexual offences against the person should be applied.[81] The term 'sexual' is defined by section 78 SOA 2003:

> **78**. ...penetration, touching or any other activity is sexual if a reasonable person would consider that—
>
> (a) whatever its circumstances or any person's purpose in relation to it, it is because of its nature sexual, or
>
> (b) because of its nature it may be sexual and because of its circumstances or the purpose of any person in relation to it (or both) it is sexual.

As the section 2 offence requires D to have penetrated the vagina or anus of V, it is likely that a jury will consider D's acts as being sexual because of their nature (s78(a)). This is where D's acts are self-evidently (objectively) sexual irrespective of the circumstances or purposes of D, and irrespective of whether D would consider them to be sexual. For example, in *Hill*[82] D forcefully inserted his fingers into his partner's vagina during a violent argument. Although the Court of Appeal described his acts as violent 'rather than sexual', D pleaded guilty to a sexual offence and it is likely that his acts would have been viewed as sexual under section 78(a) without consideration of his purposes.

Where D's act of penetration is not sexual by its nature (eg because of a medical context), section 78(b) should be considered. As penetration of the vagina or anus always '*may* be sexual', the jury will consider whether the circumstances or D's purposes make it sexual. For example, if D (a doctor) recommends certain penetrative examinations of V in circumstances in which such examinations have no medical role, and/or for reasons of personal sexual gratification, his conduct will be sexual under section 78(b).

> *Extra detail...*
> Where D's acts may be sexual and the sexual requirement is satisfied by his accompanying purposes (s78(b)), this is an example where an actus reus requirement seems to be satisfied by D's mind as opposed to an external fact.[83]

---

[81] **Chapter 7.**

[82] [2006] EWCA Crim 2575.

[83] Sullivan, 'Bad Thoughts and Bad Acts' [1990] Crim LR 559. Cf Child, 'The Structure, Coherence and Limits of Inchoate Liability: The New Ulterior Element' (2014) 34 LS 537.

8.3.2 Mens rea of s2

The mens rea for the section 2 offence is exactly the same as for rape, discussed earlier. When penetrating V, D must:

- intend the act of penetration (see **8.2.2.1**); and
- lack a reasonable belief that V is consenting (see **8.2.2.2**).

There is no corresponding mens rea to the actus reus requirement that D's conduct is 'sexual'. D's liability does not require him to be aware (or even negligent) that his conduct is sexual.[84]

8.4 SOA 2003, s3: sexual assault

Section 3 of the SOA 2003 criminalises a broad range of conduct under the offence of sexual assault, carrying a maximum sentence of ten years on indictment.[85]

3. A person (D) commits an offence if —
  (a) he intentionally touches another person (V),
  (b) the touching is sexual,
  (c) V does not consent to the touching, and
  (d) D does not reasonably believe that V consents.

The elements of sexual assault are set out in **Table 8.3**.

Table 8.3 SOA 2003, s3

	Actus reus	Mens rea
Conduct element	Any conduct that causes the result	Voluntary
Circumstance element	V does not consent	D lacks a reasonable belief in consent
	Touching is sexual	No mens rea
Result element	Touching of V	Intention

8.4.1 Actus reus of s3

As with section 1 and 2 offences, a central element of sexual assault is that V does not consent to the contact from D. Again, this will involve consideration of the conclusive

---

[84] Although, of course, where D's conduct is only potentially sexual, it may be made sexual by D's purposes (s78(b)).
[85] SOA 2003, s3(4).

presumptions of non-consent (s76), rebuttable presumptions (s75), and (if necessary) the general definition of consent (s74).

However, beyond non-consensual penetration, sexual assault also includes non-consensual sexual touching of any kind. D and V may be male or female.

8.4.1.1 Touching

The label 'sexual *assault*' implies that D must commit a technical assault or battery,[86] however, this is not the case. Rather, a 'touching' is all that is required. Touching is defined broadly within section 79(8) to include 'touching, (a) with any part of the body, (b) with anything else, (c) through anything.' Touching does not need to be firm or prolonged, and may be satisfied even where V is unaware of it.[87] The leading case is *H*.

> 🔲 ***H*** [2005] EWCA Crim 732
>
> D approached V as she walked across some fields and asked her 'Do you fancy a shag?' D then grabbed her tracksuit bottoms by the fabric and attempted to pull her towards him. V escaped. D was charged with sexual assault.
>
> - Crown Court: guilty of sexual assault. Touching V's clothes amounted to touching V.
> - Court of Appeal: conviction upheld on appeal.

Although it is clear that touching 'through' clothes will amount to touching V,[88] *H* confirms that it also includes cases where D *only* makes contact with V's clothes. This interpretation is to be welcomed, and is consistent with the interpretation of touching in relation to battery.[89] As with battery, it is also likely that 'touching', sufficient for sexual assault, can be performed by omission if D omits to act in breach of a recognised duty (eg, where D allows a child to touch his genitals).[90]

Despite this broad interpretation of 'touching', it will not include cases where D makes no contact with V even where this amounts to an assault. For example, if D threatens V and makes her remove her clothes, this will not be a sexual assault unless he also makes some physical contact.

8.4.1.2 Touching must be sexual

We have already discussed the meaning of 'sexual' in the context of section 2,[91] and the same two-stage approach (set out in s78) is also applied here. Thus, D's conduct will be 'sexual' if (a) the jury consider it to be sexual by its 'nature' independent of other factors, or (b) if they consider it to be potentially sexual and made sexual by the 'circumstances' or D's 'purposes'.

In the context of the section 2 offence involving penetration of the vagina or anus, it is common for D's conduct to be considered sexual by its nature. However, as sexual

---

[86] See **7.2**.
[87] *Bounekhla* [2006] EWCA Crim 1217.
[88] *Swinscoe* [2006] EWCA Crim 2412: D touched an 8-year-old girl through her underwear.
[89] *Thomas* (1985) 81 Cr App R 331. See **7.2.2**.
[90] *Speck* [1977] Crim LR 689.
[91] See **8.3.1.1**.

assault encompasses any sexual touching, the full definition of 'sexual' becomes much more important. A classic illustration of this is *Court*.

***Court* [1989] AC 28**

In a case pre-SOA 2003, D, a shop assistant pulled a 12-year-old girl across his knee and spanked her clothed bottom. When asked why, he said 'buttock fetish'. D was charged with indecent assault (equivalent to sexual assault).

- Crown Court: guilty of indecent assault—assault was made indecent (sexual) by D's sexual purpose.
- Court of Appeal: conviction upheld on appeal.
- House of Lords: appeal dismissed.

Court is a useful example where D's touching is unlikely to be considered sexual by its nature, but is potentially sexual, and made sexual by the purposes of D. Similarly, in *H* (discussed earlier[92]), grabbing V's clothing is not sexual by its nature, but it is potentially sexual, and made sexual by the circumstances: D asking V for 'a shag'.

This second possibility for satisfying the sexual element, set out in section 78(b), has an interesting construction. This is because, before we look at the circumstances and purposes of D, it must first be satisfied that D's conduct 'may' potentially be sexual. This is illustrated in **Table 8.4**.

Table 8.4 Defining 'sexual'

A) D's conduct is sexual by its nature = sexual
B) D's conduct may be sexual + made sexual by circumstances or D's purposes = sexual

The two-part approach within (b), however, creates some uncertainty in relation to odd sexual fetishes. In *George*,[93] for example, D had a foot fetish and attempted to remove a girl's shoe for reasons of sexual gratification. If decided today, as D's conduct is not sexual by its nature (a), it could only come within the offence if it satisfied the sexual element through (b). In cases of this kind, it is clear that the second part of (b) would be satisfied as D is acting for sexual gratification. However, would the case get beyond the first part of the test in (b)? Objectively viewed, without considering D's purposes, is the removal of a shoe potentially sexual? If the answer is 'yes', and such conduct may be sexual, then it is difficult to imagine any form of touching that would not satisfy this part of the test. As fetishism knows no bounds, the first part will be redundant and we will always look to the circumstances and D's purposes. If the answer is 'no', and such conduct is not considered potentially sexual, then this first part of the test will maintain an active role. However, if this approach were taken, it will be very difficult to see where the line should be drawn: what is required for conduct to be potentially sexual?[94]

---

[92] See **8.4.1.1**.

[93] [1956] Crim LR 52.

[94] Bantekas, 'Can Touching Always be Sexual When There is No Sexual Intent?' (2008) 73 J Crim L 251.

8.4.2 Mens rea of s3

The mens rea for sexual assault includes two main elements. First, D's conduct (touching) must be intentional. Thus, for example, if D *accidentally* makes contact with V on a busy train he will not commit sexual assault even if the touching is sexual in nature (as where his hand touches her breast). Secondly, as with the section 1 and 2 offences earlier, D must lack a reasonable belief that V is consenting to the touching. This is discussed previously in relation to rape (see **8.2.2.2**).

Again, although the actus reus of section 3 includes a sexual element, D does not require any corresponding mens rea to this element.[95]

8.5 SOA 2003, s4: causing a person to engage in sexual activity without consent

Section 4 of the SOA 2003 criminalises D where he or she causes V to engage in sexual activity without consent. The offence carries a maximum life sentence where sexual penetration is involved, or ten years on indictment for other cases.

(1) A person (D) commits an offence if —

    (a) he intentionally causes another person (V) to engage in an activity,

    (b) the activity is sexual,

    (c) V does not consent to engaging in the activity, and

    (d) D does not reasonably believe that V consents.

The elements of section 4 are set out in **Table 8.5**.

Table 8.5 SOA 2003, s4

	Actus reus	**Mens rea**
Conduct element	Any conduct that causes the result	Voluntary
Circumstance element	V does not consent	D lacks a reasonable belief in consent
	The activity is sexual	No mens rea
Result element	V engages in an activity	Intention

8.5.1 Actus reus of s4

Unlike offences under sections 1–3, section 4 does not require D to have any physical contact with V or even be present at the time of the sexual activity. Rather, the offence

---

95 Although, of course, where D's conduct is only potentially sexual, it may be made sexual by D's purposes (s78(b)).

focuses on D who causes V to complete some form of non-consensual sexual activity. The offence will cover D (a woman) who causes V (a man) to penetrate her without consent, as well as cases of sexual activity with a third party,[96] or even self-masturbation.[97] In each case, although D need not make physical contact with V, a causal link must be proven between D's conduct (which could be words alone) and V engaging in the sexual activity.

Beyond D's causal role, other elements of the actus reus must be demonstrated that have already been discussed in relation to sections 1–3. These include:

- V's activity as caused by D must be 'sexual' (s78). As discussed in relation to section 2 (**8.3.1.1**) and sexual assault (**8.4.1.2**), conduct may be sexual because of its nature, or be potentially sexual and made sexual by the circumstances or D's purposes;

- the sexual activity must also be without V's consent. As discussed in relation to rape (**8.2.1.4**), this element requires consideration of the conclusive presumptions of non-consent (s76), rebuttable presumptions (s75), and (if necessary) the general definition of consent (s74).

It should be remembered that the actus reus of section 4 will only be satisfied when all of these elements are complete. Thus, for example, if D threatens V and causes V to perform a sexual activity at some point in the future, the actus reus is not satisfied until that future activity is completed.

8.5.2 Mens rea of s4

The mens rea for section 4 includes two central elements. First, D must intend the conduct which causes V to engage in a non-consensual sexual activity. Secondly, as with offences under sections 1–3, D must lack a reasonable belief that V will consent to the sexual activity. This is discussed earlier in relation to rape (**8.2.2.2**).

Again, although the actus reus of section 4 includes a sexual element, D does not require any corresponding mens rea to this element.

Assessment matters…
Unlike sections 1–3, the actus reus of section 4 allows for the possibility of a gap in time between D's conduct and the sexual activity carried out by V (eg where D threatens V over the phone or internet to complete sexual acts with another person on a later date the offence occurs when that activity on the later date occurs). It should be remembered from our discussion of mens rea in **Chapter 3** that although the actus reus of an offence can be spread in this manner, the same is not true of the mens rea. As with all offences, we must identify all of the mens rea requirements at the time that D completes the conduct element of the actus reus. Thus, while performing the acts that cause V's later sexual activity, D must be intending to cause that activity and lack the belief that V will consent to it.

8.6 Sexual offences against children under 13 years

The four offences in this category (ss5–8) closely mirror the four offences discussed earlier (ss1–4). However, crucially, these offences do *not* require the prosecution

---

[96] *Basherdost* [2009] EWCA Crim 2883.
[97] *Devonauld* [2008] EWCA Crim 527.

to prove that V lacked consent or that D lacked a belief in V's consent. In cases where V is aged 12 or younger, D can be prosecuted under these offences regardless of consent.[98]

Don't be confused...
Offences in this category are not claiming that a child under 13 is incapable of consent. Rather, they are constructed to make the issue of consent irrelevant; it is not an offence element.

8.6.1 SOA 2003, s5: rape of a child under 13

The section 5 offence is commonly referred to as 'statutory rape', criminalising D who penetrates the vagina, anus, or mouth of V *aged 12 or under* with his penis. The offence carries a maximum sentence of life imprisonment.[99]

(1) A person commits an offence if—

   (a) he intentionally penetrates the vagina, anus or mouth of another person with his penis, and

   (b) the other person is under 13.

The elements of section 5 are set out in **Table 8.6**.

Table 8.6 SOA 2003, s5

	Actus reus	**Mens rea**
Conduct element	Penile penetration of V's vagina, anus, or mouth	Intention
Circumstance element	V is aged 12 or under	No mens rea
Result element	None	None

8.6.1.1 Actus reus of s5

In common with rape (s1), this offence requires penile penetration of V's vagina, anus, or mouth. These elements share the same meaning as they do for the section 1 offence, and are discussed earlier. The actus reus of section 5 differs from section 1 in that V's consent or non-consent is irrelevant. Also, although D may be of any age,[100] V must be aged 12 or younger.

8.6.1.2 Mens rea of s5

As with section 1, D must intend to penetrate V. However, beyond this, there are no mens rea requirements. As V's consent is irrelevant, there is no mens rea requirement in

---

[98] Spencer, 'The Sexual Offences Act 2003: Child and Family Offences' [2004] Crim LR 347.
[99] SOA 2003, s5(2).
[100] As long as he is over the age of criminal responsibility (10 years old).

relation to it. V must be under 13, but mens rea as to this element is strict: no mens rea need be demonstrated. This was confirmed in G.[101]

> **G** [2008] UKHL 37
>
> D (15) had sexual intercourse with V (12). V consented to the intercourse, and D reasonably believed that V was over 13. D was charged with a section 5 offence.
>
> - Crown Court: guilty of section 5 offence.
> - Court of Appeal: conviction upheld on appeal.
> - House of Lords: appeal dismissed. Issues of consent and D's belief in V's age are irrelevant to the offence. Also confirming that section 5 is compatible with Article 6 ECHR (right to a fair trial) and Article 8 (right to respect for family life).

8.6.2 SOA 2003, s6: assault of a child under 13 by penetration

Section 6 mirrors s2 by criminalising any sexual penetration of V's vagina or anus but does so *where V is aged 12 or under.*

(1) A person commits an offence if—

    (a) he intentionally penetrates the vagina or anus of another person with a part of his body or anything else,

    (b) the penetration is sexual, and

    (c) the other person is under 13.

The elements of section 6 are set out in **Table 8.7.**

Table 8.7 SOA 2003, s6

	Actus reus	**Mens rea**
Conduct element	Penetration of V's vagina or anus	Intention
Circumstance element	Penetration is sexual	No mens rea
	V is aged 12 or under	No mens rea
Result element	None	None

In common with the section 2 offence (discussed previously in that context), section 6 targets the intentional sexual penetration of V's vagina or anus with any part of D's body or anything else. In contrast with section 2, however, this offence does not require V to lack consent to penetration or for D to lack a belief in V's consent. As long as D sexually penetrates V in the proscribed manner, and V is under 13 years old, D will be liable for

---

[101] Ashworth, 'Commentary on *G*' [2008] Crim LR 818.

the offence. Again, D will be liable even if he reasonably believes that V is aged 13 or over: mens rea as to the age of V is strict.

8.6.3 SOA 2003, s7: sexual assault of a child under 13

Section 7 (mirroring s3) criminalises the sexual touching of V but does so *where V is aged 12 or under.*

(1) A person commits an offence if—

   (a) he intentionally touches another person,

   (b) the touching is sexual, and

   (c) the other person is under 13.

The elements of section 7 are set out in **Table 8.8**.

Table 8.8 SOA 2003, s7

	Actus reus	Mens rea
Conduct element	Any conduct that causes the result	Voluntary
Circumstance element	Touching is sexual	No mens rea
	V is aged 12 or under	No mens rea
Result element	Touching of V	Intention

As with section 3, this offence requires D to have intentionally touched V and for that touching to be sexual. The definitions of these terms are common between the offences, and have been discussed previously. However, as with the other child sex offences, this offence will only apply where V is aged 12 or under. V's non-consent and D belief as to V's consent and/or V's age are irrelevant to liability.

8.6.4 SOA 2003, s8: causing or inciting a child under 13 to engage in sexual activity

Section 8 (mirroring s4) criminalises D who causes *or incites* sexual activity with V but does so *where V is aged 12 or under.*

(1) A person commits an offence if—

   (a) he intentionally causes or incites another person (V) to engage in an activity,

   (b) the activity is sexual, and

   (c) V is under 13.

Section 8 creates two separate offences, set out in **Tables 8.9** and **8.10**.[102]

---

[102] *Walker* [2006] EWCA Crim 1907.

Table 8.9 SOA 2003, s8

	Actus reus	Mens rea
Conduct element	Any conduct that causes the result	Voluntary
Circumstance element	V is under 13	No mens rea
	The activity engaged in by V is sexual	No mens rea
Result element	V engages in an activity	Intention

The first of these offences mirrors the section 4 offence discussed earlier: criminalising D who causes V to engage in any sexual activity. As with the other child sexual offences, the offence is only committed where V is under 13 years old, and issues of non-consent, belief in consent, and belief in age are irrelevant.

Table 8.10 SOA 2003, s8

	Actus reus	Mens rea
Conduct element	Any conduct that causes the result	Voluntary
Circumstance element	V is under 13	No mens rea
	D's communication with V incites her to engage in an activity	No mens rea
	The activity incited is sexual	No mens rea
Result element	Communication with V	Intention

The second offence within section 8 (set out in Table 8.10) does not mirror the section 4 offence. Rather, it criminalises D for inciting (encouraging) V to engage in sexual activity where V is aged under 13. D is liable as soon as he has completed the conduct of encouragement, and there is no requirement that sexual activity ever takes place. Further, although D's communication with V must be voluntary, there is no additional mens rea: D's beliefs in relation to V's willingness to engage in the activity; her age; and even whether he truly intends the sexual activity to ever come about, are all irrelevant to liability. This construction of section 8 was charged in *Walker*.

Walker [2006] EWCA Crim 1907

D spoke on the phone to a child he was watching telling her 'show us your fanny'. He was charged with a section 8 offence of inciting sexual activity.

• Court: guilty of section 8 offence.

> • Court of Appeal: conviction upheld on appeal. Whether D intended the sexual activity to happen (disputed in this case) is irrelevant to D's liability.[103]

It is also clear from the case of *Jones*[104] that incitement under section 8 does not require the targeting of a particular child: in this case, a note left in a public toilet asking for sex with any children who read it.

Although the incitement offence provides additional protection against those encouraging children to perform sexual acts,[105] the broad nature of the actus reus and the use of strict liability has the potential to cause problems. For example, what if D writes on an open internet blog about the joys of sex and comments that people should have sex as soon as they are in a relationship. D is not intending to encourage children to have sex and he may not foresee that children will even be reading his post. However, he has voluntarily completed an act that has the potential to encourage those aged 12 or under to engage in a sexual activity. D's conduct satisfies the elements of the offence, and he must rely on prosecutorial discretion to avoid liability.[106]

8.6.5 Sexual offences against children under 13 by children

The offences within sections 5–8 can only be committed against children aged 12 or under. However, as long as D is over the age of criminal responsibility (10 years old), his age is irrelevant. Therefore, although paradigm examples of these offences will focus on adult offenders, the offences will apply equally where D is a similar age (or even younger) than V. As a result, because the consent of V is irrelevant to these offences, they have the potential to criminalise sexual experimentation between young people that we may wish to keep outside the criminal law. For example, at the extreme end, it would be possible to view a kiss between two consenting 12-year-olds as acts *from both parties* of sexual assault against someone aged 12 or under (contrary to s7).[107]

Foreseeing this possibility when the SOA 2003 first gained Royal Assent, the Home Secretary stated in a press release that there would be no prosecutions of children under 16 years old where sexual activity was genuinely consensual. This restriction seems sensible. However, by not including the restriction within the offences themselves *which would have been quite straightforward* to do, it relies on the much less consistent process of prosecutorial discretion.[108] The result has been unwelcome and unnecessary inconsistency. In certain cases (eg *R(S) v DPP*[109]) prosecutors have been willing to abandon charges of this kind against young

---

[103] The correctness of this decision should be doubted, but it remains a valid precedent.
[104] [2007] EWCA Crim 1118.
[105] The problems in this area for the general offence of incitement (now assisting and encouraging) are discussed at **11.4**.
[106] See discussion of the CPS at **1.1.6.1**.
[107] Bohlander, 'The Sexual Offences Act 2003 and the *Tyrrell* Principle Criminalising Victims' [2005] Crim LR 703.
[108] See discussion of the CPS at **1.1.6.1**.
[109] [2006] EWHC 2231 (Admin).

people where consent has been found. However, in others, such as G^{110} (discussed earlier[111]), prosecutors have pursued cases through to conviction despite the presence of consent.

Assessment matters...
If a problem question includes facts of this kind (ie a young person charged with an offence under ss5–8 in circumstances where V consents to the conduct) some mention of prosecutorial discretion would be useful. Although we do not usually discuss prosecutorial discretion in the context of the substantive law, the statement by the Home Secretary provides a clear guide that will limit the substantive application of these offence. However, in light of *G* and other prosecutions in conflict with the guidance, you should also highlight the possibility of a prosecution being brought. If it is brought, the issue of consent is irrelevant (it is not an element of the offence) and so as long as the elements of the crime are satisfied then D will be liable.

8.7 Sexual offences against children under 16 years

Offences in this category target offending against victims under 16 years old which is the age of sexual consent. Victims of this age are also covered by the offences in sections 1–4, and the lower end of the age range (under 13 years old) are also covered by the offences in sections 5–8. In this manner, we will often see considerable overlap between offences: cases where a single event could lead to liability under a number of different offences.

Extra detail...
The extent of overlap in offences within the SOA 2003 is very high. However, some overlap is common in many areas of the criminal law. The advantage of overlap is that there is much less likely to be any gaps between offences where D's conduct (although wrongful) does not quite come within the elements of an offence. However, on the other side, overlap can create confusion for prosecutors (and students!) trying to choose which offence to apply, and also lead to a lack of precise labelling of different wrongful acts in different ways.[112]

As with the offences against children discussed earlier (ss5–8), the consent or non-consent of V and D's belief in that consent, if any, are not relevant to these offences. As a result, the protection of young victims where consent is irrelevant is extended beyond those aged 12 and under (ss5–8) to include those up to 15 years old.

However, as we will see, these offences include two major differences from those within sections 5–8. First, where the victim is aged between 13 and 15, D will only be caught by the offence if he does not reasonably believe that V is aged 16 or over. Secondly, for the first time in this chapter, offences in this category are classified differently depending upon the age of D. We summarise the offences in the following sections with reference to those age restrictions.

---

[110] [2008] UKHL 37.
[111] See **8.6.1.2**.
[112] See 'Eye on assessment' at **8.10.1** for guidance on choosing the appropriate offence.

8.7.1 Adults offending against children under 16

The four offences set out in sections 9–12 apply to adults (aged 18 or over) who offend against children (aged under 16).

8.7.1.1 SOA 2003, s9: sexual activity with a child

Mirroring some of the substance from offences under sections 3 and 7, section 9 focuses on sexual touching. The maximum sentence varies depending upon the nature of the touching.[113]

> (1) A person aged 18 or over (D) commits an offence if—
>> (a) he intentionally touches another person (V),
>> (b) the touching is sexual, and
>> (c) either—
>>> (i) B is under 16 and A does not reasonably believe that B is 16 or over, or
>>> (ii) B is under 13.

The elements of section 9 are set out in **Table 8.11**.

Table 8.11 SOA 2003, s9

	Actus reus	**Mens rea**
Conduct element	Any conduct that causes the result	Voluntary
Circumstance element	D is aged 18 or over	No mens rea
	Touching is sexual	No mens rea
	V is aged 12 or under	No mens rea
	Or	
	V is aged 13–15	Lack of reasonable belief that V is aged 16 or over
Result element	Touching of V	Intention

Where V is aged 12 or under, the elements of this offence mirror the offence under section 7 precisely other than as to the restriction on D's age. D is liable if he intentionally touches V; the touching is sexual;[114] and V is aged 12 or under. Again, D and V may be male or female.[115] Issues of consent (actus reus or mens rea) are irrelevant, as are D's beliefs as to the sexual nature of his conduct, and the age of V.

---

[113] SOA 2003, s9(2) and (3).
[114] *Lister* [2005] EWCA Crim 1903: confirming again that passionate kissing will suffice.
[115] *Angela C* [2006] EWCA Crim 1781: 43-year-old lady having sex with 14-year-old boy.

Where V is between 13 and 15, D will avoid liability if when completing the conduct element he held a reasonable belief that V was aged 16 or over. Aside from this additional element of mens rea, the other elements of the offence are the same as where V is aged 12 or under.

8.7.1.2 SOA 2003, s10: causing or inciting a child to engage in sexual activity

Mirroring much from the offences under sections 4 and (more closely) 8, section 10 focuses on D's causing V to engage or inciting V to engage in sexual activity. Again, the maximum sentence will vary in line with the type of activity caused or incited.[116] The offence is commonly used to prosecute the senders of explicit text messages,[117] and in certain cases of sexual grooming.[118]

(1) A person aged 18 or over (D) commits an offence if—

    (a) he intentionally causes or incites another person (V) to engage in an activity,

    (b) the activity is sexual, and

    (c) either—

        (i) V is under 16 and D does not reasonably believe that V is 16 or over, or

        (ii) V is under 13.

Again, it is useful to view this section as two separate offences, set out in **Tables 8.12** and **8.13**.

Table 8.12 SOA 2003, s10

	Actus reus	**Mens rea**
Conduct element	Any conduct that causes the result	Voluntary
Circumstance element	D is aged 18 or older	No mens rea
	The activity in which V engaged is sexual	No mens rea
	V is aged 12 or under	No mens rea
	Or	
	V is aged 13–15	Lack of reasonable belief that V is aged 16 or over
Result element	V engages in an activity	Intention

---

116 SOA 2003, s10(2) and (3).
117 *Howell* [2007] EWCA Crim 1863.
118 Gillespie, 'Indecent Images, Grooming and the Law' [2006] Crim LR 412.

Table 8.13　SOA 2003, s10

	Actus reus	Mens rea
Conduct element	Any conduct that causes the result	Voluntary
Circumstance element	D is aged 18 or older	No mens rea
	D's communication with V incites her to engage in an activity	No mens rea
	The activity incited is sexual	No mens rea
	V is aged 12 or under	No mens rea
	Or	
	V is aged 13–15	Lack of reasonable belief that V is aged 16 or over
Result element	Communication with V	Intention

Where V is aged 12 or under, the elements of this offence mirror section 8 precisely except that D must be over 18. D will be liable either because he has intentionally caused V to engage in a sexual activity that has come about (offence in Table 8.12); or because he has incited (encouraged) V to engage in a sexual activity whether or not it later comes about (offence in Table 8.13). In each case, the consent of V; D's belief as to consent; D's belief as to the sexual nature of the conduct; and D's belief as to V's age are all irrelevant.

Where V is between 13 and 15, D will avoid liability if when completing the conduct element he held a reasonable belief that V was aged 16 or over. Aside from this additional element of mens rea, the other elements of the offence are the same.

8.7.1.3　SOA 2003, s11: engaging in sexual activity in the presence of a child

Moving away from the types of conduct criminalised in the sections we have discussed so far in this chapter, section 11 criminalises D who engages in a sexual activity in order to gain sexual gratification from being witnessed by a young person. For example, it will apply to D who masturbates in front of a child,[119] as well as 'doggers' (individuals who have sex in public because they enjoy being observed) where the activity can be viewed by children.[120]

> (1) A person aged 18 or over (D) commits an offence if—
>
>　(a) he intentionally engages in an activity,
>
>　(b) the activity is sexual,
>
>　(c) for the purpose of obtaining sexual gratification, he engages in it—
>
>　　(i)　when another person (V) is present or is in a place from which D can be observed, and
>
>　　(ii)　knowing or believing that V is aware, or intending that V should be aware, that he is engaging in it, and

---

[119] *Chevron* [2005] All ER 91: D masturbating in view of a 12-year-old on the beach.

[120] *WT* [2005] EWCA Crim 2448: husband and wife having their 9-year-old daughter photograph them during sex.

(d) either—

    (i)   V is under 16 and D does not reasonably believe that V is 16 or over, or

    (ii) V is under 13.

The elements of section 11 are set out in **Table 8.14**.

Table 8.14 SOA 2003, s11

	Actus reus	**Mens rea**
Conduct element	Any activity	Voluntary
Circumstance element	D's activity is sexual	No mens rea
	D is aged 18 or over	No mens rea
	V is present or can observe D	No mens rea
	V is aged 12 or under	No mens rea
	Or	
	V is aged 13–15	Lack of reasonable belief that V is aged 16 or over
Result element	None	None
Ulterior mens rea element	*	Intends, knows, or believes that V is aware he is engaging in the activity
		Intends to gain sexual gratification from V's presence and awareness

Actus reus of s11

The actus reus of section 11 catches D (aged 18 or over) where he performs a sexual activity whether alone or with another, and V is present or can observe D. The construction of 'present' *or* can 'observe' is important: allowing for liability where V is viewing the activity on a webcam, for example, where she is not present but can observe. It is unclear whether V must be viewing the activity in real time, and this will have to be clarified by the courts: for example, will it apply where D posts images of his sexual activity on the internet for children to view at a later point? The actus reus also requires that V is aged 15 or under.

Mens rea of s11

The mens rea of section 11 contains three core elements. First, D must be acting intentionally. Secondly, D must at least believe (note that recklessness is not sufficient) that V is aware that he is engaging in the activity. Thirdly, D must intend to gain sexual gratification from V's presence and awareness. These second two elements are examples of ulterior mens rea because they do not correspond to elements within the actus reus: D must believe that V is aware and must intend to gain sexual gratification, but it is *irrelevant* whether V actually is aware or whether D actually is sexually gratified.

Where V is aged 12 or under, no further mens rea is required. However, where V is between 13 and 15, it must be proved that D lacked a reasonable belief that V was aged 16 or over.

Don't be confused...
Where V unexpectedly walks in on her parents having sex, her parents do not commit an offence. Although several elements of the offence are likely to be satisfied, and the parents may even believe that the child is aware of what they are doing, they would only be liable if they intended to gain sexual gratification from their child's presence and awareness.

8.7.1.4 SOA 2003, s12: causing a child to watch a sexual act

Section 12 criminalises D, aged 18 or over, who causes V, aged 15 or younger, to view the sexual activity of another or view the image of a sexual act, doing so in order to gain sexual gratification. The primary target of this offence will be paedophiles who use sexual imagery whether of themselves or others as part of a grooming process.[121]

(1) A person aged 18 or over (D) commits an offence if—

  (a) for the purpose of obtaining sexual gratification, he intentionally causes another person (V) to watch a third person engaging in an activity, or to look at an image of any person engaging in an activity,

  (b) the activity is sexual, and

  (c) either—

    (i) V is under 16 and D does not reasonably believe that V is 16 or over, or

    (ii) V is under 13.

The elements of section 12 are set out in **Table 8.15**.

Table 8.15 SOA 2003, s12

	Actus reus	**Mens rea**
Conduct element	Any conduct that causes the result	Voluntary
Circumstance element	The activity viewed (directly or through an image) is sexual	No mens rea
	D is aged 18 or over	No mens rea
	V is aged 12 or under	No mens rea
	Or	
	V is aged 13–15	Lack of reasonable belief that V is aged 16 or over
Result element	V watches a third party engage in an activity or looks at an image of an activity	Intention
Ulterior mens rea element	*	Intends to gain sexual gratification from V's presence and awareness

---

[121] *L* [2006] EWCA Crim 2225: D sent images of himself masturbating to V's phone.

Actus reus of s12

D completes the actus reus where he (aged 18 or over) causes V (aged 15 or under) to watch an activity or view images of an activity; and that activity is sexual. Where D causes V to view an image of a person engaging in a sexual activity, the term 'image' has been defined broadly to include moving or still images, 3D images,[122] and even cartoons, etchings, and computer-generated pseudo-images.

Mens rea of s12

To complete the mens rea, at the time of acting D must intend that his conduct will cause V to watch another engage in an activity or to view images of an activity. The statute does not specify mens rea as to the 'sexual' nature of the conduct/image, implying that as long as it is considered sexual by the court (actus reus) then D's belief is irrelevant.[123] However, D must intend to gain sexual gratification from V viewing the activity. Interestingly, 'intention to gain sexual gratification' has been interpreted very broadly to include both the intention to gain immediate gratification (eg from viewing the child or knowing that the child is viewing the activity), as well as the intention to gain sexual gratification later (eg where causing V to view the activity is part of a grooming process leading to a possible sexual encounter with D).[124]

8.7.2 Young people offending against children under 16

A common feature of the offences in sections 9–12 is that D must be aged 18 or over. However, through section 13 of the SOA 2003, the same conduct will also be an offence if committed by someone under 18 years old.

8.7.2.1 SOA 2003, s13: child sex offences committed by children or young persons

Section 13 creates an offence for D (aged 17 or under) where he completes any of the conduct proscribed by sections 9–12. The difference between liability under section 13 and liability under sections 9–12 is that the maximum sentence for section 13 is considerably lower.[125]

> (1) A person under 18 commits an offence if he does anything which would be an offence under any of sections 9 to 12 if he were aged 18.

The elements of this offence are exactly the same as discussed in relation to sections 9–12, the only difference being the age of D.

Returning to the issue of overlapping offences and prosecutorial discretion, it will be interesting to see the extent to which this offence with its lower maximum sentence is used in favour of more serious offences where D is under 18 years old. It is contended that this offence (s13) should usually be preferred. However, this does not rule out the possibility of other offences being used *which may be a criticism of overlapping*

---

[122] SOA 2003, s97(4).
[123] This could cause problems, particularly in relation to artwork.
[124] *Abdullahi* [2006] EWCA Crim 2060.
[125] SOA 2003, s13(2).

offence. A good illustration of this is the case of *G*,[126] discussed earlier,[127] where D (aged 15) had consensual intercourse with V (aged 12), believing that she was over 13 years old. D was convicted with the offence of raping a child (s5), where issues of consent and the age of D are both irrelevant. On appeal, D claimed that if he was to be prosecuted at all, which he claimed would be contrary to the Home Office guidance,[128] it should have been for an offence under section 13. This was rejected by the House of Lords: D satisfied the elements of the section 5 offence, and it was not for him to decide which offence to charge.

Assessment matters...

Where an event within a problem question could be charged as more than one offence, the general rule is that you discuss the most serious of the potential offences first, and stop your discussion if you find the offence elements to be satisfied (eg if D stabs and kills V, within this single act D may have committed assault; battery; ABH; GBH; manslaughter; etc, but you should begin with a discussion of murder, and if murder is committed you do not need to discuss the others). However, where D is under 18 years old and committing a sexual offence, because of the prosecutorial guidance it is best to begin with a discussion of section 13. You should highlight if D may be alternatively guilty of a section 5 offence, for example, and note the possibility and the case of G, but it is likely that section 13 will usually be preferred.

8.7.3 Preparatory offences against children under 16

The final two offences in this category (ss14 and 15) are preparatory in nature: they criminalise behaviour that is likely to lead to sexual contact with a child, looking to intervene at the stage of preparation before any sexual contact has occurred.

8.7.3.1 SOA 2003, s14: arranging or facilitating commission of a child sex offence

Section 14 criminalises D (of any age) who arranges or facilitates conduct that would amount to an offence under sections 9–13 by himself or another, intending or believing that that future offence will come about. This offence is targeted at those who facilitate sexual offences against children, either by arranging meetings (eg transporting the child) or in other ways (eg providing a venue).

(1) A person commits an offence if—

    (a) he intentionally arranges or facilitates something that he intends to do, intends another person to do, or believes that another person will do, in any part of the world, and

    (b) doing it will involve the commission of an offence under any of sections 9 to 13.

The elements of section 14 are set out in **Table 8.16**.

---

[126] [2008] UKHL 37.
[127] See **8.6.1.2**.
[128] See **8.6.5**.

Table 8.16 SOA 2003, s14

	Actus reus	Mens rea
Conduct element	Any conduct that causes the result	Voluntary
Circumstance element	The activity would amount to an offence under ss9–13	No mens rea
Result element	Arranging or facilitating an activity	Intention
Ulterior mens rea element	*	Intention to carry out the activity personally Or Intention or belief that another person will carry out the activity

Actus reus of s14

The actus reus of section 14 requires D to have arranged or facilitated a future activity that will amount to an offence within sections 9–13, whether this future offence is to be committed by D or another. As with all preparatory or inchoate offences, this future offence does not need to come about for D to be liable for the offence under section 14: he is liable for the separate wrong of arranging or facilitating it.

The central terms of 'arranges' and 'facilitates' are not defined in the statute, but are likely to be interpreted widely to include a broad range of behaviour leading to potential future offences. For example, in the case of R,[129] D asked an adult prostitute (X) whether she could arrange a 12-year-old prostitute for him. D was eventually convicted of 'arranging' under section 14 despite reaching no agreement with X, and despite asking her to do the arranging for him. Making contact in this manner was sufficient. On this basis, it seems that the offence is even wide enough to catch D (aged 18) who asks to meet his girlfriend (aged 15) for sex, even where she says no.

Mens rea of s14

D satisfies the mens rea where he intends to arrange or facilitate the activity, and where he either intends to carry it out himself or intends or believes that another will do so. The mens rea will not be satisfied if D arranges or facilitates merely foreseeing a risk that the offence will come about: for example, D rents a hotel room to a man and young girl foreseeing that it *may* be used for abuse.

---

[129] [2009] EWCA Crim 1472. See Gillespie, 'Case Comment: Attempting to Find a Child Prostitute' (2009) 73 J Crim L 378.

Statutory exception to s14

Following concern that section 14 might criminalise youth or health workers and teen magazine columnists providing advice to teens on safe sexual practices, Parliament inserted a wide-ranging exception into the statute.

(2) A person does not commit an offence under this section if—

    (a) he arranges or facilitates something that he believes another person will do, but that he does not intend to do or intend another person to do, and

    (b) any offence within subsection (1)(b) would be an offence against a child for whose protection he acts.

(3) For the purposes of subsection (2), a person acts for the protection of a child if he acts for the purpose of—

    (a) protecting the child from sexually transmitted infection,

    (b) protecting the physical safety of the child,

    (c) preventing the child from becoming pregnant, or

    (d) promoting the child's emotional well-being by the giving of advice,

    and not for the purpose of obtaining sexual gratification or for the purpose of causing or encouraging the activity constituting the offence within subsection (1)(b) or the child's participation in it.

Terms such as 'emotional well-being' are ambiguous and will require interpretation by the courts. However, it seems that as long as D is acting with the intention to assist V in an accepted context, and does not actively want V to engage in sexual practices for reasons of personal sexual gratification or otherwise, he will avoid liability under section 14.

8.7.3.2 SOA 2003, s15: meeting a child following sexual grooming, etc

The much publicised grooming offence under section 15 criminalises D (aged 18 or over) who communicates with V (aged 16 or under) on at least two occasions and then travels or arranges to meet V with the intention to commit a sexual offence. The offence is primarily targeted at adults who groom children through internet chat forums etc.

(1) A person aged 18 or over (D) commits an offence if—

    (a) D has met or communicated with another person (V) on at least two occasions and subsequently—

        (i)   D intentionally meets V,

        (ii) D travels with the intention of meeting V in any part of the world or arranges to meet V in any part of the world, or

        (iii) V travels with the intention of meeting D in any part of the world,

    (b) D intends to do anything to or in respect of V, during or after the meeting mentioned in paragraph (a)(i) to (iii) and in any part of the world, which if done will involve the commission by D of a relevant offence,

    (c) V is under 16, and

    (d) D does not reasonably believe that V is 16 or over.

The elements of section 15 are set out in **Table 8.17**.

Table 8.17 SOA 2003, s15

	Actus reus	Mens rea
Conduct element	Any conduct that causes the result	Voluntary
Circumstance element	D is aged 18 or over V is aged 15 or younger	No mens rea Lack of reasonable belief that V is aged 16 or over
Result element	Meeting or communicating with V on at least two occasions Meeting V, travelling to meet V, or V travelling with the intention to meet	Intention Intention
Ulterior mens rea element	*	Intention to commit a sexual offence with V at the meeting or after it

Actus reus of s15

To satisfy the actus reus of section 15, D (aged 18 or over) must first meet or communicate with V (aged 15 or younger) on two separate occasions. It is not clear whether two internet posts within the same conversation will count as two occasions. It is clear, however, that despite the offence label of 'sexual grooming', these initial communications do not need to be sexual.[130]

Following this initial contact, it must also be proved that D subsequently met V *or* travelled to meet V *or* V travelled to meet D. In this manner, the offence can be completed without D ever meeting V.

Mens rea of s15

D has the requisite mens rea where he intends the prior meetings/communications with V; intends to meet V on the subsequent occasion; and intends to commit a sexual offence at the time of or after this final occasion. Additionally, D must lack a reasonable belief that V is over 16 years old: required (unlike other offences) even where V is aged 12 or under.

8.8 Status and relationship-based sexual offences

Just as offences in the previous category (ss5–15) are constructed to protect a V who is vulnerable due to their youth, other categories of sexual offences are designed in relation to similar vulnerabilities. These include cases where D is in a position of trust;

---

[130] *Gaviria* [2010] EWCA Crim 1693.

where D is a family member; as well as where V has a mental disorder impeding choice. In this section, we provide only a brief overview of these offences.

8.8.1 Sexual offences abusing a position of trust

Sections 16–19 create four offences that mirror those of sections 9–12 (discussed earlier) almost entirely, applying where D:

- sexually touches V (s16);
- causes or incites V to engage in sexual activity (s17);
- engages in sexual activity in V's presence for the purpose of sexual gratification (s18); or
- causes V to watch a sexual activity or image for the purpose of sexual gratification (s19).

Two differences at once expand and narrow liability in comparison to sections 9–12. First, expanding potential liability, sections 16–19 apply to victims up to the age of 17 (ss9–12 only apply to victims up to the age of 15).[131] Secondly, narrowing potential liability, sections 16–19 will only be committed by D who holds a position of trust over V. 'Position of trust' is defined in great detail within sections 21 and 22: including, for example, teachers, care-home workers, guardians, etc.

> **Point to remember...**
> Mirroring sections 9–12, issues of V's consent are irrelevant to D's liability under sections 16–19. Thus, where V is 16 or 17 years old, although she may legally consent to sexual intercourse, her consent to intercourse with D (who holds a position of trust) will not prevent his liability under sections 16–19.

Although offences under this category are still committed where V is aged 16 or 17, so is over the age of sexual consent, and where V consents to a sexual activity with D who is in a position of trust, there are two important exceptions to this.

A) **Marriage exception (s23):** D will not commit an offence under sections 16–19 if V is aged 16 or over and D proves that (*note the reverse burden of proof*) they are legally married.

B) **Prior sexual relationship exception (s24):** D will not commit an offence under sections 16–19 if he proves that (*note the reverse burden of proof*) they were involved in a sexual relationship immediately prior to the position of trust arising, and that V was aged 16 or over throughout this period. This will cover cases, for example, where D is involved in a legitimate sexual relationship with V (aged 17), becomes V's teacher (position of trust), and continues the relationship.

8.8.2 Sexual offences within a family relationship

There are two sets of offences within the SOA 2003 that focus on sexual activity within a family relationship: sections 25 and 26 that deal with child family relationships, and sections 64 and 65 that deal with adults. Again, in neither case is the consent of V a relevant consideration.

---

[131] *Wilson* [2007] EWCA Crim 2762: teacher engaged in sex with 15- and 16-year-olds.

Section 25 (mirroring s9, discussed earlier) criminalises D who intentionally touches V sexually. In contrast with section 9, this offence applies to D of any age, and will apply even where V is aged 16 or 17 as long as D does not reasonably believe that V is older. It must, however, be demonstrated that D and V have a family relationship (defined in s27), and that D knows or could reasonably be expected to know that they have this relationship. Section 26 is similarly constructed, but focuses on D who incites or causes V, aged 17 or under and with a family relationship, to engage in a sexual activity. As with the 'abuse of a position of trust' offences discussed previously, these offences also include exceptions where D and V are lawfully married (s28) and where they had a lawful sexual relationship prior to the family relationship (s29).

> *Terminology...*
>
> The definition of 'family relationship' in section 27 goes well beyond blood relations to include stepchildren, foster children, adopted children, and even where D and V simply cohabit in circumstances where D cares for V in the manner of a family member.[132] This demonstrates a move in these offences, away from the criminalisation of heterosexual incest, and towards gender-neutral offences based on sexual exploitation.

The second set of offences, set out in sections 64 and 65, are much more controversial.[133] These offences criminalise D (aged 16 or over) who intentionally and sexually penetrates with his penis the vagina, anus, or mouth of V (a relative aged 18 or over) or penetrates the vagina or anus of such a person with anything else: section 64. They also criminalise D (aged 16 or over) who consents to being sexually penetrated by V (aged 18 or over) in the same manner: section 65. In each case, the definition of 'adult relative' is considerably narrower than the definition of 'family relationship' discussed above, and D will avoid liability if he did not know and could not have reasonably been expected to know that he was V's relative. These offences are particularly controversial when you consider that if adult relatives D and V have a consensual sexual relationship, then they are both committing an offence: one for penetration (s64) and one for consenting to being penetrated (s65). Where this is the case, it is difficult to identify the *victim* the law is seeking to protect.

8.8.3 Sexual offences against people with a mental disorder impeding choice

There are a number of offences in this category, designed to protect those with a mental disorder from exploitation and abuse. In each case, the consent or non-consent of V, as well as the gender and ages of D and V, are not relevant offence elements.

A) Sections 30–33: These sections criminalise D where he intentionally sexually touches V (s30); intentionally incites or causes V to engage in a sexual activity (s31); intentionally engages in a sexual activity in the presence of V for the purposes of sexual gratification (s32); or intentionally causes V to watch a sexual act or view a sexual image for the purposes of sexual gratification (s33). In each case, V must have a mental disorder that makes her *unable to refuse*, and D must know or reasonably be expected to know that V has a disorder that may cause such an inability. This was discussed in C.

---

[132] Brackenridge and Williams, 'Incest in the "Family" of Sport' (2004) 154 NLJ 179.
[133] Spencer, 'Sexual Offences Act 2003: Child and Family Offences' [2004] Crim LR 347.

C [2009] 1 WLR 1786

V had a history of mental disorders manifesting in manic episodes and delusions involving irrational fears for her safety. D befriended V, gave her crack cocaine, and made her perform acts of oral sex on him and another. V claimed that she only consented out of fear for her safety.

- Crown Court: guilty of the section 30 offence. Capacity undermined by fears originating from mental illness.
- Court of Appeal: allowing D's appeal. Capacity not undermined by condition of this kind.
- House of Lords: Court of Appeal was wrong, capacity can be undermined where V understands the nature of the act but a mental condition prevents her making a real choice. Even if the inability to refuse is temporary.

B) **Sections 34–37:** These sections criminalise the same conduct as sections 30–33, but this time instead of the inability to refuse V's mental disorder must be accompanied by an agreement from V that is caused by D's *threats or deception or inducement*, in circumstances in which D knows or could reasonably be expected to know that V has a disorder. Particularly in the context of 'inducements', these offences go considerably further than the conclusive presumptions of non-consent discussed in relation to sections 1–4.

C) **Sections 38–41:** Again, these offences focus on the same range of conduct. Here, the additional factor is that V is mentally disordered, and that D is in a *relationship as a carer*.

The range of offences highlighted earlier provides the CPS with a complicated and confusing task, with one set of facts potentially coming within the elements of several overlapping offences. However, on the other hand, the ability to choose between a number of offences of this kind, all targeting slightly different wrongs, at least potentially enables the CPS to select appropriate offences that more accurately label the offender's specific conduct.

8.9 Reform

The emotive nature of sexual offences, as well as the continued low reporting[134] and conviction rates,[135] means that discussions of potential reform in this area are always high on the agenda. The SOA 2003 represents a comprehensive and still relatively recent reform, broadly welcomed for its gender neutrality, broadening of liability, specific labelling, and use of modern and appropriate language.[136] However, several problem areas remain. In this section we provide a brief discussion of three of the most important: the appropriate boundaries of liability for rape; the specific problem of voluntary intoxication and consent; and the issue of undue complexity.

A) **Boundaries of rape:** The offence of rape (s1) is one of the most well-known and highly stigmatised within the criminal law. Partly because of this central role, the

---

134 Consistently evidenced within the British Crime Survey (victims survey).
135 Consistently evidenced within Home Office Crime Statistics. Such statistics can, of course, be misleading, and should be treated with caution. For example, trial conviction rates are 55 per cent of cases that start, which is significantly higher than many other offences, eg threats to kill offences are around 16 per cent.
136 Home Office, *SOA 2003: Stocktake* (2006).

boundaries of rape (both actus reus and mens rea) are a common focus of academic attention. This has arisen particularly within two interesting debates.

The first debate of note focuses on the role of consent within the offence rape. Under the current law, as we discussed previously, the non-consent of V is central to the wrongfulness of D's conduct: consensual penile penetration is a social good, whereas non-consensual penile penetration is rape. There are two main problems with this. First, it is difficult to prove a lack of consent: in the absence of force, there will often be little evidence. Secondly, and just as importantly, 'consent' is a difficult concept to define with the degree of objectivity and consistency that is required for such a central role. The current law has attempted to mitigate this with a definition across three statutory sections (ss74, 75, and 76), but despite this the definition is rightly criticised for its lack of precision. These problems have given rise to a number of interesting academic alternatives. Some of these have focused on redefinitions of consent, attempting to provide a more robust concept for the task.[137] More radically, others have sought to reduce the centrality of non-consent by reinterpreting the act of penetration as inherently wrongful, shifting the focus to circumstances that must be observed by D to make his wrongful act acceptable as, for example, the *active* willingness of V.[138]

The second debate in this area concerns the label of 'rape' and its role within potential reform. On one side of this debate, the powerful label and its stigmatising effect can be presented as positive aspects of the criminal law: sending a clear message about unacceptable behaviour and condemning those who offend. However, on the other hand, a powerful and well-known label can constrict and hamper reform. For example, where the definition of rape has been expanded to include anal and oral penetration, there is discussion not only about whether this conduct is equivalently wrongful to be included within the offence, but also whether it will be acceptable within the common meaning of 'rape'.[139] Part of the concern is that by widening the offence beyond its common understanding, the label will be misunderstood or undermined. In extreme cases, jury members with strong impressions of what rape is may be less inclined to find liability outside this understanding, even where the legal elements are satisfied.[140] Entrenched common understandings of offences like rape can also lead to the entrenchment of rape myths (eg that stranger rape is more serious), as well as prejudicial attitudes (eg relating to V's sexual history).[141] This is part of the reasoning behind the decision in Canada, for example, to abandon the label of rape entirely.[142]

B) Voluntarily intoxicated consent: The general policy of the law towards D who acts in a state of voluntary intoxication is that an intoxicated intention is still an intention: D may regret his intoxicated actions when he is sober, he may even claim that he would not have done them if he had not been intoxicated, but as long as he displayed the

---

[137] Munro, 'An Unholy Trinity?' (2010) 63 OJLS 45; Huigens, 'Is Strict Liability Rape Defensible?' in Duff and Green (eds), *Defining Crimes* (2005) 196; Tadros, 'Rape Without Consent' (2006) 26 OJLS 515.

[138] Dempsey and Herring, 'Why Sexual Penetration Requires Justification' (2007) 27 OJLS 467; Herring, 'Mistaken Sex' [2005] Crim LR 511.

[139] Home Office, *Setting the Boundaries* (2000).

[140] Ashworth and Temkin, 'Rape, Sexual Assault and the Problems of Consent' [2004] Crim LR 328.

[141] Elvin, 'The Concept of Consent under the Sexual Offences Act 2003' (2008) 72 J Crim L 516.

[142] Gotell, 'Canadian Sexual Assault Law' in McGlynn and Munro (eds), *Rethinking Rape Law* (2010) 209.

required state of mind when intoxicated this will not affect his liability.[143] In relation to rape and other sexual offences, the law will *also* often have to deal with V who has become voluntarily intoxicated and then provides some form of consent to sexual activity with D. In such a case, should we follow the same hard line employed for defendants and hold that intoxicated consent is still consent, or should we provide additional protection for the intoxicated V who has *albeit voluntarily* become particularly vulnerable to sexual abuse?

The current law does not provide a clear answer to this question. Where V is so intoxicated that she becomes unconscious, or where she is tricked into consuming an intoxicant against her will, the SOA 2003 creates a rebuttable presumption that V is not consenting (s75). However, no presumption will apply where V has become heavily voluntarily intoxicated but not yet unconscious. In such cases, the general definition of consent in section 74 (focusing on freedom and capacity) will be applied, and the jury must decide whether V consented or not whatever level of intoxication is present.[144] Whether V in this scenario should be provided with further protection, and whether the law should send a clearer message to men (in particular) that taking sexual advantage of intoxicated people is not acceptable, is an interesting and contentious debate.[145]

C) **Undue complexity:** Modern statutes have generally become longer and this is not necessarily a bad thing: by setting out the detail of an offence, the public are more accurately warned, and there is also less need for appeal cases to clarify ambiguous offence elements. However, certain statutes have become unduly and unhelpfully complex, and this is certainly a criticism that can be levelled at the SOA 2003.[146]

The SOA 2003 does not define offences simply in relation to general harms, but rather provides multiple elements that set out each specific form of conduct that will be caught by the offence. In doing so, individual offences can become difficult to follow, and care must be taken to work methodically through the elements when applying them to factual cases. A useful example of this, from an offence we have not discussed in this chapter, is voyeurism (s67). D, for the purpose of obtaining sexual gratification, observes or records or enables another to observe (with equipment or otherwise) V doing a 'private act' knowing V does not consent to observation for that purpose. By section 68, 'private acts' are those 'in a private structure in which one would expect privacy and V's genitals, buttocks or breasts are exposed or covered only with underwear, or V is using the lavatory, or V is doing a sexual act not of a kind ordinarily done in public'! Where offences are set out in this level of detail, we may question how effectively they are providing a warning for the general public.[147] They are also likely to cause problems in practice, with prosecutors identifying the wrong offences and/or failing to apply each of the essential elements.[148]

Extra detail...

Alongside the criticism of undue complexity, it is perhaps even more glaring and unsatisfactory that central concepts such as 'consent' have been defined so briefly and ambiguously within the statute.

---

[143] The intoxication rules are discussed at **13.2**.

[144] *Bree* [2007] EWCA Crim 804.

[145] Wallerstein, 'A Drunken Consent is Still a Consent—Or Is It?' (2009) 73 J Crim L 318; Wertheimer, 'Intoxicated Consent to Sexual Relations' (2001) 20 Law & Phil 373.

[146] Spencer, 'The Drafting of Criminal Legislation: Need it Be So Impenetrable?' (2008) 67 CLJ 585.

[147] See **1.4.1**.

[148] We see this in a recent Australian case, eg, where there was a confusion of elements between non-consent offences and abuse of position offences: *Gillard v The Queen* [2014] HCA 16.

8.10 Eye on assessment

The complexity of the offences within the SOA 2003 and the quantity of offences make their application to problem facts particularly challenging. However, as long as you adopt the methodical approach that we have repeated throughout this text, they need not cause you too many problems.

STEP 1 Identify the potential criminal event in the facts

This should be simply stated (eg 'The first potential criminal event arises where D touches V'). The role of this stage is to highlight which part of the question you are answering before you begin to apply the law.

STEP 2 Identify the potential offence

Again, state this simply (eg 'When touching V, D may be liable for sexual assault'). The role of this stage is to highlight which offence you are going to apply.

STEP 3 Applying the offence to the facts

Having highlighted a possible offence, Step 3 requires you to both identify the actus reus and mens rea of that offence, *and* apply them to the facts.

In this section, we are going to focus on Steps 2 and 3. Step 2 is usually straightforward, but in the context of sexual offences (if you are not told in the question which offence to apply) the choice between a large number of potential offences can be quite challenging. We provide some guidance on this. Following this, we will discuss Step 3 in the context of sexual offences, providing an outline of how to structure your analysis of complex offences such as rape.

8.10.1 Step 2: identifying which sexual offence to apply

Certain problem questions will specify a particular offence that should be applied (eg 'Discuss D's potential liability for rape'), and where this is the case, only the specified offence should be considered. Others may specify a certain range of offences (eg 'Discuss D's potential liability under sections 1–4 of the SOA 2003') and, again, the limited range will make it much easier to identify which offence should be applied. (*Note: the rule of thumb is that you should begin with the most serious potential offence first.*)

However, there may be problem questions that simply require you to consider 'D's liability for sexual offences' generally. In this case, Step 2 (identifying which offence to apply) becomes very important. To help with this task, **Table 8.18** sets out each of the offences that have been discussed in this chapter, with a guide of how the appropriate offences can be identified quickly.

Table 8.18 Identifying which sexual offence to charge

Age of V	V consents	D is in a position of trust	D is a family member	V has a mental disorder impeding choice	V does not consent
18+	No offence	No offence	ss64–65 (requires D's MR as to familial status)	ss30–33 (requires D's MR as to disorder)	ss1–4 (requires D's MR as to non-consent)
16–17	No offence	ss16–19 (requires D's MR as to position of trust)	ss25–26 (requires D's MR as to familial status)	ss30–33 (requires D's MR as to disorder)	ss1–4 (requires D's MR as to non-consent)
13–15	ss9–15 (requires D's MR as to V's age)	(ss16–19) *But easier to apply the non-specific offences:* ss9–15	(ss25–26) *But easier to apply the non-specific offences:* ss9–15	ss30–33 (requires D's MR as to disorder) *May be easier to apply* ss9–15	ss1–4 (requires D's MR as to non-consent) *May be easier to apply* ss9–15
0–12	ss5–8 ss10–14 s15 (requires D's MR as to V's age for s15) (s9)	(ss16–19) *But easier to apply the non-specific offences:* ss5–8, 10–14, 15	(ss25–26) *But easier to apply the non-specific offences:* ss5–8, 10–14, 15	(ss30–33) *But easier to apply the non-specific offences:* ss5–8, 10–14, 15	(ss1–4) *But easier to apply the non-specific offences:* ss5–8, 10–14, 15

Using **Table 8.18**:

(a) First look to the age of V, and this will identify the correct row of potential offences in the table. Many of the sexual offences will only apply to certain ages, or apply different rules depending upon the age of V.

(b) Next you must look (in very general terms at this stage) at the sort of factors that *may* be present in the facts (ie non-consent; D is in a position of trust; D is a family member; or D has a mental disorder impeding choice). This will identify the correct column in the table.

(c) The intersection of V's age (row) and other relevant factor (column) will provide the relevant offences that should be applied. In doing so, the following should be noted:

   (i) where two or more relevant factors are present (eg D is a family member and V does not consent), then both sets of offences can be applied;

   (ii) where certain offences are emboldened and in a small box, this means that they can be applied but it will be easier to apply the non-specific offences. For example, where V is aged 12 or younger and does not consent to sexual contact, the offences within sections 1–4 can be applied, but it will be easier to apply offences such as sections 5–8 where the same conduct is criminalised (with the same maximum sentences) because there is no need to prove the absence of consent.

> **Assessment matters...**
> Even when using this table, there is likely to be more than one offence that could apply to a particular factual scenario. Where this is the case, you should follow the rule of thumb to apply the most serious offence first. If you find liability then you need not explore alternatives. Where there is a doubt (where an element of the offence may not be satisfied) it may be useful to go on to explore the next most serious offence that could apply as an alternative.
>
> The only exception to this, in the context of sexual offences, is where D is under 16 years old. In this case, although D may be liable for a more serious offence, prosecutorial guidance suggests that you should first explore the offence designed for younger defendants (s13).

8.10.2 Step 3: structuring your analysis of rape

In this section we provide an outline of how you should structure your analysis of the actus reus and mens rea of rape. The same structure is easily transferrable to the other non-consent-based offences (ss1–4), and can be adapted for the other offences as well. As we are dealing with statutory offences, your identification of the law in order to apply it to the problem facts should *always* begin with the statute. Case law can (and should) be used to inform and clarify the statute within your discussion, but the statute provides your most authoritative framework.

- **Actus reus**
  - As with all offences, you should begin with the conduct element. For rape, it is enough to ask simply whether, on the facts, D's movement has caused the penetration of V's vagina, anus, or mouth with his penis.

o Next you should consider the circumstance element of the offence: did V consent to the penetration?

– Do the facts of the case come within the conclusive presumptions of non-consent (s76)? If yes, you can conclude that V lacked consent. If not, continue to the next stage.

– Do the facts of the case come within the rebuttable presumptions of non-consent (s75)? If yes, D must provide evidence that V was consenting. If not, all burdens (legal and evidential) remain on the prosecution. However, either way, you should continue to the next stage.

– Consider the general definition of consent (s74), considering issues of freedom and capacity. The definition in section 74 leaves considerable discretion to the jury, so remember to talk in terms of *likely* outcomes.

- **Mens rea**

o The first part of the mens rea will usually be straightforward: did D penetrate V intentionally? Where the answer is a simple yes, there is no need to discuss in any great detail, although you should not leave it out entirely. Where there is some doubt (eg D was being physically manipulated by another), you should discuss in more detail.

o The second part is to question whether D lacked a reasonable belief in V's consent. Remember to keep this element (mens rea as to non-consent) separate from the issue of whether V did in fact consent (actus reus). You should again consider the presumptions of non-consent (ss76 and 75) as these are also mens rea presumptions. If these do not apply (or a s75 presumption is rebutted), the mens rea question can be usefully analysed as two questions.

– Would a reasonable person in D's position have believed that V was consenting? If no, then D satisfies the mens rea. If yes, continue to the next question.

– Did D hold this belief at the time of penetration? If no, D satisfies the mens rea. If yes, D does not satisfy the mens rea and is not liable for rape.

Beware...

Particularly when discussing consent, we have referenced several cases that pre-date the SOA 2003. These cases will often have informed the SOA 2003 and can provide a useful point of discussion where the statute is unclear. However, remember that they are no longer authoritative precedent as to what the law is now, which can only be found from the SOA 2003 itself and the cases that have come after it.

 ONLINE RESOURCE CENTRE

www.oxfordtextbooks.co.uk/orc/smithandhogan/

This chapter is accompanied by a selection of online resources to help you with this topic, including:

- **Multiple choice questions**
- **Chapter summary sheet**

- Two **sample examination questions** with answer guidance
- **Further reading**

Also available on the Online Resource Centre are:

- A selection of **videos** from the authors explaining key topics and principles
- **Legal updates**
- Useful **weblinks**

9

Property offences

9.1 Introduction

Having discussed offences against the person, fatal (**Chapters 5** and **6**), non-fatal (**Chapter 7**), and sexual (**Chapter 8**), this chapter and **Chapter 10** move onto consider offences against property. Offences within this category are many and varied, criminalising conduct such as the taking of another's property (eg theft, robbery, etc), possessing stolen or criminal property (eg handling stolen goods, money laundering, etc), as well as damaging another's property (eg criminal damage, arson, etc). Beyond such crimes, there are also a number of specific technical offences designed to protect particular property rights, such as those relating to intellectual and/or digital property, vehicle misuse, and so on. Through such offences, the criminal law provides protection for the full range of civil law property rights, enabling the system of civil ownership to exist and function.[1]

Within the wide range of property crimes, this chapter will focus on a selection of core offences.

- **Theft:** D dishonestly appropriates V's property.
- **Robbery:** D uses force to steal V's property.
- **Burglary:** D trespasses onto V's property, committing (or intending to commit) one of a number of offences.
- **Handling stolen goods:** D deals in specified ways with V's property which has been stolen.
- **Blackmail:** D threatens V in order to gain her property.
- **Criminal damage:** D damages V's property.

Each of these offences are defined by statute, and often in considerable detail. In the following sections we discuss each in turn.

In **Chapter 10**, still focusing on property crimes, we analyse the fraud offences. We discuss these separately in light of the major revisions brought by the Fraud Act 2006. The new fraud offences are also distinct from most other property offences because they are conduct crimes, focusing on D's inchoate criminal intentions: criminalising D for acting with the intention to interfere with V's property rights, rather than for actually doing so.[2]

9.2 Theft

Theft is defined in section 1(1) of the Theft Act 1968 (TA 1968), with further detail provided over sections 2–6. The maximum penalty on indictment is seven years' imprisonment.[3]

(1) A person is guilty of theft if he dishonestly appropriates property belonging to another with the intention of permanently depriving the other of it...

---

[1] Ormerod and Williams, *Smith's Law of Theft* (9th edn, 2007) and *Smith and Hogan's Criminal Law* (14th edn, 2015), Ch19.

[2] We discuss the meaning of inchoate liability at **4.2.1.2**.

[3] Theft Act 1968, s7.

The elements of theft are set out in **Table 9.1**.

Table 9.1 Theft

	Actus reus	Mens rea
Conduct element	Any conduct causing the result	Voluntary
Circumstance element	What is appropriated is property	Knowledge
	belonging to another	Knowledge
	D's appropriation is dishonest	Knowledge
Result element	D appropriates V's property	Intention
Ulterior mens rea element	*	Intention to permanently deprive V of her property

Theft may be more straightforwardly presented as five core offence elements, as in **Table 9.2**. Although consistent with **Table 9.1** (separating actus reus and mens rea), the focus on five core elements in **Table 9.2** is generally preferred: mirroring the statutory sections of the TA 1968, and reflecting the most common approach of the courts.

Table 9.2 Theft

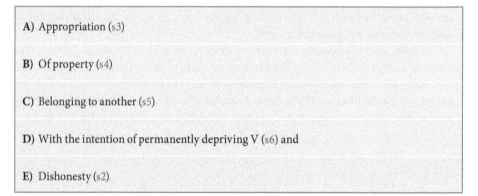

A) Appropriation (s3)

B) Of property (s4)

C) Belonging to another (s5)

D) With the intention of permanently depriving V (s6) and

E) Dishonesty (s2)

We discuss each of these offence elements in turn. It is important to remember that liability requires the prosecution to prove that D had satisfied *every* element and for these elements to occur at the same time.

9.2.1 Appropriation

Appropriation is defined in section 3 of the TA 1968. Section 3(1) states that:

Any assumption by a person of the rights of an owner amounts to an appropriation, and this includes, where he has come by the property (innocently or not) without stealing it, any later assumption of a right to it by keeping or dealing with it as owner.

Despite the relative clarity of section 3(1), the meaning of 'appropriation' has generated considerable dispute in the appellate courts, including four cases in the House of Lords. In resolving these disputes, the courts have generally preferred to interpret the term broadly. Three central points of debate have arisen: whether D must appropriate all of the rights of the owner; whether consensual appropriation will satisfy this element; and whether D appropriates where V has given the property as a valid gift in civil law.

9.2.1.1 Assuming the rights of an owner

Section 3(1) is clear that assuming the rights of an owner will amount to an appropriation. The most obvious cases will be where D takes V's property and treats it as her own. However, as we will see when discussing 'belonging to another' later, the ownership of property is made up of a bundle of associated rights, such as possession, control, legal and equitable rights, and so on. Therefore, the question emerges whether D appropriates if she simply assumes *one* of these rights as opposed to the complete bundle. The answer, confirmed in *Morris*, is that assumption of any one property right will be sufficient.

> ### *Morris* [1984] AC 320
>
> D switched labels on supermarket goods in order to purchase the more expensive goods at the (false) lower price. He proceeded to the checkout and paid the lower price. D was then charged with theft.
>
> - Crown Court: guilty of theft.
> - Court of Appeal: conviction upheld on appeal.
> - House of Lords: appeal dismissed. When swapping the labels, D assumed 'a' right of the owner (the right to price the goods) and this was sufficient (at that point) to amount to an appropriation.

It has been cogently argued that *Morris* represents an incorrect interpretation of the TA 1968 and that appropriation should only be found where D assumes all of the rights of an owner.[4] However, the approach in *Morris* has been confirmed subsequently by the House of Lords in *Gomez*[5] and so, for better or worse, this is the approach that should be applied. Importantly, this means that the taking of a single item can involve several distinct appropriations at different times. For example, if D takes an item from V with the intention of borrowing it and returning it later then she appropriates at the point of taking physical possession. It is at that point that D assumes rights of possession and control. But if she later decides to keep the item, then this later decision amounts to a further appropriation when she assumes the rights of ownership.[6]

---

[4] For discussion of this and support for the decision, see Melissaris, 'The Concept of Appropriation and the Offence of Theft' (2007) 70 MLR 581.

[5] [1993] AC 442.

[6] Indeed, this second appropriation (where D decides to keep the property) is explicitly catered for in the latter part of s3(1): 'this includes, where he has come by the property (innocently or not) without stealing it, any later assumption of a right to it by keeping or dealing with it as owner.'

Following *Morris*, it is clear that D can appropriate certain property rights by omission or through the mental 'act' of deciding to treat V's property as her own. Of course, where D discovers that she has taken possession of V's property accidentally as, for example, where it is picked up by D's child, and only discovered when the child takes it home, D will *not* be assumed to have appropriated that property if she has not treated it as her own or made a decision to keep it.[7] However, if she does so decide, this and any other assumption of rights will be sufficient to constitute the appropriation element of the actus reus.

A final point should be clarified regarding 'continuing acts' of appropriation.[8] In most cases of theft, the act of appropriation is best analysed as a single and instant event: for example, if D steals V's bag when she grabs the bag from V and runs away, she does not continue to steal it when using it several days or weeks later. However, if we follow the logic of *Morris*, we could say the appropriation starts and finishes moment that D touches the bag; so even when running away the appropriation will have already concluded. This issue can be important where there is uncertainty as to jurisdiction as, for example, where D takes V's car whilst abroad and imports it to England—is it already stolen abroad? It will also be important in the context of other offences such as robbery, where violence must be shown to accompany the act of theft. The shorter the duration of the theft, the less likely that robbery can be found.[9] In such cases, courts have sensibly interpreted appropriation as existing beyond an instant, to include the time where D is still 'on the job,' probably including D's running away but not her use of the property on following occasions.[10]

9.2.1.2 Appropriation with consent

Paradigm cases of theft will involve a non-consensual appropriation; D taking V's property without her knowledge or against her wishes. In line with this, a requirement of 'adverse' appropriation has often been assumed by the courts, such as in *Morris*.[11] However, the wording of the TA 1968 does not expressly limit the offence to these cases, stating generally that 'any assumption' of rights will constitute an appropriation. In light of this drafting, other cases such as *Laurence* have held that the consent or non-consent of V is irrelevant.[12] The question, and the inconsistent approach of previous cases, was eventually addressed by the House of Lords in *Gomez*.

---

[7] *Broom v Crowther* (1984) JP 592.

[8] For a general discussion of continuing acts, see **4.3.2.1**. See also, Williams, 'Appropriation: A Single or Continuous Act?' [1978] Crim LR 69.

[9] See **9.3**.

[10] *Atakpu* [1994] QB 69: no appropriation in England where cars were stolen in Frankfurt or Brussels and brought to England days later.

[11] [1984] AC 320. Lord Roskill (*obiter*) 'appropriation involves not an act expressly or impliedly authorized by the owner but an act by way of adverse interference with or usurpation of those rights'.

[12] *Lawrence* [1972] AC 626: D, a taxi driver, took extra money from V for a fare. V did not speak much English and 'allowed' the extra money to be taken from his wallet. The House of Lords held that there was an appropriation: it did not matter that V consented to the taking.

Gomez [1993] AC 442

D was the assistant manager of an electrical goods shop. He convinced his manager to allow a customer to buy items using cheques that D knew were stolen and therefore worthless. The manager consented to the 'sale'. D was charged with theft.

- Crown Court: guilty of theft.
- Court of Appeal: appeal allowed. Following *Morris*, the consent of V undermines the element of appropriation.
- House of Lords: appeal allowed, reaffirming D's liability and following *Lawrence*. With Lord Lowry dissenting, the Lords confirmed that, where D tricks V, appropriation will be found whenever there is an assumption of ownership rights by D, regardless of V's consent.

The decision in *Gomez* sparked considerable academic debate,[13] not least because the irrelevance of V's consent created a substantial overlap with offences of obtaining property by deception which were then in force[14] and, with fraud offences in force today.[15] Indeed, the prosecution of *Gomez* for an offence of obtaining property by deception (what would today be fraud by false representation) would have been straightforward.[16] However, for reasons unknown, the prosecutors chose to charge theft and so the question of consent in relation to theft had to be resolved. *Gomez* (again, for better or worse) confirms that as long as D assumes a right of ownership over V's property, there will be an appropriation and V's consent or non-consent is irrelevant.

9.2.1.3 Appropriation with full civil title

Gomez confirmed that D could, by deception, appropriate V's property regardless of V's consent. However, as D's appropriation was still achieved through deception when D lied about the cheques, the question remained open as to whether D's assumption of rights would still be an appropriation where V consents and there is no deception. The court in *Gomez* indicated that appropriation would be found even in the absence of deception, both through the examples they employed,[17] as well as other cases they overruled, but this did not form part of the ratio of the case.[18]

The decision that appropriation could be found despite a lack of deception was confirmed with even more controversy in the case of *Hinks*. *Hinks* provides that, where D assumes ownership rights from V, this may be an appropriation even where the property is consensually transferred from V with full title (where the transfer is valid and not

---

13 Heaton, 'Deceiving Without Thieving' [2001] Crim LR 712; Davies, 'Consent After the House of Lords: Taking and Leading Astray the Law of Theft' (1993) 13 LS 308; Cooper and Allen, 'Appropriation after *Gomez*' (1993) 57 J Crim L 186.

14 TA 1968, s15. Repealed by the Fraud Act 2006.

15 Fraud Act 2006. See **Chapter 10**.

16 We discuss the overlap between theft and fraud offences further at **10.8.3**.

17 eg of a person switching labels in a supermarket, where the court said there would be appropriation at the moment D touches the labels. At that point there is no full deception offence.

18 eg *Fritschy* [1985] Crim LR 745: D was not found to have committed theft in England where he picked up goods to transport to Switzerland and only diverted from that task after leaving this jurisdiction. Following *Gomez*, despite no deception within England, D appropriated the goods when he first had contact with them.

voidable in civil law[19]). Thus, D may be liable for theft of certain property in criminal law but be entitled to keep that same property in civil law.

◻ Hinks [2000] 4 All ER 833

D befriended V who was a man described by the court as naive, trusting and of limited intelligence. Over a six-month period she took V to his building society almost every day and was given £300 (the maximum withdrawal), eventually totalling over £60,000. At the point of arrest, D had taken almost all of V's money as well as his television. D was charged with theft.

- Crown Court: guilty of theft.
- Court of Appeal: conviction upheld on appeal.
- House of Lords: appeal dismissed, with Lord Hutton and Lord Hobhouse dissenting. Although the transfer of the money may not have amounted to a civil wrong, this does not preclude it being an appropriation and a theft.

Extra detail...

It may have been arguable that the facts of *Hinks* involved a voidable contract. In other words, it could have been argued that V was mentally incapable of making a valid gift or that there must have been some undue influence from D. If the gift was voidable then D's conviction for theft (following *Gomez*) would have been uncontroversial. However, importantly, the accepted facts at the House of Lords were such that the gift was valid in civil law.

In order to appreciate the full implications of *Hinks*, it is useful to highlight the two main arguments raised and rejected by the appeal courts.

A) Distinguishing *Hinks* and *Gomez*: The first line of argument was that *Hinks* should be distinguished from *Gomez* because *Hinks* involved a full and valid transfer of property in civil law. Indeed, even following *Gomez*, in *Mazo*,[20] it was accepted by the Court of Appeal to be 'common ground that the receiver of a valid gift *inter vivos* could not be the subject of a conviction for theft'.[21] This argument was supported by the apparent absurdity of D being potentially liable for theft and yet, as a matter of civil law, remaining the owner of the property stolen.[22] However, this argument was rejected in *Hinks*, and *Mazo* was overruled. The court found the law clearly stated in *Gomez*. On the issue of inconsistency between civil and criminal law, Lord Steyn, with the majority, stated that:

> The purposes of the civil law and the criminal law are somewhat different. In theory the two systems should be in perfect harmony. In a practical world there will sometimes be some disharmony between the two systems. In any event, it would be wrong to assume on priori grounds that the criminal law rather than the civil law is defective.

---

[19] Transfers become voidable if there is a 'vitiating factor'. These include duress, misrepresentation, undue influence and so on.

[20] [1996] Crim LR 435.

[21] In *Mazo*, this led to the acquittal of D in similar facts to *Hinks*.

[22] Beatson and Simester, 'Stealing One's Own Property' (1999) 115 LQR 372.

The House of Lords therefore recognised the inconsistency but rejected it as a reason for finding no appropriation. This is particularly interesting if we consider the rationale of property offences to be for the protection of the civil system of ownership rights. Following the decision in *Hinks*, theft is not being used to protect ownership rights; quite the opposite, it is punishing D for gaining valid ownership.[23] Theft is now targeting dishonesty or exploitation more generally. Whether this is the correct role for the offence of theft remains an open debate.[24]

B) **Challenging Gomez:** The second line of argument within *Hinks* was that consistent academic criticism of *Gomez* should have led the court to reconsider the definition of appropriation. Alongside the issue of conflict between civil and criminal law, it was argued that *Gomez* had undermined the role of appropriation within the offence of theft by rendering that element of negligible significance. Any touching by D of V's property would suffice for that element of the actus reus, with the effect being that the full offence of theft turns on mens rea: it become something akin to a thought crime.[25] Alongside this was the argument that the element of 'dishonesty' (discussed later) was not suitable on its own to focus the offence on only those deserving of liability. However, the court reasoned that any fundamental change of this kind (reconsidering *Gomez*) could lead to the offence becoming unacceptably narrow. It is clear that the court wanted to find liability in cases such as *Hinks* so, taking some comfort from one alternative academic opinion,[26] they dismissed this line of argument as well.

> **Point to remember...**
> *Gomez* and *Hinks* led to considerable debate about the appropriate role and construction of theft, and some of these points will be discussed further in the 'reform' section later in the chapter. However, by avoiding technical distinctions based on the civil law, the requirement of appropriation is usually straightforward to apply: we ask simply, did D assume any right of ownership over V's property? For example, if D goes to a supermarket to steal an item, she will have appropriated (and committed theft) at the first moment she comes into contact with the item. The fact that D is permitted by the shop to touch the item at this point (ie the shop's consent) is irrelevant.

9.2.1.4 The bona fide purchaser exception

Section 3(2) of the TA 1968 creates an exception where no appropriation will be found. This arises where D purchases property in good faith (bona fide), believing that she is gaining full civil title, it then transpires that full title has not been transferred (eg because the goods were stolen) but D continues to treat the item as her own. In such a case, D appears to have assumed the rights of the owner and thus come within the definition of appropriation: this section prevents that from being the result in law.

It should be remembered that this exception only applies to property acquired by D for value so it does not apply to gifts received by D. Further, even though D is excused from theft by section 3(2), she remains potentially liable for handling stolen

---

[23] For an alternative view, that *Hinks* provides indirect protection for property rights, see Shute, 'Appropriation and the Law of Theft' [2002] Crim LR 445.

[24] Bogg and Stanton-Ife, 'Protecting the Vulnerable: Legality, Harm and Theft' (2003) 23 LS 402. We discuss this in the reform section later in the chapter.

[25] Smith, 'Theft or Sharp Practice: Who Cares Now?' (2001) 60 CLJ 21.

[26] Gardner, 'Appropriation in Theft: The Last Word' (1993) 109 LQR 194.

property[27] and/or fraud if she presents herself as the owner, for example to sell the property to another.[28]

9.2.2 Property

To commit theft, what D appropriated must be legally recognised as 'property'. Unlike the definition of appropriation, the definition of property is generally not controversial. However, care must be taken to understand exactly what is included. Section 4 of the TA 1968 provides a general definition of property (founded on civil law concepts) and then specific exclusions relating to land, things growing wild, and wild creatures.

> (1) 'Property' includes money and all other property, real or personal, including things in action and other intangible property.

Before moving to consider the specific exceptions to this definition, its key terms require some unpacking.

Real property is a reference to land. Thus, subject to the specific exclusions discussed later, D can be liable for the theft of certain land rights.

Personal property is a reference to all property that is not land and that includes property that is illegal or prohibited. For example, D commits theft where she appropriates drugs from V, even where they are illegally possessed by V.[29]

Things in action is a reference to a category of intangible property where D has the right to sue another for a particular sum. This is most commonly associated with bank accounts. Although we commonly refer to having 'money in the bank' this is, of course, not accurate: there is no specific pile of money in a bank belonging to us.[30] Rather, depositing money to a bank creates a form of intangible property, our right to sue the bank for that specific sum. This property right is a 'thing in action'. Therefore, where D dishonestly causes the bank to transfer funds from V's account, D does not steal any physical money belonging to V, she steals a thing in action (ie she steals part of V's right to sue V's bank for a sum of money).[31] The same is true where D has transferred money from V's overdraft.[32] The only exception in such cases is where D has transferred funds from V's account that V had no right to sue for (ie where V had no thing in action). This can arise where D has transferred funds in excess of V's overdraft, or where D takes from her own account in excess of her overdraft.[33]

Other intangible property allows the definition of intangible property to extend beyond the most common things in action. An example can be seen in *AG of Hong Kong*

---

[27] See **9.5**.
[28] *Wheeler* (1990) 92 Cr App R 279.
[29] *Smith* [2011] EWCA Crim 66.
[30] Discussed in *Davenport* [1954] 1 All ER 602.
[31] *Chan Man-sin v AG for Hong Kong* [1988] 1 All ER 1.
[32] *Kohn* [1997] 2 Cr App R 445.
[33] *Hilton* (1979) 69 Cr App R 395; Griew, 'Stealing and Obtaining Bank Credits' [1986] Crim LR 356.

v Chan Nai-Keung,[34] in which D, a director of company A and company B, sold export quotas from one company to the other at a gross undervalue. Although the export quotas did not represent a thing in action, they were held to constitute other intangible property and were therefore subject to theft.

An interesting problem of categorisation has emerged in relation to the stealing of cheques.[35] A cheque which is given by V for consideration creates a thing in action as it creates the right to sue V's bank for the specified sum. So if V is tricked, for example, into writing a cheque in D's favour, that creates a right for D to sue V's bank but D has not taken V's right to sue, unlike electronic bank transfers discussed earlier. Instead, the thing in action which D has gained is not property which has ever belonged to V and cannot be the subject of theft.[36] What D gains is her own brand new right to sue V's bank. We could wait for a theft to arise when D presents the cheque and thereby causes a bank transfer so that V's bank account—a thing in action—is diminished. The problem is that D does not commit theft until she presents the cheque and causes the transfer, which seems too late. Alternatively, we could focus on the cheque as a piece of paper (tangible property) and say that D stole that from the outset. However, as D does not intend to keep the paper, in fact she intends to present it to the bank, she does not satisfy a different offence element (intention to permanently deprive) in relation to the paper: so this cannot ground our case for theft either.[37] Our final option to find liability in theft[38] is to say the cheque is a 'valuable security', a piece of property that creates or guarantees certain financial rights.[39] This approach has been accepted in Australia by the Supreme Court of Victoria[40] and, although not yet accepted in this jurisdiction, may well (and should) be followed in the future.

> *Extra detail...*
> The decline in the use of cheques generally has made this problem less acute. However, the same issues can arise in relation to the stealing of paper tickets.

9.2.2.1 Exceptions

Section 4 highlights a number of specific exceptions to the definition of property.

Land

The first specific exclusion in the definition of property relates to land (s4(2)). Thus, where D takes some of V's land without severing it as, for example, where D moves her garden fence a few inches into V's garden, she may have appropriated property within the civil law, but this will not constitute property for the purposes of theft.[41] Only certain specified land rights will amount to property within the offence of theft.

---

[34] [1987] 1 WLR 1339, exploring identical provisions in the law of Hong Kong.
[35] Smith, 'Obtaining Cheques by Deception or Theft' [1997] Crim LR 396.
[36] *Preddy* [1996] AC 815.
[37] *Graham* [1997] 1 Cr App R 302.
[38] D may commit fraud if she dishonestly induces V to write the cheque for her, see **Chapter 10**.
[39] *Arnold* [1997] 4 All ER 1.
[40] *Parsons* [1998] 2 VR 478.
[41] It was felt that civil remedies would be more appropriate to deal with cases of this kind.

First, section 4(2)(a) allows for theft of land by a trustee of property.

> (a) when he is a trustee or personal representative, or is authorised by power of attorney, or as liquida-
> tor of a company, or otherwise, to sell or dispose of land belonging to another, and he appropriates
> the land or anything forming part of it by dealing with it in breach of the confidence reposed in him

Thus, where D is the trustee of property and disposes of that property dishonestly for her own advantage, she may commit theft.

Secondly, section 4(2)(b) allows for theft of land by someone whose interest in the land is not that of ownership who severs part of the land.[42]

> (b) when he is not in possession of the land and appropriates anything forming part of the land by
> severing it or causing it to be severed, or after it has been severed

The moving fence example was not theft because D was not severing (not removing) the part of V's land that she appropriated. Where there is such severance however these items will constitute property for the purposes of theft as, for example, where D takes some of V's topsoil, her plants, her garden shed, etc.

Thirdly, section 4(2)(c) allows for theft of land by a tenant who appropriates a fixture or structure from the land.

> (c) when, being in possession of the land under a tenancy, he appropriates the whole or part of any
> fixture or structure let to be used with the land.

Unlike D with no rights to the land, a tenant will not commit theft where she removes minor fixtures (eg topsoil).[43] However, where she appropriates a fixture (eg bath, sink, etc) or a structure (eg garden shed, greenhouse, etc), these items will constitute property for theft. In such cases, simple appropriation is all that is required, there is no additional requirement for severance.

Wild mushrooms and flowers

The second exclusion, where property in civil law will not amount to property for the purposes of the TA 1968, relates to wild mushrooms and flowers (s4(3)). This is defined liberally to include all fungi, and any plant or tree.

> (3) A person who picks mushrooms growing wild on any land, or who picks flowers, fruit or foliage
> from a plant growing wild on any land, does not (although not in possession of the land) steal what
> he picks, unless he does it for reward or for sale or other commercial purpose.

As the section makes clear, this exclusion from theft includes important exceptions. Although D may pick 'flowers, fruit or foliage', she may not take or dig up the whole plant, and to do so could be theft. The exclusion also only applies to things growing wild, and so cultivated plants or fungus are not included. Finally, the exclusion will only apply to those picking for non-commercial reasons.[44] Thus, where D picks berries in order to

---

42 This includes, eg, the children of a tenant.
43 Although she has appropriated the property of another (the landlord) in civil law.
44 Welstead, 'Season of Mists and Mellow Fruitfulness' (1995) 145 NLJ 1499.

make jam for sale, she is picking property and may commit theft. However, where she is picking for her own use only, the berries are not property within the offence. How D makes use of the items picked is a useful indication of her intentions at the time of picking, but remember that it is her intention at this point (regardless of what happens later) that is crucial to liability. For example, if D picks berries for her own use then she does not commit theft, even if she *later* decides to sell the jam.

Wild creatures

The final specified exclusion relates to wild creatures (section 4(4)).

> (4) Wild creatures, tamed or untamed, shall be regarded as property; but a person cannot steal a wild creature not tamed nor ordinarily kept in captivity, or the carcase of any such creature, unless either it has been reduced into possession by or on behalf of another person and possession of it has not since been lost or abandoned, or another person is in course of reducing it into possession.

Although wild creatures will generally not constitute property for the purposes of theft, the provision makes clear that this will not be the case with tamed creatures, or wild creatures that have been killed or trapped because these become the property of the person who killed or trapped them. Thus, for example, if D kills and removes a wild animal from V's property, such as a pheasant, whilst D may be guilty of a poaching offence,[45] she will not be guilty of theft. To keep a creature in 'captivity', thus making it property for the purposes of the TA 1968, requires more than the regular feeding of a wild creature, even if the eventual aim is to trap and/or kill the creature.[46]

Other common law exclusions

Alongside the specific statutory exclusions within section 4, the common law has also developed to exclude other areas from the definition of property in theft. These include the following.

A) **Electricity:** Electricity is not property for the purposes of theft[47] but there is a separate offence within section 13 of the TA 1968 of wasting or diverting another's electricity.

B) **Confidential information:** Information does not amount to property within section 4.[48] Thus, in *Oxford v Moss*,[49] a university student who unlawfully acquired an examination paper, read and returned it, could not be liable for theft. There may be alternative offences under the Computer Misuse Act 1990, where the information is taken from a computer, and the Law Commission once provisionally proposed a new offence of misuse of trade secrets.[50] However, there is no theft in these cases.

C) **Services:** A service (eg a manicure, taxi journey, a theatre performance, etc) is not property within section 4 and so failure to pay for a service is not theft. Such conduct is likely to be an offence of obtaining services dishonestly under section 11 of the Fraud Act 2006.

---

[45] Night Poaching Act 1828; Game Act 1831.

[46] *Cresswell v DPP* [2006] EWHC 3379 (Admin): involving the feeding of wild badgers.

[47] *Low v Blease* [1975] Crim LR 513.

[48] Christie, 'Should the Law of Theft Extend to Information?' (2005) 69 J Crim L 349; Davies, 'Protection of Intellectual Property—A Myth?' (2004) 68 J Crim L 398.

[49] (1978) 68 Cr App R 183.

[50] Law Commission, *Misuses of Trade Secrets* (Consultation 150, 1997).

D) Bodies: Traditionally, human bodies and/or parts of bodies have not been classed as property within section 4.[51] However, this view is changing in a number of areas. For example, it has been held that bodily products which are intended to be held or controlled can amount to property (eg urine samples,[52] sperm deposits,[53] etc). Thus, stealing blood from a blood bank, for example, is likely to constitute theft.

9.2.3 Belonging to another

Theft is not designed simply to prevent D dishonestly assuming property rights (ie appropriating property) but more broadly to protect the ownership rights of others. Thus, it is always essential to demonstrate that the property appropriated belonged to another at the point of appropriation. The general rule is set out in section 5(1) of the TA 1968.

> (1) Property shall be regarded as belonging to any person having possession or control of it, or having in it any proprietary right or interest (not being an equitable interest arising only from an agreement to transfer or grant an interest).

Before commenting on the individual terms used, it is important to recognise that it is not necessary that the person from whom D appropriates the property had exclusive ownership; it is sufficient that V had at least one of the relevant ownership rights at the time of appropriation. For example, V lends a book to X, X then gives the book to Z to hold, and D then snatches the book from Z and makes off with it. Here, D appropriates property belonging to V (proprietary ownership), X (possession ownership) and Z (control ownership). Even if only one of these could be proved, D's charge for theft of property belonging to another would be satisfied. What matters is that there is someone who has *some* proprietary right or interest in the property other than D.

9.2.3.1 Possession or control

V has possession or control of property where she intends to control or possess it, and maintains some degree of control over it in fact. Thus, for example, the owners of a vending machine will possess the coins inside the machine even if they do not know the quantity; and a landowner will possess the contents of their buildings even if they are not aware of every item.[54] The question in each case, turning on civil law concepts, is whether V demonstrates a sufficient claim of possession. This is illustrated in *Rostron*.

> **Rostron** [2003] All ER 269
>
> D and others trespassed onto a golf course at night, with diving apparatus, and took lost golf balls from a lake which was part of the course driving range. D was charged with theft of the balls.
>
> - Crown Court: guilty of theft.
> - Court of Appeal: conviction upheld on appeal. The jury were entitled to find that the balls belonged to the golf course. Although the course owners did not intend to collect the balls themselves, they still maintained possession and control over them.

---

[51] *Sharpe* (1857) D & B 160.
[52] *Welsh* [1974] RTR 550.
[53] *Yearworth v North Bristol NHS Trust* [2009] EWCA Civ 37.
[54] *Woodman* [1974] QB 754.

An interesting problem emerges where D is the owner of the property and she takes it from another who has possession or control. Does D commit theft of her own property? The requirement of dishonesty (discussed later) makes theft in these circumstances very unlikely. However, where there is dishonesty, the basic rule is that, if V holds a proprietary interest in D's property, then D's taking of the property may amount to theft. This is illustrated in *Turner (No 2)*.

Turner (No 2) [1971] 2 All ER 441

D had his car repaired by V at a garage. On collecting his car, D used a spare set of keys to take his car without paying the bill. D was charged with theft of the car.

- Crown Court: guilty of theft.
- Court of Appeal: conviction upheld on appeal. The garage was in possession and control of the car and so, although D was the legal owner, he was still taking property that belonged to another (the garage).

The reasoning in *Turner (No 2)* was expressed too widely, indicating that appropriation in all such circumstances would amount to the taking of property belonging to another (note that theft requires mens rea not just appropriation). This cannot be right. For example, if V snatches D's bag in the street and D takes it back, even though V takes brief control of the bag, D's re-taking is not taking property belonging to another: D has every right to take it back. This was recognised in *Meredith*, where D's dishonest appropriation of his car from a police compound was not theft.[55] *Turner (No 2)* does provide a useful illustration, however, of theft in circumstances where D does not have the right to demand his car be returned in civil law (until he pays the bill).

9.2.3.2 Proprietary interest

Proprietary interests are determined in reference to civil law rules of ownership. In most cases, the ownership of property will be clear as with the owner of the book in our opening example. However, the civil law rules are not always straightforward, as illustrated in *Marshall*.[56]

Marshall [1998] 2 Cr App R 282

D obtained part-used tickets from Underground users and resold them. London Underground Ltd (V) claimed ownership of the part-used tickets, making D's reselling an appropriation of their property. D was charged with theft.

- Crown Court: guilty of theft.
- Court of Appeal: conviction upheld on appeal. The question was whether a clause on the back of the ticket stating V's continued ownership of the ticket was sufficiently clear to buyers. If yes, then it remained V's property in civil law but if not, then V has no interest. The court found that the clause was sufficiently clear.

---

[55] [1973] Crim LR 253.
[56] Smith, 'Stealing Tickets' [1998] Crim LR 723.

As with *Marshall*, decisions in this area will often turn on the subtle rules of civil ownership. Thus, for example, property may be found to belong to the Crown if it comes within the rules of 'treasure',[57] property may belong (in equity) to beneficiaries of a trust,[58] property ownership may pass on contract despite V never receiving the goods,[59] and so on. Although identifying the proprietary interest may involve close scrutiny of civil rules, once such an interest is identified, it will always satisfy this element of theft. This will be the case even where D also has a proprietary interest in the property, as where one business partner takes all of the value out of a corporate partnership.[60]

9.2.3.3 Specific examples within s5

Alongside the general definition of 'belonging to another' in section 5(1), the rest of the section goes on to clarify certain potentially problematic examples.

A) **Section 5(2):** This subsection clarifies that where D, a trustee, dishonestly appropriates from that trust, she takes property of another. This is true where the trust has individual beneficiaries (overlapping with s5(1)), as well as purpose trusts (eg charitable trusts) where others have the ability to enforce the trust.[61]

B) **Section 5(3):** This subsection deals with property given to D for a particular purpose as, for example, where V provides D (her cleaner) with money to buy cleaning products. In such cases, even though the property is passed to D, if she deals with it in an improper manner by keeping it for herself, this will constitute taking the property of another.

> **Point to remember...**
> There is an obvious overlap with section 5(1) and (2) where the agreement between D and V creates a trust or V retains equitable proprietary rights. In such a case, either provision may be used.[62]

In order to come within this subsection, D must be under a legal, as opposed to a merely moral, duty to deal with the property in a particular way. This is a question of law for the judge.[63] In the context of money, the question is often whether D was expected to use that specific money for a specific purpose (s5(3) applies), or whether the money was a general payment to D in exchange for future conduct that may be paid for from other funds (s5(3) does not apply). For example, where a travel agent receives deposits for a trip, there is an expectation that the agent will organise and pay for the trip, but no expectation that they will do so with the particular money provided. Thus, even where the company dishonestly fails to provide the trip or a

---

[57] *Waverley Borough Council v Fletcher* [1995] 4 All ER 756: using a metal detector, D found a gold broach on the council's land.

[58] *Clowes (No 2)* [1994] 2 All ER 316; Davies, 'After *R v Clowes No 2*' (1997) 61 J Crim L 99.

[59] *Rose v Matt* [1951] 1 KB 810.

[60] *Bonner* [1970] 1 WLR 838.

[61] *Dyke and Munro* [2002] Crim LR 153. In the context of charitable trusts, the Attorney General has the right of enforcement.

[62] *Hallam* [1995] Crim LR 323.

[63] *Clowes (No 2)* [1994] 2 All ER 316.

refund, there is a breach of civil/contractual obligation but there is no theft.[64] Just on the other side of this fine line are cases where D receives money in sponsorship, on the understanding that it will be passed to the relevant charity. These cases are now likely to fall within section 5(3): those sponsoring are not paying D, they expect her to pass that money to the charity.[65]

C) **Section 5(4):** This subsection applies where D receives property by mistake and is under an obligation to return it or its value: a good example is where D receives an overpayment of wages. In such cases, where D appropriates the property and refuses to make restoration, she takes the property of another. This is illustrated in *Gresham*.[66]

Gresham [2003] EWCA Crim 2070

D's mother died and yet D, who had power of attorney, did not inform her pension provider (V) who continued to make payments for ten years. D used this money as his own. D was charged with theft.

- Crown Court: guilty of theft.
- Court of Appeal: conviction upheld on appeal.[67] D had a duty under section 5(4) to return the money to V, and so his use of it amounted to the taking of another's property.

Where V mistakenly transfers property to D, this will *also* often result in V retaining some equitable proprietary ownership. In such cases, section 5(4) *and* (1) will apply.[68]

D) **Section 5(5):** This subsection clarifies that a legal person (a corporation) can own property. Therefore, for example, if directors of the company dishonestly appropriate company property, they are taking the property of another (the company).[69]

9.2.3.4 Abandonment

Where property is owned by another, it is capable of theft but it may nevertheless become abandoned, thus ownerless and no longer capable of theft. However, it should be emphasised that such abandonment is very rare: V must leave the property and be indifferent as to any future appropriation. Thus, where V throws property into the bin, intending it to be collected and disposed of by authorised collectors, it is not abandoned and if D, who is not an authorised collector, takes it from V's bin then D appropriates it.[70] Hence, in *Rostron* (discussed earlier), the golf course had not abandoned lost golf balls even though they had no intention of collecting the balls themselves. The same applies if V loses a valuable piece of jewellery and gives up the search, the jewellery is not actually abandoned; and so on. The same is true where V leaves property for specific charities to collect.

---

64 *Hall* [1972] All ER 1009.
65 *Wain* [1995] 2 Cr App R 660.
66 See also *AG's Reference (No 1 of 1983)* [1985] QB 182: theft of overpaid wages.
67 Two of the 12 counts were overturned for lack of appropriation but these are not relevant to the current discussion.
68 *Shadrokh-Cigari* [1988] Crim LR 465; MacCormack, 'Mistaken Payments and Proprietary Claims' [1996] Conv 86.
69 *A v Snaresbrook Crown Court* (2001) 165 JPN 495.
70 *Williams v Phillips* (1957) 121 JP 163.

9.2.3.5 The *Hinks* problem

The case of *Hinks*, discussed earlier (see **9.2.1.3**), provides an interesting problem in relation to this element: that the property must belong to another. It will be remembered that in *Hinks* the money given to D from V, who was a vulnerable adult, though dishonestly appropriated, amounted to a valid gift in civil law. Thus, at the moment the property was passed to D, D gained full ownership rights: it was no longer property of another. The question arises whether, at the moment of appropriation, the property belonged to D or to V. If it belonged to D, then there is no appropriation of another's property—no coincidence in time—and, therefore, no theft.

In *Hinks*, this point was given little consideration and the property was assumed to belong to V at the moment of transfer. This is a useful indication that, when appropriation and the passing of property ownership are simultaneous, the courts will take a permissive approach to potential problems of coincidence. However, facts could arise that test such indulgence. For example, what if V in *Hinks* had sent the money to D by post, with D only appropriating it when later picking up her mail inside her house. In such a case, if the money is a valid gift, then when it sits in D's house it is entirely her property: thus, her appropriation of it could not, surely, be theft.

9.2.4 Intention to permanently deprive

The next major element of theft is the requirement that, when appropriating the property of another, D does so with an intention to permanently deprive V of it. Section 1(2) of the TA 1968 explicitly clarifies that theft need not be for D's benefit, so it is enough that D gives away V's property—that is still theft. However, V must be deprived of her property and, D must intend that deprivation to be permanent.

The requirement of an intention to permanently deprive is an ulterior mens rea element.[71] There is no corresponding actus reus element: whether D permanently deprives V in fact is irrelevant. Indeed, D's conduct after the appropriation, whether she returns the property and/or how she deals with it, is only relevant insofar as it provides evidence of D's intention at the moment of appropriation. For example, if D takes V's watch intending to keep it, but later discovers the sentimental value of the watch to V and returns it, she still commits theft: all the elements of the offence coincide at the moment of appropriation. Conversely, where D takes the watch intending to return it, but later loses it or changes her mind, there is no theft at the moment the watch is taken.[72]

> **Beware...**
> It is very easy to slip up in your discussion of this element by focusing on whether D has permanently deprived V or not. Remember, *all* discussion of this element should be focused on D's intentions at the point of appropriation only.

---

[71] See **4.2.1.2**.

[72] In such a case, prosecution for theft would rely on finding a second act of appropriation at the stage D decides to keep the watch.

9.2.4.1 TA 1968, s6(1): extensions

Section 6(1) of the TA 1968 sets out a broad, and not entirely clear,[73] definition of what it means to intend to permanently deprive.

> (1) A person appropriating property belonging to another without meaning the other permanently to lose the thing itself is nevertheless to be regarded as having the intention of permanently depriving the other of it if his intention is to treat the thing as his own to dispose of regardless of the other's rights; and a borrowing or lending of it may amount to so treating it if, but only if, the borrowing or lending is for a period and in circumstances making it equivalent to an outright taking or disposal.

Several areas of uncertainty have arisen in the application of this section and it is useful to trace how the courts have responded to them.

A) **Ransoming or selling property back to V:** Where D appropriates V's property with the intention of selling it back, or ransoming it to V, it is arguable that D does not intend to *permanently* deprive V of it. However, not surprisingly, the courts have consistently held this to come within section 6(1): D intends to treat the property as her own, and this is equivalent to the intention of an outright taking.[74] The same principle applies, for example, where D steals a ticket from a theatre, intending to return the ticket only when granted entry to the theatre (ie only when the theatre provides consideration).

B) **Replacing with identical property:** A problem emerges where D takes property intending to replace it with an identical equivalent. This can arise with any property, for example, where D takes a celebrity's sunglasses and replaces them with an identical pair. It is relatively easy to see how that amounts to theft. However, it is most troublesome in the context of money. For example, where D takes money from a till at work, intending to replace it the following day with equivalent money, albeit not exactly the same notes or coins taken. All such cases will satisfy section 6(1), as clarified in *Velumyl*.

Velumyl [1989] Crim LR 299

D, an employee, took money from the company safe, intending to return it after the weekend. D was charged with theft.

- Crown Court: guilty of theft.
- Court of Appeal: conviction upheld on appeal. D did not intend to return the exact notes or coins taken, so he must have intended to permanently deprive his employers of them.

It should be noted that, although liability was found in *Velumyl*, many cases of this kind will fail for lack of dishonesty (discussed later).

C) **Removing value from the property:** If D's intention is to take property and return it to V with *all* of its value removed, then there is, straightforwardly, an intention to permanently deprive as, for example, when D returns an animal after killing it; a car after setting it on fire; a sports season ticket at the end of the season; etc. Such conduct

---

[73] Spencer, 'The Metamorphosis of Section 6 of the Theft Act' [1977] Crim LR 653.
[74] *Raphael* [2008] EWCA Crim 1014: D stole V's car and then offered to sell it back.

may be described, within section 6(1), as borrowing equivalent to an outright taking or disposal.[75] However, as illustrated in *Lloyd*, difficult questions of degree emerge where D intends only to take *some* of the value from the property.

📁 *Lloyd* [1985] 3 WLR 30

D, who worked as a cinema projectionist, appropriated films with the intention of making illegal copies to sell elsewhere, but to return the originals. D was charged with theft.

- Crown Court: guilty of theft.
- Court of Appeal: appeal allowed. D's intention was merely to remove some of the value from the films, and was not sufficient to be equivalent to an outright taking.

Each case will turn on its facts. Where, for example, D intends to return the sporting season ticket halfway through the season, or the car when damaged but not destroyed, the question for the court will be one of degree: did D's intended conduct amount to an intention to remove sufficient value to be equivalent to an outright taking?

D) **Abandoning the property:** There will be clear cases where an intention to abandon V's property will amount to an intention to dispose of it, as where D demonstrates his intention by throwing V's pin into a haystack. However, where D's intended abandonment may allow V to regain her property, the question is again one of degree. This is illustrated in the case of *Mitchell*.

📁 *Mitchell* [2008] EWCA Crim 850

D and three others forcibly took V's car, having crashed their own, whilst attempting to escape from the police. The car (largely undamaged) was later abandoned on the road with its hazard lights on. D was charged with robbery, which requires D to have committed theft.

- Crown Court: guilty of robbery.
- Court of Appeal: appeal allowed. The circumstances of the intended abandonment made it likely that the car would be returned to V and thus did not amount to an intention to permanently deprive.

The question in each case will focus on how D *intended* to abandon the property at the moment of appropriation.

E) **Conditional intentions:** This final problem case emerges where D appropriates property with a conditional intention to permanently deprive V of it. Examples include intention to keep V's jewellery only if the stones are genuine; to keep V's season ticket only if the team keep winning; etc. Despite doubt created by early case law,[76] it is now clear that, consistently with the general approach,[77] D's conditional intention will constitute a valid intention. This was confirmed in *AG's References (Nos 1 and 2 of 1979)*.

---

[75] *DPP v J* [2002] EWHC 291 (Admin): intention to return headphones after breaking them.
[76] *Easom* [1971] 2 QB 315; *Husseyn* (1977) 67 Cr App R 131.
[77] See **3.4.1.3**.

> 🗂 *AG's References (Nos 1 and 2 of 1979)* [1980] QB 180
>
> Combined cases involving Ds who were arrested whilst trying to break into buildings. Both were charged with burglary, requiring an intention to steal.
>
> - Crown Court: not guilty of burglary, a conditional intention to steal (if there was anything worth taking) is insufficient.
> - Court of Appeal: the Crown Court was wrong: both Ds had an intention to steal, even if they had no specific property in mind. The court explicitly extended its judgment to standard theft cases.

The older case of *Easom* provides useful facts to explain how the current law should be applied. In that case, D picked up a woman's handbag and looked through it for valuables, but then replaced it having taken nothing. Pre-*AG's References (Nos 1 and 2 of 1979)*, D's conviction for theft of the handbag and its contents was quashed because of D's conditional intention. Following *AG's References*, there remains no theft of the bag: D never intended (even conditionally) to permanently deprive V of the bag. There will, however, be theft of the bag's contents: although D decided not to keep the contents because of their lack of value, he still appropriated them with the conditional intention of keeping them had they been valuable. Finally, if the bag had been empty, there would be no property for D to conditionally intend to permanently deprive, and therefore no theft. There would, however, be liability for attempted theft.[78]

9.2.4.2 TA 1968, s6(2): intention to risk the property

Although most borderline cases were left to the courts, one such area has been clarified by section 6(2) of the TA 1968.

> (2) Without prejudice to the generality of subsection (1) above, where a person, having possession or control (lawfully or not) of property belonging to another, parts with the property under a condition as to its return which he may not be able to perform, this (if done for purposes of his own and without the other's authority) amounts to treating the property as his own to dispose of regardless of the other's rights.

This subsection makes clear that where D intends to part with the property and cannot be sure of its return, her intention amounts to an intention to permanently deprive. For example, where D intends to risk V's money by gambling with it, or pawning it in circumstances where she is not positive of its return, her intention amounts to an intention to permanently deprive even if she hopes to be successful and give the property back.[79]

9.2.5 Dishonesty

The final element of theft is the requirement of dishonesty. D must appropriate property belonging to another, with the intention to permanently deprive, and that appropriation must be dishonest. With many of the other elements (discussed earlier) being interpreted widely by the courts, and potentially applying to apparently innocent conduct, the role of dishonesty in focusing the offence on only wrongful conduct is crucial.[80]

---

[78] **Chapter 13**.
[79] *Fernandes* [1996] 1 Cr App R 175.
[80] Griew, 'Dishonesty: The Objections to *Feely* and *Ghosh*' [1985] Crim LR 341.

Unfortunately, despite its importance, dishonesty is not defined in the TA 1968. However, section 2 does provide three situations when D is *not* dishonest. These will always be the starting point for a discussion of dishonesty: if the case comes within one of the examples then the discussion stops there—there is no dishonesty and therefore there is no theft.

9.2.5.1 Statutory examples of no dishonesty

The first situation applies to cases where D believed she had a legal right to the property she appropriated (s2(1)).

> (a) if he appropriates the property in the belief that he has in law the right to deprive the other of it, on behalf of himself or of a third person;

D's belief need not be reasonable,[81] and it does not have to be based on an accurate understanding of the law.[82] As long as D *honestly* believed she had a legal (and not merely moral) right to the property, she will not be dishonest. Most commonly, this will arise where D takes V's property believing that it is hers as, for example, where D takes the wrong umbrella when leaving a restaurant.

The second example applies where D believed that V would have consented to the appropriation (s2(1)).

> (b) if he appropriates the property in the belief that he would have the other's consent if the other knew of the appropriation and the circumstances of it;

Again, D's belief need not be accurate or reasonable. As long as D honestly believed at the time of appropriation that V would have consented, then her conduct is not dishonest. Circumstances of this type are common as, for example, with family or friends using each other's property in the belief that the other would consent.

The final example applies where D appropriates property believing that the owner is undiscoverable (s2(1)).

> (c) (except where the property came to him as trustee or personal representative) if he appropriates the property in the belief that the person to whom the property belongs cannot be discovered by taking reasonable steps.

This example is intended to deal with those who discover seemingly abandoned property: D is not dishonest if she appropriates that property, as long as she honestly believes that the owner could not be found using reasonable steps. D's belief does not have to be reasonable. D comes within this example even if she believes that the owner is potentially discoverable in certain circumstances. For example, D may believe she could find the owner of a watch if she spent weeks searching and paid for television adverts, but this is clearly more than would be reasonably expected. The value of the property will obviously affect what constitutes reasonable steps in each case.[83]

---

[81] *Terry* [2001] EWCA Crim 2979.
[82] *Bernhard* [1938] 2 KB 264.
[83] *Sylvester* (1985) CO/559/84: D unsuccessfully raised s2(1)(c) in relation to a car he was stripping for parts.

As the subsection makes clear, this example does not apply to trustees and trust property. In such a case, D may attempt to rely on one of the other examples, or the general common law definition of dishonesty.

> **Point to remember…**
> Section 2(2) also clarifies that D may be dishonest even where she pays for the property. This is necessary to criminalise situations such as D taking her neighbour's barbeque on a hot day, but leaving some money to compensate the neighbour. However, the subsection only provides that D 'may' be dishonest in such cases; thus, the common law definition must be applied.

9.2.5.2 Common law definition of dishonesty

In the absence of a statutory definition of what *is* dishonest, the test has been left to the common law. The question of dishonesty is one of fact for the jury: the jury must find what D did and what she was thinking, and whether that was dishonest.[84] In doing so, the jury are not given a legal definition to apply, but they are instead told to apply the common understanding of 'dishonesty' by 'ordinary decent people'.

> **Judge and jury…**
> Where the jury are not given a legal definition to apply, there is always a risk of inconsistency between juries in identical cases: one jury's understanding of dishonesty may be different from another's. This is mitigated by asking the jury to apply the standard of 'ordinary decent people' as opposed to their own individual understandings, but the potential for inconsistency remains. We consider this further in the reform section later in the chapter.

The leading case, providing the test for dishonesty, is *Ghosh*.

> **Ghosh** [1982] QB 1053
>
> D, who was working as a surgeon, claimed fees for carrying out certain operations where this was not appropriate. D was charged with obtaining property by deception (since repealed as an offence under the TA 1968, s15), an offence where D must act dishonestly.
>
> • Crown Court: guilty of section 15 offence.
> • Court of Appeal: conviction upheld on appeal. D acts dishonestly where (a) D's conduct is dishonest according to the standards of reasonable and honest people; and (b) D realised (at that point) that the conduct would be seen as dishonest according to those standards.

In many cases, it will not be necessary for the jury to be directed by reference to the *Ghosh* test.[85] For example, if D accepts that the conduct would be dishonest but denies the conduct;[86] or where D accepts that she performed apparently dishonest conduct but claims to have done so absentmindedly (ie, so the question is whether we believe her);[87] and so on. However, where dishonesty is at issue, both parts of the *Ghosh* test must be applied.

---

[84] *Feely* [1973] QB 530.
[85] *Roberts* (1985) 84 Cr App R 177.
[86] *Cobb* [2005] EWCA Crim 1549: D denied taking money from a till.
[87] *Atkinson* [2004] Crim LR 226.

Step 1: Is D's conduct dishonest according to the standards of reasonable and honest people? The first step of the *Ghosh* test is commonly referred to as a mens rea test, although this is not strictly accurate: the jury are considering the potential fault in the form of dishonesty of what D has done rather than her internal state of mind.[88] If they consider both at this stage, the second step of the test is redundant.[89] We are not looking for particular specified movements but rather for an external demonstration of fault.

The first step of the test is therefore objective. The jury must consider what D has done and apply the objective standards of reasonable people in deciding whether that conduct is dishonest. Such standards may change over time, and leaving this question to the jury allows the legal standard to change with society. The question will not always be obvious. For example, in *Gohill v DPP*,[90] although magistrates found D's behaviour not to be dishonest (D allowed customers to borrow tools from a hire shop for short periods without payment, and sometimes for a personal tip), this was reversed on appeal.

Step 2: Does D realise that her conduct would be considered dishonest by the standards of honest and reasonable people? As well as being dishonest by the standards of honest and reasonable people, D must *also* realise that her conduct would be so considered to satisfy the full test. The construction of this second step is important. It is a subjective question, asking what D believes, but the question relates back to an objective standard: we do not ask D if she considers her behaviour dishonest by her own standards of honesty; we ask if she knew that others would consider her conduct dishonest by the objective standard of reasonable and honest people. Thus, an animal rights protester might believe it is not dishonest to take equipment from an animal testing lab by her own standards (believing it is justified to disrupt the industry), but she is likely to concede that her conduct would be perceived as dishonest by the standards of the community.

Two common examples may be useful. The first example involves D who does not pay for public transport because, having recently arrived in the country, she does not believe payment is required. D's conduct in this case by not paying for public transport is likely to be seen as dishonest by the standards of reasonable people: likely to satisfy the first step of the *Ghosh* test. However, D is likely to avoid liability on the second step: she did not realise that payment was expected, and so is unlikely at that time to have appreciated that others would consider her conduct dishonest. The second example is that of Robin Hood, and this example is useful to demonstrate some of the test's uncertainties. On the first step, it is not certain that every jury would consider that robbing from the rich to give to the poor to be dishonest, although it is likely that most would. On the second step, we would have to distinguish between the perceptive folk hero, who appreciates that most people would think her dishonest but carries on regardless (satisfying the second test), and, the more self-obsessed folk hero, who believes (however unreasonably) that she is acting in a way that reasonable and honest people would not think dishonest (failing the second step).

[88] See our separation of actus reus and mens rea at **9.2**. See also the discussion of dishonesty at **3.6.1**.

[89] Campbell, 'The Test of Dishonesty in *Ghosh*' (1994) 43 CLJ 349.

[90] [2007] EWHC 239 (Admin).

9.3 Robbery

Robbery is defined in section 8(1) of the TA 1968. The maximum sentence on indictment is life imprisonment.[91]

> (1) A person is guilty of robbery if he steals, and immediately before or at the time of doing so, and in order to do so, he uses force on any person or puts or seeks to put any person in fear of being then and there subjected to force.

The elements of robbery are set out in **Table 9.3**.

Table 9.3　Robbery

	Actus reus	**Mens rea**
Conduct element	Any conduct causing the results	Voluntary
Circumstance element	What is appropriated is property	Knowledge
	What is appropriated does not belong to D	Knowledge
	D's appropriation is dishonest	Knowledge
Result element	D appropriates V's property	Intention
	(D uses unlawful force against another, or causes another to apprehend immediate unlawful force)	Intention or recklessness
Ulterior mens rea element	*	Intention to permanently deprive V of her property
		Intention that force or threat of force will facilitate the theft
		(Where D does *not* use or cause another to apprehend unlawful force, she may still be liable if seeking to make another so apprehend)

---

[91] TA 1968, s8(2).

The elements of robbery may be more simply illustrated in line with **Figure 9.1**.

Figure 9.1 Robbery

9.3.1 Theft

D must commit theft as an essential part of the offence of robbery.[92] If D does not commit theft due to the absence of any of the elements of theft as discussed previously, then D does not commit robbery. Of course, where there is no theft but D has used unlawful force, she may still be liable for an offence against the person,[93] or for an offence of assault with intent to rob,[94] but not for robbery.

We have already discussed the elements of theft at **9.2**, so we will not repeat them again here. It is important to remember that every element of theft must be satisfied.

9.3.2 Force or the threat of force

The requirement of 'force' can be satisfied in any one of three ways: actual infliction of force; causing an apprehension of force; and/or seeking to cause the apprehension of force. We discuss each in turn.

> **Beware...**
> The requirement of force or threat of force shares several similarities with the offences of assault and battery discussed at **7.2**. However, as we will see, these similarities are not complete, and so the requirement of force within robbery should not equated with assault and battery.

9.3.2.1 Force

Most straightforward cases of robbery will involve D using force against V in the course of theft. Such force must be bodily and not simply against V's property. It must be more than negligible, but need not be serious.[95] For example, minor bodily contact when picking V's pocket will not satisfy this element[96] but any pushing or shoving of V is likely to do so.[97] This is illustrated in *P v DPP*.

---

[92] *Guy* (1990) 93 Cr App R 108.
[93] **Chapter 7.**
[94] TA 1968, s8(2).
[95] It has been argued that different levels of force should lead to different levels of liability: Ashworth, 'Robbery Reassessed' [2002] Crim LR 851.
[96] *Monaghan and Monaghan* [2000] 1 Cr App R 6: pickpocketing and 'jostling' charged as theft.
[97] *Dawson* (1976) 64 Cr App R 170: theft and a 'nudge' charged as robbery.

🗂 *P v DPP* [2012] EWHC 1657 (Admin)

D snatched a lit cigarette from V's hand. No contact was made with V. D was charged with robbery.

• Youth Court: guilty of robbery.
• High Court: appeal allowed, and convictions for theft substituted. D's snatching of the cigarette did not amount to sufficient 'force' to satisfy robbery.

D's appeal was allowed in *P v DPP* because of a lack of sufficient force, not because of the lack of direct bodily contact. It has been recognised for some time that although force against another's body is required, such force may be inflicted indirectly. For example, where D wrenches a shopping basket or a handbag from V's grip, causing force to be inflicted despite the lack of direct physical contact, robbery may be found.[98]

9.3.2.2 Fear of force

Section 8 describes putting V in 'fear' of being subjected to force. However, the term 'fear' is problematic to the extent that it suggests something beyond the apprehension of force. It would not be desirable, for example, for D's liability to depend on the robustness or bravery of V. Therefore, courts have interpreted 'fear' in line with a simple apprehension that force will be used.[99] In line with section 8, V must be caused to apprehend that force will be used 'then and there'. Thus, there was no robbery in *Khan*[100] where V handed money to D fearing that if he did not do so D would be in trouble with a third party (X) and then D may return and use force against V: the apprehension was of future, not present force. Where D threatens force in the future in order to gain V's property, the appropriate charge is blackmail.[101]

9.3.2.3 Seeking fear of force

D can alternatively satisfy this element of robbery if she 'seeks' to put V in fear of force. Thus, even where D does not use force against V or cause V to apprehend the use of force (both actus reus) D may still be liable if she acts with the intention to cause V to so apprehend (ulterior mens rea).[102] For example, robbery will be committed if D uses a fake gun to threaten V and take property, even if V realises the gun is fake.

Point to remember...
Where D causes another to apprehend force, or seeks to do so, the person threatened must be aware of it. For example, where D threatens V directly, or where D threatens V's family member X whilst X is present, the offence may be committed. However, where D threatens V with the attack of one of her family, and that family member is not present and not aware of the threat, robbery is not committed.[103]

---

[98] *Clouden* [1987] Crim LR 56; *Symons* [2009] EWCA Crim 83.
[99] *R v DPP* [2007] EWHC 739 (Admin): robbery despite evidence from V that he was not afraid.
[100] [2001] EWCA Crim 923.
[101] See **9.6**.
[102] *Tennant* [1976] Crim LR 133.
[103] *Taylor* [1996] 10 Arch News 2.

9.3.3 Link between theft and force

To amount to robbery, as opposed to separate offences of theft and an offence against the person, the two major parts of the offence must be linked. This does not mean that force must *necessarily* be aimed at the owner of the property stolen. For example, there will be robbery where D overpowers a security guard of shop A to prevent her seeing and reporting D's thefts from shop B. However, there must be temporal and intentional links.

A) **Temporal link:** Section 8 states that the force must be 'immediately before' or 'at the time of' the theft. This means that there is no robbery where there is a large time gap between the two. However, a commonsense application of the law, as in *Hale*, allows some minor gaps in time, even where the force comes after the act of appropriation.

◻ *Hale* (1978) 68 Cr App R 415

D1 and D2 broke into V's house. Whilst D1 stole V's jewellery, D2 tied V up. D1 and D2 were charged with robbery.

- Crown Court: guilty of robbery.
- Court of Appeal: convictions upheld on appeal. Even if the appropriation by D1 might have occurred fractionally before the force used by D2, the act of theft could be interpreted as a continuing act: the elements coincided in time.

Just as the courts have interpreted the 'act' of theft broadly to find that the elements coincide in time, the same has been true of the element of 'force', particularly in threat of force cases. For example, there will be robbery where D threatens V on day one and then takes property from V on day two, knowing that the threat is still operating on V (ie V, due to the earlier threat, apprehends immediate force if she refuses).[104]

B) **Intentional link:** D must use the force 'in order to' steal. Therefore, accidental infliction of force during a theft is not robbery. Indeed, even where D assaults V with no intention to steal but then takes the opportunity to take V's property, there is no robbery: there may be a theft and an assault in such a case but there is no intentional link between them.[105]

9.4 Burglary

Burglary is set out in section 9 of the TA 1968. The maximum sentence on indictment is ten years' imprisonment, or 14 years where the burglary takes place in a dwelling.[106]

(1) A person is guilty of burglary if—

    (a) he enters any building or part of a building as a trespasser and with intent to commit any such offence as is mentioned in subsection (2) below; or

---

[104] *Donaghy and Marshall* [1981] Crim LR 644.
[105] *James* [1997] Crim LR 598.
[106] TA 1968, s9(3).

(b) having entered any building or part of a building as a trespasser he steals or attempts to steal anything in the building or that part of it or inflicts or attempts to inflict on any person therein any grievous bodily harm.

(2) The offences referred to in subsection (1)(a) above are offences of stealing anything in the building or part of a building in question, of inflicting on any person therein any grievous bodily harm therein, and of doing unlawful damage to the building or anything therein.

As is clear from the statute, the offence of burglary is more complex than its common (mis)understanding as simply breaking and entering to commit theft. In fact, the offence is best understood by splitting it into two separate offences, both leading to conviction for burglary. The first offence is set out in section 9(1)(a); the second in section 9(1)(b).

9.4.1 TA 1968, s9(1)(a): burglary because of intent at time of trespass

Section 9(1)(a) creates a form of inchoate offence: targeting D who trespasses: with *intent* to commit theft, cause GBH, or commit criminal damage. D is liable at the point of entry provided she has the requisite intent. Whether she goes on to commit the intended offence is irrelevant to her liability under this subsection. As with other inchoate offences,[107] the rationale for this offence is to facilitate early intervention by the police, imposing liability *before* the harms associated with theft, GBH, or criminal damage have come about. The offence is set out in **Table 9.4**.

Table 9.4 Burglary: TA 1968, s9(1)(a)

	Actus reus	**Mens rea**
Conduct element	Any conduct causing the results	Voluntary
Circumstance element	D is a trespasser	Intention or recklessness
Result element	Entry into a building or part of a building	Intent
Ulterior mens rea element	*	Intent to commit theft; cause GBH; or commit criminal damage

9.4.1.1 Actus reus of s9(1)(a) burglary

The actus reus of section 9(1)(a) burglary is deceptively simple: entry to a building, or part of a building, as a trespasser. However, within this, areas of complication have arisen.

---

[107] **Chapter 11.**

A) **Entry:** D 'enters' a building, or part of a building, if any part of her person crosses the threshold. In the case of *Collins*,[108] discussed in the following section, Edmund Davis LJ said that entry must be 'effective and substantial'. However, such terms are not useful, they erroneously suggest that D must have fully entered or that her entry must be such that she could commit the intended offence. As illustrated in *Ryan*, following *Brown*,[109] such a degree of entry is not required.

> **Ⓘ** *Ryan* [1996] Crim LR 320
>
> D attempted to break into V's house but became wedged in the kitchen window with his arm and head inside the building. D was charged with section 9(1)(a) burglary.
>
> • Crown Court: guilty of burglary.
> • Court of Appeal: conviction upheld on appeal. Although most of D's body was not inside the building and, although he was not in a position to commit the intended offence, the jury were still entitled to find a valid entry.

Under the (pre-1968) common law, entry could also be found indirectly as where D uses an instrument such as a long hook rather than her body to enter the building. It is uncertain whether such conduct could constitute entry under the current law, and there is no authority directly on this point. In such cases, where D uses the instrument to commit the intended offence, it is better to simply charge that offence rather than burglary, or an attempt of that offence where the offence is not carried out.[110]

B) **Building or part of a building:** The word 'building' is given its ordinary meaning by the courts.[111] However, a judge must still advise the jury whether the structure entered by D is capable of being found to be a building. This is not always straightforward. A standard house is clearly a building whether occupied or not, as are work buildings; outhouses; sheds; and so on. The term has been interpreted broadly to include part-built or damaged structures, as well as semi-permanent containers.[112] Section 9(4) also extends the term to include 'inhabited' vehicles or vessels whether occupied or not, which includes caravans, houseboats, and so on. However, where the vehicle or vessel is not inhabited, or the structure is insufficiently permanent (eg a tent), a court may find that there is no building and therefore no burglary.[113]

> *Don't be confused...*
> A building is standardly interpreted to include the entire structure. Thus, where D breaks into Flat 1 in order to gain access to Flat 2 in order to steal, D commits section 9(1)(a) burglary at the point of entry to the building that houses the two flats (we do not have to wait until she enters Flat 2).[114]

---

[108] [1973] QB 100.

[109] [1985] Crim LR 212: there was entry where D stood outside a shop, but was reaching through a window.

[110] **Chapter 11**.

[111] *Brutus v Cozens* [1973] AC 854. Laird, 'Conceptualising the interpretation of "dwelling" in section 9 of the Theft Act 1968' (2013) Crim LR 656.

[112] *B & S v Leathley* [1979] Crim LR 314: a freezer container disconnected from its chassis could be a building.

[113] *Norfolk Constabulary v Seekings and Gould* [1986] Crim LR 167: a freezer container that was still connected to its chassis was a (non-inhabited) vehicle and not a building.

[114] *Headley v Webb* [1901] 2 Ch 126: two semi-detached houses can constitute a single building.

Reference to 'part of a building' is included to deal with cases where D has permission to enter the building (eg the shop) but not into certain areas (eg behind the counter).[115] Where such areas constitute 'part of a building', D may be liable under section 9(1)(a) for entering them with the required mens rea. As with the definition of 'building', there are core examples such as separate rooms within a house or hotel; behind a shop counter; etc, but there will also be areas of uncertainty as with a roped-off area within a shop.[116]

C) **As a trespasser:** Where D enters a building without permission of the owner or possessor, or the owner or possessor's family, or some other legal authorisation,[117] she enters as a trespasser. Trespass is a tortious concept, but its definition in the criminal law need not be identical to that in tort.[118] Whether D is a trespasser will usually be clear. Where it is not, two rules are particularly important. First, where V mistakenly permits D to enter, D enters as a trespasser, for example, if V thinks D is the plumber.[119] Secondly, where D enters in excess of her permission, she is also trespassing. This is illustrated in *Jones and Smith*.

▯ *Jones and Smith* [1976] 3 All ER 54

D and another entered his father's house, at night, with the intention to steal. D had a general permission to enter, but not for the purposes of stealing. D was charged with burglary.

- Crown Court: guilty of burglary.
- Court of Appeal: conviction upheld on appeal. D entered the building in excess of the general permission given by his father, thus as a trespasser.

The logical conclusion to this second rule is that D commits burglary whenever she enters a shop with intent to steal: she is a trespasser because her permission to enter does not extend to entry for the purposes of theft.[120] This seems correct on the law. However, prosecutors have been, and are likely to remain, reluctant to prosecute shoplifting as burglary unless D enters a specifically restricted area within a shop.[121]

Extra detail...
Interesting problems emerge where D enters with permission but the permission is then withdrawn. Where D fails to leave in a reasonable time, she becomes a trespasser. However, as she has not 'entered' as a trespasser, we would still need some kind of crossing (eg into a new area of the building) as a trespasser in order to potentially catch D within burglary.

---

[115] *Walkington* [1979] 2 All ER 716: D trespassed behind a shop counter.
[116] Discussed in *Walkington*. Where the barrier is clear, it is likely to create a separate part of the building.
[117] eg police entering property pursuant to a warrant.
[118] *Collins* [1973] QB 100.
[119] Ibid. Discussed at **9.4.1.2**.
[120] Smith, 'Shoplifting and the Theft Acts' [1981] Crim LR 586.
[121] *Walkington* [1979] 2 All ER 716.

9.4.1.2 Mens rea of s9(1)(a) burglary

There are two major elements within the mens rea of section 9(1)(a) burglary. First, D must be at least reckless as to the facts that make her a trespasser. Secondly, D must intend to commit one of the offences listed in section 9(2).

A) **Intent/Reckless as to trespass:** In most cases D will be well aware when she enters the building as a trespasser. However, particularly in relation to mistaken consent cases, and cases of entry in excess of permission, mens rea may be harder to demonstrate. Take the case of *Collins*.

Collins [1973] QB 100

D, naked apart from his socks, climbed a ladder up to V's window. D's intention was to have sex with V. Seeing the silhouette of D in her window, V mistook D for her boyfriend, invited him in, and they engaged in sexual intercourse. V turned on the light and discovered her mistake. D was charged with burglary (at this time burglary included entry as a trespasser with 'intent to rape').

- Crown Court: guilty of burglary.
- Court of Appeal: appeal allowed. Although V's mistake meant that D entered without true permission, the jury were not directed to ask the separate mens rea question: was D at least reckless as to V's mistake (ie did he at least foresee a risk of the mistake and continue unreasonably to run such a risk)?

Although *Collins* avoided liability due to (possible) lack of mens rea, this will not always be the case. For example, in *Jones and Smith* (discussed in the previous section), the fact that the boys waited to enter D's dad's house at night provided evidence that they realised that they were entering in excess of their permission.

B) **Intent to steal, cause GBH, or commit criminal damage:** This element is an example of ulterior mens rea: D must intend to commit one of these offences at the time of entry, but whether she goes on to carry it out is irrelevant.[122] This element is pivotal to the wrong under section 9(1)(a). Without this intention, D merely commits the civil wrong of trespass; with the intention, D commits burglary, a serious criminal offence. As a form of ulterior intention, it is clear that a conditional intention is sufficient, as where D intends to steal if she finds anything worth stealing.[123] However, nothing short of intention as to every element of the future offence will suffice.[124]

Assessment matters...
What if D intends to take an item from the building and damage it elsewhere (does D intend to commit criminal damage 'therein'?), or to take a person from the building and cause GBH elsewhere (does D intend to cause GBH 'therein'?). These questions have not arisen in the case law, but provide an interesting problem. As with all legal unknowns, if arising in a problem question, you should highlight the lack of authority and say what you think the likely outcome would be, based on the rationale of the offence and the general approach of the courts.[125]

---

[122] See **4.2.1.2**.
[123] *AG's References (Nos 1 and 2 of 1979)* [1979] 3 All ER 143.
[124] *A v DPP* [2003] All ER 393: recklessness is not sufficient.
[125] White, 'Lurkers, Draggers and Kidnappers' (1986) 150 JP 37.

9.4.2 TA 1968, s9(1)(b): burglary following trespassory entry

Section 9(1)(b) burglary will often overlap with section 9(1)(a), but is quite different. Section 9(1)(b) applies where D enters a building or a part of a building as a trespasser and then commits theft, attempted theft, causes GBH, or attempts to cause GBH. Where D enters with the intent to commit one of these offences, and then does so, she commits burglary under *both* sections 9(1)(a) and 9(1)(b). However, where she enters with intent to commit one of the listed offences, but does not commit or attempt to commit it, there is a section 9(1)(a) burglary only. Where she enters without the intent to commit one of the listed offences, but then does commit such an offence after having entered, there is a section 9(1)(b) burglary only.

To come within section 9(1)(b), D must complete the offence of theft, attempted theft, a GBH offence, or an attempted GBH offence. The elements of these offences are discussed elsewhere in this book.[126] In addition to this base offence, the other elements of section 9(1)(b) are set out in **Table 9.5**.

Table 9.5 Burglary: TA 1968, s9(1)(b)

	Actus reus	Mens rea
Conduct element	Any conduct causing the results	Voluntary
Circumstance element	D is a trespasser	Recklessness
Result element	Entry into a building or part of a building	Intent

Section 9(1)(b) burglary may be more simply illustrated, as in **Figure 9.2**.

Figure 9.2 Burglary: TA 1968, s9(1)(b)

Beware…
The listed offences in relation to sections 9(1)(a) and 9(1)(b) are different. Importantly, criminal damage is a listed offence under section 9(1)(a), but not under section 9(1)(b). So, where D trespasses without the intention to commit criminal damage, but then does so whilst inside the building, she does not commit burglary. She will, of course, be liable for criminal damage.

---

126 Theft (**9.2**); GBH (**7.5–7.6**); Attempt (**Chapter 11**).

9.4.2.1 Actus reus of s9(1)(b) burglary

D must enter a building or a part of a building as a trespasser. These elements were discussed above in the context of section 9(1)(a).

When inside the building, D must then complete the actus reus of theft, a GBH offence, or attempt either. We discuss the elements of theft at **9.2**; GBH offences at **7.5–7.6**; and criminal attempts at **Chapter 11**.

9.4.2.2 Mens rea of s9(1)(b) burglary

D must be at least reckless as to the facts that make her entry a trespass. We discussed this previously in relation to the case of *Collins*.

When committing one of the listed offences within the building, D must act with the mens rea required for that offence. For example, if committing theft, D must intend to permanently deprive V of her property, and do so dishonestly. We discuss the elements of theft at **9.2**; GBH offences at **7.5–7.6**; and criminal attempts at **Chapter 11**.

> *Extra detail…*
>
> As section 9(1)(b) does not specify a particular GBH 'offence', it was held in *Jenkins*[127] that as long as D caused GBH there was no need to demonstrate any mens rea. However, this interpretation has been heavily criticised and is unlikely to be followed by future courts. For example, D trespasses into V's house, thinking V is away. V hears someone in the house and suffers a shock-induced heart attack. D has committed the trespass, but surely not burglary.

9.4.3 Aggravated burglary

A burglary becomes aggravated burglary under section 10 of the TA 1968 if it is committed with the use of a listed weapon. The maximum sentence for aggravated burglary on indictment is life imprisonment.[128]

> (1) A person is guilty of aggravated burglary if he commits any burglary and at the time has with him any firearm or imitation firearm, any weapon of offence, or any explosive; and for this purpose—
>
> (a) 'firearm' includes an airgun or air pistol, and 'imitation firearm' means anything which has the appearance of being a firearm, whether capable of being discharged or not; and
>
> (b) 'weapon of offence' means any article made or adapted for use for causing injury to or incapacitating a person, or intended by the person having it with him for such use; and
>
> (c) 'explosive' means any article manufactured for the purpose of producing a practical effect by explosion, or intended by the person having it with him for that purpose.

The structure of the offence is illustrated in **Figure 9.3**.

---

127 [1983] 1 All ER 1000.
128 TA 1968, s10(2).

Figure 9.3 Aggravated burglary

We have already discussed the elements of burglary, and much of the possession require-ment is self-explanatory from the text of section 10. However, three points should be stressed.

First, it will not always be clear if what D possesses is a 'weapon' within the mean-ing of section 10. Section 10(1)(b) is particularly ambiguous, but has been interpreted broadly. For example, even an otherwise innocent item such as a screwdriver will become a weapon within this section if D is carrying it to use as a weapon.[129] Note that section 10(1)(b) also extends to 'incapacitation'. Thus, carrying sleeping pills to drug the owner of the building, or socks to tie her up, etc, will all be caught by the offence.

Secondly, the requirement that D must have the weapon 'at the time' of committing the burglary means that it is important to identify whether D is committing burglary under section 9(1)(a) or 9(1)(b). D commits section 9(1)(a) burglary at the point of entry to the building with the requisite intention. Thus, for aggravated section 9(1)(a) burglary, D must have the weapon at this point.[130] D commits section 9(1)(b) burglary at the point she commits theft, a GBH offence, or attempts either. Thus, for aggravated section 9(1)(b) burglary, D must have the weapon at this point.[131]

Thirdly, the requirement of possession ('has with him') simply means that D must be in control of the weapon and must be aware of it.[132] It is irrelevant whether D intends to use the weapon in the course of the burglary. For example, in *Stones*,[133] D's conviction was upheld where he was carrying a kitchen knife, even though he claimed to have the knife for defensive purposes only.

9.5 Handling stolen goods

The offence of handling stolen goods is set out in section 22 of the TA 1968. The maxi-mum sentence on indictment is 14 years' imprisonment.[134]

(1) A person handles stolen goods if (otherwise than in the course of the stealing) knowing or believ-ing them to be stolen goods he dishonestly receives the goods, or dishonestly undertakes or assists in their retention, removal, disposal or realisation by or for the benefit of another person, or if he arranges to do so.

[129] *Kelly* [1993] Crim LR 763.
[130] *Wiggins* [2012] EWCA Crim 885.
[131] *Chevannes* [2009] EWCA Crim 2725.
[132] *Russell* (1985) 81 Cr App R 315.
[133] [1989] 1 WLR 156.
[134] The high maximum of 14 years (theft carries a maximum of seven years) is set to discourage trade in stolen goods and thereby discourage future thefts. *Shelton* (1993) 15 Cr App R 415.

The elements of the offence are illustrated in **Table 9.6**.

Table 9.6 Handling stolen goods

	Actus reus	Mens rea
Conduct element	Any conduct causing the result	Voluntary
Circumstance element	The goods are stolen	Knowledge or belief
	D's conduct is dishonest	Knowledge/dishonesty
Result element	D receives the goods,	Intention
	Or undertakes or assists in their retention, removal, disposal, or realisation by or for the benefit of another person, or arranges to do so	Intention

9.5.1 Actus reus of s22

Handling stolen goods is an extremely wide-ranging offence, extending well beyond the paradigm where D takes physical possession of V's recently stolen goods from the thief (P). Core questions within the actus reus relate to the meaning of 'goods'; the meaning of 'stolen'; and the meaning of 'handling'.

9.5.1.1 Goods

The definition of 'goods' for the purpose of this offence is set out in section 34(2)(b) of the TA 1968.

> (b) 'goods', except in so far as the context otherwise requires, includes money and every other description of property except land, and includes things severed from the land by stealing.

This section explicitly links the definition of 'goods' to that of 'property', defined within section 4 and discussed earlier.[135] Therefore, (almost) everything that qualifies as property under section 4 will also be 'goods' for the purposes of section 22. Although there has been some doubt whether things in action (eg bank account credit) can constitute goods for the purpose of this offence, it is now clear that they can.[136] The only exception to the equivalence between property and goods is in relation to land: certain non-severed fixtures are capable of constituting property, whereas they will not be goods for the purpose of this offence unless severed.

9.5.1.2 Stolen

In order for the handling offence to apply, it must be demonstrated that the property was in fact 'stolen'.[137] This is set out in section 24 of the TA 1968.

---

[135] See **9.2.2**.

[136] *AG's Reference (No 4 of 1979)* [1981] 1 All ER 1193.

[137] If the goods are not stolen, but D believes they are, she may be liable for an attempted handling offence (*Haughton v Smith* [1975] AC 476), see **Chapter 11**.

(4) For purposes of the provisions of this Act relating to goods which have been stolen…goods obtained in England or Wales or elsewhere either by blackmail or…by fraud…shall be regarded as stolen; and 'steal', 'theft' and 'thief' shall be construed accordingly.

The types of property that are classed as stolen goods for the purposes of this offence extends beyond those that are acquired by theft. In line with this section, goods can be stolen through theft,[138] robbery,[139] burglary,[140] blackmail,[141] or fraud.[142] Although D need not steal the goods personally, it must be demonstrated that one of these offences was carried out by someone. This is discussed in *Defazio v DPP*.

 Defazio v DPP [2007] EWHC 3529 (Admin)

V's missing credit card was found in D's house. D was charged with handling stolen goods.

- Magistrates' court: guilty of handling stolen goods.
- High Court: appeal allowed. The fact that the card was found does not mean that it was stolen: D had claimed that he found the card on the street and merely forgot to hand it in.

Where as in *Defazio* goods are found and there is some doubt as to their status, the fact that D has been told by another that they are stolen is not sufficient to demonstrate that they are stolen in fact.[143] However, other material evidence, such as D witnessing the goods being stolen; buying them in extremely suspicious circumstances; and/or for an unrealistically low price, may be sufficient.[144]

The types of property that can be classed as stolen under this section also extend beyond the property that was originally acquired through theft, robbery, etc. This is set out in section 24(2) of the TA 1968.

(2) For purposes of those provisions references to stolen goods shall include, in addition to the goods originally stolen and parts of them (whether in their original state or not),—

(a) any other goods which directly or indirectly represent or have at any time represented the stolen goods in the hands of the thief as being the proceeds of any disposal or realisation of the whole or part of the goods stolen or of goods so representing the stolen goods; and

(b) any other goods which directly or indirectly represent or have at any time represented the stolen goods in the hands of a handler of the stolen goods or any part of them as being the proceeds of any disposal or realisation of the whole or part of the stolen goods handled by him or of goods so representing them.

This means that, in certain cases, it will be necessary to trace the stolen goods, or their proceeds. The operation of this subsection is best illustrated by way of an example.

---

138 See **9.2**.
139 See **9.3**.
140 See **9.4**.
141 See **9.6**.
142 **Chapter 10**.
143 This is evidence of D's belief only: *Marshall* [1977] Crim LR 106.
144 *Korniak* (1983) 76 Cr App R 145: D buying jewellery from a stranger for a very low price.

Let us imagine that P steals an iPhone and then sells it to X for £100, and X then sells the phone to D. In line with section 24(2)(a), despite gaining the phone third-hand, D may still be liable for handling stolen goods if she has the requisite mens rea. This will be the case even if X did not commit the offence of handling because her conduct in relation to the phone was not accompanied by mens rea. In line with section 24(2)(b), it is also possible to trace the proceeds of stolen goods. Thus, where P sells the phone he stole to X for £100, the money P receives from X (the proceeds of the stolen goods) becomes stolen property in its own right. This will also be the case for D if she goes on to sell or exchange the goods bought from X. However, D's money received by X (who did *not* commit a handling offence in relation to the original goods) does not constitute stolen goods: the money received by X is not money 'in the hands of a handler of stolen goods'.

Section 24(3) sets out when goods cease to be stolen, and thus cannot form the basis of the offence when handled.

(3) But no goods shall be regarded as having continued to be stolen goods after they have been restored to the person from whom they were stolen or to other lawful possession or custody, or after that person and any other person claiming through him have otherwise ceased as regards those goods to have any right to restitution in respect of the theft.

The result of this section is that where the police (or owner) regain lawful possession, the goods cease to be stolen. In such a case, where D retakes control of the goods, she is guilty of theft rather than handling stolen goods. Interesting questions emerge about what constitutes being 'restored' to an owner or custody, as in *AG's Reference (No 1 of 1974)*.

> **AG's Reference (No 1 of 1974)** [1974] 2 All ER 899
>
> A police officer immobilised D's car while D was absent from it and kept watch for D's return, correctly suspecting the car contained stolen goods. D returned, and was questioned by the officer. In view of his unsatisfactory responses, D was arrested and the car searched. D was charged with handling stolen goods.
>
> - Crown Court: not guilty of handling stolen goods. When immobilising the car, the police officer effectively took control of (restored) the goods. Thus, when D came to the car, the goods were no longer stolen.
> - Court of Appeal: whether the officer had restored the goods was a question of fact for the jury, taking account of the officer's intentions. Thus, the judge at first instance was wrong not to allow this issue to be decided by the jury.

9.5.1.3 Handling

The section 22 offence specifies a number of ways (as many as 18) through which the stolen goods may be handled.

(1) A person handles stolen goods if…he…receives the goods, or…undertakes or assists in their retention, removal, disposal or realisation by or for the benefit of another person, or if he arranges to do so.

Several of these terms require explanation.

A) **Receives or arranges to receive:** This is the only form of handling that does not have to be 'by or for the benefit of another person'. Thus, where D is not acting for another, this is the only potential route to liability. D receives goods where she gains possession or control from another.[145] This will typically involve physical possession, but is wide enough to include joint control as where the goods are held by X, but X is acting as an agent of D.[146] Acts of arranging to receive will also be included as where D agrees to receive the goods from X.[147] However, the simple fact that the goods are found on D's premises will not be sufficient; it must be shown that they are there by D's invitation or agreement: receiving requires D's active participation.[148]

B) **Retention, removal, disposal, realisation:** Alongside receiving, these terms represent the other form of handling. 'Retention' requires D to act in a manner that will make it more likely that stolen goods are kept (eg storing them for X).[149] Simple use of the goods is not sufficient.[150] 'Removal' requires D to assist with moving the goods from one location to another even if D never gains possession or control.[151] 'Disposal' requires D to destroy or sell/exchange the stolen goods.[152] 'Realisation' requires D to exchange the goods for money or other property, and as such, overlaps with disposal.[153]

C) **Arranging or assisting:** Just as 'receiving' extends to arranging to receive, the same is true of the other forms of handling defined above, as where D arranges to dispose when she agrees with another to sell the stolen goods. However, beyond that which is applicable to receiving, D may also handle stolen goods under these other headings through acts of assisting or encouraging the retention, removal, disposal, or realisation of the goods such as lying to the police to allow the goods to be retained by X.[154] To assist, it must be shown that D actively encouraged or helped X; simply benefiting from another's handling is not sufficient.[155] When combined, these qualifications even allow for handling where D arranges to assist X to retain, remove, dispose, or realise.

D) **For the benefit of another:** Apart from in cases of receiving or arranging to receive (as in point A above), it must be shown that D has acted (handled) for the benefit of another. This requirement keeps the offence within limits, avoiding every theft also being an incident of handling. With this in mind, the requirement has been interpreted narrowly in *Bloxham* to apply only where D is acting on behalf of another.

---

[145] 'From another' is important. Where D simply finds stolen goods, she does not receive them: *Haider* (1985) unreported.

[146] *Miller* (1854) 6 Cox CC 353; *Smith* (1855) Dears CC 494.

[147] *King* [1938] 2 All ER 662.

[148] *Cavendish* [1961] 2 All ER 856.

[149] *Pitchley* (1972) 57 Cr App R 30.

[150] *Sanders* (1982) 75 Cr App R 84: D used a stolen heater and battery charger in his father's garage.

[151] *Gleed* (1916) 12 Cr App R 32.

[152] *Watson* [1916] 2 KB 385.

[153] *Bloxham* [1983] 1 AC 109.

[154] *Kanwar* (1982) 75 Cr App R 87.

[155] *Coleman* [1986] Crim LR 56: D's knowledge that his wife was using stolen money to pay their joint solicitor's fees did not, of itself, amount to assisting.

> **Bloxham** [1983] 1 AC 109
>
> D purchased a car from P, unaware that it was stolen. D later came to suspect that the car was stolen and sold it to X. D was charged with handling stolen goods.
>
> - Crown Court: guilty of handling stolen goods.
> - Court of Appeal: conviction upheld on appeal.
> - House of Lords: appeal allowed. D clearly disposed of the stolen goods, but did not do so for the benefit of another. Although the buyer of the car (X) may have benefited, it was not sold by D for X's benefit.

9.5.2 Mens rea of s22

There are two main mens rea elements: knowledge or belief that the goods are stolen, and dishonesty.

9.5.2.1 Knowledge or belief that the goods are stolen

D must know or believe that the goods are stolen. These are subjective mens rea terms and, as such, it will not be sufficient to show that a reasonable person would have believed or known.[156] It must be proved that D believed or knew.[157]

It is clear that suspicion or recklessness that the goods are stolen will never be sufficient.[158] Interestingly, it has also been held that wilful blindness will not be sufficient either.[159] Thus, where D is suspicious but actively avoids looking deeper in order to remain ignorant, although this may amount to a form of knowledge in other contexts,[160] it will not be the case for the purposes of handling stolen goods.

9.5.2.2 Dishonesty

The requirement of dishonesty requires us to apply the *Ghosh* test discussed previously.[161] It must be demonstrated that (a) D's acts of handling were dishonest by the standards of honest and reasonable people; and (b) D realised that her actions would be so regarded. In most cases where D handles stolen goods knowing or believing that they are stolen, it will not be difficult to demonstrate dishonesty. The exception may be where D handles the goods with an intention to return them to the owner or the police.[162]

> **Extra detail...**
> Similar and overlapping offences of money laundering are used in tandem with the offence of handling stolen goods. The main offences of money laundering are found in the Proceeds of Crime Act 2002. We do not discuss these offence further in this book.

---

[156] See **3.4.2–3.4.3**. Griew, 'States of Mind, Presumptions and Inferences' in P Smith (ed), *Criminal Law: Essays in Honour of JC Smith* (1987) 63.
[157] *Atwal v Massey* [1971] 3 All ER 881.
[158] *Forsyth* [1997] Crim LR 581.
[159] *Griffiths* (1974) 60 Cr App R 14.
[160] See **3.4.2.1**.
[161] See **9.2.5**.
[162] *Matthews* [1950] 1 All ER 137.

9.6 Blackmail

The offence of blackmail is defined in section 21 of the TA 1968. The maximum sentence on indictment is 14 years' imprisonment.[163]

(1) A person is guilty of blackmail if, with a view to gain for himself or another or with intent to cause loss to another, he makes any unwarranted demand with menaces; and for this purpose a demand with menaces is unwarranted unless the person making it does so in the belief—

    (a) that he has reasonable grounds for making the demand; and

    (b) that the use of the menaces is a proper means of reinforcing the demand.

The elements of blackmail are set out in **Table 9.7**.

Table 9.7 Blackmail

	Actus reus	Mens rea
Conduct element	D makes demands	Voluntary
Circumstance element	D uses menaces	Knowledge
Result element	None	None
Ulterior mens rea element	*	D intends to make a gain or cause a loss to another D does not believe that she has reasonable grounds to make the demands, *or*, D does not believe that the use of menaces is a proper means of reinforcing the demand

There is no single rationale for the offence of blackmail. It can be seen as needed to protect the person from threats of unpleasant consequences; their privacy from invasive demands;[164] and their property which is the subject of the demand.[165] Blackmail also has an interesting structure: criminalising harmful conduct (the demand with menace), but also a significant inchoate or ulterior element: D must intend to make a gain or cause a loss, but this need never come about, the offence requires no actual results at all.

9.6.1 Actus reus of s21

The actus reus of blackmail is formed of two principal elements: the making of a demand, and the use of menaces.

---

[163] TA 1968, s21(3).

[164] Alldridge, 'Attempted Murder of the Soul: Blackmail, Privacy and Secrets' (1993) 13 OJLS 368.

[165] Lamond, 'Coercion, Threats and the Puzzle of Blackmail' in Simester and Smith (eds), *Harm and Culpability* (1996) Ch10.

> **Don't be confused…**
> Although the 'unwarranted' nature of D's demand may appear to be an actus reus element, and is often described by courts in these terms, it is better understood as part of D's mens rea. This is because the question of whether D's demands are unwarranted depends solely upon her intentions and beliefs (ie her state of mind).

9.6.1.1 Demands

It must be proved that D made a demand in relation to another's property. This can be express or implied, as where D points a gun and asks if V might like to hand over her wallet, and it can be by any means of communication: orally, written, gesture, via an intermediary, etc.[166] Also, although the word demand might imply some form of harsh words, it is clear that the manner of the request, however polite, will still constitute a demand. In *Robinson*,[167] for example, 'Sir, I am now only making an appeal to your benevolence' was capable of being a demand. The requirement of a demand is satisfied as soon as it is made, regardless of whether V is aware of it, such as in cases where a letter is lost in the post, where V is deaf, etc.[168]

The lack of a demand as to property will be fatal to the offence. Where D catches V committing a crime (or doing anything she would rather keep secret), and V asks D if she will accept some property in exchange for her silence, there is no demand from D and therefore no blackmail. Equally, even where there is a demand from D, but that demand does not relate to property such as where D demands sexual acts from V, again there is no blackmail.[169]

9.6.1.2 Menaces

A menace has been defined as 'any action detrimental to or unpleasant to the person addressed'.[170] Therefore, beyond threats of violence to persons or property, any threat of an unpleasant character (eg to reveal compromising information, etc) can amount to a menace. The only restriction, preventing the offence applying in trivial circumstances, is that the menace must be 'of such a nature and extent that the mind of an ordinary person of normal stability and courage might be influenced or made apprehensive so as to accede unwillingly to the demand.'[171] This is a relatively low threshold (note the use of 'might'), but it is an objective one. Three situations should be distinguished.

A) **V does not accede, but a reasonable person would:** The use of an objective standard means that D's threats constitute a menace even if V is not intimidated in fact because, for example, she is particularly brave.[172]

B) **V accedes, but a reasonable person would not:** Again, the objective standard means that V's reaction is largely irrelevant and the question is whether a reasonable

---

166 *Treacy v DPP* [1971] AC 537.
167 (1796) 2 East PC 1110.
168 *Treacy v DPP* [1971] AC 537: the demand was made when the letter was posted.
169 Although D may be committing a sexual offence: **Chapter 8**.
170 *Thorne v Motor Trade Association* [1937] AC 797, 817.
171 *Clear* [1968] 1 All ER 74, 80.
172 *Moran* [1952] 1 All ER 803.

person *might* have acceded. Thus, in this context there will be no menace, and therefore no blackmail.[173]

C) **V accedes due to unique vulnerabilities, but a reasonable person would not:** As with (B), the result here is likely to be no menace. However, there is an exception. This arises where D has personal knowledge of V's vulnerability, such as V's infirmity, youth, timidity, etc, and so D realises that her threat will be particularly menacing to V. In this case, a menace will be found.[174]

As long as D's threats meet the objective standard required, it is irrelevant whether the menace is directed at V or another, whether the menace is carried out, or even whether it is possible for D to carry it out. This is illustrated in *Lambert*.

 Lambert [2009] EWCA Crim 2860

D phoned his grandmother pretending to have been kidnapped, and asking her to send money to have him freed. D was charged with blackmail.

- Crown Court: guilty of blackmail.
- Court of Appeal: conviction upheld on appeal. D communicated a menace to V. The fact that D was also the victim of that menace, and that the whole scenario was untrue, did not matter.

9.6.2 Mens rea of s21

There are two core mens rea elements: D's demands must be unwarranted, and they must be made with the intention to make a gain or cause a loss. Both of these requirements are ulterior in the sense that they do not correspond to elements within the actus reus.[175]

Point to remember…
Unlike the property offences discussed earlier, blackmail does not require an element of dishonesty.

9.6.2.1 Unwarranted demands

Not all demands with menaces will constitute blackmail, for example, D's demands for payment of a debt from V and threats of civil legal action will not suffice. Demands will only come within blackmail if they are unwarranted. In order to apply this element, we do not look to the content of the threat or the demands, although these will be useful evidence but, rather, we look to the state of mind of D. It must be demonstrated that (A) D did not believe that she had reasonable grounds to make the demands *or* (B) that D did not believe that the use of menaces was a proper means of reinforcing the demand: lack of either belief will suffice.

---

173 *Harry* [1974] Crim LR 32: V felt threatened by a note from a student charity event offering shopkeepers immunity from 'inconvenience' for payment: not sufficiently menacing.
174 *Garwood* [1987] 1 All ER 1032: where D must have been aware of V's extreme timidity.
175 See **4.2.1.2**.

Extra detail...
The unwarranted requirement attempts to mitigate what some describe as the 'blackmail paradox'. The paradox is evident because D is legally entitled to make certain demands of V (eg ask V for money). D is also legally entitled to do certain things that are unpleasant for V (eg expose V's immoral activities). However, where D threatens the latter in exchange for the former, her conduct becomes criminal.[176]

A) Lack of belief in reasonable grounds for the demand: Even where D believes that it is proper to use menaces, she must also believe that she has reasonable grounds for her demands. The question is not whether she thinks her demands are correct, but whether she believes that others would agree they are reasonable.

B) Lack of belief in the propriety of menaces: More common is the case where D believes that her demands are reasonable, but lacks belief in the propriety of her menaces. For example, in *Kewell*,[177] although D believed in the reasonableness of demanding the return of a debt, it was easy for the prosecution to show that D did not honestly believe that threatening to reveal embarrassing photos of V was a proper means of enforcing that debt. It has been argued that whenever D realises that her threat will involve committing a criminal offence, such as threats of unlawful violence, this will automatically undermine any claim of belief in propriety.[178] However, although this is undoubtedly very strong evidence that D did not believe that her threats were proper, it is unlikely to be conclusive in every case.

Extra detail...
Structuring this element in terms of mens rea can lead to two interesting results. First, even where (objectively) D's demands and use of menaces are entirely reasonable, if D lacks belief as to either she will still satisfy this element. Conversely, even where (objectively) D's demands and use of menaces are entirely unreasonable, unless the Crown can disprove D's claim that she honestly believed that both were proper, she will not satisfy this element.

9.6.2.2 A view to a gain or a loss

Although D need not make a gain or cause a loss in fact,[179] it is necessary that she made the demands with this intention. Gain and loss are defined in section 34(2)(a) of the TA 1968, refining the offence to focus on property only.[180]

(a) 'gain' and 'loss' are to be construed as extending only to gain or loss in money or other property, but as extending to any such gain or loss whether temporary or permanent; and—

(i) 'gain' includes a gain by keeping what one has, as well as a gain by getting what one has not; and

(ii) 'loss' includes a loss by not getting what one might get, as well as a loss by parting with what one has;

---

[176] Lindgren, 'Unraveling the Paradox of Blackmail' (1984) 84 Col L Rev 670.
[177] [2000] 2 Cr App R 38.
[178] *Harvey, Ulyett and Plummer* (1981) 72 Cr App R 139.
[179] *Moran* [1952] 1 All ER 803. The leading case on this element is *Dooley* [2005] EWCA Crim 3093, see commentary [2006] Crim LR 544.
[180] As stated earlier, a demand of a sexual nature or other non-property demand will not come within the offence.

An intention to make a gain *or* cause a loss is sufficient. Thus, for example, this element will be satisfied where D intends to cause a loss to V even though D makes no gain by, for example, demanding that V destroys an item of property. The same is also true where D intends to make a gain but not to cause a loss by, for example, demanding to be promoted, but intending to do a good job. It has been argued that where D demands something to which she is legally entitled, such as the payment of a debt, she cannot be intending to make a gain or cause a loss.[181] However, the court in *Lawrence and Pomroy*,[182] without specific discussion, seem to have assumed that such demands will still satisfy this element.

9.7 Criminal damage

In this section we discuss offences of criminal damage, arson, and aggravated criminal damage.[183] The basic offence of criminal damage is contained in section 1(1) of the Criminal Damage Act 1971.[184] The maximum sentence on indictment is ten years' imprisonment.[185]

(1) A person who without lawful excuse destroys or damages any property belonging to another intending to destroy or damage any such property or being reckless as to whether any such property would be destroyed or damaged shall be guilty of an offence.

The elements of criminal damage are set out in **Table 9.8**.

Table 9.8 Criminal damage

	Actus reus	**Mens rea**
Conduct element	Any conduct causing the result	Voluntary
Circumstance element	What is damaged is property	Intention or recklessness
	The property belongs to another	Intention or recklessness
Result element	Damage or destruction	Intention or recklessness

Following the enactment of the TA 1968 just three years earlier, the Criminal Damage Act 1971 attempts to create a coherent scheme of liability where D damages as opposed to appropriates another's property.

---

[181] Hogan, 'Blackmail' [1966] Crim LR 474.

[182] (1971) 57 Cr App R 64.

[183] There are also various offences of threatening criminal damage (Criminal Damage Act 1971, s2), possession of anything with intent to commit criminal damage (Criminal Damage Act 1971, s3), as well as more specific offences relating to dangerous materials such as explosives. These offences will not be discussed in this book.

[184] Following Law Commission recommendations: *Offences of Damage to Property* (No 29, 1970).

[185] Criminal Damage Act 1971, s4(2).

9.7.1 Actus reus of s1(1)

D commits the actus reus of criminal damage where she: (a) damages; (b) property; (c) belonging to another. Each requires discussion.

9.7.1.1 Damage

Damage is not defined in the statute, and is intended to carry its ordinary meaning.[186] Short of destruction, courts have generally discussed damage in terms of rendering property unusable and/or physical interference that reduces the value of property or costs money to repair. The utility of this open-textured approach has been necessary flexibility, allowing similar acts to be considered as damage in one context but not another. For example, we may want to say that spitting in food is damage, but spitting on the pavement is not. However, the courts have struggled to maintain coherence.

A) **Undermining usability:** In *Drake v DPP*,[187] it was held that wheel clamping did not amount to damage because, although it prevents use of the vehicle, the physical integrity of the vehicle is not affected. Contrast *Fiak*,[188] where D stuffed blankets from his prison cell in the toilet and flushed repeatedly to cause a small flood. The fact that the blankets and the cell were rendered temporarily unusable led the courts to find that damage was caused.

B) **Reduction in value:** Other cases have found damage from a reduction in value.[189] This seems apt in examples such as the scratching of a car: the car remains usable, but there is clearly some damage. However, this approach has been criticised,[190] and has largely fallen out of favour.

C) **Cost of repair:** Recent cases have tended to focus on the cost of repair as opposed to any reduced value of the property. However, again, courts have struggled for coherence. In *A (A Juvenile)*,[191] there was no damage where D spat on a policeman's raincoat because the spittle could be easily removed with a damp cloth. Contrast *Samuels v Stubbs*,[192] where D jumped on a policeman's hat, and whilst the hat could be restored to its original state with little difficulty, the court still found that damage was caused. A useful case, demonstrating the problems for the court, is *Hardman v Chief Constable of Avon and Somerset Constabulary*.

Hardman v Chief Constable of Avon and Somerset Constabulary [1986] Crim LR 330

D painted silhouettes on the pavement using water-soluble paints. The paint would have washed away in a few days, but the council paid for a jet wash to remove it. The issue was whether the painting constituted damage.

- Crown Court: taking account of the cost of removal, the painting constituted criminal damage.

---

186 *Roe v Kingerlee* [1986] Crim LR 735.
187 [1994] RTR 411. Note, this may now constitute a separate offence.
188 [2005] EWCA Crim 2381.
189 *Foster* (1852) 6 Cox CC 25.
190 Smith, *Property Offences* (1994) para 27.16.
191 [1978] Crim LR 689.
192 [1972] 4 SASR 200.

This case seems correct in that the paint did cost the council money to remove. However, it opens several unanswered questions. For example, would it still have been damage if the council had left the paint to be removed by the rain? What about other mess that we leave for the council (or rain) to clear up?[193] What about graffiti that people appreciate, and D anticipates will be appreciated?[194]

Assessment matters...
When applying this element to problem facts, it is important to acknowledge the inconsistent approach of the courts and areas of uncertainty. Compare the facts of your case with those of decided cases, discuss relevant academic debate, and conclude whether you think it is likely that damage will be found or not.

9.7.1.2 Property

Property is defined by section 10(1) of the Criminal Damage Act 1971.

(1) In this Act 'property' means property of a tangible nature, whether real or personal, including money and—

   (a) including wild creatures which have been tamed or are ordinarily kept in captivity, and any other wild creatures or their carcasses if, but only if, they have been reduced into possession which has not been lost or abandoned or are in the course of being reduced into possession; but

   (b) not including mushrooms growing wild on any land or flowers, fruit or foliage of a plant growing wild on any land.

   For the purposes of this subsection 'mushroom' includes any fungus and 'plant' includes any shrub or tree.

This definition, particularly subsections (a) and (b), is broadly consistent with the definition of property in the TA 1968.[195] However, there are three important differences.

- Land cannot generally be the subject of theft. However, the same logic does not apply to criminal damage. For example, D may not be able to steal her neighbour's garden, but can certainly damage it. Land is property in this context.

- Intangible property, such as bank account credit, copyright, etc, is property for theft, but will not constitute property for criminal damage. Criminal damage is isolated to physical damage to tangible property only.

- Wild plants/fungi can be property for theft if picked with a commercial intention, but this will not be the case for criminal damage. Plants/fungi growing wild will not be property for the purposes of criminal damage.

9.7.1.3 Belonging to another

It is not an offence under section 1(1) for D to damage her own property. There are exceptional situations where the law creates separate offences to prevent even an

---

[193] Alldridge, 'Incontinent Dogs and the Law' (1990) 140 NLJ 1067.
[194] Edwards, 'Banksy's Graffiti: A Not So Simple Case' (2009) 73 J Crim L 345.
[195] See **9.2.2**.

owner from damaging their property, as with the offences dealing with cruelty to animals. Belonging to another is defined in section 10(2)–(4) of the Criminal Damage Act 1971.

(2) Property shall be treated for the purposes of this Act as belonging to any person—

    (a) having the custody or control of it;

    (b) having in it any proprietary right or interest (not being an equitable interest arising only from an agreement to transfer or grant an interest); or

    (c) having a charge on it.

(3) Where property is subject to a trust, the persons to whom it belongs shall be so treated as including any person having a right to enforce the trust.

(4) Property of a corporation sole shall be so treated as belonging to the corporation notwithstanding a vacancy in the corporation.

As with 'belonging to another' in the context of theft, discussed earlier,[196] it is not fatal to conviction if D had some proprietary interest in the property, as long as another party also had some proprietary interest. Thus, this element will be satisfied where D damages property that she co-owns with another, or in which another has even a minor proprietary interest as, for example, where the property is loaned to V.[197]

9.7.2 Mens rea of s1(1)

There are two principal elements to the mens rea. First, it must be shown that D intended, or was at least reckless, as to causing damage to the property. Secondly, D must also have intended/known or been reckless as to the fact that the property belonged to another. This second element of the mens rea should not be forgotten, as illustrated in *Smith*.

Smith [1974] QB 354

At the end of D's tenancy, he removed a length of wiring that he had installed, causing £130 worth of damage. Under civil law, following its installation, the wiring belonged to D's landlord. However, D was unaware of this, believing that it belonged to him. D was charged with criminal damage.

• Crown Court: guilty of criminal damage.

• Court of Appeal: appeal allowed. D did not know, and did not foresee a risk, that the wiring did not belong to him. Thus, he lacked an essential element of the mens rea.

The mens rea terms 'intention' and 'recklessness' were discussed at **Chapter 3**. It will be remembered that much of the debate and flux relating to the definition of recklessness has focused on criminal damage cases, including the leading case of G.[198]

---

[196] See **9.2.3**.

[197] This does not extend to insurers of goods, as they hold no proprietary interest: *Denton* [1982] 1 All ER 65.

[198] [2004] AC 1034.

9.7.3 Defences to criminal damage

In addition to the general defences such as duress, necessity, etc,[199] section 5 of the Criminal Damage Act 1971 also provides two specific defences: belief in consent; and protection of property.

> (2) A person charged with an offence to which this section applies, shall,... be treated for those purposes as having a lawful excuse—
>
> > (a) if at the time of the act or acts alleged to constitute the offence he believed that the person or persons whom he believed to be entitled to consent to the destruction of or damage to the property in question had so consented, or would have so consented to it if he or they had known of the destruction or damage and its circumstances; or
> >
> > (b) if he destroyed or damaged... in order to protect property belonging to himself or another or a right or interest in property which was or which he believed to be vested in himself or another, and at the time of the act or acts alleged to constitute the offence he believed—
> >
> > > (i) that the property, right or interest was in immediate need of protection; and
> > >
> > > (ii) that the means of protection adopted... were... reasonable having regard to all the circumstances.
>
> (3) For the purposes of this section it is immaterial whether a belief is justified or not if it is honestly held.
>
> (4) For the purposes of subsection (2) above a right or interest in property includes any right or privilege in or over land, whether created by grant, licence or otherwise.

9.7.3.1 Belief in consent defence

Section 5(2)(a) provides a belief in consent defence. As confirmed by section 5(3), the test is simply whether D honestly believed that the owner did or would have consented to her causing damage, even if that belief was not reasonable. In *Denton*,[200] for example, there was no criminal damage where D honestly believed that the owner of a mill had encouraged him to burn it down, even though the reason for that belief was based on insurance fraud. Although, note that belief (however honest) that God is the owner, and would have consented, will not be sufficient.[201]

It should be remembered that even where the owner would not have consented and/or the person consenting does not have the authority to do so, and even where this would have been clear to a reasonable person, D may still satisfy the defence if she *honestly* believes that both requirements are satisfied. One of the more controversial mistake cases is *Jaggard v Dickinson*.[202] In this case, D had permission from X to treat X's house as her own. However, when arriving heavily intoxicated at what she mistakenly believed was X's house, D broke a window to V's house in order to gain entry. Her defence to criminal damage under section 5(2)(a) was accepted. Although rather shocking, the problem with this case may be the court's treatment of her intoxicated

[199] **Chapters 13 and 14.**
[200] [1982] 1 All ER 65.
[201] *Blake v DPP* [1993] Crim LR 586.
[202] [1981] 3 All ER 716.

state (concluding that it made no difference) rather than the defence itself. We discuss this further in **Chapter 13**.

9.7.3.2 Belief in protection of property defence

Section 5(2)(b) creates a defence for belief in the protection of property as where D damages a fence in order to protect/enforce her right of way, or shoots a dog to protect cattle, etc.[203] There are three main elements to this defence: belief that D or another has a vested interest in the property protected; belief that that property is in immediate need of protection; and belief that the means of protection (ie the damage caused) is reasonable. Each must be satisfied.

A) **Belief in vested interest:** D must believe that she or another has a vested interest in property that she is acting to protect by damaging other property.[204] She must also believe that her action is necessary 'in order to' protect that property. This sounds like a subjective requirement (did D honestly believe?), but following *Hunt*, has been given a mixed subjective/objective meaning.

Hunt (1977) 66 Cr App R 105

D, who was assisting his wife as a warden at a set of retirement flats, set fire to some bedding in order to draw attention to the defective fire alarms. D claimed a section 5(2)(b) defence, saying that he was acting to protect the properties from future risks. D was charged with arson which requires proof of criminal damage.

- Crown Court: guilty of arson.
- Court of Appeal: conviction upheld on appeal. Whether D's acts were capable of protecting the property (were 'in order to') is an objective question. Here, D's acts provide no protection.

It is counterintuitive to interpret a requirement of 'belief' in an objective way; however, this case has been confirmed in further judgments.[205] What is necessary, therefore, is to ask what D believes (subjectively), and then to ask if this belief in protection has any reasonable (objective) basis.

Extra detail…

It is open to future courts to interpret this element subjectively, which would be preferable. These cases should also be ruled out due to the apparent lack of 'immediate' need.

B) **Belief in immediate need:** Again, this element has been interpreted to be part subjective and part objective. First, the court must ascertain the subjective beliefs that D held at the time: how soon did she believe, reasonably or not, that the property would be in danger? Secondly, the court must decide (objectively) whether D's belief amounted to a belief of an 'immediate' need but note that whether D would classify it as immediate is irrelevant.[206]

---

[203] The 'threat' protected from need not be a criminal act: *Jones* [2005] QB 259.

[204] *Cresswell v DPP* [2006] EWHC 3379 (Admin).

[205] *Hill and Hall* (1988) 89 Cr App R 74: D could not use the defence when damaging an air-force base in order to protect surrounding properties from being targeted by enemy forces.

[206] *Jones* [2005] QB 259.

C) **Belief in reasonableness of methods:** This is a subjective requirement: we ask whether D believed her methods were reasonable, not whether they were reasonable or whether others would so regard them. Thus, even where D cuts down large parts of her neighbour's trees in order to protect her right to light, if she honestly believes that this is a reasonable method and the jury believe she is or may be telling the truth, then the defence will be available.[207]

9.7.4 Arson

Arson is preserved as a separate offence from simple criminal damage by section 1(3) of the Criminal Damage Act 1971. The maximum penalty on indictment is life imprisonment.[208]

(3) An offence committed under this section by destroying or damaging property by fire shall be charged as arson.

The structure of arson is illustrated simply in **Figure 9.4**.

Figure 9.4 Arson

All elements of the criminal damage offence must be satisfied. Additionally, it must be demonstrated that D caused the damage by fire, and that her intention or recklessness was as to cause the damage by fire. Thus, where D causes damage other that by fire, such as smoke damage, or intentionally causes damage to property that results unexpectedly in fire, there will be no liability for arson although D may still be liable for criminal damage.[209]

9.7.4.1 Defences to arson

D may rely on the general defences such as duress, necessity, etc.[210] D may also rely on the specific defences under section 5 discussed earlier.[211]

9.7.5 Aggravated criminal damage

Aggravated criminal damage and aggravated arson are also separate offences under section 1(2) of the Criminal Damage Act 1971. The maximum sentence on indictment is life imprisonment.[212]

---

[207] *DPP v Unsworth* [2010] EWHC 3037 (Admin).
[208] Criminal Damage Act 1971, s4(1).
[209] *Drayton* [2006] Crim LR 243.
[210] **Chapters 13** and **14**.
[211] See **9.7.3**.
[212] Criminal Damage Act 1971, s4(1).

(2) A person who without lawful excuse destroys or damages any property, whether belonging to himself or another—

(a) intending to destroy or damage any property or being reckless as to whether any property would be destroyed or damaged; and

(b) intending by the destruction or damage to endanger the life of another or being reckless as to whether the life of another would be thereby endangered;

shall be guilty of an offence.

The structure of aggravated criminal damage/arson is illustrated simply in **Figure 9.5**.

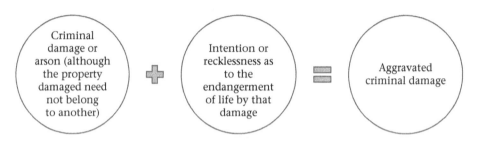

Figure 9.5 Aggravated criminal damage

As illustrated in Figure 9.5, aggravated criminal damage can be constructed upon either criminal damage or arson, even where the damage is to D's own property. The aggravating element is that D must intend or be reckless as to the endangerment of life by the damage she intended to, or was reckless about causing.

9.7.5.1 Actus reus of aggravated criminal damage

The actus reus of aggravated criminal damage, for the most part, simply mirrors that of criminal damage or arson. However, crucially, the actus reus of this offence may also be satisfied where damage is caused to D's own property. Thus, even where D burns down her own house, for example, or takes a hammer to her own car, she will complete the actus reus.[213]

Although, as we discuss later, D must intend or be reckless as to the endangerment of life, there is no need for endangerment of life in fact. This is not part of the actus reus. In *Parker*,[214] for example, D was liable for aggravated criminal damage where he started a fire in his semi-detached house and foresaw a risk to the lives of his neighbours. This was the case even though his neighbours were unharmed, and even though they were not even in their house at the time such that the fire could not have actually endangered them.

9.7.5.2 Mens rea of aggravated criminal damage

The mens rea of aggravated criminal damage requires D to satisfy all the mens rea requirements of the base offence of criminal damage or arson discussed previously.

---

213 *Merrick* [1996] 1 Cr App R 130: D, with the owner's permission, exposed a cable reckless as to endangerment. There are also several cases of attempted suicide reckless as to endangerment, e.g. where D burns down her own house, eg, *Brewis* [2004] EWCA Crim 1919.

214 [1993] Crim LR 856.

Additionally, it must also be proved that D acted with the intention or was reckless as to the possibility of another person's[215] life being endangered.

D must intend or foresee endangerment arising from the damage of property (this is the nexus to the property offence), and so foresight of endangerment from D's acts alone is not sufficient: it has to be *by* the damage D intended/was reckless about. This was discussed in *Steer*.

 Steer [1988] AC 111

D shot a rifle at the windows of V's house, against whom he had a grudge, breaking the windows (criminal damage) and foreseeing the endangerment of V. D was charged with aggravated criminal damage.

- Crown Court: guilty of aggravated criminal damage.
- Court of Appeal: appeal allowed. D was reckless as to the endangerment of V from his acts (ie shooting the rifle), he was not reckless as to the endangerment of V 'by the destruction or damage of property' (ie from the broken glass from the window). Aggravated criminal damage is only satisfied by the latter.
- House of Lords: appeal dismissed, confirming the reasoning of the Court of Appeal.

The result of this case is that D will be liable for aggravated criminal damage where she foresees the endangerment of life *by* the damage she intended (eg demolishing a building that might fall on someone, breaking a gas pipe that might poison someone, etc[216]), but not where the damage is simply incidental (eg throwing a bat that might hit someone, and may also damage property). This may seem a fine and perhaps unnecessary distinction but the House of Lords recognised that to hold otherwise would lead to undesirable results. Lord Bridge in *Steer* provided the following example:

If A and B both discharge firearms in a public place, being reckless as to whether life would be endangered, it would be absurd that A, who incidentally causes some trifling damage to property, should be guilty of an offence punishable with life imprisonment, but that B, who causes no damage, should be guilty of no offence.

The point being made here is that our criminal law does not recognise a general offence of endangerment which would apply to reckless acts where no harm is caused,[217] and aggravated criminal damage should not be manipulated/misapplied into filling that role.

Extra detail…
Criminal damage under section 1(1) can alternatively be aggravated if it is accompanied by racial or religious hatred.[218] The mechanism for such aggravation is discussed at **7.9.2** in relation to offences against the person, and applies in the same way for racially or religiously aggravated criminal damage.[219]

---

215 Foresight of self-endangerment is not sufficient. *Thakar* [2010] EWCA Crim 2136: D set fire to his car when depressed following divorce.
216 *Cunningham* [1957] 2 QB 396: breaking a gas pipe.
217 Duff, 'Criminalising Endangerment' in Duff and Green (eds), *Defining Crimes* (2005) Ch3.
218 Crime and Disorder Act 1998, s30.
219 *DPP v M* [2005] Crim LR 392.

9.7.5.3 Defences to aggravated criminal damage

D may rely on the general defences such as duress, necessity, etc.[220] However, the specific defences under section 2 do not apply to aggravated criminal damage: belief in the owner's permission and/or protection of property will not excuse causing damage that might endanger a person's life.

9.8 Reform

There are numerous areas of confusion and seeming incoherence in relation to property offences, and many of the academic articles referred to in this chapter are calling for some manner of reform. In this section we focus on just one of these debates: how to define the offence of theft, although we use it to highlight questions that are common among many of the property offences.

When considering reform of property offences it is important to remember that, despite some quite powerful criticism in certain specific areas and, despite a flurry of appeals cases between the 1970s and 1990s in particular, the law has been relatively settled during the last ten or 15 years. This is not to say that reform is no longer desirable but that stability should caution against reform that is likely to result in renewed uncertainty.

9.8.1 Defining theft

The discussion here is whether the elements of theft, as currently interpreted, are fairly and coherently targeting their intended wrongs. There are two parts to this debate.

The first part of the debate is to identify the wrongs of theft: what is the offence designed to target? The most obvious answer to this, and the one we began the chapter with, is that theft is designed to protect property rights. Thus, the wrongs of theft are any violation of those rights. However, this is not sufficient. Where V lends D her car, for example, D gains possession and so interferes with V's property rights, but there is nothing wrongful here, and certainly nothing deserving of criminalisation. Thus, there must be something more, beyond simple interference with property rights, that justifies the use of criminal law.

At one time, this additional wrong or harm may have been identified in D's 'manifestly criminal' appropriation: theft being a *non-consensual* interference with property rights.[221] However, following *Gomez*,[222] an appropriation can be found even where V consents. Without this additional 'wrong' within the actus reus of the offence much of the work necessary to isolate theft to those deserving of criminalisation is instead done within the mens rea, and particularly the requirement of dishonesty. Some believe that this has led to the offence becoming unacceptably broad in its application, potentially applying to minor acts of preparation that outwardly suggest little wrongdoing such as touching an item in the supermarket with the requisite mens rea.[223]

---

[220] **Chapters 13 and 14.**
[221] The term manifest criminality was coined by Fletcher, *Rethinking Criminal Law* (1978) 82. It means that D's external conduct is obviously wrongful.
[222] [1993] AC 442.
[223] For a good summary of the debate, see Shute, 'Appropriation and the Law of Theft' [2002] Crim LR 445.

Perhaps the most controversial point of this debate, however, relates to cases where theft has been found even though there has been no breach of civil law and no property rights have been infringed. The clearest example of this is *Hinks*,[224] where D dishonestly took advantage of a vulnerable person although the gifts from V were valid in civil law. Cases like *Hinks* are central to our identification and understanding of the wrongs of theft, suggesting that the offence is targeting dishonest appropriation more generally, and not as had generally been assumed, being structured by civil property rules. Academics have responded to *Hinks* in three main ways. For some, the inconsistency with civil law is unproblematic, and the criminal law of theft should go beyond the wrongs of civil law to protect against dishonest appropriation more generally.[225] However, a majority of commentators have seen the developing split from civil law as problematic. Within this group, many have criticised *Hinks* as a wrong turn, losing sight of the specific wrongs (anchored by civil law breaches) that theft should be targeting.[226] However, also within this group, there has developed an interesting line of analysis that sees the split as problematic but places the fault for that split with unduly narrow interpretations of the civil law.[227]

A final, but vital part of this first debate relates to the overlap between the expanding wrongs of theft and fraud offences. We discuss fraud in **Chapter 10** and will return to this debate there. Basically, the argument is that theft and fraud are designed to protect property rights in different ways targeting and separately labelling different wrongs: theft should target non-consensual appropriation, whereas fraud should target deceptive consensual appropriation. On this view, the expansion of theft in *Gomez* and *Hinks* has broken down the distinction, potentially leading to inappropriate convictions and labelling.[228] The argument against this, from Gardner in particular, has been that overlapping offences are useful to ensure all criminally deserving cases are covered, particularly in relation to protection of the vulnerable where it may be difficult to demonstrate deception.[229] Although this argument is well put, following the reform of fraud offences within the Fraud Act 2006, where proof of deception is no longer required, it is debatable whether this justification for overlap still holds.

Point to remember…

Debate about the identification of wrongs (the rationale for the offence) is also central to academic discussion of several other property offences discussed in this chapter. This is particularly true where the offence contains a requirement of harm or endangerment of a person, leading us to consider whether the gravamen of the offence is the protection of property or the person.[230]

---

[224] [2000] 4 All ER 833.

[225] Bogg and Stanton-Ife, 'Theft as Exploitation' (2003) 23 LS 402.

[226] Simester and Sullivan, 'The Nature and Rationale of Property Offences' in Duff and Green (eds), *Defining Crimes* (2005).

[227] Green, 'Theft and Conversion—Tangibly Different' (2012) 128 LQR 564: discussing the interpretation of 'property' within the two regimes.

[228] Shute and Horder, 'Thieving and Deceiving: What is the Difference?' (1993) 56 MLR 548; Melissaris, 'The Concept of Appropriation and the Offence of Theft' (2007) 70 MLR 597.

[229] Gardner, 'Appropriation in Theft: The Last Word?' (1993) 109 LQR 194.

[230] eg robbery. Ashworth, 'Robbery Reassessed' [2002] Crim LR 851.

The second part of the debate, having discussed what the offence is attempting to achieve, is to analyse the appropriateness of its elements. If we agree that theft should be protecting against the dishonest appropriation of all property rights, or dishonest appropriation more generally, then it may be contended that the current rules are too narrowly drawn. Glanville Williams, for example, makes the case that even where D's intention is to temporarily, as opposed to permanently, deprive V of her property, this may still have a similarly detrimental effect on V's rights, and be deserving of criminalisation.[231] Lacey, Wells, and Quick go even further to suggest that the elements of theft could be expanded to protect other rights, such as environmental and welfare rights.[232] Where the wrongs of theft are identified broadly in terms of dishonest appropriation, even this level of broadening may seem appropriate.

A related discussion, if the wrong of dishonesty lies at the heart of theft and many other property offences, is whether the current definition of dishonesty is sufficient to distinguish between those deserving and not deserving of liability. When discussing the definition of dishonesty and the *Ghosh* test mentioned earlier,[233] we highlighted several problems with relying on the jury to identify common standards of honesty without legislative guidance. In the most thorough critique of the current approach, Edward Griew highlights several problems including the lack of consistency, the lack of objectivity, a tendency towards longer and more complex trials, etc.[234] However, despite these problems, it is interesting to note the even greater emphasis on dishonesty within the Fraud Act 2006, implying that perhaps the current definition of dishonesty (although flawed) lacks a more acceptable alternative.

Finally, a further discussion relating to the construction of theft and other property offences contends that there should be some distinction between amounts or types of property appropriated. In this regard, it is interesting to note that whilst offences against the person (**Chapters 5–7**) are standardly constructed to take account of the *degree* of harm suffered by V, and only exceptionally in terms of the *method* of that infliction, property offences tend to be the opposite. And this is despite research showing that the public does see a moral difference between different degrees of theft, such as the values of the property taken and/or types of property.[235] Rearranging property offences to reflect degrees of harm would represent a fundamental shift from current practice.

9.9 Eye on assessment

In this section we consider the potential application of property offences within a problem question, using the same structure of analysis discussed in previous chapters.

---

[231] Williams, 'Temporary Appropriation Should Be Theft' [1981] Crim LR 129.
[232] Lacey, Wells, and Quick, *Reconstructing Criminal Law* (4th edn, 2010) 399.
[233] See **9.2.5**.
[234] Griew, 'Dishonesty: The Objections to *Feely* and *Ghosh*' [1985] Crim LR 341.
[235] Green and Kugler, 'Community Perceptions of Theft Seriousness' (2010) 7 J Em S 511.

> **STEP 1 Identify the potential criminal event in the facts**
>
> This should be simply stated (eg 'The first potential criminal event arises where D takes the iPhone). The role of this stage is to highlight which part of the question you are answering before you begin to apply the law.

For most criminal offences, this stage is quite straightforward. However, particularly in relation to property offences, you need to take extra care. This is because, as well as obvious potential criminal events (eg D snatches V's wallet, D smashes V's vase, etc), many of the offences discussed can arise from what might appear to be quite innocent conduct when accompanied by mens rea so, for example, any touching of another's property could be theft, any trespass could be section 9(1)(a) burglary, and so on. Take care not to miss potential crimes; read the question facts carefully.[236]

In addition, when dealing with a potential theft, it should be remembered that a single taking might include more than one act of appropriation. For example, where D takes physical control of the property (appropriation by control) and then later decides to keep it (appropriation of ownership rights). In such a case, although there may be only one crime, you are given a choice of conduct elements: a choice of where to identify the potentially criminal event. You should focus on the one that is most likely to find liability. Thus, in our example, if the first act of taking control was not accompanied with an intention to keep the item, then this appropriation will not be theft because D did not, at this point, have an intention to permanently deprive. You should therefore highlight the second act of appropriation (D's decision to keep the item) as the one that is most likely to lead to liability, and therefore focus your discussion of the offence on that moment.

> **STEP 2 Identify the potential offence**
>
> Again, state this simply (eg 'When taking V's iPhone, D may be liable for theft'). The role of this stage is to highlight which offence you are going to apply.

Identifying the relevant offence can also be quite challenging in relation to property offences, partly because of the overlap between offences and partly because of the common use of aggravating elements. Where more than one offence could apply to the same potentially criminal event, our advice in previous chapters has been to apply the most serious potential offence first. This advice also holds true for property offences. However, a distinction should be made between entirely separate and more serious offences (eg the difference between battery and murder), and more serious offences that include the lesser offence with the addition of an aggravating element (eg the difference between section 20 GBH and racially aggravated section 20 GBH). Where you are dealing with a choice between offences in the first category, it always makes sense to apply the more serious offence first. However, where you are dealing with aggravating elements, it is often clearer to apply the base offence first and then to consider whether the aggravating factor applies to satisfy the more serious offence.

In relation to the property offences discussed in this chapter, this approach is illustrated in **Table 9.9**.

---

[236] Also, as always, be guided by the question as well as the facts (eg if the question asks you to consider theft only, then these potential criminal events are the only relevant ones to highlight).

Table 9.9 Identifying and applying property offences

Starting offence	Offence following aggravation
Where D appropriates property—first consider liability for **theft**	If D satisfies the elements of theft, go on to consider the following potential aggravations: • Does D use force—robbery • Is D trespassing—s9(1)(b) burglary • Where there is s9(1)(b) burglary, does D use a weapon—aggravated burglary
Where D trespasses into another's building or part of a building—first consider liability for **s9(1)(a) burglary**	If D satisfies the elements of s9(1)(a) burglary, go on to consider the following potential aggravations: • Does D use a weapon—aggravated burglary
Where D has trespassed into another's building or part of building, and then harms someone or attempts to harm someone or attempts to steal—first consider liability for **s9(1)(b) burglary**	If D satisfies the elements of s9(1)(b) burglary, go on to consider the following potential aggravations: • Does D use a weapon—aggravated burglary
Where D comes into possession of stolen property, or the proceeds of stolen property—consider liability for **handling stolen goods**	*
Where D threatens V, making demands in relation to property—consider liability for **blackmail**	*
Where D damages another's property—first consider liability for **s1(1) criminal damage**	If D satisfies the elements of s1(1) criminal damage, go on to consider the following potential aggravations: • Is there any racial or religious hatred—racial or religiously aggravated criminal damage • Is the damage caused by fire—arson • Is D at least reckless as to the endangerment of others' lives—aggravated criminal damage
Where D damages her own property—first consider liability for **s1(2) aggravated criminal damage**	If D satisfies the elements of s1(2) aggravated criminal damage, go on to consider the following potential aggravations: • Is the damage caused by fire—aggravated arson

When applying the law to problem facts, you therefore need to choose between the 'starting offences' in the left-hand column, applying the most serious potential offence. Then, if the elements of that offence are satisfied, you should go on to consider whether that offence can be upgraded by one of the aggravating elements detailed in the right-hand column.

When discussing aggravating elements, it is common for courts and commentators to describe the process as 'constructing' upon the base offence. This is accurate, but you should take care not to confuse it with 'constructive liability', which is a specific label given to offences that include a constructive strict liability element.[237] The offences discussed in this chapter are not constructive crimes in this more specific sense. To avoid confusion and mislabelling, it may be best to avoid the language like 'construction' in the context of property offences entirely.

STEP 3 Applying the offence to the facts

Having identified the relevant offence make sure you discuss each of the required elements.

Actus reus: What does the offence require? Did D do it?

Mens rea: What does the offence require? Did D possess it?

STEP 4 Consider defences

The word 'consider' here is important as you should not discuss every defence for every question. Rather, think whether there are any defences (eg duress) that *could* potentially apply. If there are, discuss those only.

When considering and discussing potential defences, remember to consider any specific defences (ie those statutory defences that only apply to certain offences) as well as the general defences (discussed at **Chapters 13** and **14**).

STEP 5 Conclude

This is usually a single sentence either saying that it is likely that D has committed the offence, or saying that it is not likely either because an offence element is not satisfied, or, because a defence is likely to apply. It is not often that you will be able to say categorically whether D has committed the offence or not, particularly when applying concepts such as dishonesty, so it is usually best to conclude in terms of what is more 'likely'.

STEP 6 Loop

Go back up to Step 1, identifying the next potential criminal event. Continue until you have discussed all the relevant potentially criminal events.

---

[237] See **4.2.1.1**.

ONLINE RESOURCE CENTRE

www.oxfordtextbooks.co.uk/orc/smithandhogan/

This chapter is accompanied by a selection of online resources to help you with this topic, including:

- **Multiple choice questions**
- **Chapter summary sheet**
- Two **sample examination questions** with answer guidance
- **Further reading**

Also available on the Online Resource Centre are:

- A selection of **videos** from the authors explaining key topics and principles
- **Legal updates**
- Useful **weblinks**

10

Fraud

10.1 Introduction

Fraud offences are designed to criminalise D's dishonest conduct—her lies, her withholding of information, and/or her abuse of position—where she intends V to lose property and/or to gain property herself. This has been contrasted with theft where, put simply, D dishonestly appropriates the property of another. However, the extent to which these offences operate to target *distinct* wrongs, is a matter of contention, particularly since theft has been held to include consensual appropriation.[1]

Fraud is an offence under section 1 of the Fraud Act 2006 (FA 2006).[2] Prior to the FA 2006, conduct that we would now charge as fraud was criminalised through a variety of deception offences within the Theft Act 1968 (TA 1968), which have now been repealed.[3] Those deception offences were heavily and consistently criticised, both for their unnecessary complexity as well as their overly restrictive application. For example, for D to be guilty of one of these offences, the prosecution had to demonstrate a 'representation' from D; that her representation *caused* V to form a false belief; that that false belief *caused* V to act in a specified manner, such as transferring property; and that V's behaviour thereby benefited D or another. Demonstrating each causal link within this chain was very difficult for prosecutors, and, more importantly, it was argued that D's behaviour may have been equally blameworthy even when certain elements were missing (eg where D failed to deceive V, but still gained the advantage[4]).

The various problems with the pre-2006 deception offences were fully explored by a Law Commission consultation in 1999.[5] However, at that stage, despite academic calls for significant reform,[6] the Commission proposed only the limited amendment of existing offences.[7] It was only later, in the Commission's 2002 report,[8] followed by a government consultation in 2004,[9] that fundamental reform recommendations were made. These led to the FA 2006. Each of these reform papers provides a useful overview of the failings of the pre-2006 deception offences. They are also useful for explanations and justifications for the new offence created by the FA 2006. Moving away from the previous result-based offences requiring the prosecution to demonstrate deception and loss, the new fraud offence focuses on D's dishonest conduct and intentions, looking to punish those intentions whether her acts of deception are successful or not. The new offence is a conduct crime, committed regardless of whether any consequences were caused or not by D's conduct. In this manner, the new fraud offence represents a move away from the property harms discussed in the previous chapter (eg theft, criminal damage, etc), and shares many more characteristics with the inchoate offences discussed at **Chapter 11**.

The offence of fraud is set out in section 1 of the FA 2006. The maximum sentence on indictment is ten years' imprisonment (three years more than theft).[10]

(1) A person is guilty of fraud if he is in breach of any of the sections listed in subsection (2) (which provide for different ways of committing the offence).

(2) The sections are—

    (a) section 2 (fraud by false representation),

    (b) section 3 (fraud by failing to disclose information), and

    (c) section 4 (fraud by abuse of position).

---

[1] We pick up on this debate further in the reform section later in the chapter (**10.8.3**).
[2] The FA 2006 came into force from 15 January 2007.
[3] Other deception offences were also contained in the Theft Acts 1978 and 1996.
[4] *Edwards* [1978] Crim LR 49.
[5] Law Commission, *Fraud and Deception* (Consultation 155, 1999).
[6] eg Sullivan, 'Framing an Acceptable General Offence of Fraud' (1989) 53 J Crim L 92.
[7] Ormerod, 'A Bit of a Con' [1999] Crim LR 789. See also *Smith and Hogan's Criminal Law* (14th edn, 2015), Ch23.
[8] Law Commission, *Fraud* (No 276, 2002).
[9] Home Office, *Fraud Law Reform* (Consultation, 2004).
[10] FA 2006, s1(3)(b).

As made clear in section 1(1), although fraud can be committed in three different ways, it represents a single offence. However, in order to analyse the offence, it is useful to look at each of these different ways separately.

After discussing the central fraud offence, we will also go on to discuss the related offences of obtaining services dishonestly (FA 2006, s11) and possession of articles for use in frauds (FA 2006, s6). We will also provide a brief overview of other related fraud and deception offences.

> **Extra detail ...**
> As the FA 2006 is still relatively new, there are fewer appeal cases to discuss in relation to its interpretation than was the case with the TA 1968. As a result, in order to predict the likely approach of the court, when interpreting certain ambiguous sections of the statute, there is considerable scope for discussion: drawing on the intentions of the drafters (from the Law Commission papers, etc), from pre-2006 cases, and from contemporary academic discussion.

10.2 FA 2006, s2: fraud by false representation

Fraud by false representation is defined in section 2 of the FA 2006. The requirements of this 'route' to fraud are exceptionally wide, and in practice section 2 is likely to be the most often prosecuted.[11]

(1) A person is in breach of this section if he—
   (a) dishonestly makes a false representation, and
   (b) intends, by making the representation—
      (i) to make a gain for himself or another, or
      (ii) to cause loss to another or to expose another to a risk of loss.

The elements of section 2 are illustrated in **Table 10.1**.

Table 10.1 FA 2006, s2

	Actus reus	**Mens rea**
Conduct element	Making a representation	Voluntary
Circumstance element	D's representation is false	Knowledge or foresight of a possibility
	D's representation is dishonest	Knowledge
Result element	None	None
Ulterior mens rea element	*	Intention, by the making of the representation, to make a gain or cause a loss to another or expose another to a risk of loss

---

[11] Ormerod, 'The Fraud Act 2006—Criminalising Lying' [2007] Crim LR 193.

There is, under section 2, fraud where D makes a false representation dishonestly, with the intention thereby to make a gain or cause a loss, or risk of loss, to another. Whether V is actually deceived by D's representation, and/or whether V loses or D gains, is irrelevant (ie no results need to be demonstrated).

10.2.1 Actus reus of s2

The actus reus of section 2 requires D to have made a representation, and for that representation to be false.

10.2.1.1 Making a representation

It must be shown that D made a representation. Therefore, where D dishonestly takes advantage of a false representation made by another, X, where X is not acting as an agent of D,[12] then unless D also makes some representation as to its truth, she will not commit the offence. Three important aspects of a 'representation' require comment: the subject of the representation; the recipient; and the method.

A) **The subject of the representation:** Paradigm cases will involve false representations as to facts. For example, D assures V that the painting is genuine; that the car is not stolen; that she has sufficient funds to pay for the meal; and so on. However, section 2 is not limited to representations as to facts.

> (3) 'Representation' means any representation as to fact or law, including a representation as to the state of mind of—
>
> (a) the person making the representation, or
>
> (b) any other person.

D makes a representation as to law where she informs someone about a legal detail, such as a contractual matter; and as to a state of mind where she states her intentions or beliefs or those of another: for example, her intention to pay for goods on delivery.

Difficulty has arisen in relation to statements of opinion where D is not stating a fact but, for example, exaggerates the quality of sale goods; tells V that her roof would benefit from retiling; etc. Under the pre-2006 law, cases of this kind were decided inconsistently, with certain cases falling short of a representation,[13] whilst others were caught.[14] It is submitted that under the current law matters of opinion should always be treated as representations of D's belief as to facts. The focus then shifts, in such cases, to whether that opinion was honestly held.

B) **The recipient of the representation:** Representations will usually be made to a person (V). Where this is the case, there may be a question whether V must be aware of the representation for it to be complete. For example, what if V does not hear D's spoken comments, perhaps because, unknown to D, she is deaf, or if written, what if D's letter or email never arrives as, for example, because it is blocked by V's email filters.

---

[12] We discuss the use of agents in section (C) 'The method of the representation'.

[13] *Bryan* (1957) Dears & B 265: saying watch components were as good as Elkington's (a famous brand) was a mere exaggeration.

[14] *Smith v Land and House Property Corporation* (1884) 28 Ch D 7: saying a tenant was 'most desirable' where there was a consistent history of non-payment of rent.

This issue did not arise under the old law with its focus on results, as without receiving the representation, V could not be deceived by it. However, under the current law, where D's actus reus is complete at the point the representation is made, such cases are quite possible. There is no case yet directly on this point, but it is likely that the courts will interpret 'representation' broadly to be satisfied even where V remains oblivious. This is supported by a similarly broad interpretation given to 'communication' in other areas of the law,[15] a term which is arguably more likely than 'representation' to require acknowledgement from V.

> **Point to remember ...**
> Although V does not need to be aware of the representation, this does not mean that D will commit the offence when she makes intentionally private representations (eg notes something inaccurate in her diary). Other elements of the offence, such as the required intention to thereby make a gain or cause a loss, mean that the offence will only catch representations that are aimed at influencing others (ie D must intend to make a representation to another or a machine).

Although D's representations will usually be aimed at a person, this need not be the case. Under the pre-2006 law, it was held that 'deception' entailed the deception of a person, and so liability in cases where D deceived a machine, such as a banking system, became highly problematic.[16] Under the current law, this is addressed by section 2(5).

> (5) For the purposes of this section a representation may be regarded as made if it (or anything implying it) is submitted in any form to any system or device designed to receive, convey or respond to communications (with or without human intervention).

Despite rather complex drafting, this subsection clearly allows for fraud by false representation where there is no intended human recipient. Indeed, if anything, it may be too broadly drafted. Read literally, it may even apply where D drafts a misrepresenting email and saves it to her computer: has she 'submitted' it to 'any system' within the meaning of the provision?

C) **The method of the representation:** As we intimated earlier, section 2 can apply regardless of how D chooses to communicate with V, whether orally; in writing; or by gestures; etc. D may even make a representation indirectly via an agent. This is illustrated in *Idrees v DPP*.

> **Idrees v DPP** [2011] EWHC 624 (Admin)
>
> Having failed his driving theory test on multiple occasions, D arranged for another person (P) to impersonate him, and pass the test on his behalf. D was charged with fraud by false representation, the false representation being that of P's impersonation whilst acting as D's agent.
>
> • Magistrates' court: guilty of fraud.
> • High Court: appeal dismissed. D was making a false representation (via P), and was doing so with the intention to make a gain (pass the test).

---

[15] *Collins* [2006] UKHL 40: discussing the offence of grossly offensive communications.
[16] *Holmes* [2004] EWHC 2020 (Admin).

As well as catching different methods of physical communication, section 6(2) also clarifies that both express and implied representations will be caught. Thus, just as D telling a shop assistant falsely that she has authority to use a credit card is a false representation, the same is also true where D simply presents the card for payment, thereby implying that she has authority to do so.[17] The case of *Barnard*, although pre-FA 2006, provides a memorable illustration.

> **Barnard** (1837) 7 C & P 784 (pre-FA 2006)
>
> D entered an Oxford cobblers and requested boots and straps. D was wearing a cap and gown (of the type then worn by Oxford University students), and requested the associated discount. D was not a student of the university, and was charged with a deception offence.
>
> • Crown Court: guilty. D clearly deceived through an express note which claimed that he was a student. However, Bolland B went on to say that even if D did not present the note, his dress provided an implied deception sufficient for liability.

Despite the section being wide enough to encompass different methods of representation, one area of uncertainty has emerged: does section 2 cover implied representation by omission? (Note that fraud by omission is covered by section 3 of the FA 2006.) It is contended that for section 2, two omissions scenarios can, and should, be distinguished.

In the first scenario, D makes a true representation to V, the facts then change but D omits to inform V of this change. In these circumstances, it is possible that D's representation will be interpreted as a continuing act to include her failure to inform V after the facts change. Pre-FA 2006 Act, such implied representations were found whether D was responsible for the change of facts, or simply became aware of them.[18] This is illustrated in *DPP v Ray*.

> **DPP v Ray** [1974] AC 370 (pre-FA 2006)
>
> D and others ordered and consumed a meal at a Chinese restaurant. D did so intending to pay. However, at the end of the meal they changed their minds. They continued to sit in the restaurant until the waiter left the room, and then ran out. D was charged with a deception offence relating to his debt to the restaurant.
>
> • Crown Court: guilty of the deception offence.
> • High Court: appeal allowed—D's omission was not a deception.
> • House of Lords: (3:2) appeal allowed. D's representations to be a paying customer continued from his ordering and eating the food (positive acts) and included his continuing to sit in the restaurant after he had decided not to pay (omission). Thus, there was coincidence of deception and mens rea.

In cases such as *Ray*, recognition of an implied continuing representation is essential to liability and, post-FA 2006, the potential for implied representations of this kind

---

[17] For a similar interpretation pre-2006, see *Lambie* [1982] AC 449.
[18] *Rai* [2000] 1 Cr App R 242: D failed to inform the council his mother had died, and allowed them to install the disability aids to which he was no longer entitled.

has been confirmed in *Government of the United Arab Emirates v Allen*.[19] However, in this case the Court of Appeal cautioned that implied continuing representations would only be found where it was 'reasonable' to read such a representation into the conduct of another. Stressing the fact-specific nature of this inquiry, the court rejected that a representation was made where D failed to inform her bank that she was no longer able to honour a security cheque deposited when she received a loan.

In the second scenario, D becomes aware that V is mistaken about a certain fact, but fails to correct her mistaken belief. For example, V says 'it will be great to buy a car which has only had one owner', where D who is selling the car knows the car has had many more owners. In such cases it could be argued that, despite no express false representation, D's silence could amount to an implied representation that V's beliefs are correct. However, it is contended that this route to liability should be avoided. In line with CPS charging guidelines,[20] the criminal law should take care not to undermine the civil rules of *caveat emptor* (buyer beware), and maintain a difference between active representations and a simple failure to report faults. In the most serious cases of this kind there will generally be a legal duty upon D to disclose the omitted information, and in such cases section 3 of the FA 2006, and not section 2, provides the appropriate route to fraud liability.

10.2.1.2 The representation must be false

Section 2(2) defines what is meant by a 'false' representation.

(2) A representation is false if—

    (a) it is untrue or misleading, and

    (b) the person making it knows that it is, or might be, untrue or misleading.

The first part of this provision, dealing with the actus reus, extends the meaning of 'false' beyond core cases of outright untruth to include representations that are misleading. A representation may be misleading, and thus come within this part of the actus reus, even if it is literally true. For example, if V asks D, a car dealer, if there has been any reported problem with a particular model in the last year, and D answers honestly that there have not, this may still be misleading if D omits to mention the several hundred reported problems every other year. Equally, where D displays a fake painting among genuine classics, although she may not state that the fake is genuine, her choice of display may still be misleading.[21]

Where D believes that her statement is false, but it is in fact true, there will be no fraud. This was the case in *Deller* (pre-FA 2006),[22] where D agreed to sell his car 'free of encumbrances' in the belief that he had mortgaged the car (ie it was encumbered). However, as the proposed mortgage was unsuccessful, his statement turned out to be true. In such cases, the appropriate charge is attempted fraud.[23]

---

[19] [2012] EWHC 1712 (Admin).
[20] www.cps.gov.uk/legal/d_to_g/fraud_act/
[21] *Hill v Gray* (1816) 1 Stark 434.
[22] (1952) 36 Cr App R 184.
[23] **Chapter 11.**

10.2.2 Mens rea of s2

The mens rea of section 2 is made up of three core elements: D must at least foresee a risk that her representation is false; she must act dishonestly; and she must intend to make a gain or to cause a loss or risk of loss to another. Each element must coincide with (ie must be present at the point in time of) D's act of false representation.

10.2.2.1 Knowledge that the statement is, or might be, false

This element is satisfied where D *either* knows her representation is false or misleading, *or* foresees that it might be (s2(2)(b)). In either case, subjective mens rea is required: simple negligence (ie a reasonable person would have foreseen) will not be sufficient. This has been confirmed in *Augunas*,[24] and will include cases where D *deliberately* closes her eyes to a risk or D deliberately avoids confirming facts when D has at least foreseen a risk of falsity.

Including the foresight of a risk makes this element of mens rea very wide indeed. For example, it will be satisfied where an art dealer, D, advertises a painting for sale as an original, being aware of the risk, which seems unavoidable in the art world, that it might be a fake. As a result, the requirement of 'dishonesty' is once again crucial for avoiding liability in such cases.

10.2.2.2 Dishonesty

The FA 2006 does not provide a definition of dishonesty.[25] There is also no equivalent to section 2 of the TA 1968, stating that certain scenarios will not be dishonest: such as where D thinks she has a legal right; where she thinks V would consent; and where she thinks V is untraceable. Therefore, in the absence of any statutory guidance, the term is left exclusively to the common law definition and the *Ghosh* test.[26]

The *Ghosh* test for dishonesty is discussed in detail at **9.2.5.2**. To apply the *Ghosh* test, the jury are required to answer two questions. If the answer to both is 'yes', then the element is satisfied.

- **Question 1:** Is D's false representation dishonest according to the standards of reasonable and honest people?
- **Question 2:** Does D realise that her false representation would be considered dishonest by the standards of honest and reasonable people?

At **9.2.5.2** we discuss several criticisms of the *Ghosh* test, not least the unpredictability of asking a jury to identify a common standard of honesty. The same criticisms apply equally here.

An important question has emerged within the academic literature: is lying always dishonest?[27] If the answer were 'yes', then the section 2 offence would be rendered hopelessly wide. When television adverts, for example, imply that the spraying of a deodorant will

---

[24] [2013] EWCA Crim 2046.
[25] 'Dishonesty' is a hybrid term that requires elements of both actus reus (that D's conduct is dishonest) and mens rea (that D is aware her conduct is perceived by others as dishonest). We discuss this at **3.6.1**. However, dishonesty is commonly applied by the courts as a mens rea element and so both parts of the term are discussed together here. This is also true for the other fraud offences later.
[26] [1982] QB 1053.
[27] Ormerod, 'Criminalising Lying' [2007] Crim LR 193.

make the wearer sexually irresistible, or that an energy drink can make you play sport like a professional, such representations are clearly false, but it is unlikely that they would be considered dishonest by the reasonable person. Ironically in such cases, the more dramatic the lie, and thus the less plausible, the less likely it is to be found dishonest. However, there is a clear grey area, for example occupations such as market trading and used car dealerships where trade patter and exaggeration is common. Such cases will be left to the case-by-case application of the *Ghosh* test, with the likely outcomes far from clear.

10.2.2.3 Intention to make a gain or cause a loss (or risk of loss)

Section 2 does not require D to make a gain, or to cause or risk a loss to another in fact. However, D must act with the ulterior intention to do so. Either intention, to gain or to cause or risk a loss to another, will be sufficient. For example, where D starts a false rumour about a competitor's business, this element of the offence will be satisfied as long as D at least intends to risk causing a loss to that competitor even if she does not intend to gain anything.

The definitions of 'gain' and 'loss' are important, and set out in section 5 of the FA 2006.

> (2) 'Gain' and 'loss'—
>
> > (a) extend only to gain or loss in money or other property;
> >
> > (b) include any such gain or loss whether temporary or permanent;
> >
> > and 'property' means any property whether real or personal (including things in action and other intangible property).
>
> (3) 'Gain' includes a gain by keeping what one has, as well as a gain by getting what one does not have.
>
> (4) 'Loss' includes a loss by not getting what one might get, as well as a loss by parting with what one has.

As made clear in section 5(2)(a), D's intentions must relate to property, so an intention to gain something other than property, eg sexual favours, will not be sufficient. However, the definition of property here is very wide, including all tangible and intangible property, and without the exclusions that exist under the TA 1968.[28]

The final point to remember is one that is easily overlooked: D's intention must be causal. D must intend to *cause* the gain or loss *by* her conduct. This is illustrated in *Gilbert*.

Gilbert [2012] EWCA Crim 2392

D and others set up a bank account in order to facilitate their company (developing and selling real estate). In doing so, they made false representations about their financial position. D was charged with fraud by false representation.

- Crown Court: guilty of fraud.
- Court of Appeal: appeal allowed. Although a false representation was made, the court failed to direct the jury clearly that D must intend to make a gain *from* that representation.

Importantly, in *Gilbert* the court did not rule out the possibility that D intended by her false representation to cause a gain in allowing her to finance the company, that

---

[28] eg land and wild creatures. These (and other examples) are not property in the context of theft because they are excluded by the TA 1968, s4. However, they are property in the context of fraud.

would then allow her to make a profit. However, D's conviction in the Crown Court was unsafe because the need to demonstrate this intention-based causal link was not clarified for the jury.

> **Point to remember ...**
>
> The requirement for D to intend her conduct to 'cause' a gain or a loss provides a further (potential) tool for limiting liability. Consider the problem examples of extreme advertising, market traders, and used car salesmen discussed earlier in the context of dishonesty. In such cases, where the trader makes an extreme puff (eg 'these sunglasses are the same as those worn by David Beckham'), it may be contended that she does not intend this representation to 'cause' V to buy the goods. Rather, perhaps, such comments are intended simply as friendly trade banter or humour.[29]

10.3 FA 2006, s3: fraud by failure to disclose information

The second route to liability for fraud under section 1 of the FA 2006 is fraud by failure to disclose information. Fraud by failure to disclose is set out in section 3 of the FA 2006.

3. A person is in breach of this section if he—

   (a) dishonestly fails to disclose to another person information which he is under a legal duty to disclose, and

   (b) intends, by failing to disclose the information—

       (i) to make a gain for himself or another, or

       (ii) to cause loss to another or to expose another to a risk of loss.

The elements of section 3 are illustrated in **Table 10.2**.

Table 10.2 FA 2006, s3

	Actus reus	**Mens rea**
Conduct element	Failing to disclose information	Voluntary
Circumstance element	D has a legal duty to disclose the information	None
	D's failure to disclose is dishonest	Knowledge
Result element	None	None
Ulterior mens rea element	*	Intention, by failing to disclose, to make a gain or cause a loss to another or expose another to a risk of loss

---

[29] Ormerod and Gardner discuss this point in [2007] Crim LR 660.

As with section 2, section 3 does not require any results. D must dishonestly fail to disclose information where there is a legal duty to do so, D must intend thereby to make a gain or cause a loss or risk of loss to another, but no such gain or loss needs to be demonstrated in fact.

10.3.1 Actus reus of s3

The actus reus of section 3 requires a failure to disclose information where D has a legal duty to do so.

10.3.1.1 Identifying a legal duty to disclose information

The question of whether a legal duty exists is one of law for the judge. There is no definition of 'legal duty' in the statute. However, quoting from the original Law Commission report,[30] the FA 2006 explanatory notes make clear that 'legal duty' should be interpreted in line with the civil law.

> 7.28 …Such a duty may derive from statute (such as the provisions governing company prospectuses), from the fact that the transaction in question is one of the utmost good faith (such as a contract of insurance), from the express or implied terms of a contract, from the custom of a particular trade or market, or from the existence of a fiduciary relationship between the parties (such as that of agent and principal).

> 7.29 For this purpose there is a legal duty to disclose information not only if the defendant's failure to disclose it gives the victim a cause of action for damages, but also if the law gives the victim a right to set aside any change in his or her legal position to which he or she may consent as a result of the non-disclosure. For example, a person in a fiduciary position has a duty to disclose material information when entering into a contract with his or her beneficiary, in the sense that a failure to make such disclosure will entitle the beneficiary to rescind the contract and to reclaim any property transferred under it.[31]

The second paragraph of this guidance is particularly informative, making it clear that a legal duty to disclose will arise whenever D's failure to disclose information would render a contract, or relevant part of a contract, voidable. Clear examples will include a failure to disclose medical conditions when taking out life insurance; failure to disclose a criminal record when applying for a job; failure, as in *Mashta*, to reveal a change of financial position when in receipt of state benefits; and so on.[32]

🔲 *Mashta* [2010] EWCA Crim 2595

D continued to receive asylum support on the grounds of destitution whilst in gainful employment. Among other charges, D was charged with fraud by failing to disclose his employment.

- Crown Court: guilty of fraud.
- Court of Appeal: appeal on sentence allowed, reducing D's sentence from 15 to eight months' imprisonment.

---

[30] Law Commission, *Fraud* (No 276, 2002) paras 7.28–7.29.

[31] FA 2006 Explanatory Notes, s3.

[32] Salter, 'It's Criminal Not to Disclose' (2007) 37 Fam L 432: discussing divorce proceedings where D fails to disclose the true extent of her assets. See also *Razoq* [2012] EWCA Crim 674: D (a doctor) failed to disclose disciplinary hearings and suspension from hospital to other locum (ad hoc medical work) agencies.

Although the Law Commission had recommended that the 'legal duty to disclose' should also include 'moral duties', this extension was rejected by the Home Office.[33] This makes the court's job easier: narrowing their search for a duty to legal concepts only. However, the court will still have to grapple with complex areas of civil law in order to decide whether or not a particular duty arises on the facts.

> **Assessment matters ...**
>
> In most cases D's failure to disclose could also be presented as a false representation (a representation that there is nothing to disclose), and so could be prosecuted under section 2. In clear cases of a failure to disclose, section 3 is likely to be preferred because it provides the most accurate label for D's conduct. However, where the presence of a duty is more difficult to identify, it is likely that section 2 will generally be preferred. We discuss this further in the 'Eye on assessment' section later in the chapter.

10.3.1.2 When does D fail to disclose

In many cases, D's failure to disclose will be obvious on the facts. For example, D has a duty in *Mashta* to disclose any gainful employment whilst receiving benefits; D does not disclose, so D has 'failed' to do so. However, it is important to remember that a failure to disclose is satisfied not only where D discloses nothing at all, but also where D fails to disclose *sufficient* information that relevant parts of the contract are voidable. Thus, even partial disclosure may still satisfy the actus reus of this offence. Again, this question will involve the judge in a detailed analysis of the relevant civil law obligation.

10.3.2 Mens rea of s3

The mens rea of section 3 requires D to have acted dishonestly, and to have intended by her failure to disclose to make a gain or to cause a loss or risk of loss to another. These two core elements have been discussed above in relation to section 2 (**10.2.2**), and should be interpreted in exactly the same way for section 3.

It should be noted that whilst the section 2 offence required mens rea of knowledge or awareness of a risk that D's representation was false, section 3 does not contain any equivalent requirement in relation to the required duty to disclose. Therefore, D may be liable under section 3 even if she did not know or even foresee a possibility that she was under a legal obligation to disclose information. However, although this seems unacceptably broad, the possibility for unfairness is limited by the requirement of dishonesty and the *Ghosh* test. This is because where D is unaware of a legal duty to disclose, her failure to do so is much less likely to be considered dishonest by the standards of reasonable and honest people, and even where it was she is unlikely to realise that it would be so considered.

[33] Home Office, *Fraud Law Reform* (Consultation, 2004) paras 18–25.

10.4 FA 2006, s4: fraud by abuse of position

The final route to liability for fraud under section 1 of the FA 2006 is fraud by abuse of position. Fraud by abuse of position is set out in section 4 of the FA 2006.

(1) A person is in breach of this section if he—

(a) occupies a position in which he is expected to safeguard, or not to act against, the financial interests of another person,

(b) dishonestly abuses that position, and

(c) intends, by means of the abuse of that position—

(i)   to make a gain for himself or another, or

(ii) to cause loss to another or to expose another to a risk of loss.

The elements of section 4 are illustrated in **Table 10.3.**

Table 10.3 FA 2006, s4

	Actus reus	**Mens rea**
Conduct element	Acts or omissions	Voluntary
Circumstance element	D occupies a position in which she is expected to safeguard the financial interests of another	None
	D abuses that position	None
	D's abuse of position is dishonest	Knowledge
Result element	None	None
Ulterior mens rea element	*	Intention, by abuse of position, to make a gain or cause a loss to another or expose another to a risk of loss

As with sections 2 and 3, section 4 does not require any results. D must dishonestly abuse a position in which she is expected to safeguard the financial interests of another, D must intend thereby to make a gain or cause a loss or risk of loss to another, but no such gain or loss needs to be demonstrated in fact.

10.4.1 Actus reus of s4

The actus reus of section 4 requires D, by act or omission,[34] to abuse a position in which she is expected to safeguard the financial interests of another.

---

[34] FA 2006, s4(2).

10.4.1.1 Identifying the relevant positions

The first element of the actus reus requires D to occupy a position in which she is expected to safeguard the financial interests of another. Unfortunately, again, this core element is not defined in the statute.

The most obvious interpretation of the required 'position' is where D owes a 'fiduciary duty' to another (ie a civil law duty to act within the interests of another). Indeed, most of the examples provided by the Law Commission and government have involved such duties. For example, employees using insider knowledge to make secret profits; those taking advantage of vulnerable people whose finances they have agreed to administer; and so on. *Marshall* provides a useful illustration.

> ### *Marshall* [2009] EWCA Crim 2076
>
> D was a manager of a residential care home for people with extreme learning difficulties, and in that position had control over a particular resident's (V's) finances. Over a period of time, D withdrew over £7,000 from the resident's account and used it for her own benefit. D was charged with fraud by abuse of position.
>
> - Crown Court: guilty of fraud.
> - Court of Appeal: appeal on sentence (12 months) dismissed.

Beyond cases of this kind, however, the government have made it clear in the FA 2006 Explanatory Notes that the offence will not be limited to abuse of a fiduciary duty.

> The necessary relationship will be present between trustee and beneficiary, director and company, professional person and client, agent and principal, employee and employer, or between partners. It may arise otherwise, for example within a family, or in the context of voluntary work, or in any context where the parties are not at arm's length. In nearly all cases where it arises, it will be recognised by the civil law as importing fiduciary duties, and any relationship that is so recognised will suffice. We see no reason, however, why the existence of such duties should be essential. This does not of course mean that it would be entirely a matter for the fact-finders whether the necessary relationship exists. The question whether the particular facts alleged can properly be described as giving rise to that relationship will be an issue capable of being ruled upon by the judge and, if the case goes to the jury, of being the subject of directions.[35]

The guidance maintains that the question is one for the judge, but by breaking away from the civil law concept of fiduciary duty, the task for the judge when identifying a relevant position will be very difficult. Potentially, whenever D is in a position of trust, or expresses some form of loyalty to another, they may satisfy this element. If it is accepted that breach of loyalty, broadly conceived, is a wrong deserving of criminalisation, then such a wide interpretation may be welcome.[36] However, on the other hand, we must ask whether such a serious offence (maximum ten-year sentence) is an appropriate tool to police loyalty within potentially unstructured, social, or family relationships.

---

[35] FA 2006, Explanatory Notes, s4. Quoting from Law Commission, *Fraud* (No 276, 2002) para 7.38.
[36] Collins, 'Fraud by Abuse of Position: Theorising Section 4 of the Fraud Act 2006' [2011] Crim LR 513.

Don't be confused ...

The breadth of section 4 will ultimately depend on how it is interpreted by the courts. One further layer of uncertainty, and (again) one that should have been made clear in the legislation, is that the phrase 'expected to safeguard' does not tell us whose expectations we should focus on. For example, is it a position from which V would expect D to safeguard her interests; from which D expects; from which a reasonable person would expect; etc? It is likely that the latter (objective) test will be preferred.

10.4.1.2 When does D abuse this position

Once it is established to the satisfaction of the judge that the position D occupies qualifies in law as a relevant one, it is then a question of fact for the jury whether she abused this position. Where D owes a fiduciary duty to V, establishing abuse will involve directing the jury on potentially complex civil law rules relating to breach of duty. And beyond this, as the offence extends beyond formal relationships of this kind, the term 'abuse' has had to remain flexible. As a result, the term is undefined, justified in the Explanatory Notes as a conscious choice to maintain flexibility.[37] Unfortunately, what is gained in flexibility from not defining such a crucial term is almost certainly lost in lack of certainty and consistency when the offence is applied by the courts. This is illustrated in *Pennock and Pennock*.

Pennock and Pennock [2014] EWCA Crim 598

D1 and D2 (husband and wife) opened a joint bank account with an uncle (V) aged 90. £100,000 of V's money was subsequently transferred into the account and later used to buy a house to be owned by D1 and D2's daughter (X). V later claimed to have no knowledge of the account, the transfer, or the use of the money. D1 and D2 were charged with fraud under section 4 as to (a) the money transfer, and (b) transferring the title of the property to X.

- Crown Court: guilty of fraud.
- Court of Appeal: appeal allowed. The evidence and detail of abuse was not sufficiently clear on the facts, the judge at first instance having failed to direct the jury that D1 and D2 were free to make use of funds from a joint account (where this was free of restrictions) and that the transfer of property title did not undermine V's equitable interest because X was not a bona fide purchaser. Although the court made clear that the facts could have resulted in liability under section 4, the lack of clear direction from the trial judge as to the civil law involved rendered the convictions unsafe.

10.4.2 Mens rea of s4

The mens rea of section 4 requires D to have acted dishonestly, and to have intended *by* her abuse of position to make a gain or to cause a loss or risk of loss to another. These two core elements have been discussed previously in relation to section 2 (**10.2.2**), and should be interpreted in exactly the same way for section 4.

In line with section 3, the additional circumstance elements for the section 4 offence are strict liability elements (they require no mens rea). Thus, although D must occupy

---

[37] FA 2006, Explanatory Notes, s4.

a position in which she is expected to safeguard the financial interests of another, and although D must abuse that position, D does not require any specific mens rea as to either of these actus reus elements. D may therefore come within the offence even where she is unaware that she holds such a position.[38] However, as with section 3, although this seems unacceptably broad, the possibility for unfairness is limited by the requirement of dishonesty and the *Ghosh* test. This is because where D is unaware that she occupies a relevant position, her potential abuse of it is much less likely to be considered dishonest by the standards of reasonable and honest people, and even where it was, she may not realise that it would be so considered.

> **Point to remember ...**
> We discussed in **Chapter 9** the central role of 'dishonesty' within most of the property offences, and highlighted criticism of its inability to perform this role effectively. Within the core fraud offences discussed earlier, that same, and arguably even greater, reliance should again be apparent.

10.5 FA 2006, s11: obtaining services dishonestly

Obtaining services dishonestly is set out at section 11 of the FA 2006.[39] The maximum penalty on indictment is five years' imprisonment.[40]

(1) A person is guilty of an offence under this section if he obtains services for himself or another—

(a) by a dishonest act, and

(b) in breach of subsection (2).

(2) A person obtains services in breach of this subsection if—

(a) they are made available on the basis that payment has been, is being or will be made for or in respect of them,

(b) he obtains them without any payment having been made for or in respect of them or without payment having been made in full, and

(c) when he obtains them, he knows—

(i) that they are being made available on the basis described in paragraph (a), or

(ii) that they might be,

but intends that payment will not be made, or will not be made in full.

The elements of section 11 are set out in **Table 10.4.**

---

[38] The term 'abuse' implies some form of conscious or intentional wrongdoing. However, there is nothing in the statute to make such mens rea a requirement. Eg we may say D is abusing her position in a workplace simply by her laziness, even where it may be hard to demonstrate that such laziness is intentional.

[39] Replacing the old offence 'obtaining services by deception' (TA 1978, s1). Unlike this old offence, s11 does not require deception to be demonstrated: Withey, 'The Fraud Act 2006—Some Early Observations and Comparisons with the Former Law' (2007) 71 J Crim L 220.

[40] FA 2006, s11(3).

Table 10.4 FA 2006, s11

	Actus reus	Mens rea
Conduct element	Acts causing the result	Voluntary
Circumstance element	D's obtaining of services is dishonest	Knowledge
	Payment is required for the services	Knowledge or foresight of a chance
	No (or insufficient) payment is provided	Intention
Result element	Services are obtained for D or another	Intention

Unlike the offence of fraud discussed earlier, section 11 creates a result crime: D's dishonest acts must *cause* services to be obtained in circumstances where payment is knowingly withheld.

10.5.1 Actus reus of s11

The actus reus of section 11 requires D to have acquired services for which payment is required, but not to have paid for these services in full. Paradigm examples will include cases where D uses an illegal device (decoder) to watch satellite TV without paying; where D takes goods on hire without intending to pay for them; where D gains entry to a sporting or music event by climbing over a fence; and so on. Indeed, where the service requires payment, the offence will even cover D who opens a bank account using false details, or continues to use her account having had her authority to do so removed.[41]

Two points should be emphasised. First, unlike with fraud, section 11 is a result crime: causation is crucial. Thus, for example, where D obtains services, for example gaining entry to a sporting event, with the intention of paying, but decides after the event that she will not do so, she does not commit a section 11 offence. This is because, at the time she acts to *cause* the services to be obtained, she is not yet dishonest; and when she is later dishonest, she has already obtained the services. The correct charge in these circumstances, discussed later, would be making off without payment.[42]

Secondly, it must be shown that D acquired a 'service'. This is not defined in the statute, but is clearly considerably wider than 'property'. The only restriction is that the service must be one for which payment is required. Thus, where D acts dishonestly to gain a gratuitous service D does not commit a section 11 offence: as, for example, where D lies about his age to obtain a free car wash for the elderly.

10.5.2 Mens rea of s11

To satisfy the mens rea of section 11, D must know that payment for the service is or might be required; must intend to obtain the service without paying; and must act dishonestly.

---

[41] *Sofroniou* [2003] EWCA Crim 3681.

[42] See **10.7**. Where D has obtained the services and continues to represent that she is willing to pay, there will be an alternative charge under the FA 2006, s2.

The first two of these requirements are relatively straightforward, but should be carefully applied. For example, where D lies about her religion or postcode in order to access a selective fee-charging school, she will not commit a section 11 offence if she intends to pay the fees: she acts dishonestly to obtain a service, but she does not intend to avoid payment.[43] The final element of dishonesty requires us to apply the standard *Ghosh* test. This is discussed earlier in the context of section 2 (**10.2.2.2**), and the same approach applies here.

10.6 Fraud preparation offences

Sections 6 and 7 of the FA 2006 criminalise acts in preparation for fraud. Section 6 proscribes possession of articles for fraud; and section 7 proscribes the making or supplying of articles for use in frauds. In both cases, the law is trying to facilitate early intervention by the police, targeting D before she has caused or attempted to cause harm.

> *Extra detail ...*
> It should be remembered that, under the current law, the principal fraud offence is also drafted in an inchoate or pre-emptive fashion, criminalising D where she falsely represents, fails to disclose, or abuses her position with the intent to make a gain or cause a loss, but not requiring that gain or loss (the substantive harm) to be caused. The offences under sections 6 and 7 provide even earlier criminalisation. Is this fair?

10.6.1 FA 2006, s6: possession of articles for use in frauds

The maximum penalty for section 6 on indictment is five years' imprisonment.[44]

> (1) A person is guilty of an offence if he has in his possession or under his control any article for use in the course of or in connection with any fraud.

The elements of section 6 are set out in **Table 10.5**.

Table 10.5 FA 2006, s6

	Actus reus	**Mens rea**
Conduct element	Possessing or controlling an article	Voluntary Knowledge
Circumstance element	None	None
Result element	None	None
Ulterior mens rea element	*	Intention to use the article in connection with fraud

---

[43] Monaghan, 'Fraudsters? Putting Parents in the Dock' (2010) 174 CJLW 581.
[44] FA 2006, s6(2).

As **Table 10.5** illustrates, section 6 creates an extremely broad offence, criminalising the possession or control of any article with the intention to use it in connection with fraud. Again, this is a conduct crime, and it is irrelevant for this offence whether any future fraud is completed or not.

10.6.1.1 Actus reus of s6

The two core elements of the actus reus are that D (a) has possession or control of (b) an article.

A) **Possession or control:** Straightforward cases will involve physical possession of an article on D's person. This will include, for example, where D is found with fake bank notes; with a decoding machine facilitating the illegal viewing of paid satellite television; etc.[45] It will also include, as in *Nimley*, items that might be otherwise innocent such as an iPhone.

□ *Nimley* [2010] EWCA Crim 2752

D was caught videoing cinema films on his iPhone. D had already successfully recorded and uploaded three previous films to the internet for free consumption. D was charged with offences including possession of articles (the iPhone) for use in fraud.

- Crown Court: guilty of section 6 offence.
- Court of Appeal: appeal against sentence allowed, removing the custodial element of the sentence and replacing it with community service.

Possession or control are not, however, limited to examples of physical possession. For example, where D has relevant articles stored in her house, in her office, or in other premises, these too will be in her possession or control. In this manner, we are in possession or control of many thousands of articles at any one time.[46]

B) **Articles:** As noted earlier, relevant articles found in D's possession may be otherwise innocent as long as D intends to use them in connection with fraud. Thus, the iPhone in *Nimley* constituted a relevant article just as much as an item, such as a decoding machine, where the sole function is to facilitate fraud. This means that everyday articles such as pens and paper will constitute relevant articles as long as D possesses them with the required mens rea. Section 8(1) of the FA 2006 also expressly includes 'any program or data held in electronic form' as articles. Thus, where D possesses certain software or a document held in electronic form, and intends to use it in connection with fraud, she commits a section 6 offence.

Extra detail ...

We wait to see how widely these terms will be interpreted by the courts. For example, does D have possession of all the information on the internet simply by her ability to access it?

---

[45] *Kazi* [2010] EWCA Crim 2752: possession of paper that was to be used to make fake banknotes; *Ciorba* [2009] EWCA Crim 1800: possession of a memory stick used to download data from ATM machines.
[46] *Montague* [2013] EWCA Crim 1781.

10.6.1.2 Mens rea of s6

The two core elements of the mens rea are D's (a) knowledge of possession of control, and (b) intention to use the article in connection with fraud.

A) **Knowledge of possession:** It is not clear from the statute whether D must have knowledge, or indeed any mens rea, as to the fact of possession. However, in line with other possession offences, particularly drug offences, it is contended that such a requirement should be found by the courts. In most cases, the fact that D must intend to use the article in connection with fraud will require in effect that D has knowledge of possession; but not always. For example, where D plans to use a piece of software without realising that the software is already installed on her computer. In such cases, it is contended that D should avoid liability under section 6.

B) **Intention to use the article in connection with fraud:** This requirement is not defined further in the statute, and may be interpreted very widely. For example, the phrase 'in connection' clearly allows for cases where D does not plan to use the article as a tool for the fraud, but simply in some related role as, for example, to help to cover her tracks; or to gain access to the necessary tools; etc. It is also unclear how widely 'fraud' should be interpreted: the term clearly covers an intention to commit an offence under sections 1–4, and most likely sections 9 and 11, but beyond this it remains uncertain. However, it has been clarified in *Sakalauskas*[47] that D's intention must relate to *future* acts of fraud, it being insufficient to show that the items were intended for past acts.

10.6.2 FA 2006, s7: making or supplying articles for use in frauds

The maximum penalty for section 7 on indictment is ten years' imprisonment.[48]

(1) A person is guilty of an offence if he makes, adapts, supplies or offers to supply any article—

  (a) knowing that it is designed or adapted for use in the course of or in connection with fraud, or

  (b) intending it to be used to commit, or assist in the commission of, fraud.

The elements of section 7 are set out in **Table 10.6.**

Table 10.6 FA 2006, s7

	Actus reus	**Mens rea**
Conduct element	Making, adapting, supplying, or offering to supply an article	Voluntary
Circumstance element	None	None

---

[47] [2013] EWCA Crim 2278.
[48] FA 2006, s7(2).

Result element	None	None
Ulterior mens rea element	*	Knowing the article is designed or adapted for use in connection with fraud
		Or
		Intending the article to be used to commit or assist the commission of fraud

Section 7 creates an offence capable of numerous constructions (eg making; adapting; supplying; offering; with knowledge; with intent; etc.) As such, it should be applied carefully, ensuring that the correct construction is identified in relation to the particular factual event. However, at its core, the offence is designed to criminalise D who is either preparing articles for the commission of fraud herself, or doing so to assist another.

10.7 Related fraud and deception offences

There are a number of fraud-related offences within the criminal law, including false accounting;[49] making false statements as company directors;[50] suppression of documents;[51] and the common law offence of cheating the public revenue.[52] However, in this section we provide only a brief account of two such offences: conspiracy to defraud and making off without payment.

10.7.1 Conspiracy to defraud

Conspiracy to defraud is a common law offence that criminalises D who agrees with another (D2) on a dishonest course of conduct that risks prejudice to another's property rights.[53] This is a spectacularly wide offence, with the potential to criminalise an agreement to complete conduct that may not be a crime or even a civil wrong if simply undertaken by an individual. Beyond this, the exact boundaries of the offence are far from certain. As a result, unsurprisingly, it has attracted considerable criticism.[54] The Law Commission recommended abolition of conspiracy to defraud within its recommendations for the FA 2006.[55] However, concerned about possible lacunae within the new statute, and bearing in mind the popularity of the offence with prosecutors, the

---

[49] TA 1968, s17.

[50] TA 1968, s19.

[51] TA 1968, s20.

[52] Ormerod, 'Cheating the Public Revenue' [1998] Crim LR 627.

[53] Defined in *Scott v Metropolitan Police Commissioner* [1975] AC 919.

[54] ATH Smith, 'Conspiracy to Defraud' [1988] Crim LR 508; JC Smith, 'Conspiracy to Defraud: Some Comments on the Law Commission's Report' [1995] Crim LR 209.

[55] Law Commission, *Fraud* (No 276, 2002) Draft Bill, s9.

government favoured retention.[56] There are currently no signs that the offence will be abolished.

The elements of the conspiracy to defraud are set out in **Table 10.7**. The maximum sentence is ten years' imprisonment.

Table 10.7 Conspiracy to defraud

	Actus reus	**Mens rea**
Conduct element	Agreement with D2	Voluntary
Circumstance element	Agreement involves a risk to V's property interests or deception in a public duty	Knowledge
	D's agreement is dishonest	Knowledge
Result element	None	None
Ulterior mens rea element	*	Intention that the course of conduct is completed

10.7.1.1 Actus reus of conspiracy to defraud

The core elements of the actus reus of conspiracy to defraud are (a) an agreement between two or more (b) on a course of conduct that risks the property interests of another or deception in a public duty. This is a conduct-based inchoate offence: the agreement must involve a risk to property interests or deception, but it is irrelevant whether the parties go through with their agreement and whether any property interests are imperilled or not.

A) **Agreement between two or more:** As with other conspiracy offences (**Chapter 11**), conspiracy to defraud requires an agreement (a meeting of minds) between two or more people. However, the agreement need not involve one of the defendants doing the defrauding themselves. For example, in *Hollinshead*[57] the House of Lords found a conspiracy to defraud where D1 and D2 agreed to produce devices designed to corrupt electricity meters making them undercount the electricity used even though the defrauding would be done by unidentified third parties—the customers using the device.

B) **Risks the property interests of another or deception of someone's public duty:** Agreements to a course of conduct that would amount to an offence under the Theft Acts and/or the FA 2006 would clearly satisfy the requirement of risking another's property interests. Conspiracy to defraud has also been used to criminalise agreements that if carried out would not amount to an offence. For example, agreements relating to the 'temporary' deprivation of another's property (short of theft);[58] to shifting land

---

[56] See commentary in Ormerod and Williams, *Smith's Law of Theft* (2007) paras 5.65 et seq.
[57] [1985] AC 975.
[58] *Scott v Metropolitan Police Commissioner* [1975] AC 919: temporary deprivation of cinema tapes.

boundary fences; to inducing another to take a financial risk they would not other-wise have taken;[59] and so on. However, the case of *Evans*[60] has clarified that something unlawful is required under this route: either that the object of the agreement was unlaw-ful, or if the object was lawful, that the means of achieving that object were unlawful.[61]

Alongside agreements that risk property interests, it has long been accepted that the deception of V to act against her public duty will also satisfy this element of the offence. Examples include D deceiving a public official to supply export licences,[62] supply informa-tion,[63] employ unqualified staff,[64] and so on. Certain cases suggest that this construction will also apply outside public officials to those deceived into acting against any contractual duties.[65]

10.7.1.2 Mens rea of conspiracy to defraud

The mens rea of conspiracy to defraud requires: (a) knowledge of the risks involved in the agreement; (b) intention that the course of conduct will be carried out; and (c) dis-honesty. As with all conspiracy offences, at least two of the parties to the agreement must *both* satisfy the mens rea (ie there must be a meeting of minds).

A) Knowledge of the risks: D must recognise the risks posed to the property inter-ests of another or the possible deception of V acting in a public duty.[66] D's motives, in this regard, are irrelevant. Thus, in *Wai Yu-tsang*[67] the Privy Council found that D had conspired to defraud the bank he worked for by failing to reveal financial information even though he was acting, he claimed, to protect the bank's interests.

B) Intention that the course of conduct will be completed: If the parties agree on a course of conduct, but do not intend that the course of conduct will actually be carried out, then no offence is committed. For example, where D agrees, but plans to 'whistle-blow' and prevent the course of conduct happening.

C) Dishonesty: The *Ghosh* test applies here, as discussed previously at **10.2.2.2**. Perhaps even more than with other offences, the potential for other elements of the offence to catch ostensibly innocent conduct makes the role of dishonesty centrally important.

10.7.2 TA 1978, s3: making off without payment

Making off without payment is an offence contrary to section 3 of the TA 1978. The maximum penalty on indictment is two years' imprisonment.[68]

(1) Subject to subsection (3) below, a person who, knowing that payment on the spot for any goods supplied or service done is required or expected from him, dishonestly makes off without having

---

[59] *Allsop* (1976) 64 Cr App R 29.
[60] [2014] 1 WLR 2817. Upheld by Fulford LJ when the SFO sought a voluntary Bill: [2014] EWHC 3803 (QB).
[61] Jarvis, 'Conspiracy to Defraud: A Siren to Lure Unwary Prosecutors' [2014] Crim LR 738.
[62] *Board of Trade v Owen* [1957] AC 602.
[63] *DPP v Withers* [1975] AC 842.
[64] *Bassey* (1931) 21 Cr App R 160.
[65] *Welham* [1961] AC 103.
[66] *Cooke* [1986] AC 909.
[67] [1992] 1 AC 269.
[68] TA 1978, s4.

paid as required or expected and with intent to avoid payment of the amount due shall be guilty of an offence.

(2) For purposes of this section 'payment on the spot' includes payment at the time of collecting goods on which work has been done or in respect of which service has been provided.

(3) Subsection (1) above shall not apply where the supply of the goods or the doing of the service is contrary to law, or where the service done is such that payment is not legally enforceable...

The elements of section 3 are set out in **Table 10.8**.

Table 10.8 TA 1978, s3

	Actus reus	**Mens rea**
Conduct element	Making off	Voluntary
Circumstance element	On the spot payment is required	Knowledge
	Payment is not supplied in full	Intention
	D's making off is dishonest	Knowledge
Result element	None	None
Ulterior mens rea element	*	Intention to avoid payment

Making off without payment was intended to provide a simple offence to target cases where D tries to avoid payment for goods or services by taking flight by, for example, running out of a restaurant without paying the bill, jumping out of a taxi without paying the fare, etc. Importantly, there is no need to demonstrate any deception, and no need to show that D has successfully avoided payment. The offence simply requires D to have dishonestly made off without paying for goods or services that she knows require payment, and doing so with the intention to avoid payment.[69]

10.7.2.1 Actus reus of s3

The actus reus of section 3 requires D to: (a) make off; (b) without payment; where (c) on-the-spot payment is required.

A) **Making off:** Making off simply requires D to have physically moved from the location in which payment is required. This will be the case whether D leaves surreptitiously as where D climbs out of a restaurant's bathroom window, or whether she leaves to the 'sound of trumpets'.[70] However, D must have fully left the relevant location. For example, if D is stopped before leaving the restaurant where payment is required she will not have committed the section 3 offence, although there may be liability in attempt.[71]

---

[69] *Vincent* [2001] 1 WLR 1172.
[70] *Brooks and Brooks* (1982) 76 Cr App R 66.
[71] *McDavitt* [1981] Crim LR 843.

One point remains unresolved in the literature—does D 'make off' if V gives her permission to leave?[72] This question is further complicated by the possibility that permission may be gained by deception as, for example, where D gives a false name and address, or by telling the truth by, for example, giving a genuine name and address. It was held in *Hammond*[73] that, however obtained, the presence of permission was incompatible with the notion of 'making off', and it is contended that this approach is correct. Where D is honest, then V has allowed her to leave and liability would seem inappropriate; where D is dishonest we may want liability, but again V has allowed her to leave, and section 3 is not appropriate. In this second case, liability can be found under fraud by false representation.[74]

B) Without payment: This element simply requires that D has not paid for the goods or services, or has not paid in full.

C) On-the-spot payment is required: There are two parts to this requirement. First, for payment to be 'required or expected', it must be that goods or services have been supplied.[75] This will include where D has taken goods that are supplied via self-service display in a supermarket, or fuel at a self-service forecourt.[76] However, where goods have not yet been supplied there will be no offence under section 3[77] as, for example, where D tries unsuccessfully to trick V out of goods and then runs away. Equally, where goods or services are supplied, but they are of a sufficiently low quality or provided in breach of contract, such that D is not legally obliged to pay for them, there will again be no liability under this section.[78] Section 3(3) also makes it clear that there will be no offence under this section where D makes off without paying for illegal goods or services, for example from a brothel, or having been supplied with illegal drugs, etc.

The second part of this element is that the payment for goods or services must be required or expected 'on the spot'. This was the focus of the court in *Vincent*.

🗋 *Vincent* [2001] EWCA Crim 295

D did not settle his bill in full when leaving two different hotels. On each occasion, he dishonestly assured the owners (V) that he was about to come into some money and would pay them later, and on each occasion V allowed him to leave on this basis. D was charged with making off without payment.

• Crown Court: guilty of section 3 offence. Even though V consented to D leaving, D's dishonest obtaining of that consent meant that he still 'made off' for the purposes of section 3.

• Court of Appeal: appeal allowed. Where V consents to D leaving without payment, even where this is procured by dishonesty, D is not 'making off' for the purpose of section 3.

---

[72] Spencer, Letter, 'Making Off Without Payment' [1983] Crim LR 573.
[73] [1982] Crim LR 611.
[74] See **10.2** if the making off related to property.
[75] 'Goods' are defined by the TA 1968, s34 (made applicable to the TA 1978 by s5(2)). 'Services' are not defined in statute.
[76] For an alternative view, see, Smith 'Shoplifting and the Theft Acts' [1981] Crim LR 586.
[77] The charge here, if any, would be for fraud or attempted theft.
[78] *Troughton v Metropolitan Police* [1987] Crim LR 138: taxi driver in breach of contract so payment was not required.

In *Vincent*, V's consent to later payment meant that payment was no longer required or expected on the spot (ie at that time, in that hotel). Therefore, D's leaving that spot could not amount to making off without payment. Where D acts in this manner, dishonestly avoiding immediate payment with the intention to make a gain or cause a loss, the appropriate charge would be fraud by false representation (**10.2**).

10.7.2.2 Mens rea of s3

The mens rea of section 3 requires D to have: (a) known that on-the-spot payment was required; (b) intended to avoid payment; and (c) acted dishonestly.

A) Knowledge that on-the-spot payment is required: It will often be clear to D that payment for goods or services is required of her on the spot. However, the element will be lacking where, for example, D may leave thinking that another party is going to pay, or believing that payment is only required at some later stage.[79] In such cases, D lacks this requirement of knowledge and is also unlikely to be dishonest.

B) Intention to avoid payment: The text of section 3 required D to intend to avoid payment, but is unclear whether this means an intention to *permanently* avoid payment or whether intention to avoid payment temporarily will suffice. This was clarified in *Allen*.

Allen [1985] AC 1029

D left a hotel without settling his bill. His intention was to pay the bill later when he could afford to do so. D was charged with making off without payment.

- Crown Court: guilty of section 3 offence. The trial judge directed the jury that D need only intend to default from payment at that time.
- Court of Appeal: appeal allowed. D must intend to make permanent default.
- House of Lords: appeal dismissed, endorsing the Court of Appeal's reasoning.

Thus, it is now clear that D will not come within section 3 unless she makes off with the intention to permanently avoid payment.

C) Dishonesty: The *Ghosh* test applies here, as discussed earlier at **10.2.2.2**. It is important to remember that we are looking for dishonesty at the point D makes off.

10.8 Reform

Despite the relatively recent reform of fraud offences in the FA 2006, the government has kept the exercise of these offences under review and further legislative change remains possible.[80] In this section, we discuss three areas of debate: the drafting of the FA 2006; the move to conduct crimes; and the disappearing distinction between theft and fraud.

---

[79] *Brooks and Brooks* (1982) 76 Cr App R 66.
[80] Sarker, 'Fighting Fraud—A Missed Opportunity' (2007) 28 Comp Law 243.

10.8.1 The drafting of the FA 2006

There has been a trend in modern statutes to define offences in an unhelpfully complex manner.[81] We were critical of this in relation to the Sexual Offences Act 2003 (**8.9**), and we will discuss similar criticisms in relation to inchoate offences of assisting and encouraging and the Serious Crime Act 2007 (**Chapter 11**). In comparison to these other statutes, the FA 2006 is remarkably straightforward, defining the three core routes to fraud liability over just five brief sections. It should also be recognised that in the early years of the statute, despite extensive use in the lower courts, there have been very few appeal cases, demonstrating its general success. The question emerges, however, whether this apparent simplicity and success has come at any cost? Two points should be highlighted.

First, in order to remove complex details from the statute, a number of key terms have been left undefined. We saw this earlier, for example, with terms such as 'dishonesty',[82] 'service',[83] 'position',[84] 'abuse',[85] and so on. With terms of this kind, where ordinary meanings are not self-evident, the choice not to provide a statutory definition creates uncertainty in the law.[86] In this manner, complexity is not avoided but is rather hidden within the case law. Secondly, in looking to simplify the fraud offences, removing complex requirements within the old law of 'deception' and resulting losses or gains, the current law has defined the core fraud offences in an inchoate manner, criminalising D's dishonest conduct which is *intended* to interfere with property rights as opposed to criminalising successful interferences. Attempting to simplify the law by broadening offence definitions has also been a common practice in recent years (eg sexual offences; inchoate liability; terrorism offences; etc). The disadvantage of this is the potential for over—or inappropriate—criminalisation, and the burden placed on elements such as 'dishonesty' to focus liability only on those acts deserving of it. We discuss this further in the following sections.

10.8.2 Fraud and the irrelevance of results

Although the fraud offences are undoubtedly simpler than their equivalents were prior to the FA 2006, the move from deception-based result crimes to dishonesty-based conduct crimes has considerably widened the range of conduct caught.[87] Unlike the old deception offences, and unlike other property offences discussed in **Chapter 9**, the actus reus of fraud does not require D to gain property or cause a loss of property to another. For example, for section 2 of the FA 2006, D commits fraud as soon as she makes a false representation with the required mens rea.

---

[81] Spencer, 'The Drafting of Criminal Legislation: Need It Be So Impenetrable?' (2008) 67 CLJ 585.

[82] This term is central to most property offences.

[83] Central to the offence of making off without payment (**10.7.2**) and obtaining services dishonestly (**10.5**).

[84] Required for fraud by abuse of position (**10.4**).

[85] Ibid.

[86] Including potential for challenge under Art 7 ECHR.

[87] See **2.4.1**.

The irrelevance of results has broadened liability in two important ways. First, the offence will be committed earlier when the false representation is made rather than when property is transferred. Although this change will affect all cases, it will have a particular impact on cases in which D fails to deceive V and no property is passed. Under the old law, D either commits an attempt offence or no offence at all. Under the FA 2006, D has completed the full offence of fraud.

Secondly, at the other end of the scale, the irrelevance of results also expands the offence to capture later acts. Under the pre-2006 law, it had to be demonstrated that D's deception caused property to be transferred. Thus, D could not be liable for deceptive conduct that came after the transfer of property. This caused problems in cases such as where D fills her car with petrol intending to pay, but then changes her mind and deceives the station attendant (V) to avoid payment. The ownership of the petrol passes to D at the moment it mingles with other petrol in her car. Therefore, by the time D deceives V there are no property rights to be passed.[88] This has traditionally been dealt with through the offence of making off without payment, and this continues to apply. However, D's conduct will now *also* be fraud by false representation: D dishonestly makes a false representation after filling her tank when she deceives V (this might be as simple as continuing to act as a paying customer), and does so to make a gain (which includes keeping what one has[89]).

Recognising the expansion of liability under the FA 2006, two questions should be considered. First, is the expansion of liability justified: are these cases criminal wrongs that we want to label as fraud? Secondly, but related to the first, are the central terms of the new expanded offence, particularly 'dishonesty', fit for the purpose of identifying and targeting only the conduct deserving of criminalisation?

10.8.3 Distinguishing theft and fraud

Having discussed the definition of the fraud offences, it is useful to briefly return to the debate about overlap between theft and fraud. As we highlighted at the end of the last chapter (**9.8.1**), there is a concern that the offences of fraud and theft overlap to an unacceptable degree.[90] The argument here is that where theft should target D who takes V's property without consent, fraud should target those who deceive V into parting with their property voluntarily. However, as we have seen, the current law does not reflect this neat division. Rather, following *Gomez* and *Hinks*, as long as D acts dishonestly, theft can now extend to cases in which V consents to the appropriation of her property.[91] And, alongside this, fraud now requires no transfer of property at all.

The question emerging from this is whether the current law is well served maintaining these two separate offences? If the wrong of both offences is now simply

---

[88] *Collis-Smith* [1971] Crim LR 716.

[89] FA 2006, s5(3).

[90] Shute and Horder, 'Thieving and Deceiving: What is the Difference?' (1993) 56 MLR 548; Melissaris, 'The Concept of Appropriation and the Offence of Theft' (2007) 70 MLR 581.

[91] See discussion at **9.1**.

focused on dishonest conduct, would a single dishonesty offence provide a more coherent way forward?[92]

10.9 Eye on assessment

In this section we consider the potential application of fraud offences within a problem question, using the same structure of analysis discussed in previous chapters.

> **STEP 1 Identify the potential criminal event in the facts**
>
> This should be simply stated (eg 'The first potential criminal event arises where D makes a false benefit claim'). The role of this stage is to highlight which part of the question you are answering before you begin to apply the law.

When identifying a potential criminal event, it is important to remember that the main fraud offence is a conduct crime: the relevant point of potential liability is where D makes the representation (s2), fails to disclose (s3), or abuses her position (s4), not at the point if and when property rights are affected. Of course, where D possesses articles for use in fraud (s6) or makes or supplies such articles (s7) the potential event may be even earlier.

> **STEP 2 Identify the potential offence**
>
> Again, state this simply (eg 'When claiming false benefits, D may be liable for fraud by false representation'). The role of this stage is to highlight which offence you are going to apply.

Identifying the appropriate offence in this area is not easy, and you need to take time to consider your options. Chiefly, this is because many of the offences overlap with one another, and so you will usually have more than one available route to liability. One issue arising here is that it can be possible, and tempting, to answer a whole problem with reference to only one offence. Although accurate, you need to consider that assessments are about demonstrating knowledge, as well as the fair labelling of D, and so it is useful to acknowledge and discuss potential liability under different offences. The one caveat here, as always, is that if the problem question specifies a certain offence (eg 'Discuss Dave's potential liability for fraud by failure to disclose') then you should *only* do what the question asks of you.

Table 10.9 sets out the offences we have discussed in this chapter (with the addition of theft), ordered in terms of when they might arise within a problem scenario. On the right, we indicate why you might discuss this offence as opposed to other overlapping options.

---

[92] This possibility is discussed (and rejected) by the Law Commission, *Fraud* (No 276, 2002) paras 5.20–5.57.

Table 10.9 Identifying and applying fraud offences

Possession of articles for use in frauds	• This offence is useful to criminalise acts where D is in possession of something with the required intent before he has done any more towards a full fraud offence. • These offences are useful to consider where, for whatever reason, D does not go on to commit the fraud or theft.
Making or supplying articles for use in frauds	• This offence is useful where D makes or supplies articles for fraud with the required intent. • Again, these offences are useful to consider where, for whatever reason, D does not go on to commit the fraud or theft.
Conspiracy to defraud	• This offence is useful where D agrees with another person to commit fraud, with the required intent. • Again, these offences are useful to consider where for whatever reason D does not go on to commit the fraud or theft.
Fraud by false representation	• This offence applies at the point D makes a false representation. • This offence is extremely wide, covering most of the conduct targeted by the two offences below. If in doubt, this is probably the one to focus on.
Fraud by failure to disclose	• This offence applies at the point D fails (omits) to disclose information where she has a legal duty to do so. • Where there is an omission and a clear legal duty, such as a failure to disclose a criminal record when applying for a job, you should try to apply this offence in preference to fraud by false representation.
Fraud by abuse of position	• This offence applies at the point D abuses her position with a view to making a gain or causing a loss. • Again, although these cases will usually involve a false representation, it is useful to apply this offence in preference to s2 where the facts are clear (eg a carer taking money from her vulnerable patients).
Theft	• Theft applies later than the offences discussed above, occurring only when property has been appropriated by D. • Remember that theft requires potentially problematic elements that fraud does not: appropriation; intention to permanently deprive. • Where you could apply theft or fraud, you should consider which offence provides the most accurate label for what D has done, but also that fraud is the more serious offence and so should usually be applied in preference.

Obtaining services dishonestly	• Like theft, this offence only applies where results are caused: the obtaining of a service. • Remember that theft does not apply to services. Thus, where services are obtained, you should either apply this offence or one of the fraud offences.
Making off without payment	• This offence comes last in our timeline, applying where D has received the goods and then makes off. • This offence is useful where D's dishonesty does not arise until after the goods have been transferred to D. In such a case, theft will not apply due to a lack of coincidence in time of actus reus and mens rea. However, at the time of making off D will be dishonest and so will come within this offence.

Where, as is likely, you identify more than one possible offence, it is good practice to focus your analysis on the most appropriate, but also to (briefly) acknowledge the other possible routes.

STEP 3 Applying the offence to the facts

Having identified the relevant offence, make sure you discuss each of the required elements.

Actus reus: What does the offence require? Did D do it?

Mens rea: What does the offence require? Did D possess it?

When applying the offences, it is important to recognise areas of uncertainty in the law, and particularly the failure of the FA 2006 to define several key terms. You are also hindered by a lack of appellate court judgments on the FA 2006 to help you to resolve these areas of uncertainty. The best way to deal with this is too look to other sources in order to predict how the courts are *likely* to apply the law to your problem facts: academic discussion of the offences; pre-2006 case law that remains influential; policy documents (including the Law Commission report) and how it intended the law to be interpreted; etc. Remember that none of these sources are conclusive, they do not create binding precedent, but they are all influential and will help you to predict the likely way forward.

STEP 4 Consider defences

The word 'consider' here is important, as you should not discuss every defence for every question. Rather, think whether there are any defences (eg duress) that *could* potentially apply. If there are, discuss those only.

STEP 5 Conclude

This is usually a single sentence either saying that it is likely that D has committed the offence, or saying that it is not likely either because an offence element is not satisfied or because a defence is likely to apply. It is not often that you will be able to say categorically whether D has committed the offence or not, particularly when applying concepts such as dishonesty, so it is usually best to conclude in terms of what is more 'likely'.

STEP 6 Loop

Go back up to Step 1, identifying the next potential criminal event. Continue until you have discussed all the relevant potentially criminal events.

ONLINE RESOURCE CENTRE

www.oxfordtextbooks.co.uk/orc/smithandhogan/

This chapter is accompanied by a selection of online resources to help you with this topic, including:

- **Multiple choice questions**
- **Chapter summary sheet**
- Two **sample examination questions** with answer guidance
- **Further reading**

Also available on the Online Resource Centre are:

- A selection of **videos** from the authors explaining key topics and principles
- **Legal updates**
- Useful **weblinks**

11

General inchoate offences

11.1 Introduction

'Inchoate', as we have introduced elsewhere,[1] is a term used to describe offences that are in some sense not complete. Standard (non-inchoate) principal offences are designed to target

---

[1] See **4.2.1.2**.

'wrongs' based on D's mens rea and, crucially, her manifestation of some harmful conduct. Inchoate offences, in contrast, will generally *not require* a significant physical harm to have come about in the form of harm to a person or property, but will target D who has made some progress towards a harmful end, intending that harm to come about. D's conduct may be inchoate ('just begun'; 'undeveloped'), but it is also deserving of criminalisation.

The general inchoate offences are not defined in relation to one type of potential harm, but apply across multiple offences.

- **Attempt:** D is criminalised for trying to commit a principal offence.
- **Conspiracy:** D is criminalised for agreeing with another to commit a principal offence.
- **Assisting or encouraging:** D is criminalised for assisting or encouraging another (P) to commit a principal offence.

Terminology...

The following will be used throughout this chapter and **Chapter 12**:

- principal offence—this refers to the offence (eg murder; theft; etc) that D is attempting/conspiring/ assisting or encouraging. This is also commonly referred to as the 'substantive offence' or the 'full offence';

- principal offender (P)—where D is assisting or encouraging another to commit a principal offence, this party is referred to as the principal offender (P).

The most important thing to remember about inchoate offences is that they only operate in combination with a principal offence. Thus, for example, D could not be liable for 'attempt', she would be liable for 'attempted murder' or 'attempted theft' or 'attempted rape', etc. This is also true of the other inchoate offences. In such cases, D's liability arises as soon as she satisfies the elements of the inchoate offence, with no requirement that the intended principal offence should ever come about. If the principal offence does later come about, this will not prevent D being liable for the inchoate offence, but may lead to liability for the principal offence directly where it is completed by D, or as a secondary party where it is completed by P. We discuss secondary liability in **Chapter 12**.

It is universally accepted that the criminal law should include some form of general inchoate liability. For example, if D shoots at V with an intention to kill, the criminal law would rightly be criticised if it did not consider D's conduct worthy of criminalisation just because, as a matter of luck,[2] D misses her target. However, the challenge with these offences is setting the point at which D's conduct justifies criminal intervention. We return to this when we consider reform of the law[3] but it is useful to keep in mind from the start of our discussion. As we move into a discussion of the different inchoate offences, you should note that there is a necessary and obvious balancing of legal priorities, and you should consider which of these priorities you believe intuitively is most important in order to start thinking about your evaluation of the current law. We can present this balancing as the relationship between fairness to D and the protection of society.

---

[2] On the role of 'luck', see Ashworth, 'Criminal Attempts and the Role of Resulting Harm' (1988) 19 Rutgers LR 725.

[3] See **11.6**.

A) **Fairness to D:** At the stage D commits one of the inchoate offences, the principal offence attempted/conspired/assisted or encouraged has not yet come about and may never come about. Thus, in order to identify sufficient blameworthiness to fairly criminalise D, we are not looking for the same wrongs as the principal offence, but rather some kind of equivalent in terms of moral blameworthiness. Following this approach, we are likely to favour higher mens rea requirements by only criminalising D where she has fully committed with intention as to the future principal offence. We are also likely to favour restrictive actus reus requirements for blameworthy conduct, or conduct very close to the point of committing the principal offence. These constraints limit the possibility that D might have changed her mind if uninterrupted.

B) **Protection of society:** If we follow the 'fairness to D' approach to its natural extremes, we end up with a narrow set of inchoate offences that only target conduct very close to the commission of the principal offence. The problem with this is that, in many cases, it will be dangerous to limit the offence so narrowly. It would mean that investigators would have to wait for D to have progressed a long way on her criminal enterprise to committing the principal offence before she could be arrested for an inchoate offence. Particularly with the rise of intelligence-led policing, where we might have very good evidence of D's future intentions and planning well before the attack, there are obvious benefits to an intervention at the earliest (and therefore safest) opportunity.

The balancing of these and other[4] considerations is central to the set of offences discussed in this chapter. It is a balancing that shifts over time due to political preferences, changes in policing and public attitudes. Thinking about your views at this stage can be useful: individual cases may influence your view one way or the other but it should be remembered that these are *general* offences; therefore, the approach taken within the law has to be defensible as it applies across multiple principal offences.

11.2 Criminal attempts

The offence of attempt[5] criminalises D at the point where, in trying to commit the principal offence, D does more than merely preparatory acts. It does not matter whether D has failed to commit the principal offence or not.[6] D may have failed for a variety of reasons; including where D changes her mind before completing the offence or is stopped from doing so, as well as where D has done everything she thought necessary but fails, for example, because she misses her shot or V is saved by medical intervention. The reason for D's failure to complete the principal offence, whether it reflects well on her character or not, is irrelevant to her liability (although it may be relevant at the sentencing stage).

---

[4] We discuss the principles of criminalisation at **1.4**.

[5] See generally Law Commission, *Conspiracy and Attempts* (Consultation 183, 2007) Parts 12–16; *Conspiracy and Attempts* (No 318, 2009) Part 8; Duff, *Criminal Attempts* (1996); Yaffe, *Attempts* (2010). See also *Smith and Hogan's Criminal Law* (14th edn, 2015), Ch13.

[6] If D succeeds in committing the principal offence, she remains liable for the earlier attempt, but it would be inappropriate to charge both: *Webley v Buxton* [1977] QB 481.

Exactly when D's 'trying to commit' a principal offence becomes a criminal attempt is defined in section 1(1) of the Criminal Attempts Act 1981 (CAA 1981). The maximum sentence for attempt mirrors that of the principal offence which is being attempted.[7]

(1) If, with intent to commit an offence to which this section applies, a person does an act which is more than merely preparatory to the commission of the offence, he is guilty of attempting to commit the offence.

The elements of criminal attempt are set out in **Table 11.1a**.

Table 11.1a Criminal attempts

	Actus reus	**Mens rea**
Conduct element	Any action	Voluntary
Circumstance element	D's action goes beyond mere preparation towards the commission of a principal offence (on the facts as she believes them to be)	None
Result element	None	None
Ulterior mens rea element	*	*Set out in Table 11.1b*

Table 11.1b Ulterior mens rea element for criminal attempts

Principal offence	**Actus reus of the principal offence**
Conduct element	D must intend to complete the conduct required for the principal offence
Circumstance element	*Possible attempts*: D must intend/know the circumstances required for the principal offence, or where the principal offence requires less than intention or knowledge, D must be at least reckless as to those circumstances Or *Impossible attempts*: D must intend/know the circumstances required for the principal offence
Result element	D must intend to cause the results required (if any) for the principal offence

---

[7] CAA 1981, s4(1).

As **Table 11.1b** demonstrates, a major part of the offence of attempt is forward-looking: examining D's ulterior mens rea as to the principal offence which D is trying to commit.

11.2.1 Actus reus of attempts

The sole requirement within the actus reus of attempt is that D's conduct has gone beyond mere preparation towards completing the principal offence. Although this sounds relatively simple, the task of identifying the line between 'mere preparation' and 'beyond mere preparation' is extremely controversial.

11.2.1.1 Can D attempt by omission?

The wording of section 1(1) ('a person does an act') suggests that a criminal attempt cannot be committed by omission.[8] There is also an absence of case law to contradict this. However, it is contended that section 1 can and should be interpreted to allow for this possibility where D is under a legal duty to act. For example, where D starves her child (V) with the intention of killing V, it is clear that she may be liable for murder.[9] Where V is discovered prior to death and given life-saving treatment, it would surely be appropriate to charge D with attempted murder.[10]

> *Assessment matters...*
> If faced with an attempt by omission in a problem question, it should be highlighted that liability may be barred. However, if there is a duty to act, as there would be in our example above, you should also acknowledge that a court may choose to interpret the CAA 1981 to allow for omissions liability.

11.2.1.2 Which principal offences cannot be attempted?

Our starting point is that all principal offences may be subject to an attempt. However, from this starting point, there are a number of exceptions.

A) **Summary only offences:** Attempts liability will only apply to indictable and either way offences, excluding summary only (those triable only in the magistrates' court) offences.[11] Notable examples of summary only offences, that cannot be subject to attempt, include assault and battery.[12]

B) **Conspiracy and secondary liability:** To avoid criminalising events too far removed from the principal offence, there can be no liability for D who attempts to conspire or attempts to aid and abet another.[13] We discuss this further in the double inchoate liability section later.[14]

---

[8] Palmer, 'Attempt by Act or Omission: Causation and the Problem of the Hypothetical Nurse' (1999) 63 J Crim L 158.

[9] *Gibbins and Proctor* (1918) 13 Cr App R 134.

[10] The Law Commission has recommended amending the CAA 1981 to make it clear that omissions liability should be possible: Law Commission, *Conspiracy and Attempts* (No 318, 2009) paras 8.142–8.151.

[11] See **1.1.7.3**.

[12] The Law Commission has recommended that attempts should not be extended to include summary only offences: Law Commission, *Conspiracy and Attempts* (No 318, 2009) paras 8.154–8.161.

[13] CAA 1981, s1(4). On the exclusion of attempting to aid and abet, see Bohlander, 'The Conflict Between the Serious Crime Act 2007 and Section 1(4)(b) Criminal Attempts Act 1981—A Missed Repeal?' [2010] Crim LR 483; Child, 'The Differences Between Attempted Complicity and Inchoate Assisting and Encouraging—A Reply to Professor Bohlander' [2010] Crim LR 924.

[14] See **11.5**.

C) **Other exceptional cases:** There are a few examples where attempt liability would be impossible, or at least unlikely, to arise. For example, it is impossible to attempt to commit an involuntary manslaughter offence. This is because attempt requires D to intend the result element of the principal offence (ie, in this case, death), and if D intends this element she has committed attempted murder.

11.2.1.3 When are D's acts more than merely preparatory?

The crux of the actus reus of attempt, as we have said, is that D's acts must go beyond mere preparation towards the commission of a relevant principal offence. The term is not defined further in the CAA 1981 and should be given its natural meaning.[15] However, it is useful to take some time to understand the intentions of the drafters of the law, before considering how it has been applied in the courts.

The intended role of 'more than merely preparatory'
Before the CAA 1981, the actus reus of the old common law offence of attempt was simply that D needed to have 'attempted'. However, without further guidance on what conduct constituted such an attempt, the law was open to interpretations across a wide spectrum of behaviour. At either end of this spectrum were what have been termed the last act test and the series of acts test. The current law seeks a middle ground.

A) **Last act test:** The last act test would only allow for attempt liability where D has completed all acts that she believes are necessary to commit the principal offence.[16] Thus, where D sets out to shoot and kill V, D would only attempt after having pulled the trigger. Allowing D every opportunity to change her mind and desist, this approach would only criminalise D where she has passed the point of no return, when she has 'crossed the Rubicon and burnt h[er] boats'.[17] The downside of this approach, of course, is that it may not provide adequate protection for society: where the police can intervene prior to D's 'last act' we would surely want them to do so, and yet we could not always rely on an alternative offence to charge them with.

B) **Series of acts test:** The series of acts test, formulated by Stephen, would find D to have attempted where her act is done towards committing a principal offence 'forming part of a series of acts which would constitute its actual commission if it were not interrupted.'[18] In our attempted murder by shooting example, this would allow for liability well before the firing of the gun, potentially back to the buying of the gun, planning the killing, etc. This approach allows for early criminalisation and thus early intervention by the police to protect society (not least V!). However, as recognised by Lord Lane in *Gullefer*,[19] the downside of this is that D's actions at these very early stages may not yet be sufficiently proximate to the principal offence to be deserving of liability. As D's conduct may also be objectively innocent (eg legally buying a gun), there is also a problem with potential over-reliance on confession evidence and the associated risks of encouraging police malpractice.[20]

---

[15] *Jones* [1990] 3 All ER 886.
[16] Applied in the early case of *Eagleton* (1855) 6 Cox CC 559.
[17] *Stonehouse* [1978] AC 55. Reference to the 'Rubicon' is to the river at the edge of the ancient city of Rome: when the Rubicon was crossed with armed men, war was declared.
[18] *Digest of Criminal Law* (5th edn, 1894) Art 50.
[19] [1990] 3 All ER 882.
[20] Ashworth and Horder, *Principles of Criminal Law* (7th edn, 2013) 462.

C) **The CAA 1981 test:** Within this spectrum of proximity to the principal offence, the CAA 1981 formulation—'more than merely preparatory'—tries to forge a midway path.[21] The idea is that, although strictly speaking all acts prior to the last act are done in preparation, there are certain acts leading to a principal offence that are sufficiently proximate as to go beyond 'mere' preparation, and are deserving of attempts liability.[22] Although somewhat vague in its construction, the test is necessarily general in its terms because it has to be adaptable to multiple offences across the criminal law. The ideal of this approach is illustrated in *Jones*.[23]

> **Jones** (1990) 91 Cr App R 351
>
> D got into the back seat of a car with V, and pointed a sawn-off shotgun at him. Following a struggle, V escaped unharmed. D was charged with attempted murder.
>
> - Crown Court: guilty of attempted murder.
> - Court of Appeal: conviction upheld on appeal. Even though D was at least three steps away from completing the principal offence (he still had to remove the safety catch, put his finger on the trigger and pull it), his acts were still capable of being 'more than merely preparatory'.

Applying 'more than merely preparatory' in practice

The aims of the CAA 1981 formulation are relatively clear. The problem, however, is that as the test is applied in practice across multiple offences and across an infinite variety of factual circumstances, there is potential for it to be applied in unwanted and inconsistent ways.[24] In relation to 'complete attempts,' where D has completed the last acts she believes are necessary to commit the principal offence, then there is no problem as D clearly satisfies the actus reus requirement of going beyond mere preparation.[25] However, problems do emerge in the context of 'incomplete attempts,' where D still has a number of acts to complete before she commits the offence. Three areas of concern are apparent within the literature: (a) the test is being applied too narrowly; (b) the test is being applied inconsistently *between* offences; and (c) the test is being applied inconsistently *within* offences.

> *Judge and jury…*
>
> What D has done, and whether these acts are more than merely preparatory, are ultimately questions of fact for the jury. However, the judge has an important filtering role, only allowing the question to go to the jury if the prosecution has provided evidence that is capable of fulfilling the test. This legal decision on the part of the judge is invariably the subject of the appeal cases discussed later.[26]

The first area of concern is that the 'more than merely preparatory' test is being interpreted too narrowly, inadequately weighing the need to protect society from harms and

---

[21] There is a useful discussion of this in the Law Commission report leading to the CAA 1981: *Attempt, and Impossibility in Relation to Attempt, Conspiracy and Incitement* (No 102, 1980) paras 2.19–2.52.

[22] *Tosti* [1997] Crim LR 746: the court held that D's acts were 'preparatory, but not merely so'.

[23] Discussed in Smith, 'Proximity in Attempt: Lord Lane's Midway Course' [1991] Crim LR 576.

[24] Law Commission, *Conspiracy and Attempts* (Consultation 183, 2007) Parts 1, 12–14.

[25] The only exception to this can arise where D is a secondary party to a principal offence.

[26] CAA 1981, s4(3). Discussed in *Wang* [2005] UKHL 9.

failing to identify the desired midway course. This was the view of the Law Commission in its recent consultation[27] although it has subsequently chosen not to recommend reform of the current formulation. **Table 11.2** provides an overview of cases that have been used to illustrate this criticism.

Table 11.2 Is the actus reus of attempt applied too narrowly?

Case	Facts	Outcome on appeal
Gullefer [1990] 3 All ER 882	D tried to stop a dog race (in which the dog he bet on was losing) by jumping onto the track. He hoped the race would be declared a 'no race' and he would be able to reclaim his bet. D was charged and convicted of attempting to steal the money.	Appeal allowed. D's acts were not beyond mere preparation: he would still have had to go to the bookmakers, demand his money, etc.
Campbell [1991] Crim LR 268	D was arrested a yard away from the door of a Post Office that he intended to rob. He was carrying an imitation firearm, a threatening note and he confessed to the planned robbery. D was charged and convicted of attempted robbery.	Appeal allowed. D's acts were not beyond mere preparation: he had not yet entered the Post Office or made any demands of the cashier.
Geddes [1996] Crim LR 894	D was found in the boys' toilet of a school with various kidnapping paraphernalia. D was charged and convicted of attempted false imprisonment.	Appeal allowed. D's acts were not beyond mere preparation: D was lying in wait but he had not confronted a potential victim.
K [2009] EWCA Crim 1931	D approached a 6-year-old boy playing near his work and asked him if he wanted to watch pornography on the laptop in his office. D was charged and convicted of attempting to cause a child to watch a sexual act (Sexual Offences Act 2003, s12).	Appeal allowed. D's acts were not beyond mere preparation: D had not yet led the child to the laptop (if indeed it was there).

The second area of concern is that the 'more than merely preparatory' test is being applied inconsistently between categories of offences where, despite the restrictive approach exemplified in the cases in **Table 11.2**, certain categories of offences seem to have attracted a considerably broader approach.[28] An example of this is the offence of attempted rape. Although the actus reus of rape is only completed when D achieves penile penetration of V's vagina, anus, or mouth, convictions for attempted rape have been secured on the basis of conduct well short of this. In most such cases, D will be

---

[27] Law Commission, *Conspiracy and Attempts* (Consultation 183, 2007).

[28] For useful discussion of this, see Clarkson, 'Attempt: The Conduct Requirement' (2009) 29 OJLS 25.

found to have attempted rape at the stage of physical confrontation with V. This is illustrated in the case of *Dagnall*.[29]

> **Dagnall** [2003] EWCA Crim 2441
>
> D grabbed V with the intention of raping her and forced her against a fence. Fortunately, a passing police car saw D and intervened. There was no evidence that D had begun to remove V's clothes, let alone attempted the act of penetration. D was charged with attempted rape.
>
> - Crown Court: guilty of attempted rape.
> - Court of Appeal: conviction upheld on appeal.

The third area of concern is that the 'more than merely preparatory' test is being applied inconsistently within individual offence groups, and even within individual offences. For example, in the case of *K*, summarised earlier (Table 11.2), it was held that discussing watching pornography with a child was not beyond mere preparation towards the offence of causing a child to watch a sexual act. However, in a case which was appealed in the same year, *R*,[30] it was held that there could be attempt liability where D sent a text message to a prostitute asking her if she knew of any 12-year-olds available for sex.[31] Similarly, although the court held in *Geddes* (also summarised in Table 11.2) that D was not beyond mere preparation to kidnapping when he was found in a school toilet, a quite different approach was taken in *Tosti* just a year later.

> **Tosti** [1997] Crim LR 746
>
> D was found examining the lock of a barn. D's car was also found nearby, containing metal-cutting equipment. D was charged with attempted burglary.
>
> - Crown Court: guilty of attempted burglary.
> - Court of Appeal: conviction upheld on appeal.

For those who believe that the approach in *Geddes* was applied too narrowly, then the decision in *Tosti* is to be welcomed. However, bearing in mind that D (in *Tosti*) was simply examining the lock, and would have had to have gone back to his car to collect the cutting equipment, etc, the two decisions are difficult to reconcile.

Assessment matters...

When applying the actus reus of attempts to facts in a problem question, it is important to acknowledge that the test is relatively uncertain and that case law thus far has shown signs of inconsistency. From here, draw on the normal meaning of the words from the test itself, combined with a discussion of relevant case law and tell your reader what you think the most likely outcome would be.

---

[29] See also *AG's Reference (No 1 of 1992)* (1992) 96 Cr App R 298; *Paitnaik* [2000] 3 Arch News 2; *MH* [2004] WLR 137.

[30] [2009] 1 WLR 713.

[31] An attempt to arrange a sexual offence with a child (Sexual Offences Act 2003, s14).

11.2.1.4 What if the crime D is attempting would be impossible for her to commit?

This question arises where D tries to commit a principal offence, *but unknown to her*, the commission of that offence would be impossible. An offence may be impossible for a variety of reasons. However, there are two broad categories that should be distinguished: legal impossibility and factual impossibility.

Legal impossibility
D's attempt is *legally* impossible where she tries to commit a principal offence which, contrary to her belief, is not actually an offence known to the law. For example, if D comes from a country where adultery is illegal, and D believing the same is true in England, tries to seduce one of her husband's friends, we could describe her actions as an impossible attempt: she has gone beyond mere preparation towards the commission of what she believes is a principal offence. She has also revealed a criminal character: a willingness to break the law. However, as adultery is not a crime known to English law and, because the actus reus of attempt requires D to have attempted to commit 'an offence', there can be no liability in these circumstances. This was confirmed in *Taaffe*.[32]

Factual impossibility
D's attempt is factually impossible where she tries to commit a principal offence which does exist in English law, but the circumstances surrounding her attempt mean that that offence could not come about. This includes cases of physical impossibility as, for example, where she is trying to kill V who is already dead; trying to steal from an empty safe; etc, as well as cases of inadequate means, such as where D is trying to kill V by putting pins in a voodoo doll; trying to shoot V with an unloaded gun; etc. In these cases, D has not only demonstrated a general willingness to break the law but has gone beyond mere preparation—on the facts as she believed them to be—towards committing a valid principal offence. In recognition of this culpability, the current law will find attempts liability. This is confirmed in section 1(2) of the CAA 1981.

> (2) A person may be guilty of attempting to commit an offence to which this section applies even though the facts are such that the commission of the offence is impossible.

This subsection does not undermine the requirement for D's acts to have been more than merely preparatory towards the commission of an offence. Rather, it provides an alternative route to satisfy this element. Let us take the example where D tries to shoot V with a gun that is, unknown to her, not loaded. Applying the actus reus of attempted murder, we first ask whether D's acts in pulling the trigger have gone beyond mere preparation of killing V in reality? The answer here may be 'no': D cannot cause an unloaded gun to fire and so, in reality, the intended shooting still requires D to go and buy bullets etc (ie it is insufficiently proximate). However, where the answer to this first question is 'no', section 1(2) allows us to ask a second question: have D's acts gone beyond mere preparation *on the facts as she believed them to be*? Where the answer to this second question is 'yes', as it would be in our example, D will have satisfied the

---

[32] [1983] 2 All ER 625: D attempted to import foreign currency, believing (incorrectly) that this was a crime. No liability for attempt.

actus reus of the attempt. Where the answer to both questions is 'no', of course, there will be no attempts liability.

In certain, and perhaps even most, cases, the application of this rule appears uncontroversial. In our unloaded gun case, for example, D has shown herself willing to complete all the acts she believes are necessary to kill another person, demonstrating her culpability, and the mere fact of failure on this occasion does not prevent her future dangerousness, thereby demonstrating the continued need to protect. However, isolated from D's intentions/beliefs, impossible attempts will often involve seemingly innocent conduct, such as clicking the trigger of an unloaded gun, putting sugar in tea (believing it is poison), handling goods (believing them to be stolen) and so on. Because such cases can seem so innocuous, despite the terms of section 1(2) of the CAA 1981, the courts initially wavered when applying the new test. We see this in *Anderton v Ryan*.

Anderton v Ryan [1985] UKHL 5

D admitted to police that she was in possession of a stolen video recorder. However, the police could not trace the origin of the recorder in order to prove that it was stolen. D was charged with attempting to handle stolen goods.[33]

- Magistrates' court: not guilty of attempting to handle stolen goods—ruled out by impossibility.
- Divisional Court: appeal allowed. The case was sent back with an instruction to convict—an impossible attempt is still an attempt.
- House of Lords: appeal against conviction allowed (Lord Edmund-Davies dissenting)—the majority held that section 1(2) only extended attempts liability to certain cases of factual impossibility and this was not one of them.

However, when the House of Lords readdressed the issue of impossible attempts in *Shivpuri* just a year later, the opposite conclusion was reached and *Anderton v Ryan* was overruled. It was confirmed, in line with section 1(2), that factual impossibility would never undermine attempts liability.[34]

Shivpuri [1987] AC 1

D was arrested by customs officials with a suitcase which he 'confessed' contained prohibited drugs. However, analysis of the contents showed that it actually contained simple vegetable matter (ie not prohibited drugs). D was charged with attempting to be knowingly concerned in dealing with a prohibited drug.[35]

- Crown Court: guilty of attempting the drugs offence.
- Court of Appeal: conviction upheld on appeal.
- House of Lords: appeal dismissed—*Anderton v Ryan* overruled.

---

[33] The offence of handling stolen goods is discussed at **9.5**.

[34] The court was heavily influenced by Williams, 'The Lords and Impossible Attempts' (1986) 45 CLJ 33.

[35] Customs and Excise Management Act 1979, s170(1)(b).

Post-*Shivpuri*, the legal position on impossible attempts is clear. Even where D's acts do not go beyond mere preparation in fact, they may still satisfy the actus reus of attempts if they go beyond mere preparation on the facts *as D believed them to be*.[36]

11.2.2 Mens rea of attempts

As with the other inchoate offences, and as illustrated in **Table 11.1**, the major part of D's mens rea relates to her completion of the future principal offence. This is an ulterior mens rea: mens rea as to a principal offence (eg murder, theft, handling stolen goods etc) that need never be completed in fact. Such mens rea is vital to D's liability, representing the gravamen of inchoate liability. Without such mens rea, D has simply completed acts that may appear entirely innocent, particularly in the context of impossible attempts. With proof of her mens rea, however, D's acts are revealed as culpable acts in pursuit of a principal offence and deserving of criminalisation. For example, D puts sugar in V's tea believing that that sugar is poison and intending to kill.

It is on this basis that section 1(1) of the CAA 1981 explicitly requires D to act 'with intent to commit an offence'. In the Law Commission's work preceding the CAA 1981, it was believed that D would only be correctly held liable for an attempt where she was fully committed (ie where she *intended*) to go on to commit every element of the offence attempted.[37] This approach was adopted within the statute. However, as we will discuss in the following section, applying the requirement that D intends the principal offence has not always been straightforward.

11.2.2.1 Intending the principal offence

When asking if D intends the principal offence, we need to examine whether D (when acting) intended to bring about the elements of the actus reus of the principal offence. The mens rea term 'intention' here carries the same meaning as it does at common law: including both direct (purposive) and oblique (defined in *Woollin*) intention.[38] Thus, for example, where D is charged with attempting to cause GBH, D must have intended the actus reus of that offence (to cause GBH) to be liable.

The requirement of an intention to commit the actus reus of the principal offence (subject to the discussion later) applies regardless of the mens rea requirements of that principal offence. This is illustrated in the case of *Whybrow*.

Whybrow (1951) 35 Cr App R 141

D wired up a soap dish in his bathroom in order to give his wife an electric shock. D was charged with attempted murder.

- Crown Court: guilty of attempted murder. The trial judge directed the jury that the mens rea for attempted murder is the same as for murder: intention to kill or cause GBH.

---

[36] For a more recent case, see *Pace* [2014] EWCA Crim 186: D handling and converting non-stolen goods but suspecting them to be stolen, and thus satisfying the actus reus of attempt.

[37] Law Commission, *Attempt, and Impossibility in Relation to Attempt, Conspiracy and Incitement* (No 102, 1980).

[38] Confirmed in *Pearman* (1984) 80 Cr App R 259; *Walker* (1989) 90 Cr App R 226. For a discussion of 'intention', see **3.4.1**.

- Court of Criminal Appeal: appeal dismissed. The direction was wrong to include 'intention to cause GBH' but the misdirection did not render the verdict unsafe. The mens rea for attempted murder requires D to intend to kill.

As clarified in *Whybrow*, although the mens rea of murder allows for an intention to kill *or to cause GBH*, the mens rea for attempted murder requires D to intend to complete the actus reus of the principal offence. Thus, as the actus reus for murder requires D to kill V (ie GBH is not sufficient), only an intention to kill will satisfy the mens rea of attempted murder. The same rule applies in relation to principal offences that require a mens rea of less than intention: for attempts liability, D must act with the *intention* to complete the actus reus. For example, attempted criminal damage requires an intention to cause damage despite the principal offence requiring only recklessness as to damage;[39] attempted ABH requires an intention to cause ABH despite the principal offence requiring no mens rea as to this harm at all;[40] and so on.[41]

As with all ulterior mens rea, an intention to commit the principal offence includes a conditional intention to do so. A conditional intention, as we have discussed,[42] arises where D decides to do something (ie in this case, to commit a principal offence) but *only* if a certain condition arises or, alternatively, *unless* certain conditions arise. This was discussed in *AG's References (Nos 1 and 2 of 1979)*.

🔲 *AG's References (Nos 1 and 2 of 1979)* [1980] QB 180

Combined cases in which D (in each case) was arrested in the process of trying to steal non-specific items from another's premises. In the first case, D had entered the building and was searching for items of value (charged with s 9(1)(a) burglary[43]); in the second, D was arrested when trying to enter the building (charged with attempted s9(1)(a) burglary).

- Crown Court: not guilty in either case—D did not have an intention to steal specific items but merely a conditional intention to steal items if there were any worth taking.
- Court of Appeal: Crown Court was wrong. D could have been convicted in either case. A conditional intention to steal is still an intention to steal.

The clarification of the law in *AG's References (Nos 1 and 2 of 1979)* seems entirely sensible: just as D intends to steal if she has specific items in mind, so she intends to steal if she has a conditional intention to steal unspecified items.

Confusion pre-*AG's References (Nos 1 and 2 of 1979)*, concerning how such cases should be charged, provides a useful reminder that care must be taken to identify exactly what D is intending. For example, in *Easom*,[44] D rummaged through a woman's handbag in a theatre and then, finding nothing worth taking, put it back. The bag was connected to a policewoman's wrist by a thread. D was charged with attempted theft of the bag and its contents such as

---

[39] *Millard and Vernon* [1987] Crim LR 393. See **9.7**.

[40] See **7.4**.

[41] Horder, 'Varieties of Intention, Criminal Attempts and Endangerment' (1994) 14 LS 335.

[42] See **3.4.1.3**.

[43] See **9.4.1**.

[44] [1971] 2 QB 315; followed in *Husseyn* (1977) 67 Cr App R 131. The way to avoid the problem in both cases was provided in *AG's References (Nos 1 and 2 of 1979)*.

tissues. D was correctly acquitted of these charges because he was not intending to steal by permanently depriving D of the bag or those specified contents. Rather, D was attempting to steal items of value that he did not find; these were the items he intended to permanently deprive from V. If the charging indictment had reflected this by stating 'attempting to steal contents of the handbag' then he could and should have been found liable.[45]

> **Don't be confused...**
> Try to remember, simply, that a conditional intention as to future acts is still an intention. Indeed, all future intention can be described as conditional to some degree, whether D makes this explicit or not. Taking the example of attempted theft, if we asked any would-be thief if she intends to steal if she discovers she is being watched by the police; if she wins the lottery and becomes a millionaire; etc, the answer is likely to be 'no'—her intention to steal is conditional on these facts not arising. In this way, just because D is explicit about certain conditions in a case will not undermine her intention.

11.2.2.2 Expanding what it means to intend the offence

So far, so good: D must act with the intention, including conditional intention, to commit the actus reus of the future principal offence. However, unfortunately, the application of this approach in practice has revealed an apparent unfairness, and the courts have reacted to this by reinterpreting the statute.

This apparent unfairness arose in the context of attempted rape, in the case of *Khan*.

> **Khan** [1990] 2 All ER 783
>
> D and others tried to have sex with V (a 16-year-old girl) who was not consenting. Each of the defendants was reckless as to her non-consent. The defendants who had achieved penetration were straightforwardly guilty of rape. However, D did not achieve penetration and was charged with attempted rape.
>
> • Crown Court: guilty of rape—the mens rea for attempted rape is the same as for the principal offence of rape.
> • Court of Appeal: *The judgment of the Court of Appeal is discussed below...*

Applying section 1(1) of the CAA 1981 literally, the judgment of the Crown Court in *Khan* appears to be wrong. If, for attempt liability, D must intend *every* element of the actus reus of the principal offence, then the mens rea for attempted rape is not the same as the mens rea for rape. The principal offence of rape is satisfied by an intention to cause penile penetration of V's vagina, anus or mouth, but it requires a lesser mens rea as to the circumstance requirement of V's non-consent (recklessness when *Khan* was decided; a lack of reasonable belief in consent under the current law[46]). Simply, it is a nonsense to say that attempts liability requires intention as to every element, rape liability requires less than intention as to the circumstance element, and the mens rea of the two are the same. If the CAA 1981 is followed, attempted rape should require a mens rea of intention as to every element of the actus reus, including intention or knowledge as to the circumstance element.[47]

---

[45] Campbell, 'Conditional Intention' (1982) 2 LS 77.

[46] See **8.2**.

[47] As discussed at **3.4.2**, in the context of circumstance elements, knowledge and intention are applied as equivalent states of mind.

The problem with this conclusion in relation to *Khan*, is that it would undermine his liability for attempted rape. D was *reckless* as to V's non-consent; he did not *intend* that she was not consenting. However, what D did in trying to have non-consensual intercourse with V, being reckless as to her non-consent, was so similar to those defendants who were liable for rape that a lack of liability for attempted rape would appear to expose a problem with the law.[48] The Court of Appeal chose to avoid this problem by reinterpreting what it means to intend to commit the offence.

> **Khan** [1990] 2 All ER 783
>
> • Court of Appeal: conviction upheld on appeal. Attempts liability requires D to *intend* the physical parts of the principal offence (ie in this case, the act of penetration), but need not include an intention as to attendant circumstances (ie in this case, V's lack of consent). Thus, in relation to such attendant circumstances, it is sufficient for D to have the same mens rea as required for the principal offence (ie in this case, recklessness).

For the Court of Appeal, 'with intent to commit an offence' should be interpreted as requiring an intention to commit the physical parts of the principal offence—that is, any act and result elements—but allows for mens rea less than intention as to any circumstance elements. On this basis, the court was able to find D liable for attempted rape. Indeed, following this case, the Law Commission has not only endorsed the approach in *Khan*, but has also recommended the CAA 1981 to be amended to make this approach clearer.[49] The *Khan* approach needs to be applied with care and requires separation of the elements of the principal offence which D has attempted in order to identify the correct mens rea. Applied to an offence of attempted criminal damage, for example, this would require D to intend the result element of causing damage, even though the principal offence would be satisfied by recklessness. However, it would allow for recklessness as to the circumstance element that the property damaged belongs to another, thereby mirroring the mens rea of the principal offence.

Khan represents the current law. We discuss this approach and others in the reform section later in the chapter.[50] However, even at this stage, it is useful to have an idea of some of the problems with the *Khan* approach in practice. Four criticisms should be noted.

A) **Difficulty in separating offence elements:** The approach taken in *Khan* had been mooted by the Law Commission when it was making its recommendations which led to the CAA 1981. However, the approach was rejected at that time, chiefly because of the difficulty of separating principal offences into conduct, circumstance, and result elements.[51] In order to apply the *Khan* approach, such separation is essential: although mens rea as to the circumstance element can mirror that required for the principal offence, mens rea as to the conduct and result elements are fixed at intention.

---

[48] Williams, 'The Problem of Reckless Attempts' [1983] Crim LR 365.

[49] Law Commission, *Conspiracy and Attempts* (No 318, 2009) paras 8.87–8.141.

[50] See **11.6**.

[51] Law Commission, *Attempt, and Impossibility in Relation to Attempt, Conspiracy and Incitement* (No 102, 1980) paras 2.11–2.13. Buxton, 'The Working Paper on Inchoate Offences' [1973] Crim LR 656; Buxton, 'Circumstances, Consequences and Attempted Rape' [1984] Crim LR 25.

> *Assessment matters…*
>
> When applying the *Khan* approach to facts in a problem question, you will have to separate the circumstance element of the principal offence. The tables that we use in this book (setting out elements in this way) should help you. However, it is important to remember that the choices we have made in these separations are matters of judgement and would not necessarily be shared by others. With this in mind, when you apply the approach in practice, it is perfectly acceptable to identify what is likely to be considered the circumstance element but to remark that such a choice is not an objective one.

B) **Lack of clarity regarding mens rea for the circumstance element:** Where the principal offence requires subjective mens rea as to the circumstance element (eg intention, recklessness etc) then it is clear from *Khan* that the mens rea for attempt should mirror this standard. However, it remains unclear whether the courts will allow a similar mirroring if the circumstance element of the principal offence allowed for negligence or strict liability. For example, in a case similar to *Khan* today (ie post-Sexual Offences Act 2003) would D have to be reckless as to V's non-consent, or would it be sufficient to mirror the principal offence mens rea (ie a lack of reasonable belief in consent)? The answer to this is uncertain. However, it is likely that courts would follow the Law Commission's interpretation that there should be a minimum mens rea of recklessness even where the circumstance element of the principal offence would require less.[52]

C) **What if the principal offence includes an ulterior mens rea element?** *Khan* helps us to identify the mens rea for an attempt in relation to the conduct, circumstance, and result elements of an offence, but does not tell us what mens rea will be required as to an ulterior mens rea element within the principal offence. This issue arose in *AG's Reference (No 3 of 1992).*

> **AG's Reference (No 3 of 1992)** (1993) 98 Cr App R 383
>
> D (and others) threw petrol bombs towards a car containing V, reckless as to the endangerment of V. The throws missed. D was charged with attempted aggravated arson.[53]
>
> - Crown Court: not guilty of attempted aggravated arson. Although the principal offence allowed for liability where D is merely reckless as to the endangerment of life (ulterior mens rea requirement), an attempt requires D to intend to endanger life.
> - Court of Appeal: Crown Court was wrong. D should have been found guilty. Following *Khan*, it is sufficient for D's mens rea in attempt to reflect the mens rea required for the principal offence.

This case is highly problematic. Although the Court of Appeal claimed to be following *Khan*, the element of the principal offence they were dealing with (recklessness as to the endangerment of life) is poorly characterised as a circumstance element. However, if we see it as anything other than a circumstance element (eg, as a result element) then *AG's Reference (No 3 of 1992)* represents a further extension of the *Khan* precedent (ie allowing

---

[52] Law Commission, *Conspiracy and Attempts* (No 318, 2009) para 8.133.
[53] See **9.7.5**.

less than intention) outside circumstances. The general confusion surrounding what this case represents makes it unlikely to be followed. It is contended that where a principal offence includes an ulterior mens rea element, this must be *intended* for attempts liability.[54]

D) What if the offence D is attempting is impossible? The potential scenario where D's attempt is impossible, *and* where D was reckless as to the circumstances, was another reason for the Law Commission's rejection of a *Khan*-like approach prior to the CAA 1981.[55] For example, if D intentionally breaks a vase, being reckless as to whether she owns it (ie recklessness as to circumstances), and where we later discover that she did own it, the crime is impossible and thus it would seem inappropriate to find liability for attempted criminal damage.[56] It is this final area of concern that has led to the latest twist in the case law, discussed in the following section.

11.2.2.3 Re-narrowing what it means to intend the offence?

As feared, a case has come before the courts that combines an impossible attempt with potential recklessness as to circumstances: *Pace*.

Pace [2014] EWCA Crim 186

Undercover police officers sold scrap metal at a scrap metal yard to D and another, intimating that the metal was stolen. As the metal was not in fact stolen, D was charged with attempting to convert criminal property.[57]

- Crown Court: guilty of attempting to convert criminal property. The fact that the attempt was impossible, because the metal was not criminal property, does not bar liability; and following *Khan* it is sufficient that D had a mens rea of suspicion as to the circumstance element of the principal offence (ie suspicion rather than intention that the property was stolen).
- Court of Appeal: appeal allowed. Attempts liability requires D to intend every element of the actus reus of the principal offence, including any circumstance elements.

The Court of Appeal in *Pace* explicitly rejected the reasoning that led to the judgment in *Khan*, drawing on a number of the criticisms of *Khan* listed earlier. However, crucially, *Pace* could not overrule *Khan*, so distinguishes it on the dual basis that: (a) *Khan* was not intended to create a general rule for attempts; and (b) *Khan* did not involve an impossible attempt.[58]

11.2.2.4 Intending the offence under the current law

The current law, following *Khan* and *Pace*, is at something of a crossroads (see **Table 11.3**). Despite the efforts to distinguish the two cases in *Pace*, it is difficult to avoid the conclusion that the two approaches are irreconcilable, representing different interpretations of the 'wrongs' of attempt liability. We must therefore wait for an appeal to the Supreme

---

54 Child, 'The Structure, Coherence and Limits of Inchoate Liability: The New Ulterior Element' (2013) 34 LS 537.

55 Law Commission, *Attempt, and Impossibility in Relation to Attempt, Conspiracy and Incitement* (No 102, 1980) paras 2.99–2.100.

56 Williams, 'The Government's Proposals on Criminal Attempts—III' (1981) 131 NLJ 128.

57 Contrary to the Proceeds of Crime Act 2002, s327(1).

58 *Pace* [2014] EWCA Crim 186, [52].

Court or for the very unlikely eventuality of legislative reform to decide between them. In this regard, there is academic opinion encouraging the court in either direction.[59]

In the meantime, for the lower courts (*and for answers to problem questions*), we may see the mens rea of attempts diverging between impossible and possible attempts: impossible attempt cases applying *Pace* and requiring intention as to every element of the principal offence attempted, and attempts that are possible applying *Khan* and requiring intention as to conduct and results, but allowing mens rea as to circumstances to mirror that required for the principal offence. To illustrate this distinction, we can use the example of attempted criminal damage. Remember that the principal offence of criminal damage has a mens rea of recklessness, both as to circumstances (ownership of the property) and results (damage to the property).[60]

Table 11.3 Applying *Khan* and *Pace*

Facts	Which case to apply?
D intentionally tries to damage property, being reckless as to whether it belongs to her. The property belongs to V.	Possible attempt = apply *Khan* D is liable for attempted criminal damage because she intended the conduct and result, and her mens rea as to the circumstance mirrored that of the principal offence.
D intentionally tries to damage property, being reckless as to whether it belongs to her. The property does belong to her.	Impossible attempt = apply *Pace*. D is not liable for attempted criminal damage because she does not intend or know every element of the principal offence.
D intentionally tries to damage property that she knows belongs to V.	D is liable for attempted criminal damage (whether the attempt is possible or not) because she intends every element of the principal offence.
D is reckless as to causing damage to property that she knows belongs to V.	D is not liable for attempted criminal damage (whether the attempt is possible or not) because she does not intend the result element of the principal offence.

Distinguishing the mens rea of possible and impossible attempts in this way is no more than a temporary position until one approach (*Khan* or *Pace*) is chosen definitively over the other. Not only does the distinction make the law overly complex, but it is also unprincipled, as the reasoning in the two cases clash; not being isolated to possible or impossible attempts. It will also be very difficult to apply in practice since it will not always be clear whether an attempt is possible or impossible.[61]

---

[59] In support of the approach in *Pace*, see Child and Hunt, '*Pace and Rogers* and the Mens Rea of Criminal Attempt: *Khan* on the Scrapheap?' (2014) 78 J Crim L 220; in support of the approach in *Khan*, see Dyson, 'Scrapping *Khan*' [2014] Crim LR 445.

[60] See **9.7**.

[61] Child and Hunt, '*Pace and Rogers* and the Mens Rea of Criminal Attempt: *Khan* on the Scrapheap?' (2014) 78 J Crim L 220.

11.2.3 Defences to criminal attempts

The general defences discussed in **Chapters 13** and **14** apply to criminal attempts in the same way that they apply to other offences. Beyond this, there are no specific defences.

Certain jurisdictions have recognised a defence of withdrawal, where D has gone beyond mere preparation with the required mens rea (ie she has committed an attempt) but then voluntarily desists from carrying it out.[62] It is an illogical defence, D's exculpatory acts coming after the offence has been committed and it has never been incorporated into English law.[63]

11.3 Conspiracy

Conspiracy is defined in section 1 of the Criminal Law Act 1977 (CLA 1977).[64] Under this section, it is an offence for two defendants or more (D1 and D2) to agree to commit a future principal offence. As with attempts, D's liability for conspiracy is tied to the principal offence: D is not guilty of conspiracy *simpliciter*, but of conspiracy to murder, conspiracy to commit theft, conspiracy to rape and so on. D is liable as soon as the agreement is formed with the required mens rea, and whether the agreement is carried out and the principal offence is committed in fact is irrelevant to D's liability for conspiracy.

> *Extra detail...*
> It is common to see prosecutions for conspiracy even where D has completed the principal offence agreed upon. There is nothing to bar this approach, and it can be advantageous for prosecutors in relation to the rules of evidence.[65] However, it has been consistently criticised by the courts[66] and has led to problems in practice.[67]

Alongside statutory conspiracy under the CLA 1977, there also remains a small subset of common law conspiracies. A legacy from the old law of conspiracy pre-CLA 1977, these conspiracies can apply even where D1 and D2 have agreed to do something that may not be a principal offence in its own right. The common law conspiracies which are still recognised within the law are conspiracy to defraud,[68] and conspiracy to corrupt public morals or to outrage public decency. These common law conspiracy offences are highly controversial and the Law Commission has repeatedly recommended their abolition.[69] Each will be discussed briefly, after we have explored the central statutory offence of conspiracy.

The rationale for criminalising conspiracy, as with attempts, is based around a dual logic: allowing for early police intervention to prevent future criminal harms, whilst targeting those whose conduct and mens rea is such that it demonstrates a sufficient

---

[62] Stuart, 'The Actus Reus in Attempts' [1970] Crim LR 505, 519–521.

[63] First rejected in *Taylor* (1859) 1 F & F 511. See also Wasik, 'Abandoning Criminal Intent' [1980] Crim LR 785.

[64] As amended by the CAA 1981, s5.

[65] Klein, 'Conspiracy—The Prosecutor's Darling' (1957) 24 Brook LR 1.

[66] We see such criticism as far back as *Boulton* (1871) 12 Cox CC 87.

[67] Jarvis and Bisgrove, 'The Use and Abuse of Conspiracy' [2014] Crim LR 261.

[68] Already discussed at **10.7.1**.

[69] eg Law Commission, *Fraud* (No 276, 2002).

wrong to be deserving of liability in its own right, even though the full principal offence is not committed. Of course, unlike an attempt which requires a close degree of proximity to the completion of the principal offence, a conspiracy is formed by agreeing to commit an offence and may take place considerably earlier than attempt. However, it has been argued that conspirators still demonstrate sufficient blameworthiness to be deserving of criminalisation. As the Law Commission has highlighted,[70] the conduct of a conspiracy—reaching an agreement—provides useful evidence of D's firm intentions to commit the principal offence.[71] Agreements to commit crimes pose a particular danger due to increased potential for coordinated attacks, for example gang violence, organised property offences, etc. There is also a psychological aspect to an agreed intention, as opposed to an individual intention, which makes D more likely to go through with what she has agreed with another.

The maximum sentence for statutory conspiracy mirrors that of the principal offence which D1 and D2 have conspired to commit.[72] For example, conspiracy to murder carries life, conspiracy to steal is seven years, etc.

(1) …if a person agrees with any other person or persons that a course of conduct shall be pursued which, if the agreement is carried out in accordance with their intentions, either—

(a) will necessarily amount to or involve the commission of any offence or offences by one or more of the parties to the agreement, or

(b) would do so but for the existence of facts which render the commission of the offence or any of the offences impossible,

he is guilty of conspiracy to commit the offence or offences in question.

The elements of conspiracy are set out in **Tables 11.4a** and **11.4b**.

Table 11.4a Statutory conspiracy

	Actus reus	Mens rea
Conduct element	Any action that causes the agreement	Voluntary
Circumstance element	The agreement involves a course of conduct that will necessarily amount to the commission of an offence (on the facts as D1 and D2 believe them to be)	None
Result element	D1 forms an agreement with D2 to pursue a course of conduct	Intention of D1 and D2
Ulterior mens rea element	*	*Set out in Table 11.4b*

---

[70] Law Commission, *Conspiracy and Attempts* (Consultation 183, 2008) Part 2.
[71] Something that is more likely to be lacking in the context of attempts liability.
[72] CLA 1977, s3.

Table 11.4b Ulterior mens rea element for statutory conspiracy

Principal offence	Actus reus of the principal offence
Conduct element	D1 and D2 must intend that the conduct element required for the principal offence is completed by at least one of them
Circumstance element	D1 and D2 must intend/know the circumstances required for the principal offence
Result element	D1 and D2 must intend that the results required (if any) for the principal offence will be completed by at least one of them

As Tables 11.4a and 11.4b makes clear, conspiracy is an offence that requires actus reus and mens rea of at least two defendants: it requires a meeting of minds. As with attempt, the focus of the wrongs involved relate principally to the ulterior mens rea. The criminal liability of each defendant is separate. For each defendant, it is necessary to prove her mens rea. D1 can be guilty even of D2 is never traced or never prosecuted (perhaps she has fled abroad or died).

11.3.1 Actus reus of conspiracy

The actus reus of conspiracy requires an agreement between D1 and D2 to pursue a course of conduct that will necessarily amount to the commission of a principal offence. These requirements are not defined in any detail within the CLA 1977, but have been the subject of several appellate cases.

11.3.1.1 Agreement to a course of conduct

At its core, the actus reus of conspiracy consists of an agreement between D1 and D2. This does not require the formalities of a contractual agreement valid in civil law, but a *decision* to pursue the criminal course of conduct must have been made.[73] This is illustrated in *Walker*.

 Walker [1962] Crim LR 458

D1 discussed with D2 and D3 the proposition that they should steal a payroll, but D1 later withdrew from the negotiation. Charged with conspiracy to rob.[74]

- Crown Court: guilty of conspiracy to rob.
- Court of Criminal Appeal: appeal allowed. There was no evidence of a decision, of an agreement being reached.

---

[73] Orchard, 'Agreement in Criminal Conspiracy' [1974] Crim LR 297.
[74] Robbery is discussed at **9.3**.

Negotiation, encouragement, or assistance, even actively pursuing a common goal,[75] all fall short of an agreement and cannot amount to conspiracy. However, once an agreement is found, there is no need to go beyond this to show that D has begun any further preparation towards committing the principal offence: the agreement is sufficient.[76] Such agreements may be oral, written, or by any other means. In charging D with conspiracy, it is obviously desirable to have identified D2 and to have direct evidence (eg observation) of their agreement. However, it should be remembered that neither of these are essential, as long as there is sufficient evidence to show that an agreement was reached between D1 and another.[77]

Care should be taken when identifying the relevant agreement, especially where the agreement involves multiple principal offences and/or multiple defendants. In the context of multiple principal offences, such as an agreement to rob *and* to murder V, it is usually appropriate to treat them as two separate conspiracies, even though they are contained within a single agreement.[78] Where there are multiple defendants, the situation may be more complex. It is not essential for every defendant within a conspiracy to have agreed with every other defendant, or even to have made contact with them. We see this, as in **Table 11.5**, in so-called wheel and chain conspiracies.

Table 11.5 Identifying wheel and chain conspiracies

Wheel conspiracies	Wheel conspiracies take place where there is a core individual or group who make agreements with a series of others. Like spokes on a bicycle wheel, these 'others' do not have contact with one another directly, but they are all joined within a single agreement (conspiracy) by the central figure. This may arise, for example, where D plans a bank robbery and contacts several others in order to play their parts as, for example, get away drivers, lookouts etc.
Chain conspiracies	Chain conspiracies take place where D1 agrees with D2, who agrees with D3, who agrees with D4 and so on. Again, although there is no direct communication between defendants beyond those either side of them in the chain, they are all signing up to a single common venture. This may arise, for example, where individuals contact others in order to organise a riot.

The examples in **Table 11.5** involve single conspiracies between multiple defendants where, although not all of the defendants are in communication with one another, they have all agreed to a course of conduct with *at least* one other, and they are all aware of the common nature of the enterprise and share the common intention to commit that offence. In such cases, the agreement between all the defendants can be charged as a single conspiracy. However, where there are parallel but separate

---

[75] eg where both D1 and D2 are trying to kill V.
[76] *Hussain, Bhatti and Bhatti* [2002] Crim LR 407.
[77] *Mehta* [2012] EWCA Crim 2824: conspiracy with persons unknown to defraud the NatWest bank, where there was CCTV evidence of others being involved. See also Smith, 'Proving Conspiracy' [1996] Crim LR 386; Smith, 'More on Proving Conspiracy' [1997] Crim LR 333.
[78] *Taylor* [2002] Crim LR 205.

agreements, those separate agreements should be charged as separate conspiracies. This is discussed in *Shillam*.[79]

> **Shillam** [2013] EWCA Crim 160
>
> There was evidence of a central figure (D2) who supplied illegal drugs and cutting equipment to several others including D1 (the appellant), D3 and D4. Each were charged with a single conspiracy to supply cocaine.
>
> • Crown Court: guilty of conspiracy to supply cocaine.
> • Court of Appeal: appeal allowed. D1, D3, and D4 were not parties to a single grand conspiracy to supply cocaine across the network of dealers. Rather, they were each party to separate conspiracies with D2 in relation to their own supply of cocaine and equipment. Conviction for a conspiracy that spanned all defendants was therefore unsafe.

The same point is made within a useful example from *Griffiths*.[80]

> I employ an accountant to make out my tax return. He and his clerk are both present when I am asked to sign the return. I notice an item in my expenses of £100 and say: 'I don't remember incurring this expense'. The clerk says: 'Well, actually I put it in. You didn't incur it, but I didn't think you would object to a few pounds being saved.' The accountant indicates his agreement to this attitude. After some hesitation I agree to let it stand. On those bare facts I cannot be charged with 50 others in a conspiracy to defraud the Exchequer of £100,000 on the basis that this accountant and his clerk have persuaded 500 other clients to make false returns, some being false in one way, some in another, or even all in the same way. I have not knowingly attached myself to a general agreement to defraud.

In this hypothetical scenario, as in *Shillam*, there is evidence of several separate conspiracies. Multiple defendants can only be grouped within a single conspiracy where they are all agreeing to a *common* course of action (as in Table 11.5).

Excluded agreements: parties to the agreement

Certain classes of agreement cannot give rise to conspiracy liability. For example, although a company can be party to a conspiracy,[81] there can be no conspiracy between a company and the sole controlling director of that company. This is because where the director (D) acts as the sole controlling mind of the company, any conspiracy between the two would involve D effectively conspiring with herself.[82] Section 2(2) of the CLA 1977 also makes three further specific exclusions.

A) **Spouses or civil partners:** Originating from the common law idea of a married couple as a single person and, currently justified on the basis of preserving the stability of marriage, there is no conspiracy where spouses or civil partners agree with one another to commit a principal offence. Of course, where there are other co-conspirators in addition to the spouses, any agreement with these others will qualify as a relevant

---

[79] Jarvis and Bisgrove, 'The Use and Abuse of Conspiracy' [2014] Crim LR 261.
[80] [1966] 1 QB 589.
[81] *ICR Haulage Co Ltd* [1944] KB 551.
[82] *McDonnell* [1966] 1 QB 233.

agreement.[83] Despite Law Commission recommendations to abolish this exclusion, it remains effective.[84]

B) Persons under the age of criminal responsibility: Where D1 agrees with a child under the age of 10, there can be no meeting of criminal minds because an infant is not legally capable of forming a criminal intent.[85]

C) The intended victim of the principal offence: There is no conspiracy where D1 agrees with D2 to commit an offence where D2 is the intended victim, and the offence involved is one designed to protect D2. For example, there is no conspiracy where D1 and D2 agree to kidnap D2, or to cause GBH to D2.[86]

Excluded agreements: principal offences

Agreements may also be excluded if they relate to certain principal offences. Care should be taken here, as the exclusions do not mirror those in relation to attempts discussed earlier. Most importantly, it is possible for D to conspire to commit a summary only offence (although it is not possible to attempt summary only offences).[87] This was thought necessary, in the context of conspiracy, to guard against the planning of multiple summary only offences on a widespread scale.[88] It is also possible to conspire to commit other inchoate offences.[89]

The only major exclusion, in the context of conspiracy, is that D cannot conspire to commit an offence as a secondary party. We discuss complicity in **Chapter 12**. For example, where D1 and D2 agree to send a letter to P to encourage her to kill V, and P goes on to kill V, D1 and D2 may be liable for conspiring to commit the inchoate offence of assisting or encouraging murder (discussed later), but they will not be liable for conspiracy to commit murder as a secondary party.[90]

11.3.1.2 Necessarily amount to or involve the commission of a crime

Having established that D1 and D2 have agreed to a course of conduct, it must then be demonstrated that that course of conduct would necessarily amount to or involve the commission of the principal offence by one of the parties to the agreement.

> *Point to remember…*
> The last part of this is simple, but easily forgotten. Where D1 and D2 agree that someone outside the agreement will commit an offence, there is no conspiracy. There is only a conspiracy where it is agreed that (at least) one of those who are party to the conspiracy will be committing the future principal offence.

The most troublesome part of this requirement is to understand what it means for an agreement to *necessarily* amount to or involve the commission of an offence. Three issues in particular have arisen: (a) where D1 and D2's agreement is vague and imprecise;

---

[83] *Chrastny* [1991] 1 WLR 1381.

[84] Law Commission, *Conspiracy and Attempts* (No 318, 2009) para 5.16.

[85] Discussed by the Law Commission (No 318) para 5.45.

[86] Ibid., para 5.35.

[87] Although consent of the DPP is required: CLA 1977, s4(1).

[88] *Blamires Transport Services Ltd* [1964] 1 QB 278: involving a conspiracy over two years to contravene certain (summary only) Road Traffic Act provisions on multiple occasions.

[89] Discussed at **11.5**.

[90] *Kenning* [2008] EWCA Crim 1534.

(b) where the agreement is conditional; and (c) where the agreement is impossible to carry out. In each of these cases, there are grounds to argue that D1 and D2's agreement will not necessarily amount to or involve the commission of a principal offence. However, a blanket exclusion of this kind would not be in the interests of justice, and so the provision has been interpreted to allow for liability.

What if the agreement is imprecise?

The rule here is relatively simple, but must be applied with care. To be sure that D1 and D2 have agreed to commit a principal offence, there must be sufficient detail within that agreement to be sure that they have agreed to do something criminal (eg an agreement to 'get revenge on James' would not be sufficient) and to identify the offence they have agreed to commit so, an agreement to 'break the law' would not be enough. On the latter, it should be remembered that conspiracy requires a principal offence to which to attach (eg conspiracy to murder) and so, unless we can identify that principal offence, there can be no liability in conspiracy. The agreement must, therefore, cover every element of the principal offence, including any results. For example, an agreement to put poison in V's tea is not a conspiracy to murder unless the agreement is to kill V with that poison: causing death is an essential element of murder and so, for conspiracy to murder, it must be part of the agreement.

Providing it can be proved that D1 and D2 have agreed that all of the elements of a particular offence will be completed, there is no requirement for the agreement to have settled the details of that offence. For example, where D1 and D2 agree to kill V, there may be a conspiracy to murder even though they have not decided when, how or where the killing will be undertaken. Indeed, as long as they have decided that the principal offence will be carried out by one of the parties to the agreement, they need not have decided which one of them will do it. All that is required is for the agreement to have decided upon completing the elements of the principal offence.[91]

What if the agreement is conditional?

Alongside the issue of conditional mens rea, discussed later, conspiracies may also involve explicitly conditional agreements.[92] For example, where D1 and D2 agree to rob a bank *if the coast is clear*, their agreement is conditional on an external factor and, therefore, it could be argued that the agreement is not one that will *necessarily* amount to or involve the commission of the robbery (ie if the coast is not clear, there will be no robbery). Where there is an agreement between multiple actors to commit a future principal offence, conditions of this kind are very likely to be present.

The basic rule here is that, as long as the condition does not fully undermine the potential for the principal offence being completed, then a conditional agreement will still satisfy the actus reus of conspiracy. For example, if D1 and D2 agree to smash a vase *only* if they discover that the vase belongs to them, or to have sexual intercourse with V *only* if V consents, then there can be no conspiracy to commit criminal damage or rape: in each case, the agreement is only to act if an essential element of the principal offence is absent. On the other hand, where the condition does not eliminate the potential for the principal offence (ie specifies a condition under which, or in the absence of

---

[91] Ormerod, 'Making Sense of Mens Rea in Statutory Conspiracies' (2006) 59 CLP 185.

[92] Discussed by the Law Commission in *Conspiracy and Attempts* (Consultation 183, 2007) paras 5.18–5.26.

which, it *will* be committed) then this element of the actus reus of conspiracy will be satisfied. This is illustrated in *O'Hadhmaill*.

> **⬜ *O'Hadhmaill* [1996] Crim LR 509**
>
> D, who was a member of the IRA, was found in possession of explosives and planned targets. D was charged with conspiracy to cause explosions. D claimed that there was no conspiracy, because the plan was not to use the explosives unless the ceasefire, which was then in operation, came to an end.
>
> - Crown Court: guilty of conspiracy to cause explosions.
> - Court of Appeal: conviction upheld on appeal—a conditional agreement to commit an offence is sufficient for liability.

In *O'Hadhmaill*, although the agreement might not have led to the use of explosives if the ceasefire held, there remained a conditional agreement to use the explosives if the ceasefire ended: this is sufficient. Indeed, even if the condition that leads to the principal offence being committed is unlikely, as long as there is a genuine agreement that, if that condition came about, it would be committed, then there can be a conspiracy.[93]

Crucial to conditional agreements is that D1 and D2 are not still negotiating in relation to a future decision, they are pre-empting and making that future decision in advance: they are deciding that under a certain condition, they *will* commit the principal offence. Thus, for example, where D1 and D2, who work in a bureau de change, agree to 'transfer money if it is not criminal property' then there can be no conspiracy: there is no agreed position on what they will do if the money is criminal property. However, if they agree to 'transfer the money even if it turns out to be criminal property' then there will be a conspiracy: they have decided that if a certain condition comes about (that the property is criminal) they *will* commit the principal offence.[94]

The case of *Reed*[95] is useful to exemplify a correct decision by the court, but a faulty hypothetical. In this case, D and others conspired to aid and abet suicide.[96] The agreement was that D would visit suicidal individuals, and either discourage them or actively help them to commit suicide, depending upon Vs' needs. The agreement was conditional on Vs' state, but sufficient for conspiracy, because D would necessarily commit the principal offence if the condition arose. However, the court provided a hypothetical where they claimed no conspiracy would be found.

> D1 and D2 agree to drive from London to Edinburgh in a time which can be achieved without exceeding the speed limits but only if the traffic which they encounter is exceptionally light.

The court in *Reed* commented that this would not be a conspiracy to exceed the speed limits, even if the parties agree that they will do so if it is necessary as where they are delayed on certain parts of the journey. Presumably, the court would like to distinguish

---

[93] *Jackson* [1985] Crim LR 444: conspiracy to pervert the course of justice where D1 and D2 agreed to shoot V in the leg if V was found guilty of a separate crime, the idea being to encourage judicial lenience at sentencing.

[94] Campbell, 'Conditional Intention' (1982) 2 LS 77.

[95] [1982] Crim LR 819.

[96] Discussed at **11.4.6**.

this hypothetical from the facts of *Reed* because the agreement to speed under certain conditions is incidental to the central agreement to meet in Edinburgh at a certain time. However, it can be argued that this reasoning is faulty, and if accepted will only encourage uncertainty and incoherence. Just as D1 and D2 foreclose a future decision in *Reed* (ie agree to commit the principal offence under certain conditions), exactly the same is true within the hypothetical scenario, and a conspiracy to exceed the speed limit should be found.

> **Assessment matters...**
>
> If you encounter similar facts in a problem question to the hypothetical scenario in *Reed* or any other conditional agreement where the principal offence is both conditional and incidental, you should discuss the approach suggested (*obiter*) in *Reed*. You should then decide what you think is more likely for the court to do (ie follow the guidance in *Reed* or apply the rule on conditional agreements strictly suggest).

What if the agreement is impossible?

Just as D may attempt the impossible as, for example, trying to kill V, being unaware that she is already dead, so D1 and D2 may also conspire to commit an impossible offence by agreeing to kill V, being unaware that she is already dead. In the context of attempts, we found that D would have no liability for attempting to do an act that D wrongly believes amounts to a criminal offence. However, factual impossibility would not prevent D satisfying the actus reus of attempt as long as it was satisfied on the facts as D believed them to be so, for example, D is liable for attempting to kill V if D believes V is alive and capable of being killed.[97] In line with the approach to attempts, section 1(1)(b) of the CLA 1977 (as amended by s5 of the CAA 1981) makes it clear that factual impossibility also does not undermine liability for conspiracy.

> (1) ...if a person agrees with any other person or persons that a course of conduct shall be pursued which, if the agreement is carried out in accordance with their intentions, either—
>
> (a) will necessarily amount to or involve the commission of any offence or offences by one or more of the parties to the agreement, or
>
> (b) would do so but for the existence of facts which render the commission of the offence or any of the offences impossible,
>
> he is guilty of conspiracy to commit the offence or offences in question.

As section 1(1) makes clear, the actus reus requirement, that the agreement must necessarily amount to or involve the commission of a principal offence, can be satisfied either on the objective facts of the case (s1(1)(a): possible conspiracies) or on the facts as D wrongly believes them to be (s1(1)(b): impossible conspiracies). Mirroring the approach to attempts, this means that D may be liable even if the principal offence is factually impossible, although it will be undermined by legal impossibility.[98] D1 and D2 can be guilty of conspiring to kill V who is, unknown to them, already dead. They cannot be guilty of conspiring to commit adultery (an offence unknown to English law).

[97] See **11.2.1.4**.
[98] The old law (pre-amendment by the CAA 1981) had barred liability for conspiracy where the principal offence was impossible: *DPP v Nock* [1978] AC 979.

11.3.2 Mens rea of conspiracy

In comparison to the other general inchoate offences, the mens rea for conspiracy[99] is relatively straightforward and does not require us to identify the separate elements of the principal offence in order to apply it. In relation to her own immediate actions, the sole requirement is that D must intend to form the agreement.[100] It is irrelevant whether D realises that what she is agreeing to is a principal offence; ignorance of the law is no excuse.[101] In relation to the future principal offence, D must intend or know that, in accordance with their agreement, *every* element of that offence will be completed, whether by D or one of her co-conspirators. Crucially, for there to be a conspiracy, it must be demonstrated that D and *at least one other party* to the agreement satisfy this mens rea.

As with attempts, the aspect of mens rea that has caused the courts the most problems has been the ulterior mens rea requirements relating to the future principal offence. Four main issues should be highlighted.

11.3.2.1 At least two defendants must intend the principal offence

It is clear in section 1(1) of the CLA 1977 that D and at least one of the other people that she is alleged to have conspired with must intend that it will be carried out 'in accordance with their intentions'. Some care must be taken when applying this in practice, and it should be remembered that we are looking at the parties' intentions at the point they form the agreement. A useful case to illustrate this is *Yip Chiu-Cheung*.

> **Yip Chiu-Cheung** [1995] 1 AC 111
>
> D1 arranged with D2 (an undercover police officer) to traffic illegal drugs between Hong Kong and Australia. D2 intended to carry out the plan but to also inform the authorities in both countries in order to identify both the suppliers and the recipients of the drugs—so both could be arrested. However, D2 missed his flight and the plan failed. D1 was charged with conspiracy to traffic dangerous drugs.
>
> - Hong Kong court: guilty of conspiracy to traffic dangerous drugs.
> - Hong Kong Court of Appeal: conviction upheld on appeal.
> - Privy Council: appeal dismissed. Although D2's aim was to arrest D1 at a later stage, at the time of agreeing with D1, he was intending that the principal offence (drug trafficking) would happen, thus we have a common intention. D2's motive for his intention is irrelevant.

This case is discussed at length by the Law Commission.[102] D1 is liable for conspiracy to traffic dangerous drugs because he made an agreement with D2 to do so, which satisfies the actus reus of conspiracy. At *the time of that agreement* both D1 and D2 intended that the principal offence would be carried out, thereby satisfying the mens rea of conspiracy. D2's motives are irrelevant. Equally, the fact that D2 later changed his mind after missing his flight is also irrelevant, what matters is the state of mind of both parties at the time of the agreement.

---

[99] Ormerod, 'Making Sense of Mens Rea in Statutory Conspiracies' (2006) 59 CLP 185.
[100] *Prior* [2004] Crim LR 849.
[101] *Broad* [1997] Crim LR 666.
[102] *Conspiracy and Attempts* (Consultation 183, 2007) paras 8.11–8.26.

If the undercover police officer, D2, had made the original agreement with the intention of intervening *before* the principal offence took place then there would be no conspiracy. On these amended facts, the actus reus of the conspiracy may have been completed by the agreement but the mens rea would be absent, as they would not *both* intend that the principal offence be completed. If D1 and D2 were the only parties to the potential conspiracy, a lack of mens rea from D2 would mean that neither party commits the offence: even though D1 intended the principal offence, if D2 did not then there can be no common intention. Of course, if there was another party to the agreement who did intend the principal offence (D3), then there could still be a conspiracy between D1 and D3, but D2 would not be liable.[103]

Don't be confused...
Although this example involves undercover police officers, the same rules apply where anyone agrees with another to commit a principal offence, without the intention that it should be completed.

11.3.2.2 A conditional intention is still an intention

Earlier (**11.3.1.2**) we discussed conditional agreements as part of the actus reus of conspiracy. In line with this, where the agreement is conditional, D is likely to have a conditional intention: an intention to commit the principal offence *only* if certain conditions are present/absent. For example, where D1 and D2 agree to rob a bank as long as the coast is clear, we have both a conditional agreement and, if D1 and D2's intentions are in line with that agreement, a conditional intention. Even where the agreement between D1 and D2 is unconditional (eg simply agreeing to rob the bank), it is still possible for either or both to have a conditional intention, as where D1 agrees but only intends to go ahead with the plan if she can get a gun. Indeed, as the House of Lords recognised in *Saik*, 'In the nature of things, every agreement to do something in the future is hedged about with conditions, implicit if not explicit.'[104]

In line with the approach taken to conditional agreements, the core point here is that a conditional intention to commit a principal offence still amounts to an intention to commit it, and will satisfy the mens rea of conspiracy. What we are looking for is a decision from D, at the point of agreement, that if a certain condition arises/ is absent then she intends the principal offence to be completed. Again, D is foreclosing a future choice (eg whether to rob the bank) by deciding in advance that if the condition is satisfied she will have the required intention.

11.3.2.3 The parties must intend *every* element of the principal offence

The wording of the statute—'in accordance with their intentions'—carries the clear implication that D1 and D2 must intend every part of the principal offence will be carried out. This was also the stated policy at the time the 1977 Act was created.[105]

---

[103] *McPhillips* (1990) 6 BNIL: D not liable for conspiracy (although others were) when he intended to intervene to prevent the principal offence taking place.

[104] [2006] UKHL 18, [5].

[105] Law Commission, *Report on Conspiracy and Criminal Law Reform* (No 76, 1976) paras 1.41–1.43.

However, as we just saw, the court in *Khan* reinterpreted the CAA 1981 to be satisfied by something less than intention as to every element of the principal offence,[106] and the wording of the CLA 1977 could be interpreted similarly. The facts of *Khan* itself provides a useful example. *Khan*, it will be remembered, involved a number of defendants raping V, and D trying to do so. Each one was reckless as to V's non-consent which was the circumstance element of the principal offence of rape as it was then defined. On these facts, as we discussed, the Court of Appeal held that, even though D did not intend or know that V was not consenting, he could still be liable for attempted rape on the basis of his intention to complete the physical elements of rape (penile penetration of V's vagina), combined with a mens rea as to the circumstance element (V's non-consent) which satisfied that required by the principal offence. Adjusting these facts, what would happen if the parties had agreed their plan in advance? If conspiracy requires intention or knowledge as to *every* element of the principal offence then there would be no conspiracy to rape: the parties lack intention or knowledge as to the circumstance of V's non-consent. However, if the *Khan* approach were applied to conspiracy, liability for conspiracy to rape could be found.

The difference between attempts and conspiracy, however, is that beyond the general requirement of intention, section 1(2) of the CLA 1977 addresses mens rea as to circumstances specifically:

> (2) Where liability for any offence may be incurred without knowledge on the part of the person committing it of any particular fact or circumstance necessary for the commission of the offence, a person shall nevertheless not be guilty of conspiracy to commit that offence by virtue of subsection (1) above unless he and at least one other party to the agreement intend or know that that fact or circumstance shall or will exist at the time when the conduct constituting the offence is to take place.

Under this subsection, a *Khan*-like approach to conspiracy is ruled out: where the principal offence requires a mens rea as to circumstances of anything less than intention or knowledge, D1 and D2 must still intend or know that circumstance for conspiracy liability.

Despite the language of section 1(2), however, in a series of conspiracy cases post-*Khan*, the potential for conspiracy liability, where D did not intend or know the circumstance element of the principal offence, began to gain traction.[107] For example, in *Sakavickas*[108] D was convicted of conspiracy to assist another to retain the benefit of criminal conduct following involvement with a tobacco-importing operation.[109] D claimed that he lacked intention or knowledge that the tobacco had been imported without duty being paid (the circumstance element of the principal offence) but this was held not to be necessary by the Court of Appeal, as long as he had the mens rea required by the principal offence. This line of cases finally came to a head in *Saik*.

---

[106] See **11.2.2.2**.
[107] Ormerod, 'Making Sense of Mens Rea in Statutory Conspiracies' (2006) 59 CLP 185.
[108] [2004] EWCA Crim 2686.
[109] Contrary to the Criminal Justice Act 1988, s93A.

Saik [2006] UKHL 18

D operated a bureau de change with a turnover of around £1,000 a week. However, from 2001 this increased dramatically to over £8 million in a year. Surveillance of D also witnessed him meeting his alleged co-conspirators in parked cars, rather than in the office, to exchange large sums of money. D was charged with conspiracy to launder the proceeds of crime.[110] D intended the physical elements of the principal offence and had a mens rea of 'suspicion' as to the criminal origins of the money (the circumstance element of the principal offence). Suspicion was sufficient mens rea for the principal offence.

- Crown Court: guilty of conspiracy to launder the proceeds of crime.
- Court of Appeal: conviction upheld on appeal. Mens rea as to circumstances can mirror those required by the principal offence.
- House of Lords (Baroness Hale dissenting): appeal allowed, quashing D's conviction. The mens rea of conspiracy requires D to intend or know *every* element of the principal offence and this is confirmed (in relation to circumstances) in section 1(2).

The House of Lords in *Saik* have brought much needed clarity to the law of conspiracy. To be liable, D and at least one other conspirator must intend every element of the principal offence. In this manner, unlike with attempts, it is not necessary to separate the principal offence into its elements in order to identify the mens rea required by D: whether act, circumstance or result, all elements must be intended.

> *Extra detail…*
> Baroness Hale dissented in *Saik* on the basis that liability could be found using conditional intention: within D's intention to convert the money, he intended, both, to launder if the money was criminal and to convert the money if it was not. A counter argument is that this analysis is faulty because D was not making a decision to pre-empt and decide upon a future choice to intend to launder money; he was simply intending the physical parts of the offence foreseeing a risk that the money might be criminal. Indeed, he did not foresee a choice to act with intention in the future at all. Therefore, D did not intend the circumstance, even conditionally. He was reckless.[111]

11.3.2.4 A problem case: *Anderson*

In *Anderson*, the House of Lords created a great deal of uncertainty for the mens rea of conspiracy from which the current law is still recovering. The case has not been overruled. However, its conclusions have been consistently overlooked and/or ignored to the extent that it should no longer be applied.

 Anderson [1986] AC 27

D was part of a group planning to effect the escape of one of them from prison. D was paid to supply diamond wire capable of cutting through metal bars. D was charged with conspiracy to effect

---

[110] Contrary to the Criminal Justice Act 1998, s93C(2); and now an offence under the Proceeds of Crime Act 2002, s327.

[111] Law Commission, *Conspiracy and Attempts* (Consultation 183, 2007) Part 5.

the escape of a prisoner. D claimed that he only wanted to be paid and did not intend the principal offence to be completed. In fact, he did not believe that it would be successful.

- Crown Court: guilty of conspiracy to effect the escape of a prisoner.
- Court of Appeal: conviction upheld on appeal.
- House of Lords: appeal dismissed. Lord Bridge, with whom the other Lords concurred, stated that conspiracy requires an agreement to commit a principal offence and an intention for D to play his part. However, it does not require an additional intention that the principal offence will be committed.

Anderson suggests that an intention to commit the principal offence is not required for conspiracy but that D must intend to play a role towards that principal offence. Both of these conclusions are highly problematic.

A) **D need not intend the principal offence:** If the parties to an agreement do not need to intend to commit the principal offence then we have the prospect of a conspiracy to commit an offence where no party actually wants it to come about; this is absurd. The approach has not been applied in subsequent cases.[112] For example, in *Ashton*,[113] the Court of Appeal found that there would be no conspiracy to murder where D did not intend the murder to take place: D had agreed the plan to kill V but did not intend that it should come about.

B) **D must intend to play an active role in the principal offence:** The idea that D must intend to play an active role in the principal offence is equally problematic; it would mean having to prove in every case exactly what D's role was going to be beyond simple agreement. This could lead to problems where D orders others (eg those in a gang) to commit an offence but does not plan to play any active role herself. Again, subsequent decisions have reinterpreted the words of Lord Bridge to, effectively, dismiss this requirement. In *Siracusa*,[114] for example, the Court of Appeal attempted to empty the requirement of any real meaning, holding that it would be satisfied where D does not actively intend to take steps to prevent the offence taking place.

The approach in *Anderson* is not likely to be followed and, we suggest, should not be followed in future cases. D1 and at least one other conspirator must intend the principal offence be committed in order for them to be liable for conspiracy. Beyond their agreement, as long as it is intended that one of them will commit the principal offence, there is no need to show that all parties will play an active role.[115]

Assessment matters…

If you encounter facts similar to *Anderson* in a problem question then the case should be discussed—remember that it is a House of Lords judgment and it has not been overruled. However, it is important that your discussion should acknowledge the criticisms of *Anderson* and the approach of subsequent cases, concluding that it is unlikely to be applied.

---

[112] *McPhillips* (1990) 6 BNIL; *Edwards* [1991] Crim LR 45; *Harvey* [1999] Crim LR 70; etc.

[113] [1992] Crim LR 667.

[114] (1989) 90 Cr App R 340.

[115] This corresponds to the Law Commission's analysis of the current law: Law Commission, *Conspiracy and Attempts* (Consultation 183, 2007) paras 4.22–4.41.

11.3.3 Defences to conspiracy

The general defences discussed in **Chapters 13** and **14** apply to conspiracies in the same way that they apply to other offences. Beyond this, there are no specific defences.[116] As with attempts, a defence of withdrawal has been mooted (ie a defence where D conspires but then acts in order to cancel her agreement) but this has not found favour.[117]

As conspiracy is a multi-party offence, it is possible for situations to arise where D1 alone has a defence such as duress, insanity etc. Where this is the case, D1 will not be liable. However, the same is not necessarily true for D2, even where she has only agreed with D1. D2's liability will depend upon whether D1's defence undermines her ability to form an agreement and to share an intention to commit the principal offence. For example, where D1's defence is insanity, and it is accepted that she was not able to appreciate the nature or quality of her conduct, then it is clear that there could not have been any agreement and neither party will have committed conspiracy. However, where D1's defence is duress, for example, whereby D1 was threatened by a third party to conspire with D2, it is still possible for D1 to have agreed and to have shared the required intention. Thus, D2 may still be liable for conspiracy.[118]

11.3.4 Common law conspiracies

Alongside the statutory offence of conspiracy, two examples of common law conspiracy remain active. Preserved by section 5 of the CLA 1977, these offences can apply even where the object of the parties agreement is not in itself an offence.

- **Conspiracy to defraud:** An agreement between two or more to dishonestly deprive or interfere with the property rights of another.
- **Conspiracy to corrupt public morals or to outrage public decency:** An agreement between two or more to act in an highly offensive way.

Conspiracy to defraud remains a frequently used offence and is discussed at **10.7.1**. Conspiracy to corrupt public morals or to outrage public decency is also retained but lacks clear definition in statute or in case law. Rather, in the rare cases where it is applied, the reasoning tends to focus on extreme moral distaste for the subject of the agreement.[119] Examples include *Shaw v DPP*,[120] where D was liable for conspiracy to corrupt public morals when publishing a 'Ladies' Directory' detailing the names, addresses and sexual activities available from various prostitutes; and *Knuller*,[121] where, despite the legalisation of homosexual acts, D was convicted of conspiracy to corrupt public morals when publishing adverts facilitating homosexual encounters. The continued existence

---

[116] The Law Commission has recommended a defence of 'acting reasonably': Law Commission, *Conspiracy and Attempts* (No 318, 2009) Part 6.

[117] *Thomson* (1965) 50 Cr App R 1: confirming that there is no such defence; *McPhillips* (1990) 6 BNIL: providing some support for such a defence.

[118] *Matusevich* (1977) 51 ALJR 657.

[119] This may be unlikely to survive an Art 7 ECHR challenge for lack of certainty.

[120] [1962] AC 220.

[121] [1973] AC 435.

of this offence is further complicated by the debate as to whether corrupting public morals and outraging public decency is itself a principal offence capable of being the subject of conspiracy under the CLA 1977.

> *Extra detail...*
> Although factual impossibility does not undermine liability for statutory conspiracy, it will undermine liability for a common law conspiracy.[122]

11.4 Assisting or encouraging

Offences of assisting or encouraging[123] are contained within Part 2 of the Serious Crime Act 2007 (SCA 2007). As with the other inchoate offences, D is not liable for assisting or encouraging *simpliciter*, but rather for assisting or encouraging a principal offence, for example assisting murder; encouraging theft; etc. In such cases, D is not trying to commit the offence herself (as in attempts) or necessarily agreeing that it should be committed (as in conspiracy) but she is, nevertheless, criminally blameworthy for her conduct in support of the potential principal offender.[124]

The SCA 2007 offences replace the old common law of incitement, where D encouraged P to commit a principal offence with the intention that it should be completed. The SCA 2007 offences cover this conduct but also reach considerably further than the old offence, and considerably further than the Law Commission recommendations that led to the reform.[125] In this regard, although Law Commission material can be useful in understanding the offences, care must be taken to identify points of departure between the Commission's report and the final form of the statute.

Three separate offences are created within Part 2 of the SCA 2007. The maximum penalty for each mirrors that of the principal offence which D has assisted or encouraged.[126]

- Section 44: Intentionally encouraging or assisting an offence.
- Section 45: Encouraging or assisting an offence believing it will be committed.
- Section 46: Encouraging or assisting offences believing one or more will be committed.

As the actus reus of each offence is the same, we will deal with this collectively. We will then explore the different mens rea requirements of each offence in turn. The offences have been rightly criticised for being overly complex in their formulation and have yet to be usefully clarified in the courts; it is therefore essential to work methodically through the offence elements as presented in the statute.

---

122 *DPP v Nock* [1978] AC 979.
123 Fortson, *Blackstone's Guide to the Serious Crime Act 2007* (2008) Ch6; Ormerod and Fortson, 'Serious Crime Act 2007: Part 2 Offences' [2009] Crim LR 389.
124 For a discussion of the rationale of these offences, see Law Commission, *Inchoate Liability for Assisting and Encouraging Crime* (No 300, 2006) Part 4.
125 Law Commission, *Inchoate Liability for Assisting and Encouraging Crime* (No 300, 2006).
126 SCA 2007, s58.

11.4.1 Actus reus of assisting or encouraging

Offences under sections 44, 45, and 46 require the following actus reus:

44 (1)(a) and **45** (a) …an act capable of encouraging or assisting the commission of an offence.

46 (1)(a) …an act capable of encouraging or assisting the commission of one or more of a number of offences.

As with attempts and conspiracy, as soon as D completes this actus reus with the required mens rea, D is liable for assisting or encouraging the offence: it is irrelevant whether P (the person assisted or encouraged) goes on to commit the principal offence.[127]

> **Point to remember…**
> Although irrelevant for the inchoate charge, where P goes on to commit the principal offence, D may be liable as an accomplice. We discuss this in **Chapter 12**.

Several aspects of the actus reus are clarified at other points in the statute. For example, section 65(2)(b) clarifies that D may assist or encourage by act *or omission*, as where a disgruntled security guard assists by omission if she omits to turn on an alarm system in order to assist a robbery.[128] Section 65(2)(a) clarifies that assisting or encouraging an offence includes taking steps to reduce the chance of criminal proceedings being brought against P, as where D acts as a lookout or intimidates witnesses of P's offence. Section 67 clarifies that the actus reus may be a 'course of conduct' as well as a one-off act, as where D sends P a series of weapons components over a period of time.

However, despite these useful points of clarification, the central terms 'encouraging' and 'assisting' are not fully defined.

A) **Encouraging:** Encouraging is intended to mean the same as 'inciting' under the pre-SCA 2007 law.[129] This includes positive acts of instigation, persuasion, or emboldening, as well as negative acts such as threats.[130] Encouraging can be express or implied,[131] and can be targeted at a particular person or addressed to the world at large.[132] Examples under the old law, demonstrating the breadth of the term, include D responding to an advert which invited readers to buy indecent pictures of children, thereby encouraging P to distribute such photos;[133] and where D subscribed to a website showing indecent pictures of children, thereby encouraging the owner of the website to continue their publication.[134]

---

[127] SCA 2007, s49(1).

[128] For omissions liability, D must have a duty to act. See **2.6.2**.

[129] Law Commission, *Inchoate Liability for Assisting and Encouraging Crime* (No 300, 2006) paras 5.32–5.45.

[130] SCA 2007, s65(1).

[131] *Jones* [2010] EWCA Crim 925: implied encouragement to grow cannabis where D gave coded advice on 'growing tomatoes'.

[132] *Parr-Moore* [2003] 1 Cr App R 425: advertising the sale of speed trap blockers, inciting speeding offences.

[133] *Goldman* [2001] Crim LR 894.

[134] *O'Shea* [2004] Crim LR 948.

B) **Assisting:** The SCA 2007 extends the old common law of incitement to include assisting as well as encouraging. This will be useful where D provides P with a tool or with advice, etc, to help with, but not necessarily encourage, the principal offence.[135] As with encouragement, there is no need for D's assistance to be substantial: any act capable of providing any assistance will suffice.

Perhaps the most important qualification of the actus reus is that D does not need to assist or encourage P in fact: D must simply perform acts *capable* of assisting or encouraging P. Thus, for example, where D encourages P to kill V, it does not matter whether this convinces P; whether it has no effect on P at all; or even if P is never aware of it; as long as D's acts were capable of encouraging P to kill then the actus reus is satisfied.[136] In the latter case, the Law Commission use the example of D who places a ladder outside V's house to assist P to commit burglary. Even if P fails to discover the ladder, and knows nothing of D's efforts, D's acts are still capable of assisting P to burgle, and so the actus reus of the SCA offence is complete.

> *Extra detail...*
> Despite extending the offence to cover 'assisting', the SCA 2007 has left a gap where D 'procures' an offence (causes it to happen) without assisting or encouraging. For example, D spikes P's drink intending for P to commit an offence of driving over the prescribed alcohol limit. Where P goes on to commit the offence then D will be liable as a secondary party (discussed in **Chapter 12**). However, where P does not (eg because she realises what has happened), it will be difficult to show that D has assisted or encouraged the offence.[137]

11.4.2 Mens rea of s44: intentionally encouraging or assisting an offence

As with attempts and conspiracy, the gravamen of assisting and encouraging lies in the mens rea.[138] Unfortunately, the unnecessarily complex drafting of the SCA 2007 expresses this requirement across two sections: sections 44 and 47.

> **44** (1) A person commits an offence if...
>
> (a) he intends to encourage or assist its commission...
>
> **47** (1) Sections 44, 45 and 46 are to be read in accordance with this section.

---

[135] Law Commission, *Inchoate Liability for Assisting and Encouraging Crime* (No 300, 2006) paras 5.46–5.51; Sullivan, 'Inchoate Liability for Assisting and Encouraging' [2005] Crim LR 1047

[136] Law Commission, *Inchoate Liability for Assisting and Encouraging Crime* (No 300, 2006) paras 5.27–5.31.

[137] Child, 'The Differences Between Attempted Complicity and Inchoate Assisting and Encouraging—A Reply to Professor Bohlander' [2010] Crim LR 924, 929. D would be liable for a poisoning offence.

[138] Child, 'Exploring the Mens Rea Requirements of the Serious Crime Act 2007 Assisting and Encouraging Offences' (2012) 76 J Crim L 220; Ormerod and Fortson, 'Serious Crime Act 2007: Part 2 Offences' [2009] Crim LR 389.

(2) If it is alleged under section 44(1)(b) that a person (D) intended to encourage or assist the commission of an offence, it is sufficient to prove that he intended to encourage or assist the doing of an act which would amount to the commission of that offence...

(5) In proving for the purposes of this section whether an act is one which, if done, would amount to the commission of an offence—

(a) if the offence is one requiring proof of fault, it must be proved that—

(i) D believed that, were the act to be done, it would be done with that fault;

(ii) D was reckless as to whether or not it would be done with that fault; or

(iii) D's state of mind was such that, were he to do it, it would be done with that fault; and

(b) if the offence is one requiring proof of particular circumstances or consequences (or both), it must be proved that—

(i) D believed that, were the act to be done, it would be done in those circumstances or with those consequences; or

(ii) D was reckless as to whether or not it would be done in those circumstances or with those consequences.

The elements of the section 44 offence are illustrated in **Tables 11.6a and 11.6b.**

Table 11.6a SCA 2007, s44: assisting or encouraging

	Actus reus	**Mens rea**
Conduct element	Any action or omission	Voluntary
Circumstance element	D's conduct is capable of assisting or encouraging P to commit an offence	Intention to assist or encourage the conduct element of P's offence
Result element	None	None
Ulterior mens rea element	*	Set out in **Table 11.6b**

Table 11.6b Ulterior mens rea element for s44 assisting or encouraging

	D's mens rea as to P's principal offence
Conduct element	D must intend that P will complete the conduct element of the principal offence
Circumstance element	D must intend, believe, or be reckless as to the circumstance element of P's principal offence

(Continued)

Table 11.6b Continued

	D's mens rea as to P's principal offence
Result element	D must intend, believe, or be reckless as to whether P will cause the results (if any) required by the principal offence
P's mens rea	D must intend, believe, or be reckless as to whether P will act with the mens rea required by the principal offence Or D must have the mens rea for the principal offence herself

Terminology...
The SCA 2007 uses the term 'fault' to mean the same as 'mens rea'; the term 'consequences' to mean the same as 'results'; and the term 'intention' is used to mean direct intention only.[139]

When considering the mens rea for these offences, it is useful to separate what is required by D in relation to her own conduct and what is required by D in relation to the future conduct and mind of P.

11.4.2.1 D's mens rea as to her own conduct

Section 44(1)(b) states that D must intend that her conduct will assist or encourage P's principal offence. This implies that D must intent to assist or encourage every element of P's offence. However, as sections 47(1) and 47(2) clarify, this is not the case. Rather, 'it is sufficient to prove that [she] intended to encourage or assist the *doing of an act* which would amount to the commission of a crime.'[140]

Therefore, D will satisfy this part of the mens rea if she intends to assist or encourage P, even minimally, to complete the conduct element of the future principal offence. For example, where D is charged with assisting murder in having provided P with a gun, it is sufficient to prove that D intended her conduct to assist P to shoot that gun (the conduct element of P's offence). There is no additional need within this element to show that D intended to assist P to shoot a person (circumstance), or cause death (result).

11.4.2.2 D's mens rea as to P's principal offence

As well as D's intentions as to the impact of her own conduct, D must also have a certain ulterior mens rea as to the future principal offence of P. Unlike conspiracy, and to a lesser extent attempts, D need not intend that *every* element of the principal offence should be completed.

Section 44 is silent on this part of D's mens rea, and so (again) we look to section 47. To identify the required mens rea, and to apply it to case facts, it is necessary to separate the elements of P's principal offence.

---

[139] Oblique intention (discussed at **3.4.1.2**) plays no role with these offences: SCA 2007, s44(2).
[140] Emphasis added.

A) D's mens rea as to P's conduct element: Even section 47 provides no mention of D's mens rea as to the conduct element of P's offence. However, as D must intend to assist or encourage this conduct element (**11.4.2.1**), the most likely interpretation is that D must also *intend* that P will complete it.[141] Using our assisting murder example: D must not only intend, that is, have mens rea as to her own conduct in assisting P's shooting of the gun, she must also intend that P will shoot the gun in fact (ie have mens rea as to P's conduct).

B) D's mens rea as to the circumstances of P's principal offence: This is provided by section 47(5)(b): requiring a minimum of *recklessness*. Thus, D must intend for P to shoot the gun and be at least reckless as to whether P shoots a person (the circumstance element of murder).

C) D's mens rea as to the results of P's principal offence: This is also provided by section 47(5)(b): requiring a minimum of *recklessness*. Thus, D must intend for P to shoot the gun and be at least reckless as to whether P shoots a person (circumstance) and causes their death (the result element of murder).

D) D's mens rea as to P's mens rea when completing the principal offence: This is provided by section 47(5)(a): requiring a minimum of *recklessness*. Thus, D must intend for P to shoot the gun, be at least reckless as to whether P shoots a person (circumstance) and causes their death (result) and be at least reckless as to whether P will do so with the intention of causing death or GBH (the mens rea of murder).

Where, in an exceptional case, D lacks recklessness as to P's mens rea, D may still be liable if she possesses the mens rea for the principal offence herself. This clause (s47(5)(a)(iii)) will rarely arise but is designed to address a potential loophole. For example, knowing that V is asleep, D provides P with a gun and encourages her to shoot V, but telling P that V is already dead. In considering whether D could be charged with assisting and encouraging murder: D clearly possesses mens rea as to her own conduct by intending to encourage P to shoot the gun, has mens rea as to the conduct, circumstances and results of P's future conduct (by intending that P will shoot the gun), and is at least reckless as to whether that will cause the death of a person. However, D is not reckless as to P's mens rea; D knows that P thinks V is dead and therefore lacks recklessness as to P acting with the mens rea for murder. In such a case, D will be liable because, although she knows that P lacks the mens rea for the murder of V, D acts with that mens rea.[142]

> **Beware...**
> As with attempts, we must separate the elements of the principal offence in order to identify D's required mens rea in relation to each. However, in this case, our main focus is not separating the circumstance element. Rather, the most important element to separate for special treatment is the

---

[141] For an alternative possibility, see Child, 'Exploring the Mens Rea Requirements of the Serious Crime Act 2007 Assisting and Encouraging Offences' (2012) 76 J Crim L 220.

[142] This will also apply to encouraging rape where, eg, D encourages P to have sex with V knowing that V will not consent. Even if D assures P that V is consenting, and even if P believes D and so would lack mens rea when completing the principal offence, D remains liable for encouraging rape because D has the mens rea for rape him/herself.

conduct element as there is a common requirement of recklessness as to the other elements. In many ways, separating the conduct element is even more troublesome than separating the circumstance element.

11.4.3 Mens rea of s45: encouraging or assisting an offence believing it will be committed

Moving beyond intentional assisting or encouraging, this offence expands liability to cases of belief.[143] The mens rea requirements for this offence are spread across sections 45 and 47.

45 A person commits an offence if...

    (b) he believes—

        (i)   that the offence will be committed; and

        (ii) that his act will encourage or assist its commission.

47 (1) Sections 44, 45 and 46 are to be read in accordance with this section...

    (3) If it is alleged under section 45(b) that a person (D) believed that an offence would be committed and that his act would encourage or assist its commission, it is sufficient to prove that he believed—

        (a) that an act would be done which would amount to the commission of that offence; and

        (b) that his act would encourage or assist the doing of that act...

    (5) [Extracted at **11.4.2**]

The elements of the section 45 offence are illustrated in **Tables 11.7a** and **11.7b**.

Table 11.7a SCA 2007, s45: assisting or encouraging

	Actus reus	**Mens rea**
Conduct element	Any action or omission	Voluntary
Circumstance element	D's conduct is capable of assisting or encouraging P to commit an offence	Belief that it will assist or encourage the conduct element of P's offence
Result element	None	None
Ulterior mens rea element	*	Set out in **Table 11.7b**

---

[143] Child, 'Exploring the Mens Rea Requirements of the Serious Crime Act 2007 Assisting and Encouraging Offences' (2012) 76 J Crim L 220; Ormerod and Fortson, 'Serious Crime Act 2007: Part 2 Offences' [2009] Crim LR 389.

Table 11.7b Ulterior mens rea element for s45 assisting or encouraging

	D's mens rea as to P's principal offence
Conduct element	D must believe that P will complete the conduct element of the principal offence
Circumstance element	D must believe or be reckless as to the circumstance element of P's principal offence
Result element	D must believe or be reckless as to whether P will cause the results (if any) required by the principal offence
P's mens rea	D must believe, or be reckless as to whether P will act with the mens rea required by the principal offence Or D must have the mens rea for the principal offence herself

11.4.3.1 D's mens rea as to her own conduct

Section 45(b)(ii) states that D must believe that her act will assist or encourage P's principal offence. Again, although this appears to apply to the whole of that offence, it must be read in accordance with sections 47(1) and 47(3). Section 47(3)(b) clarifies that, as with the s44 offence, D's mens rea need only apply to the conduct element of P's offence.

Therefore, this part of D's mens rea merely requires her to believe that her conduct will assist or encourage the conduct element of P's principal offence. Using our assisting murder example, this might apply where D sells P a gun simply in order to make a profit. In this case, D may not intend to assist P to fire the gun, indeed she may actively not want her to and so D will not come within the section 44 offence. However, if she believes that she is assisting P to fire the gun, she will satisfy this part of section 45.

11.4.3.2 D's mens rea as to P's principal offence

Section 45(b)(i) states that D must believe that the principal offence will be completed, implying that D must have belief as to each element. However, as section 47(3)(a) subsequently clarifies, this only applies to P's conduct element. Thus, again, it is necessary to separate the elements of P's principal offence in order to identify the mens rea required of D in relation to each.

A) **D's mens rea as to P's conduct element:** This is provided by a combination of sections 45(b)(i) and 47(3)(a): requiring a minimum of *belief*. Thus, using our gun-selling example, D not only has to believe that her conduct will assist P to shoot the gun (D's mens rea as to her own conduct) but must also believe that P will shoot the gun in fact.

B) **D's mens rea as to the circumstances of P's principal offence:** This is provided by section 47(5)(b): requiring a minimum of *recklessness*. Thus, D must believe that P will shoot the gun and be at least reckless as to whether P shoots a person (the circumstance element of murder).

C) **D's mens rea as to the results of P's principal offence:** This is also provided by section 47(5)(b): requiring a minimum of *recklessness*. Thus, D must believe that P will shoot the gun and be at least reckless as to whether P shoots a person (circumstance) and causes their death (the result element of murder).

D) **D's mens rea as to P's mens rea when completing the principal offence:** This is provided by section 47(5)(a): requiring a minimum of *recklessness*. Thus, D must believe that P will shoot the gun, be at least reckless as to whether P shoots a person (circumstance) and causes their death (result), and be at least reckless as to whether P will do so with the intention of causing death or GBH (the mens rea of murder). Again, D may alternatively satisfy this element if she has the mens rea for the principal offence herself.

> *Point to remember…*
> Much of the mens rea between the section 44 and 45 offences are the same. The only difference (intention/belief) relates to the conduct element of the principal offence.

11.4.4 Mens rea of s46: encouraging or assisting offences believing one or more will be committed

Section 46 applies where D does acts capable of assisting or encouraging P to commit a number of principal offences but is unsure which offence P will choose.[144] The mens rea is set out over sections 46 and 47.

46 (1) A person commits an offence if…

    (b) he believes—

        (i) that one or more of those offences will be committed (but has no belief as to which); and

        (ii) that his act will encourage or assist the commission of one or more of them.

47 (1) Sections 44, 45 and 46 are to be read in accordance with this section…

    (2) If it is alleged under section 46(1)(b) that a person (D) believed that one or more of a number of offences would be committed and that his act would encourage or assist the commission of one or more of them, it is sufficient to prove that he believed—

        (a) that one or more of a number of acts would be done which would amount to the commission of one or more of those offences; and

        (b) that his act would encourage or assist the doing of one or more of those acts.

    (5) [Extracted at **11.4.2**]

The elements of the section 46 offence are illustrated in **Tables 11.8a** and **11.8b**.

---

[144] Child, 'Exploring the Mens Rea Requirements of the Serious Crime Act 2007 Assisting and Encouraging Offences' (2012) 76 J Crim L 220; Ormerod and Fortson, 'Serious Crime Act 2007: Part 2 Offences' [2009] Crim LR 389.

Table 11.8a SCA 2007, s46: assisting or encouraging

	Actus reus	**Mens rea**
Conduct element	Any action or omission	Voluntary
Circumstance element	D's conduct is capable of assisting or encouraging P to commit one or more of a number of offences	Belief that it will assist or encourage the conduct element of one or more of P's offences (but must have no belief as to which)
Result element	None	None
Ulterior mens rea element	*	Set out in *Table 11.8b*

Table 11.8b Ulterior mens rea element for s46 assisting or encouraging

	D's mens rea as to P's principal offence
Conduct element	D must believe that P will complete one or more conduct elements of one or more principal offences
Circumstance element	D must believe or be reckless as to the circumstance elements of P's principal offences
Result element	D must believe or be reckless as to whether P will cause the results (if any) required by the principal offences
P's mens rea	D must believe, or be reckless as to whether P will act with the mens rea required by the principal offences Or D must have the mens rea for the principal offences herself

In order to explain the mens rea of this offence, it is useful to employ an example. As before, let us imagine that D sells V a gun, motivated purely by profit from the sale. D believes that P will use the gun to attack V. However, D is unsure whether P will use the gun as a blunt object with which to strike V causing ABH,[145] or whether P will use the gun to shoot and kill V. In such a case, D may be charged under section 46 with assisting ABH and murder. Again, in respect of D's inchoate liability

---

[145] OAPA 1861, s47. See **7.4**.

under section 46, it is irrelevant whether P goes on to commit neither, either or both offences.

11.4.4.1 D's mens rea as to her own conduct

Section 46(b)(ii) states that D must believe that her act will assist or encourage P to commit one or more principal offences. Read in accordance with sections 47(1) and 47(4)(b), this requires D to believe that her conduct will assist or encourage (at least) the conduct element of those possible offences. Thus, using the previous example, D must believe that she has assisted one or both offences of ABH and murder.

11.4.4.2 D's mens rea as to P's principal offence

Section 46(b)(i) states that D must believe that one or more of P's principal offences will be completed, implying that D must have belief as to each element of those offences. However, as section 47(4)(a) subsequently clarifies, this only applies to P's conduct elements. Thus, again, it is necessary to separate the elements of P's principal offences in order to identify the mens rea required of D in relation to each.

A) **D's mens rea as to P's conduct elements:** This is provided by a combination of sections 46(b)(i) and 47(4)(a): requiring a minimum of *belief.* Thus, using our example, D must believe that D will *either* use the gun to hit with *or* to shoot. D does not intend either (so s44 would be inappropriate), does not believe that P will commit one act over the other (so s45 would be inappropriate), she believes that P *will* commit one of the acts but is unsure which.

B) **D's mens rea as to the circumstances of P's principal offences:** This is provided by section 47(5)(b): requiring a minimum of *recklessness.* D must believe that P will shoot or hit with the gun and be at least reckless as to whether P shoots or hits a person (the circumstance element of murder and ABH).

C) **D's mens rea as to the results of P's principal offences:** This is also provided by section 47(5)(b): requiring a minimum of *recklessness.* D must believe that P will shoot or hit with the gun, be at least reckless as to whether P shoots or hits a person (circumstance) and at least reckless as to whether D will cause death or ABH (the result elements of murder and ABH).

D) **D's mens rea as to P's mens rea when completing the principal offences:** This is provided by section 47(5)(a): requiring a minimum of *recklessness.* D must believe that P will shoot or hit with the gun, be at least reckless as to whether P shoots or hits a person (circumstance), be at least reckless as to whether D will cause death or ABH (result) and be at least reckless as to whether P will do so with the mens rea required for murder or ABH. Again, D may alternatively satisfy this element if she has the mens rea for the principal offence herself.

11.4.4.3 Applying s46: the Court of Appeal's guidance in *Sadique*

There is, arguably, a need for an offence like section 46 to cater for assisting and encouraging where D believes an offence will be committed but is unsure which offence it will be. However, as the previous section sets out, the structure of this offence is highly complex. The offence was discussed in *Sadique.*

> **Sadique** [2011] EWCA Crim 2872
>
> D supplied cutting agents including benzocaine and hydrochloric acid to assist the production and supply of illegal drugs. D was charged with a section 46 offence of assisting the supply of Class A or Class B drugs.
>
> • Crown Court: appeal against charges in preparatory hearing, contending that section 46 is incompatible with Article 7 ECHR.
> • Court of Appeal: appeal dismissed.

In confirming that the section 46 offence is sufficiently clear to be compatible with Article 7 ECHR, the Court of Appeal set out their interpretation of the provision. However, their analysis was problematic in two main areas.

A) **Confusing ss45 and 46:** The court held that section 46 requires D to believe that each of the possible offences, assisted or encouraged, *will* be committed by P. Thus, in *Sadique*, D must believe that his acts will assist the supply of Class A drugs and Class B drugs and an indictment should ideally separate these offences into separate counts. The problem with this, as highlighted by several academics,[146] is that although it makes the sentencing exercise clearer, it undermines the purpose of section 46. Although section 45 requires D to believe that an individual offence will come about, section 46 is designed to deal with cases where D only believes that one of a number of offences will be committed (but does not know/believe which). This interpretation (consistent with our discussion at **11.4.4.1–11.4.4.2**) was later accepted by the Court of Appeal following a further appeal in 2013.[147]

B) **Mens rea as to circumstances, results and mens rea of the principal offence:** Seeking to clarify the requirements of the offence, the court set out the mens rea in simple terms.[148] However, they do so inaccurately, suggesting that D must believe that P will complete *all* elements of the principal offence. As we set out earlier, the statute in fact requires a minimum of recklessness as to P's circumstances, results and mens rea. The court's confusion on this point is a useful illustration of over-reliance on the Law Commission report which had recommended a minimum of belief, a recommendation that was not accepted within the SCA 2007.

Despite these problems with *Sadique*, much of the blame must be placed with the unnecessary complexity of the legislation. Without significant amendment, further confusions of this kind are inevitable.

11.4.5 Defences to assisting or encouraging

As well as the general defences (discussed in **Chapters 13** and **14**), the SCA 2007 creates two specific defences: acting reasonably and protection of the victim.[149]

---

[146] Virgo, 'Encouraging or Assisting More Than One Offence' [2012] 2 Arch Rev 6.
[147] *Sadique* [2013] EWCA Crim 1150. Commentary by Fortson [2014] Crim LR 61.
[148] *Sadique* [2011] EWCA Crim 2872, [87].
[149] Law Commission, *Inchoate Liability for Assisting and Encouraging Crime* (No 300, 2006) Part 6.

> **Point to remember...**
> These defences only apply to offences under sections 44–46 of the SCA 2007. They do not apply to attempts or conspiracy, or any other offences.

Section 50 of the SCA 2007 creates a specific defence of 'acting reasonably'. This applies where circumstances exist, or D reasonably believes they exist, and these circumstances make it reasonable to act as D did.

This defence is essential in order to narrow liability to acceptable limits. For example, D is driving at 70mph in the outside lane of a motorway but moves in when she sees P's car approaching from behind at greater speed. In this case, without the defence of acting reasonably, the Law Commission recognise that because of the astonishing breadth of the offences created, D may be liable for assisting P's speeding offence: D's act is capable of assisting by clearing the way; D believes that she will assist P to continue speeding; D believes that P will continue speeding; and D is at least reckless as to whether P will be over the speed limit, etc.

Although such examples are used to illustrate the role of the defence, they may also be employed to demonstrate the overbroad scope of the original offences. As we discussed from the start of **Chapter 1**, the purpose of a criminal offence is to define and punish a criminal wrong. The fact that the assisting and encouraging offences apply to conduct such as moving motorway lanes, as in the example above, shows that these offences are not satisfying that task and are effectively switching the burden: requiring D, through the specific defence, to demonstrate the reasonableness of her own conduct to avoid liability. The criminal law would be much simpler for the prosecution if all acts were presumed criminal unless D could justify their reasonableness!

Less controversially, section 51 provides a specific defence where D assists or encourages an offence for which she is the intended victim. For example, if D (12 years old) encourages her boyfriend (16 years old) to have sex with her, *she* has a defence to a charge of encouraging rape of a child under 13.

11.5 Double inchoate liability

So-called double (or infinite) inchoate liability arises where D's inchoate offence is targeted at a principal offence which is itself inchoate.[150] For example, where D provides P with access to her house so that P can plan a robbery with a third party, D may be liable for assisting a conspiracy to commit robbery. Although, as in our example, liability of this kind may be justified, it must also be recognised that D's conduct is extremely remote from the potential future harm, being at least two steps removed. Concern that such remoteness will lead to inappropriate criminalisation is limited in two ways.

First, not all combinations of inchoate offences are possible. The potential combinations, illustrated in **Table 11.9**, have been expanded dramatically by the SCA 2007. They have developed in the absence of a clear principle. For example, the Law Commission has recently rejected the potential for an attempt to conspire as an overextension of the law, yet conceded that such conduct will almost always amount to encouraging a

---

150 Law Commission, *Conspiracy and Attempts* (No 318, 2009) Part 3.

conspiracy, which is an offence.[151] Table 11.9 must be read by looking to the left-hand column before identifying the possible inchoate in the row.

Table 11.9 Double inchoate liability

	Attempt	Conspiracy	SCA 2007, s44	SCA 2007, s45	SCA 2007, s46
Attempt	No offence	No offence CAA 1981, s1(4)(a)	D may attempt a s44 offence	D may attempt a s45 offence	D may attempt a s46 offence
Conspiracy	D1 and D2 may conspire to attempt	D1 and D2 may conspire to conspire	D1 and D2 may conspire to commit a s44 offence	D1 and D2 may conspire to commit a s45 offence	D1 and D2 may conspire to commit a s46 offence
SCA 2007, s44	D may assist or encourage an attempt	D may assist or encourage a conspiracy	D may assist or encourage a s44 offence	D may assist or encourage a s45 offence	D may assist or encourage a s46 offence
SCA 2007, s45	No offence SCA 2007, s49(4–5)	No offence SCA 2007, s49(4–5)	No offence SCA 2007, s49(4–5)	No offence SCA 2007, s49(4–5)	No offence SCA 2007, s49(4–5)
SCA 2007, s46	No offence SCA 2007, s49(4–5)	No offence SCA 2007, s49(4–5)	No offence SCA 2007, s49(4–5)	No offence SCA 2007, s49(4–5)	No offence SCA 2007, s49(4–5)

The second way in which double inchoate liability could be limited is through requiring D to intend the future offence. For example, where D assists a conspiracy to commit robbery, she must intend that the robbery is completed. To ensure that this second limitation is applied, courts must require that for D to commit an inchoate offence, she must intend any ulterior mens rea requirement within the principal offence. As noted previously when discussing *AG's Reference (No 3 of 1992)*,[152] however, this has not always been the case with attempts and appears contrary to the wording of the SCA 2007 in relation to the assisting and encouraging offences. Therefore, despite some comments to the contrary, it seems that this second limitation is largely absent from the current law.[153]

---

[151] Law Commission, *Conspiracy and Attempts* (No 318, 2009) para 3.22.
[152] (1993) 98 Cr App R 383. See **11.2.2.2**.
[153] Child, 'The Structure, Coherence and Limits of Inchoate Liability: The New Ulterior Element' (2013) 34 LS 537.

11.6 Substantive offences in an inchoate form

We have discussed several offences in this book that could be described as inchoate and there are a considerable number of such offences within the criminal law. These include, for example, the new fraud offences where D acts with the dishonest intention of making a gain or causing a loss, but need not do so in fact to be liable;[154] several of the new sexual offences such as specific offences of inciting sexual activity and grooming, where no sexual contact is required;[155] several possession offences such as D's possession of illegal drugs or weapons, although not itself harmful, but posing an obvious future risk of their use; endangerment offences such as driving over the speed limit, with excess alcohol; as well as D acting in criminal violation of health and safety legislation: again, we are criminalising D for causing the *potential* for future harms.

11.6.1 Assisting or encouraging suicide

The offence of assisting or encouraging suicide, under section 2 of the Suicide Act 1960,[156] is included here by way of contrast to the assisting or encouraging offences discussed previously (see **Table 11.10**). The general inchoate offences in the SCA 2007 do not apply to suicide, simply because suicide is not a criminal offence. However, section 2 of the Suicide Act makes special provision for the criminalisation of acts which assist or encourage it. The most controversial aspect of this offence relates to the likelihood of prosecution being brought where, for example, D assists P's travel to a jurisdiction in which euthanasia is legal.[157]

Table 11.10 Assisting or encouraging suicide

	Actus reus	**Mens rea**
Conduct element	Any action	Voluntary
Circumstance element	D's conduct is capable of assisting or encouraging P to commit suicide (on the facts as D believes them to be)	Intention to assist or encourage suicide
Result element	None	None

It should be noted that the offence contains no result element so it is irrelevant whether P is in fact assisted or encouraged, or whether P commits suicide. There is also no ulterior mens rea requiring D to intend that P will, as a result, commit suicide, so a suicide website owner whose posts intend to assist P, but does not necessarily desire that P will commit suicide, will be caught by the offence.

---

[154] **Chapter 9.**
[155] **Chapter 8.**
[156] Amended by the Coroners and Justice Act 2009, s59.
[157] O'Sullivan, 'Mens Rea, Motive and Assisted Suicide: Does the DPP's Policy Go Too Far?' (2014) LS 96.

11.7 Reform

The general inchoate offences criminalise conduct at the very fringes of the criminal law and so it should be no surprise that there has been, and remains, considerable debate about their appropriate construction. Much of this debate relates to the overarching clash between those who would like to facilitate earlier intervention, in order to mini-mise the risk of future harms, and those who are concerned about the over-expansion of criminalisation to remote conduct, such that may be insufficient to demonstrate suf-ficient wrongfulness. In this section, we do not attempt to discuss these debates in full. Rather, we provide a brief summary combined with references to academic material that should be followed in order to get a fuller picture.

11.7.1 The actus reus of attempts

Debate surrounding the actus reus of attempts is probably the most straightforward to understand, but may also be the most intractable. Defensible academic arguments can be made for a wide variety of approaches from very early to very late criminal intervention.

A) **Early intervention with attempts:** If we believe that the 'wrong' targeted by crim-inal attempts is D's mental commitment to completing the principal offence, rather than any physical signs of that commitment, then we can justify very early intervention by the criminal law as soon as we have sufficient evidence of that commitment.[158] However, for many the term 'attempt' is problematic here, requiring D to do more than form an inten-tion. It was on this basis that the Law Commission proposed the creation of a new offence of 'criminal preparation' in 2007.[159] This proposal was problematic and was ultimately rejected following consultation.[160] However, for those who favour early intervention through a general offence, the case for a preparation offence may still be appealing.[161]

B) **Refining the current midway course:** Most academics, and most other jurisdic-tions, favour something of a midway option between first and last act attempts. In this regard, it may be that an alternative form of words (eg 'substantial step' or 'unequivo-cal act') might be preferred to the current formulation.[162] Alternatively, or in addition, several academics recommend the use of statutory examples, as used in the US Model Penal Code[163] to supplement the statute. These could, for example, make it clear that lying in wait, as in *Geddes*,[164] should satisfy the actus reus.[165] However, this approach has been resisted in this country, partly because of the problem with agreeing suitable examples, and partly because statutory examples have not been part of the drafting his-tory in England and Wales.[166]

---

[158] Robinson, 'The Modern General Part: Three Illusions' in Shute and Simester (eds), *Criminal Law Theory* (2003) 92–93.

[159] Law Commission, *Conspiracy and Attempts* (Consultation 183, 2007) Part 16.

[160] Law Commission, *Conspiracy and Attempts* (No 318, 2009) Part 8.

[161] Rogers, 'The Codification of Attempts and the Case for "Preparation"' [2008] Crim LR 937.

[162] There is a very useful discussion of this in Law Commission (No 102, 1980) Part 2D.

[163] Model Penal Code, §5.01(2).

[164] See **11.2.1.3**.

[165] Duff, *Criminal Attempts* (1996) 57.

[166] Law Commission, *Conspiracy and Attempts* (No 318, 2009) para 8.74.

C) Narrowing the actus reus to later acts: It may also be argued that attempts liability should be narrowed from the current formulation to apply only to the most blameworthy cases. For example, a subtle narrowing has been recommended by Duff, who conceptualises attempts as 'attacks' on protected interests, and so would only find an attempt where D's conduct could be described as an attack.[167] More radical, Alexander, Kessler, and Morse have recommended that attempts should be narrowed to cases in which D has unleashed a risk, an approach that comes close to the 'last act' test discussed earlier.[168]

11.7.2 The mens rea of attempts and conspiracy

Although the current mens rea requirements for attempts and conspiracy differ, it is generally accepted that overlap between the offences means that a consistent approach would be preferable. It was partly on this basis that the court in *Pace* rejected *Khan*, and chose to adopt a position for the mens rea of impossible attempts in line with conspiracy.[169] However, a preference for consistency does not tell us what that consistent approach should be. Some of the main options for reform include the following:

A) Intention approach: This approach requires D to intend every element of the principal offence. This approach was preferred and adopted within the CAA 1981 and the CLA 1977. Its benefits include its simplicity, as well as its narrowing of inchoate liability to cases where D is fully committed to completing the principal offence. However, as discussed in *Khan*, it may be too narrow: preventing liability for (eg) attempted rape, where D intends the physical parts of the offence but is reckless as to the circumstance of V's non-consent. An alternative may be to offer a standard mens rea requirement of belief, or even recklessness, as to every element.[170]

B) Khan approach: This approach allows D's mens rea as to circumstances to mirror that of the principal offence. This approach has been recommended, with clarification, by the Law Commission for both attempts and conspiracy.[171] Problems with this approach have been highlighted earlier.[172] To these we may also add that this approach seems to be conceptually confused: requiring less than intention as to circumstances, but not telling us why circumstances as elements of an offence warrant special treatment (beyond the desired result in the individual case).[173]

C) Conditional intention approach: This approach stretches a traditional understanding of conditional intention to find intention where D intends to act in the knowledge that her action may be criminal.[174] This has the advantage of focusing on intention,

---

[167] *Criminal Attempts* (1996) Ch13.

[168] *Crime and Culpability: A Theory of Criminal Law* (2009).

[169] See **11.2.2.2–11.2.2.3**.

[170] Belief is preferred in Child and Hunt, 'Mens Rea and the General Inchoate Offences: Another New Culpability Framework' (2012) 63 NILQ 247.

[171] Law Commission, *Conspiracy and Attempts* (No 318, 2009).

[172] See **11.2.2.2**.

[173] Child and Hunt, 'Mens Rea and the General Inchoate Offences: Another New Culpability Framework' (2012) 63 NILQ 247.

[174] Williams, 'Intents in the Alternative' (1991) 50 CLJ 120.

but also allowing for liability in *Khan*-like cases. However, it is problematic, labelling what is essentially recklessness as conditional intention, and struggling to explain why recklessness as to results (as opposed to circumstances) should be treated differently.[175]

D) **Missing element approach:** Stannard has recommended an approach in which D need only intend elements of the principal offence that are not completed despite his trying (eg in *Khan*, V is not consenting and the only missing element is the sexual penetration; so D must intend the latter, but need not intend the former).[176] This approach was preferred in *AG's Reference (No 1 of 1992)*.[177] However, this case may be too broad. For example, D borrows V's tools to do a job that risks damaging them; however, in his confusion, he uses his own tools and causes damage. D would be liable for attempted criminal damage: intending the missing element (ownership) and reckless as to the non-missing element (damage).[178]

E) **Mirroring approach:** The Irish Law Commission has recommended that mens rea should mirror that required for the principal offence as to every element (with the exception of murder).[179] This has the advantage of simplicity but is highly problematic. For example, if D asks a drunken P for a lift home, D may be liable for the strict liability offence of encouraging P to drive with excess alcohol, even if D was not aware that P was intoxicated.[180]

11.7.3 The future of assisting and encouraging

Whatever the merits of the Law Commission's recommendations on assisting and encouraging,[181] the final scheme of offences created within the SCA 2007 is not fit for purpose. Spread over multiple complex sections, the current law lacks clarity and has already caused problems for the appellate courts.[182] Additionally, although its complex drafting seems to have discouraged its extensive use, the breadth of the offences as drafted (both in terms of actus reus and mens rea) provides for the possibility of inappropriate criminalisation—with only the uncertain defence of 'acting reasonably' to restrain it.[183]

The Justice Committee of the House of Commons has recently engaged a review of these offences with a view to post-legislative scrutiny, a process that could end in reform or even repeal of the offences.[184] This has already revealed a consistent dissatisfaction with the law amongst those consulted. However, the Committee concluded that a full review should be delayed to see if the current law can be clarified by future court judgments.

---

[175] Duff, *Criminal Attempts* (1996) 15–16.
[176] Stannard, 'Making Up for the Missing Element—A Sideways Look at Attempts' (1987) 7 LS 194.
[177] (1992) 96 Cr App R 298.
[178] Duff, *Criminal Attempts* (1996) 14–15.
[179] Irish Law Reform Commission, *Report on Inchoate Offences* (No 99, 2010).
[180] Child and Hunt, 'Mens Rea and the General Inchoate Offences: Another New Culpability Framework' (2012) 63 NILQ 247.
[181] Law Commission, *Inchoate Liability for Assisting and Encouraging Crime* (No 300, 2006).
[182] See **11.4.4.3**.
[183] Ormerod and Fortson, 'Serious Crime Act 2007: Part 2 Offences' [2009] Crim LR 389.
[184] House of Commons, *Post-Legislative Scrutiny of Part 2 of the Serious Crime Act 2007* (2013).

11.7.4 The inconsistency of law reform

To help provide a critique of the current state of the law, it is useful to observe the inconsistent approach taken to the reform of the general inchoate offences. As we have highlighted at various points of this chapter, the codification of attempts (CAA 1981) and conspiracy (CLA 1977) resulted from a fundamental review of inchoate offences by the Law Commission at that time. Between 2006 and 2009, we have seen a similar review by the Law Commission and recommendations for a consistent change of direction—particularly through the broadening of mens rea.[185] However, this time, these recommendations have not been consistently taken forward into legislation. Rather, the only offences to be reformed on the basis of this latest review have been those of assisting or encouraging, those in least need of reform and for which reform has proved least satisfactory.

As a result, the current general inchoate offences are imbalanced. Despite the overlap between the offences (eg it is hard to think of an agreement to commit an offence that does not also involve one party encouraging the other), the approach codified within the SCA 2007 is fundamentally different from the current law of attempts and conspiracy. And as the courts seek to bridge this gap, both sides risk further confusion and incoherence. In **Chapter 12**, we discuss a similar inconsistency caused by the reform of inchoate assisting and encouraging, and the lack of complementary reform of secondary liability, (again) despite Law Commission recommendations. Finally, a similar criticism can be made in relation to the creation of specific inchoate offences, such as those relating to sexual offences and terrorism, which again do not seem to have been created with a view to consistent coexistence with the general inchoate offences.[186]

11.8 Eye on assessment

As with previous chapters, this section provides advice for applying the offences discussed in practice. Although the elements of the general inchoate offences are very different from the offences discussed in previous chapters, the basic structure to follow within a problem question remains the same.

STEP 1 Identify the potential criminal event in the facts

This should be simply stated (eg 'The first potential criminal event arises where D tries to shoot V'). The role of this stage is to highlight which part of the question you are answering before you begin to apply the law.

STEP 2 Identify the potential offence

Again, state this simply (eg 'When shooting at V, D may be liable for attempted murder'). A useful way to identify the principal offence attempted/conspired/assisted or encouraged

---

[185] No 300, 2006; Consultation 183, 2007; No 318, 2009.
[186] Child and Hunt, 'Risk, Pre-Emption, and the Limits of the Criminal Law' in Doolin, Child, Raine, and Beech (eds), *Whose Criminal Justice? State or Community?* (2011) 51.

> **STEP 2 Continued**
>
> is to think about what offence D (or D2) would have committed if her plan had been successful. The role of this stage is to highlight which offence you are going to apply.

When answering a question on the general inchoate offences, it is easy to become overwhelmed by the detail. Steps 1 and 2 should be useful reminders to start simply. While looking for a potential offence, keep the basic descriptions of the offences in your mind: for example, has D tried to commit an offence (attempt); has D agreed with another to commit an offence (conspiracy); has D assisted or encouraged another to commit an offence (assisting and encouraging)?

Remember that these offences overlap and so a single action may amount to more than one of the general offences. In this case, highlight the overlap to your reader and then proceed with your analysis of the offence you think is most appropriate: either because it more accurately describes what D has done, or because you think there is more chance of finding liability for that offence. Again, tell your reader *why* you have made the choice.

> **STEP 3 Applying the offence to the facts**
>
> Having identified the relevant offence, make sure you discuss each of the required elements.
>
> Actus reus: What does the offence require? Did D do it?
>
> Mens rea: What does the offence require? Did D possess it?

This is the most challenging part of problem questions in relation to the general inchoate offences because there are several stages of analysis that you need to lead your reader through. The most important advice here is to be clear; to separate each part of your discussion; and to be methodical. With reference to our detailed discussion of the offences earlier, the checklist approach in **Tables 11.11, 11.12,** and **11.13** can provide a useful guide to structuring your answer.

Table 11.11 Applying attempts

Attempts
D decides to cut down a tree, unsure whether it belongs to her or her neighbour V. The tree belongs to V, who stops D just before the first chop of her axe. If she was successful, she would have committed the principal offence of criminal damage.
When D tries to cut down the tree, she may have committed attempted criminal damage • Actus reus: Has D's act gone beyond mere preparation towards damaging or destroying V's tree (the actus reus of criminal damage), either in reality or on the facts as D believes them to be? • Mens rea: D's attempt is not impossible (ie if D continued as planned, she would have committed criminal damage); therefore we need to apply the mens rea of attempts as set out in *Khan*. Does D *intend* the conduct she has performed? Does D *intend* the conduct element of the criminal damage (ie the chopping)? Does D *intend* the result element of the criminal damage (ie causing damage)? Does D have the same mens rea as criminal damage requires (ie *recklessness*) as to the circumstance element (ie that the tree belongs to another)?

Table 11.12 Applying statutory conspiracy

Conspiracy
D1 and D2 agree to smash the window of V's car. If their plan had been carried out, the principal offence of criminal damage would have been committed.
When D1 and D2 make their plan, they may be liable for conspiracy to commit criminal damage • Actus reus: Has D (whichever D you are considering) formed an agreement with another that will necessarily amount to or involve the commission of criminal damage by one of them, either in reality or on the facts as they believe them to be? • Mens rea: Does D (whose case you are considering) intend to form the agreement? Does D (whose case you are considering) *intend* that every element required for criminal damage will be completed by a party to the agreement?

Table 11.13 Applying assisting or encouraging

Assisting or encouraging
D sells a can of spray paint to P in her shop. D is concerned that P might use it for graffiti. If P did use it she would commit the offence of criminal damage.
When D sells the spray paint to P, she may commit an offence of assisting criminal damage. As she does not intend the principal offence to come about, and has only one principal offence in mind, the most likely charge would be SCA 2007, s45 • Actus reus: Has D done an act which is capable of assisting P to commit criminal damage? • Mens rea: Does D *believe* that her act will assist P to complete the conduct required for criminal damage (ie assist spraying the paint)? Does D *believe* that P will complete the conduct element of criminal damage (ie spraying the paint)? Is D at least *reckless* as to whether P will complete the other elements of the principal offence: the results (ie causing damage), circumstances (ie that the damaged property belongs to another), the mens rea (ie that P will be at least reckless as to causing damage to another's property)?

Remember that with the exception of conspiracy and impossible attempts, you will need to split the principal offence into conduct, circumstances, and results in order to identify and apply the mens rea required of D in relation to each. You will find this division relatively straightforward for certain offences, as with the criminal damage examples in Tables 11.11, 11.12, and 11.13. Where you struggle to find a clear separation, try and do the best you can but highlight to your reader that the separation is not clear, and reflect on this as a criticism of the changes to the law in this area that makes such separation essential.

> **STEP 4 Consider defences**
>
> The word 'consider' here is important, as you should not discuss every defence for every question. Rather, think whether there are any defences (eg duress) that *could* potentially apply. If there are, discuss those only.

As well as the general defences, remember that there are also a number of specific defences (as discussed earlier). Remember that where a specific defence applies to a certain offence, it only applies in this context and should *never* be applied to a different offence.

STEP 5 Conclude

This is usually a single sentence either saying that it is likely that D has committed the offence, or saying that it is not likely either because an offence element is not satisfied, or because a defence is likely to apply. It is not often that you will be able to say categorically whether D has committed the offence or not, so it is usually best to conclude in terms of what is more 'likely'.

STEP 6 Loop

Go back up to step 1, identifying the next potential criminal event. Continue until you have discussed all the relevant potentially criminal events.

ONLINE RESOURCE CENTRE

www.oxfordtextbooks.co.uk/orc/smithandhogan/

This chapter is accompanied by a selection of online resources to help you with this topic, including:

- **Multiple choice questions**
- **Chapter summary sheet**
- Two **sample examination questions** with answer guidance
- **Further reading**

Also available on the Online Resource Centre are:

- A selection of **videos** from the authors explaining key topics and principles
- Legal updates
- Useful **weblinks**

12

Parties to crime

12.1 Introduction

Crimes are rarely committed by a single defendant in perfect isolation. Where P robs a bank, for example, she may have enlisted X as a getaway driver, Y as a lookout, Z to assist gathering the loot, and so on. Even before the robbery begins, these parties and others may also have encouraged P or helped her to make plans. In **Chapter 11** we discussed the potential for inchoate liability in these circumstances. Under those inchoate offences, provided they have the required mens rea, X, Y, and Z and any others involved will be liable for assisting or encouraging robbery or conspiracy to rob at the first moment of assisting, encouraging, or agreeing with P. Those offences apply whether the principal offence (the robbery) ever comes about or not, for whatever reason.

Where the principal offence *is* completed by P, the other parties are no longer simply liable for their inchoate roles,[1] but may now be additionally liable as accomplices. There is no need to prove that X, Y, and Z have done anything more than they had to trigger inchoate liability, but their liability as accomplices reflects the additional blameworthiness that is derived from the completion and associated harms of the principal offence. In this way, their accessorial liability is triggered by or derives from the completion of P's principal offence. Where X, Y, and Z are liable as accomplices, they are labelled and punished in the same way as P. In the example given, each will be charged with 'robbery', and if convicted, sentenced as a 'robber'.

> **Extra detail...**
> P may also be assisted after the principal offence (eg to hide the money or to disrupt the police investigation). There are a number of offences to deal with such acts,[2] but they will not be discussed in this chapter. Rather, our focus is on the actions of the parties before P's crime is completed or during its continuance.

Complicity, like the general inchoate offences, creates a form of general liability, applying across the criminal law unless expressly[3] or impliedly[4] excluded. Therefore, just as D may commit an offence as a principal offender, D may alternatively commit that offence as an accomplice. Although complicity is largely a common law doctrine, this basic structure is codified within section 8 of the Accessories and Abettors Act 1861.[5]

> **8**. Whosoever shall aid, abet, counsel, or procure the commission of any indictable offence, whether the same be an offence at common law or by virtue of any Act passed or to be passed, shall be liable to be tried, indicted, and punished as a principal offender.

Where D acts as an accomplice, she does not commit the offence as a principal, but her assistance or encouragement of P's offence ('aiding, abetting, counselling, or procuring'), and her mens rea, connect her to P's crime. Where P commits murder, for example, her accomplice D will also be labelled as a murderer, and will be subject to the same mandatory life sentence. Where P commits rape, his accomplice, D, will be labelled and punished as a rapist, even if D is a woman and therefore unable to commit rape as a principal because rape requires penile penetration.[6] Indeed, where D acts as an accomplice, her liability will derive directly from whatever offence is committed by P.

---

[1] Although each will remain liable for the inchoate offences committed.

[2] Examples include impeding the apprehension or prosecution of offenders (Criminal Law Act 1967, s4); compounding an offence (Criminal Law Act 1967, s5); and the common law offence of refusal to aid a constable.

[3] eg the Corporate Manslaughter and Corporate Homicide Act 2007 expressly excludes complicity of individuals.

[4] *Farr* [1982] Crim LR 745, and commentary.

[5] The Magistrates' Courts Act 1980 s44 creates an equivalent provision for summary offences.

[6] *Ram and Ram* (1893) 17 Cox CC 609. For the exceptional cases where a woman can commit rape as a principal, see **8.2**.

Despite the important role played by complicity, and perhaps partly because of it, the rules governing liability have not developed consistently within the common law. Rather, as the Law Commission has observed, the current law has 'developed haphazardly and is permeated with uncertainty'.[7] There are two main reasons for the current unsatisfactory state of the law.

- **Inevitable complexity:** Complicity, like the general inchoate offences, is particularly complex and challenging because it requires discussion of D's actus reus; D's mens rea as to her own conduct; and D's mens rea as to a future principal offence being committed by P. However, beyond inchoate liability, complicity also involves the *commission* of that principal offence by P. Therefore, complicity includes an additional requirement: D's mens rea as to P's principal offence must be sufficiently similar (factually) to that principal offence to ground D's increased liability. Maintaining a consistent and coherent approach to each of these separate requirements, especially within the common law, is exceptionally difficult.

- **Problem of policy:** The doctrinal rationale of complicity, as we discuss in the reform section later in the chapter,[8] remains uncertain, and so provides little structure for how complicity should be interpreted by the courts. However, at its simplest, there is a strong intuitive sense in which P's completion of the principal offence assisted or encouraged by D increases D's blameworthiness from a position where P does not commit the offence and D's liability is therefore inchoate. In other words, results matter. In addition to this, the political will to tackle gang violence and other forms of coordinated law breaking, even where the individual roles of each member are unclear, creates a powerful incentive towards expansive interpretations of the law to facilitate findings of liability.[9]

As a result of these problems and uncertainties, the appellate courts have faced a consistent and unabated flow of cases questioning the operation of the law. However, such cases have only provided limited assistance, as we see from the Supreme Court's recent offering in *Gnango*.

Gnango [2011] UKSC 59

D and P (who was unidentified, but referred to in court as 'Bandana Man') got into a gun fight with each other following a chance meeting in a London estate. Both shot at the other with the intention to kill or to cause GBH. One of P's shots missed D and hit and killed V, an innocent pedestrian passing by. D was charged with murder through the doctrine of complicity.

- Crown Court: D guilty of murder on the basis that D and P were jointly concerned with an affray, and D foresaw the chance of murder being committed within this venture.

- Court of Appeal: appeal allowed, quashing D's conviction. There was no common purpose between D and P, and thus no way of connecting P's crime with D.

---

[7] Law Commission, *Participating in Crime* (No 305, 2007).

[8] See **12.7**.

[9] See eg the House of Lords case of *Powell and English* [1999] AC 1 where Lord Hutton makes repeated reference to 'practical concerns' outweighing 'strict logic', and the Law Commission similarly in their discussion of joint enterprise (Law Commission, *Participating in Crime* (No 305, 2007) Parts 2–3).

- Supreme Court: appeal allowed, restoring liability (Lord Kerr dissenting). D was liable because he assisted or encouraged P to shoot (Lords Phillips, Judge, and Wilson); or because he was a principal offender (Lord Clark); or because he was a joint principal with P (Lords Brown, Clark, and Dyson).

We discuss this important case at several points later. However, for present purposes it is sufficient to highlight that despite a general agreement that liability should have been found, the case leaves open four distinct bases for that liability, all of which are revealed to be questionable and imprecise.[10] Cases of homicide involving accomplices are depressingly common, and the law requires clarification and codification. As we discuss in the reform section later, a statutory scheme for reform was recommended by the Law Commission in 2007.[11] Unfortunately, at the time of writing the government has stated no intention to take these recommendations forward into legislation, either in whole or in part.

This chapter provides a route to understanding and applying the current law of complicity. The challenge, as it is for courts, academics, and students alike, is to find sufficient coherence within the law to be able to discuss and apply it logically, whilst also to acknowledge an inevitable lack of certainty as to the law in practice.

12.2 Principal or accomplice?

Where a criminal event involves multiple actors, the division between principal offenders and accomplices is not always obvious. However, as the rules governing the liability of principals and accessories are different, identifying the role of D may be crucial.

12.2.1 D as a principal offender

D is a principal offender if she completes the actus reus and mens rea elements of the principal offence. This is the standard form of liability assumed in our discussion of the substantive offences in previous chapters.

12.2.2 D as a co-principal

Where there is more than one actor involved in an offence, this does not necessarily mean that there is a single principal offender and that the other parties are accessories. Rather, where D and another (or others) each complete the actus reus and mens rea of an offence, they commit the offence as co-principals. For example, where D1 and D2 attack V with the intention to kill or cause GBH, and V dies as a result of this combined attack, both D1 and D2 will be liable for murder as principal

---

[10] See Lord Kerr's dissent. See also Buxton, 'Being an Accessory to One's Own Murder' [2012] Crim LR 275; Virgo, 'Joint Enterprise Liability is Dead: Long Live Accessorial Liability' [2012] Crim LR 850; Sullivan, 'Accessories and Principals after *Gnango*' in Reed and Bohlander (eds), *Participating in Crime* (2013).

[11] Law Commission, *Participating in Crime* (No 305, 2007).

offenders.[12] D1 and D2 have both caused the result (death) in fact and in law, even though there were multiple causes.[13]

This contrasts with the situation where D does not commit the actus reus of the offence with P, but she does assist or encourage it. For example, where D hires P as a contract killer to murder V. In this scenario, it may be thought by a lay person that D has caused V's death, but this is not the result in law. Rather, because P has taken the free and informed choice to kill V after D's assistance or encouragement, P's free and voluntary act breaks the chain of causation between D and the killing.[14] Legally, D has not caused P's voluntary acts or their results: P is their sole author. As stated in *Kennedy (No 2)*:

> Principals cause, accomplices encourage (or otherwise influence) or help. If the instigator were regarded as causing the result he would be a principal, and the conceptual division between principals (or, as I prefer to call them, perpetrators) and accessories would vanish. Indeed, it was because the instigator was not regarded as causing the crime that the notion of accessories had to be developed. This is the irrefragable argument for recognising the *novus actus* principle as one of the bases of our criminal law. The final act is done by the perpetrator, and his guilt pushes the accessories, conceptually speaking, into the background. Accessorial liability is, in the traditional theory, 'derivative' from that of the perpetrator.[15]

Despite the foundational importance of the distinction between principals and accessories, because both parties (if found guilty) will be labelled and punished in the same way, it is one that is often confused.

In *Gnango*,[16] for example, where P shoots V when aiming at D during a shoot-out with D, it is clear that D is not a principal cause of V's death: D does not shoot V himself, and P's shots are not caused by D, they are free and voluntary acts.[17] In short, D does not commit the actus reus of murder. However, in the Supreme Court, Lords Brown,[18] Clarke,[19] and Dyson[20] each express support for the view that D could be liable as a principal offender; and in the latter's case, this was even after recognising a break in the chain of causation.[21] If this dicta were accepted it would represent a significant change to the law, collapsing the distinction between principals and accessories set out in *Kennedy (No 2)*, and rewriting the rules of causation.[22] It cannot be correct. It is an understandable, but regrettable, confusion of distinct concepts.[23]

---

[12] *Macklin and Murphy's Case* (1838) 2 Lew CC 225.
[13] See **2.7.1**.
[14] *Kennedy (No 2)* [2007] UKHL 38.
[15] [2007] UKHL 38, [17], quoting Williams, '*Finis* for *Novus Actus*?' (1989) 48 CLJ 391.
[16] [2011] UKSC 59.
[17] Unlike in *Pagett* (1983) 76 Cr App R 279, where return fire from police was held not to break the causal chain, P's shots were not involuntary self-defence. See **2.7.2.3**.
[18] At [71].
[19] At [81].
[20] At [105].
[21] At [106].
[22] Sullivan, 'Accessories and Principals after *Gnango*' in Reed and Bohlander (eds), *Participating in Crime* (2013).
[23] Buxton, 'Being an Accessory to One's Own Murder' [2012] Crim LR 275.

12.2.3 D as a principal via innocent agency

Although the free and voluntary acts of a third party will break the chain of causation, this is not the case where the actions of that party are uninformed. Where D uses a party (X) as a tool to commit an offence, and that party is unaware of the circumstances that would make her acts criminal, D may still be liable as a *principal* offender via the doctrine of innocent agency.[24] For example, D gives X a letter bomb to deliver to V, X does so, and V is killed. In this scenario, if D had informed X that the letter contained a bomb then X's act of delivery becomes a free and voluntary act that breaks the chain of causation between D's acts and the death of V (X becomes the principal to the murder; D the accessory). In contrast, if X is unaware of the letter's contents, then her delivery to V is not an informed act and D remains the cause of V's death (D becomes the principal to the murder; X the innocent agent).

The doctrine of innocent agency is illustrated in *Michael*.[25]

Michael (1840) 9 C & P 356

D, intending to kill her baby (V), gave the nurse caring for the child (Y) a bottle of 'medicine' which she asked Y to administer. The bottle actually contained laudanum, a drug that would kill V if administered at the dose instructed by D. In the event, Y did not administer the drug but left it on the mantelpiece. Whilst Y was absent, her 5-year-old son (X) took the drug and administered it to V, causing death. X had no understanding of the drug or its danger. D was charged with murder.

- Assizes: guilty of murder. The actions of Y and X were uninformed (ie they were innocent agents) and so D's act remained the cause of V's death.

A third party will qualify as an innocent agent if she acts without essential knowledge (as with X and Y in *Michael*); where she is under the age of criminal responsibility (as X was in *Michael*); or where she is legally insane. In each case the third party becomes, in effect, a tool of D as opposed to an autonomous agent.

The doctrine of innocent agency works well with types of offence for which the principal does not require a particular attribute, such as murder. However, for certain offences, it seems inappropriate to characterise D as a principal offender when acting through an innocent agent. For example, where D tells X to have sex with his wife (V) knowing that V will not consent, and X does so (V not making her lack of consent apparent to X because of D's threats), can we say that D rapes V as a principal offender?[26] The doctrine of innocent agency would suggest that this is possible, with X's uninformed acts not breaking the chain of causation. However, section 1 of the Sexual Offences Act 2003 defines rape in terms of D penetrating V's vagina with 'his penis', an act D has not performed. Similar problems arise in the context of bigamy: if D knows Y is married, but induces X (unaware of Y's marital status) to marry Y, it is problematic to say that D has 'married during the lifetime of his wife' (the actus reus of bigamy). In each case, the courts have preferred to describe D as 'procuring' the offence as an accomplice. This

---

[24] Williams, 'Innocent Agency and Causation' (1992) 3 Crim L Forum 289.
[25] See also *Stringer and Banks* [1991] Crim LR 639: fraud via an innocent agent.
[26] This example is based on the facts of *Cogan and Leak* [1976] QB 217, where there was some support for an innocent agency approach.

affords liability, and avoids the linguistic problems described in relation to rape and big-amy above, but it also begs an obvious question: how can D be an accomplice to X when X has not committed an offence? We return to this in our discussion of 'procuring' later.

> **Extra detail...**
> The Law Commission has recommended that the doctrine of innocent agency should be codified and reformed to include problematic cases such as those discussed earlier. Thus, for the Commission, D should be liable for rape and bigamy as a principal offender in the examples given despite the linguis-tic problems applying offence definitions. This would resolve the current need to resort to procuring. However, this recommendation does not represent the current law.[27]

12.2.4 D as an accomplice

D is an accomplice to a principal offence where, rather than completing the actus reus of the offence herself, she aids, abets, counsels, or procures P to commit the offence, and P does so. In modern language, this requires D to have assisted or encouraged P, to have caused P's offence to come about, *or* to have coordinated behaviour with P as part of a joint enterprise. D needs only to have done one of these.[28] Each will be discussed in detail later.

> **Terminology...**
> Several terms are used interchangeably in the literature.
> • Complicity: the doctrine of complicity is also commonly referred to as accomplice liability; acces-sorial liability; and secondary liability.
> • Accomplices: accomplices are also commonly referred to as accessories and secondary parties.
> • Principals: principal offenders are sometimes referred to as perpetrators.

D's liability for the principal offence is derivative of, or parasitic on, P's conduct. This does not mean that P must be convicted of the principal offence before D can be liable, or even that P must be identified. D's liability derives from proof of the principal offence, not from P's conviction for it. Thus, D's liability depends on proof that her acts were rel-evant to a principal offence that has been committed by another party: D's liability *does* derive from P's criminal conduct.[29] This is crucial where, for example, P is unidentified (eg *Gnango*) or even deceased.

12.2.5 Uncertainty whether D is a principal or an accomplice

Even when the greatest care is taken to distinguish between principals and accessories,[30] there are two circumstances where uncertainty can emerge. One is legal, and the other is factual.

---

[27] Law Commission, *Participating in Crime* (No 305, 2007) paras 4.8–4.27. See, Taylor, 'Procuring, Causation, Innocent Agency and the Law Commission' [2008] Crim LR 32.

[28] *Ferguson v Weaving* [1951] KB 814.

[29] *Thornton v Mitchell* [1940] 1 All ER 339: no principal offence, and therefore not accessory liability.

[30] See criticism of the Supreme Court in *Gnango* at **12.2.2**.

A) **Legal:** Legal problems separating principal offenders and accomplices can emerge, as we have highlighted, in the context of innocent agency.[31] Although the doctrine of innocent agency operates logically in relation to most offences, it struggles to apply to certain offences such as rape and bigamy. As a result, despite D acting through an innocent agent (ie acting as a principal), the courts are more likely to characterise D's conduct as procuring (ie acting as an accomplice). We discuss this further later.

B) **Factual:** Factual problems separating principal offenders and accomplices can emerge in cases where D's role in the principal offence is unclear. For example, it might be common ground that both D1 and D2 were present at the time V was attacked and killed, but it may be disputed whether both attacked V, or whether only one of the parties attacked V, and disputed between them as to which. Where this is the case, there are two possible outcomes.

First, if it can be proved that D *either* killed V as a principal offender *or* was an accomplice to the killing of V by another because D must have, at least, assisted or encouraged the offence, then D may be convicted of the principal offence without the prosecution having to prove which role she played. *Giannetto* provides a useful illustration.

Giannetto [1997] 1 Cr App R 1

D threatened to kill his wife (V) and hired another party (Y) to kill her. V was killed, but it could not be proved who killed her. D was charged with murder on the basis that he *either* killed V himself as a principal *or* she was killed by someone on his behalf (ie he was an accomplice).

- Crown Court: guilty of murder.
- Court of Appeal: conviction upheld on appeal. D may be liable in these circumstances even where the jury are not unanimous on what role he played, as long as they were sure that he was either a principal or an accessory.

Despite uncertainty as to D's role, because conviction as principal or accessory leads to the same result in the shape of liability for the principal offence, it has been held that this rule does not breach D's right to a fair trial under Article 6 ECHR.[32] This is often referred to as the forensic advantage of complicity, and provides a crucial route to liability in a number of cases.[33] The ability to charge and convict D as principal or accessory in the alternative is particularly important. For example, in the context of gang violence and other group offences it may be impossible to prove which member committed the actus reus of the principal offence, namely which member struck the fatal blow, but it is clear that each member was sufficiently involved.[34] It is also useful for domestic situations involving mistreatment of children: a parent's duty to prevent harm to their child may be enough to implicate them as an accomplice to abuse carried out by the other parent, avoiding the need to identify which parent is the principal offender.[35]

---

[31] See **12.2.3**.
[32] *Mercer* [2001] All ER 187.
[33] Law Commission, *Participating in Crime* (No 305, 2007) paras 2.5–2.6 and 3.3–3.4.
[34] *Bristow* [2013] EWCA Crim 1540: D convicted of manslaughter where there was uncertainty which of the group (jointly committing burglary) killed V in their escape. Commentary by Ormerod [2014] Crim LR 457.
[35] Glazebrook, 'Insufficient Child Protection' [2003] Crim LR 541.

For the second possibility of factual confusion, we may again have two or more parties and know that one of them must have committed the principal offence, but this time the evidence may be inadequate to demonstrate that if D was not the principal then in the alternative D must have been an accomplice. In other words, although D may have committed the principal offence, or may have acted as an accomplice, she may also be an innocent party; the evidence is inconclusive. In such a case, D must be acquitted. Where this is the case for both/all parties involved, even though we know one of them must have committed the offence, both/all must be acquitted: simply, guilt cannot be proved *beyond reasonable doubt*.[36] This principle was recently reaffirmed by the Court of Appeal in *Banfield*.[37]

12.3 Complicity by aiding, abetting, counselling, or procuring

Where D aids, abets, counsels, or procures P to commit a principal offence, and P does so, D is labelled and punished *as if* she committed the principal offence herself. As we have said, D's liability goes beyond inchoate liability (discussed in **Chapter 11**) because the principal offence has been committed. Equally, D does not commit the principal offence as a principal offender because P's choice to commit the offence breaks the chain of causation between D's acts and that offence. D is an accomplice, a secondary party.

Although the precise elements for liability (as an accomplice) remain uncertain within the common law, **Table 12.1** provides an overview of the likely requirements.

Table 12.1 Complicity by aiding, abetting, counselling, or procuring

	Actus reus	**Mens rea**
D's conduct element	Any acts or omissions causing the result	Voluntary
D's circumstance element	Aiding, abetting, or counselling: D's conduct is capable of assisting or encouraging P to commit the principal offence	Knowledge
	Or	
	Procuring: D's conduct is capable of causing P's principal offence	Knowledge
D's result element	Aiding, abetting, or counselling: D's conduct assists or encourages P to commit the principal offence	Intention
	Or	
	Procuring: D's conduct causes P's principal offence	None

[36] *Abbott* [1955] 2 QB 497; Williams, 'Which of You Did It?' (1989) 52 MLR 179.
[37] [2013] EWCA Crim 1394.

D's ulterior mens rea element	*	Recklessness whether P will commit the principal offence
P's principal offence	P's principal offence must be completed, and must be of the type that D foresaw (ie, not fundamentally different).	

Unlike the general inchoate offences, as P's offence is completed we do not analyse D's actus reus and mens rea in the abstract. Rather, cases will begin by identifying the crime that P has committed, and will then discuss D's actus reus and mens rea *in relation to* that principal offence.

12.3.1 Actus reus of aiding, abetting, counselling, or procuring

As illustrated in **Table 12.1**, D's actus reus requires us to distinguish between aiding, abetting, or counselling on the one hand, and procuring on the other. It should be reiterated that D's conduct only needs to satisfy one of these terms to complete the actus reus.[38]

In *AG's Reference (No 1 of 1975)*,[39] Lord Widgery CJ stated that the terms 'aid', 'abet', 'counsel', and 'procure' should be given their 'ordinary meaning'. However, this is somewhat misleading, particularly in the context of counselling which should not be interpreted in line with common parlance,[40] and abetting and procuring which are not terms in common use. Rather, we need to identify legal definitions.

12.3.1.1 Aiding, abetting, or counselling

Aiding, abetting, and counselling have been interpreted in modern times[41] to mean no more than assisting or encouraging. This will include, for example: D providing P with tools, with information, acting as a lookout, positively emboldening P, threatening P to commit the principal offence, and so on.

A) **Aiding:** 'Aiding' should be read as 'assisting'. D may assist at the time P commits the principal offence (eg acting as a lookout, driving the getaway car, etc), or in advance of the offence (eg providing tools, weapons, etc).[42] D may satisfy this requirement even where the assistance is unwanted by P, or even unknown as where D, without P's knowledge, restrains a policeman who would have intervened to stop P's offence.[43]

---

[38] *Ferguson v Weaving* [1951] KB 814.

[39] [1975] 2 All ER 684, 686.

[40] We are not talking about D providing P with emotional support or therapy.

[41] Historically, these terms have been interpreted in different ways.

[42] *Nedrick-Smith* [2006] EWHC 3015 (Admin): D was an accessory when driving P to the scene of the crime.

[43] Discussed in *Fury* [2006] EWCA Crim 1258.

B) Abetting: 'Abetting' should be read as 'encouraging'. As we saw in the context of inchoate liability,[44] D can encourage positively by emboldening or instigating; or negatively by threatening.

An important line of case law has developed in relation to encouraging by 'mere presence' at the scene of P's offence. This is not the same as omissions liability (discussed later) because D must have *actively* gone to the scene: simply finding yourself at the scene of a crime and doing nothing will not be sufficient[45] to make you an accomplice. However, even accepting the qualification that D must have been active in her choice to be present, it may still be doubted whether the effect of mere presence should be recognised as capable of encouraging. Nevertheless, it has been consistently held that mere presence is *capable* of constituting an act of encouragement. This is illustrated in *Clarkson*.

> ### *Clarkson* [1971] 3 All ER 344
>
> D1 and D2 entered a room in their barracks in which a woman was being raped by other soldiers. There was no evidence that they provided any assistance or encouragement beyond their choice to enter and remain present. They were charged with rape as accomplices.
>
> • Court-Martial: guilty of rape.
> • Court-Martial Appeal Court: appeal allowed. Voluntary presence is *capable* of satisfying the actus reus of complicity. However, there was insufficient proof as to mens rea: the prosecution did not prove that D1 and D2 intended to assist or encourage rape by their presence.

Clarkson provides useful clarification on the actus reus of complicity, as well as a reminder to be mindful of mens rea requirements (discussed later). Although voluntary presence is capable of constituting an act of encouragement, such encouragement should not be assumed, and must still be demonstrated on the particular facts. For example, in *Coney*,[46] D's presence at an illegal prize-fight was clearly capable of encouraging those taking part because such fights would not happen without an audience, but his conviction was quashed because the jury were incorrectly directed that such presence was *conclusive* of encouragement.[47] In fact, where encouragement is found, D has often done more than being *merely* present. For example, in *Wilcox v Jeffery*,[48] where D was complicit in P's offence of playing an illegal jazz concert,[49] D was present at the concert, but had also arranged the concert and transported P from the airport.

> *Point to remember…*
> Issues relating to mere presence are only necessary where there is no evidence of D's conduct at the scene or there is evidence of inactivity. Where there is evidence of D encouraging P at the scene (eg clapping at the concert in *Wilcox*), then it will be much easier to find liability.

---

[44] See **11.4.1**.

[45] eg *Kousar* [2009] EWCA Crim 139: D was not liable for possession of counterfeit goods simply because her husband was found storing them in the loft of their matrimonial home.

[46] (1882) 8 QBD 534.

[47] *Allen* [1965] 1 QB 130: D's presence at an affray did not constitute encouragement, even though he held a secret intention to help P if needed.

[48] [1951] 1 All ER 464.

[49] Paid employment was not allowed on the terms of P's permission to visit the UK.

C) **Counselling:** 'Counselling' should also be read as 'encouraging'. At one time counselling and abetting were distinguished on the timing of D's encouragement with abetting occurring at the time of the offence and counselling in advance, but this distinction no longer operates.[50]

Can D assist or encourage by omission?

As with inchoate assisting and encouraging, D may also become complicit in P's offence by omission. This arises in two circumstances, both of which are usually analysed as providing P with tacit encouragement.

The first, and most straightforward case applies where P's omission arises as a breach of a recognised duty to act. We highlighted such duties in our general discussion of omissions liability (ie familial duties; contractual duties; assumed duties; duties arising from the creation of a dangerous situation; and so on).[51] This will include, for example, D who does nothing whilst his wife drowns their child,[52] or a disgruntled security guard who omits to turn on an alarm system.

In the context of an offence by encouragement under the SCA 2007, where the offence is inchoate, this is the end of the matter. However, controversially, complicity also recognises a second category of omission-based encouragement. It applies where D has a *power or right to control* the actions of P, but deliberately refrains from doing so. The rule is illustrated in *Du Cros v Lambourne*.

📄 *Du Cros v Lambourne* [1907] 1 KB 40

D was charged with driving a motor vehicle at a dangerous speed. However, it could not be proved whether he was driving or was a passenger.

- Petty Sessions: guilty of driving at a dangerous speed. Conviction in the alternative that he was either driving, or was (as owner of the car) assenting to P's speeding by failing to intervene.
- Quarter Sessions: conviction upheld on appeal.
- King's Bench: appeal dismissed.

More recent cases, confirming the rule, include *Tuck v Robson*, where D (a pub licensee) allowed customers to drink after hours;[53] *Webster*, where D allowed an intoxicated P to drive his car;[54] *Gaunt*, where D (a manager) failed to prevent P (his employee) racially harassing another employee;[55] and *Martin*, where D (supervising a learner driver) allowed P to drive dangerously, resulting in the deaths of P and that of a passenger.[56] It should be remembered that liability under this rule, although potentially extensive, is restrained by the requirements of mens rea (discussed later), including that D must intend by her acts or omissions to assist or encourage P.

---

[50] Discussed in *NCB v Gamble* [1959] 1 QB 11.
[51] See **2.6.2**.
[52] *Russell* [1933] VLR 59.
[53] [1970] 1 WLR 741.
[54] [2006] EWCA Crim 415: P crashed the car causing death. D was liable as an accomplice for causing death by dangerous driving.
[55] [2003] EWCA Crim 3925.
[56] [2010] EWCA Crim 1450.

Extra detail...

The Law Commission recommend abolishing omissions liability where D is not in breach of a duty to act, contending that the current law demands too much of D to act as a 'good Samaritan'. The Commission uses the example of D who fails to prevent an assault happening on his front lawn when woken by it in the middle of the night.[57]

Must D cause P's offence?

Having established that D's conduct is *capable* of assisting or encouraging P's principal offence, the next question is whether it must do so in fact. We have already highlighted that a strict causation between D's conduct and P's offence could never be required: where P acts voluntarily she breaks the chain of causation, and therefore there is no causal link from D's conduct; where P does not act voluntarily (ie she is an innocent agent), then D is a principal rather than an accomplice.[58] It will also be remembered that no causal link is necessary for inchoate assisting or encouraging.[59] However, as D's liability in complicity derives from P's completion of a crime, it might be thought that some causal role is essential to justify that derivation.[60] As stated in *Stringer*:[61]

> It is well established that D's conduct need not cause P to commit the offence in the sense that 'but for' D's conduct P would not have committed the offence.... But it is also established by the [common law] that D's conduct must have some relevance to the commission of the principal offence; there must, as it has been said, be some connecting link. The moral justification for holding D responsible for the crime is that he has involved himself in the commission of the crime by assistance or encouragement, and that presupposes some form of connection between his conduct and the crime.

It is on this rather vague basis that the current law of complicity requires *some* causal effect from D's conduct, but does not require full causation of the kind discussed in **Chapter 2**. So what does this mean in practice?

A) **D assists P (eg provides tools, acts as a lookout, etc):** It must be demonstrated that D's assistance contributed to P's offence in some way. For example, where D provides P with a gun to kill V, but P ignores the gun and kills V with a knife, there is no assistance: D's acts were capable of assisting P, but provided no assistance in fact. Thus, although D satisfies the actus reus for inchoate liability by her acts capable of assisting or encouraging,[62] D does not assist P for the purposes of complicity.

Assessment matters...

Where P rejects D's assistance (as in our example), the offer of help may nevertheless encourage P to commit the principal offence. With this in mind, even where D's acts look like potential assistance, remember to consider whether they also (or alternatively) encourage P (ie abet or counsel). In the absence of actual assistance or encouragement, you should remember that D may still be liable under the SCA 2007 if her acts were capable of assisting or encouraging.

---

[57] Law Commission, *Participating in Crime* (No 305, 2007) paras 3.39–3.41.

[58] See **12.2**.

[59] See **11.4.1**.

[60] Some have argued that this causal connection is/should be the basis for complicity liability. See **12.6**.

[61] [2011] EWCA Crim 1396, per Toulson LJ at [48].

[62] See **11.4.1**.

Once it is established that D has provided some assistance the actus reus of complicity will be satisfied. There is no need to show that D's assistance was substantial. For example, D acts as a lookout but no one appears to disturb the crime being committed by P; D supplies weapons that P could have acquired elsewhere; D drives P to the scene but gets lost and is late: in each case D's assistance is minimal, but will still satisfy the actus reus for complicity in P's offence. The issue of causation is usefully discussed in *Bryce*.

Bryce [2004] EWCA Crim 1231

D drove P to a place to enable P to kill V. D foresaw that P would kill V. P did kill V, but a full 12 hours after D's involvement, and only following discussion with another party. D was charged with murder as P's accomplice.

- Crown Court: guilty of murder.
- Court of Appeal: conviction upheld on appeal. Despite the time delay between D's acts and the killing, and despite other contributory facts, D's acts continued to provide some assistance to the murder.

B) **D encourages P (eg emboldens, threatens, etc):** To establish a connection between D's encouragement and P's offence, it must be proved that D's encouragement was communicated to P.[63] In other words, P must know that D is encouraging her. For example, if D shouts in a football stadium for one player (P) to punch another player (V), and P does so, D will only be complicit in P's offence if P hears the shout. If P does not hear, D remains liable for inchoate encouragement (ie her act is *capable* of encouraging P), but will not satisfy the actus reus of complicity.[64]

However, once it is demonstrated that P was aware of D's encouragement, even where that encouragement had little effect on P, D will satisfy the actus reus of complicity. The trial judge in *Giannetto*, discussed earlier,[65] provided a useful and often repeated example.

If…[D] knew that somebody else intended to kill his wife and he just did nothing at all, then he is not guilty because he has not participated…Supposing somebody came up to [D] and said, 'I am going to kill your wife', if he played any part, either in encouragement, as little as patting him on the back, nodding, saying, 'Oh goody', that would be sufficient to involve him in the murder, to make him guilty, because he is encouraging the murder.

As this example illustrates, D's encouragement will be sufficient even where P has already decided to commit the principal offence. It is assumed that D's encouragement, although not changing D's settled plan, still emboldens or fortifies her intention. This assumption is only rebutted if there is evidence that P gained no encouragement from D. For example, where D encourages P to punch V, but before doing so P tells D to 'mind your own business'.[66]

---

[63] *Caelham* [1985] 1 QB 808.
[64] Example taken from the Law Commission, and discussed in *Stringer* [2011] EWCA Crim 1396, [49].
[65] See **12.2.4**.
[66] Law Commission, *Participating in Crime* (No 305, 2007) para B.62.

12.3.1.2 Procuring

In the alternative to aiding, abetting, or counselling, the actus reus of complicity can be satisfied where D 'procures' P's offence. To procure is to 'produce by endeavour'. Procuring will apply even where D has not assisted or encouraged P, as long as D has played a causal role in the principal offence coming about. The leading case is *AG's Reference (No 1 of 1975)*.

AG's Reference (No 1 of 1975) [1975] 2 All ER 684

D surreptitiously laced P's drink with alcohol knowing that P would be driving home. P was unaware of this. P later committed an offence of driving with excess alcohol[67] as the principal offender and D was charged as an accomplice.

- Crown Court: not guilty of driving offence, because P was unaware of D's role.
- Court of Appeal: on a reference from the AG, D should have been liable. D procured P's offence.

In line with this case, it is clear that D can procure an offence where P is unaware of D's actions, and even though D is not encouraging or assisting P's acts (ie in this case, P's driving). It is enough that D caused the necessary circumstances of the offence to be present (ie in this case, for P to be over the proscribed alcohol limit), and thus caused P to commit the offence.

Subject to the problem cases discussed in the following section, procuring requires D to have caused P's offence. Thus, liability for procuring will be undermined by any break in the causal chain. In *AG's Reference (No 1 of 1975)*, P chose only to drink soft drinks and then to drive. Those acts do not break the chain of causation because they are not informed acts (ie P is unaware of the alcohol lacing his drink). If P was aware and chose to continue, his acts would break the chain, and D would only be liable as an accomplice if it could be shown that his acts also assisted or encouraged P. In *Beatty v Gillbanks*,[68] for example, the Salvation Army knew that a proposed meeting would provoke a violent reaction from a hostile organisation known as the 'Skeleton Army'. Although this proved to be correct, the Salvation Army could not be said to have procured the violence. This is because the free, voluntary, and informed choice of Skeleton Army members broke any potential causal chain. Provocation is not causation.

Extra detail...
Although D may assist or encourage by omission, it is very unlikely that D could procure an offence (produce by endeavour) without positive movement.

Problem cases and procuring

Difficulties can arise in certain cases involving procuring. Ideally, procuring cases can be logically distinguished from other cases in the following way.

- **D assists or encourages P who knowingly commits a principal offence:** This is *not* a procuring case because D has not caused P to commit the principal offence. This is a standard case of complicity by D assisting or encouraging P.

---

[67] Contrary to the Road Traffic Act 1972, s6(1), now replaced by the Road Traffic Act 1988, s5.
[68] (1882) 9 QBD 308.

- **D causes the unknowing P to complete the actus reus of an offence that also requires mens rea:** This is not a procuring case because P commits no crime. D will be liable as the principal offender via the doctrine of innocent agency.

- **D causes the unknowing P to commit a strict liability offence:** This *is* a procuring case. P does commit the principal offence, and D has caused her to do so.

Unfortunately, within the innocent agency category in the second bullet point, certain cases have been decided under the heading of procuring. Thus, as well as standard cases of procuring in the last bullet point, a further category must be added.

- **D causes the unknowing P to complete the actus reus of an offence that also requires mens rea, but the offence cannot be committed by an innocent agent:** As highlighted earlier,[69] there are a number of offences that cannot be committed via an innocent agent (eg rape and bigamy). Therefore, for these cases, even though innocent agency might appear the correct approach because D causes P's actus reus but P does not commit an offence because she lacks mens rea, the courts are more likely to describe D's liability as complicity by procuring. This is an unfortunate description. P has not committed an offence and so it cannot be said that D's liability derives from another's crime. This is not to say that D does not warrant liability—D has caused P to commit the actus reus of that crime, and D has mens rea[70]—it is simply that the approach used to find liability (ie procuring) seems inappropriate.

The case of *Cogan and Leak* provides a useful illustration.

> **Cogan and Leak** [1976] QB 217
>
> D told his wife (V) to have sexual intercourse with his friend (P). V was scared of D and so, although she did not consent, she did not resist P. P was unaware that V was not consenting. P was charged with rape, with D as his accomplice.
>
> - Crown Court: guilty of rape (both D and P).
> - Court of Appeal: P's appeal allowed—there was a misdirection relating to the mens rea required of P for rape.[71] D's conviction upheld—although P was innocent, D nevertheless procured the offence of rape.

Cogan and Leak is a useful case because the Court of Appeal discusses the possibility of finding liability on the basis of innocent agency, but eventually prefers the procuring approach. Similar reasoning was adopted in *Millward*.[72] In this case D instructed an employee (P) to drive a tractor and trailer knowing that the hitch mechanism connecting them was defective. The hitch broke in transit, and the detached trailer killed the driver of an oncoming car (V). P did *not* commit an offence of causing

---

[69] See **12.2.3–12.2.4**.
[70] See the discussion later in the chapter.
[71] See **8.2**.
[72] [1994] Crim LR 527.

death by reckless driving[73] because he lacked mens rea. However, D *was* convicted of procuring that offence.

> **Point to remember...**
> Although these cases allow for complicity by procuring even though P does not commit a principal offence, it is essential that P completes the actus reus of the offence and that D has caused P to do so. We see this in *Cogan and Leak*, and in *Millward*, where D instructs or permits conduct from P knowing (but not telling P) that such conduct satisfied the actus reus of an offence. Where the actus reus of the offence is not completed by P, whatever D's role, there can be no complicity.[74]

12.3.2 Mens rea of aiding, abetting, counselling, or procuring

The mens rea for complicity has not been consistently identified or applied by the courts. Indeed, the Law Commission has highlighted four different (and inconsistent) approaches to mens rea within the current law.[75] Therefore, although this section discusses the dominant interpretation of the law, this should not imply a settled interpretation.

When discussing D's mens rea, it is useful to separate (a) D's mens rea as to her own conduct, and (b) D's mens rea as to the future conduct and state of mind of P. We discuss each in turn.

> **Point to remember...**
> Separating our discussion of D's mens rea in this way was also recommended in relation to inchoate assisting and encouraging.[76] However, the important difference here is that we assess D's mens rea with regard to a principal offence which has been committed by P. We do not ask generally whether D had mens rea as to P committing an offence but, rather, whether D had mens rea as to P committing the offence completed. As you will see later, this difference becomes very important where P's offence varies from D's expectation.

12.3.2.1 D's mens rea as to her own conduct

This part of D's mens rea contains two requirements. First, as with all criminal liability, D's conduct (ie D's assisting, encouraging, or procuring) must be performed voluntarily. For example, there will be no liability where D inadvertently drops a tool which P then uses to commit a crime, and/or no omissions liability where D omits because she is tied up and unable to move.[77]

Secondly, D must intend that her conduct will assist or encourage P to commit the principal offence, or in the context of procuring, that her conduct will cause the

---

[73] Since replaced by the offence of causing death by dangerous driving, discussed at **6.4.2.1**.

[74] *Loukes* [1996] 1 Cr App R 444: D was not an accomplice to causing death by careless driving because P (the driver) was not careless and therefore did not satisfy the actus reus of the offence.

[75] Law Commission, *Participating in Crime* (No 305, 2007) para 1.16.

[76] See **11.4.2–11.4.4**.

[77] *Bryce* [2004] EWCA Crim 1231, [41]–[42].

principal offence.[78] Importantly, this is not to say that D must intend that P will commit the principal offence (we discuss D's mens rea as to P's offence later). Of course, where D intends to assist, encourage, or cause an offence she will usually also intend that that offence should be committed, but this is not necessarily the case. For example, if D sells P a gun knowing that P could use it to kill V, D may be motivated purely by payment for the gun and may hope that P does not commit the offence, but she is still 'intentionally assisting' P to commit murder.[79] This was discussed in *National Coal Board v Gamble*.

National Coal Board v Gamble [1959] 1 QB 11

D supplied coal to P. At the weigh-station, before P was able to leave with the coal, P's lorry was overladen to the extent that taking the lorry on the road became an offence.[80] Nevertheless D allowed P to leave with the overladen lorry. D was charged as an accomplice to P's offence.

- Court: guilty of overladen offence.
- Divisional Court: conviction upheld on appeal by case stated. Although D may have been indifferent as to P's offence, he must have obliquely intended to assist (knowing that his action, supplying the coal and allowing P to leave, was virtually certain to assist). Slade J dissented, stating that D should only be found to have intended to aid where this is his direct intention (ie oblique intent was insufficient).

Following *Gamble*, another useful example of obliquely intending to assist or encourage is supplied by *Gnango* where the gunfight between D and P resulted in V being shot.[81] In *Gnango* it was clearly not D's direct intention that P would shoot at him with the intention to kill, D would have actively not wanted this, but such encouragement was a foreseen virtual certainty from D's conduct (ie D obliquely intended it).[82] In summary, then, this element will satisfied where D directly intends to assist, encourage, or procure P's offence because it is D's desire or purpose, *or* where it is D's oblique intention because although she may not desire it, D recognises that assistance or encouragement is the virtually certain consequence of her conduct.

The requirement of an intention to assist or encourage is particularly important in cases where D performs only minor acts of assistance or encouragement, such as in mere presence cases.[83] This is because where D's conduct provides only minor assistance or encouragement there is more reason to doubt whether she intended to assist or encourage.[84] Recklessness is never sufficient for this element. For example, it is not enough that D left a weapon foreseeing that it might be taken and used by another.

---

[78] Duff, 'Can I Help You? Accessorial Liability and the Intention to Assist' (1990) 10 LS 165.
[79] Even if assisting P is not D's purpose, she is aware that her conduct is virtually certain to assist. See **3.4.1**.
[80] Motor Vehicles (Construction and Use) Regulations 1955, regs 68 and 104.
[81] See **12.1**.
[82] See also *Lynch v DPP for Northern Ireland* [1975] AC 653, 678: knowingly driving P to murder V is sufficient even where D would prefer the murder not to happen.
[83] See **12.3.1.1**.
[84] *Coney* (1882) 8 QBD 534: confirming that mere presence during P's crime was not conclusive evidence of an intention to encourage.

> **Don't be confused...**
>
> In most cases, D's intention to assist, encourage, or procure P's offence can be discussed and applied in general terms. However, this is not always required. The following represents the minimum mens rea to satisfy this element.
>
> - Assisting or encouraging: as with the inchoate equivalent, D need not intend to assist or encourage every part of P's offence as long as she intends to assist or encourage P's conduct. For example, where D provides P with a gun, it is sufficient (for this element) that D intends to assist P to shoot the gun, she need not also intend to assist P to cause death.[85]
> - Procuring: D must intend to cause the principal offence, but again, she need not intend to cause every element. For example, in *AG's Reference (No 1 of 1975)*,[86] where D laced P's drink with alcohol, it was enough that D intended to cause the circumstance element (alcohol level) to come about, there was no additional requirement to intend to cause D's conduct (driving).

The requirement that D must intend to assist, encourage, or procure P's offence is a settled element of D's liability, but problem cases have emerged. For example, it has been argued that where D supplies P with an article for use within a principal offence, D may be excused accessorial liability if the supply was required under civil law, for example where P demands the return of a gun which was lent to D.[87] However, although liability in these circumstances can appear harsh,[88] it is unlikely that such an exclusion exists.[89] As long as D intends directly or obliquely to assist, encourage, or procure P's crime, she will satisfy this element.

12.3.2.2 D's mens rea as to P's principal offence

This element of D's mens rea is the most complex.[90] Unlike inchoate assisting or encouraging where we assess D's mens rea as to a *potential* principal offence in the abstract, complicity requires us to examine D's mens rea in relation to a principal offence that has come about. Therefore, as well as exploring D's state of mind at the time of the assistance or encouragement, we must also assess whether that mens rea will be sufficient in cases in which P's actual offence is less serious than D anticipated; more serious; or simply very different. We discuss each of these separately. However, we begin with the simplest case in which P completes the offence in line with D's expectations.

A) **P commits the principal offence D foresaw:** The general rule, taken from *Johnson v Youden*,[91] is that at the time of assisting, encouraging, or procuring D must 'know the essential matters' that constitute P's offence. This implies that D must have knowledge of what P will go on to do. However, despite consistent endorsement of the quotation from *Johnson*, it has been interpreted to mean something quite different. Rather than a requirement of knowledge, or even belief, it is now clear that D will

---

[85] See discussion in *Bryce* [2004] EWCA Crim 1231.

[86] See **12.3.1.2**.

[87] Discussed in *National Coal Board v Gamble* [1959] 1 QB 11, 20.

[88] Williams, 'Obedience to Law as a Crime' (1990) 53 MLR 445.

[89] Not least because withholding property in these circumstances would not be a breach of civil law: *K v National Westminster Bank* [2006] EWCA Civ 1039. Discussed in *Bryce* [2004] EWCA Crim 1231, [63].

[90] Law Commission, *Participating in Crime* (No 305, 2007) paras B.79–B.152.

[91] [1950] 1 KB 544, 546.

satisfy this element of complicity even where she is merely reckless as to P's offence coming about. This includes cases of wilful blindness, where D intentionally avoids discovering knowledge of P's potential future offending.[92] However, crucially, recklessness is the minimum mens rea required; negligence (or less) will not be sufficient.[93]

The test is illustrated in *Carter v Richardson*.

> **Carter v Richardson** [1974] RTR 314
>
> D was supervising a learner driver (P). P was charged with driving with excess alcohol and D was charged as an accomplice. D was aware that P had been drinking, but did not know he was over the prescribed limit.
>
> • Court: guilty of driving over the prescribed limit.
> • High Court: conviction upheld on appeal by case stated. As long as D foresaw a risk that P was over the limit (ie D was reckless), this is sufficient for liability.

In *Carter v Richardson*, D *knew* that P would complete the conduct element of the offence (driving), and was *reckless* as to whether he will satisfy the circumstance element (being over the alcohol limit). The reverse of this arose in *Blakely and Sutton v DPP*,[94] where D laced P's drink with alcohol and so *knew* that D was over the limit, but did not want him to drive. D escaped liability in this case due to potential confusion over the definition of recklessness applied in the lower court, but the High Court made clear that recklessness (properly defined) as to P's future conduct (ie driving) would have been sufficient for D's accomplice liability. Thus, as these cases demonstrate, as long as D is at least reckless as to P completing the elements of the principal offence then this requirement of D's mens rea will be satisfied.

> **Point to remember…**
> The offence of driving over the prescribed alcohol limit is one of strict liability (ie P may be liable even though she does not know she is over the limit). However, although P need not have mens rea as to this essential element of her crime, D (for complicity liability) must be reckless as to every essential element.[95] In *Callow v Tillstone*,[96] P (a butcher) committed a strict liability offence by selling tainted meat. P was liable despite genuinely believing that the meat was fit for sale, a belief based on D's negligent veterinary examination. D was not liable as an accomplice because he was not reckless as to the tainted status of the meat. The important point here is that although not every element of P's offence requires P to have mens rea, D must be at least reckless as to all the essential elements for complicity liability.

Just as the actus reus elements of P's offence constitute 'essential elements' that must be foreseen by D, the same is also true of the mens rea elements of P's offence. As with inchoate assisting and encouraging, to be an accomplice to P's offence, D must be at least reckless as to whether P will commit the actus reus of the principal offence with the required mens rea. This was discussed in *ABCD*.[97]

---

[92] See **3.4.2.1**.
[93] *Webster* [2006] EWCA Crim 415, [25]–[26].
[94] [1991] RTR 405.
[95] The only exception relates to constructive liability offences, discussed later.
[96] (1900) 83 LT 411.
[97] See also *Rahman* [2008] UKHL 45.

> **ABCD** [2010] EWCA Crim 1622
>
> C organised an attack on V in his home, carried out by A, B, and D. Unable to prove which of the defendants inflicted the fatal blows, they were each charged with murder as a principal or an accomplice.
>
> - Crown Court: that would suffice to make them guilty of murder.
> - Court of Appeal: appeal allowed. Although the trial judge had made it clear that (for accomplice liability) D must be at least reckless as to another causing death, it was not made clear that D must also be at least reckless as to that other doing so with the mens rea required for murder (ie D must foresee as a real possibility that P might act *with the intention* to kill or cause GBH).

As this case demonstrates, where the principal offence requires mens rea D can only be liable as an accomplice where she was at least reckless as to P acting with this mens rea. P's mens rea is an essential element to which D must be reckless.

   Although D must be at least reckless as to the essential elements of P's principal offence, there is no requirement beyond this for D to foresee the precise details of that offence. Thus, in *Bainbridge*,[98] D was liable as an accessory to bank robbery even though, when supplying cutting equipment to P, he was unaware which premises would be targeted and when. The Court of Criminal Appeal clarified that although D did not know the details of the specific offence committed by P, his conviction remained safe because he did foresee when supplying the equipment that P might use the equipment for breaking and entering. In other words, D was reckless as to the *essential* elements of P's offence. Similar reasoning is also evident in *DPP for NI v Maxwell*.

> **DPP for NI v Maxwell** [1978] 1 WLR 1350
>
> D was a member of the proscribed organisation UVF in Northern Ireland and he assisted P by driving him to a pub. D knew that P intended to attack the pub, but was unsure whether this would involve planting explosives, murder, or robbery. In the event, P damaged the pub using pipe bombs. D was charged as an accessory to the explosives offence.[99]
>
> - NI Crown Court: guilty of explosives offence.
> - NI Court of Appeal: conviction upheld on appeal.
>
> - House of Lords: appeal dismissed. D does not need to know the details of P's offence, as long as he knows the essential matters.

Maxwell is a particularly useful case in two regards. First, it provides House of Lords endorsement for the principle in *Bainbridge* that D need not know the details of P's offence. Secondly, it also confirms that where D foresees the possibility of multiple different offences, this will be sufficient foresight where P commits one of those offences. Of course, where P commits an offence that was not foreseen, for example in this scenario rape, then D would not be an accomplice to this offence.

---

[98] [1960] 1 QB 129.
[99] Explosive Substances Act 1883, s3(1)(a).

B) P commits a less serious principal offence than D foresaw: This situation arises where D assists, encourages, or procures P to commit an offence such as intentional GBH, but P commits a less serious offence such as battery. Regardless of P's conduct, D is likely to be liable for the inchoate offence of assisting or encouraging the more serious offence.[100] D is also likely to be complicit in the offence committed by P. For the latter, it would have to be shown that D either foresaw that P might commit the less serious offence, or as with our example that the less serious offence is a lesser included offence within the one foreseen.[101] However, there are certain cases in which D may be liable as an accomplice to the more serious offence foreseen, even though this offence is not completed by P. It is useful to separate our analysis into the three reasons why P may not have committed the more serious offence foreseen by D.

P lacks actus reus: this was the case in our example, where P commits battery rather than GBH. Here, D's liability is limited by P's actus reus and will not go beyond it. D may therefore be an accessory to battery, but not to intentional GBH in our example. This is a logical outcome, and one that remains faithful to the idea of complicity as derivative from P's offence. However, it can appear rather generous to D, particularly where P causes harm as a result of D's assistance or encouragement, but does not complete the actus reus of an offence. This was the issue in *Thornton v Mitchell*.[102]

Thornton v Mitchell [1940] 1 All ER 339

A bus conductor (D) negligently signalled for a bus driver (P) to reverse. Two pedestrians were knocked down by the bus, one of whom (V) was killed. P was charged with careless driving, D as an accomplice.[103]

- Court: P not guilty, as his driving was not careless. D was found guilty, and appealed.
- High Court: appeal by case stated allowed. Where P does not commit the actus reus of an offence, there can be no accomplice liability.

P's commission of the actus reus may therefore limit D's accomplice liability, and where no actus reus is performed by P, it may undermine it altogether. In such cases, however, remember that inchoate liability may still be available.

P lacks mens rea: Mirroring cases of incomplete actus reus, a lack of mens rea from P is also likely to minimise or even extinguish her liability; with D's derivative liability following suit. However, there is an important exception. This applies where, although P lacks mens rea for the principal offence and although D may know that P will lack mens rea, D will nevertheless be guilty as an accomplice to that offence if she herself

---

[100] See **11.4**.

[101] A 'lesser included' offence is one where all of its elements are included within the more serious offence (with the more serious offence also requiring further elements). Thus, eg, where D foresees P committing intentional GBH it is very likely that she foresaw P making unlawful physical contact with V (ie battery) as part of that greater offence.

[102] See also *Loukes* [1996] Crim LR 341: lack of actus reus element undermining D's accomplice liability for dangerous driving.

[103] The relevant offence under the current law is causing death by careless driving (see **6.4.2.2**).

acted with the mens rea required for it. Lord Mackay approved the following example in the House of Lords:[104]

> [D] hands a gun to [P] informing him that it is loaded with blank ammunition only and telling him to go and scare [V] by discharging it. The ammunition is in fact live, as [D] knows, and [V] is killed. [P] is convicted only of manslaughter, as he might be on those facts. It would seem absurd that [D] should thereby escape conviction for murder.

In this example, P has not committed murder, and D did not foresee the possibility that P would do so because D knew that P lacked mens rea. However, although P's lack of mens rea negates his murder liability, it would seem unfair if it also undermined D's liability for murder as an accomplice: P did not intend to kill or cause GBH (the mens rea of murder), but D certainly did. This is the crux of the exception.[105] Indeed, it is an exception that is closely mirrored in the context of inchoate assisting and encouraging as well.[106]

Where P lacks mens rea for any crime, it is possible for D to be liable as an accomplice even though P has not committed an offence. Such cases will usually more appropriately be treated within innocent agency: where P lacks any mens rea, she becomes a tool of D's offence, and her conduct does not break the causal chain.[107] However, as we have discussed, there are linguistic problems with innocent agency in the context of offences such as rape and bigamy, and so the doctrine of complicity has been preferred. *Cogan and Leak*, discussed earlier,[108] provides a useful example: D made his wife V submit to sex with P, where P was unaware that V was not consenting. In this case, P was not liable for rape or any other offence because he lacked mens rea. However, D qualifies within the exception and was liable as an accomplice to rape[109] because D acted with the mens rea for rape: D knew that V was not consenting[110].

Alternatively, as in Lord Mackay's example, P may have mens rea for a lesser offence, with D complicit in a more serious one. These examples are more troublesome than those in which P has *no* mens rea, because P's knowledge of the lesser crime is enough to undermine her potential status as an innocent agent. Commentators have characterised P's conduct as a form of semi-innocent agency,[111] but this terminology raises more questions than it answers. Rather, as we did previously, the better approach is to apply the exception, and to ask if D had mens rea for the more serious principal offence. Where she does, as with the murder in Lord Mackay's example, she should be liable as

---

[104] *Burke* [1987] AC 417, 457.

[105] Taylor, 'Complicity, Legal Scholarship and the Law of Unintended Consequences' (2009) 29 LS 1. See critique of the exception in Kadish, 'Complicity, Cause and Blame' in *Essays in Criminal Law* (1987) 180.

[106] See **11.4.2.2**.

[107] See **12.2.3**.

[108] See **12.3.1.2**.

[109] See also *Millward* [1994] Crim LR 527: D instructed P to drive a vehicle he knew was unfit for the road. P did so, and an accident led to the death of V. D was complicit in causing death by reckless driving, but P committed no offence.

[110] The minimum mens rea for rape at this time was recklessness as to non-consent. The current law has a minimum of a lack of reasonable belief in consent. See **8.2**.

[111] Williams, *Textbook of Criminal Law* (1978) 373.

an accomplice to that more serious offence, even though P is only guilty of the minor one. This approach was rejected in *Richards*,[112] but following judicial criticism of that case in *Burke*,[113] it is contended that the exception should (and would) be applied in these circumstances today.

> **Don't be confused...**
> Standard cases involve an assessment of D's recklessness as to P's mens rea. Only when this breaks down, because P lacks mens rea, do we go on to explore the possible exception. The exception finds complicity liability where D has the mens rea required for the principal offence (ie the mens rea P lacks).

P has a defence: The last possibility, where D is complicit to a more serious offence than P has committed, arises where P has a defence. In this case, as P has committed the anticipated principal offence assisted, encouraged, or procured by D, our starting point is that they are both liable for that offence. If P then satisfies a defence, P's liability will be reduced or removed. If D does not satisfy the defence, she will remain complicit in the principal offence, even if P has been acquitted.

This rule applies both to partial and complete defences. For the partial defences to murder, the potential for D to be liable for murder despite P's satisfaction of a partial defence has been codified.[114] For the other defences, the rule exists at common law. *Bourne* provides an example in the context of duress.[115]

> **Bourne** (1952) 36 Cr App R 125
>
> D compelled his wife (P) to have sex with a dog. D was charged as an accomplice to P's offence of buggery. P was not charged because she would have had a defence of duress.
>
> • Court of Assizes: guilty of buggery.
> • Court of Criminal Appeal: conviction upheld on appeal. The fact that P had a defence, and so was not liable for the principal offence, does not undermine D's liability as an accomplice.

This rule has the same effect as the last one discussed (where P lacks mens rea) but it applies very differently. In the present case, the standard complicity rules are applied, with the only difference being that P's liability (but not D's) is reduced by a defence. Where P lacks mens rea, as discussed earlier, the standard complicity rules would not result in D's liability because D will know that P will act without mens rea and so D lacks an essential part of the mens rea for complicity. However, in that context only, there is an exception that allows D to remain liable as an accomplice if, despite P not having mens rea for the principal offence (and despite D potentially realising this), D herself has the mens rea required for the principal offence.

C) P commits a more serious offence than D foresaw: At the other extreme from the cases just discussed, P may act in a way which goes beyond that anticipated by D. For example, D assists P to commit a simple battery, but P intentionally causes GBH.

---

[112] [1974] QB 776.
[113] [1987] AC 417, 457. Cf Kadish, 'Complicity, Cause and Blame' (1985) 73 Cal L Rev 323, 329.
[114] Diminished responsibility, Homicide Act 1957, s2(4); loss of control, Coroners and Justice Act 2009, s54(8).
[115] **Chapter 14.**

Most cases of this kind can be resolved relatively simply. Since D must be at least reckless as to the essential elements of P's offence, D's liability cannot exceed that of the offences which D foresaw. In our example, as P's causing of GBH is likely to have included a battery in the form of some unlawful contact between P and V, D will be complicit in that battery as foreseen by D, but only P will be liable for the more serious GBH offence since that was not foreseen by D.

There is an exception, however, and this applies where P commits a constructive liability offence—an offence, such as unlawful act manslaughter, where an unforeseen result increases P's liability from the base offence intended to a more serious offence.[116] Where P commits an offence of this kind, because P is not required to foresee the result element for liability (in manslaughter that is the death of V), it has been consistently held that D can also be liable as an accomplice where she does not foresee the result either. For example, D encourages P to punch V, with both expecting the punch to result in no more than minor bruising amounting to only a battery. However, when P punches V and commits the base offence of battery, V unexpectedly falls backwards and hits her head on the hard floor, dying as a result. P is now liable for unlawful act manslaughter despite not foreseeing the death.[117] D is liable for unlawful act manslaughter as an accomplice; as with P, despite her lack of foresight that P might cause death.

> **Don't be confused...**
> You may have noticed an inconsistency—where P commits a strict liability offence that does not require her to have mens rea, it has been held that D must nevertheless be reckless as to P completing the actus reus of that offence to be liable as an accomplice; however, where P does not require mens rea as to the result element of a constructive liability offence, we are told that D may be liable as an accomplice even where she too lacks mens rea as to that result. The best explanation for this inconsistency, explained by the Law Commission,[118] is that (unlike complicity in strict liability offences) complicity in a constructive crime still requires D to be reckless as to P committing the base offence. Thus, her foresight of the base offence means that D is not an innocent party, and she (like P) should accept even the unforeseen consequences of her actions.

The application of this rule in manslaughter cases is exemplified in *Bristow*.[119]

> **Bristow** [2013] EWCA Crim 1540
>
> D and others undertook a planned robbery of an off-road vehicle repair yard. The owner of the yard (V) attempted to prevent the robbery and was killed, run over by one or more of the vehicles used for the robbery. It was unclear who was driving the vehicle that hit V. D and the others were charged with unlawful act manslaughter (as principal or accessory).
>
> - Crown Court: guilty of unlawful act manslaughter.
> - Court of Appeal: conviction upheld on appeal. D either (a) completed the dangerous and unlawful act (burglary) and caused death (ie acted as a principal), or (b) he assisted others to commit burglary and they caused V's death. D was liable under (a) or (b) even if he did not foresee the chance of death being caused.

---

[116] See **4.2.1.1**.
[117] See **6.3.1**.
[118] Law Commission, *Participating in Crime* (No 305, 2007) para B.97.
[119] [2014] Crim LR 457 and commentary.

Extending the mens rea of constructive liability crimes into complicity liability has been criticised for being too harsh on D. This has been particularly true for accomplices to murder, another example of a constructive liability offence.[120] As P commits murder where she kills with the intention to kill or to cause GBH, D may be liable for murder and subject to the mandatory life sentence having done some act of assistance or encouragement and simply foreseen that P *might* act to harm V (ie D is reckless as to P's conduct) and *might* do so with an intention to cause GBH (ie D is reckless as to P's mens rea). This is exemplified in *Bryce*, discussed earlier, where D drove P to V's house, reckless as to whether P would attack V with the intention (at least) of causing GBH. P later murdered V, and D was liable for murder as P's accomplice.

Whether the harshness of the current law is the fault of the complicity rules, or simply a result of the harshness of constructive liability in general, is a moot point. However, in either case, the main basis for defence challenges has become the claim that in causing the more serious result (eg death), P's actions were fundamentally different from those foreseen and assisted, encouraged, or procured by D. On this basis, D attempts to show a break in the nexus between her acts and the eventual crime of P, to negate her complicity liability. We move to cases of this kind now.

D) P commits an offence which is different from that D foresaw: As we have discussed, D's foresight or lack of foresight about the details of P's offence will not affect her liability as long as she foresees the essential elements. For example, if D provides P with a gun to murder V on Tuesday, but P kills V on Wednesday, D remains liable for murder as P's accomplice. However, there are occasions where P's crime is so fundamentally different from that assisted, encouraged, or procured by D that complicity liability would be inappropriate. D remains inchoately liable for her acts of assistance or encouragement, but is not complicit in P's offence. The leading case, establishing this rule, is *English*.[121]

> **English** [1999] AC 1
>
> D and P attacked a police sergeant, V, with wooden posts. P produced a knife which D had not foreseen that P might carry and fatally stabbed V. D was charged with murder as an accomplice.
>
> - Crown Court: guilty of murder.
> - Court of Appeal: conviction upheld on appeal.
> - House of Lords: appeal allowed. Even though D was reckless as to P causing GBH with intent (ie sufficient mens rea for complicity in murder), P's conduct (stabbing with a knife) was fundamentally different from that anticipated by D (hitting with posts). Thus, D is not an accomplice to P's offence.

The 'fundamental difference' rule remains faithful to the idea of complicity as a derivative form of liability: D only derives liability from P's offence if it is not fundamentally different from that which she foresaw and associated herself with.

---

[120] Mitchell and Roberts have researched public attitudes to liability in these circumstances, finding an unease at the harshness of liability, *Public Survey of the Mandatory Life Sentence for Murder* (2010).

[121] The appeal of *English* was combined with *Powell and Daniels*.

> **Judge and jury...**
> Whether P's conduct was fundamentally different from D's foresight is a question of fact for the jury.[122]

There are always likely to be differences between D's foresight and the eventual crime of P. Therefore, the detail of how the rule is applied becomes crucial. The following questions should be born in mind.

What qualifications are there to the fundamentally different rule? Before we consider the detail of the fundamentally different rule, it is first necessary to identify the two main circumstances where it will *not* apply.

First, the rule will not apply where D performs acts of assistance or encouragement and *intends* that P should kill V, and P does so by an unexpected means. Where D is *reckless* as to P killing V or causing GBH, as in *English*, we see that the means of killing can lead to a finding of fundamental difference. However, where D intends that P should kill, this route is removed. Thus, for example, where D hires a contract killer (P) to murder V with a bat, but P murders V with a gun or any other means, D will be complicit in the murder regardless of the difference. This rule was established by the House of Lords in *Rahman*,[123] and confirmed with useful discussion in *Yemoh*.[124]

Secondly, the rule will not apply where P *mistakenly* targets the wrong victim.[125] Where P attempts to kill X, but accidentally kills V, P commits murder because her mens rea—her intention to kill X—is transferred to V.[126] Just as the doctrine of transferred malice operates to secure P's liability, the same is true for D: her mens rea (ie foresight of P killing X) is also transferred to V. However, although transferred malice applies where P misses her target by accident, it does not extend to an intentional change. As illustrated by *Saunders and Archer,* and discussed further later, an intentional change of target is likely to constitute a fundamental difference and relieve D of complicity liability.

📋 **Saunders and Archer** (1573) 2 Plowd 473

P planned to kill his wife, X. D advised P, and on this advice P gave X a poisoned apple. X ate some of the apple, but gave the rest to their child, V, who ate it and died. P saw what happened and did not intervene.

- Court: P is guilty of murder, his intention to kill X being transferred to V. X is an innocent agent. D is also not guilty of murder as an accomplice.

Although dicta in *Saunders and Archer* suggest that D will never be liable as an accomplice where P kills the wrong victim, this does not represent the current law. Rather, in line with the *outcome* of this case, D is likely to escape liability because P was aware of the change of victim, had the power to intervene, and did not do so. In such a case the change of target was controllable, and therefore not fully unintentional. If the same facts occurred but P was not present when X passed the apple to V, then D would also be liable for murder via transferred malice.

What constitutes a fundamental difference? The fundamental difference rule has evolved from case law, and particularly cases involving constructive crimes such as

---

[122] *Greatrex* [1999] 1 Cr App R 126.
[123] [2008] UKHL 45.
[124] [2009] EWCA Crim 930. See also *Mendez* [2010] EWCA Crim 516.
[125] Lanham, 'Accomplices and Transferred Malice' (1980) 96 LQR 110.
[126] We discuss transferred malice at **4.3.1**.

murder. D commonly argues that even if she did foresee the chance of P harming V, the manner in which P carried out the principal offence was so different from that foreseen and assisted, encouraged, or procured, that it would be inappropriate for D to derive any liability from it. Various types of 'difference' have been mooted.

> **Point to remember...**
> The key to the fundamental difference rule is not simply looking for extreme factual differences. Rather, we are looking for factual differences that break the nexus of responsibility between D and the principal offence. For example, a long time delay might appear a significant difference, but is unlikely to undermine D's liability.[127] On the other hand, a change of weapon which makes P's conduct more dangerous than that foreseen is considerably more likely to establish such a break.
>
> It should also be remembered that the more specific D's foresight of P's offence (eg specific weapon, victim, etc), the more likely a finding of fundamental difference. For example, if D encourages P to kill others in general, and P goes on to kill, there is very little basis upon which D can claim that P's offence was fundamentally different from her foresight.

The most straightforward cases of fundamental difference arise where P *intentionally* changes the target of her offence. For example, D encourages P to kill X, but P intentionally kills V; D assists P to damage X's car, but P intentionally damages V's car; and so on. In these circumstances, P's intentional change of target will probably constitute a fundamental difference, and D will not be liable as an accomplice to P's offence.[128] However, three qualifications should be noted. First, as discussed earlier, there will be no fundamental difference where P's change of target is unintentional. Secondly, even if intentional, there will also be no fundamental difference if the change is insubstantial. For example, in *Dunning and Graham*,[129] following a grievance between D and V, P offered to set fire to V's house. D accepted, and supplied V's address. In the event, P changed his mind and set fire to V's car instead. Although this was a clear change of target, the court found that it was not a substantial change from the plan envisaged by D, and so he remained complicit. Thirdly, there is unlikely to be a fundamental difference where P carries out the principal offence as planned *and* goes on to commit an additional offence of the same type. For example, D provides P with a jemmy to assist burglary, and P burgles multiple properties; or D supplies a knife for P to kill someone, and P kills two people with it; and so on.[130] In these cases, D is likely to be complicit in the foreseen offence and the additional offence.

The second basis for establishing a fundamental difference, and the most commonly litigated, arises where P uses an unforeseen tool or weapon. The rule will not apply where the new weapon is equivalent to the one foreseen, for example where P uses a knife to kill V rather than a gun.[131] And, as highlighted earlier, will also not apply where D *intends* P to commit the principal offence as opposed to being reckless as to P's offence. However, the rule has applied in a number of cases. The test, set out in *Rahman*,[132] requires:

(a) change of weapon (or P uses a weapon where none was foreseen);

---

127 *Bryce* [2004] EWCA Crim 1231.
128 Recognised in *Powell* [1999] AC 1, and *Reardon* [1999] Crim LR 392.
129 Unreported, December 1985.
130 *Reardon* [1999] Crim LR 392: D was complicit in two murders committed with his knife, despite only foreseeing one of them.
131 *Powell and Daniels; English* [1999] AC 1, 30.
132 [2008] UKHL 45.

(b) no knowledge from D about the new weapon or its potential use;[133]

(c) the new weapon is more lethal than that foreseen; and

(d) because of the change, P's acts are fundamentally different from those foreseen.

Examples of the rule in operation include *English*, discussed earlier, where P's use of a knife was fundamentally different from the wooden posts foreseen; *Rafferty*,[134] where P's drowning of V was fundamentally different from the hitting and kicking foreseen; *Mendez*,[135] where P's use of a knife was fundamentally different from the wooden posts and metal bars foreseen; etc. Each of these cases was decided on its specific facts, and so overly formulaic interpretations assuming that certain weapons will *always* be fundamentally different should be avoided. However, the four-step test set out in *Rahman* still provides useful guidance when applying the rule in practice.

A third basis for establishing fundamental difference arises where, although D foresaw the type of tools/weapons, she did not foresee the more dangerous manner in which they would be used by P.[136] This is a logical extension from the change of weapon rule. For example, if D foresees P using a knife to cut off one of V's fingers, but P uses it to cut V's throat, the fact that the same weapon is used does not detract from the extreme difference between the two actions. *AG's Reference (No 3 of 2004)* provides useful illustration.

> **AG's Reference (No 3 of 2004)** [2005] EWCA Crim 1882
>
> D recruited P and another to intimidate V by discharging a firearm near (but not at) him. P intentionally shot and killed V. D was charged with murder as P's accomplice.
>
> • Crown Court: not guilty of murder.
> • Court of Appeal: judge was correct to rule as he had to find no liability, as P's act (shooting at V) was fundamentally different from the act foreseen by D (shooting near V).

Along with clear examples of this kind, however, are cases that have presented more challenging facts. In *Gamble*,[137] for example, D foresaw that an attack on V would result in GBH by kneecapping (ie shooting V in the knee joints). In the event, P killed V by cutting his throat and shooting him in the chest. As a result of this, despite D intending that P should cause GBH, the fundamental difference in P's acts meant that D was not liable for murder.

> Although the rule remains well entrenched that an intention to inflict grievous bodily harm qualifies as the mens rea of murder, it is not in my opinion necessary to apply it in such a way as to fix an accessory with liability for a consequence which he did not intend and which stems from an act which he did not have within his contemplation. I do not think that the state of the law compels me to reach such a conclusion, and it would not in my judgment accord with the public sense of what is just and fitting.[138]

---

[133] This criterion is controversial. If D knows that P has a weapon, but does not foresee its use, why should she be liable if it is used? The answer is clearly policy-based.

[134] [2007] EWCA Crim 1846.

[135] [2010] EWCA Crim 516.

[136] *Mendez* [2010] EWCA Crim 516, [42]–[47].

[137] [1989] NI 268.

[138] Per Carswell J at 284.

As V was killed by the throat cutting, this case also involves a change of weapon. However, as the weapon used (knife) was not more lethal than the one foreseen (gun), the finding of a fundamental difference is clearly located in the change of P's actions which become more lethal rather than a change of weapon. Thus, the case would be decided in the same way if P had shot V in the head rather than using the knife: in either scenario P's acts are significantly more life threatening than the kneecapping foreseen by D.

A fourth *potential* basis for finding a fundamental difference relates to D's foresight of P's mens rea. For example, D foresees P shooting V being reckless as to causing GBH, but P actually shoots with an intention to kill. The change in mens rea is important for P's liability since in our example, if V dies, P becomes liable for murder rather than manslaughter. However, the courts have taken the consistent line that a change in P's mens rea will not result in a fundamental difference such as to undermine D's complicity. Rather, in cases like our example, D remains complicit, albeit for the lesser charge of manslaughter.[139] This was established in *Rahman*.[140] A change of P's mens rea will only constitute a fundamental difference if it also affects her conduct: transforming it into one of the cases discussed previously.

Although the four examples here are those that have been most widely discussed, the open-textured nature of the 'fundamental difference' test means that alternative bases may be recognised. The advantage of this is that the law remains flexible to different factual scenarios; the cost is a lack of predictability. The South African case of *Robinson* provides a useful example.[141] D, P, and V agreed that P would kill V, allowing D to claim V's life insurance and to avoid V's upcoming fraud prosecution. At the last moment V withdrew consent to being killed, but P killed V regardless. Applying an equivalent to the fundamental difference rule, the South African court found that D was not complicit in the murder because the withdrawal of consent made P's act of killing very different from that agreed to and foreseen by D. Whether the same approach would be adopted in this jurisdiction is not certain.

Extra detail...

The Law Commission propose codifying the fundamental difference test, but maintaining the wide discretion of the current law. For the Commission, the question should be whether P's actions were within the 'scope of her venture' with D.[142]

12.4 Complicity by joint enterprise

Alongside standard cases of complicity by assisting, encouraging, or procuring,[143] D may also be liable for the common law offence of complicity by joint enterprise.[144] In

---

139 D is complicit in manslaughter rather than murder because she did not foresee P acting with the mens rea for murder.

140 [2008] UKHL 45. See also *Yemoh* [2009] EWCA Crim 930; *Bristow* [2013] EWCA Crim 1540.

141 1968 (1) SA 666.

142 Law Commission, *Participating in Crime* (No 305, 2007) paras 3.153–3.166.

143 'Standard' because this form of complicity is codified within the Accessories and Abettors Act 1861.

144 Krebs, 'Joint Criminal Enterprise' (2010) 73 MLR 578.

essence, joint enterprise describes a coordination of behaviour between D and P towards a common criminal end. For example, D and P take part in a fight with a rival gang, and P kills one of its members (V). D is not a co-principal with P in the murder of V because D does not commit the actus reus of the principal offence of murder. It may well also be that D did not provide any obvious assistance or encouragement to the acts of P in killing, and if so the standard route to accomplice liability becomes difficult to establish: D has not assisted or encouraged murder directly. However, through her coordinated conduct, the doctrine of joint enterprise provides the basis for accomplice liability.

> **Terminology...**
> Joint enterprise is also commonly and interchangeably referred to as joint criminal enterprise, joint venture, and/or joint criminal venture.

The problem with joint enterprise is that as soon as one begins to explore the actus reus and mens rea in any detail, it begins to merge back into standard complicity by assisting, encouraging, or procuring. Take our gang murder example, it is difficult to see how D can coordinate behaviour with P in any meaningful way without either committing the offence with her as a co-principal, or by assisting, encouraging, or procuring her. Where D does none of these, where her conduct is simply being proximate to P, complicity liability should not be found.[145]

This raises the question whether joint enterprise represent one form of secondary liability or a separate type of complicity liability altogether. There has been much academic debate over the last two decades. Several commentators, not least the Law Commission, have argued that it is (or should be) distinguished.[146] There has been limited judicial support for this view.[147] For such commentators, joint enterprise represents a different wrong from complicity by assisting, encouraging, or procuring, focused more directly on collaborative criminality and therefore requiring separate treatment. The alternative view, followed in all recent appeal decisions, is to analyse joint enterprise in line with the standard rules of assisting, encouraging, or procuring.[148] As Toulson LJ stated in *Stringer*:[149]

> Joint enterprise is not a legal term of art. In *R v Mendez* [2011] QB 876 , the court favoured the view that joint enterprise as a basis of secondary liability involves the application of ordinary principles; it is not an independent source of liability. Participation in a joint criminal adventure involves mutual encouragement and assistance.

In line with this view, our earlier discussion of complicity by assisting, encouraging, and procuring has included several cases where courts have used the language of joint enterprise. Rather than distinguishing such cases for discussion in this section alone,

---

[145] We would not want to criminalise as accomplices all those within a certain distance of a criminal offence!

[146] Law Commission, *Participating in Crime* (No 305, 2007); Simester, Spencer, Sullivan, and Virgo, *Simester and Sullivan's Criminal Law Theory and Doctrine* (2013) 244–249.

[147] *Stewart and Schofield* [1995] 1 Cr App R 441.

[148] *ABCD* [2010] EWCA Crim 1622; *Mendez* [2011] QB 876; *Stringer* [2011] EWCA Crim 1396; *Gnango* [2011] UKSC 59. See also *Smith and Hogan's Criminal Law* (14th edn, 2014), Ch 14.

[149] [2011] EWCA Crim 1396, [57].

the term 'joint enterprise' in these cases does not distinguish them as a separate form of complicity liability.

If this were the end of the story, it would be a mercifully simple one: joint enterprise is not a separate form of complicity liability, so the term should simply be viewed as short-hand for complicity by assisting, encouraging, or procuring.[150] However, although this is clearly the direction the law is taking, it is arguable that a complete absorption of joint enterprise into standard forms of complicity has not yet been achieved. To understand this, it is necessary to distinguish standard joint enterprise cases where D and P coordinate conduct towards a primary principal offence (eg D and P rob a bank together), and cases where D foresees that P might commit a further collateral offence (eg D and P rob a bank together, and P murders a bank security guard). It is the latter cases, often described as 'parasitic liability',[151] where some academics argue that joint enterprise may still retain a role independent of complicity by assisting, encouraging, or procuring.

12.4.1 Joint enterprise and a single primary offence

No difficulty arises where D and P coordinate their conduct towards a mutual criminal end, for example to rob a bank together, or murder V, etc. D will only be liable for the offence as P's accomplice if she has assisted, encouraged, or procured its completion. The language of joint enterprise may be used, but the elements of the offence will be identical to those discussed earlier in standard cases of complicity.[152]

The fact that joint enterprise is simply a form of accomplice liability in this context does not significantly narrow the breadth of complicity liability. Where D intentionally coordinates her conduct with P towards a common criminal end, it is difficult to imagine a scenario in which D does not thereby provide some manner of intentional assistance or encouragement. However, such cases are possible.[153]

It is arguable that *Gnango* represents just such a case, where D and P coordinated their conduct, but D does not intentionally assist or encourage P to commit murder.[154] The facts of *Gnango*, it will be remembered, involved a shoot-out between D and P, where P shot and killed a passerby (V). In Lord Kerr's powerful dissenting judgment, the point is made that D's intentional conduct within the gunfight did not include an intention to assist or encourage P to return fire so D was not intending to assist or encourage P's conduct as required for the principal offence, the murder of V. It is a convincing point: D's plan was to shoot P and thereby *stop* him shooting back, not to encourage it. Hence D lacked an essential element of mens rea, and liability could not have been found applying the normal rules of complicity discussed above.[155] However, this approach was not accepted, and a majority within the Supreme Court found that D

---

[150] Virgo, 'Joint Enterprise Liability is Dead: Long Live Accessorial Liability' [2012] Crim LR 850.

[151] *Gnango* [2011] UKSC 59. Smith, 'Criminal Liability of Accessories: Law and Law Reform' (1997) 113 LQR 453. See also Wilson and Ormerod, 'Simply Harsh to Fairly Simple' [2015] Crim LR 3.

[152] *Mendez* [2011] QB 876.

[153] An exception might be where P testifies that, although D's acts were capable of assisting or encouraging, she was not assisted or encouraged in fact. Law Commission, *Participating in Crime* (No 305, 2007) paras 3.42–3.45.

[154] Discussed at **12.1**.

[155] See **12.3.2.1**.

did intend to encourage P to shoot back thereby finding D liable as an accessory to his own attempted murder by P.

If a separate doctrine of joint enterprise existed for single primary offences, this would have applied in *Gnango*. A better view is that adopted in the Crown Court where joint enterprise was the basis for D's conviction. D assisted P in affray with murder as a collateral offence. This analysis, although ultimately rejected within the Court of Appeal and the Supreme Court, provides a justifiable basis for D's liability for murder: D has participated in the affray and lent himself to the enterprise of murder foreseeing P might intentionally kill or do GBH. An alternative approach, favoured by some academics, is that such collateral joint enterprise cases should be seen as a separate form of liability. They argue that this would have provided a more coherent basis for D's complicity in *Gnango*. Although it is difficult to maintain that D intended to assist or encourage P, an intentional coordination of behaviour within the gunfight is comparatively clear.[156] However, this approach was not favoured by the Supreme Court. In finding that D *did* intend to encourage P to shoot back at him (at least obliquely), the majority's approach is not the most intuitive, but it is sufficient to find liability, and it therefore avoids the court having to address whether joint enterprise is a separate route to liability.

12.4.2 Joint enterprise and the collateral offence

Collateral offences arise when P commits an additional offence in the course of committing the primary offence assisted, encouraged, or procured by D: for example, D and P rob a bank and, whilst doing so, P kills a security guard.[157] If D has *both* foreseen that this additional offence might occur and provided assistance or encouragement to that additional offence then it is not a collateral offence, it is simply an additional offence for which D is complicit by the standard route. The category of offences we are concerned with here are those where D is reckless as to P committing the additional offence, but has *not* provided any assistance or encouragement for it; indeed D may even have specifically instructed P not to do it. Where this is the case, the current law will find accomplice liability and the terminology of 'joint enterprise' will generally be used. *Powell* provides a useful example.[158]

> **Powell and Daniels** [1999] AC 1
>
> D, X, and P went to the house of a drug dealer (V) to buy drugs (the primary offence). At the door, one of them shot V dead (the collateral offence). D was charged with murder either as a principal offender or as an accessory.
>
> • Crown Court: guilty of murder.
> • Court of Appeal: conviction upheld on appeal.
> • House of Lords: appeal dismissed.

[156] Virgo discusses something like this (which he calls 'association') as a proposal for a 'new' basis for liability. Virgo, 'Joint Enterprise Liability is Dead: Long Live Accessorial Liability' [2012] Crim LR 850.

[157] This will also include cases where D is the principal offender to the primary offence jointly committed with, or assisted or encouraged by, P.

[158] *Powell* was combined with *English* on appeal.

The issue in *Powell* was not whether D assisted or encouraged the collateral offence, but simply whether having embarked upon the primary offence D continued whilst being reckless as to whether P might commit murder. On the basis that D must have been aware of the gun, and must have foreseen the chance of P using it to kill V, D's liability was established.

Despite no obvious assistance or encouragement in relation to a collateral offence, the courts have imposed liability without accepting a separate doctrine of joint enterprise. *Stringer*,[159] for example, supports the idea that by assisting or encouraging the primary offence, and going ahead with it foreseeing that P might commit a collateral offence, D's conduct in itself will constitute some encouragement for that collateral offence. On this approach, as currently accepted by the courts, there is no 'separate' basis of joint enterprise liability; it is part of accomplice liability.

However, there is an alternative view favoured by some academics, holding that joint enterprise should be seen as a separate ground for complicity in relation to collateral offences. In cases like *Powell* and *Stringer* it may not be essential because the collateral offences are broadly consistent with the aims of the primary offences, such that the encouragement of one could plausibly be described as the encouragement of both. However, in cases where D foresees the potential collateral offence and specifically instructs P not to commit it, but P does so, it may be artificial to describe D's role as assisting or encouraging that collateral offence. Unless we are prepared to say that D has assisted or encouraged by lending his support and not withdrawing, to maintain liability in these circumstances, then acknowledging joint enterprise as a separate ground for complicity is argued by some academics to be more appropriate.[160]

The requirements for joint enterprise collateral liability are set out in **Figure 12.1**.

Figure 12.1 Complicity by joint enterprise in a collateral offence

We will discuss each of these steps in turn.

12.4.2.1 Complicity in the principal offence

In order for the issue of 'collateral' offences to arise, first there must be complicity liability for a primary offence. Taking our bank robbery and murder example, the primary offence is the burglary: the principal offence that D has assisted, encouraged, or procured P to commit. D must satisfy all of the offence elements discussed at **12.3** to be liable for this offence.

---

159 [2011] EWCA Crim 1396.
160 Law Commission, *Participating in Crime* (No 305, 2007) paras 3.46–3.59.

D's participation within the primary offence is essential to her liability for the collateral offence because it serves as the basis for her liability in the collateral offence. Where we analyse liability for a primary offence alone, we are looking for assistance, encouragement, or procurement in order to identify a nexus between D's conduct and P's offence. Where P commits a collateral offence (ie one that has not been directly assisted, encouraged, or procured), the nexus is provided instead by D's participation in the primary offence: D is not an innocent party, she is someone engaged in a criminal venture who foresees the potential for additional crimes being committed.[161]

D only has that nexus to P's collateral offences, for the span of time in which D and P are 'on the job' in relation to the principal offence, so where D and P rob the bank, and P commits murder a week later, D will not be complicit in the later offence. Establishing when the primary offence starts and finishes can be difficult: for example, where P shoots someone outside the bank when making his escape, is this in the course of the robbery? It can also be problematic where D assists or encourages multiple offences: for example, where D provides P with a jemmy to help her rob a bank, and two years later when robbing her tenth bank P kills a security guard, should D be liable for the murder as P's accomplice? Unfortunately, such grey areas may be inevitable, and will be left to the jury.[162]

> **Don't be confused...**
> The Supreme Court and many Court of Appeal decisions (and the Law Commission) describe the primary offence as a 'meeting of minds', an 'agreed offence', and/or involving a 'common intention'. They hold that there can only be joint enterprise liability for a collateral offence where there is a common purpose between D and P. These expressions are unfortunate. They are trying to explain that through complicity in the primary offence D has associated herself with a crime. However, they misleadingly imply that D must 'intend' P's primary offence, agree to it, or have the same mens rea as P. As yet, in practice, the courts have not required such intention.[163] D's mens rea for complicity in the primary offence is as discussed at **12.3.2**: intention to assist, encourage, or procure; recklessness as to P committing the offence.

12.4.2.2 Recklessness as to the collateral offence

It is not necessary for D to assist, encourage, or procure the collateral offence, but it is necessary for her to be at least reckless as to its commission during the course of the primary offence.[164] As discussed in *Willet*, D must foresee the collateral offence in advance of its occurrence: D must have chosen to continue with the primary offence knowing that there is a risk that P will commit the further offence with mens rea.

> **Willet** [2010] EWCA Crim 1620
>
> D and P set out to steal from V's van (primary offence). Their theft was disturbed by V, and in trying to get away, P drove their vehicle into V causing death (collateral offence). D was charged with murder as P's accomplice.
>
> • Crown Court: guilty of murder.

---

[161] Simester, 'The Mental Element in Complicity' (2006) 122 LQR 578, 598–600.
[162] Law Commission, *Participating in Crime* (No 305, 2007) paras 3.153–3.166.
[163] On agreement, see *Hyde* [1991] 1 QB 134. On common intentions, see *Chan Wing-siu* [1985] AC 168.
[164] *Lewis* [2010] EWCA Crim 496.

- Court of Appeal: appeal allowed. D could only be liable if he either (a) assisted or encouraged murder (ie through basic complicity), or (b) having participated in the theft he had foreseen that P might commit murder. If D did not foresee P committing murder until seconds before it happened, there would be no opportunity to make a decision about continuing with the venture with this knowledge in mind.

If D had foreseen the chance of P committing murder at an earlier point and chosen to continue with the venture, he would be liable for murder as P's accomplice. It is worth highlighting again the harshness of liability in these circumstances: D is liable for murder (and thus subject to a mandatory life sentence) despite not assisting, encouraging, or procuring murder, and despite not intending P to kill or cause GBH. In *English*, Lord Hutton describes this as 'not based solely on logic' but justified by 'public policy' and 'practical concerns' in relation to group criminality.[165]

12.4.2.3 No fundamental difference

Finally, D's complicity in P's collateral offence requires that there be no fundamental difference between D's foresight and the collateral offence as committed. We have already discussed this rule in the context of primary offences,[166] and the law should be applied in the same way here. In fact, most of the cases discussed earlier involved collateral offences. This is no surprise, where D is reckless as to an offence which she has not assisted, encouraged, or procured, it is much more likely that there will be differences in fact between D's foresight and the offence committed.

Assessment matters…

As we have explained, the status of joint enterprise as a separate form of complicity (even in relation to collateral offences) is only supported by a minority academic and judicial opinion. Therefore, you should only look to explore this potential route after you have concluded that it is unlikely that D has assisted, encouraged, or procured the relevant offence. In other words, it should be treated as an uncertain last resort to finding liability.

12.5 The relationship between complicity and inchoate liability

Just as D may be complicit in substantive offences such as rape or murder, for example, D may also be complicit in an inchoate offence such as conspiracy to rape, or assisting murder. This arises where D assists, encourages, or procures (or forms a joint enterprise to commit) the inchoate offence, and P goes on to commit that inchoate offence.[167]

---

[165] *English* [1999] AC 1.

[166] See **12.3.2.2(D)**.

[167] Smith, 'Secondary Participation and Inchoate Offences' in Tapper (ed), *Crime, Proof and Punishment* (1981) 21.

However, it is *no* offence to inchoately conspire, or to assist or encourage P to act as an accomplice.[168] There is also *no* offence of attempted complicity.[169]

12.6 Defences

The general rules about denial of criminal responsibility and the general defences apply to complicity as they do across other criminal offences. These will be discussed in **Chapters 13** and **14** respectively. Here we discuss two established specific defences,[170] and one that has not yet been recognised by the courts. These are defences to complicity offences only, and will not necessarily relieve D of inchoate liability.[171]

12.6.1 Withdrawal

Where D assists or encourages P to commit a principal offence (with mens rea) she is immediately liable for an inchoate offence regardless of P's future conduct.[172] D cannot negate such inchoate liability even if she later 'withdraws' by removing or renouncing her assistance or encouragement.[173] However, if D successfully withdraws in the time between her conduct and P committing the principal offence, D will be able to limit her liability to the inchoate charge and avoid complicity liability. The ability to withdraw and prevent complicity liability in this way provides a useful incentive for D to negate or at least mitigate the effects of her criminal conduct.

What is required of D to establish an effective withdrawal is not entirely clear within the law, and will vary between case facts, but rules have developed to help us to apply the defence. A useful starting point is that mere repentance, without any action, is not sufficient.

Rook [1993] 2 All ER 955

D and another were recruited by X to kill his wife (V). D further recruited P. On the day of the murder, D was unexpectedly absent but P went ahead with the plan and murdered V. D was charged with murder as P's accomplice.

- Crown Court: guilty of murder.
- Court of Appeal: conviction upheld on appeal. D's absence was not sufficient to withdraw from P's offence.

---

[168] *Kenning* [2008] EWCA Crim 1534.
[169] Criminal Attempts Act 1981, s1(4)(b). For discussion, see Bohlander, 'The Conflict Between the Serious Crime Act and s4(1)(b) of the Criminal Attempts Act 1981' [2010] Crim LR 483 and Child, 'The Differences Between Attempted Complicity and Inchoate Assisting and Encouraging: A Reply to Professor Bohlander' [2010] Crim LR 924.
[170] Law Commission, *Participating in Crime* (No 305, 2007) Part 5.
[171] See **11.4.5**.
[172] See **11.4**.
[173] Reed, 'Repentance and Forgiveness: Withdrawal From Participation Liability and the Proportionality Test' in Reed and Bohlander (eds), *Participation in Crime* (2013); Smith, 'Withdrawal and Complicity' [2001] Crim LR 769.

The court in *Rook* does not specify what D should have done to successfully with-draw, but does state a minimum that he must have served 'unequivocal notice' of his withdrawal to P.[174] The focus of the defence is not the withdrawal of D as an indi-vidual, but the withdrawal of D's assistance or encouragement, and this will always require action.

The most important detail to remember, discussed in *O'Flaherty*,[175] is that the courts will balance the weight of D's assistance or encouragement against the action taken to withdraw. Thus, the more substantial D's involvement in P's offence,[176] and the closer to P's commission of the offence that D attempts to withdraw,[177] the more the courts will require. Where D's assistance or encouragement is relatively minimal, for example where D has simply expressed the view that P's plan is a good one, it may be sufficient for D to withdraw by retracting these comments to P or removing the assistance. Where D's conduct is more substantial, she will have to do more. This does not necessarily mean that she must try and prevent P's crime taking place by going to the police, for example,[178] although this will obviously be useful evidence of withdrawal.

In cases where D is withdrawing from a joint enterprise and a collateral offence, the requirements may be slightly different. As well as the standard routes to withdrawal discussed in the previous cases, D may also claim something equivalent to withdrawal by establishing that the primary offence was completed and that she provided no assis-tance or encouragement to the collateral offence: that the collateral offence did not occur within the scope of the primary venture. This can occur where D joins an attack on V foreseeing that P might kill V, the attack ends and D leaves, and then P returns to kill V.[179] D's argument, on these facts, would be that the second attack was not col-lateral to the first, but was a separate event.

12.6.2 The victim rule

Where an offence is designed for the protection of a specific class of victim,[180] someone within that class is not complicit where they assist, encourage, or procure the offence to be committed *against themselves*. This mirrors similar defences discussed in the context of inchoate assisting or encouraging and conspiracy.[181] Often referred to as the '*Tyrrell* defence', it originated in this case.

---

[174] Following *Becerra* (1975) 62 Cr App R 212.

[175] [2004] EWCA Crim 526.

[176] *Gallant* [2008] EWCA Crim 111: comparing withdrawal of instigators within gang violence compared to peripheral members.

[177] *Becerra* (1975) 62 Cr App R 212: failure to withdraw at a very late stage.

[178] *Otway* [2011] EWCA Crim 3.

[179] *Mitchell* [1999] Crim LR 496; *Robinson* [2000] 5 Arch News 2 (restricting the approach in *Mitchell*); *O'Flaherty* [2004] EWCA Crim 526.

[180] Williams, 'Victims and Other Exempt Parties in Crime' (1990) 10 LS 245.

[181] See **11.3.1.1** and **11.4.5**.

> **Tyrrell** [1894] 1 QB 710
>
> D (a girl between 13–16 years) encouraged a P to have sexual intercourse with her. D was charged under section 5 of the Criminal Amendment Act 1885 (now the Sexual Offences Act 2003, s9) as P's accessory.
>
> • Central Criminal Court: guilty of the sexual offence.
> • Crown Case Reserved: appeal allowed. The statute was passed for the protection of young girls, not to criminalise them.

How far the victim rule extends, and exactly which offences it applies to, has not been settled. Indeed, modern statutes such as the Sexual Offences Act 2003 can be criticised for not taking full account of the rule.[182] However, it remains an important defence, and one that the Law Commission would like to codify in statute.

Two exceptions to the rule should be noted. First, the defence will only apply to offences designed to protect a specific sub-group of the population, not the population as a whole. Thus, for example, the defence will not apply to D who encourages P to kill her, as the offence of murder is designed to protect all people.[183] Secondly, the defence will not apply to D within the protected class if she assists or encourages P to commit the offence against *another* person within that class (eg D would have been liable in *Tyrell* had she encouraged P to have sexual intercourse with another girl of 13).

12.6.3 Acting reasonably?

The courts have not recognised a defence of acting reasonably within the current law, although the Law Commission has recommended a defence of acting to prevent crime or limit harm.[184] Such a defence has also been accepted in the context of inchoate assisting or encouraging.[185] It would be open to the courts to recognise a defence of this kind where, for example, D encourages P to damage V's car in order to convince P not to attack V herself. In the absence of this as a specific defence, D would have to rely on the uncertain general defence of necessity.[186]

12.7 Reform

Any student studying the law of complicity will be struck by its complexity and (in several areas) its incoherence. The number of appellate court cases in recent years

---

[182] Bohlander, 'The Sexual Offences Act 2003—The *Tyrrell* Principle—Criminalising the Victim' [2005] Crim LR 701.
[183] *Gnango* [2011] UKSC 59.
[184] Law Commission, *Participating in Crime* (No 305, 2007) paras 5.10–5.23.
[185] Serious Crime Act 2007, s50.
[186] **Chapter 14.**

provides further demonstration of the uncertainties within the current law; and the judgments themselves seem to have done little to stem the flow. Parliamentary reform and clarification are long overdue.[187]

When seeking legal coherence, however, it is important to understand the base principles underlying liability (ie what is the 'wrong' complicity seeks to criminalise?). And it is here that we locate the source of the current law's confusion. There are at least two competing rationales for complicity, neither of which is entirely satisfactory. These are the causal theory and the derivative theory.

A) The causal theory: The causal theory holds that D is complicit in P's offence because she has materially contributed to its commission. There is support for this theory within the current law. For example, unlike inchoate assisting and encouraging where D is merely required to perform acts 'capable' of assisting or encouraging, complicity will *not* be found where there is evidence that (despite conduct capable of encouraging or assisting P) D has not assisted or encouraged in fact.[188] Indeed, in *Mendez*, Toulson LJ stated that 'at its most basic level secondary liability is founded on the principle of causation'.[189] There is also support for a version of this theory from Gardner, who highlights the benefits of a causal theory in terms of respect for D's autonomy: D is liable for what she has done, not simply for her association with the actions of another.[190]

The obvious (and potentially fatal) problem with this theory, however, is that most complicity cases do not require D to have caused P's offence. Where D has caused P's offence, D has either procured P's offence or committed it as a principal via the doctrine of innocent agency.[191] For most complicity cases involving assistance or encouragement P's free, voluntary, and informed choice to commit the principal offence will break any chain of causation between D's conduct and that offence.[192] In view of this, causal theories are forced into the murky realms of 'substantial contribution' rather than full causation. This is problematic: it does not provide clarity on what the offence should require of D, and if less than causation, as must be the case, it is arguable that it undermines the benefits of the theory highlighted earlier.

B) The derivative theory: The derivative theory holds that D's liability is a product of P's liability; D assuming co-responsibility with P because of her association with P's conduct. Again, advocates of the derivative theory can find support within the current law's treatment of D (ie labelling and punishing her in the same way as P), as well as the fact that D's liability hangs on P's completion of the principal offence. It is this theory that underlies the Law Commission's most recent recommendations on complicity.[193]

---

[187] cf Wilson and Ormerod [2015] Crim LR 3.
[188] See **12.3.1.1.**
[189] [2010] EWCA Crim 516, [18].
[190] Gardner, 'Complicity and Causality' (2007) 1 Crim L & Phil 127, 136.
[191] See **12.2.**
[192] *Kennedy (No 2)* [2007] UKHL 38.
[193] Law Commission, *Participating in Crime* (No 305, 2007) paras B.8–B.27.

However, the derivative theory is also problematic. In contrast to the causal theory, the derivative theory can be criticised for being too harsh to D and not respecting the principal of autonomy: D seems to be punished for P's choices rather than her own. And it may also be too generous to D. Where P commits a less serious offence than that foreseen by D, the current law allows for D's liability for the more serious offence, but surely if we fully respect a derivative theory this should not be possible. Finally, the grounding of any derivative theory, if not located within D's conduct, must be her mens rea; and yet the current law only requires D to be reckless as to P's offending: how can mere foresight establish association deserving of equal treatment with P?

The current doctrinal uncertainty makes useful reform almost impossible. As Wilson comments, 'the range of problems left uncatered for by this fudging of the theoretical basis to accessorial liability spreads across the whole field of doctrine.'[194]

12.7.1 Abolishing complicity

In view of the doctrinal uncertainty discussed in the previous section, for some commentators the abolition of complicity liability becomes an attractive proposition. This would not result in a complete lack of liability for D, as the inchoate offences of assisting or encouraging and conspiracy would cover almost all cases.[195] Indeed, it is an approach that once found favour with the Law Commission.[196]

However, the most recent Law Commission report has rejected this approach for two main reasons.[197] First, it was contended that cases where P goes on to commit the principal offence assisted or encouraged are different (ie more serious) than cases where P does not, such that only inchoate liability in both cases would fail to mark the distinction in culpability. Secondly, it was highlighted that abolition of complicity would undermine the forensic advantage of (in appropriate cases) being able to charge D as a principal *or* an accessory where D's exact role is uncertain. On both of these grounds, we agree that the Commission were right to rethink their original proposal. Interestingly, a variation on the abolition proposal has been mooted by Sullivan in a manner which seeks to address some of these concerns.[198]

---

[194] Wilson, *Central Issues in Criminal Theory* (2002) 221.

[195] The only exception might be cases of procuring. Child, 'The Differences Between Attempted Complicity and Inchoate Assisting and Encouraging: A Reply to Professor Bohlander' [2010] Crim LR 924.

[196] Law Commission, *Assisting and Encouraging Crime* (Consultation 131, 1993).

[197] Law Commission, *Participating in Crime* (No 305, 2007) paras 1.38–1.40.

[198] Sullivan, 'Doing Without Complicity' [2012] JCCL 199.

12.7.2 Law Commission 2007 recommendations

We have made reference to the latest Law Commission recommendations[199] at several points during this chapter, and it is contended by some commentators that they represent the best route available to reform of this area. However, despite codification of inchoate assisting or encouraging within the Serious Crime Act 2007 (intended to work in tandem with the Commission's complicity recommendations), the Commission's complicity report remains unimplemented. Embracing the derivative theory of complicity liability, the Commission recommend the codification of three main offences.

- Clause 1: Complicity liability where D assists or encourages P to commit an offence that P goes on to commit, intending to assist or encourage, and intending that P should complete at least the act element of that offence. The requirement that D should *intend* the principal offence (absent from the current law) would shrink complicity liability to only those cases where D wants to affect P's conduct, where she fully associates herself with P, and where the derivative theory justifying liability is most convincing.[200] Cases falling out of complicity liability will be caught by the Commission expanded inchoate offences, now codified within Part 2 of the Serious Crime Act 2007.

- Clause 2: Complicity liability where D forms a joint enterprise with P, and P goes on to commit the principal offence. This clause provides for a separate basis for complicity liability, applying to *both* primary and/or collateral offences where D coordinates her behaviour with P and is reckless as to P committing the offence. The fact that only recklessness is required (both as to the primary and/or collateral offence) does not marry with the derivative theory employed by the Commission and is essentially a concession to public policy. The different and lesser mens rea for joint enterprise cases would make the distinction between clause 1 and clause 2 very important.

- Clause 3: A new offence of 'causing a no-fault offence' where D causes (ie not just assists or encourages) P to commit a strict liability offence. This new offence provides a coherent response to cases where D causes P's offence, but P is not an innocent agent because the conduct she is caused to complete is an offence despite her lack of mens rea.

Academic responses to the Commission's recommendations have been mixed.[201] In 2015, the Justice Committee of the House of Commons recomended that the Law Commission start a further project on joint enterprise, not adopting its 2007 report.

---

199 Law Commission, *Participating in Crime* (No 305, 2007).
200 The Commission draw heavily on similar recommendations from Simester, 'The Mental Element in Complicity' (2006) 122 LQR 578.
201 Wilson welcomes the proposals in 'A Rational Scheme of Liability for Participating in Crime' [2008] Crim LR 3, but they are criticised in Sullivan, 'Participating in Crime' [2008] Crim LR 19 and Taylor, 'Procuring, Causation, Innocent Agency and the Law Commission' [2008] Crim LR 32. Horder (Criminal Law Commissioner at the time of the Complicity Report) responds to Sullivan's criticism in Chapter 6 of *Homicide and the Politics of Law Reform* (2012).

12.8 Eye on assessment

Answering problem questions on complicity is challenging, but the structure is no different to any other essay of this kind. The focus should be on clarity, leading your reader through your analysis, and keeping your discussion as simple as possible (there is no need to add to the complexity!). The starting point is to identify a criminal offence from P, and then to work backwards to D's potential liability for complicity in that offence.

STEP 1 Identify the potential criminal event in the facts

This should be simply stated (eg 'The first potential criminal event arises where P murders V, having been encouraged to do so by D'). The role of this stage is to highlight which part of the question you are answering before you begin to apply the law.

STEP 2 Identify the potential offence

Again, state this simply (eg 'When P kills V, following D's encouragement, D may be liable for murder as P's accomplice'). The role of this stage is to highlight which offence you are going to apply.

STEP 3 Applying the offence to the facts

Having identified the relevant offence, make sure you discuss each of the required elements.

Actus reus: What does the offence require? Did D do it?

Mens rea: What does the offence require? Did D possess it?

In order to apply steps 2 and 3, you need to do two things. First, you need to lead your reader through the most likely route to liability (ie principal offender; complicity by assisting or encouraging; by procuring; by joint enterprise; etc) and, secondly, you need to apply the elements of that offence.

In **Figure 12.2** we set out a flowchart to help you to make sense of the different routes to complicity liability. Within each stage represented in the figure, you will need to take account of the detailed commentary set out in the chapter (ie this is a rough guide, not a substitution for engagement with the case law).

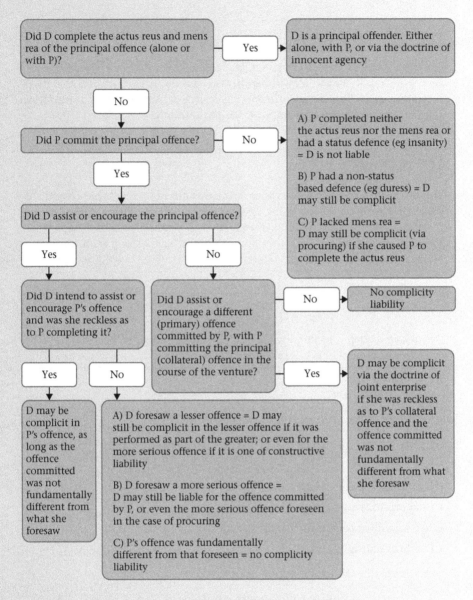

Figure 12.2 Guide to multi-party offending

If the outcome of your discussion is that D may be complicit in an offence, we must then move to Step 4.

STEP 4 Consider defences

The word 'consider' here is important, as you should not discuss every defence for every question. Rather, think whether there are any defences (eg duress) that *could* potentially apply. This includes the specific defences of withdrawal and the victim rule. If there are any potential defences, discuss those only.

STEP 5 Conclude

This is usually a single sentence either saying that it is likely that D has committed the offence, or saying that it is not likely either because an offence element is not satisfied or because a defence is likely to apply. It is not often that you will be able to say categorically whether D has committed the offence or not, so it is usually best to conclude in terms of what is more 'likely'.

STEP 6 Loop

Go back up to Step 1, identifying the next potential criminal event. Continue until you have discussed all the relevant potentially criminal events.

 ONLINE RESOURCE CENTRE

www.oxfordtextbooks.co.uk/orc/smithandhogan/

This chapter is accompanied by a selection of online resources to help you with this topic, including:

- **Multiple choice questions**
- **Chapter summary sheet**
- Two **sample examination questions** with answer guidance
- **Further reading**

Also available on the Online Resource Centre are:

- A selection of **videos** from the authors explaining key topics and principles
- **Legal updates**
- Useful **weblinks**

13

Denials of an offence

13.1 Introduction

In **Chapters 13** and **14** we shift focus from the discussion of substantive offences (ie issues of inculpation), to denials of liability (ie issues of exculpation). We have already discussed a number of specific defences in relation to particular crimes (eg withdrawal for complicity, belief in an owner's consent for criminal damage, etc). The rules discussed in these two chapters are different because, if they apply, they provide a complete[1] defence for (almost[2]) any criminal offence.

The classification of criminal law defences is controversial, not least because the term 'defence' is often employed non-specifically to describe all manner of arguments raised by a defendant.[3] In this book, between **Chapters 13** and **14**, we distinguish two sets of rules which continue to be commonly referred to as defences. This chapter focuses on the rules regulating D's denial of an offence, a denial of one or more actus reus or mens rea elements. **Chapter 14**, in contrast, focuses on defences properly so called. These rules apply where D *has* committed the actus reus and mens rea of the offence charged, but seeks to rely on an independent set of rules (ie a defence) to escape liability.

We begin with denials of an offence. Where D has not completed every element of the offence charged, strictly speaking, she does not need a defence: she has not committed the offence. We might talk loosely of a 'defence' where D states an alibi (eg that she was somewhere else when the bank was robbed), or where D denies specific offence elements (eg that she did not foresee a risk of causing criminal damage), but such statements are not appealing to independent rules beyond the terms of the offences themselves. However, there are three sets of rules that, whilst falling within this category, require specific examination.

- **Intoxication:** D explains her lack of mens rea (including, in extreme cases, her lack of voluntary movement) on the basis of intoxication. For example, when drunk D stabs what she thinks is a theatrical dummy which is in fact her sleeping friend.[4] D, in this example, lacks subjective mens rea for any offence against the person.

- **Sane automatism:** D explains her lack of voluntary movement (and associated lack of mens rea) on the basis that she was rendered totally incompetent by some *external* circumstances affecting her. For example, D drives dangerously when attacked by a swarm of bees, or punches V whilst suffering concussion following a blow to the head.[5] D, in these examples, lacks an essential element for all offences.

- **Insanity (as a denial of offending):** D explains her lack of mens rea (including, in extreme cases, her lack of voluntary movement) on the basis of what the law labels insanity.[6] This includes all medical conditions which cause some bodily malfunctioning which prevents D understanding the nature or quality of her acts, or not to know they are wrong. For example, D kills V under the insane delusion that she is breaking a jar.[7]

---

[1] Unlike the 'partial' defences to murder discussed at **6.2**, the rules discussed in **Chapters 13** and **14** lead to an acquittal.

[2] The only exception is the defence of duress (**Chapter 14**) which does not apply to murder and a small number of related offences.

[3] Williams, 'Offences and Defences' (1982) 2 LS 233.

[4] Example from Lord Denning in *AG for Northern Ireland v Gallagher* [1963] AC 349, 381.

[5] Examples from Lord Goddard in *Hill v Baxter* [1958] 2 WLR 76, 82–83.

[6] The insanity rules can apply *both* as a denial of offending, and as a defence where D has committed the offence. This chapter discusses the former only, **Chapter 14** discusses the latter.

[7] Example from Stephen, *A Digest of the Criminal Law* (8th edn, 1947) 6.

These three sets of rules require separate discussion from other denials of offending for three main reasons. First, unlike most denials (eg simple alibis), D cannot raise issues of intoxication, automatism, and/or insanity without bringing some evidence that the relevant condition or circumstances applied to her at the time of the alleged offence.[8] This is because although there is a general burden on the prosecution to prove D's liability, there are legal presumptions that our movements are voluntary, that we are sane, etc.[9] Secondly, where D successfully pleads insanity, this will not result in an unqualified acquittal, but rather in the special verdict of 'not guilty by reason of insanity'. Thirdly, and most importantly, these rules are special because in certain circumstances they can provide alternative routes to liability where D lacks mens rea for the offence charged. In other words, if D uses evidence of her intoxication to explain the absence of mens rea or actus reus, the evidence might then be capable of being used by the prosecution to justify her conviction despite the missing offence element(s). The evidence is used as a method of *inculpation*. In the context of intoxication, D's voluntary choice or negligence in losing control (through intoxication) might excuse her conduct for one offence but will itself provide evidence from which the Crown prosecution can construct liability for a different offence. For example, D who is too drunk to form an intent to kill will be not guilty of murder, but her causing V's death in an intoxicated state will render her liable for manslaughter.

13.1.1 Denials, defences, or constructors of liability?

Where the rules in this chapter apply to inculpate D for an offence, there is a potentially confusing inconsistency in the terminology used by courts and within academic writing. This is because many commentators still prefer to discuss denials of liability as 'defences'. You are likely to come across two methods of presentation.

- D completes the offence because, although she lacks mens rea, the relevant rules substitute for that mens rea.
- D completes the offence because the relevant rules prevent D denying liability (ie prevent her using a defence).

We prefer the first method of analysis because we believe it provides a more accurate description of D's liability. Where D lacks mens rea through intoxication, for example, it seems odd to say that she completes the offence because she is not allowed to raise the defence of intoxication—not being allowed to raise the issue of intoxication does not mean that D somehow acted with mens rea. Rather, if we are finding D liable, it must be because D's intoxication is substituting for her lack of mens rea.[10] We return to this discussion at several points in the chapter in relation to voluntary intoxication, prior-fault automatism, and prior-fault insanity.

---

[8] The nature of this burden differs between the rules, discussed later.

[9] The use of reverse burdens in these areas is another reason why the terminology of 'defences' has been common.

[10] Simester, 'Intoxication is Never a Defence' [2009] Crim LR 3; Child and Reed, 'Automatism is Never a Defence' (2014) 65 NILQ 167; Child, 'Prior Fault: Blocking Defences or Constructing Crimes' in Reed and Bohlander (eds), *General Defences* (2014).

13.2 Intoxication

There is an obvious and well-documented link between intoxication,[11] particularly alcoholic intoxication, and crime.[12] Intoxicants can lower inhibitions, warp moral and practical judgements, encourage unpredictable behaviour, and so on. In short, D's conduct when intoxicated may not be a reflection of her character when sober. This is not, however, and never has been, a defence to criminal offences. D's claim that 'it was the drink' may provide some moral mitigation, and may become relevant at sentencing, but it is not an answer to a criminal charge. If it were, there would be a lot more space in prisons!

The intoxication rules *only* become relevant where, as a result of intoxication, D lacks the prescribed mens rea for the crime charged. This is illustrated in *Kingston* where, although intoxicated, D still had the mens rea for the crime at the time of the actus reus.

> ### *Kingston* [1994] 3 All ER 353
>
> Y and X hired P to take compromising photos of D to use for blackmail. P invited V (a 15-year-old boy) to his flat, gave him alcohol and drugs, and left him asleep. He then drugged D's coffee, and encouraged D to indecently assault V as he slept. D did so. D was charged with indecent assault.[13]
>
> - Crown Court: guilty of indecent assault.
> - Court of Appeal: appeal allowed. No liability: D only committed the offence as a result of P surreptitiously drugging him and thus lowering his inhibitions.
> - House of Lords: appeal allowed, and D's conviction reinstated. A drunken intention is still an intention.

In *Kingston*, the mens rea was proved irrespective of the intoxication, so there is no need (or scope) to rely on special rules of intoxication (discussed later). Despite the disinhibiting effect of the drugs in this case, D was still able (and did in fact) form an intention to assault V, and so D satisfied all elements of the offence charged. D acted with the mens rea required for the offence. There is no defence of intoxication where D has committed an offence; a drunken intent is still an intent; an intoxicated mens rea is still a mens rea.[14] This is illustrated in **Figure 13.1**.

Figure 13.1 An intoxicated mens rea is still a mens rea

---

[11] This chapter only discusses the intoxication of D. The intoxication of a victim may affect D's liability (eg where it affects V's consent in sexual offences) but this is a separate issue, discussed elsewhere. See also *Smith and Hogan's Criminal Law* (14th edn, 2015), Ch11.

[12] Dingwall, *Alcohol and Crime* (2005).

[13] D's conduct would now be charged under the Sexual Offences Act 2003.

[14] Horder has recommended an alternative approach for cases like *Kingston* based on temporary insanity: Horder, 'Sobering Up? The Law Commission on Criminal Intoxication' (1995) 58 MLR 534.

In contrast, where D raises her extreme intoxication to explain that she completely lacked the mens rea (eg 'I was *so* drunk I did not intend to touch V' or 'to cause damage', etc), there are special legal rules on intoxication that apply. The same rules also apply where, in an extreme case, D relies on intoxication to explain her lack of voluntary movement (eg 'I was high on hallucinogenic drugs, I didn't understand what I was doing').[15]

> **Don't be confused...**
> In this book we have analysed a lack of voluntariness in movement as a lack of mens rea (mens rea as to the conduct element of a crime). However, as we explained at **3.3**, it is common to analyse 'voluntary movement' as a single actus reus element. Thus, where D uses intoxication to explain a lack of voluntary movement, some courts and commentators will describe this as explaining a lack of actus reus. The difference between the two descriptions does not affect the application of the intoxication rules, but should be noted to avoid confusion.

These special rules apply where D does not form the mens rea because of the intoxication. It is wrong to say, as some cases have, that the intoxication rules will only apply where D is rendered 'incapable' of forming a mens rea as opposed to simply not forming one as a result of intoxication.[16] For example, if D mistakenly kills V thinking (due to intoxication) that V is a theatrical dummy, D may be 'capable' of forming an intention to kill, but her intoxication still provides an explanation for her lack of mens rea in relation to V. The intoxication rules apply therefore when D is claiming that she did not have the mens rea for the offence charged because she was intoxicated by drink or drugs at the time of the offence.

Once engaged, our starting point, as set out in **Figure 13.2**, is that D has not committed an offence.

Figure 13.2 Lacking mens rea due to intoxication

When considering cases involving the intoxication rules, bear in mind that the overriding question is whether, despite D lacking the mens rea for the offence at the time of the commission of the actus reus (what we will call time T2), the court is interested in whether D's earlier conduct at the time of becoming intoxicated (what we can call T1) is sufficiently blameworthy that we can use D's 'prior fault' at T1 to replace or substitute for the missing offence elements at T2?[17] **Table 13.1** sets out the elements of the intoxication rules in a logical order it is worth following. If the conditions in these rules apply, D will be guilty of a criminal offence even though she lacked mens rea at T2 when committing it.

---

[15] *Lipman* [1970] 1 QB 152: D took LSD (a hallucinogenic drug). Believing that he was fighting snakes at the centre of the earth, D killed V.

[16] *Beard* [1920] AC 479, 501–502; *Kingston* [1994] 3 All ER 353; cf *Sheehan and Moore* [1975] 2 All ER 960.

[17] Simester, 'Intoxication is Never a Defence' [2009] Crim LR 3.

Table 13.1 Intoxication rules

A) D's intoxication at T1 must have been voluntary;
B) D's offence at T2 must have been one of 'basic intent', as opposed to one of 'specific intent';
C) D's intoxicant at T1 must have been 'dangerous' in the sense that it is commonly known to lead to unpredictability or aggression; and
D) D must lack mens rea at T2 *because* of that intoxication

Where these elements are satisfied, D's lack of mens rea (including a potential lack of voluntariness) at T2 will be substituted for by the intoxication rules, and D will be liable as if the missing elements were satisfied.[18] This is illustrated in **Figure 13.3**.

Figure 13.3 Intoxication replacing a lack of mens rea

Extra detail...

Unless D claims to have lacked voluntariness, there should be no burden on D to prove she lacked mens rea through intoxication.[19] However, intoxication is usually raised by D to explain a lack of mens rea that would otherwise be difficult for a jury to believe (eg 'I thought my sleeping friend was a theatrical dummy'). Indeed, in certain cases, the courts have begun to require specific evidence of intoxication from D before she is allowed to raise the issue.[20] This reflects policy concerns about allowing D to claim a lack of mens rea on the basis of intoxication too easily, and may also reflect the language of defences commonly used when discussing the intoxication rules. However, it is submitted that no specific evidence should be required: it is for the prosecution to prove mens rea, and the law should avoid any rules requiring D to prove her innocence.

13.2.1 Was D's intoxication voluntary or involuntary?

D's voluntariness in becoming so intoxicated at T1 that she lacks mens rea for the crime at T2 is fundamental to establishing any kind of blameworthiness. The law is looking for equivalence between D's conduct in becoming intoxicated at T1 and her lack of mens

---

[18] The alternative way of expressing this, using the language of defences, is to say that if the elements of the intoxication rules are satisfied D will *not* be able to raise intoxication as a defence. See **13.1.1**.

[19] We discuss the presumption of voluntary movement in the context of automatism later.

[20] *McKnight* (2000) The Times, 5 May; *P* [2004] EWCA Crim 1043.

rea at T2. Only if D became intoxicated voluntarily can we say that she *chose* to run the associated risks.[21]

13.2.1.1 Involuntary intoxication

Where D's intoxication was involuntary,[22] it would not be fair for the courts to say she has chosen to run the risks associated with intoxication, and it would be inappropriate to blame her if her subsequent conduct involves criminal acts. Where D is not responsible for her intoxicated state (ie involuntary intoxication at T1), there is no liability for any offence if the involuntary intoxication caused her to lack the relevant mens rea at the time of the offence (T2). Involuntariness, however, has been narrowly defined. The leading case is *Kingston* (discussed earlier), where D was drugged by a third party, and then sexually assaulted a minor. Understandably, the House of Lords in *Kingston* had some sympathy for D: he was aware of and claimed to be in control of his paedophilic tendencies when sober, only losing control as a result of the drugs involuntarily administered by P. Where such involuntary intoxication leads to a lack of mens rea at T2, there is no blameworthy conduct at T1 or T2 and D will not be liable for an offence. D was only liable in *Kingston* because his conduct at T2 *was* accompanied by mens rea. Thus, although there was no prior fault at T1, D was liable at T2 without the need for such substitution.

D's intoxication is clearly involuntary in cases like *Kingston* where D's drinks are surreptitiously laced with alcohol or other intoxicating drugs,[23] and the same may be true where D is forced to take drugs under duress. However, as illustrated in *Allen*, where D knows that she is consuming a dangerous intoxicant (eg alcohol), this does not qualify as involuntary simply because she is unaware of its quantity or possible effects.

Allen (1988) The Times, 10 June

D committed the actus reus of buggery and indecent assault.[24] He lacked mens rea (he claimed he was not acting voluntarily) because he had consumed a large amount of wine supplied by a friend. D claimed this was involuntary intoxication because he did not realise the strength of the wine. D was charged with the sexual offences.[25]

- Crown Court: guilty of the sexual offences.
- Court of Appeal: convictions upheld on appeal. D's intoxication was voluntary.

A more difficult case arises where D voluntarily consumes an intoxicant, but a further intoxicant is added without her knowledge (eg X gives D a double shot of alcohol rather than the single requested, or X laces D alcoholic drink with another intoxicating drug). In cases of this kind, the question for the court is likely to be whether the *in*voluntary proportion of D's intoxication overrides the voluntary, such to make it trivial.[26]

---

[21] Note the important role of 'choice'. See our discussion of the principle of autonomy at **1.4.3**.

[22] Law Commission, *Intoxication and Criminal Liability* (No 314, 2009) Part 4.

[23] *Ross v HM Advocate* 1991 SLT 564: D's drink was involuntarily laced with various drugs including LSD, under the influence of which D injured several people. His conviction for offences against the person was quashed on appeal.

[24] Commentary at [1988] Crim LR 698.

[25] For such acts performed today D would be charged under the Sexual Offences Act 2003.

[26] Law Commission, *Intoxication and Criminal Liability* (No 314, 2009) paras 3.126–3.127.

As illustrated in **Figure 13.4**, where D's intoxication is involuntary and she is intoxicated to the extent that she has no mens rea then there is no liability. This is because there is no prior fault in her becoming intoxicated at T1 which can provide the culpability for conduct at T2.

Figure 13.4 Involuntary intoxication

13.2.1.2 Voluntary intoxication

Where D has voluntarily consumed the intoxicant (T1) and subsequently, because of that voluntary or self-induced intoxication, she lacks mens rea when she commits the actus reus of an offence (T2), the intoxication rules may apply depending on the further two questions which we must now address: (a) was the crime D was charged with one of basis intent or specific intent; and (b) was the drug D voluntarily consumed known to be a 'dangerous one'.

13.2.2 Offences of basic intent and specific intent

Having established that D was voluntarily intoxicated at T1, and lacked mens rea for the offence charged at T2, we have to ask what nature of crime was involved at T2. If the crime D is charged with is one classified by the law as 'specific intent', then D is not guilty of that crime—irrespective of the type of drug.[27] If the crime D is charged with at T2 is one classified by the law as of 'basic intent' then D may be liable for that offence on the basis of her prior fault in voluntarily intoxicating herself at T1 subject to the type of intoxicant involved.

The common law has developed this crucial two-part classification between basic and specific intent offences.

> **Terminology...**
> The terms 'basic intent' and 'specific intent' are misleading, as they do not describe types of intention. Rather, they are simply labels that have been used to distinguish two classifications of offences. We discuss the basis of this distinction later, but suffice to say, it has nothing to do with different types of intention.[28]

A) **Basic intent offences:** The prior fault in D's voluntary intoxication at T1 *may be* sufficient to replace her lack of mens rea at T2 subject to the final element of the intoxication rules discussed later. Malicious wounding or inflicting GBH,[29] for

---

[27] Unless D had voluntarily intoxicated herself in order to commit the offence—'Dutch courage', see later.

[28] For discussion of the origin of these terms, as well as a more general critique, see Gough, 'Intoxication and Criminal Liability: The Law Commission's Proposed Reforms' (1996) 112 LQR 335, 342.

[29] Offences Against the Person Act 1861, s20.

example, is a basic intent offence. Thus, where D wounds V or causes GBH, but lacks mens rea (and even, potentially, lacks voluntariness in her movement) because of her voluntary intoxication, she will still be liable for the offence.[30] This is illustrated in **Figure 13.5**.

Figure 13.5 Basic intent offences

Terminology...
Where intoxication is discussed using the language of defences, Figure 13.5 would be described as the defence of intoxication not being permitted to apply.

B) **Specific intent offences:** D's prior fault in voluntary intoxication at T1 will *not* be sufficient to replace her lack of mens rea at T2. Wounding or causing GBH with intent,[31] for example, is a specific intent offence. Thus, where D wounds V or causes GBH, but lacks mens rea (and even, potentially, lacks voluntariness in her movement) because of her voluntary intoxication, she will not be liable for this offence.[32] This is illustrated in **Figure 13.6**.

Figure 13.6 Specific intent offences

Terminology...
Where intoxication is discussed using the language of defences, Figure 13.6 would be described as the defence of intoxication being permitted to apply.

The logic of separating basic and specific intent offences is that D's voluntary intoxication at T1 is only sufficiently wrongful to replace a lack of mens rea for certain offences and not others. However, there are two major problems with this.

The first problem is that the culpability in D's voluntarily becoming intoxicated is not truly equivalent to D's culpability had she had the subjective mens rea for the offence charged. Such equivalence is assumed within the current law in the context of basic intent

---

[30] *Aitken* [1992] 1 WLR 1006.
[31] Offences Against the Person Act 1861, s18.
[32] *Davies* [1991] Crim LR 469.

offences,[33] but it is difficult to justify logically.[34] Even if we accept that voluntarily taking a dangerous drug means that D *chose* to risk committing a harmful act, that choice is necessarily non-specific. In contrast, subjective mens rea requires D to intend or be reckless as to specific elements of an offence before she is liable for it. In the context of criminal damage, for example, foresight of possible danger is not sufficient for liability, D must be reckless as to the specific risk of causing damage, and to the specific fact of ownership as to the property damaged. The criticism, therefore, is that when the intoxication rules are used to replace a lack of subjective mens rea (including voluntariness in movement at T2), we are finding liability on the basis of an objective (negligence-based) standard at T1.[35]

The second problem is that the common law has struggled to create a clear set of rules to distinguish basic intent and specific intent offences. It should be acknowledged that in the absence of a justified equivalence between intoxication and a certain level of mens rea a principled test of this kind is almost impossible, but the law requires one in order to function.

13.2.2.1 Distinguishing between basic and specific intent offences

The leading case discussing the separation of basic and specific intent offences is *Majewski*.[36]

◻ DPP v Majewski [1977] AC 443

Intoxicated by a range of dangerous drugs, including alcohol, D was involved in a bar brawl where he assaulted several people. D also assaulted a number of police officers during the course of his arrest. D was charged with assault occasioning ABH, and assaulting a police officer.[37] D claimed that he lacked mens rea due to intoxication.

- Crown Court: guilty of assault offences.

- Court of Appeal: appeal dismissed.

- House of Lords: appeal dismissed. These were basic intent offences, and so D's voluntary intoxication can be used as a substitute for the mens rea he lacks at the time of his conduct.

Although *Majewski* is clear in its categorisation of assault as a basic intent offence, the Lords do not provide a unified test to apply to other offences. Following the older case of *Beard*,[38] there is general discussion of the equivalence of intoxication with certain species of mens rea, but the Lords fall short of a precise test. To the extent that a test is discernible, the Lords seem to equate offences that can be satisfied by recklessness

---

[33] *Majewski* [1977] AC 443.

[34] Horder, 'Sobering Up? The Law Commission on Criminal Intoxication' (1995) 58 MLR 534.

[35] Robinson, 'Causing the Conditions of One's Own Defence: A Study in the Limits of Theory in Criminal Law Doctrine' (1985) 71 Vir LR 1, 14–17; Husak, 'Intoxication and Culpability' (2012) 6 Crim L & Phil 363, 366–368; Williams, 'Voluntary Intoxication—A Lost Cause?' (2013) 129 LQR 264, 266–271.

[36] Law Commission, *Intoxication and Criminal Liability* (No 314, 2009) paras 2.2–2.74; Horder, 'The Classification of Crimes and the General Part' in Duff and Green (eds), *Defining Crimes* (2005).

[37] Offences Against the Person Act 1861, s47; Police Act 1996, s89.

[38] [1920] AC 479.

as basic intent, and those requiring intention as specific intent. It is noted by Lord Edmund-Davis that this distinction 'illogical though…it may be' has an advantage of 'compromise' where offences are laddered on the basis of mens rea.[39] For example, where D in her voluntary intoxicated state causes GBH she is not liable for a section 18 offence (specific intent), but is liable for a section 20 offence (basic intent);[40] where she causes death she is not liable for murder (specific intent), but is liable for manslaughter (basic intent); and so on. However, where the Lords attempted to be more specific, they ran into problems. For example, Lord Simon discusses a test based on intention as to consequences (ie where D must intend the consequence element of the offence, it is a specific intent offence).[41] But this cannot be right: murder, the paradigm example of a specific intent offence, can be committed without an intention to kill (ie where D intends to cause GBH).

An alternative, but equally flawed, method of distinction was considered in *Heard*.

Heard [2007] EWCA Crim 125

Whilst drunk, D exposed his penis and rubbed it on a police officer's leg. D claimed to lack mens rea due to intoxication (ie a lack of *intentional* touching). D was charged with sexual assault.[42]

- Crown Court: guilty of sexual assault, holding that sexual assault is a basic intent offence.
- Court of Appeal: conviction upheld on appeal.

Extra detail…

Heard should not have been a difficult case. The fact that D did not remember his actions the following day is not a basis for claiming that he did not intend to touch V when intoxicated. There was no need to discuss the classification of sexual assault as a basic or specific intent offence because his appeal to the intoxication rules should have fallen at the first hurdle: an intoxicated mens rea is still a mens rea.

Although *Heard* should not have been a difficult case, it does raise a number of important issues. First, in classifying sexual assault as a basic intent offence, despite a mens rea of *intentional* touching, it runs counter to the intention/recklessness distinction in *Majewski*. Secondly, by extension, it implies that all sexual offences will be classified as basic intent where D's mens rea (as with sexual assault) relates solely to D's intentional contact with V and V's non-consent to that contact. Thirdly, and most importantly, *Heard* provides an alternative test for identifying basic and specific intent offences.

crimes of specific intent are those where the offence requires proof of purpose or consequence, which are not confined to, but amongst which are included, those where the purpose goes beyond the actus reus (sometimes referred to as cases of 'ulterior intent').

---

[39] [1977] AC 443, 495.
[40] Offences Against the Person Act 1861.
[41] [1977] AC 443, 478–479.
[42] Sexual Offences Act 2003, s3.

In this passage, Hughes LJ accepts Lord Simon's test in *Majewski* (despite the problems outlined earlier), and also builds upon it with reference to ulterior mens rea.[43] For Hughes LJ, any offence which requires ulterior mens rea, even ulterior mens rea of recklessness (eg criminal damage being reckless as to the endangerment of life[44]) will be one of specific intent. However, this test is no less problematic than Lord Simon's. First, as with Lord Simon's test, applying this test would mean murder was not a specific intent offence because D need not intend the result (ie it is sufficient if she intends to cause GBH), and murder does not require any ulterior mens rea. But, more importantly, by holding that intention-based offences like sexual assault can be basic intent offences, and recklessness-based offences like aggravated criminal damage should be specific intent offences, any theoretical underpinning claiming equivalence between recklessness and voluntary intoxication falls away.

Without guidance beyond these two equally unattractive alternatives, the current law remains in a state of uncertainty. The reaction of several other common law jurisdictions has been to reject the *Majewski* distinction between specific and basic intent.[45] However, we have not yet taken that step in England and Wales.[46] Rather, in the absence of a clear test, the law has developed by categorising offences as they emerge in case law. There is a pattern, with most intention-based offences being classified as specific intent, but this is not systematic.

- **Basic intent:** Manslaughter,[47] malicious wounding or causing GBH (s20),[48] assault occasioning ABH (s47),[49] assault and battery,[50] rape,[51] sexual assault,[52] criminal damage (where only recklessness is alleged),[53] etc.

- **Specific intent:** Murder,[54] wounding or causing GBH with intent (s18),[55] theft,[56] robbery,[57] section 9(1)(a) burglary,[58] attempt to commit a specific intent offence,[59] complicity,[60] etc.

---

[43] Mens rea going beyond the actus reus of the offence: see **4.2.1.2**.
[44] Criminal Damage Act 1971, s1(2). See **9.7.5**.
[45] eg Canada in *Daviault* (1994) 118 DLR (4th) 469; Australia in *O'Connor* (1980) 146 CLR 64; New Zealand in *Kamipeli* [1975] 2 NZLR 610; South Africa in *Chretien* 1981 (1) SA 1097.
[46] See the discussion of reform at **13.6**.
[47] *Beard* [1920] AC 479.
[48] *Aitken* [1992] 1 WLR 1006.
[49] *Bolton v Crawley* [1972] Crim LR 222.
[50] *Majewski* [1977] AC 443.
[51] *Grout* [2011] EWCA Crim 299.
[52] *Heard* [2007] EWCA Crim 125.
[53] *Caldwell* [1981] 1 All ER 961.
[54] *Beard* [1920] AC 479.
[55] *Davies* [1991] Crim LR 469.
[56] *Majewski* [1977] AC 443.
[57] Ibid.
[58] *Hutchins* [1988] Crim LR 379.
[59] *Clarkson* [1971] 3 All ER 344.
[60] *Clarkson* [1971] 3 All ER 344, although note some doubt in *Lynch* [1975] AC 653.

13.2.2.2 Dutch courage

Where an intoxicated D lacks mens rea for a specific intent offence, this is usually the end of the matter: D's intoxication cannot replace her lack of mens rea, so there is no liability for that offence.[61] However, there is one possible exception to this rule. This relates to (so-called) 'Dutch courage' cases, where D becomes intoxicated at T1 *in order to* commit the specific intent offence at T2. In such cases, D's blameworthy conduct is not merely her choice to become voluntarily intoxicated, but her choice to do so in order (ie with intention) to commit the offence. This was discussed in *AG for Northern Ireland v Gallagher*.

AG for Northern Ireland v Gallagher [1963] AC 349

D decided to kill his wife. D drank most of a bottle of whisky and then did so. D claimed that, due to his intoxication, he lacked mens rea for murder as a specific intent offence. D was charged with murder.

- Crown Court: guilty of murder.
- Northern Ireland Court of Appeal: appeal allowed. The court found that D had been wrongly convicted on the basis of his mens rea at T1, rather than focusing on T2.
- House of Lords: appeal allowed, restoring D's conviction. Contrary to the Court of Appeal, the House of Lords held that the trial court had correctly focused on D's mens rea at T2. Thus, this was simply a case where intoxicated mens rea is still mens rea.

D's conviction in this case did not require an examination of 'Dutch courage' because, despite D's intoxication, it was found that D intended to kill at the time (T2) of killing his wife. However, Lord Denning went on to say that even if the Court of Appeal's interpretation was correct (ie that D only had mens rea when becoming intoxicated at T1), it would still be correct in law to find liability, even for a strict liability offence.

> I think the law on this point should take a clear stand. If a man, whilst sane and sober, forms an intention to kill and makes preparation for it…and then gets himself drunk so as to give himself Dutch courage to do the killing, and whilst drunk carries out his intention, he cannot rely on this self-induced drunkenness as a defence to a charge of murder, nor even as reducing it to manslaughter…The wickedness of his mind before he got drunk is enough to condemn him, coupled with the act which he intended to do and did do. A psychopath who goes out intending to kill, knowing it is wrong, and does kill, cannot escape the consequences by making himself drunk before doing it.

The logic of this statement is compelling. However, it bunches together two situations which are quite different. In one, D intends to become intoxicated in order to kill when drunk. In the other, D intends to kill at some point in the future, and the killing of V when drunk is not part of her plan.

For the latter, where D does not plan to kill when intoxicated, she should not be liable for murder (or any specific intent offence). Although D plans to kill V at T1, she does not intend to kill V through becoming intoxicated and losing control. Thus, her case is akin to D who drives to V's house to kill her, accidentally hits a pedestrian on the way, and it turns out to be V. D is not liable for murder in this case because she does not intend to

---

[61] See **Figure 13.6**. D may be liable for an alternative basic intent offence.

kill by that act.[62] The fact of intoxication does not seem to make any meaningful difference to this conclusion.

However, in the former case, where D becomes intoxicated *in order to* kill whilst in that state, it seems correct that D should be liable for murder even if she lacked mens rea at the moment she caused V's death (due to her intoxication). This can be presented as an exception to the rule that intoxication cannot replace a lack of mens rea for specific intent offences. But it is not necessary to analyse it in that way. An alternative way of analysing these (rather unlikely) facts, is that D's conduct in becoming intoxicated is the conduct element of her offence. Under this analysis, D's conduct in becoming intoxicated is akin to the shooting of a bullet or the release of a stampeding herd of cattle towards V. In each case, D is in control of the release (ie becoming intoxicated; pulling the trigger; releasing the cattle) and then loses control of the weapon before it makes contact with V (ie her involuntary body; the bullet; the cattle). Analysed in these terms, there is no issue of coincidence, as D has the mens rea for murder whilst completing the conduct element (becoming intoxicated). And there is nothing to break the chain of causation. Thus, whether we recognise an exception to the intoxication rules or we rely on standard rules of liability, D is guilty of murder.[63]

13.2.3 Voluntary intoxication by a dangerous drug

In cases where D has become voluntarily intoxicated at T1,[64] has then gone on to commit the actus reus of the offence at T2, and the offence is one of basic intent,[65] we have a further question to ask before we can determine whether her prior fault in becoming so intoxicated is sufficient to be treated in law as a substitute for the mens rea that she lacks for the offence at T2.

Where the drug consumed is 'dangerous', such that it is known (commonly, or at least to D) to cause unpredictability and/or aggression, D's voluntary intoxication by that drug at T1 will be sufficient prior fault to be treated as a substitute for the mens rea of a basic intent offence at T2. Alcohol is a clear example where such effects are commonly known. And, as established in *Lipman*,[66] other drugs such as LSD will come within the same category.

Where the intoxicant consumed by D at T1 is *not* commonly known to have effects of this kind, and it is not known to D personally (eg from previous use), D's prior fault in her voluntary consumption of that drug will not be a sufficient substitute for the mens rea of the basic intent offence at T2. This was recognised in *Bailey*,[67] where D (a diabetic) failed to take sufficient food after insulin, and committed a series of serious attacks whilst in an intoxicated state.

> It is common knowledge that those who take alcohol to excess or certain sorts of drugs may become aggressive or do dangerous or unpredictable things, they may be able to foresee the risks of causing

---

[62] See **5.4**.

[63] Child, 'Prior Fault: Blocking Defences or Constructing Crimes' in Reed and Bohlander (eds), *General Defences* (2014).

[64] Of course, if D is involuntarily intoxicated there is no criminal liability if that causes her lack of mens rea at T2 (see **13.2.1**).

[65] Of course, as discussed, if the offence is one of specific intent D is not guilty irrespective of the kind of drug (see **13.2.2**).

[66] [1970] 1 QB 152.

[67] [1983] 1 WLR 760.

harm to others but nevertheless persist in their conduct. But the same cannot be said without more of a man who fails to take food after an insulin injection.[68]

The same reasoning was later applied in *Hardie*.

Hardie [1985] 1 WLR 64

D took five valium tablets (a sedative drug) to calm himself after being told to leave the house by his partner. D returned, intoxicated by the tablets, and set fire to a wardrobe in the house. D was charged with arson with intention or recklessness as to the endangerment of life.

- Crown Court: guilty of arson. D's lack of mens rea (due to intoxication) was replaced by his voluntary intoxication.
- Court of Appeal: appeal allowed. Valium was not a dangerous drug, and D had no reason to believe it would lead to the actions it caused.

The prior fault of voluntarily consuming the drug will only suffice as a substitute for mens rea if the intoxicant is either commonly known to be dangerous (eg alcohol, LSD, etc), or D knows or is reckless as to its dangerousness (eg from previous use). Where the intoxicant is non-dangerous in the sense that it does not come within one of these categories, even where it results in potentially criminal harms, there will be no liability. This is illustrated in **Figure 13.7**.

Figure 13.7 Intoxication with a non-dangerous intoxicant

Where it is established that D has *voluntarily* taken a *dangerous* intoxicant, we have a blameworthy choice.

13.2.4 D must lack mens rea because of intoxication

Having established that D was voluntarily intoxicated by a dangerous drug at T1, and that she lacked mens rea for the basic intent offence at T2, the final stage of the intoxication rules looks for a nexus to connect the two. In short, D's prior fault by voluntary intoxication at T1 will only be sufficient substitute for her lack of mens rea at T2, creating liability, if her intoxication was the reason she lacked that mens rea. For example, if a voluntarily intoxicated D who has taken a dangerous drug trips on a hidden tripwire and smashes V's vase in the fall (basic intent offence of criminal damage), it would be inappropriate to use D's voluntary dangerous intoxication to substitute for a lack of mens rea in criminal damage. Even if D was sober, she would have done the same thing (ie her blameworthiness at T1 has not affected conduct her at T2).

---

[68] Griffiths LJ at 764–765.

This point was at issue in *Richardson and Irwin*.

Richardson and Irwin [1999] 1 Cr App R 392

D and others (university students) picked up V whilst heavily intoxicated and dropped him over a balcony. D fell 10–12 feet, and was injured. D claimed that he did not foresee the potential for injury, because of his intoxication. D was charged with maliciously inflicting GBH (basic intent offence).[69]

- Crown Court: guilty of section 20 offence.
- Court of Appeal: appeal allowed. D was convicted because a *reasonable* sober person would have foreseen the risk of injury (satisfying the mens rea of s20). However, the correct question was whether *D* would have foreseen the risk of injury if sober.

In some cases, as with *Richardson and Irwin*, it may be difficult to predict what D (as opposed to a reasonable person) would have foreseen if sober. This is a question for the jury.

13.2.5 Intoxication and defences

Just as D's voluntary intoxication can create liability where she lacks mens rea, it can also affect her use of various defences. This does not mean that defences become entirely unavailable: an intoxicated person may still have good reason to act in self-defence, for example. Problems arise, however, where D makes a mistake due to intoxication. For instance, where D assaults V with the intoxicated belief that she is acting in self-defence, where in fact no defensive force was necessary.

The general rule is that D may not use a defence where, in order to satisfy the elements of that defence, she is forced to rely on an intoxicated mistake. D can rely on self-defence,[70] for example, where she believes that force is required to protect herself or property, and where the amount of force used is objectively reasonable. If sober, D's belief in the necessity for force does not need to be correct, or even reasonable, as long as it is honestly held.[71] However, as stated in *Hatton*, D's belief will be disregarded if it is based on an intoxicated mistake.[72]

Hatton [2005] EWCA Crim 2951

Heavily intoxicated, having drunk more than 20 pints of beer, D killed V with several blows of a sledgehammer. D raised self-defence on the grounds that he thought V (who had told D that he was an SAS officer) had attacked him with a stick that he thought was a samurai sword. D was charged with murder.

- Crown Court: guilty of murder. The court did not allow D to rely on his intoxicated mistake as a basis for self-defence.
- Court of Appeal: conviction upheld on appeal. The lower court was correct not to allow D to rely on his intoxicated mistake.

---

[69] Offences Against the Person Act 1861, s20.
[70] **Chapter 14**.
[71] *Gladstone Williams* [1987] 3 All ER 411.
[72] Following *O'Connor* [1991] Crim LR 135, and *O'Grady* [1987] QB 995.

The decision in *Hatton*, and the policy it follows, have been subject to criticism.[73] It seems strange, for example, that although other unreasonable beliefs can ground self-defence, an intoxicated mistake is singled out for special treatment. However, it is a public policy decision (reflecting a general concern about intoxicated offenders) that has been endorsed by subsequent legislation,[74] as well as by the Law Commission.[75]

The only exception to this rule has arisen in the context of criminal damage, where D raises the specific statutory defence that she believed the owner was consenting or would have consented to the damage.[76] As shown in *Jaggard v Dickinson*, here at least D *is* able to rely on her intoxicated mistake.[77]

Jaggard v Dickinson [1981] QB 527

D was told by X, a friend, to use his house as her own. Returning home drunk, D mistakenly tried to enter an identical house on the same street, and when her way was blocked by the owner she gained access by breaking windows. D was charged with criminal damage, and raised the defence that she believed (at the time) that the house belonged to X, and he would have consented to the damage if he had known the circumstances.

- Crown Court: guilty of criminal damage. D may not rely on an intoxicated mistake.
- Divisional Court: appeal allowed. D may use the defence, even if her belief is based on an intoxicated mistake.

This decision is anomalous, and cannot be reconciled with the general rule discussed previously. The Law Commission's proposals would reverse it.[78]

Assessment matters...
If something similar to *Jaggard v Dickinson* were to arise in problem facts, it is important to remember that this case remains authoritative (ie the Commission's recommendations have not been codified into legislation). However, it would be correct to stress the criticism of this case as anomalous, and recognise that a case on similar facts may choose to overrule it and apply the general rule.

13.3 Sane automatism

The 'defence' of sane automatism,[79] as it is commonly referred to, is structured in broadly the same way as the intoxication rules.[80] Where D raises sane automatism, she is making the claim that some external factor affected her body at T1 and caused her to lack voluntariness at T2. For example, 'I drove dangerously at T2 because I was knocked

---

[73] Dingwall, 'Intoxicated Mistakes About the Need for Self-Defence' (2007) 70 MLR 127; Spencer, 'Drunken Defence' (2006) 65 CLJ 267.
[74] Criminal Justice and Immigration Act 2008, s76(5).
[75] Law Commission, *Intoxication and Criminal Liability* (No 314, 2009) para 3.53.
[76] Criminal Damage Act 1971, s5(2).
[77] Williams, 'Two Nocturnal Blunders' (1990) 140 NLJ 1564.
[78] Law Commission, *Intoxication and Criminal Liability* (No 314, 2009) paras 3.81–3.83.
[79] Law Commission, *Insanity and Automatism* (Discussion Paper, 2013).
[80] Child and Reed, 'Automatism is Never a Defence' (2014) 65 NILQ 167.

unconscious at T1'; 'I omitted to feed my child because I was tied up'; I struck out at the paramedic causing injury at T2 because I was suffering the effects of having taken insulin and not having eaten at T1'. As we discussed at **3.3**, all criminal offences require voluntary conduct (actions or omission). Thus, D's claim of involuntariness at T2 is a claim that she did not commit an offence. However, even where D successfully denies offending in this way, it is possible for D to be held liable on the basis of her prior fault in becoming an automaton. We are again dealing with a two-part set of rules: providing a shorthand for D's claim to lack voluntariness, and providing a possible tool of inculpation for the prosecution.

Despite similarities with the intoxication rules, there are three major differences. First, the automatism rules will not apply where D's automatic state is caused by a dangerous drug (as defined within the intoxication rules). Here, only the intoxication rules will apply.[81] Secondly, automatism will *only* apply where D loses voluntary control of her conduct. If something external causes D to lack mens rea, but not to lack voluntariness, then the automatism rules will not apply. Thus, automatism arises in many fewer cases than the intoxication rules, which apply whenever D's intoxication causes *any* lack of mens rea. Thirdly, as automatism lacks the commonly understood link to violence associated with intoxication, the potential of prior fault and inculpation is considerably more limited.

13.3.1 Automatism as a denial of offending

Automatism is shorthand for the claim that D *totally* lacked voluntary control of her conduct at the time of her potential offence. Therefore, where D acts voluntarily, even if her conduct has been influenced by external factors, automatism will not be found.[82] Just as 'an intoxicated mens rea is still mens rea', so irrational or erratic voluntariness is still voluntariness.[83]

> *Extra detail...*
> Although there is a general burden on the prosecution to prove that D completed the elements of the offence charged, there is a legal presumption that a person's movements are voluntary. This creates an evidential burden for D, if she wants to raise automatism, to provide some evidence of involuntariness. After she satisfies this evidential burden, it is then for the prosecution to prove to the criminal standard that her acts were voluntary.[84]

The clearest cases of sane automatism will involve D being rendered fully unconscious at T1, as with our dangerous driving example earlier. Where D is fully unconscious, it is clear that she lacks any voluntary control of her body, and so any harm her body causes cannot be the product of voluntary movement.

However, sane automatism is not limited to states of unconsciousness. Indeed, there are several clear examples of conscious automatic behaviour. For example, where X overpowers D and physically manipulates her body to complete certain movements (eg to plunge a knife into V); where D's body spasms uncontrollably (eg causing her to strike V); where D reacts to a sudden noise (eg causing her to drop another's property);

---

[81] Mackay, 'Intoxication as a Factor in Automatism' [1982] Crim LR 146.
[82] *AG's Reference (No 4 of 2000)* [2001] Crim LR 578: accidental, but not automatic, conduct.
[83] *Coley* [2013] EWCA Crim 223, [22].
[84] Jones, 'Insanity, Automatism and the Burden of Proof on the Accused' (1995) 111 LQR 475.

where D thrashes her arms in response to an attack by a swarm of bees (eg causing her to drive dangerously);[85] and so on. In each of these cases, even though D is conscious she is not in control of her actions. As Lord Denning describes in *Bratty*:

> No act is punishable if it is done involuntarily: and an involuntary act in this context—some people nowadays prefer to speak of it as 'automatism'—means an act which is done by the muscles without any control by the mind, such as a spasm, a reflex action or a convulsion. [86]

Having accepted that conscious behaviour can satisfy automatism, however, the challenge is then to identify the line between automatism on the one hand, and non-automatic conduct brought about by external factors on the other hand.

Automatism, particularly where it arises in driving offences, has been defined very narrowly. This is illustrated in *Broome v Perkins*.

Broome v Perkins [1987] Crim LR 271

D (a diabetic) failed to take sufficient food after an injection of insulin, and slipped into a hypoglycaemic episode.[87] Whilst in this trance-like state, he drove erratically and collided with another car. D was charged with driving without due care and attention.[88]

- Magistrates' court: not guilty of driving offence due to automatism.
- Divisional Court: appeal (by way of case stated) allowed. The fact that D was able to coordinate his movements to drive, even though severely impeded, meant that he could not have been in a fully automatic state.

This extremely narrow definition of automatism was later confirmed in *AG's Reference (No 2 of 1992)*,[89] where a lorry driver was charged with causing death by reckless driving having suffered a condition known as 'driving without awareness' as a result of long hours on the road. Following D's acquittal on grounds of automatism, the Court of Appeal held that automatism should not have been left to the jury, and that only a 'total destruction of voluntary control' would suffice.

It could be that these decisions reflect policy considerations unique to driving offences (ie a reaction to the commonality of people driving when tired or otherwise impaired).[90] This view may be supported, to some extent, by non-driving cases such as *Charlson*,[91] where a broader view of automatism seems to have been employed: D's

---

85 Example from *Hill and Baxter* [1958] 1 QB 277, 286.

86 [1963] AC 386, 409.

87 Diabetes can lead to involuntariness in two main ways: (a) *hypo*glycaemia—this results from taking insulin (an external cause) and then failing to eat sufficiently; (b) *hyper*glycaemia—this results from failing to take insulin (and so the diabetes acts as an internal cause). As we discuss later, the distinction between these two is vital. This is because although hypoglycaemia causing involuntariness will be treated as a standard form of sane automatism (now under discussion), hyperglycaemia causing involuntariness (because of its internal cause) will be dealt with under the insanity rules.

88 Road Traffic Act 1988, s3.

89 [1994] Crim LR 692.

90 Simester, Spencer, Sullivan, and Virgo, *Criminal Law: Theory and Doctrine* (5th edn, 2013) 112.

91 [1955] 1 All ER 859.

cerebral tumour caused him to act as an 'automaton without any *real knowledge* of what he was doing.'[92] However, a number of recent cases have reasserted the narrow view of automatism for both driving[93] and non-driving cases.[94] In *Coley*,[95] a non-driving case in which doctors agreed that D would not have been conscious of his movements, the Court of Appeal has asserted a particularly restrictive approach.

> [D] was plainly not unconscious, in the sense of comatose. But automatism does not require that, and if it did it would be even more exceptional than it undoubtedly is. On the other hand, his mind may well, if the doctors were right, have been affected by delusions or hallucinations and in that sense his detachment from reality might be described by some as an absence of conscious action. Such condition, however, clearly falls short of involuntary, as distinct from irrational, action.... [T] he defendant would, despite their hypothesis of psychotic episode, have been capable of complex organised behaviour. It is plain that a person acting under a delusion may act in such a way, and clearly this defendant did. ... The doctor said 'He is conscious in a way but it is conscious in the belief that he is a character [in a computer game]. He does not have an awareness of what he is doing.' That is a description of irrational behaviour, with a deluded or disordered mind, but it is not a description of wholly involuntary action.

If automatism is interpreted in line with this statement, it will rarely (if ever) apply outside the context of unconsciousness or physical manipulation. This makes the law easier to apply (ie it creates a clear line between sane automatism and voluntariness), but raises serious questions of fairness. When discussing the voluntariness requirement at **3.3**, we explain its importance to a conscious link between D and the harmful or wrongful events attributed to her; an essential ingredient in the law's respect for individual autonomy. In the circumstances discussed in *Coley*, where D's brain is guiding movement, but that guide is not conscious or rational, it is questionable whether there is a sufficient nexus through which to blame D in criminal law for any harm caused. The current narrow view of sane automatism has therefore attracted considerable academic criticism.[96]

In view of this narrow approach, it will be little surprise that claims of *moral* involuntariness have been consistently rejected as a basis for automatism. We may feel some moral sympathy for D who commits an offence because of an 'irresistible impulse', 'hysterical amnesia', 'hysterical fugue', or where she is unaware of a legal restriction. But D is not treated as acting in an automatic manner in a legal sense.[97] Where D steals alcohol because of an irresistible craving for drink, she still commits theft;[98] where D is provoked to attack V, this is still an assault. These circumstances will be considered as relevant mitigation at sentencing, but they do not affect the liability stage.[99]

---

[92] Emphasis added.

[93] *C* [2007] EWCA Crim 1862.

[94] Law Commission, *Insanity and Automatism* (Discussion Paper, 2013) paras 5.24–5.31.

[95] [2013] EWCA Crim 223, [23].

[96] Horder, 'Pleading Involuntary Lack of Capacity' (1993) 52 CLJ 298; Sullivan, 'Making Excuses' in Simester and Smith (eds), *Harm and Culpability* (1996) 131.

[97] *Isitt* [1978] Crim LR 159.

[98] *Dodd* (1974) 7 SASR 151; Tolmie, 'Alcoholism and Criminal Liability' (2001) 64 MLR 688.

[99] The only exceptions to this are extreme cases which engage defences such as duress (discussed in **Chapter 14**) or loss of control as a partial defence to murder (discussed in **Chapter 6**).

To summarise, where D's conduct is fully involuntary at T2 due to an external factor at T1, as long as the intoxication rules do not apply and there is an absence of other prior fault, she will not be guilty of an offence at T2. This is illustrated in **Figure 13.8**.

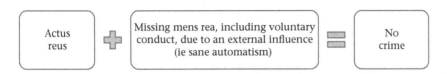

Figure 13.8 Automatism as a denial of offending

Where D's conduct is affected by external stimuli but her movements remain voluntary, there is no automatism. As discussed previously, the narrow interpretation of automatism makes this scenario increasingly likely. This is illustrated in **Figure 13.9**.

Figure 13.9 External impact not causing automatism

13.3.2 Prior fault automatism as a method of inculpation

Where D's conduct is involuntary at T2 due to an external factor at T1 (ie where she is in a state of automatism), we need to examine whether D's conduct at T1 was sufficiently blameworthy to serve as a substitute for the voluntary fault required for the offence at T2 which D lacks.

- Where D is a sane automaton (ie suffers a total loss of control at the time of T2 owing to some external factor at T1) and the cause of the automatism is some involuntary external factor (a swarm of bees, someone knocking D unconscious by a blow to the head, etc), there is no liability for any offence whether specific intent or basic intent.
- Where D is charged with a specific intent offence, if she is an automaton at the time of that offence there is no liability for it, even if she has become automaton by her prior fault. The definition of specific intent is dealt with earlier.
- Where D is charged with a basic intent offence and is an automaton at the time of the offence, we must apply the 'prior fault doctrine' mirroring the approach we have described in relation to intoxication. Where D has become an automaton due to her

own prior fault, the automatism rules (as with the intoxication rules) are capable of substituting for the missing offence elements and creating liability. In this way, the automatism rules do not work as a defence, but as a method of inculpation.[100]

Table 13.2 sets out the elements of the automatism rules.

Table 13.2 Automatism rules

A) The automatism must have resulted from D's prior fault (ie D must have foreseen at T1 the risk of becoming involuntary at T2);
B) The automatism must have caused the lack of offence elements for a basic intent offence

We discuss each element further in the following sections.

> **Don't be confused…**
>
> As with the intoxication rules, the inculpatory work of the automatism rules is most commonly described by courts and commentators as a denial of a defence (see **13.1.1**). For example, in *Coley*,[101] Hughes LJ states that 'the defence of automatism is not available to a defendant who has induced an acute state of involuntary behaviour by his own fault.' We avoid this terminology because it is misleading: saying that D cannot raise the issue of automatism does not make her conduct voluntary or mean that she had mens rea. Rather, as we describe the same phenomenon, the automatism rules are replacing a lack of voluntariness and other mens rea with (what the law considers) equivalent prior fault. The rules are not denying a defence, they are constructing a crime.[102]

13.3.2.1 Prior fault at T1

For the intoxication rules, the issue of prior fault at T1 (ie when becoming intoxicated) was relatively straightforward to establish because of the commonly understood link between intoxication and certain crimes. Thus, where D voluntarily becomes intoxicated with a dangerous drug (one commonly known to create states of unpredictability), we may attribute prior fault. For automatism, in contrast, there is no equivalent common understanding (and no link in fact) between a lack of voluntariness and the causing of criminal harms.[103] Therefore, more must be required at T1 to establish sufficient prior fault that might later substitute for missing offence elements.[104]

The law in this area, however, is unfortunately vague and inconsistent. On the one hand, cases such as *Bailey*[105] suggest that D will only have sufficient prior fault where she has *subjectively* foreseen at T1 the potential for involuntariness at T2. This

---

[100] Child and Reed, 'Automatism is Never a Defence' (2014) 65 NILQ 167.

[101] [2013] EWCA Crim 244, [24].

[102] Child and Reed, 'Automatism is Never a Defence' (2014) 65 NILQ 167.

[103] *Bailey* [1983] 2 All ER 503, 764–765. For academic discussion of this, see Horder, 'Sobering Up? The Law Commission on Criminal Intoxication' (1995) 58 MLR 534, 544–555.

[104] Law Commission, *Insanity and Automatism* (Discussion Paper, 2013) Ch6.

[105] [1983] 2 All ER 503.

would be the case, for example, where D decides to drive foreseeing the chance of an (insulin-induced) hypoglycaemic episode, and foreseeing the chance that this might lead to unconsciousness whilst at the wheel. This approach is endorsed by the Law Commission,[106] and seems to be the most appropriate if D's fault is going to be used to construct liability at T2.[107] On the other hand, cases such as *Quick*[108] state that D will have sufficient fault if she *objectively* should have foreseen such risks. Thus, where D is negligent in the management of her diabetes before driving (eg fails to eat sufficiently after a dose of insulin), then this negligence will constitute sufficient prior fault even where she does not subjectively foresee the risk of hypoglycaemia herself. The Australian case of *Ryan*[109] provides a further example of the objective approach. In this case, D pointed a loaded shotgun at V (whom he had robbed) with one hand, whilst attempting to tie him up with the other. V moved, startled D, and D (according to his account) involuntarily pulled the trigger as a reflex. On Windeyer J's view, D remained liable because of the obvious danger created by his actions at T1, even if D did not subjectivly foresee the risk of the involuntary reflex which followed.

> *Assessment matters...*
> Where there is inconsistent case law of this kind, you need to take particular care when applying it to problem facts. Do not just choose certain cases and ignore others. Rather, where D subjectively foresees a risk of involuntariness in dangerous circumstances then you can be sure that this is sufficient prior fault. Where D does not foresee the risk, but was potentially negligent in not doing so, you should highlight cases such as *Quick* and *Ryan* that suggest that this too might be sufficient, but also (ideally) note the academic criticism.

13.3.2.2 Causing a lack of offence elements

Having established some prior fault by D at T1 (when losing voluntary control), our next question is to consider whether the law is prepared to treat that prior fault as sufficient to replace or substitute for the missing element of the offence at T2 (when D commits the potential offence). Clearly, D's prior fault at T1 must be capable of replacing a lack of voluntary conduct at T2: as all cases of automatism include a lack of voluntariness, the ability to substitute for this missing element is essential for automatism to perform any inculpatory role at all. This has been consistently confirmed in all the case law involving prior fault and automatism.[110]

But what about other mens rea elements beyond voluntary conduct? Where D is effectively (or in fact) unconscious, she is unlikely to possess any mens rea as to any aspect of the harm she causes at T2. If the automatism rules are *only* able to substitute prior fault at T1 for a lack of voluntary conduct at T2, then they could only produce liability in the context of strict/absolute liability offences (ie offences that require no mens rea beyond

---

[106] Law Commission, *Insanity and Automatism* (Discussion Paper, 2013) paras 6.12–6.28.

[107] Rumbold and Wasik, 'Diabetic Drivers, Hypoglycaemic Unawareness and Automatism' [2011] Crim LR 863.

[108] [1973] QB 910.

[109] (1967) 40 ALJR 488; Elliott, 'Responsibility for Involuntary Acts: *Ryan v The Queen*' (1968) 41 ALJ 497.

[110] Although, as we noted at **13.3.2** ('Don't be confused...'), the phenomenon will generally be described as the denial of a defence.

voluntariness). But we know from the case law that prior fault is used as a substitute for liability for offences beyond this, most commonly for driving offences that often require mens rea as to the dangerous circumstances of D's driving.

Perhaps the most obvious question, in view of the intoxication rules, is whether prior fault automatism also makes a distinction between basic and specific intent offences (ie that D's prior fault can replace a lack of mens rea for a basic intent offence but not for a specific intent offence).[111] The early case law on prior fault and automatism did not recognise a basic/specific intent distinction; implying a very broad potential for the substitution of missing mens rea elements.[112] However, this position was later clarified (to some extent) in *Bailey*:[113] a case involving the specific intent offence of wounding or causing GBH with intent.[114] The court highlighted that *Quick* should not be interpreted to allow prior fault automatism to substitute for missing mens rea elements in crimes of specific intent. Unfortunately, following this useful clarification, the court then went further to cast doubt on its ability to substitute for similar elements in crimes of basic intent as well.

In our judgment, self-induced automatism, other than that due to intoxication from alcohol or drugs, may provide a defence to crimes of basic intent. The question in each case will be whether the prosecution have proved the necessary element of recklessness. In cases of assault, if the accused knows that his actions or inaction are likely to make him aggressive, unpredictable or uncontrolled with the result that he may cause some injury to others and he persists in the action or takes no remedial action when he knows it is required, it will be open to the jury to find that he was reckless.[115]

In view of this confused position, it is likely (and hoped) that the courts will take a lead from the recent Law Commission Discussion Paper on automatism and insanity.[116] For the Commission, despite reservations as to the specific/basic intent distinction, there is a useful recognition that prior fault for automatism should be consistent with prior fault for intoxication. Thus, contrary to *Bailey*, D's conduct in voluntarily rendering herself an automaton should be capable of serving as a sufficient substitute fault for a lack of mens rea of basic intent offences, even where D merely foresees (at T1) a potential loss of voluntariness as opposed to future results or circumstances. D's conduct in voluntarily rendering herself automaton should *not* be capable of serving as a sufficient substitute fault for a lack of mens rea of specific intent offences.[117] This is illustrated in **Figure 13.10**.

---

[111] See discussion at **13.2.1** in the context of intoxication.
[112] *Quick* [1972] QB 910: 'A self-induced incapacity will not excuse...nor will one which could have been reasonably foreseen as a result of either doing, or omitting to do something, as, for example, taking alcohol against medical advice after using certain prescribed drugs, or failing to have regular meals while taking insulin' at 922. Criticised in Mackay, 'Intoxication as a Factor in Automatism' [1982] Crim LR 146.
[113] [1983] 2 All ER 503.
[114] Offences Against the Person Act 1861, s18.
[115] *Bailey* [1983] 1 WLR 760, 765 (Griffiths LJ).
[116] Law Commission, *Insanity and Automatism* (Discussion Paper, 2013).
[117] This is the necessary implication from the flowchart at p 95, and para 6.77.

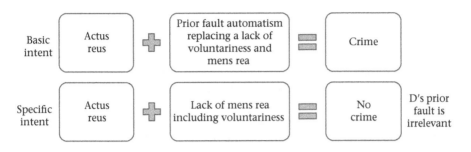

Figure 13.10 Prior fault automatism

13.3.3 Automatism and defences

Subject to the rules of prior fault we have just discussed, where D causes harm while in a state of sane automatism, she will not be liable for a criminal offence, and will not therefore require a defence. However, where she does so in circumstances of prior fault, and the offence is one of basic intent, she will be liable even though she was an automaton unless there is some other defence available to her. In such cases, we do not focus on D at T2: D's involuntariness is incompatible with the elements of criminal defences (discussed in **Chapter 14**). Instead, our focus is on D at T1, asking whether she became involuntary in circumstances that give rise to a defence (eg where D was threatened, was under duress, to drive even though she foresaw the chance of losing consciousness). In such circumstances, D's defence will undermine any finding of prior fault, and thereby undermine any construction of liability at T2.

13.4 Insanity as a denial of mens rea

The final category of denial of offence discussed in this chapter relates to the rules of insanity.[118] This will arise where (unlike intoxication and automatism) D claims not to have fulfilled all the elements of the offence because of some malfunctioning of her body—an *internal* factor (eg where D's insane delusions prevent her from appreciating that the thing she is stabbing is a person). This analysis of the insanity rules should be distinguished from two other related discussions elsewhere in this text.

- **Unfitness to plead:** This arises where D is mentally and/or physically unfit to stand trial, and was discussed at **1.5.3**. In contrast, the rules of insanity discussed in this chapter relate to insanity at the time of the potential offence in circumstances where D is now able to stand trial.

- **Insanity as a defence:** This arises where D *has* completed the actus reus and mens rea of an offence, and raises insanity as a way to avoid liability. This is discussed in **Chapter 14**. In contrast, the rules of insanity discussed in this chapter relate to a claim that D's insanity meant that she did not complete an offence.

---

[118] Law Commission, *Insanity and Automatism* (Discussion Paper, 2013).

Don't be confused...
Insanity as a defence, and insanity as a denial of offending, are often discussed together. This is because the same rules will apply to the application of insanity in either context. We separate them here (between **Chapters 13** and **14**), not to suggest that different rules apply, but to reflect the different role played by the insanity rules in the two different contexts.

As with intoxication and automatism, where D raises insanity to deny the mens rea it is not useful (although entirely commonplace) to refer to this as a defence. In this context, D raises insanity to explain her lack of mens rea (potentially, but not necessarily, including a lack of voluntariness), attempting to avoid liability for any offence.[119]

Extra detail...
We have seen earlier that one of the reasons the language of defences is employed has been because of the use of reverse burdens, and insanity is no different. Just as the law presumes that D is sober and in control of her conduct, so the law also presumes that D is sane. Indeed, the presumption of sanity is much more severe. Presumptions of sobriety and voluntariness only create evidential burdens on D, whereas the presumption of sanity creates a legal burden such that D must (on the balance of probabilities) prove that she was insane at the time of the offence.[120] This is extremely controversial, and the Law Commission has proposed a reverse evidential burden for insanity instead.[121] Where D is claiming not to have committed the offence, it is one thing to require evidence to rebut a presumption of common behaviour, but quite another to ask D to prove her innocence![122] But this is what the current law requires.

Where insanity arises as a denial of mens rea, and D succeeds in proving that to the civil standard, the verdict will be one of 'not guilty by reason of insanity'. Where the insanity rules are satisfied, even where this involves a denial of offence elements, and even where there is no prior fault at issue, D will be denied an unqualified acquittal. Rather, D will be found 'not guilty by reason of insanity': a technical acquittal which still allows the court to impose a range of compulsory orders (eg hospitalisation, supervision).[123] The inculpatory status of the special verdict is acknowledged by the fact that D (uniquely) can appeal if found not guilty on this basis.[124]

The special verdict, and the disposal options which follow, mark the insanity rules out from other denials of offending which may result in an unqualified acquittal. This is not to say that D who lacks mens rea due to insanity is blameworthy; she has not committed the offence, and is rightly acquitted. However, the rationale of the insanity rules is that where D lacks mens rea as a result of insanity, as opposed to an external

---

[119] It was held in *DPP v Harper* [1998] RTR 200 that the insanity rules do not apply to strict liability offences, the court reasoning that insanity amounted to a denial of mens rea and strict liability offences do not require mens rea. However, commentators agree that this decision must be wrong. First, insanity can also involve a denial of voluntary movement, which is required for strict liability offences and, secondly, because (as we discuss in **Chapter 14**) insanity can act as a defence as well as a simple denial of offending.

[120] *M'Naghten* (1843) 10 Cl & Fin 200, 210, confirmed in *Bratty* [1963] AC 386.

[121] Law Commission, *Insanity and Automatism* (Discussion Paper, 2013) para 4.163.

[122] Jones, 'Insanity, Automatism, and the Burden of Proof on the Accused' (1995) 111 LQR 475.

[123] See **13.4.1**.

[124] Criminal Appeals Act 1968, s12.

influence, then D's condition is more likely to reoccur and so the special verdict is required to ensure that the public are protected.[125] How effectively the current insanity rules achieve this rationale can be criticised, and is discussed later. But at this point it is important to highlight the unique status of the insanity rules as far as defendants are concerned. Faced with the uncertain outcome of the special verdict, as well as the stigma of the insanity label, defendants will generally attempt to deny liability without engaging the insanity rules. Indeed, where they are engaged, many will prefer to plead guilty.

Judge and jury...
Due to its inculpatory effects, defendants will rarely try to raise insanity directly. Rather, it is the judge's role to identify whether D's denial of offence elements amounts to a denial based on insanity.[126] Where this is the case, the judge will then inform D, who will choose whether to proceed with a claim of insanity or to change her plea to guilty.

The leading case on insanity is *Sullivan*.

Sullivan [1984] 1 AC 156

Whilst visiting an 80-year-old friend (V), D had an epileptic seizure during which he kicked V in the head and caused GBH. D was charged with GBH offences.[127]

• Crown Court: guilty of ABH offence.[128] D attempted to rely on automatism, but the court ruled that his condition amounted to insanity. On this basis, to avoid the insanity rules, D pleaded guilty to ABH.
• Court of Appeal: conviction upheld on appeal.
• House of Lords: appeal dismissed.

Sullivan is unfortunately a typical application of a set of rules which, as we will see, are not fit for purpose. A seemingly innocent man would rather plead guilty than be treated under a set of rules designed to acknowledge and protect those not deserving of blame. We offer a critique of these rules in the following sections.

13.4.1 The special verdict of 'not guilty by reason of insanity'

Where D satisfies the insanity rules (discussed later) she will be acquitted, but the verdict will be 'not guilty by reason of insanity'.[129] The judge will then choose from a range of disposal orders appropriate to D's case.

Terminology...
Although disposal orders can be compulsory, this is not a matter of sentencing. D has been acquitted, and so the terminology of 'disposal' is important.

---

125 *Sullivan* [1984] AC 156, 172.
126 *Roach* [2001] EWCA Crim 2698.
127 Offences Against the Person Act 1861, s18 and s20. See **7.5** and **7.6**.
128 Offences Against the Person Act 1861, s47. See **7.4**.
129 Trial of Lunatics Act 1883, s2.

Before 1991, those found not guilty by reason of insanity (as well as those unfit to plead) had to be ordered to be detained indefinitely in a hospital. Fortunately, with the exception of cases involving murder,[130] this is no longer the case. Disposal is now governed by section 5 of the Criminal Procedure (Insanity and Unfitness to Plead) Act 1991.[131] Under this Act, the judge is provided with three disposal options:

(a) a hospital order (with or without a restriction order);

(b) a supervision order; and

(c) an order for an absolute discharge.

Although the insanity plea remains underused in the courts, there is evidence that the rationalisation of disposal orders has begun to correct this.[132]

A second reason for underuse, which has not been addressed in legislation, is the enduring label 'insanity'. Insanity can be a stigmatising term for those with severe mental conditions, but as will be clear from *Sullivan* (and expanded later) the insanity rules apply well beyond those within this group. When so much progress has been made regarding public attitudes to mental illness more generally, it is staggering that the criminal law retains a label of this kind. The Law Commission has proposed that the special verdict should be amended, holding D 'not criminally responsible by reason of a recognised medical condition.'[133] The sooner the law is amended in these terms, the better.

13.4.2 Elements of legal insanity

The rationale of the insanity rules, as a denial of mens rea, is essentially forward-looking: D has not committed an offence, and this must be acknowledged with an acquittal, but D has revealed herself as someone who could pose a danger to the public in the future and so may warrant compulsory treatment and/or supervision. Despite some unease about the compulsory treatment of those who have not committed an offence, most commentators accept the public need for a set of rules of this kind.[134] For example, in *Bratty*[135] D removed a girl's stockings and strangled her with them, in circumstances where (according to medical evidence) his psychomotor epilepsy could have prevented him understanding his actions. Were this to have been the case, D might have been acquitted, but it is surely right that the courts are empowered to put compulsory measures in place to protect others in the future.

The devil, of course, is in the detail; whilst compulsory treatment may be acceptable under certain conditions, those conditions involve the complex weighing of legal and medical priorities, and will inevitably shift alongside medical advancement. However, the

---

130 In this case, a fixed hospital order is mandated: Criminal Procedure Act 1991, s5(3).

131 As amended by the Domestic Violence, Crime and Victims Act 2004.

132 Mackay and Kearns, 'The Continued Under Use of Unfitness to Plead and the Insanity Defence' [1994] Crim LR 546; Mackay, Mitchell, and Howe, 'Yet More Facts About the Insanity Defence' [2006] Crim LR 399.

133 Law Commission, *Insanity and Automatism* (Discussion Paper, 2013) para 10.15.

134 For a contrary view, see Slobogin, 'An End to Insanity: Recasting the Role of Mental Illness in Criminal Cases' (2000) 86 Vir LR 1199.

135 [1963] AC 386.

criminal law has not created a dynamic set of rules capable of balancing these priorities and shifting in line with medical progress. Rather, the insanity rules remain products of the common law, and remain principally based on a set of Law Lord opinions from 1843.

The current law of insanity was set out in relation to *M'Naghten*. This case involved insanity as a defence (ie D had committed an offence), but the same rules apply where D uses insanity to deny offending.

> *M'Naghten* (1843) 10 Cl & Fin 200
> D attempted to murder Sir Robert Peel, who was then Home Secretary, and killed Edward Drummond (Peel's secretary) by mistake. D was charged with murder.
>
> • Crown Court: not guilty of murder by reason of insanity. D was suffering from morbid delusions about the Conservative Party.

M'Naghten's acquittal provoked controversy and was debated in the legislative chamber of the House of Lords, where the Law Lords were asked questions on the insanity rules.[136] It was the answers given to those questions, and not the case itself, which provide the basis for the modern law on insanity. The '*M'Naghten* Rules', as they have come to be known, were given binding authority by their endorsement in *Sullivan*.[137]

The *M'Naghten* Rules, crucially, are not based on a medical definition of insanity. Rather, they provide a set of legal rules to determine if D will be caught within a legal definition of insanity, and directed towards the special verdict. These rules are set out in **Table 13.3**.

Table 13.3 The *M'Naghten* Rules

A) D must suffer from a disease of the mind;
B) This must have caused a defect of reason; and
C) This must have caused a lack of responsibility, *either* because D did not know the nature or quality of her act, *or* she did not know it was wrong

We explore each in turn.

13.4.2.1 Disease of the mind

The first requirement, that D must have been suffering from a disease of the mind, sounds very much like a medical question. However, although medical experts will be required to provide evidence,[138] the definition they are asked to apply ('a disease of the mind') is a legal one. This is illustrated in *Kemp*.

---

[136] (1843) 4 St Tr NS 847.
[137] [1984] 1 AC 156.
[138] Criminal Procedure (Insanity and Unfitness to Plead) Act 1991, s1. This section prevents a jury returning a verdict of not guilty by reason of insanity except on the evidence of two or more registered medical practitioners, of whom at least one must be approved as having special expertise in the field of mental disorder.

Kemp [1957] 1 QB 399

D made a motiveless and irrational attack upon his wife with a hammer, causing GBH. D was suffering from arteriosclerosis, a condition which caused a congestion of blood in his brain and caused him to lapse into unconsciousness at the time of the attack. D was charged with a GBH offence.

• Court of Assizes: not guilty by reason of insanity. The fact that D's condition was physical rather than mental does not prevent the insanity rules applying.

Later confirmed in *Sullivan, Kemp* provides important clarification that D may be suffering from a disease of the mind (in legal terms) even where there is no degeneration of brain cells. As Devlin J stated:

In my judgment the condition of the brain is irrelevant and so is the question of whether the condition of the mind is curable or incurable, transitory or permanent. There is no warranty for introducing those considerations into the definition in the M'Naghten Rules. Temporary insanity is sufficient to satisfy them. It does not matter whether it is incurable and permanent or not.[139]

Moving away from a medical understanding of mental illness, the legal definition of 'disease of the mind' is rather more concerned with marking the distinction between insanity (leading to the special verdict) and sane automatism or simple lack of mens rea (leading to an acquittal in the absence of prior fault). In doing so, the law focuses on a sole criterion: does D's involuntariness (and/or lack of other mens rea) stem from an internal bodily condition or from an external factor. Where D's condition is internally caused, whatever its medical classification, it will be deemed a disease of the mind for the purposes of the insanity rules.

Although most insanity cases will involve medically recognised mental illnesses (eg schizophrenia being the most common basis[140]), the central role of the internal/external test has led to a number of unfortunate (and largely indefensible) classifications. Perhaps the most striking of these has arisen in relation to diabetes, where a diabetic coma (and associated involuntariness) can be brought on *internally* by a lack of treatment with insulin (hyperglycaemia), or *externally* by treatment with insulin followed by an insufficient intake of food (hypoglycaemia). The origins of these conditions and their impact upon D are almost identical, but they sit either side of the internal/external divide.[141] This was discussed in *Quick*.

Quick [1973] QB 910

D, a nurse in a mental hospital, attacked a paraplegic patient causing ABH. D called evidence that he was diabetic and, at the time of the attack, was suffering from hypoglycaemia caused by a lack of food after insulin. D was told that this would amount to a claim of insanity, and so he changed his plea to guilty.

• Crown Court: guilty of assault occasioning ABH.[142]

---

[139] At 407.
[140] Mackay, Mitchell, and Howe, 'Yet More Facts About the Insanity Defence' [2006] Crim LR 399.
[141] Rumbold, 'Diabetes and Criminal Responsibility' (2010) 174 CLJW 21.
[142] Offences Against the Person Act 1861, s47.

• Court of Appeal: appeal allowed. D's hypoglycaemia was externally caused, and so he should have been allowed to raise automatism rather than insanity.

Quick can be contrasted with *Hennessy*,[143] where D who was charged with taking a conveyance and driving while disqualified also raised automatism on the basis of a diabetic coma. However, in this case D's coma was induced by a lack of insulin. The ruling, therefore, was that automatism was unavailable because D's condition was internally caused: D could rely on the insanity rules, or (as he did) change his plea to guilty.

Beyond diabetes, a number of other conditions have also been (morally inappropriately) caught within the insanity rules. This means the individuals treated in criminal law as insane include epileptics,[144] pre-menstrual syndrome suffers,[145] sleepwalkers,[146] and so on. These examples are problematic for the simple reason that the term 'insanity' is so obviously inappropriate both medically as well as to the ordinary citizen. But they can also be problematic for a test which seeks a neat (or at least consistent) divide between internal and external causes. In the context of sleepwalking, for example, which has attracted particular attention,[147] it is not always obvious that the cause is purely internal. For example, D's sleepwalking may arise from the external influence of hypnosis or, more trivially, it may be triggered from disturbed sleep or from eating certain foods before sleeping.[148]

Another example of uncertain classification arises in so-called psychological blow cases, where D tries to explain an internal loss of faculties on the basis of an external psychologically traumatic event, hoping through this to ground a claim of sane automatism rather than insanity. One of the first cases where this line of argument was attempted was the Canadian case of *Rabey*.[149] D, a student who became infatuated with a girl (V), discovered that she was not interested in him, and reacted by hitting her on the head with a rock that he had taken from the geology laboratory. D was initially acquitted on the basis of automatism, the court accepting that the psychological blow of rejection had caused him to experience a dissociative state. However, (not surprisingly) the prosecution's appeal was later accepted, with the Canadian Supreme Court clarifying that 'the common stresses and disappointments of life which are the common lot of all mankind do not constitute an external cause'.[150] The dissociative state it seems, if accepted, should have constituted evidence of insanity. A more difficult case is *T*.

---

[143] (1989) 89 Cr App R 10.
[144] *Sullivan* [1984] AC 156; Mackay and Reuber, 'Epilepsy and the Defence of Insanity—Time for a Change' [2007] Crim LR 782.
[145] *Smith* [1982] Crim LR 531; Edwards, 'Mad, Bad or Pre-Menstrual' (1988) 138 NLJ 456.
[146] *Burgess* [1991] 2 All ER 769; Mackay, 'The Sleepwalker is Not Insane' (1992) 55 MLR 714.
[147] Wilson et al, 'Violence, Sleepwalking and the Criminal Law' [2005] Crim LR 601 and 614; Mackay and Mitchell, 'Sleepwalking, Automatism and Insanity' [2006] Crim LR 901.
[148] Law Commission, *Insanity and Automatism* (Discussion Paper, 2013) para 1.44.
[149] (1977) 37 CCC 461.
[150] (1980) 54 CCC at 7.

> **⊓** *T* [1990] Crim LR 256
>
> D, a young woman, took part in a violent robbery with two others. She was charged with robbery. It emerged that D had been raped at some point prior to the robbery took place, and the issue of automatism was raised by the defence: that D was acting in a dissociative state (akin to sleepwalking) as a result of the rape.
>
> • Crown Court: guilty of robbery. Crucially, the court found that the case gave rise to the potential for automatism rather than insanity, and thus accepted the psychological blow as an external cause. However, the jury did not accept that D's conduct was fully involuntary.

This case is useful for two main reasons. First, it demonstrates that psychological blows stemming from extreme circumstances can ground a claim of automatism rather than insanity. But, secondly, it also provides a reminder of how narrowly the law has interpreted involuntariness in the context of automatism, leading to liability in a case of this kind.[151]

Finally, not only can the current internal/external test be criticised for leading to inappropriate labelling and uncertainty, but its practical application is also out of line with its rationale of public protection. The fact that D's condition is internally caused does not necessarily make her more likely to be dangerous in the future. This is clear when we compare states of hyper- and hypoglycaemia, where D suffers an internal congestion of blood to the brain that can be treated to prevent reccurrence, where D's external blow to the head creates permanent brain injury, and so on. Indeed, so well acknowledged is this list of criticisms that the law applied at Crown Court level has increasingly failed to apply the rules set down by the appellate courts in favour of a more commonsense approach (ie allowing automatism to run in sleepwalking cases).[152]

> *Assessment matters...*
> Where problem facts involve D causing harm whilst sleepwalking, for example, it is important to follow the established authorities: D's state is internally caused, and thus gives rise to the insanity rules. Acknowledging that the law 'in practice' will often see courts allowing automatism to be run will be an impressive addition to your answer, but should be a secondary point.

13.4.2.2 Causing a defect of reason

Having established that D's denial of offending is based on an internal cause (a disease of the mind), ruling out the potential application of intoxication and/or sane automatism, our next question is whether D was thereby caused to have a defect of reason. This stage is important. If D's defect of mind caused her to behave absent-mindedly, so she had the ability to reason but did not do so, or simply contributed to an attitude where she chose not think about the dangerous nature of her conduct, then the insanity rules will not apply. The leading case here is *Clarke*.

---

[151] Horder, 'Pleading Involuntary Lack of Capacity' (1993) 53 CLJ 298, 313–315.
[152] *Lowe* (2005, unreported) and *Pooley* (2007, unreported); Mackay and Mitchell, 'Sleepwalking, Automatism and Insanity' [2006] Crim LR 901.

> *Clarke* [1972] 1 All ER 219
>
> D took articles from a supermarket without paying for them. Evidence was raised that she did so absent-mindedly, partly as a result of mild depression. D was charged with theft. When told that her denial amounted to a plea of insanity, D changed her plea to guilty.
>
> • Crown Court: guilty of theft.
> • Court of Appeal: appeal allowed. D's condition did not prevent her being able to reason, and so the insanity rules were not satisfied. D was simply denying mens rea.

Where (as in *Clarke*) D is denying mens rea, her defence representatives will want to avoid the insanity rules. This is because insanity would direct D to the uncertain outcome of the special verdict[153] and, if insanity does not apply, D will be acquitted on the simple basis of lack of mens rea. However, where D raises insanity as a defence to a completed crime (discussed in **Chapter 14**), she will be arguing that the internal condition *did* deprive her of an ability to reason as avoiding the insanity rules will lead to liability. Where the insanity rules can operate as both a denial of mens rea and as a defence, context is everything.

13.4.2.3 Causing a lack of responsibility

The final stage of the insanity rules requires D's defect of mind to have caused D to lack responsibility for the harms caused, *either* because she did not understand the nature or quality of what she was doing (a denial of mens rea) *or* because she did not know it was wrong (a defence). Our focus in this chapter is the former, but both will be discussed.

The insanity rules will not apply in situations other than these two alternatives. Thus, for example, where D commits an offence as a result of an 'irresistible impulse', if she understands what she is doing and that it is wrong, she will not satisfy the insanity rules. This was considered in *Kopsch*,[154] where D admitted killing his uncle's wife, but evidence was raised that he was acting under the uncontrollable direction of his subconscious mind. The court held that such evidence provided no basis for a denial of criminal responsibility. An irresistible impulse will only be relevant to the insanity rules where it causes D to lack understanding of her actions, or not to know they are wrong.[155]

D does not know the nature or quality of her act
In modern language, this is a claim that D 'did not know what he was doing'.[156] It is a reference to the physical nature of D's conduct, and will not include lesser states of inadvertence (eg to the moral or legal quality of the conduct).[157] It will clearly apply where D is unconscious, but will also include cases where D is acting under a delusion. Often-repeated examples include where D kills V under the insane delusion that she is breaking a jar,[158] or cuts V's throat believing it is a loaf of bread.[159] However, cases

---

153 At the time of *Clarke* it would have led to hospitalisation.
154 (1925) 19 Cr App R 50.
155 *AG for South Australia v Brown* [1960] AC 432.
156 *Sullivan* [1983] 2 All ER 673, 678.
157 *Codere* (1916) 12 Cr App R 219; Mackay, 'Some Observations on the Second Limb of the M'Naghten Rules' [2009] Crim LR 80.
158 Stephen, *A Digest of the Criminal Law* (8th edn, 1947) 6.
159 Kenny, *Outlines of Criminal Law* (2007) 76.

outside clear examples of this kind will be more testing. For example, in the case of B,[160] a paranoid schizophrenic defendant had sex with his wife (without her consent) believing that he had sexual-healing powers. D was rightly convicted of rape on the facts, but interestingly for present purposes, the Court of Appeal also considered what would have happened if D's condition had led him to believe that V was consenting. The court said that nothing would change. But surely this would be an example of D not knowing the nature or quality of his act, consensual intercourse being categorically different from non-consensual intercourse.

In cases where D does not know the nature or quality of her act, the rejection of the insanity rules will generally lead to D's unqualified acquittal: not understanding the nature or quality of one's act is to deny mens rea. With the public's protection in mind, it will be interesting to see if a case with the amended facts of B postulated by the court would end, as the Court of Appeal suggest, outside these rules.[161]

D does not know that her act is wrong

Even where D *does* understand the nature and quality of her conduct, the insanity rules will still apply if her defect of reason caused her not to know that what she was doing was wrong. This limb of the insanity rules will usually arise where D has committed an offence (both actus reus and mens rea), and raises insanity as a defence. Insanity as a defence (as opposed to a denial of offending) will be discussed further in **Chapter 14**. However, it is useful to provide an overview here.

The basic, but controversial rule is that D will only satisfy this limb of the insanity rules where she is caused to not know the *legal* wrongfulness of her acts. Where her condition causes her to believe her actions are morally right, but she still understands that they are criminal, she will not come within the insanity rules. This was established in *Windle*.

Windle [1952] 2 QB 826

D's wife was mentally ill, and often spoke to him of suicide. D, described as 'weak willed', became obsessed with this idea. Having discussed it repeatedly with his workmates, one suggested that D should give her a dozen aspirin. D gave his wife 100 aspirin tablets, which she took, and died. Reporting her death, D told the police 'I suppose they will hang me for this'. D was charged with murder.

- Crown Court: guilty of murder. The defence of insanity was withdrawn from the jury because, although there was medical evidence of a defect of mind, it was agreed that D knew that what he did was legally wrong.
- Court of Criminal Appeal: conviction upheld on appeal.

The position in *Windle* has been confirmed *Johnson*,[162] and so its narrow interpretation continues to apply.

Criticism of *Windle*, however, has been telling. Bearing in mind that the special verdict still allows for compulsory treatment and therefore restraint, it is difficult to see

---

160 [2013] EWCA Crim 3.
161 Child and Sullivan, 'When Does the Insanity Defence Apply? Some Recent Cases' [2014] Crim LR 787.
162 [2007] EWCA Crim 1978.

why a defendant such as Windle should be denied a defence which would recognise his lack of meaningful choice in offending. Other common law jurisdictions, notably Australia,[163] have refused to follow *Windle* in their application of the insanity rules. Indeed, even within this jurisdiction, it seems that the lower courts will often apply the wrongfulness limb without distinction between D's legal and moral awareness.[164]

Assessment matters...

As with the 'disease of the mind' discussion earlier, the potential inconsistency between appellate court authority and the 'law in practice' in lower courts needs to be handled with care. When applying to problem facts, always begin by applying the binding authority, which in this context is *Windle*. However, where D is unable to appreciate the moral wrongfulness of her acts, but knows that they are against the law, it is good practice to mention that although *Windle* suggests that the insanity rules will not apply, Mackay et al have found that they are often applied in practice.

13.4.3 Insanity and defences

Where insanity is raised as a denial of offending (ie to explain D's lack of mens rea), D will not require a defence. D has not committed an offence. The only exception to this, potentially, could arise were the courts to recognise a rule of prior fault for insanity in line with intoxication and automatism. Thus, if D's prior fault resulted in a state of insanity and criminal conduct, D would be liable for the full offence rather than not guilty by reason of insanity. In such a case, with D now facing liability, defences would come back into play. D could claim a defence to undermine her prior fault at T1 and thus undermine liability (eg duress, where D is threatened to not take her medication).

Where D commits an offence and raises insanity as a defence (discussed in **Chapter 14**), a potential clash with other defences may arise. This is because if D also satisfies the elements of an alternative complete defence, she will naturally prefer that option (leading to an unqualified acquittal) rather than insanity (leading to the special verdict). We explore this potential for multiple applicable defences in **Chapter 14**. However, importantly, where insanity is raised as a denial of offending, this issue does not arise.

13.5 Combining intoxication, automatism, and insanity

The three denials of offending discussed in this chapter are mutually exclusive in their application, and will (in most cases) lead to different outcomes. Identifying which set of rules (if any) should apply is therefore crucial. If D's lack of mens rea stems from an internal factor then *only* the insanity rules should be applied; where it stems from voluntary consumption of a dangerous drug then *only* the intoxication rules should be applied; where D's conduct is involuntary as a result of an external factor (other than a dangerous drug) then *only* the automatism rules should be applied.

---

[163] *Stapleton* (1952) 86 CLR 358.

[164] Mackay and Kearns, 'More Fact(s) About the Insanity Defence' [1999] Crim LR 714, 722; Mackay, Mitchell, and Howe, 'Yet More Facts About the Insanity Defence' [2006] Crim LR 399.

Certain cases, however, will test these neat divisions. Causes can be consecutive: for example, D's voluntary intoxication may cause her to fall and hit her head, causing her to commit a criminal act whilst in a state of automatism;[165] repeat intoxication can lead to addiction and a disease of the mind;[166] and so on. Causes can also be concurrent: for example, where an external blow causes automatism by aggravating an internal condition;[167] where D is suffering from a disease of the mind and is intoxicated;[168] and so on. Cases of this kind expose the problems of relying on the internal/external distinction. Courts have tended to take a pragmatic approach, looking for the dominant cause.

13.6 Reform

The rules on insanity, automatism, and intoxication have attracted sustained academic criticism, and have each been discussed recently by the Law Commission in terms of potential reform.[169] In this section we provide a brief overview of those reform proposals.

Before dividing our analysis between the three sets of rules, however, it is useful to highlight an underlying debate that is common to them. The major function of the rules discussed in this chapter are inculpatory in nature.[170] Where D has not completed all of the elements of an offence, our starting point must be to assume that there will be an unqualified acquittal: D's behaviour is not proscribed by the criminal law (or at least not by the offence charged). The rules governing prior fault automatism, the potential for what we might call 'prior fault insanity', and the intoxication rules, and to a more limited extend the rules covering insanity in general,[171] each operate to construct liability (or the grounds for compulsory treatment) that would not otherwise be available. The underlying debate, then, particularly when we are discussing the construction of liability, is the question of when and how such liability should be constructed.

The dominant language of the current law, discussing automatism, insanity, and intoxication as *defences*, only serves to disguise and confuse this underlying question.[172] If we think of these rules in terms of defences, then it is natural to think about what is required of D to excuse or justify her avoidance of liability (ie liability becomes the default). In contrast, when we accept that these rules are designed to construct liability (or in the context of insanity, at least to provide a route to orders for public protection),

---

[165] *Stripp* (1979) 69 Cr App R 318.
[166] *Beard* [1920] AC 479.
[167] *Roach* [2001] EWCA Crim 2698.
[168] *Burns* (1973) 58 Cr App R 364.
[169] Law Commission, *Intoxication and Criminal Liability* (No 314, 2009); Law Commission, *Insanity and Automatism* (Discussion Paper, 2013).
[170] Outside this, the rules simply provide a shorthand terminology for saying that D lacks essential elements for the offence charged.
[171] The special verdict of not guilty by reason of insanity provides an acquittal, but its qualified nature (including the potential for compulsory treatment) means that it is still inculpatory in effect.
[172] Simester, 'Intoxication is Never a Defence' [2009] Crim LR 3; Child and Reed, 'Automatism is Never a Defence' (2014) 65 NILQ 167; Child and Sullivan, 'When Does the Insanity Defence Apply? Some Recent Cases' [2014] Crim LR 787; Child, 'Prior Fault: Blocking Defences or Constructing Crimes' in Reed and Bohlander (eds), *General Defences* (2014).

the question changes to consider what D has done wrong to deserve liability. The difference between these two may be subtle, but it has a real impact on our interpretation (and potential reform) of the law. For example, whilst the use of objective mental states is common among defences (discussed in **Chapter 14**), the modern trend within offences has been to require subjective mens rea, holding D liable only where she has *chosen* to commit an offence.[173] Thus, when we come to consider D's prior fault for intoxication (objectively based where the drug is a dangerous one) or automatism (case law is uncertain), our perception of the rules as defences or offence constructors is crucial.

13.6.1 Intoxication

The intoxication rules in general, and the *Majewski* principle in particular, have been consistently criticised for their lack of a theoretical basis and their confused application in practice.[174] Where other jurisdictions have abandoned the principle, the English courts have become isolated in clinging to it. It is clear that if reform is to come, it will need to be through Parliament.

When the Law Commission first considered the intoxication rules in 1992, they proposed that the *Majewski* principle should be abolished and replaced with an intoxication offence.[175] This would have meant that rather than D's intoxication (at T1) being used to construct liability for offence where D lacks mens rea (at T2), D's intoxication plus harm would itself constitute a separate offence. However, following criticism on consultation,[176] the Commission changed their minds and recommended codification (with only slight amendment) of the current law.[177] This recommendation was never taken forward into legislation, being widely viewed as unnecessarily complex.

The latest Law Commission project on intoxication was completed in 2009.[178] In their report, the Commission recommended the abandonment of the *Majewski* distinction between offences of basic and specific intent. However, the Commission did not reject the basic logic underlying the current law that voluntary intoxication with a dangerous drug is equivalent (in culpability terms) to a missing mens rea of recklessness. For the Commission, the main problem with the law was that this principle was not consistently or specifically applied. Thus, rather than distinguishing between offences that might include various mens rea requirements, the Commission recommended that each element of each offence should be analysed separately: where the missing element of mens rea is recklessness or less, then D's intoxication can substitute for it (the Commission labels these 'non-integral' elements), but if the element requires a higher mens rea than recklessness (eg intention, knowledge, etc) then the absence of this cannot be replaced by D's intoxication (the Commission labels these 'integral' elements). There are a number of merits to this policy as a rationalisation of the current law. However, they have also attracted criticism,[179] and have been rejected by government.

---

[173] *G* [2003] UKHL 50.
[174] Williams, 'Voluntary Intoxication—A Lost Cause?' (2013) 129 LQR 264.
[175] Law Commission, *Intoxication and Criminal Liability* (Consultation 127, 1992).
[176] Gardner, 'The Importance of *Majewski*' (1994) 14 OJLS 279.
[177] Law Commission, *Intoxication and Criminal Liability* (No 229, 1995).
[178] Law Commission, *Intoxication and Criminal Liability* (No 314, 2009).
[179] Child, 'Drink, Drugs and Law Reform' [2009] Crim LR 488.

As more commentators have accepted that the intoxication rules are essentially inculpatory, and that the debate should be about what is required to construct liability, the prospect of an intoxication offence to replace the current intoxication rules has regained popularity.[180] Rather than the fiction of the current law, pretending that D possessed mens rea where she did not, the advantage of an intoxication offence is that it could accurately label and punish D for what she has done: become intoxicated and caused a criminal harm. The detail of such an offence remains contested,[181] but it is contended that this approach offers the best way forward.

13.6.2 Sane automatism

The automatism rules have attracted less academic attention than intoxication, but many of the same debates and criticisms can be applied. Again, the approach of the Law Commission (within its recent Discussion Paper[182]) has been an attempt to rationalise the current law in the context of other denials of offending, most notably intoxication and insanity. For example, the Commission explores the wider concept of prior fault, and looks to identify consistent approaches across the three sets of rules. Focusing on automatism specifically, the Commission also looks to resolve some of the main areas of uncertainty within the current law (discussed earlier) relating to the type of foresight required by D in the context of prior fault, as well as the degree of involuntariness required to give rise to automatism at all.[183]

As with intoxication, however, if we see the automatism rules as designed to construct liability, an alternative approach could be the creation of a prior fault automatism offence.[184] This option is not discussed by the Commission. It will be interesting to see what approach is eventually recommended by the Commission.

13.6.3 Insanity

The most widely criticised rules discussed in this chapter relate to insanity.[185] That the law remains governed by the outlined opinions of Law Lords over 170 years ago is nothing short of remarkable; that this should be the case despite dramatic strides in medical and public understanding of mental illness is nothing short of disgraceful.

We have already discussed a number of specific problems with the insanity rules, and there is also a useful summary of these in the Law Commission's recent Discussion Paper.[186] One of those we have not yet discussed, but a major pressure for reform

---

[180] Simester, 'Intoxication is Never a Defence' [2009] Crim LR 3.

[181] Williams, 'Voluntary Intoxication—A Lost Cause?' (2013) 129 LQR 264; Child, 'Prior Fault: Blocking Defences or Constructing Crimes' in Reed and Bohlander (eds), *General Defences* (2014).

[182] Law Commission, *Insanity and Automatism* (Discussion Paper, 2013).

[183] Ibid., Ch5.

[184] Child and Reed, 'Automatism is Never a Defence' (2014) 65 NILQ 167.

[185] Dell, 'Wanted: An Insanity Defence That Can Be Used' [1983] Crim LR 431; Loughnan, 'Manifest Madness: Towards a New Understanding of the Insanity Defence' (2007) 70 MLR 379; Hathaway, 'The Moral Significance of the Insanity Defence' (2009) 73 J Crim L 310.

[186] Law Commission, *Insanity and Automatism* (Discussion Paper, 2013) paras 1.30–1.79.

derives from the potential incompatibility of the current law with the ECHR.[187] There are three main areas of potential challenge.

- **Articles 2 and 3:** Articles 2 and 3 provide for the right to life and the prohibition of inhuman or degrading treatment. In this regard, the insanity rules have a crucial role to protect mentally disordered individuals from inappropriate prosecution, and also to protect society from potentially dangerous individuals. Where the current law fails in these roles, it is open to challenge in relation to both groups.[188]

- **Article 5:** Article 5 provides the right to liberty and security unless certain circumstances apply, such as where D has committed an offence or requires detention in relation to an 'unsound mind'. Where D lacks mens rea she has not committed an offence, and where the cause of this lack of mens rea is a condition such as diabetes (or sleepwalking, etc), it is highly questionable whether this satisfies the Article 5 exception of an unsound mind.[189] Thus, where D (in these circumstances) is caught within the insanity rules and potentially detained against her will, this may be a breach of her Article 5 right.[190] This ground centres on the current disconnect between legal definitions of insanity and medical definitions of mental illness.

- **Article 6:** Article 6 provides the right to a fair trial, including the presumption of innocence. The presumption of innocence entails placing the burden upon the prosecution to prove the elements of liability. However, where D's denial of offending is based upon a disease of the mind (ie caught within the insanity rules) the current law reverses the legal burden of proof; requiring D to prove her innocence.[191]

In light of the various criticisms levelled at the current law, it is little surprise that it has attracted several reform proposals (almost from its inception[192]). The most recent of these is again contained in the Law Commission's 2013 Discussion Paper.[193] Some of the Commission's main proposals include the following.

- **Proposal 1:** Abolition of the common law rules on insanity.

- **Proposal 2:** Creation of a new statutory test, labelled as 'not criminally responsible by reason of recognised medical condition'.

- **Proposal 3:** Creation of a three-limbed test, where D's recognised medical condition must have caused D to lack capacity: (a) to rationally form a judgement about her conduct or their circumstances; (b) to understand the wrongfulness of what she is charged with (not isolated to legal wrongfulness); or (c) to control her conduct in the relevant circumstances.

---

[187] Mackay and Gearty, 'On Being Insane in Jersey—The Case of *AG v Jason Prior*' [2001] Crim LR 560; Mackay, 'On Being Insane in Jersey—Part Two' [2002] Crim LR 728; Mackay, 'On Being Insane in Jersey—Part Three' [2004] Crim LR 219.

[188] Law Commission, *Insanity and Automatism* (Discussion Paper, 2013) paras 1.65–1.72.

[189] For discussion of this definition, see *Winterwerp v Netherlands* (1979) 2 EHRR 387.

[190] Although, of course, detention of this kind will require the advice of two medical experts.

[191] *Bratty* [1963] AC 386.

[192] As early as 1923 a committee chaired by Lord Atkin recommended a test based on 'mental disease [which] in substance deprived [D] of any power to resist': Cmd 2005.

[193] Law Commission, *Insanity and Automatism* (Discussion Paper, 2013) paras 4.158–4.168.

- **Proposal 6:** Placing an *evidential* burden on D when raising the reformed rules, but placing the legal burden on the prosecution.

As with the Commission's proposals for automatism, it is important to remember that these are only the provisional proposals of a discussion paper.

13.7 Eye on assessment

In this section we consider how denials of offending based on intoxication, automatism, and insanity should be applied to problem facts. The same basic structure is employed as discussed in previous chapters.

> **STEP 1 Identify the potential criminal event in the facts**
>
> This is unlikely to take more than a sentence, but it is essential to tell your reader where in the facts you are focusing. For example, 'The first potential criminal event appears where Mary drunkenly shoots and kills Amir.'

It is important to take care at this stage. Where you note from the facts that D may be intoxicated (as in our example) or may be acting involuntarily or may have a mental disorder, it is correct that this should alert you to the potential application of the rules discussed in this chapter. However, this (Step 1) is not the time to discuss those rules! Many students make the mistake of launching into a discussion of intoxication, automatism, or insanity at this stage, but without having told the reader why these rules need to be discussed, their analysis is likely to be confused.

Rather than discussing rules of denial at this stage, you first need to identify a potential offence (Step 2) and discuss if the elements of that offence are satisfied (Step 3).

> **STEP 2 Identify the potential offence**
>
> Having identified the facts (eg D potentially killing V), you must now identify the offence you are going to apply. Usually, this means identifying the most serious offence that D might have committed, which in this case would be murder.

> **STEP 3 Applying the offence to the facts**
>
> Actus reus: What does the offence require? Did D do it?
> Mens rea: What does the offence require? Did D possess it?

If you conclude that D satisfies all the actus reus and mens rea elements of the offence, then the intoxication and automatism rules have no role. This can be highlighted to your reader, for example: 'Although Mary was drunk when she killed Amir, she remains liable for murder because (despite her intoxication) she still possessed the required mens rea.' As the House of Lords confirmed in *Kingston*, 'a drunken intent is still an intent'. The insanity rules as a denial of mens rea will also have no application, although insanity as a defence (discussed in **Chapter 14**) may be relevant.

It is *only* when D lacks elements of the offence that the rules discussed in this chapter become relevant. Here, having identified the missing elements, your next question is which set of rules (if any) could apply.

(1) D lacks mens rea (potentially including a lack of voluntary conduct) because of her consumption of drugs = apply the intoxication rules;

(2) D lacks voluntary movement (potentially including other mens rea) because of an external factor other than within the intoxication rules = apply the automatism rules;

(3) D lacks mens rea (potentially including a lack of voluntary conduct) because of an internal condition = apply the insanity rules;

(4) D lacks actus reus elements, or mens rea elements for any reason other than the above = D has not completed the offence and should be acquitted.

We provide detailed analysis of how each set of rules should be applied within this chapter. Here, we include **Figures 13.11, 13.12,** and **13.13** to help with the basic structuring of this application, to be used alongside the more detailed discussion.

Figure 13.11 Intoxication flowchart

Figure 13.12 Automatism flowchart

(Continued opposite)

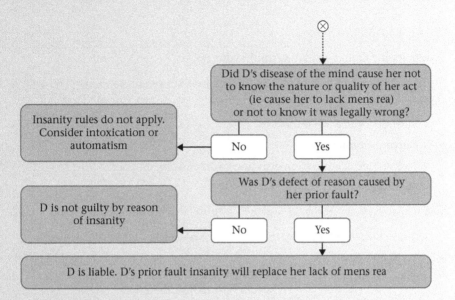

Figure 13.13 Insanity as a denial of offending flowchart (*Continued*)

Where no liability is found, you can move to Step 5. Where liability is found, remember to consider Step 4.

STEP 4 Consider defences

The word 'consider' here is important, as you should not discuss every defence for every question. Rather, think whether there are any defences that *could* potentially apply. If you conclude there are, then discuss those only.

Where liability has been constructed on the basis of D's prior fault at T1, D may rely on a defence to undermine that fault. For example, D may rely on the defence of duress (discussed in **Chapter 14**) to deny responsibility for a failure to take medication (leading to insanity), or for taking something that causes a lack of voluntariness (leading to automatism, or the intoxication rules).

STEP 5 Conclude

This is usually a single sentence either saying that it is likely that D has committed the offence, or saying that it is not likely either because an offence element is not satisfied or because a defence is likely to apply. It is not often that you will be able to say categorically whether D has committed the offence or not, so it is usually best to conclude in terms of what is more 'likely'.

STEP 6 Loop

Go back up to Step 1, identifying the next potential criminal event. Continue until you have discussed all the relevant potentially criminal events.

ONLINE RESOURCE CENTRE

www.oxfordtextbooks.co.uk/orc/smithandhogan/

This chapter is accompanied by a selection of online resources to help you with this topic, including:

- **Multiple choice questions**
- **Chapter summary sheet**
- Two **sample examination questions** with answer guidance
- **Further reading**

Also available on the Online Resource Centre are:

- A selection of **videos** from the authors explaining key topics and principles
- **Legal updates**
- Useful **weblinks**

14

General defences

14.1 Introduction

In this chapter we discuss general complete defences. Unlike denials of offending discussed in **Chapter 13**, defences, properly so called, accept that D has committed the elements of an offence, but provide an additional set of rules that D can rely on so as to avoid liability. For example, D accepts that she intentionally pushed V to the ground thereby committing assault occasioning ABH,[1] but denies liability on the basis that she did so only to stop V attacking her child, and is relying on the public and private defence.[2] We have discussed

---

[1] Offences Against the Person Act 1861. See **7.4**.

[2] Commonly referred to as self-defence. See **14.5**.

a number of 'specific' defences in previous chapters—defences that only apply to a single offence or a cluster of offences, such as the belief in owner's consent for criminal damage.[3] In contrast, the defences discussed in this chapter, as 'general' defences, can apply, with one exception,[4] to offences throughout the criminal law. We have also previously discussed the 'partial' defences to murder—defences which have the potential to reduce liability for murder to manslaughter as, for example, where D was suffering from diminished responsibility.[5] The defences discussed in this chapter in contrast, as 'complete' defences, will result in D's acquittal.

> **Terminology…**
> When discussing defences, the language of actus reus (guilty act) and mens rea (guilty mind) is no longer relevant. This is because these terms are used to describe offences only. What is under discussion now are defences, and we only talk of elements of defences and not the actus reus or mens rea of a defence.

Defences, and the general defences in particular, play a vital role within the criminal law. On one level, they can be viewed as a concession to the bluntness of the criminal offence. Offence definitions attempt to isolate and identify criminal wrongs, but, within the infinite variety of circumstances in the real world, it is almost impossible for these definitions to account for every eventuality. Criminal defences provide the next layers of detail; allowing the law to account for the exceptional. Indeed, the same analysis can be presented in more positive terms. If criminal offences have a role in guiding the behaviour of society, then relative bluntness in offence definitions is a good thing: offences can provide clear messages about conduct to be avoided, leaving defences to act as a safety net where D commits the offence in exceptional circumstances such that liability would be inappropriate.[6]

Defences can be problematic, however, and it is useful to highlight a few common issues at this stage. First, defences are often criticised for being drawn too narrowly and for failing to exculpate a defendant who does not deserve to be held liable. They are also often criticised for being drawn too widely thereby allowing blameworthy conduct, inappropriately, to escape liability. Such criticisms are also common of criminal offences, but they may be felt particularly keenly in the context of defences as the 'last line' or the last set of legal rules that stand between D and a criminal conviction. Indeed, it may be partly because of this that many defences lack clarity in their definitions; opening the potential for inconsistent application and criticism, but also providing flexibility to account for different factual circumstances. A second issue which often arises, although mostly in the context of specific, as opposed to general, defences, is a confusion of roles between offence and defence. We discussed this, for example, in the context of offences of 'assisting and encouraging' and the defence of 'acting reasonably'.[7] The

---

[3] Criminal Damage Act 1971, s5(2)(a). See **9.7.3**.
[4] The exception is duress, which does not provide a defence to murder and certain related offences. See **14.3** and **14.4**.
[5] Homicide Act 1957, s2. See **6.2.2**.
[6] Duff, *Answering for Crime* (2007) Ch11; Wilson, 'The Structure of Criminal Defences' [2005] Crim LR 108.
[7] See **11.4.5**.

problem here is that although defences enable the law to provide a safety net to account for exceptional circumstances, they should not be doing the work of the offence definition: an offence should still identify blameworthy conduct requiring a defence to excuse or justify it; defences are not a licence to criminalise large amounts of reasonable behaviour, forcing D to raise defences to exculpate herself.[8]

In this chapter, we discuss the following defences.

- **Insanity (as a defence):** This arises where a medical condition caused a defect in reason, and prevented D understanding her conduct or understanding that it was wrong. For example, where D kills V under the insane delusion that she is required by law to do so.

- **Duress by threats:** This arises where D was threatened by someone that unless she committed the offence she is now charged with she would suffer serious injury or death, and D reasonably believed that the threat would be carried out imminently, and a reasonable person in those circumstances would have reacted as D did. For example, D may plead duress when charged with robbery if she was told by X to rob a bank or else D would be killed.

- **Duress by circumstances:** This arises where D faces a threat of death or serious injury, but with the threat arising from D's circumstances rather than explicitly from a person. For example, where D sees a tidal wave coming her way, and realises that breaking into a car to drive away is her only means of escape, she would have a defence to a charge of criminal damage to the car.

- **The public and private defence (commonly known as self-defence):** This arises where D uses force against another in the genuine belief that she needs to do so to protect herself or others, or to prevent crime, and the amount of force used is reasonable in the circumstances as D believed them to be. For example, D assaults V where D believes she needs to do so in order to stop V harming her child.

- **Necessity:** This arises where D acts for the greater good, or the lesser evil. This defence, as we will see, is poorly defined and rarely applied. An example of its rare use has been to justify the separation of conjoined twins, killing one to give the other a chance of life.

These defences are not denials of actus reus or mens rea. In order to explain the moral permissibility of D's offending in circumstances of a defence, courts and commentators have occasionally referred to D's conduct as 'involuntary', or 'morally involuntary'.[9] This terminology is unhelpful. If D's conduct is involuntary then she does not commit an offence, and we apply the rules discussed in **Chapter 13**. Here, D may have been subject to an impossible choice, such that her voluntary commission of an offence is not blameworthy, but her appeal to defences properly so called marks an acceptance that she has committed an offence.[10]

---

[8] Duff, *Answering for Crime* (2007) Ch11. See also *Smith and Hogan's Criminal Law* (14th edn, 2015), Ch12.

[9] *Perka* (1984) 13 DLR (4th) 1: Canadian court discussing duress by threats.

[10] *Hasan* [2005] UKHL 22, [18].

14.1.1 Excuses and justifications

Much of the theoretical writing in this area has focused on categorising types of defences in order to understand the basis upon which D is exculpated; particularly the division between excusatory and justificatory defences. The language of excuses and justifications originates from a historical question of forfeiture on acquittal: historically a justified killer would not have her goods forfeited, but a merely excused killer would. This question has not been relevant since the abolition of forfeiture in 1828, but academic interest in the division continued, and was re-sparked by the seminal work of George Fletcher.[11]

The division between excuses and justifications can be stated quite simply, but the detail of its application and relevance to today's law is highly contested. Essentially, an excusatory defence accepts that D's actions were wrongful but challenges the idea that D can be blamed because of circumstances personal to her, whereas justifications challenge the wrongfulness of D's actions.[12] As Fletcher put it:

> A justification speaks to the rightness of the act; an excuse, to whether the actor is accountable for a concededly wrongful act.[13]

An excuse, then, tends to focus on D herself rather than her actions. For example, if D explains that she committed the offence because voices in her head compelled her to do so, we do not question whether her acts were wrongful (they clearly were), but we may question whether it is right to blame D for those acts, and this is done through the excusatory defence of insanity. As Hart notably stated, 'unless a man has the capacity and fair opportunity or chance to adjust his behaviour to the law, its penalties ought not to be applied to him'.[14] This is the essence of an excusatory defence; whether due to a physical or mental restraint, or whether due to extreme circumstances, D did not have a *fair* opportunity to obey the law.[15] Justifications, on the other hand, focus on D's acts. For example, where D assaults V in order to stop V harming her child, D may have completed the elements of an offence, but her acts were permissible.[16]

There is an appealing logic to the separation of excuses and justification, but outside core examples, it can also be problematic.[17] Take the simple example of D who assaults V in order to stop V harming D's child. Although this is a clear example of the justified defence of another, known as 'the public and private defence', D could also rely on this defence if she made a mistake, if she thought V was trying to harm her child but was wrong and V was actually no threat at all. In this case, D's actions are *justified on her beliefs*, but

---

[11] Fletcher, *Rethinking Criminal Law* (1978) Ch10.

[12] For criticism, see Gardner, 'Wrongs and Faults' in Simester (ed), *Appraising Strict Liability* (2005) 6–67.

[13] Fletcher, *Rethinking Criminal Law* (1978) 759.

[14] Hart, *Punishment and Responsibility* (1968) 181.

[15] See generally Horder, *Excusing Crime* (2004).

[16] It is problematic to say we 'approve' of D's acts because they still involved the commission of a criminal wrong. However, here acts should not be condemned; they were permissible: Duff, *Answering for Crime* (2007) Ch11; Westen, 'Offences and Defences Again' (2008) 28 OJLS 563.

[17] Even within them there is a question of hierarchy, Husak, 'On the Supposed Priority of Justification to Excuse' (2005) 24 Law & Phil 557.

few would call them justified in light of the objective facts. Rather, if we accept the use of the public and private defence on these amended facts, it appears to be *excusing* D's blameworthy conduct on the basis of her mistake. Countless examples of this kind, as Duff acknowledges, have been difficult to categorise within the excuse/justification framework, and 'bred needless confusion' in the law.[18] This has prompted two main responses, with certain commentators questioning why we should talk of these distinctions at all,[19] whilst others have attempted to resolve the issue by becoming ever more fine-grained in their theorising, separating subcategories of excuses and justification.[20] This latter approach can be useful to resolve problematic scenarios, but does so at the expense of simplicity and therefore at the expense of one of the initially appealing elements of the separation.

The current law does not rely on the explicit separation of excuses and justifications; the practical result of D's acquittal is the same for both. However, an outright rejection of these classifications, despite their critics, would be premature.[21] First, this is because the debate about these theories is useful; it forces us to question the basis upon which a defence operates. This aids our evaluation of current defences, questioning their coherence, and leads us towards potential reform options.[22] Secondly, where a separation can be made, it does seem to have certain practical consequences. For example, it seems that it is legitimate for D to use force to defend herself against an excused attacker (eg where V is attacking D under an insane delusion), but it is not legitimate for D to use force to protect herself where the attacker's conduct is justified (eg where V uses force on D in the belief that D is harming her child).[23] Further, whilst D may be an accomplice to an offence committed by P who is excused from liability, in contrast D is absolved of liability as an accessory where P was justified in committing the offence.[24] Thirdly, and finally, the distinction seems to make a difference in what the law is trying to communicate to society. Robinson, for example, has discussed the role of defences as rule 'articulators'; that is, telling the public what they should and should not do.[25] For Robinson, whilst excuses are essential concessions to human frailty, they are not rules that the public need to know, they are not designed to adjust behaviour. Justifications, in contrast, should be communicated clearly because they tell people when it is permitted to commit certain offences for the greater good.

Assessment matters...

As we have said, the current law does not require an explicit identification of defences as excusatory or justificatory. Therefore, when applying a defence to problem facts, this terminology is unlikely to be useful. However, when evaluating the law, either within a problem question or a more general essay, the terminology will be very useful.

---

18 Duff, *Answering for Crime* (2007) 263.

19 Williams, 'The Theory of Excuses' [1982] Crim LR 732.

20 For a particularly useful model, see Simester, 'On Justifications and Excuses' in Zedner and Roberts (eds), *Principles and Values in Criminal Law and Criminal Justice* (2012) 95.

21 Robinson, 'Four Distinctions that Glanville Williams Did Not Make' in Baker and Horder (eds), *The Sanctity of Life and the Criminal Law* (2013).

22 This is a common structure within academic writing. See eg Stark 'Necessity and *Nicklinson*' [2013] Crim LR 949.

23 Fletcher, *Rethinking Criminal Law* (1978) para 10.1.1.

24 *Bourne* (1952) 36 Cr App R 125.

25 Robinson, *Structure and Function in Criminal Law* (1997) Ch5.

14.2 Insanity as a defence

We have already discussed the insanity rules as a denial of offending (**13.4**), where D raises insanity to explain her lack of mens rea including in extreme cases her lack of voluntary conduct. However, uniquely, the insanity rules can *also* apply as a defence, exculpating D from liability even when she has completed the actus reus and mens rea of the offence charged. The elements of insanity as a defence are the same as those for insanity as a denial of offending. Therefore, our discussion in this section should be read in the context of our more detailed analysis of the insanity rules in the previous chapter. Rather than repeating details from **13.4**, this section provides a brief overview of insanity as a defence, before highlighting a few areas where the difference between denial of offending and defence will affect our application of the law.

The insanity rules were set out in *M'Naghten*,[26] and confirmed in the House of Lords in its judicial capacity in *Sullivan*.[27] They are illustrated in **Table 14.1**.

Table 14.1 Insanity defence

A) D must suffer from a disease of the mind;
B) This must have caused a defect of reason; and
C) This must have caused a lack of responsibility, *either* because D did not know the nature or quality of her act, *or* she did not know it was legally wrong

Where D satisfies these elements, even though she may have committed an offence, she is entitled to a special acquittal. The burden of proof is on D on the balance of probabilities. D will be found 'not guilty by reason of insanity' (which is known as the special verdict), and the court will then choose from a range of disposal orders.[28] The special verdict ensures that D is protected from inappropriate liability through conviction, but also that the public can be protected from future danger through disposal options which include compulsory treatment and/or supervision.

Where insanity is raised as a defence, as opposed to a denial of mens rea, two main theoretical differences should be noted from our discussion at **13.4**. The first relates to the application of the elements of the insanity rules, and the second to their interaction with other defences.

14.2.1 The elements of insanity as a defence

The three elements of the insanity defence, set out in **Table 14.1**, were discussed at **13.4.2**. It should be noted here, in relation to the third element, that the either/or between 'not knowing the nature or quality of her act' and 'not knowing it was wrong' will often mark the difference between insanity as a denial of offending and insanity as a defence.

---

[26] (1843) 4 St Tr NS 847.

[27] [1984] 1 AC 156.

[28] See **13.4.1**.

Where D caused harms without an understanding of her acts as, for example, where D killed V thinking she was breaking a jar, she will not have possessed mens rea. Thus, if mens rea is required for the offence (remember that all offences require at least voluntary conduct), D's plea to the insanity rules will be a denial of offending. In contrast, where D has capacity to understand her acts, but her disease of the mind causes her not to know they are legally wrong, she may well possess mens rea. Indeed, understanding the legal wrongfulness of one's conduct is rarely relevant to the mens rea of an offence: ignorance of the law is no excuse.[29] Thus, an appeal to the insanity rules on this basis is likely to be an appeal to insanity as a defence.

A second point that should be noted relates to the first element of the insanity rules, which requires D to suffer from a disease of the mind and the internal/external cause distinction. Importantly, the need to show an internal cause is common to insanity as a denial of offending and insanity as a defence. However, there is likely to be an interesting switch in the priorities of the defendant. Where the plea is one amounting to a denial of offending, D will be particularly keen for the insanity rules not to be applied to her because, if the cause of her lack of capacity is external, she will receive an *unqualified* acquittal. This is why, for example, there is so much litigation around the borderline between automatism resulting in an unqualified acquittal and insanity resulting in the special verdict of not guilty by reason of insanity. In contrast, where the plea arises as a defence, the default position if the insanity rules do not apply is likely to be full criminal liability. Thus, although issues of stigma may still put off D from raising insanity, she is much more likely to do so in hope of the special verdict.

14.2.2 Insanity and other defences

Where insanity arises as a denial of offending, it will rarely come into conflict with defences.[30] However, where insanity arises as a defence, other alternative defences may also be applicable. For example, suppose a situation where D is visiting V and has a psychotic delusion that V is possessed by the devil and is about to launch a deadly attack upon her. She makes a pre-emptive strike and is charged with assault. D will seek to raise mistaken self-defence (the public and private defence) in this case because, if successful, it would result in an unqualified acquittal. Alongside this, however, it is also clear that D's delusion will qualify for the insanity defence within the *M'Naghten* Rules. This is because D's delusion of self-defence is likely to mean that she did not know that what she was doing was wrong, and the *M'Naghten* Rules also make explicit reference to catching delusions of this kind.[31] For example, Lord Chief Justice Tindal remarked that D:

> must be considered in the same situation as to responsibility as if the facts with respect to which the delusion exists were real. For example, if under the influence of his delusion he supposes another man to be in the act of attempting to take away his life, and he kills that man, as he supposes, in self-defence, he would be exempt from punishment.[32]

---

[29] *Grant v Borg* [1982] 2 All ER 257; Ashworth, 'Ignorance of the Criminal Law, and Duties to Avoid It' (2011) 74 MLR 1.

[30] See **13.4.3**.

[31] This is sometimes referred to as a third limb of *M'Naghten*: the delusion limb: Williams, *Criminal Law: The General Part* (2nd edn, 1961) 497–507.

[32] *M'Naghten* [1843] UKHL J16, 211.

The reference to being 'exempt from punishment' in this extract is intended to mean that the insanity defence will apply. But this is very much a second best outcome for D. The insanity defence will result in acquittal, but also in the special verdict and the uncertainty of the various disposal options.

The question for the insanity rules is whether D should be allowed to rely on an alternative defence in priority to insanity, or whether the insanity rules should exclude and take preference over alternative options in order to ensure compulsory treatment and/or supervision where it is required. If D claims that her belief in the need to use force to protect herself is a belief based on her psychotic state, should D be treated as pleading self-defence, or should the fact that her claim raises insanity mean that self-defence is no longer available to her? Following the approach taken to insanity as a denial of offending, it seems right in principle and in policy that the latter option should be preferred. Whether D would favour an alternative basis for denying offending, or an alternative defence, if her satisfaction of these alternatives relies upon a defect of reason arising from a disease of the mind then the insanity rules should be applied in preference. Just as D is prevented from relying on a simple denial of mens rea where that denial is based on what the law calls insanity, the same forward-looking rationale must apply equally to a choice between multiple defences: there remains a strong interest in protecting the public from future potential harm.

This issue arose recently in the case of *Oye*.

Oye [2013] EWCA Crim 1725

D became gripped by delusions that police officers were agents of evil spirits out to kill him, and launched a series of attacks on officers causing serious harm. D was charged with affray and maliciously inflicting GBH.[33] D raised the self-defence (the public and private defence), and the judge instructed that insanity should *also* be left to the jury.

- Crown Court: guilty of affray and GBH offence. The jury rejected both defences.
- Court of Appeal: appeal allowed, substituting a special verdict of not guilty by reason of insanity.

The correct decision was reached in *Oye*, but it remains a problematic case. This is because the trial judge was in error in allowing the defences of mistaken self-defence and insanity to run in parallel. Although he was saved by the jury having rejected both defences, allowing both to run together is surely wrong in principle: if D was found not guilty on the basis of self-defence, thereby leading to an unqualified acquittal, this should be the end of the matter, and if a judge then wished to impose compulsory treatment under the separate heading of insanity this would give rise to some interesting issues under Article 5 ECHR. The Court of Appeal could have held, in line with our earlier discussion, that raising self-defence on the basis of an insane delusion amounted to raising the defence of insanity alone. However, the court achieved this same result by an alternative route. Focusing on the rules governing self-defence, the Court of Appeal held that insane delusions should be added to the list of grounds which the jury should

---

[33] Offences Against the Person Act 1861, s20.

ignore when considering whether D's use of force was reasonable (an element of the public and private defence).[34]

> **Don't be confused...**
> The *Oye* case is problematic, but the result (at least) is clear. Where D raises multiple defences including insanity, the insanity defence should be applied ahead of the other options. Following the approach in *Sullivan*[35] (discussing insanity as a denial of offending), it is hoped that future courts will provide clarity as to the priority of defences.

14.3 Duress by threats

Duress, like insanity, is commonly understood as an excusatory defence.[36] D has committed an offence, but she has done so because she was threatened by X with death or serious injury if she refused. Thus, we do not agree with her conduct, the commission of the crime was not a justified act, but we can accept that she was placed in an impossible position, and so we can excuse her.

Some commentators go further and describe D's impossible position as a species of involuntariness, and it may be that D herself would protest that she 'had no choice' but to offend.[37] However, as we highlighted earlier, this kind of terminology is unhelpful in the context of defences. Where D appeals to the defence of duress, she is not claiming that she was not in control of her conduct, that would be automatism, nor is she claiming any other lack of mens rea. And this has been consistently recognised by the courts.[38] Rather, the defence of duress represents a concession to human frailty,[39] an acceptance that although D *did* have a choice between offending or suffering serious harm from X, her decision to offend does not reveal a dangerous character deserving of criminal punishment. We accept, essentially, that D did no more than most of us would have done in her position, and we acquit on the basis that, as the adage goes, 'there, but for the grace of God, go I'.

The defence of duress has developed at common law, and remains uncodified. As illustrated in **Table 14.2**, it consists of three main elements,[40] each of which will be explored later.

---

[34] Child and Sullivan, 'When Does the Insanity Defence Apply? Some Recent Cases' [2014] Crim LR 787.

[35] [1984] AC 156.

[36] Westen and Mangiafico, 'The Criminal Defense of Duress: A Justification, Not an Excuse' (2003) 6 Buff Crim L Rev 833; Huigens, 'Duress is Not a Justification' (2004) 2 Ohio St J Crim L 303.

[37] The Australian court in *Perka* (1984) 13 DLR (4th) 1 describe it as 'moral involuntariness'. See Wasik, 'Duress and Criminal Responsibility' [1977] Crim LR 453.

[38] *Fisher* [2004] EWCA Crim 1190; *Hasan* [2005] UKHL 22, [18].

[39] *Howe* [1987] 1 All ER 771, 779–780; *Hasan* [2005] UKHL 22, [18].

[40] Duress by threats is inconsistently presented as containing anything between two and eight elements. This inconsistency does not represent disagreement on the substance of the defence, but simply the presentation.

Table 14.2 Duress by threats

A) Exclusions: duress is not a defence to murder, attempted murder, and certain treason offences, and will not apply in circumstances of prior fault;
B) X's threat and demand: D must have reasonably believed that she or another was threatened with death or serious injury by X unless D committed the offence; and
C) D's response: committing a crime as D did must be something that a reasonable person in her circumstances would have done. D must show reasonable steadfastness in response to the threat, only committing the offence because her will was overborne.

It is commonly accepted that a defence of duress is necessary within the law. For example, where X holds a gun to a bank manger's head and forces her to open the vault, few would want to hold D, the manager, liable as X's accomplice.[41] However, it should be highlighted from the start that there is also great concern about the limits of the defence, and scepticism about those raising it. Particularly in the context of criminal organisations and gangs, where threats and intimidation between members is common, duress can be claimed quite easily and can be very difficult for the prosecution to disprove.[42] The reaction to this has been twofold. First, as with other defences, D must provide some evidence of duress (D bears an evidential burden) before it will be considered in court, and before the prosecution are then under a legal burden to disprove it.[43] Secondly, and more controversially, scepticism about the defence's overuse has led courts, in recent years in particular, to interpret the elements of the defence increasingly narrowly. This has led to criticisms in the other direction, claiming that the defence has now become overly restrictive and thus unable to apply in certain deserving circumstances.[44]

Extra detail...
The narrowing of duress in recent years can be witnessed across multiple cases. However, it is best illustrated by the speech of Lord Bingham in *Hasan*.[45] This speech should be carefully read in full. The minority speech of Baroness Hale, in the same case, provides useful illustration of arguments in favour of a wider interpretation.

14.3.1 Exclusions

There are two areas where duress will be excluded: (a) in relation to certain offences; and (b) in circumstances of prior fault.

---

[41] On accomplice liability, see **Chapter 12**.
[42] Law Commission, *Murder, Manslaughter and Infanticide* (No 304, 2006) paras 6.101–6.111.
[43] *Hasan* [2005] UKHL 22, [37]. The Law Commission has recommended reversing the legal burden of proof where duress is raised as a defence to murder (see discussion at **14.7**).
[44] For a useful discussion of this in the context of defendants suffering from domestic abuse, see Loveless, 'Domestic Violence, Coercion and Duress' [2010] Crim LR 93.
[45] [2005] UKHL 22.

14.3.1.1 Offences to which D cannot raise duress

Unlike the other general defences discussed in this chapter, which potentially apply across all criminal offences, the defence of duress (by threats and by circumstance) contains a few important exclusions. Duress is not a defence to certain offences.

A) **Treason:** The term 'treason' refers to a bundle of offences against the state. Duress *can* be defence to certain of these offences. In *Purdy*,[46] for example, a British prisoner of war (D) was forced to assist with German propaganda during the Second World War. In doing so, D committed a treason offence, but it was held that he could rely on duress as a defence. However, other more serious treason offences will not allow duress as a defence.[47]

B) **Murder:** More controversially, duress is not a defence to murder.[48] As Blackstone put it, under duress a person 'ought rather to die himself than escape by the murder of an innocent.'[49] This was recognised by a bare majority of the Privy Council in *Abbott*,[50] and later by the House of Lords in *Howe*,[51] where it was also established that duress was no defence to murder as a secondary party.[52] The harsh results of this exclusion are most clearly illustrated in the case of *Wilson*.[53]

📖 *Wilson* [2007] EWCA Crim 1251

D, a 13-year-old boy, assisted his father to murder his neighbour, fetching an axe and starting a fire on his father's instruction. D claimed that he only did so because of fear of his father's violence. D was charged with murder as his father's accomplice.[54]

- Crown Court: guilty of murder. The defence, being unable to rely on duress, had tried to claim that D was so swept up in fear of his father that he was not able to form mens rea.
- Court of Appeal: conviction upheld on appeal.

The Court of Appeal in *Wilson* accepted that the law could be criticised for not providing a defence of duress where a 13-year-old is forced to commit murder by a dominant and violent parent,[55] but were obliged to follow the clear precedent from *Howe*.

C) **Attempted murder:** It was recognised in *Gotts*,[56] that if duress was no defence to murder then it would be illogical to recognise it as a defence to attempted murder.[57] If the court had found otherwise, the results would have been bizarre: allowing D's acts

---

[46] (1946) 10 JCL 182.
[47] *Steane* [1947] KB 997, 1005.
[48] Law Commission, *Murder, Manslaughter and Infanticide* (No 304, 2006) Ch6.
[49] Blackstone, *Commentaries on the Laws of England* (1765–69) Book 4, 30.
[50] [1977] AC 755.
[51] [1987] AC 417.
[52] Walters, 'Murder Under Duress and Judicial Decision Making in the House of Lords' (1988) 18 LS 61.
[53] Ashworth, 'Commentary on *Wilson*' [2008] Crim LR 138.
[54] **Chapter 12**.
[55] At [18].
[56] [1992] 2 AC 412.
[57] Gardner, 'Duress in Attempted Murder' (1991) 107 LQR 389.

to be excused, but not the results. This would have been particularly odd if V died some time after D's attack, where D would be allowed her excused freedom until the moment of V's death.

Unfortunately, the law remains illogical in allowing duress to apply where D commits the offence of intentionally causing GBH.[58] This is because, as the mens rea of murder includes both an intention to kill or an intention to cause GBH,[59] the same potential for problems arises here as it did in the context of attempted murder. For example, D attacks V under duress, causing V serious injury. D is not prosecuted because she has clearly acted under duress. Months later, or even longer, V dies from the injuries caused by D's original attack. D is now liable for murder, is prosecuted, and has no defence of duress.

It was confirmed in *Ness* that duress remains a valid defence for conspiracy to murder, and presumably assisting or encouraging murder.[60] Unlike attempted murder, these offences will never involve the direct application of force to V as part of their actus reus. Thus, the defence can be safely recognised in this context without encountering the potential problems just discussed.

> **Point to remember...**
> The exclusion of duress as a defence to murder and attempted murder is one of the most controversial aspects of the defence. Echoing academic criticisms, the Law Commission has recommended that duress should be extended to cover these offences.[61] This is discussed further in the reform section at **14.7.1.2**.

14.3.1.2 Exclusion on the basis of prior fault

The general defences are designed to protect D from liability where she has been placed in a position where her offending is either excused or justified. The reference here to 'has been placed in a position' is important. Where D, either consciously or through negligence, places herself in a position where she requires a defence, the law will be much less willing to recognise that defence.[62] The defence of duress, more than any other general defence, has applied this principle progressively strictly.

Early case law allowed D some leeway where she demonstrated prior fault by voluntarily associating with X, but reasonably did not foresee the threat and demand which followed.[63] However, more recent case law has been considerably more restrictive, illustrated in *Hasan*.

---

[58] Offences Against the Person Act 1861, s18.

[59] See **5.4**.

[60] [2011] Crim LR 645.

[61] Law Commission, *Murder, Manslaughter and Infanticide* (No 304, 2006) Ch6.

[62] Child, 'Prior Fault: Blocking Defences or Constructing Crimes' in Reed and Bohlander (eds), *General Defences* (2014).

[63] *Shepherd* (1987) 86 Cr App R 47: joining a group of burglars does not mean that D should have foreseen being threatened with a gun when trying to leave; *Lewis* (1992) 96 Cr App R 412: joining a group of armed robbers does not mean that D should have foreseen being threatened not to testify against other members when in prison.

> *Hasan* [2005] UKHL 22
>
> D committed burglary. He did so as a result of threats from X, who was known to be violent. D acted as a minder for X's girlfriend, who was a prostitute. X also acted as a minder for his girlfriend, as well as being involved in drug dealing. D was charged with aggravated burglary.[64]
>
> • Crown Court: guilty of aggravated assault.
> • Court of Appeal: appeal allowed, finding a defence of duress.
> • House of Lords: appeal allowed, reinstating conviction. D's voluntary association with X undermined any appeal to duress.

Hasan confirms that duress will be excluded where D voluntarily associated with X in circumstances where a reasonable person (note the objective standard) would have foreseen a risk of future coercion. This foresight of 'coercion' need not even be specific in nature, and not even require foresight of coercion to commit a crime. As Lord Bingham states:

> The policy of the law must be to discourage association with known criminals, and it should be slow to excuse the criminal conduct of those who do so. If a person voluntarily becomes or remains associated with others engaged in criminal activity in a situation where he knows or ought reasonably to know that he may be the subject of compulsion by them or their associates, he cannot rely on the defence of duress to excuse any act which he is thereafter compelled to do by them.[65]

The breadth of this principle was criticised in a powerful minority speech from Baroness Hale, who would prefer a test based on subjective foresight,[66] and it has also attracted cogent academic criticism.[67] However, the majority approach in *Hasan* has been confirmed in *Ali*,[68] and represents the current law.

> *Extra detail...*
> The quotation above from Lord Bingham includes reference to 'remains associated' as well as becoming associated. The potential for prior fault in these circumstances has not been well litigated, but is designed to cover cases where D joins what appears to be a non-criminal organisation, discovers that it is criminal and/or violent, but does not take an opportunity to leave. Care must be taken, however, to distinguish between cases where D has a genuine opportunity to leave (such that her choice to stay represents prior fault), and those for whom leaving the group is not a realistic or safe option (eg children brought up within a terrorist organisation) where D's decision to remain in the group might not represent prior fault.[69]

---

[64] Theft Act 1968, s10. See **9.4.3**.

[65] At [38].

[66] Hale's approach would only deny duress where D subjectively foresaw that she might be threatened to commit crimes.

[67] John Smith, 'Comment on *Heath*' [2000] Crim LR 109. Criticising objective foresight of *any* coercion: 'It is one thing...to be aware that you are likely to be beaten up if you do not pay your debts, it is another to be aware that you may be required under threat of violence to commit other, though unspecified, crimes, if you do not.'

[68] [2008] EWCA Crim 716.

[69] This issue has arisen in the context of trafficked women: *Ajayi* [2010] EWCA Crim 471.

14.3.2 X's threat and demand

When considering the threat and demand from X, three main questions should be considered: (a) how serious must the threat be; (b) who has made the threat, and who it is directed at; and (c) how detailed must the demand be?

14.3.2.1 How serious must the threat be?

It is generally accepted that X's threat must be of death or serious personal injury,[70] as confirmed by the House of Lords in *Hasan*.[71] In this manner, the gravity of X's threat works as an important threshold for the applicability of the defence. Any threat other than that of death or serious injury, even if it is vastly more serious than the offence X is demanding of D, will not qualify. For example, X threatens D that unless she commits a minor theft of V's property, she will face the much greater theft or damage of her own property. Where D succumbs to the threat and takes V's property, even if a reasonable person in D's position would have done likewise, D will have no defence of duress.[72] Duress is not a 'balance of evils' defence. In circumstances of this kind, where D commits a minor offence in fear of greater harm that does not threaten life or serious injury, D will have to appeal to the defence of necessity, discussed later.[73]

Threats of death are straightforward, but there remains some uncertainty about what constitutes a threat of serious harm. For example, a threat to cause non-psychiatric GBH will always be sufficient, although it is unlikely that a threat to cause ABH will be as, for example, where X threatens to punch D[74] unless D commits a crime. It has also been held (*obiter*) that a threat to rape D will be sufficient to meet the gravity threshold.[75] There is more uncertainty about whether a threat to cause serious psychiatric injury will be sufficient as, for example, a threat to leave D a nervous wreck;[76] however, as such harm is now recognised as being capable of constituting GBH for offences against the person,[77] the same approach may well be followed for duress.

> *Extra detail...*
>
> Although duress is not a balance of evils defence, there is some authority to suggest that where X demands that D commit a particularly serious offence, that the gravity of the threat must be even higher (ie of life-threatening harm, or even of death only).[78] The Law Commission has taken a similar approach with their recommendations for duress as a defence to murder, saying that it should only apply where D is threatened with death or 'life-threatening injury'.[79]

A problem can arise where D *believes* that she is being threatened with death or serious injury, but in fact she is not. For example, where X says she will 'do D over' unless D

---

[70] *Radford* [2004] EWCA Crim 2878.
[71] [2005] UKHL 22.
[72] *Vinh van Dao* [2012] EWCA Crim 1717 (a threat of false imprisonment); *Singh* [1973] 1 WLR 1600 (a threat of blackmail); *M'Growther* (1746) Fost 13 (a threat to property).
[73] See **14.6**.
[74] *Aikens* [2003] EWCA Crim 1573.
[75] *Ashley* [2012] EWCA Crim 434.
[76] *Baker v Wilkins* [1997] Crim LR 497.
[77] *Ireland and Burstow* [1998] AC 147. See **7.4.1.3**.
[78] *M'Growther* (1746) Fost 13; *Purdy* (1946) 10 JCL 182; *Abbott* [1976] 3 All ER 152, 152.
[79] Law Commission, *Murder, Manslaughter and Infanticide* (No 304, 2006) para 6.76.

commits a certain crime, D may take this as a threat to her life, and therefore sufficient for duress, when in fact it is a threat to destroy D's property which is insufficient for duress. It is clear that duress is not restricted to situations where there are *in fact* threats of death or serious injury, as otherwise there would be no duress where X threatens D with an unloaded gun. It is enough that D reasonably believes that there is a threat of death or serious injury. But case law has been required to determine how and when the defence can be based upon D's mistaken beliefs. *Safi and others* provides a useful illustration.

Safi [2003] EWCA Crim 1809

D and others hijacked a plan in Afghanistan, eventually landing in England at Stansted. They claimed duress on the basis that they were fleeing death or serious injury from the Taliban in Afghanistan. D was charged with various offences including hijacking.[80]

- Crown Court: guilty of hijacking offences. The jury were directed that duress was only available where there was objective evidence of a threat, which on the facts there was not, and that D's beliefs in an imminent threat were insufficient.
- Court of Appeal: appeal allowed. There is no need for objective evidence of a threat, as long as D reasonably believed it existed.

Safi clarifies that duress can be founded upon a mistaken belief. Note, however, that an honest belief will not necessarily be sufficient: the court also held that D's belief must be *reasonable*: a reasonable person in D's position would also have believed that there was a real threat of death or serious injury.[81] Whether D's belief in the threat must be (objectively) reasonable as well as (subjectively) honest has not always been clear in the case law.[82] However, more recent case law has endorsed, expressly[83] or implicitly,[84] the objective approach in *Safi*, and so it is very likely that this represents the current law.

In requiring an objectively reasonable belief in the threat from X, the defence of duress is inconsistent with the public and private defence (discussed at **14.5**) where a subjectively honest belief will suffice. This may be explained on grounds that the defences apply in different circumstances, one as an excuse and the other as a justification.[85] However, the origins of the objective approach in duress were guided by the then objective approach employed for the public and private defence.[86] It is therefore at least arguable that a consistent approach favouring one alternative or the other should be preferred.[87]

Extra detail...
A related question has emerged asking whether the threat from X must be criminal in nature. With a threshold of death or serious injury, this question is rarely relevant to duress. However, in *Jones and*

---

[80] Aviation Security Act 1982, s1(1).

[81] At [25].

[82] eg a purely subjective approach is taken by the Court of Appeal in *M* [2003] EWCA Crim 1170.

[83] *Blake* [2004] EWCA Crim 1238, [18]; *Bronson* [2004] EWCA Crim 903, [23].

[84] *Hasan* [2005] UKHL 22.

[85] Lord Bingham expressly rejected the comparison between defences in *Hasan* [2005] UKHL 22.

[86] *Graham* [1982] 1 All ER 801.

[87] Alldridge, 'Developing the Defence of Duress' [1986] Crim LR 433; Wilson, 'The Structure of Defences' [2005] Crim LR 108, 115–116.

others,[88] D raised the defence of duress of circumstance against charges of criminal damage by cutting the fence at an RAF base, claiming that his actions were to prevent the UK government waging an illegal war and killing people in Iraq. The Court of Appeal avoided engaging with the question of whether the war was illegal by holding that the defence of duress could only apply to threats of death or serious injury that amounted to 'domestic' crimes, which the war was not. This was a convenient approach for the court, but has been cogently criticised and should be seen as isolated to its facts.[89] As we will discuss later, in the context of duress of circumstance in particular, many threats will not be criminal in nature, such as an approaching tidal wave, and the courts are unlikely to follow *Jones* in requiring them to be.

14.3.2.2 Who must the threat be from, and against whom must the threat be made?

The paradigm example of duress involves X threatening D with death or serious injury unless she commits a particular offence. Cases have emerged, however, to test this paradigm.

What if, for example, the threats do not come from another person but come from D herself in the form of suicidal thoughts? This was discussed in *Roger and Rose*.

> **Roger and Rose** [1998] 1 Cr App R 143
>
> D broke out of prison following news that the tariff period (jail time) of his life sentence had been substantially increased. It was accepted that D did this because he was depressed and suicidal, and believed that he would have committed suicide if he did not escape. D was charged with breaking prison.
>
> - Crown Court: guilty of breaking prison. Duress was not open to D because the threat was not external from himself.
> - Court of Appeal: conviction upheld on appeal.

The Court of Appeal stated that to allow a defence of duress in these circumstances 'could amount to a licence to commit crime dependant on the personal characteristics and vulnerabilities of the defendant.' The case is useful, therefore, both as a clarification that the threat must come from another person, and to help to understand duress as a defence which provides a concession to *human* frailty as opposed to *individual* frailty.

The next question asks who the threat must be aimed at: for example, what if X threatens to kill D's child unless D commits an offence? Although X's threat will invariably be aimed at D herself, the same principles are engaged where D is compelled to offend in order to protect another against a threat of death or serious injury. In light of this, case law has progressively opened up the cases in which D can plead the defence based on her perception of threats of death or serious injury to others. In *Hurley and Murray* an Australian court allowed duress to apply where X's threats related to D's de facto wife;[90] in *Wright*, threats against D's boyfriend sufficed;[91] in *Conway*, threats against D's car

---

[88] [2004] EWCA Crim 1981. Affirmed in the House of Lords on other grounds [2006] UKHL 16.
[89] Ormerod, Commentary [2005] Crim LR 122.
[90] [1967] VR 526.
[91] [2000] Crim LR 510.

passenger were enough;[92] and so on. There is some suggestion in *Hasan* that this class of people, other than the defendant, may be limited to 'immediate family or someone close to [D] or for whom [D] is responsible'.[93] But if this is right, it must surely be interpreted liberally. If X, a bank robber, puts a gun to a customer's (Z's) head and instructs the bank manager (D) to open the safe, D may not have any personal connection with Z, but the fact and circumstances of the threat will surely be enough to make D feel 'responsible' for Z; and it would be very harsh to deny D the defence on the basis that she was not sufficiently attached to Z. If this is correct, as *dicta* from other cases suggest,[94] and as the Law Commission has recommended,[95] then the class of people who the threat might be aimed at has no limits at all.

> **Extra detail...**
> It is even possible for the person threatening D and the target of that threat to be the same person. This was so in *Martin*,[96] where D's wife threatened to take her own life unless D drove whilst disqualified in order to take their son to work.[97]

14.3.2.3 Does X's demand have to specify a particular offence?

Paradigm cases will involve X demanding that D commits a particular offence, for example 'open the safe or else', but this will not always be the case. Sometimes it will become clear to D that she must commit a particular offence to avoid a threat, but this may not have been communicated from X: for example, 'have the money by tomorrow or else'. Where, as in our example, X does not specify a crime, it is unlikely that D will be able to rely on duress by threats although she may be able to rely on duress by circumstances[98]. This was discussed in *Cole*.

> **Cole** [1994] Crim LR 582
>
> D robbed two building societies in order to repay a debt. The money lenders had hit D with a baseball bat and threatened him and his family unless he repaid the money, although they did not specify what he should do to get it. D was charged with robbery.[99]
>
> - Crown Court: guilty of robbery.
> - Court of Appeal: conviction upheld on appeal. Duress did not apply because: (a) D's offence was not specified by the lenders; and (b) there was a lack of immediacy between the threat and D's offence.[100]

---

[92] [1989] QB 290.

[93] [2005] UKHL 22, [21].

[94] *Shayler* [2001] 1 WLR 2206, where the Lord Chief Justice approves a statement to this effect from *Hussain*, [49].

[95] Law Commission, *Defences of General Application* (No 83, 1977) para 2.46.

[96] [1989] 1 All ER 652.

[97] The court discussed this as a duress by circumstances case, but given that there were explicit threats involved it is better analysed as one of duress by threats.

[98] See **14.4**.

[99] Theft Act 1968, s8(1). See **9.3**.

[100] We discuss this element of duress at **14.3.3.2**.

The line taken in *Cole* is a little too restrictive, suggesting that duress by threats will only apply where a single crime is clearly demanded. This line has been softened in *Ali*.

Ali [1995] Crim LR 303

D, a heroin addict, robbed a building society. D claimed that his dealer (X) had threatened him about unpaid debts, provided him with a gun, and told him to get the money from a bank or building society. D was charged with robbery.[101]

- Crown Court: guilty of robbery.
- Court of Appeal: conviction upheld on appeal. Duress did not apply because of D's prior fault in forming a relationship with X.[102] *Obiter*: the level of specificity as to the crime to be committed was sufficient for duress.

Following *Cole* and *Ali* it is clear that duress by threats requires X to have provided some indication of the type of crime that D must commit, but precise details of that crime (eg time, place, etc) are not required. Where D's defence fails on this element, the defence of duress by circumstances should be considered (see **14.4**).

14.3.3 D's response to the threat

When analysing D's response to the threat and demand, three main questions should be considered: (a) must the threat and demand have caused D's offence; (b) what if D could have avoided committing the offence; and (c) what if a reasonable person would not have acted as D did?

14.3.3.1 Must the threat and demand have caused D's offence?

The simple answer to this, unsurprisingly, is 'yes': duress only provides a defence where D's offence was compelled and therefore factually caused by X's threats and demands. If D would have done the same thing in the absence of X's threat then the defence will not apply.[103]

Problems can emerge, however, where D has several reasons for committing the offence, and only one of these constitutes a threat qualifying within the duress threshold. This was the case in *Valderrama-Vega*.

Valderrama-Vega [1985] Crim LR 220

D was involved in trafficking drugs. He claimed that he did so because of: (a) threats of serious harm from a mafia-type organisation; (b) because of financial difficulties; and (c) because of threats to expose his homosexuality. D was charged with drug trafficking offences.

- Crown Court: guilty of drug trafficking. The jury were directed that duress could only apply where D acted 'solely' due to the threats of serious injury.

---

101 Theft Act 1968, s8(1). See **9.3**.
102 We discuss this element of duress at **14.3.1.2**.
103 *DPP v Bell* [1992] Crim LR 176: in terror, D drove over the alcohol limit. D was planning to drink drive before the threat, but as he may have been talked out of it by his passengers, it was accepted that the threat was the cause.

- Court of Appeal: conviction upheld on appeal. However, the court clarified that the 'sole' motive test was wrong. The threats of serious injury had to be a sufficient cause, such that D would not have offended without them, but they need not be the sole cause.

The approach of the court is sensible, and straightforward. Duress will only apply where the qualifying threat caused D to offend. There may have been other causes, but these are irrelevant and should be discounted.

14.3.3.2 What if D could have avoided offending?

Related to the requirement of causation, is that D must have committed the offence because she had no other option to escape before the threat would be carried out. This is often referred to as a requirement of 'imminency', because the longer the time between X's threat and D's offence, the more opportunity D is likely to have had to escape the threat without offending by, for example, going to the police. Again, the interpretation of this principle in recent years has been to narrow the defence.

Historically, courts were willing to interpret this requirement quite generously for D. For example, in *Abdul-Hussain*[104] the Court of Appeal allowed the appeal of D who had hijacked a plane and come to England to escape deportation and likely execution in Iraq. Although the execution was not going to happen in the 'immediate' future,[105] the threat of execution was the 'imminent' cause of D's offence, and this was sufficient. The court illustrated their approach with a useful and convincing hypothetical:

If Anne Frank had stolen a car to escape from Amsterdam and been charged with theft, the tenets of English law would not, in our judgment, have denied her a defence of duress..., on the ground that she should have waited for the Gestapo's knock on the door.[106]

A similar approach was adopted in *Hudson and Taylor*.

> **Hudson and Taylor** [1971] 2 All ER 244
>
> D and another, aged 17 and 19, admitted committing perjury by failing to testify as to the identity of the suspect of a wounding at trial, leading to his acquittal. D claimed that she lied because she was threatened with being 'cut up' if she identified the suspect, and one of those threatening her was in the public gallery when she gave evidence. D was charged with perjury.
>
> - Crown Court: guilty of perjury. Duress did not apply because the threat was not immediate, D was safe in the court and so the threat could not have been carried out there and then.
> - Court of Appeal: appeal allowed. Although the harm threatened could not have been carried out immediately, the threat was still imminent and was the operative cause of D's offence. Duress was also not undermined by D's failure to go to the police before the trial because she believed the police could not provide adequate protection.

---

[104] [1999] Crim LR 570.
[105] This is why duress was rejected at trial.
[106] Here, again, the court is focusing on the imminence of the threat rather than the immediacy of the threatened harm.

The test as applied in these cases simply required D to have no effective means of escape. The threatened harm may not be immediate, but as long as it is imminent and operative at the time D offends, the defence will be allowed. There is much to be said for this approach. Just because the threatened harm is not immediate, this does not mean that a reasonable person in D's position would not have acted as D did: there is still a need to protect D by providing a concession to human frailty.

In more recent times, the courts have read this element narrowly. Serious doubt must now been placed on these judgments because of statements (*obiter*) in *Hasan*.[107] In this case, Lord Bingham referred to *Hudson* as having the 'unfortunate effect of weakening' the immediacy requirement, referred to as a 'cardinal feature' of duress.[108] The likelihood, therefore, is that this element will be applied more strictly in the future.[109]

14.3.3.3 What if a reasonable person would not have acted as D did?

The final element of duress applies a further objective standard; requiring that D should display a reasonable fortitude in resisting the threat and demand from X. For example, if an adult, D, is threatened with serious harm from an infant unless she commits an offence, this threat may satisfy the elements discussed previously but it is likely that D will be expected to resist the threat. Thus, where D commits the offence in these circumstances, duress will not apply. The threat may be real, but a reasonable person would not have had their will overborne by it.[110]

The objective reasonable fortitude test has been consistently highlighted in the case law,[111] and is usefully illustrated in *Graham*.

🔲   *Graham* [1982] 1 All ER 801

D lived in 'a bizarre ménage a trois' with his wife (V) and homosexual partner (X). D suffered from anxiety and took valium, making him more susceptible to bullying. X had been violent to both D and V in the past. Following a previous attack, X and D tricked V into returning home, X put a flex around V's neck and instructed D to pull. D did so in fear of X, and V died. D was charged with murder.[112] (*Note: at this time duress could be a defence to murder.*)

- Crown Court: guilty of murder.

- Court of Appeal: conviction upheld on appeal.

- House of Lords: appeal dismissed. The test for duress asks if a reasonable and sober person would have acted as D did; the fact that D's steadfastness was weakened by alcohol and valium is therefore irrelevant.

The objective nature of the test is another reflection of duress as a concession to human frailty as opposed to individual frailty. The question whether D's will was overborne is half the story; the defence is only available if a reasonable person in D's position would also have had their will overborne.

---

[107] [2005] UKHL 22.
[108] At [25]–[27].
[109] *Batchelor* [2013] EWCA Crim 2638, [15]: echoing Lord Bingham's criticism of *Hudson*, and support for stricter application of the immediacy requirement.
[110] Smith, 'Duress and Steadfastness: In Pursuit of the Unintelligible' [1999] Crim LR 363.
[111] *Howe* [1987] 1 All ER 771.
[112] **Chapter 5**.

A strictly objective test of steadfastness, however, can result in unfairness. Although duress is not a concession to *individual* frailty, there are certain general characteristics, such as age, that will affect D's ability to resist threats and demands. Interestingly, in contrast to the narrowing of other elements of duress, the courts have responded to this concern by gradually liberalising the range of D's characteristics that can be taken into account when applying the reasonable steadfastness test. This is discussed in *Bowen*.

> **Bowen** [1996] 2 Cr App R 157
>
> D obtained various electrical goods on credit by deception, with no way of making repayment. D claimed to be acting under duress, having been threatened to obtain the goods by two other men. Expert evidence showed that D had an IQ of 68, putting him in the bottom 2 per cent of the population, and likely to be extremely suggestible. D was charged with obtaining services by deception.[113]
>
> - Crown Court: guilty of obtaining services by deception. Duress steadfastness test based on a reasonable person of D's age and sex.
> - Court of Appeal: conviction upheld on appeal. Characteristics that affect D's ability to resist a threat and demand beyond age and sex may be relevant, but this does not include D's IQ.

The characteristics recognised in *Bowen* as potentially relevant include D's age and sex, pregnancy, serious physical disability, and recognised mental illness or psychiatric condition.[114] Where these are found with D, the test will be whether a reasonable and sober person *sharing these characteristics* might have also had their will overborne. In this way, although *Bowen* can be criticised for excluding the relevance of D's low IQ,[115] it has had a highly liberalising impact on this element of duress.

> *Point to remember...*
> Despite the liberalising of this element, the restrictive objectivity of other elements means that duress remains a very narrow defence. The case of *GAC* provides a useful example.[116] In this case D pleaded duress to a charge of importing drugs, having been threatened by her abusive partner (X). It was accepted that D's characteristics could be taken into account, including the fact that she was suffering from battered women syndrome. However, her defence failed on several other grounds, including the fact that the abuse she was suffering did not amount to a threat of death or serious injury.[117]

14.4 Duress by circumstances

Duress by circumstances is essentially an extension of duress by threats. It has been recognised at common law to provide a defence where there is no direct threat and/or demand from another party, but the surrounding circumstances create an equivalent

---

[113] Now obtaining services dishonestly, Fraud Act 2006, s11. See **10.5**.
[114] Buchanan and Virgo, 'Duress and Mental Abnormality' [1999] Crim LR 517.
[115] Although D's low IQ would not make him less resistant to threats, it will make him less able to identify ways of escaping them. Thus, the threat may appear more grave.
[116] [2013] EWCA Crim 1472.
[117] Loveless, 'Domestic Violence, Coercion and Duress' [2010] Crim LR 93.

overbearing of D's will. For example, if D sees a tidal wave crashing towards her on the shore, the wave does not tell her to break into a car and escape or she will be killed, but it may be very obvious that this is her choice.

> **Don't be confused...**
> Duress by circumstances has caused considerable confusion for the courts, mainly in terms of its place alongside other defences such as duress by threats and necessity. As a result, it has been inconsistently labelled as 'necessity' or 'necessity of circumstances', etc. Although, as we see later, this defence is similar to the necessity defence, it is better presented as a separate defence. This is because whereas necessity is hopelessly ambiguous in its application, duress by circumstances is relatively well defined. Therefore, even if we see it as a sub category of necessity, where duress by circumstances can be applied it provides a welcome opportunity to avoid the necessity defence.[118]

Duress by circumstances was first recognised in *Willer.*

> **Willer** (1986) 83 Cr App R 225
>
> D drove his car slowly onto a pavement in order to escape from a gang of youths who were intent on doing serious injury to him and his passenger. D was charged with reckless driving, and tried to raise the defence of necessity.
>
> • Crown Court: guilty of reckless driving. Necessity does not apply.
> • Court of Appeal: appeal allowed. Necessity is irrelevant, but D does have a defence of duress.

In recognising a defence of duress, the Court of Appeal did not distinguish it as a new form of duress by circumstances. However, this was the necessary implication: the youths were not shouting 'drive on the pavement or else', the threat and demand was not specific, they were circumstantial. This was later confirmed, and to some extent clarified, in *Conway,*[119] where D drove dangerously to escape what he believed were two assailants intent on killing his passenger.[120] It was in this case that the language of duress by circumstances (or 'duress of circumstances') began to be used.

The elements of duress by circumstances are set out in **Table 14.3.**

Table 14.3 Duress by circumstances

A) Exclusions: duress is not a defence to murder, attempted murder, and certain treason offences, and will not apply in circumstances of prior fault;
B) Circumstantial threat and demand: D must have reasonably believed that the circumstances posed a threat of death or serious injury which compelled her to commit the offence; and
C) D's response: D must have shown reasonable steadfastness in response to the threat, only committing the offence because her will was overborne

---

[118] Gardner, 'Necessity's Newest Invention' (1991) 11 OJLS 125.
[119] [1989] QB 290.
[120] They were in fact plain-clothes police officers, wishing to interview his passenger.

14.4.1 Relationship between duress by threats and duress by circumstances

When compared to other general defences, duress by circumstances is still very new to the law. However, because of its close relationship with duress by threats, it has been able to establish itself by mirroring most of the elements of that defence. This has led to some confusion in cases such as *Martin*,[121] where D's wife's threats to commit suicide unless he committed an offence were treated as duress by circumstances rather than the more appropriate defence of duress by threats. However, because of the similarities between the defences, both in substance and rationale, such confusions are not overly problematic.

The one area of difference, set out in **Table 14.3** and discussed later, relates to the second element of the defence. The same exclusions apply to duress by circumstances as for duress by threats, and the same reasonable steadfastness must be shown. However, the requirement of a threat and demand does not need to be specific and does not need to come from an individual.

14.4.2 The elements of duress by circumstances

Most of the elements of duress by circumstances mirror those for duress by threats, and so there is no need to repeat that discussion here. However, it is useful to highlight a few key points to illustrate how those elements apply in the context of duress by circumstances.

14.4.2.1 Exclusions

The same exclusions apply for duress by circumstances as apply to duress by threats.[122] Therefore, duress by circumstances is no defence to murder, attempted murder, and certain treason offences. Also, although there is no case on point, it is likely that duress by circumstances will be excluded where the circumstances were brought about by prior fault. Taking the example of D who breaks into a car to escape a tidal wave, she may therefore lose the defence if she is a storm chaser who has travelled to the coast to witness the devastation. This would be akin to a form of voluntary association in duress by threats.

14.4.2.2 Circumstantial threat and demand

This element represents the major difference between duress by threats and duress by circumstances. However, it also retains important similarities.[123]

A) **Differences from duress by threats:** Unlike duress by threats, there is no requirement to show that the threat and demand came from a person.[124] There is also no need to show that a specific crime was demanded.[125] Both of these requirements have been applied restrictively within the context of duress by threats, and so duress by circumstances provides a useful alternative.

---

[121] [1989] 1 All ER 652.
[122] See **14.3.1**.
[123] See **14.3.2**.
[124] See **14.3.2.2**.
[125] See **14.3.2.3**.

B) **Similarities with duress by threats:** Despite the differences, this element still retains two important and restrictive similarities. First, the threat must still be one of death or serious injury:[126] duress by circumstances retains this high threshold from duress by threats and is not a simple balance of evils defence. Where the circumstances threatening D fall below this threshold, this defence will not apply and D will have to appeal to the defence of necessity. Secondly, although the threat does not need to come from another person, it must still be from a person other than D.[127] Thus, the principle from *Roger and Rose* applies.[128] The restrictive application of these requirements in the context of duress by circumstances is illustrated in *Quayle*.[129]

Quayle [2005] EWCA Crim 1415

Combined cases involving possession, importation, and/or supply of cannabis for the purposes of relieving the pain of those suffering a variety of conditions. In each case, the defences of necessity and/or duress of circumstance were raised.

- Crown Court: guilty of drug offences in all but one of the cases, and rejecting D's defence. One case allowed the defence to go to the jury and D was acquitted.

- Court of Appeal: convictions upheld on appeal, and the AG's Reference (concerning the acquitted D) was answered to the effect that the defence should not have been allowed to run.

Duress by circumstances was rejected in the *Quayle* appeals for two main reasons. First, the threat, in that case the additional pain resulting from not using cannabis, was not sufficient to constitute a threat of death or serious injury. Secondly, where the drug offences related to personal use, the threat was purely internal to D and was therefore disqualified by the principle in *Roger and Rose*.

14.4.2.3 D's response to the perceived threats

The requirements are the same here as those for duress by threats.[130] D's offending must have been caused by the threats and demands of X; D must have made reasonable efforts to avoid offending; and D must have demonstrated reasonable fortitude in resisting X's threats.

One point within this, which is particularly tricky for duress by circumstances, is identifying the beginning and end of D's compelled conduct. Unlike duress by threats, where there is another party directing what D should do and when, duress by circumstances can be rather more fluid and uncertain. For example, where an intoxicated D is compelled to drive in order to escape a tidal wave or gang of youths, how far can D drive with an operative defence of duress by circumstances? A number of cases have encountered this issue, and the general approach has been to allow the defence to operate until D is clear of the danger, such that if D continues to drive she is now committing an offence (driving over the proscribed alcohol limit) without a defence.[131]

---

[126] See **14.3.2.1**.
[127] See **14.3.2.2**.
[128] [1998] 1 Cr App R 143.
[129] Watson, 'Cannabis and the Defence of Necessity' (1998) 149 NLJ 1260.
[130] See **14.3.3**.
[131] *DPP v Bell* [1992] Crim LR 176; *DPP v Jones* [1990] RTR 34; *DPP v Mullally* [2006] EWHC 3448 (Admin).

14.5 Public and private defence

The public and private defence, which is commonly referred to as self-defence,[132] provides a complete defence to any charge where D uses force to protect her public or private interests.[133] Two preliminary questions are immediately apparent: (a) what type of force can the defence justify; and (b) what are public and private interests.

As to the first, the public and private defence will only provide a defence where D's offence involved the use of force. Thus, it is most commonly applied as a defence to murder, false imprisonment, and the offences against the person more generally. For example, D appeals to the public and private defence where she hits V, causing ABH, in order to prevent V stabbing her with a knife. However, the defence is not limited to offences within certain categories, and each case will be judged on its own facts to identify whether D has used force when committing the offence. For example, although dangerous driving will not always involve force, *Renouf* established that where the particular case did involve force, the public and private defence could apply.[134] This seems logical, but can lead to some rather strange results. In *Blake v DPP*,[135] for example, D was charged with criminal damage having written in felt pen on a concrete pillar outside the Houses of Parliament in protest against the Iraq war. Denying the public and private defence, the court held that D's act was 'insufficient to amount to the use of force', suggesting that D would have had more chance of using the defence if he had caused greater damage.[136]

> *Extra detail...*
> Although the public and private defence provides a justification for the use of force in certain circumstances, there is some uncertainty over whether it can also provide a defence to preparatory acts. For example, if D knows that V is going to try and kill her in a week's time, can D purchase a gun without a licence in self-defence? Or more proximately, if D is caught in a shoot-out and picks up a discarded gun for protection, can she claim self-defence for this brief moment of unlawful possession? The law would speak with a strange moral voice if it said that D was justified in these cases to use the gun to kill or injure V in defence, but has no defence to her possession of the gun. With this in mind, courts have been willing to extend the public and private defence to cover certain preparatory acts of this kind, particularly if they are proximate to or even simultaneous with the use of force.[137] To avoid confusing the limits of the public and private defence further, it is contended that such preparatory acts are more appropriately analysed using duress of circumstance.

The second preliminary question asks what we mean by public and private interests: to come within the defence, what must D be using force to achieve? The answer requires

---

[132] The term 'self-defence' is common, but misleading. The public and private defence is not limited to the use of force to protect oneself.

[133] See generally Leverick, *Killing in Self-Defence* (2006); Sangero, *Self Defence in Criminal Law* (2006).

[134] [1986] 2 All ER 449. A case of reckless driving, now abolished as an offence. Cf the dangerous driving case of *Bailey* [2013] EWCA Crim 378 where there was no force used, and the defence could not apply.

[135] [1993] Crim LR 586.

[136] The absurdity of this was noted by Brooke LJ in *Bayer v DPP* [2003] EWHC 2567 (Admin).

[137] *AG's Reference (No 2 of 1983)* [1984] QB 456 (making and storing petrol bombs to protect shop); *McAuley* [2009] EWCA Crim 2130 (carrying a knife for self-protection).

recognition that the public and private defence is actually two defences, brought together because of substantial overlap and the common rules that apply to both.

- **Private defence:** The private defence has developed at common law, and provides a defence where D uses force to protect herself or another from physical harm,[138] or in the protection of property.[139]
- **Public defence:** The public defence is provided by section 3 of the Criminal Law Act 1967, and provides a defence where D uses force to prevent a crime[140] or in effecting or assisting a lawful arrest.

There will be cases where only one of the two applies. For example, if D uses force to protect herself from V, a 9-year-old child under the age of criminal responsibility, she may be able to rely on the private defence, but the public defence will not apply because V cannot commit a crime. Equally, where D uses force to assist police making an arrest D qualifies under the public defence, but it is quite possible that D does so despite facing no personal threat and would therefore not qualify for the private defence. However, in the majority of cases, both defences will apply simultaneously. For example, where D uses force to protect Z from attack by V, where V would commit an offence in attacking Z, D acts both to protect Z and to prevent V's crime.[141]

As a result of their common denominator—that each applies only where D uses force—and as a result of the substantial overlap between public and private interests, these defences are now best analysed as a single public and private defence. The integration of the two has been ongoing for many years within the common law, and has now been codified within section 76 of the Criminal Justice and Immigration Act 2008 (CJIA) as amended.

(1) This section applies where in proceedings for an offence—

    (a) an issue arises as to whether a person charged with the offence ('D') is entitled to rely on a defence within subsection (2), and

    (b) the question arises whether the degree of force used by D against a person ('V') was reasonable in the circumstances.

(2) The defences are—

    (a) the common law defence of self-defence; and

    (b) the defences provided by section 3(1) of the Criminal Law Act 1967...

The rules in this section, which we explore later, provide a partial restatement and codification of the common law; they do not provide for reform.[142]

The two core elements of the public and private defence, usefully characterised as trigger and response, are set out in **Table 14.4**.

---

[138] *Duffy* [1967] 1 QB 63.

[139] Where D damages property to protect other property, this is governed by the Criminal Damage Act 1971, s5(2)(b) (see **9.7.3.2**). However, the public and private defence is still necessary where D uses other force to protect property (eg against the person).

[140] This only applies to the prevention of crimes in English law (as opposed to crimes in other jurisdictions or international crimes): *Jones* [2005] Crim LR 122.

[141] *Clegg* [1995] 1 All ER 334, 343.

[142] CJIA 2008, s76(9); *Keane* [2010] EWCA Crim 2514.

Table 14.4 Public and private defence

A) Trigger: D must have believed (subjective) that force was immediately required in order to protect her public or private interests; and

B) Response: the amount of force used by D must have been reasonable (objective) on the facts as D believed them to be.

After D has raised the defence, the legal burden is then on the prosecution to prove beyond reasonable doubt that the elements of the defence are not satisfied.[143]

14.5.1 Trigger: the necessity for force

The trigger element within the public and private defence is essentially a threshold question: was it necessary to use *any* force against V on the facts as D believed them to exist? Questions concerning the *degree* of force used should be avoided until the second element. For example, if D sees V scratching her car and reacts by shooting V, she is likely to satisfy the first element since D may well have believed it was necessary to use *some* defensive force, but fail the second element: shooting V is an unreasonably excessive response.

The trigger element is almost entirely subjective: unlike duress,[144] we do not ask whether a reasonable person in D's position would have believed that force was necessary; we ask simply whether it was necessary on the facts as D believed them to be. Thus, this element can be satisfied even where D was wrong, and even where her mistake was unreasonable. This approach has raised concerns in relation to ECHR compatibility, particularly where D has killed V.[145] However, since being established in *Gladstone Williams*, it has been consistently applied in subsequent cases,[146] and is now codified in section 76(4)(b) of the CJIA.

Gladstone Williams (1984) 78 Cr App R 276

V witnessed X rob a woman in the street. V caught X and held him down, knocking X to the ground on a second occasion when X attempted to get away. D witnessed the second altercation, and thought V was assaulting X. D then punched V in the face in an attempt to defend X. D was charged with assault occasioning actual bodily harm.[147]

- Crown Court: guilty of assault occasioning actual bodily harm. The judge directed that, for self-defence, D must have honestly, and on *reasonable grounds*, believed that force was necessary.
- Court of Appeal: appeal allowed. The necessity element must be based on an honest belief, but there is no requirement of reasonable grounds.

The essential question, then, is not whether D's belief in the necessity of force was reasonable, but whether it was honest. The reasonableness of D's belief will provide useful

---

[143] *O'Brian* [2004] EWCA Crim 2900.
[144] See **14.3.2.1**.
[145] We discuss this in the reform section at **14.7**.
[146] *Beckford v R* [1988] AC 130 (Privy Council).
[147] Offences Against the Person Act 1861, s47. See **7.4**.

evidence in this regard, but it is not determinative.[148] This is the case whether D is defending against force to the person as in *Gladstone Williams*, property,[149] or in the context of crime prevention or criminal apprehension.[150]

The trigger element is not, however, purely subjective. Two objective considerations have been introduced.

A) **Voluntary intoxication:** D may not rely on mistakes (however honest) that have been caused by voluntary intoxication. For example, if D takes a hallucinogenic drug which causes her to mistakenly believe that she is being attacked, her use of defensive force will not be considered 'necessary'. We discussed this at **13.2.5** in the context of the intoxication rules, and the case of *Hatton*.[151] It has also been confirmed, and codified, within section 76(5) of the CJIA.

B) **Mental defects:** More controversially, D may also not rely on mistakes, however honest, that have been caused by mental defect or disorder. For example, in the *Martin* case,[152] D was not able to rely on psychiatric evidence that he perceived threats to be greater than a normal person would; and in *Oye*,[153] D was not able to rely on his insane delusion that he was being attacked by evil spirits. Notably, in each case this exclusion was analysed under the second element of the defence (reasonable force) rather than the first (necessary force).[154] However, it can alternatively be analysed, as it is here, under the first element. This is because the purpose of the first element of the public and private defence is to establish the facts upon which we can question the reasonableness of D's response. Therefore, if D's insane delusion (for example) is to be excluded from the reasonableness question in the second element, little is gained by allowing it to apply within the first element. In effect, there is no difference between this exclusion and that based on voluntary intoxication.

The first element, the trigger, is therefore established from the facts as D honestly believed them to be. Whether D's belief was mistaken or unreasonable is irrelevant, unless that mistake was caused by voluntary intoxication or mental defect or disorder. Saying that the trigger element is predominantly subjective, however, does not tell us how to *assess* D's subjective belief. Although the necessity question is based on subjective belief, this does not mean that we simply ask D whether she thought force was necessary. Rather, we take the facts as she subjectively believed them, and our question is then whether we accept that *any* force was necessary. In answering this question, several sub-questions have emerged within the case law.

---

[148] *Dewar v DPP* [2010] EWHC 1050 (Admin): D's recognition that his use of force was not necessary *after* the event, does not undermine his defence (based on his beliefs at the time of the event).

[149] *Faraj* [2007] EWCA Crim 1033: D forcefully detained a gas repair man (V), believing he was a burglar.

[150] *Morris* [2013] EWCA Crim 436: D injured V with his taxi, wrongly believing that V was trying to make off without payment.

[151] [2005] EWCA Crim 2951.

[152] [2002] Crim LR 136.

[153] [2013] EWCA Crim 1725.

[154] *Oye* [2013] EWCA Crim 1725, [37]–[59].

14.5.1.1 Is it ever necessary to use force pre-emptively?

The answer here is 'yes'. Although the public and private defence will usually apply where D is responding to another's attack, this need not always be the case. In *Devlin v Armstrong*,[155] for example, the Court of Appeal in Northern Ireland held that the defence could apply where D uses force to 'ward off or prevent attack' as long as she honestly believed it was 'imminent'.[156] The imminence requirement has been interpreted narrowly, and is seen as crucial to ensure that the defence does not extend to cover aggressive, as opposed to defensive, force. However, it also has the effect of limiting the defence in the context of abused women who kill their abusers in pre-emptive, but not imminent, circumstances.[157]

14.5.1.2 Is it ever necessary to use force where D could have retreated?

There is no duty to retreat, even where D knows that staying in a certain location is likely to result in attack from V and the need for defensive force. Over recent years, courts have treated a willingness to retreat as evidence in D's favour, suggesting that the force D then used was necessary, but force may still be necessary even where D has chosen to remain.[158] This is now confirmed, and codified, in section 76(6A) of the CJIA.

14.5.1.3 Is it ever necessary to use force where D instigated V's attack?

This question engages with prior fault. For duress, D's voluntary association where coercion was *objectively* foreseeable undermined D's defence.[159] However, this very strict rule is not applied to the public and private defence, and it is clear that D may appeal to the defence even where she instigated the violence with V (ie it does not matter 'who started it').[160] The only exception to this is where D has *consciously* manipulated V into attacking her in order to retaliate in 'apparent' defence. In these circumstances, confirmed in *Rashford*,[161] D's force will not satisfy the necessity element.

14.5.1.4 Is it ever necessary to use force against innocent/lawful force?

It is generally not permissible to use force against lawful actions. In other words, it is not necessary for D to use force against another party who is acting in lawful self-defence, or against a police officer making a lawful arrest. However, this rule is not absolute. Where D is attacked by a child under 10 or someone who is insane, the attacker may not be committing an offence, but it still may be necessary to use some defensive force.[162] Equally, the defence may apply where D has made a mistake, and we have to assess the events on the basis of D's honest beliefs as, for example, where D believes that she is defending against an unlawful attack or preventing crime, where in fact V is acting lawfully.[163]

---

[155] [1971] NI 13.
[156] At 33.
[157] McColgan, 'In Defence of Battered Women Who Kill' (1993) 13 OJLS 508.
[158] *Bird* [1985] 2 All ER 513, 516; *Duffy v DPP* [2007] EWHC 3169 (Admin).
[159] See **14.3.1.2**.
[160] *Keane* [2010] EWCA Crim 2514.
[161] [2005] EWCA Crim 3377.
[162] *Bayer v DPP* [2003] EWHC 2567 (Admin).
[163] *Gladstone Williams* (1984) 78 Cr App R 276.

14.5.1.5 Is it ever necessary to use force where the justifying reasons are unknown to D?

With the trigger element based on D's subjective appreciation of the facts, an interesting problem emerges where D's force is in fact objectively justified. An example would be where D uses force on V but D was not aware that V was about to launch an attack on D. D's force was, as a matter of fact, necessary. Where D uses force in these circumstances, it has been held in *Dadson* that she will not be able to rely on the public and private defence.[165] If D had been aware of the justifying circumstances (eg that she was about to come under attack, that V was about to commit a crime, etc) then her use of force would be necessary; but the focus of this defence on D's subjective knowledge (the facts as she believes them to be) means that it cannot apply where such circumstances are unknown.

14.5.2 Response: a reasonable degree of force

Having established the trigger (ie the facts as D believed them to be), and having established that *some* force was necessary on those facts, the second element of the public and private defence focuses on the degree of force used by D. This is a jury question.[166] Where the degree of force used was *reasonable*, or *proportionate*,[167] even if it equated to more force than was threatened by V,[168] the defence will be satisfied and D will be acquitted. Where D's degree of force was unreasonable the defence will fail, subject to the exceptional case of the householder discussed later.

In order to identify 'reasonable force', the courts have adopted a middle ground between subjective and objective approaches when defining the defence.

- **Subjective:** A purely subjective approach, asking whether D believed the amount of force she used was reasonable, would be inappropriate. For example, D may honestly believe that it is reasonable to shoot V to prevent her scratching D's car, but this is not justified force.

- **Objective:** A purely objective approach, asking what degree of force would have been used by a reasonable person in D's circumstances, would be equally inappropriate. This is particularly true where D has made an honest mistake (eg believing that V is about to attack her). An approach to reasonable force that only takes account of the objective facts would always deny the defence in such cases: where V is not in fact threatening or involved in an offence, then no degree force is reasonable.

---

[164] [2000] 4 All ER 961.

[165] (1850) 2 Den 35. Funk, 'Justifying Justifications' (1990) 19 OJLS 630; Christopher, 'Unknowing Justification and the Logical Necessity of the *Dadson* Principle in Self-Defence' (1995) 15 OJLS 229.

[166] *AG's Reference (No 1 of 1975)* [1976] 2 All ER 937, 947.

[167] The terms 'reasonable' and 'proportionate' can be used interchangeably in this context.

[168] The public and private defence is not a balance of evils defence.

The current law combines these approaches by asking whether the degree of force D used was *objectively* reasonable based on the *subjective* facts as D believed them to be.[169] Thus, for example, where D mistakenly believes V is about to shoot her, and so responds by stabbing V, the question for the jury is whether D's force (stabbing) was objectively reasonable based on D's belief that she was about to be shot. As confirmed and codified within section 76(3)–(4) of the CJIA, this will be the case regardless of whether D's mistaken belief was reasonably or unreasonably held, as long as it was honestly held.

When applying this element, it is important to remember that we are focusing on the degree of *force* employed by D and not the degree of *harm* caused. For example, suppose V attempts to steal D's handbag in the street, and D reacts by pushing V away. It is likely, here, that D's force (the push) is both necessary and reasonable. However, what if V trips as a result of the push, hits her head on the pavement, and dies? The answer is, from the perspective of the public and private defence, that nothing has changed: our focus is on the reasonableness of the force (the push) and not the resulting harm (death). Thus, where D's force involves an obvious risk of causing death or serious harm as, for example, where D pushes V off a cliff, shoots V, etc, then this is likely to make D's force unreasonable.[170] However, just because D's reasonable use of force results in an unforeseen unreasonable degree of harm, this will not undermine D's defence.[171]

When assessing the objective reasonableness of D's degree of force, on the facts as she subjectively believed them to be, the jury must also take account of the circumstances surrounding the use of that force. Essentially, this involves a margin of appreciation for D; acknowledging that where she was in a pressured and stressful situation, she may not have been able to think entirely rationally about the level of force to be used. This rule has been expressed by the courts in various ways, including: 'it will be recognised that a person defending himself cannot weigh to a nicety the exact measure of his necessary defensive action';[172] 'one did not use jewellers' scales to measure reasonable force';[173] and so on. It has now also be confirmed, and codified, within section 76(7) of the CJIA.

Even acknowledging D's margin of appreciation, however, it should always be remembered that where the degree of force used by D is unreasonable (subject to the householder exception) the defence will fail. This was famously illustrated in the case of *Martin*.

Martin [2001] EWCA Crim 2245

D lived in a remote farmhouse in Norfolk. He was woken by two people trying to burgle his premises, disturbed them, and then shot them as they tried to escape. One was killed, and the other seriously injured. D was charged with murder and a serious offence against the person.[174]

- Crown Court: guilty of murder and wounding offence. The public and private defence was rejected by the jury.

---

[169] *Owino* [1996] 2 Cr App R 128; *Harvey* [2009] EWCA Crim 469.
[170] It will rarely, if ever, be reasonable to use deadly force to protect property.
[171] *Keane* [2010] EWCA Crim 2514; *Noye* [2011] EWCA Crim 650, [9] and [55].
[172] *Palmer* [1971] AC 814.
[173] *Reed v Wastie* [1972] Crim LR 221.
[174] For murder, see **Chapter 5**; for offences against the person, see **Chapter 7**.

> • Court of Appeal: appeal allowed, substituting murder for manslaughter. Public and private defence was not satisfied because of the excessive force used by D. However, new evidence provided the basis for a partial defence of diminished responsibility.

Martin is an important case for a number of reasons. First, it provides a useful example of the limits of the public and private defence: D's use of force was clearly necessary both to protect himself and his property and to prevent crime, but the force he used was excessive and so the defence failed. Secondly, it demonstrates the role that the partial defences can play where D's defensive force is excessive: in this case diminished responsibility.[175] And, thirdly, the case was also a catalyst for public, and ultimately political, concern about the operation of the defence in the context of householders who use force against unlawful intruders.

14.5.2.1 Householder cases

Following *Martin*, the public, fuelled by inaccurate media commentary, became concerned that householders were not adequately protected by the public and private defence where force is used against a trespasser. This issue became politicised, and despite the enactment of the CJIA clarifying the current law, there continued to be calls for a wider defence in these circumstances.[176] The result, contained within section 43 of the Crime and Courts Act 2013, has been the amendment of section 76 of the CJIA in the context of householders (non-trespassers) who use defensive force against trespassers.

> (5A) In a householder case, the degree of force used by D is not to be regarded as having been reasonable in the circumstances as D believed them to be if it was grossly disproportionate in those circumstances.

Householders, then, may employ 'disproportionate' force in defence of themselves and their property as long as that force is not 'grossly disproportionate'. How juries will draw a line between these descriptions, and whether the amendment will have any impact on the operation of the law, is unclear. What is most likely, it is contended, is that this terminology will simply become a further expression of the margin of appreciation already recognised within the public and private defence (discussed earlier). With so many areas of the criminal law in need of scrutiny and potential reform, the political focus and response to these cases and their public misunderstanding reflects poorly on our system of law reform.[177]

14.6 Necessity

The definition of the defence of necessity in English law remains an enigma, but it is clear that the criminal law needs such a defence. It is best understood as an imperfect

---

[175] Wake, 'Battered Women, Startled Householders and Psychological Self-Defence' (2013) 77 J Crim L 433.

[176] Skinner, 'Populist Politics and Shooting Burglars' [2005] Crim LR 275.

[177] Dobinson and Elliott, 'A Householder's Right to Kill or Injure an Intruder Under the Crime and Courts Act 2013: An Australian Comparison' (2014) 78 J Crim L 80.

safety net, a complete and general defence of last resort where no other defence is available but it is clear that liability would be inappropriate. In this way, the necessity defence represents an acceptance that within the infinite variety and complexity of human events, those crafting the criminal law will never be able to predict and account for every variation. Where unexpected facts lead to an inappropriate acquittal, this is to be regretted but tolerated. In such a case there is no opportunity for a broad overarching category of offences that should be applied to catch those who might otherwise avoid liability. That would be intolerable. In contrast, where unexpected facts could lead to inappropriate liability, the law rightly sacrifices principles of coherence in order to find an acquittal. The principal vehicle for this has become the defence of necessity.[178]

> **Extra detail...**
> Alongside necessity, other approaches have been developed to achieve the same outcome. Most notably, this has included the use of prosecutorial discretion simply to avoid bringing those who commit necessary crimes within the criminal system,[179] as well as the use of necessity in the guise of other defences or legal rules.[180] However, both of these approaches can be criticised,[181] and, arguably, the defence of necessity provides a preferable route.

The defence of necessity has had an interesting history: its existence has often been denied by courts and commentators, but then gratefully deployed in times of legal need.[182] Where it has been recognised and applied, it seems to operate on a simple balance of evils: if D's evil (ie the offence she commits) is less serious than the evil avoided by committing it, then she is entitled to the defence; we might even say she has done the right thing.[183]

The problem lies in setting limits on the defence. If we define necessity in greater detail, then we risk sacrificing its utility as a safety net that can apply to unexpected facts. However, if the only rule defining the offence is a balance of evils test, then the defence becomes potentially impossibly wide, allowing D to raise the defence whenever she believes she has acted for good reason. The reaction of the courts has been pragmatic, to resist further definition and restriction, but to apply the defence reluctantly, and always with its potential indeterminate dangers in mind. The words of Lord Denning and Edmund Davies LJ in *Southwark London Borough v Williams* provide a useful illustration of this, discussing the potential

---

178 Williams, 'Necessity' [1978] Crim LR 128.
179 Following the Zeebrugge disaster, eg, no charges were brought against the corporal who ordered a man to be forcefully detached from an escape ladder (the man was frozen with fear and cold, and was blocking the escape of others): Leverick, *Killing in Self-Defence* (2006) 6–11.
180 *Gillick* [1986] AC 112 provides a notable example, where the court applied flawed reasoning about medical judgement not being compatible with a guilty mind, in order to avoid liability where D (a doctor) prescribed the contraceptive pill to an underage girl. See **3.4.1.2**.
181 On prosecutorial discretion, see Ashworth, 'Prosecution, Police and Public: A Guide to Good Gatekeeping?' (1984) 23 Howard J Crim L 65.
182 Stephen went as far as to say that rules of necessity could never be laid down in advance: *A History of the Criminal Law*, vol 2 (1883) 108.
183 Where necessity is recognised, it is generally understood to operate as a justification as opposed to an excuse.

application of necessity where a homeless person steals food or enters another's premises for shelter:

> if hunger were once allowed to be an excuse for stealing, it would open a door through which all kinds of lawlessness and disorder would pass... If homelessness were once admitted as a defence to trespass, no one's house would be safe. Necessity would open a door which no man could shut...The reason for such circumspection is clear—necessity can very easily become simply a mask for anarchy.[184]

The problem with this approach to necessity, however, is that it sends a mixed and complicated message to the public; some might even say a contradictory message. And, in this way, it can provide false hope. In recent years we have seen the defence of necessity employed on multiple occasions in an effort to justify drug offences committed to relieve severe pain,[185] and in even more extreme cases to justify assisted suicide or euthanasia.[186] Such cases, of course, were never likely to succeed. Although a case can be made for both on a balance of evils test, the courts are extremely circumspect about fundamental shifts that bring into question legislative codes and decisions. Despite its potential width, the necessity defence is only likely to succeed where a case arises where its precedent can be contained; only where there is a genuine belief that its unique facts have been missed or uncatered for within the current law; only where it is exceptional.

Despite these problems, and despite judicial reluctance, the defence of necessity has been applied within a number of exceptional cases. It has been applied, for example, to justify detention of a person suffering from a mental disorder;[187] to justify the jettisoning of cargo from a ship to save the lives of those on board;[188] to justify the force-feeding of prisoners;[189] to justify procuring an abortion to save the mother;[190] to justify a police officer instructing cars to travel the wrong way on a one-way-street to allow ambulances access;[191] and so on. The circumstances of necessity are usefully illustrated, and discussed, in *F v West Berkshire Authority*.[192]

⬛ *F v West Berkshire Authority* [1989] 2 All ER 545

V, a 36-year-old patient in a psychiatric hospital, formed a sexual relationship with another patient. Medical evidence found it would be 'disastrous' from a psychiatric perspective if she became pregnant, but there were problems ensuring the use of ordinary contraception. In order to allow V to continue her relationship, V's mother, acting as her next friend, applied for a court declaration that the performance of a sterilisation operation without V's consent (she was unable to consent) would be lawful.

- Court: declaration granted.
- Court of Appeal: appeal dismissed.

---

[184] [1971] 2 All ER 175, 179–181.
[185] *Quayle* [2005] EWCA Crim 1415.
[186] *R (Nicklinson) v Ministry of Justice* [2014] UKSC 38; Stark, 'Necessity and *Nicklinson*' [2013] Crim LR 949; Ost, 'Euthanasia and the Defence of Necessity' [2005] Crim LR 255.
[187] *Bournewood Trust* [1998] 3 All ER 289.
[188] *Mouse's Case* (1608) 12 Co Rep 63.
[189] *Leigh v Gladstone* (1909) 26 TLR 139.
[190] *Bourne* [1939] 1 KB 687.
[191] *Johnson v Phillips* [1975] 3 All ER 682.
[192] Should now be read with the Mental Capacity Act 2005 in mind.

- House of Lords: appeal dismissed. The doctors' actions would be protected by the defence of necessity. Duress by circumstances is not available here because the 'threat' (ie pregnancy) does not meet the threshold of death or serious injury.

Interestingly, following many of these cases where it has been accepted that the courts were correct to apply a defence, legislation has followed to create a specifically tailored defence to apply in the future. In many ways, this is the ideal situation for necessity: catching the exceptional case within the imperfect safety net, alerting to the need for a defence, and then for a precise defence to be created. On a slightly grander scale, this is one way to characterise the creation of duress by circumstances.

However, there remain cases where necessity has been recognised and the creation of a specific defence has not followed. For these cases, and other exceptional cases in the future, the necessity defence remains their only imperfect option. Chief among these, because of the inapplicability of duress by threats or circumstances, is necessity as a defence to murder.

14.6.1 Necessity as a defence to murder

When considering necessity as a defence to murder, it is useful to begin with the case of *Dudley and Stephens*.

> **Dudley and Stephens** (1884) 14 QBD 273
>
> D1, D2, and V were shipwrecked, and spent 18 days drifting in an open boat. After several days without food or water, D1 and D2 decided to murder V (the cabin boy) and eat him in order to survive. They did so, and four days later they were rescued. D1 and D2 were charged with murder.
>
> - Assizes: on instruction from the judge, the jury produced a special verdict, making findings of fact that D1 and D2 would probably have died if they had not eaten V, and that V (being very weak already) would certainly have died. The case was then adjourned to the Royal Courts of Justice.
> - High Court: guilty of murder, with a sentence of death. [The prisoners were afterwards respited and their sentences commuted to six months' imprisonment without hard labour.]

The rationale for rejecting the necessity defence in *Dudley and Stephens* is disputed, but two main reasons are often highlighted from the court's judgment.[193] The first is that (at this time) necessity was not thought to provide a defence to murder. Following more recent case law, although the point is not settled, it is likely that necessity can be a defence to murder. The second reason, however, has continued to influence the application of the defence. This was the fact that D1 and D2 *chose* to kill V. This is unlike the hypothetical case of the mountain climber, D, whose partner, V, has fallen from the cliff face and is pulling D with her: D must cut the rope (allowing her partner to fall) in order to prevent them both being dragged from the cliff. In contrast, the defendants in *Dudley and Stephens* picked the cabin boy to be killed when it could have been any of their number who was selected to die. There has been some discussion of whether the

---

[193] See generally Simpson, *Cannibalism and the Common Law* (1984).

drawing of lots would have led to a different result, as it was held it would have done, *obiter*, in a US case,[194] but even this was found to be unacceptable.[195]

Following this, it is notable that on the few occasions where the necessity defence has been successfully run that there has been no problem of victim selection analogous to *Dudley and Stephens*. The most famous of these is the case of *Re A*.

 Re A (Children) [2000] 4 All ER 961

J and M were conjoined twins. Although they had separate vital organs, medical evidence established that the stronger twin (J) was sustaining the life of M through their common artery. If left conjoined, J's heart would fail within months and they would both die; if separated, J had the potential for a life that was worthwhile but M would die within minutes. J and M's parents refused on religious grounds to consent to an operation to separate the twins. Doctors applied for a declaration that separating the twins (killing M) would not be unlawful.

- Court: declaration granted.
- Court of Appeal: appeal dismissed.

The reasoning of the court in *Re A* is varied, but it is clear that Brooke LJ based his decision on necessity. He set out three requirements for the defence:

(i)   the act is needed to avoid inevitable and irreparable evil;

(ii) no more should be done than is reasonably necessary for the purpose to be achieved;

(iii) the evil inflicted must not be disproportionate to the evil avoided.

These requirements provide useful points of reference for the application of necessity. However, importantly, they remain vastly over-inclusive and should not be seen as criteria for the defence: they are required, but they are not sufficient. This was confirmed in the case itself, where each of the judges was obviously keen to limit the case to its particular facts. A useful illustration of the over-inclusivity of the requirements set out by Brooke LJ is also provided by Dennis:

Suppose P, a hospital patient, urgently needs a blood transfusion to survive, but she has a very rare blood group. As it happens, Q, the patient in the next bed, has the same rare blood group, but refuses to make a donation of blood even though she could do so without risk to herself. May, D, the doctor treating P, take the blood from Q without her consent?[196]

As Dennis goes on to explain, it is arguable that if D forcefully takes blood from Q, she will satisfy the requirements set out in *Re A*. The 'rare' blood type also makes this a case, unlike *Dudley and Stephens*, where there is no problem of selection. However, if we respect the autonomy of Q, if we believe that people 'have rights to be treated as ends in themselves and not as means to the achievement of other social goals', we would surely not want to the criminal law to justify such action. In short, *Re A* confirms the presence

194 *US v Holmes*, 26 Fed Cas 360 (1841).
195 *Dudley and Stephens* (1884) 14 QBD 273, 285.
196 Dennis, 'On Necessity as a Defence to Crime' (2009) 3 Crim L & Phil 29, 44–45.

of the necessity safety net, but the problematic nature of even the barest attempt at criteria also confirms that that safety net is imperfect.[197]

> **Extra detail...**
> Although it has not been considered by a court, it is clear that the UK government (along with many others) believes that necessity can be a defence to murder where a hijacked passenger jet is shot down. Such action involves the intentional killing of innocent passengers, but is performed in order to limit the potential damage if the plane were to be crashed into a populated area or other target.[198]

14.7 Reform

The general defences have attracted considerable academic attention and criticism, as we have discussed, but parliamentary reform has often been piecemeal, as with the partial codification of the public and private defence, or non-existent. In this section, we first consider the potential reform of each of the defences covered in this chapter. We then widen out to discuss the current inconsistencies between defences and the importance of achieving coherence.

14.7.1 Reforming the individual defences

Each of the general defences has attracted individual comment and criticism. We consider each in turn.

14.7.1.1 Insanity as a defence

We have already considered the potential reform of the insanity rules at **13.6.3**, and we do not repeat that discussion here. However, when evaluating the insanity rules it is useful to bear in mind the distinction between insanity as a denial of offending and insanity as a defence. Indeed, in the context of our discussion of potential human rights compatibility, the difference can be crucial. For example:

- **Article 6:** Article 6 ECHR provides a right to fair trial including the presumption of innocence and the reverse burden of proof for insanity. This is particularly important in the context of insanity as a denial of offending: because the Crown has not established the elements of the actus reus and mens rea, then by definition the case for reversing the burden is much weaker because there is no prima facie wrong. In contrast, where D has committed an offence and raises insanity as a defence, there is stronger ground for a reverse burden: D has been found to have performed the actus reus and mens rea, and therefore no longer needs to be presumed innocent. However, a reduced evidential burden may still be preferred.[199]

---

[197] Huxtable, 'Separation of Conjoined Twins: What Next for English Law?' [2002] Crim LR 459; Rogers, 'Necessity, Private-Defence and the Killing of Mary' [2001] Crim LR 515.

[198] Hornle, 'Hijacked Planes: May They Be Shot Down?' (2007) 10 New Crim LR 582; Bohlander, 'In Extremis? Hijacked Airplanes, Collateral Damage and the Limits of Criminal Law' [2006] Crim LR 579. Also recognised in *R (Nicklinson) v Ministry of Justice* [2014] UKSC 38.

[199] Law Commission, *Insanity and Automatism* (Discussion Paper, 2013).

- **Articles 2, 3, and 5:** Criticisms under Articles 2, 3, and 5, will apply in largely the same way to insanity as a denial of offending and insanity as a defence. The defence of insanity, as with insanity as a denial of offending, is designed to protect the right to life, to liberty, and to protect against inhuman and degrading treatment. To the extent that the current law fails to do this, but drawing the defence too narrowly or too widely, or through its disconnect with medical knowledge about mental illness, it is rightly subject to criticism.[200]

14.7.1.2 Duress

The rules on duress by threats, and now duress by circumstances, are reasonably well established within the common law. However, as we have discussed previously, the current law has been criticised for being drawn too narrowly, excluding those deserving of an excuse, and even narrowing further in recent years.[201] Academic opposition to this narrowing has questioned the merits of criminalising people for failing to resist pressures that they are subjectively unequipped to resist, especially where those pressures may objectively have affected others in a similar way.[202] Following recent case law, it is clear that these concerns are only likely to be addressed, if at all, through legislation. However, such reform does not appear on the current agenda. If and when this changes, the Law Commission has already provided a useful set of reform proposals.[203]

In contrast with this general lack of legislative attention, one area within the defence has attracted considerable recent debate: whether duress should be a defence to murder. The arguments in favour of such an extension reflect the general arguments in favour of a defence of duress to *any* crime. In simple terms, if D is threatened with death or serious harm to a degree that a reasonable person in her position would have done likewise to avoid it, D's actions are still wrong, but we can excuse the actor and sympathise with the impossible position in which she was placed. Against this, a number of arguments have been formulated to reject any extension of duress. These are most clearly stated in the reasoning of the court in *Howe*.[204] However, none of these arguments seem to hold up under analysis.

- The ordinary person of reasonable fortitude should sacrifice herself rather than take the life of an innocent.[205] *If the defence of duress were extended to cover murder, it would only apply where a jury found that a reasonable person would have yielded to the threat. If the criminal law is defining a 'reasonable' person as a hero, it is surely expecting too much.*

- One who takes the life of an innocent cannot claim to be choosing the lesser of two evils.[206] *This is not necessarily the case. For example, if D takes a single life to avoid X's threat to kill multiple people, this looks like the lesser evil. Also, the defence of duress is*

---

[200] Law Commission, *Insanity and Automatism* (Discussion Paper, 2013) paras 1.30–1.79.
[201] This stems from cases such as *Hasan* [2005] UKHL 22.
[202] Lippke, 'Chronic Temptation, Reasonable Firmness and the Criminal Law' (2014) 34 OJLS 75.
[203] Law Commission, *A Criminal Code for England and Wales*, 2 vols (No 177, 1989) cll 42 and 43, and most recently *Offences Against the Person and General Principles* (No 218, 1993) Part 4.
[204] [1987] 1 All ER 771.
[205] At 779–780.
[206] At 780.

generally conceived as a concession to reasonable human frailty (an excuse) rather than a balance of evils defence (a justification).

- The Law Commission had previously recommended that duress should be a defence to murder,[207] but this was not acted upon by Parliament.[208] *This proves little, as the Commission's previous recommendations were not put before Parliament to consider. We could equally claim that the failure of Parliament to overrule the House of Lords decision in* Lynch, *which suggested duress could be a defence to murder, demonstrated their approval of that approach.*

- Hard cases can be avoided though prosecutorial discretion (ie by not prosecuting).[209] *The morally innocent should not be left to the uncertain mercy of administrative discretion.*

The Law Commission has considered these arguments and others, and has recommended that the duress defence should be extended to apply to murder.[210] However, in doing so the Commission has taken the controversial step of recommending a reversed burden of proof in cases of this kind,[211] and an increased threshold so that the defence will only apply where D is threatened with death or 'life-threatening' harm; in other words serious, non-life-threatening harm will be insufficient.[212] Whether or not the Law Commission's scheme is accepted in full, it is contended that the arguments in favour of extending the defence of duress to murder are overwhelming.[213]

14.7.1.3 The public and private defence

Unlike the other general defences, the public and private defence has attracted the recent attention of Parliament. However, as discussed earlier, the reasons for this attention have been unfortunate, being based chiefly upon public and media misunderstanding about the limits of the defence. The reaction of Parliament in partially codifying the common law within section 76 of the CJIA can be welcomed as a useful clarification, although a complete codification would have been preferable. However, the more recent amendments to this section in relation to householder cases, allowing for disproportionate force to be used in this context, demonstrates the worst features of populist unprincipled law reform.[214] This process has also distracted from two areas of potential reform that should be highlighted regarding (a) the human rights compatibility of the current law, and (b) the potential for a new defence of excessive self-defence.

Concerns have been raised about the compatibility of the current public and private defence with rights enshrined within the ECHR. In particular, this debate has focused on the potential for the defence to apply where D has killed V, and done so on the basis of an unreasonable mistaken belief that force was necessary.[215] As long as D's response

---

207 Law Commission, *Defences of General Application* (No 83, 1977).
208 At 784 and 788.
209 At 780–781 and 790–791.
210 Law Commission, *Murder, Manslaughter and Infanticide* (No 304, 2006) Ch6.
211 At paras 6.87–6.141.
212 At paras 6.73–6.76.
213 Reed, 'The Need for a New Anglo American Approach to Duress' (1996) 61 J Crim L 209. See also Arenson, 'The Paradox of Disallowing Duress as a Defence to Murder' (2014) 78 J Crim L 65.
214 Editor, 'Defending Self-Defence' [2010] Crim LR 167.
215 See **14.5.1**.

in killing V was reasonable *on the facts as she believed them to be*, the defence will apply and D will be acquitted. However, what of V's Article 2 right to life?[216] As various commentators have set out,[217] although Article 2 is not an absolute right, it only permits life to be taken when it is 'absolutely necessary',[218] with the ECtHR clarifying that this requires 'good grounds' in circumstances of self-defence.[219] Arguably, D's unreasonably mistaken belief, albeit an honest one, does not constitute good grounds. It should be highlighted that neither the ECtHR nor any domestic court has yet found the public and private defence to be in breach of Article 2,[220] and there are also good reasons for favouring the current subjective test over an objective alternative.[221] However, it should also be acknowledged that a case of killing under an unreasonable mistaken belief has not yet made its way to the European Court, and so the potential for a breach to be found is still very much alive.

A second area of topical debate is the potential for a new partial defence for murder where D acts with excessive force in self-defence. The public and private defence will not apply to D in these circumstances: although D's use of force may be necessary in the circumstances as she believes them to be, if they are excessive because the degree of force used is unreasonable, then the defence will fail.[222] The potential for a new partial defence that would reduce D's liability from murder to manslaughter was considered by the House of Lords in *Clegg*.[223] However, the court concluded that a change of this kind, if it were required, would have to come from Parliament. Such reform has not been forthcoming. However, the potential for a partial defence of this kind has found consistent favour with the Law Commission and there are sound reasons for its recommendation.[224] Under the current law, someone who kills in excessive self-defence may be able to rely on one of the existing partial defences (as in *Martin*[225]), and this potential has been increased by the expansion of the loss of control defence to include a trigger based on fear of serious violence.[226] However, there will still be defendants who kill without having lost control, and who do not qualify for the partial defence of diminished responsibility, and there remains a case to be made that these defendants also warrant partial mitigation on the basis of their (semi-)defensive motivations.[227]

---

[216] Although debate has focused on killing and Art 2, it could equally apply where D causes lesser harm in similarly unreasonable circumstances (potentially infringing Arts 3 and/or 5).

[217] Ashworth, 'Human Rights: Case Commentary on *Andronicou and Constantinou v Cyprus*' [1998] Crim LR 823; Leverick, 'Is English Self-Defence Law Incompatible with Article 2 of the ECHR?' [2002] Crim LR 347.

[218] Art 2(2) ECHR.

[219] *McCann v UK* (1996) 21 EHRR 95.

[220] *Bubbins v UK* (2005) 41 EHRR 458; *R (Bennett) v HM Coroner for Inner London* [2007] EWCA Civ 617; *Duggan* [2014] EWHC 3343 (Admin).

[221] Although mistaken, D's belief in the need for extreme force was honest and so does not reveal a blameworthy character.

[222] This is, of course, subject to the householder exception: see **14.5.2.1**.

[223] [1995] 1 All ER 334. Kaye, 'Excessive Force in Self-Defence: After *Clegg*' (1996) 61 J Crim L 448.

[224] Law Commission, *A Criminal Code for England and Wales*, 2 vols (No 177, 1989) cl59; Law Commission, *Murder, Manslaughter and Infanticide* (No 304, 2006) para 1.53.

[225] See **14.5.2**.

[226] See **6.2.1**.

[227] Smith, 'Excessive Defence—A Rejection of Australian Initiative' [1972] Crim LR 524. Australian law no longer recognises a partial defence of this kind, adopting the English position in

14.7.1.4 Necessity

At one time, the Law Commission went as far as to recommend the abolition of necessity as a defence.[228] However, as we discussed earlier, such a policy is surely ill-conceived, severely limiting the ability of the courts to deal with exceptional cases where liability is inappropriate but other defences do not apply. The recommendation was severely criticised,[229] and has been dropped. Subsequently, the Commission has recommended that necessity should remain a defence but (unlike the other defences) it should not be codified.[230] This seems to be the correct approach, allowing the necessity defence to perform its role as an imperfect safety net without the restraint of codification. Indeed, we see a similar approach in most other common law jurisdictions.[231]

14.7.2 Coherence between defences?

It is not an objection to the current general defences that they apply in variously different circumstances. However, there may be a problem where the defences are inconsistent in their approach to common issues to an extent that the overall approach of the law becomes incoherent. This is undoubtedly a problem within the current law, and one in which, within denials of defences at least, the Law Commission has begun to take an interest.[232]

It is useful to provide a brief overview of some of the main areas of inconsistency within the current general defences, each of which has been highlighted previously in the context of the individual defences. These inconsistencies can be explained on the basis of common law development that lacks a unifying theory of defences, and the conflict between excusatory and justificatory rationales.[233] However, although they can be explained on this basis, the law must still aim for coherence. After all, unifying theories are elusive in any area of the law.[234]

- **Subjective and objective approaches:** Probably the most striking area of inconsistency between the defences discussed in this chapter relates to their use of subjective and objective elements. For example, whereas duress requires D to have an *objectively* reasonable belief in the presence of a serious threat requiring D to offend, the

---

Zecevic (1987) 61 ALJR 375. See also, in the context of abused women who kill in excessive self-defence, Wake, 'Battered Women, Startled Householders and Psychological Self-Defence' (2013) 77 J Crim L 433.

[228] Law Commission, *Defences of General Application* (No 83, 1977).

[229] Williams, 'Necessity' [1978] Crim LR 128; Huxley, 'Proposals and Counter Proposals on the Defence of Necessity' [1978] Crim LR 141.

[230] Law Commission, *Offences Against the Person and General Principles* (No 218, 1992) cl36(2).

[231] eg Canada (*Perka* (1984) 13 DLR (4th) 1); Australia (*Loughnan* [1981] VR 443); across the Oceanic countries (Forsyth, 'The Divorce and Marriage of Morality and Law' (2010) 21 Crim L Forum 121); and so on. One exception, where codification has been attempted, is the United States (Model Penal Code, §3.02), on which, see Alexander, 'Lesser Evils: A Closer Look at the Paradigmatic Justification' (2005) 24 Law & Phil 611; Berman, 'Lesser Evils: A Less Close Look' (2005) 24 Law & Phil 681.

[232] Law Commission, *Insanity and Automatism* (Discussion Paper, 2013).

[233] Lacy, 'Space, Time and Function: Intersecting Principles of Responsibility Across the Terrain of Criminal Justice' (2007) 1 Crim L & Phil 233.

[234] Tadros, 'The Character of Excuse' (2001) 21 OJLS 495.

public and private defence requires the equivalent belief in the necessity of force to be *subjectively* honest. If this difference was based on stated principles then it would be acceptable, but it actually originates from the defences unsuccessfully attempting to run in tandem.[235]

- **Characteristics of the defendant:** Where an objective standard is applied, there are no obvious principles underpinning the approach to which of D's character-istics can be taken into account when applying that standard. For example, for duress, it now seems that almost all of D's physical and psychiatric characteristics can be taken into account when deciding whether a reasonable person with those characteristics would have been compelled to offend.[236] In contrast, for the public and private defence, the objective degree of force test does not allow characteristics beyond age and sex to be taken into account, and explicitly excludes psychiatric characteristics.[237]

- **Approaches to prior fault:** The question of whether D's prior fault can under-mine her appeal to a defence is equally inconsistent. For example, duress will be excluded where D voluntarily associates with others in circumstances where she *objectively* should have foreseen a risk of coercion.[238] In contrast, the public and private defence will only be similarly excluded where D has *consciously* manipu-lated the circumstances in order to attack V under the guise of defensive force.[239] Again, reasons for the inconsistency are hard to fathom.[240]

An extreme response to the issue of inconsistency would be to collapse each of the general defences into a single defence, with a single set of rules and principles. A model for this approach has been set out by Clarkson.[241] However, the problem here is that a single defence becomes nothing more than a vague statement of neces-sity, unifying only in its inevitable preference for the lowest common denominator. Although we acknowledge that a defence of this kind (necessity) is essential as an imperfect safety net below other defences, it is surely right that other defences should exist which are capable of greater clarity and precision.

A better approach, it is contended, following the lead of the Law Commission in relation to automatism, intoxication, and insanity, is to identify common elements between the defences and make sure that the reform of any one takes account of the others, whether this means principled consistency or principled inconsist-ency. Wilson's work on the structure of defences provides a good example of this approach.[242]

---

[235] The court in *Graham* [1982] 1 All ER 801 equated duress with self-defence and so adopted an objective approach in line with (what was then) the accepted approach for self-defence. How-ever, less than two years later the court in *Gladstone Williams* [1987] 3 All ER 411 opted for a subjective approach to self-defence. See also Alldridge, 'Developing the Defence of Duress' [1986] Crim LR 433.

[236] *Bowen* [1996] 2 Cr App R 157. See **14.3.3.3**.

[237] *Martin* [2001] EWCA Crim 2245. See **14.5**.

[238] *Hasan* [2005] UKHL 22. See **14.3.1.2**.

[239] *Rashford* [2005] EWCA Crim 3377. See **14.5.1.3**.

[240] Child, 'Prior Fault: Blocking Defences or Constructing Crimes' in Reed and Bohlander (eds), *General Defences* (2014).

[241] Clarkson, 'Necessary Action: A New Defence' [2004] Crim LR 81.

[242] Wilson, 'The Structure of Defences' [2005] Crim LR 108.

14.8 Eye on assessment

In this section we consider the application of the general defences to problem facts. We employ the same structure as we have discussed throughout the book. However, here perhaps more than ever, it is vital to read carefully what the question, at the bottom of the problem facts, is asking you to do. In most cases, questions involving defences will be no different from any other question: they will ask you to discuss potential liability and so you will have to go through every step of the structure (which we set out later) and remember to only discuss the potential for a defence when it becomes necessary to do so, that is *only after* you have established that D is likely to have committed the actus reus and mens rea of an offence. However, exceptionally, a question may tell you that D has committed an offence and ask you to consider potential defences only. In this case, you should skip from Step 1 (you still need to identify the criminal event) straight to Step 4 (discussion of defences).

Assuming that we are dealing with a standard question, the following structure should be applied.

STEP 1 Identify the potential criminal event in the facts

This should be simply stated (eg 'The first potential criminal event arises where D punches V'). The role of this stage is to highlight which part of the question you are answering before you begin to apply the law.

STEP 2 Identify the potential offence

Again, state this simply (eg 'When punching V, D may be liable for assault occasioning ABH'). The role of this stage is to highlight which offence you are going to apply.

STEP 3 Applying the offence to the facts

Having identified the relevant offence, make sure you discuss each of the required elements.

Actus reus: What does the offence require? Did D do it?

Mens rea: What does the offence require? Did D possess it?

STEP 4 Consider defences

The word 'consider' here is important, as you should not discuss every defence for every question. Rather, think whether there are any defences (eg duress) that *could* potentially apply. If there are, discuss those only.

Figure 14.1, on page 607, is designed to help you to identify which defence you should apply. Note that, if insanity applies, D will usually be directed to the special verdict. If insanity does not apply, you should consider duress, the public and private defence, and/or any specific defences. Remember that there is often an overlap between defences including duress and self-defence, so it may be necessary to apply more than one to the facts. Finally, if these defences do not apply, you should consider necessity as the imperfect safety net beneath. If D is liable for murder and none of the complete defences apply, you should also go on to consider the partial defences.[243]

Remember, as we note next to Step 4, analysis of the defences is mainly a mental process. Particularly in an exam, you will not have time to lead your reader through the elements of each defence and say why each does not apply. Rather, keep **Figure 14.1** in mind to help you identify any defences that might apply (ie there are facts in the problem that suggest it might apply) and lead your reader through those defences only.

STEP 5 Conclude

This is usually a single sentence either saying that it is likely that D has committed the offence, or saying that it is not likely either because an offence element is not satisfied or because a defence is likely to apply. It is not often that you will be able to say categorically whether D has committed the offence or not, so it is usually best to conclude in terms of what is more 'likely'.

STEP 6 Loop

Go back up to Step 1, identifying the next potential criminal event. Continue until you have discussed all the relevant potentially criminal events.

ONLINE RESOURCE CENTRE

www.oxfordtextbooks.co.uk/orc/smithandhogan/

This chapter is accompanied by a selection of online resources to help you with this topic, including:

- **Multiple choice questions**
- **Chapter summary sheet**
- Two **sample examination questions** with answer guidance
- **Further reading**

Also available on the Online Resource Centre are:

- A selection of **videos** from the authors explaining key topics and principles
- **Legal updates**
- Useful **weblinks**

---

[243] See **6.2.**

Figure 14.1 Applying the general defences

Index